GOLF
A GOOD WALK
& THEN SOME

GOLF
A GOOD WALK

John R. Jenchura

Second Edition Revised & Updated

& THEN SOME

A Quintessential History of the Game

A Mountain Lion Book

Library of Congress Control Number: 2010936649
ISBN 978-0-9839689-5-5

Updated through June 2015

Printed in the United States of America

Jacket and text design by Bob Antler, Antler Designworks

Every effort has been make to make
Golf–A Good Walk & Then Some
as accurate and complete as possible. I have been as diligent
as possible in giving appropriate credit. My apologies if
I have come up short in this regard. Should you have
any comments, questions, or just want to get in touch
with me, you are encouraged to do so as follows:

John Jenchura, 617 Schiller Avenue, Merion, PA 19066;
golfagoodwalk@gmail.com

Dedicated to my favorite "foursome,"
my wife, Grace, and my three daughters,
Sarah, Charlotte, and Emily

Foreword
by Gary Player

Golf has been the major part of my life for over fifty years— as a professional golfer, a golf course architect, and an international ambassador and supporter of the game. I have been blessed with the opportunity to play and design courses on five continents, and throughout my more than fifteen million miles of traveling the world, I am always amazed at the popularity of this great game.

Golf is a game that is both simple and complex. It is a game that is enjoyed by people with wide-ranging skill levels. It is a social sport played with friends. But at the same time it is the most solitary and individually challenging of all sports. It tests you physically, mentally, emotionally, and spiritually. It takes from you and gives back, and not always in equal measures. It is all of these elements and more that make it the greatest game ever invented, in my humble opinion.

The appeal of the game of golf knows no limitations. You only need to look at the advancement of the game in China and India to understand the attraction of golf. Where golf was at one time unheard of in China, that country has now embraced it. I have no doubt that it won't be too long before China, as India already has done, produces world-class golfers qualified to compete around the world on all tours. I should also point out that, in recognition of the burgeoning worldwide popularity of golf, the International Olympic Committee has seen fit to add golf to the list of sports for the Summer Olympics to be held in Rio de Janeiro, Brazil in 2016.

Since the game of golf has been so much a part of my life, I find its history a fascinating story in itself. Golf history books help cement golf's legacy and teach us about how this game came to be so special. Without such works, much about golf, its champions, and its championships would be lost in the mist of time. Oddly, and despite its popularity, there hasn't been a comprehensive telling of the game's history in some time. That is why I am so pleased to see the publication of *Golf–A Good Walk & Then Some*, the inviting work of John Jenchura. With all that has transpired in golf over the past several decades—or at least since Jack Nicklaus, Arnold Palmer, and I were branded "The Big Three"—the book you're holding in your hands could not be more timely.

His coverage from the rumored multiple origins of the game and through to the first decade of the new millennium is a testament to the author's lifelong passion for this grand game, and his goals of producing a comprehensive history of golf and its records. Hopefully, when you read this book, you will gain insights into what the title means. I expect that you will come away concluding, as I did, that there is much, much more to the wondrous game of golf than just playing it. It's the game, and then some. This rich and storied recounting of the game's history is sure to fascinate golfers and non-golfers alike.

I can heartily recommend it, and I am sure that it will quickly become a welcome addition to the lore of golf history.

Acknowledgments

A comprehensive book such as *Golf–A Good Walk & Then Some* could not be written without a lot of help along the way. I start first with thanks to my wife, Grace, who encouraged me "to just do it" and to my daughters Sarah, Charlotte, and Emily, who reminded me on more than one occasion that "you are a golf fanatic." Gratitude goes to my parents, Joe and Alice, who encouraged me to learn to play golf by letting me use their golf clubs, and by enrolling me in youth group golf lessons.

Then there were the inspirations for the book, particularly one golfer and one author. The golfer is Bobby Jones, who has been an idol of mine since I first learned of him in the late 1960s. He epitomizes the way golf should be played and respected. The late author, Herbert Warren Wind, was a fantastic golf writer. No golf book more than his masterpiece, *The Story of American Golf*, influenced my start of this project in 2006. In my opinion, his storytelling about golf knows no equal.

I must also recognize Mark Twain, who is credited with saying that "golf was a good walk spoiled." It was his remark that was the inspiration for my title.

I have admired many of those who play the game for a living. One person in particular is Ben Crenshaw who, in addition to being a fine golfer and golf architect in his own right, is recognized as a serious student of the history of golf.

Gary Player is a worldwide golfer and architect. I am deeply indebted to him for writing the foreword and the kind words contained therein. Thank you, Gary!

No golf history writing can get very far without the help of the United States Golf Association (U.S.G.A.). I want to thank librarian Nancy Stulack for making the U.S.G.A. collection of books available to me, especially those from generations past. I was able to verify many facts by visiting the World Golf Hall of Fame. Mark Cubbedge, manager of collections and research there, has assembled a trove of golf history that I mined.

Two locals bear mentioning. The late Jim Finegan's *A Centennial Tribute to Golf in Philadelphia* helped me put a Philadelphia flavor in my book where possible. The other local is the Merion Golf Club for which I developed a deep affection when I moved to Merion in 1979. I enjoyed visiting the course for two U.S. Opens, two U.S. Amateurs, a U.S. Girls Junior, and a Walker Cup. But my greatest pleasure was walking the 11th hole where Bobby Jones completed his Grand Slam in September 1930.

After I wrote the first draft in November 2007, I asked several people with mastery of the English language to give the draft a critical eye. Their edits and suggestions were invaluable, and I am indebted to my wife, Grace, Bob Gale, PhD, and Bruce Adams for their tedious work to help smooth out my rough draft. I also want to give a special acknowledgment to Bruce who, as the sports editor of our local newspaper, *The Main Line Times*, gave me the opportunity to report on golf and other sports, which helped me hone my writing skills.

For photographs, I wish to express my gratitude to Ellie Kaiser of the U.S.G.A. for guiding me through the U.S.G.A.'s large and thorough collection of photographs and making them available to me. Tom Imperial was a great source for photographs of golfers from the 1990s and 2000s. As for the earliest photographs, I was fortunate to be given access to the massive collection of Hobbs Photographs owned by Margaret Hobbs across the Pond. And Peter Horvath gave me the photograph of the eighth hole at my home course, Honeybrook Golf Club in Honey Brook, PA.

Thank you to my partners at Honeybrook for allowing me in a small way to help with opening Honeybrook, and for asking me to come along as a partner in the course. I am speaking of my good friends and partners, Donna Horvath and her twin brothers, Ted and Tom Piersol. And I want to thank my daughter, Sarah for taking the photograph of her Dad shown on the back of the jacket.

I appreciated the five years I spent coaching a high school girls' golf team—The Country Day School of the Sacred Heart in Bryn Mawr, PA. This stint allowed me to emphasize to the girls that G.O.L.F. stands for the Game of Life Forever. That motto also gave me the desire to write a history of golf. My assistant coach, Bob Battista, seconded that acronym on more than one occasion. Also, I thank my athletic director, Cindy Shay, for trusting that I would not teach the girls too many bad swing habits.

The nuts and bolts of putting a book together require much time and talent. I am indebted to my agent, John Monteleone of Mountain Lion, Inc. John, you believed in me from the beginning and have been with me every step of the way. Thank you to Peter Kollmann, editorial consultant at Mountain Lion, for helping to revise and copy edit the second edition. Turning a manuscript into a finished product is almost miraculous as I see it, and the miracle worker in my case was book designer, Bob Antler, of Antler Designworks.

If I forgot anyone who helped me, you know who you are, and I appreciate what you did to make *Golf–A Good Walk & Then Some* a reality. Thank you very much.

Photo Credits
United States Golf Association: xx, 24 (top), 27, 41, 43, 47, 48, 53, 56, 58, 63, 66, 70, 78, 81, 85, 88, 91, 94, 98, 105, 107, 112, 116, 121, 128, 139, 143, 150, 156, 159, 161, 163, 165, 166, 168, 170, 178, 190, 193, 196, 201, 203, 206, 216, 219, 224, 229, 238, 243, 257, 268, 286, 298, 328, 333. **Peter Horvath**: xviii. **Margaret Hobbs**: 3, 4, 5, 6, 8, 10, 11, 16, 17, 23, 24 (bottom), 34. **Tom Imperial**: 39, 260, 273, 291, 318, 324, 336, 350, 353, 354, 355, 361, 362, 364, 365, 366, 367, 368, 369, 372, 378, 381, 382, 383, 386, 387, 389.

Table of Contents

Foreword by Gary Player...vii
Acknowledgments...ix
Introduction...xvii

SECTION 1
Origins of the Game and Planting the Seeds in America............1

Chapter 1. Before the Scots, Where Did It All Begin?...2
Chapter 2. Modern Golf—Scotland's Gift...7
Chapter 3. The Origins of Golf Clubs and Associations...9
Chapter 4. The Early Evolution of the Golf Ball and Golf Clubs...15
Chapter 5. Inauguration of The Open Championship...19
Chapter 6. The Great Triumvirate...22
Chapter 7. The Birth of Golf in the United States...26
Chapter 8. Further Evolution of the Golf Ball...33
Chapter 9. New Equipment...38
Chapter 10. The Founding of the United States Golf Association (U.S.G.A.)...40
Chapter 11. Charles B. Macdonald—His Role in the Establishment of American Golf...42
Chapter 12. Harry Vardon's First Tour of the United States...46

SECTION 2
The Late 1800s and Early 1900s.............................49

Chapter 13. Golf For Women...50
Chapter 14. Willie Anderson—Dominance in the U.S. Open at the Turn of the Century...55
Chapter 15. Walter J. Travis and Jerome D. Travers...57

Chapter 16. John McDermott—A Native-Born American Breaks
Through at the 1911 U.S. Open...61
Chapter 17. Francis Ouimet and the 1913 U.S. Open...64

SECTION 3
Walter Hagen, Gene Sarazen, and Others................................71

Chapter 18. Following Ouimet, There Came Walter Hagen...72
Chapter 19. Chick Evans—Among Amateur Golf's Best...77
Chapter 20. The Hiatus of World War I—Exhibition Matches...80
Chapter 21. The Squire—Gene Sarazen...82

SECTION 4
Bobby Jones...89

Chapter 22. Bobby Jones—The Early Years...90
Chapter 23. Bobby Jones—The Lean Years...93
Chapter 24. Bobby Jones—The Run of Majors Leading Up to the
Grand Slam...97
Chapter 25. Bobby Jones—The Grand Slam—
"The Impregnable Quadrilateral"...103
Chapter 26. Bobby Jones—The "Retirement Years"...111

SECTION 5
The Era of Post-Bobby Jones Through World War II..............117

Chapter 27. Glenna Collett Vare and Her Battles With Joyce Wethered...118
Chapter 28. After Bobby Jones, Then Who?...126
Chapter 29. The New American Great Triumvirate...134
Byron Nelson, Sam Snead, Ben Hogan
Chapter 30. The Years Following World War II...149
Chapter 31. Mildred "Babe" Didrikson Zaharias...154
Chapter 32. Patty Berg...158
Chapter 33. The Founding of the Ladies Professional Golf Association
(L.P.G.A.)...160
Chapter 34. Mickey Wright...162
Chapter 35. Three Women Who Chased Patty Berg...164
Louise Suggs, Betsy Rawls, Betty Jameson
Chapter 36. The Late 1940s and Early 1950s:
The Era Before Arnold Palmer...169

SECTION 6
The Men's Modern "Big Four"....................................179

Chapter 37. Arnold Palmer and the Dawn of a New Era...180

Chapter 38. The 1950s Turn Into the 1960s...189
Chapter 39. Gary Player—A World Class Player...191
Chapter 40. Through the Mid-1960s...195
Chapter 41. Billy Casper—The Fourth Member (Almost)
    of the Big Three...199
Chapter 42. The Years 1966-1967...202
Chapter 43. The Golden Bear...204

SECTION 7
Champions of the 1960s, 1970s, and 1980s.............................217

Chapter 44. The Late 1960s and Early 1970s...218
Chapter 45. The Merry Mex—Lee Trevino...223
Chapter 46. The Rest of the 1970s...227
Chapter 47. Four Outstanding Women Golfers in the
    Modern Era...237
    Nancy Lopez, Kathy Whitworth, Pat Bradley,
    Joanne Gunderson Carner
Chapter 48. 1980-1984...242
Chapter 49. Tom Watson—Jack Nicklaus's Successor...251
Chapter 50. Seve Ballesteros—The Spaniard Extraordinaire...256
Chapter 51. The Rest of the 1980s...259

SECTION 8
The 1990s and Beyond..269

Chapter 52. 1990-1996...270
Chapter 53. One of Britain's Best—Nick Faldo...286
Chapter 54. The Rest of the 1990s...290
Chapter 55. 2000-2006...298
Chapter 56. International Icons...317
    Ernie Els, Vijay Singh, Padraig Harrington
Chapter 57. Phil Mickelson...323
Chapter 58. 2007-2008...329
Chapter 59. 2009-2011...335

SECTION 9
Tiger Woods..341

Chapter 60. Tiger Woods...342

SECTION 10
Women of the 1980s, 1990s, and 2000s.................................357

Chapter 61. Three Generations of Women During the 1980s,
  1990s, and 2000s...358
  Betsy King, Amy Alcott, Patty Sheehan, Beth Daniel,
  Julie Inkster, Laura Davies
Chapter 62. A Modern Women's Great Triumvirate...362
  Annika Sörenstam, Karrie Webb, Se Ri Pak
Chapter 63. The Ladies' New Blood of the New Millennium...369
  Lorena Ochoa, Cristie Kerr, Natalie Gulbis,
  Paula Creamer, Morgan Pressel, Michelle Wie

SECTION 11
2011 and Beyond.. 379

Chapter 64. The Rise of the Asian Women...380
Chapter 65. Two Rising American Stars:...385
  Stacy Lewis and Lexi Thompson
Chapter 66. The Changing of the Guard—The 20 Somethings...388
Chapter 67. Rory McIlory, Sucessor to Tiger Woods?...391
Chapter 68. The World of Golf 2011-2015...400

SECTION 12
Professional and Amateur Team Competitions....................... 409

Chapter 69. The Competitions...410
  The Ryder Cup, The Presidents Cup, The Walker Cup,
  The Solheim Cup, The Curtis Cup

Epilogue...421
Winners of Major Championships and Team Competitions...422
Bibliography...451
Index...457

Introduction

I first became acquainted with the game of golf at the age of 12 when my mother let me borrow her clubs to take group lessons at a nearby country club, Churchill Valley Country Club in Penn Hills, Pennsylvania. I became hooked immediately and couldn't wait until I was able to go out and play an actual round. Signing up as a caddy at Churchill Valley was the easiest way to gain access to a course. Caddies were allowed to play there on Mondays when the course was closed to the membership. So around the age of 13, I hit the links for the first time. Almost five decades later, I still have that boyish enthusiasm for the game, and I see no end in sight. Yes, I support the creed that G.O.L.F stands for the Game Of Life Forever.

As I grew into adulthood, other facets of the game started to intrigue me. I began modestly with learning to re-grip my golf clubs. Later, I developed an interest in making clubs and, using a self-help book, learned how to make drivers by obtaining the components from a golf supply house. To learn more about the retail side of golf and the latest in modern equipment, I took a part-time job in a golf store. When I was approaching 50, the opportunity to fulfill a life-long dream of building and owning a golf course came about unexpectedly. Through a mutual friend, I met three siblings who were building a course and volunteered to help them. This eventually led to my being asked to join the partnership which owns the course, Honeybrook Golf Club in Honey Brook, Pennsylvania. What a thrill!

Aside from these golf-related activities, how did I have the audacity to think that I could write a book on the history of this great game? Well, I have to admit that it did not happen overnight, and I did have misgivings about attempting such a project. At first, I felt that to understand the game in its entirety, I had to learn as much about the history of golf as I could possibly accomplish.

The eighth hole at Honeybrook Golf Club, Honey Brook, Pennsylvania
where the author has taken many a good walk.

The starting point for this interest was a time in my late teens when I asked myself the school-age essay question of who is the person you most admire? For me, it was somebody in the world of golf. It didn't take me long to focus on Bobby Jones, who is acknowledged as among the greatest golfers of all time and the best amateur who ever played the game. I had heard of his golfing exploits while growing up and admired not only his achievement in winning golf's Grand Slam, (winning all four of golf's Major championships in one calendar year), but his sportsmanship and love for the game.

I started to read books about Jones, including his own well-received autobiography, *Down the Fairway*, which he wrote when he was only 25. I soon wanted more than just to read about Jones. I traveled to Atlanta to see his boyhood home at East Lake and his home in the Buckhead section of Atlanta where he lived as an adult. I also visited his grave and former law offices in Atlanta. However, my greatest thrill was to play the course where he completed his Grand Slam, Merion Golf Club in Ardmore, Pennsylvania, only three miles from my home in Merion.

There, on September 27, 1930, Jones completed his Grand Slam by winning the U.S. Amateur when he defeated Eugene Homans, ending the match on the 11th hole. Exactly 100 years after his birthday, on March 17, 2002, I went to the 11th hole at Merion and, in the rain, sang "Happy Birthday" to Jones at approximately the location where the cup was when he won the Grand Slam. My wife is a witness to this act of infatuation!

Having satisfied my curiosity about Bobby Jones, I developed an interest in all of the history of golf. I began to collect golf books, especially ones relating to the history of the game. I have collected books for over 35 years, and at some point during that period I got the idea to write my own history of the game if I ever had the time to do so. That time came when I exited the full-time practice of law in 2006.

For a year and a half, I worked on the book and thoroughly enjoyed what had become the principal hobby in my "retirement" years. Aside from Bobby Jones, my inspiration was the late, esteemed golf writer Herbert Warren Wind, whose book, *The Story of American Golf*, is a classic among golf's history books. Indeed, I have long felt that it is one of the best books that I have ever read. Wind also coined the term "Amen Corner" to describe holes 11-13 at Augusta National. In November 2008, he earned a place in the World Golf Hall of Fame under the category of Lifetime Achievement, joining Bernard Darwin and Herb Graffis as the only full-time golf writers to be so honored.

As I continued writing, I wondered what it would have been like to have Mr. Wind as a mentor and advisor. I'm sure his guidance would have benefited in ways I can only imagine.

I hope my modest effort to pay homage to Bobby Jones and Mr. Wind holds your interest as much as it did while I was authoring *Golf–A Good Walk & Then Some*. Enjoy the walk and then some!

"Old" Tom Morris, along with his son "Young" Tom Morris dominated the early days of the British Open. Old Tom is still the oldest to win the British Open when he won at the age of 46 in 1867.

Origins of the Game and
Planting the Seeds in America

1

Before the Scots,
Where Did It All Begin?

Like much of history shrouded in the mist of time, no one knows precisely where the game of golf began. Not in the world. Not in America. In short, no concrete evidence exists as to its invention. How strange that it is a game of recreation that has enthralled players and observers for hundreds of years with statistics, love, and captivating events, yet historians cannot uncover its birthright with any assuredness. However, there are snippets of history, evidence and lore that challenge the imagination of students of the game so that they have at least some clue as to golf's origins.

For starters historians cannot even be sure where the term "golf" originated. One school postulates that it derived from the Dutch-Flemish word for club—"choler." Other historians say it came from the German word—"kolbe," which also means club.

If one goes back far enough there is evidence that early man, even the caveman, held a basic motivation to strike an object with a stick. Furthermore, it does not require much to believe that the skills developed in striking one's perceived enemy can be readily adapted to the art of striking a ball or other stationary object. As one backtracks through the ages there is evidence that Roman soldiers kept themselves amused and in condition by playing *paganica*, a game in which players struck a feather-stuffed ball with a curved stick. This may have occurred in what is now Great Britain, where

Dutch Golf Clubs, 1600s

they ruled from 40 to 400 AD. Fast-forwarding many centuries, during the Ming Dynasty in the 1300s, the Chinese can stake their claim to being the first to play "golf," in a game called *suignan*— a game where players strolled along while striking a ball with a stick.

Historians also note that a stained glass window in England's Gloucester Cathedral portrays a figure wielding a stick in a backswing motion preparing to strike a round object of some sort. The window in question dates back to the mid-fourteenth century. From this, it is conceivable that golf may have derived from an English game called *cambuca*.

Across the English Channel, during the sixteenth century, the French perfected a game called *jeu de mail*, played with long-handled mallets and large wooden balls. Some of the mallets resembled crude golf clubs and others were in the shape of croquet mallets. The game had several similarities to today's miniature golf, croquet, and billiards, and the object was to hit balls through hoops in the least possible number of strokes. The game was quite popular until the eighteenth century, when it seemed to have lost the interest of the French.

Next door to France the game that caught the fancy of the Belgians was once called *"chole,"* played by advancing a ball with a mallet, cross-country, up to four leagues from the starting point. *Chole* dates back to the early 1500's.

In another version, also in Belgium, teams of players wielding heavy iron mallets struck egg-shaped wooden balls toward a target perhaps 400 yards distant. This target could be a tree, a door, or almost anything. The game had similarities to croquet in that the offensive team took three strikes, and then the defensive team could swat the ball back from the target or to a difficult place, where the offensive team would have an awkward time hitting the ball toward the target. Then the teams switched roles. Each team bid on the number of strokes it estimated it would take to strike the target, with the lower bidding team having the honor of going first. *Chole*

Dutch Kolf by Aert van der Neer, 1600

still survives in Belgium, and a version is still played in Northern France under the name *"soule."*

Another neighbor of the French, the Dutch, invented a game whose origins seem to go back to the thirteenth century. Interestingly, the game's name was *"colf,"* a game that for all intents and purposes has much to establish itself as the true precursor to the acknowledged Scottish version of the game now recognized as the modern game of golf.

Another Dutch game called *"het kolven"* was in vogue for at least a hundred years, between the mid-1500s and the latter years of the 1600s. It had similarities to *colf. Het kolven* was played using a club with a straight brass face larger than the modern golf club. It was played indoors on a court with a post at either end of the court. The object was to strike the post at one end of the court in the fewest number of strokes, and to accomplish the same by striking the post at the other end of the court. Outdoors, *het kolven* was played on ice. While the game is still played in scattered locales in the Netherlands it is conceded that it bears little resemblance to golf.

Het kolven eventually was discredited as bearing any relationship to golf, in essence because it was played on ice. Casting further doubt on *het kolven's* kinship with golf is the fact that Dutch pictures show that there was little room in *het kolven* for a player to strike the ball for distance. The pictures further reveal that players held the clubs with their hands far apart, unlike golf, and used a shoving motion to advance the ball.

Evidence does suggest that, like the Belgian *chole*, the Dutch had colf courses measuring in the vicinity of up to 5000-yard "holes" or targets. The targets were anything one could imagine—doors to homes, kitchens, churches, windmills, and the like. The *colf*-happy Dutch pursued their balls around buildings, through thoroughfares, and even through the center of their towns. With the havoc *"colfers"* brought to their towns they eventually were confined to the countryside in the summers and to the frozen ponds in the winter where they struck their balls to poles imbedded in the ice. *Colf* remained the game of choice outdoors in the Netherlands for more than four hundred years, or until the early 1700's.

Where did it all go? Though the evidence is scarce it appears to have migrated to Scotland. How so? Piecing together how the Scots laid claim to the birth of golf requires some recounting of history.

Henry V's English invasion of France made him the ruler of Normandy by 1420. The French king, Charles VI, sent an emissary to Scotland to ask for help from the Scots. By 1421 the English were still trying to solidify

Jeu de mal club

Jeu de mal clubs and balls

their hold on Northern France while the pesky Scots sought to thwart that initiative by coming to the aid of the French. The Scots took advantage of lulls in battle and intermittent truces to play some form of cross-country

Crecy window in Gloucester Cathedral

game, possibly not unlike the Belgian game of *chole*. Golf historians believe that the Scottish soldiers, who learned and enjoyed *chole* while in France, continued the game upon their return home to Scotland. If the Scots did take *chole* back to Scotland following their French-Normandy campaign this would have been consistent with the timing of the aforementioned 1421 date and the advent of a transformed *chole* into golf by the mid-1400s in Scotland.

All of the foregoing incidents of history suggest a common thread among the various countries in Europe. That thread is the test to see who can strike a ball the farthest, using a stick or mallet. This feature is so elementary as to be indigenous to most—if not all—of the countries that are recognized as having a hand in the development of modern-day golf. The litmus test for golf is to uncover the domain where the fundamental concepts of golf were laid. That is to say, where were the essential features of the game configured? These fundamental components are: a designated mark or spot, striking of a ball to that mark or spot, the task of striking accomplished by an individual rather than a team, and, lastly, the absence of interference by a player's opponents.

With as much certainty as the sketchy history reveals, most golf historians conclude that it was the Scots who melded these concepts together to devise the modern game of golf. Furthermore, this belief is consistent with the character of Scots—that reserve, caution and a painstaking nature are the attributes of a quintessential Scotsman. At the end of the day, the misty search for the origin of golf still allows rival countries to claim it as theirs, but it is mostly conceded that it was the Scots who perfected the modern game of golf.

2

Modern Golf–Scotland's Gift

Some idea of the age of golf in Scotland can be gleaned from the fact that it was of national importance and popularity in Scotland by 1457. And so, to put it in some historical perspective, golf had achieved some measure of popularity before the birth of Christopher Columbus. We know this because golf was so popular in the fifteenth century that in March of 1457, the parliament of King James II of Scotland issued a decree that it be banned because it was interfering with archery practice—a necessary skill in Scotland's long war with England, its bitter enemy. This decree is the earliest written reference to the game of golf. Interestingly, thirty years previously, the game of "futeball" had been similarly banned while golf was not then prohibited. Thus golf seemingly enjoyed a surge in popularity during this period. However, it seems puzzling for a surge of this magnitude to have occurred in such a short time.

Logic would suggest that golf was likely played in Scotland at least as early as 1400 while before that the continual wars, economic circumstances and rather primitive existences would make the existence of golf somewhat, if not probably, impossible to imagine.

Subsequent Scottish kings, James III and James IV, issued similar edicts banning golf but they were honored more in the breach. All's well that ends well. When James IV married the daughter of King Henry IV of England the warring with England ended, and the Scots entered into a period of

King James IV of Scotland

peace. This boded well for golfers and the popularity of golf extended from the lower classes on up to the royal lineages. One would be remiss if mention of Mary, Queen of Scots were not made. According to legend she was so taken with the game that she played golf a few days after her husband Lord Darnley was murdered. This was purportedly one of the charges leveled against her that cost Mary the crown,

Mary, Queen of Scots returning from golf

and ultimately her head. Golf in those days was an equal opportunity venture, and anyone with clubs, some balls, and the desire for fresh air could take up the game. There were few rules, no golf associations, no member clubs and a paucity of any tournaments, except those of a localized, casual nature. This rather loose, disorganized form of golf in Scotland appears to have carried on for approximately the next three centuries. In the 1700s, the winds of change, such as those that figuratively buffeted the links lands of the Scottish coast, beckoned and progressive changes in the game of golf began to take shape. These changes were fueled by the kindred desire of the golfing community to identify the champion golfer of the land.

3

The Origins of Golf Clubs and Associations

I t is at this point that one should examine the birth of golf clubs in Scotland during the middle of the seventeenth century. During the middle of the seventeenth century golf enthusiasts in Scotland began to organize into associations. In 1744 a milestone in the advancement of organized golf occurred. It is first necessary to understand that until that time, clubs and associations were nowhere to be found. There were no written rules and no established authorities to rule over and provide structure to the game. At best each community had its own unwritten rules adapted to local conditions, and these rules were simple and few.

In March 1744 a group of golfers from the Links of Leith petitioned the city of Edinburgh to provide a silver club for an annual competition over the Links of Leith. These "several Gentlemen of Honour," skillful in the "ancient and healthful exercise of Golf," simply wanted to identify the best golfer and designate him as the "Captain of Golf." This concept in modern times would be referred to as the Champion Golfer, a new term now closely identified with the British Open. The golfer declared as the Captain of Golf would become the Arbitrator of all disputes affecting the game. These Gentlemen of Honour wanted more than a Captain of Golf, so they set about to form a club under the leadership of one William St. Clair—a club called the Gentlemen Golfers of Leith, later called the Honourable Company of Edinburgh Golfers. While this club was not formally recognized by the city of

St. Andrews Swilcan Bridge and the 18th hole

Edinburgh until 1764 many historians date the club back to 1744, since that was the year of the first golf competition—a now-recognized watershed for the establishment of early golf clubs.

Over the next 150 years the Honourable Company of Edinburgh Golfers would move around a number of times but it always kept its name intact. In 1891 it settled in its current home at Muirfield, just to the east of Edinburgh. These Gentlemen Golfers had anticipated a large contingent of golfers from the other links for their inaugural championship in Edinburgh. These "out of towners" would not be familiar with Leith's local rules. So the Gentlemen Golfers devised thirteen rules compiled in a "Golf Manual." These rules form the cornerstone of today's modern rules of golf.

The first of all formalized golf competitions could be described as disappointing. For one thing the lads who entered were all local. Only a dozen men signed up and only ten played. The Silver Club and title of Captain of Golf went to an Edinburgh surgeon named John Rattray. His score was 60 for two trips around the five-hole course. He repeated his victory the following year.

Nonetheless, the Gentlemen Golfers made their mark in three respects: 1) they are credited with establishing the first bona fide club; 2) their modest event is acknowledged as the first organized golf competition; and 3) the competition was largely organized because, for the first known time, golf was played under a set of written rules.

During the next decade or so members of the Honourable Company would take the boat from their then home at Musselburgh to a spot thirty-three miles to the northeast called St. Andrews. The "links" there, close to the sea, proved to be very popular, as the short, weedy grass allowed the ball to roll freely and smoothly. The short grass also made it easier to make contact with the ball, and there was less wear and tear on the clubs and the "featheries"—the golf balls in use at the time.

After about ten years the example of the Honourable Company was adopted by a group of golfers in St. Andrews. On May 14, 1754 twenty-two "Noblemen and Gentlemen" met together to acquire their own Silver Club, a trophy similar to the competition for the Silver Club in Edinburgh. Only four men entered this first competition.The winner was a local merchant, Bailie William Landale. As at Leith the open competition failed to attract outside competitors.

Thinking as the Leith men the St. Andrews men anticipated that outsiders would eventually join their competition, so they too drew up a set of local rules, based largely on those of the Honourable Company. The Leith and St. Andrews rules form the backbone for the Rules of Golf used today. They are translated as follows from the archaic English.

1. You must tee your ball within a club length of the hole.
2. Your tee must be upon the ground.
3. You are not to change the ball with which you strike off the tee.
4. You are not to remove stones, bones, or any break-club for the sake of playing your ball, except upon the fair green, and that only within a club length of your ball.
5. If your ball comes among water or any watery filth, you are at liberty to take out your ball and throw it behind the hazard six yards at least; you may play it with any club, and allow your adversary a stroke for so getting out your ball.
6. If your balls be found anywhere touching one another, you are to lift the first ball until you play the last.
7. At holing you are to play your ball honestly for the hole, and not to play upon your adversary's ball, not lying in your way to the hole.
8. If you should lose your ball by its being taken up or any other way, you are to go back to the spot where you struck last and drop another ball and allow your adversary a stroke for the misfortune.
9. No man at holing his ball is to be allowed to mark his way to the hole with his club or anything else.
10. If a ball is stopped by any person, horse, dog or anything else, the ball so stopped must be played where it lies.
11. If you draw your club in order to strike and proceed so far with your stroke as to be bringing down your club, if then your club should break in any way, it is to be accounted a stroke.
12. He whose ball lies farthest from the hole is obliged to play first.

13. Neither trench, ditch, nor dike made for the preservation of the links, nor the Scholars' Holes, nor the Soldiers' Lines shall be accounted a hazard, but the ball is to be taken out, teed, and played with any iron club.

The "linksland" in and about St. Andrews became the early traditional place of golf. The linksland consisted of sandy deposits left by centuries of receding oceanic tides. It was barren, undulating, wind-swept terrain that separated the beach from the arable land further inland. The wind-swept, rain-whipped courses of the linksland were for the most part not constructed—they simply evolved. St. Andrews was so old that it appeared to exist for centuries. The grasses were fertilized by the droppings of birds, and were trimmed by the likes of rabbits and other grazing animals. Bunkers were formed by sheep seeking shelter from the wind and rain. This combination of elements seems to have predestined golf as the consummate game to be played under adverse geographic and atmospheric circumstances, often with trying and exasperating consequences.

There was no set number of holes for a round of golf. A round consisted of a turn or two around what number of holes the locals happened to have in place. How the number eventually settled at eighteen has attracted one or two stories in explanation. Old lore has it that the Scotsmen played each hole in tandem with a shot of whiskey. With a bottle containing eighteen shots, it was foretold that this led to the standard eighteen holes when each player finished his bottle and his round. Alas, more explanations are founded on sounder factual footings, and St. Andrews can lay claim in its glorious history to being the catalyst for the eighteen-hole round.

In 1764 the Society of St. Andrews Golfers made a dramatic revision to the hallowed ground of their Old Course. At that time the Old Course consisted of eleven holes set out along the shore. Golfers teed off from beside the home hole and played eleven holes out to the far end of the course, then turned and played eleven holes home, playing the same holes as on the outward journey, but in the reverse direction. They finished by holing out at the home hole from which they started. Thus, at this time, a round at St. Andrews consisted of twenty-two holes. In 1764, however, the Royal and Ancient Club of St. Andrews passed a resolution that the first four holes should be converted into two holes. As this change necessarily converted the eleven holes to nine holes, a "round" became 18 holes.

In time the Links of Leith and the Honourable Golfers diminished in influence. Meanwhile, St. Andrews and the Society of St. Andrews Golfers, by a combination of design and happenstance, ascended in authority over all matters relating to golf in Scotland. Since its members felt a duty to establish what was "correct" about golf, eighteen holes in time became the accepted standard throughout Scotland, England, and eventually the world.

Over the next several years the Society of St. Andrews Golfers framed a new set of rules and positioned itself as the preeminent authority on all matters relating to golf. As an example it set the standard width of a cup at 4 ¼ inches. In 1834 King William IV became the patron of the Society and decreed St. Andrews as the "Royal and Ancient Golf Club." This royal decree thus assured that, for all intents and purposes, a lengthy period ensued in which St. Andrews was the last word on golf and all matters relating thereto. At that time, however, there wasn't much golf to oversee. Only seventeen clubs existed. There were fourteen in Scotland, two in England and one in India, where British colonists had taken the game. But the formation of the Honourable Company and the Society of St. Andrews Golfers spurred a rush to establish golf courses throughout golfdom.

Blackheath, the first golf club formed outside of Scotland, was established in England. In 1787 the Glasgow Club was formed as the first golf club west of England.

4

The Early Evolution of the Golf Ball and Golf Clubs

B etween the formation of these early clubs and associations and the invention of the gutta percha golf ball, however, the growth of golf proceeded at a relatively slow pace. One reason was the cost of golf balls.

In the earliest days of golf, balls were, in all likelihood, made of box-wood, similar to those used in the kindred games of *chole* and *jeu de mail*. While these balls had their limitations, they were at least affordable to the masses.

In the early seventeenth century a new ball was adapted. It was called a "featherie" and was slightly larger than today's golf balls, but, at ¾ of an ounce, was half the weight of the modern ball. Featheries were used until the middle of the nineteenth century when gutta percha golf balls appeared on the scene.

The basic procedure to making a featherie was as follows: using the breast feathers of a goose or chicken, boiling the feathers, cutting a sheet of tough, thick leather into three parts, stitching the leather pieces together inside out, leaving a small hole through which to turn it outside in, and then stuffing the feathers into the casing, first by using a hand "stuffer" and after stuffing in feathers much more tightly, using a long awl-like stuffer held against the chest, or under the arm, finally, closing the small hole with a single stitch tied on the outside and painting the ball with several layers

Featheries, circa 1860

of white lead paint. A final step was to soak the ball in alum, which would cause the leather to shrink as it dried, thus making the ball even harder.

It was tedious to make featheries and even the best craftsmen could produce no more than four or five balls a day. This made the featheries, at about a half crown apiece, about twelve times as expensive as wooden balls, thus having an economic effect on the caste of players who could afford to play golf during the period that featheries were in vogue. Clearly, then, only the wealthiest could sustain their passion for the game. Another dire problem with featheries was their durability. They seldom maintained a round shape, and they became waterlogged quite easily. They also often split apart with an off-centered hit by an iron club, which literally could "knock the stuffing" out of it! The advent of the featheries eventually led to the formation of golf clubs and associations, and the evolution of the rules of golf. It also turned the craft of club making into an art and raised the job of caddie (the Scottish spelling of the French word "cadet") to a professional status. Obviously what was needed to address the shortcomings of the featheries was a ball that would be resistant to water, be able to maintain its shape and be inexpensive. This would bring back the masses to the game.

These problems were addressed with the development of the gutta percha ball. The precise origin of the gutta percha golf ball is a matter of some conjecture. However, it is fairly well known that gutta percha material arrived from the Far East and was constructed from the coagulated milk of the Malayan gum tree. A golfer named Robert Paterson played a few holes on the Old Course with a gutta percha ball in April 1855. Apparently the gutta percha material had been used as packing material when Paterson's brother sent a fragile object from India. Robert fashioned the gutta percha material into a golf ball and the seeds were sown. The gutta percha material came in the form of sheets, was boiled in hot water and then formed into a sphere by hand. Then the ball was dropped in cold water where it hardened. One benefit of this ball was that a cracked ball could be repaired by again following the technique of hot and cold water.

The smooth-surfaced gutta percha balls did have a problem—they were tough to get airborne and tended to duck or dive in flight. A professional from Musselburgh named Willie Dunn, who would later be known as a champion golfer, solved this problem. He and caddies at his course noticed that the ball flew better after it had been nicked and scuffed. Thus the second generation of the ball was hammered with dimples to improve its flight. Equipped with this ball thousands of golfers took up the game or returned to it. With demand so high craftsman soon began to produce up to 100 balls a day. Scotland enjoyed a boom in the game throughout the latter part of the nineteenth century, in large part because of the improvement in and affordability of the golf ball.

The arrival of the "gutties," as gutta percha balls became known, was not without its detractors. Opposition was fueled by the featherie makers. The most prominent opponent was Allan Robertson of St. Andrews. He came from a long line of club and ball makers, and was purportedly the finest golfer in the land. He also was the game's first professional who played for money.

Among his chief rivals and his chief apprentice was Tom Morris, Sr. who eventually became the most famous of the early Scottish champions. Robertson was so opposed to the guttie that he required his employees to disavow use of the ball. Morris agreed to this restriction but in a transgression was caught using the guttie. This infraction led to a rift between the two and Morris went his separate way. He opened his own pro shop in St. Andrews making gutties and then later moved to Prestwick where he also became keeper of the green.

Early gutty hand hammered

Soon after Morris left, Robertson had a change of heart regarding the guttie. He realized he could make far more balls and income fabricating the guttie. Also, the guttie made him a better player. To his further credit he determined that the new ball would require a new style of clubs. Up to that point irons were the clubs of the day, the most popular being the cleeks, a form of today's two-iron, and the niblick, which had the loft of about a five-iron. Short pitches from over bunkers were done with a baffing spoon, a short-shafted, deep-faced wood. The guttie was much harder than the featherie and did not compress much upon impact. Consequently, the traditional wooden clubs tended to split and crack upon contact with the guttie.

As a result clubs began to be assembled with shafts of softer wood such as hickory imported from America. The new shafts had less torsion, meaning the club head did not lag so far behind the hands during the downswing. The softer-wooded shafts also were the catalyst for a somewhat radically different swing, from a round-the-body motion to a more upright swing. Changes came about in the club heads as well. Softer beech wood became the standard material for the club heads, as it allowed better absorption of the hit. The club head also became thicker to put more force behind the ball. Complementing these changes in the woods, the irons also enjoyed a transformation. No longer capable of destroying a ball they began to be used for all kinds of approach shots. The cleek took the place of a modern two- or three-iron. Not long after, the very practical golf bag came into play, and with it the increased use of caddies.

One would be remiss if, during any discussion of the advancement in balls and clubs, another invention was not mentioned. That would be the grass mower in the 1850's, which allowed golf to be played on grassland and during the growing season for grass. Another significant invention that improved grass maintenance was the introduction of the gasoline-powered grass mower around 1913.

5

Inauguration of
The Open Championship

In 1858 with his new golf clubs Allan Robertson became the first golfer to break 80 over the Old Course at St. Andrews. Sadly, the following year, Robertson died at the age of forty-four from an attack of hepatitis. In the meantime Tom Morris and his wife had a boy, named Tom, Jr., who eventually made his own mark in golf.

Robertson's untimely demise opened the way for a new group of golfers to ascend to the list of champions. So Prestwick, Tom Morris's club, reckoned it was time to announce a championship for professional golfers. Instead of the customary medal a red belt was the prize for the champions and permanent possession went to the golfer who could win it three years in a row. The initial tournament at Prestwick in 1860 attracted a field of eight professional golfers. Willie Park was the first winner. Tom Morris finished second, two shots behind. The high scores emboldened the amateurs of the day to feel that they could win the championship themselves. So the tournament was declared "open to all the world," and it has remained so ever since. Hence was born the Open Championship.

Tom Morris and Willie Park won seven of the next eight championships. The tournament was held at Prestwick from 1860 to 1872. In 1867 Morris won for the last time at the age of forty-six, which makes him still the oldest British Open Champion. Who else but Morris's son, Tom Morris, Jr., won the Championship the following year in 1868 at the age of seventeen, making him the youngest to win the Championship, and he still is to this day. This legendary father-son duo became forever known as Old Tom and Young Tom. Old Tom was the runner-up to Young Tom in 1868 and 1869. Young Tom also won in 1870, which entitled him to permanent possession of the belt. No Championship was held in 1871 because no one offered a prize to replace the belt, but Young Tom came back to win in 1872 when a claret jug was offered as the prize. Thus, he achieved the amazing feat of four championships in a row.

Young Tom might have won many more British Opens had he not died suddenly at the age of twenty-four. In 1875 his wife and child died in childbirth. On Christmas morning of the same year Young Tom was found dead in his bed. His death was caused either by pneumonia or by a broken blood vessel in his head—another bit of unresolved golf history. Lore has it that he actually died of a broken heart, and one of the largest gravestones in St. Andrews Cemetery marks Young Tom's burial site. Old Tom outlived his son by thirty-seven years, and he spent that time at The Royal & Ancient Golf Club as greenskeeper. With his long gray beard, tweed cap, and pipe Old Tom was an institution to those who stopped by the pro shop at St. Andrews. He died in 1908 at the age of eighty-six.

Soon after Young Tom's death two other professionals mounted an attack on his record of four consecutive British Open victories. It should be noted that by this time the Open Championship was being rotated among the courses at St. Andrews, Prestwick and Musselburgh. Jamie Anderson of St. Andrews won from 1877 through 1879. He was followed by Robert Ferguson from Musselburgh, who triumphed from 1880 to 1882 but missed a fourth consecutive British Open in 1883, when he lost in a play-off to Willie Fernie.

The next great player was an amateur with the apt name of John Ball. Ball's British Open victory in 1890 also made him the first Englishman to win the title. By 1890 Ball was already enjoying his second victory in the British Amateur. This gave him the unique British double of being the champion of the British Open and British Amateur. He went on to win the British Amateur a breathtaking total of eight times. Two years after Ball's win in the 1890 British Open, Muirfield was added to the Open rotation. To the consternation of Scottish professionals the winner in 1892 was another British amateur, Harold Hilton. He repeated his British Open victory in 1897, and added four British Amateur titles to his résumé. His best-known achievement occurred in 1911, when he won both the British and the U.S. Amateurs. Besides Matthew Fitzpatrick in 2013, no other Englishman has ever won the U.S. Amateur.

In 1894 the weakening of the Scottish dominance in the British Open was becoming more apparent. The winner that year was an Englishman, John Henry Taylor. J.H. Taylor, as he was known, won the British Open at Royal St. George's in Sandwich, the first time it was played in England. He played a unique style of attacking the greens with his approach shots, giving him a deadly accuracy. He successfully defended his title in 1895 at St. Andrews. One of the players in the field in both years was another Englishman, Harry Vardon. When the Open Championship moved to Muir-field in 1896 Vardon beat Taylor in a 36-hole play-off. This started Vardon's phenomenal career as part of "the Great Triumvirate" which also included James Braid and planted the seeds for the modern era of golf.

6

The Great Triumvirate

Harry Vardon was born in 1870 in the village of Grouville in Jersey, England, the first of a notable list of golfers to come from the Channel Islands. When he first appeared on the scene and made his fledgling appearance felt, he was 24. Golf and, in particular, British golf, was ready to enjoy a golden age.

In the last decade of the nineteenth century and the early part of the twentieth century the game would be dominated by three golfers known as"the Great Triumvirate." There was J.H. Taylor, a West countryman of Vardon, James Braid, a Scotsman and, of course, the indisputable leader, Vardon. The three of them dominated the Open Championships until World War I, chalking up an amazing total of sixteen wins in the twenty-one-year period between 1894 and 1914. They may have won more except that there were no Championships during the period of World War I between 1914 and 1919. At Sandwich in 1894 J.H. Taylor had, of course, opened the floodgates for the Great Triumvirate. He won again in 1895, 1900, 1909, and 1913. James Braid triumphed with a string of wins in 1901, 1905, 1906, 1908, and 1910. To the relief of his countrymen he was the heroic Scot who led Scotland's involvement in the Open Championships. Vardon, the Open record holder earned the silver claret a record six times. He was the Champion Golfer in 1896, 1898, 1899, 1903, 1911, and 1914.

The Great Triumvirate: J.H. Taylor, James Braid and Harry Vardon

Vardon brought innovation to the game. Aside from his fine play his service to the game in several aspects further secured his place in the his-

Above, *Ted Ray, James Braid, and Harry Vardon, along with J.H. Taylor dominated European golf from the 1890s to the early part of the twentieth century.*
Left, *J.H. Taylor*

tory of modern golf. Any golfer of more than a casual acquaintance with the game has heard of the Vardon grip. While of normal stature Vardon possessed enormous hands. His famous "Vardon Grip"—the little finger of the right hand crooked under the index finger of the left hand—was not his invention, (lore has it that Johnny Laidlay, a Scottish amateur, first employed the overlapping grip) but Vardon popularized it. This grip is the standard grip used today. Using this grip Vardon preferred a soft feel with the club. Before Vardon there was no standard style for hitting the ball. Many golfers adhered to a style of an exaggerated swing around the body with a severely closed stance. Vardon changed all that. First he repositioned the ball forward with a slightly open stance. This stance allowed for a sweeping upward swing to project the ball farther into the air, in contrast to the low flying shots fashioned by the likes of Old and Young Tom Morris.

Vardon also introduced the easy, simple, graceful, upright swing which is the foundation of today's modern swing. It is generally acknowledged that this swing was much more adaptable to a repeating style that promotes the consistency and accuracy necessary to play good golf. Vardon not only used the upright swing, he wrote about it, too. While he was not the first to author a golf instructional book he was among the first to produce a bestseller in which he described his methods for perfecting the golf swing. Vardon's *The Complete Golfer*, published in 1905, is still considered a classic of the genre. His writing extended to four other full-length books, ending with *Vardon on Golf*, a composite of individual chapters and other material from the four previously published books.

CHAPTER

7

The Birth of Golf
in the United States

The earliest reference to golf in the United States comes from an ordinance of Fort Orange, New York—the old name of Albany, New York. Dealing with complaints that golf was being played in the public streets and causing damage the town fathers passed an ordinance banning the playing of golf in the streets. The ordinance is dated December 10, 1659.

Rumor also has it that, based on some old pamphlets, a golf club of sorts had been formed in Charleston, South Carolina—perhaps a form of golf played on a few acres of land. The date was 1786.

Another early reference to the game of golf in the United States occurred in an advertisement by an Englishman named James Rivington. His advertisement, dated April 21, 1797, was placed in *The Royal Gazette*, published in New York City. Rivington had received a set of clubs and feathery balls from Scotland and advertised them for sale. Whether or not he sold them is unknown.

There is evidence of a club having been formed in 1796 in Savannah, Georgia. This evidence consisted primarily of an invitation from the year 1811 sent out by members of the club for a New Year's ball in honor of a Miss Eliza Johnston. The invitation came from "Members of the Golf Club." There is little other evidence that a golf club existed and, in any event, the War of 1812 may have contributed to the club's demise. Thus, like "The

John Reid, the Father of American Golf.

Lost Colony," there is no answer as to what happened to the Savannah Golf Club. Finally, there is evidence that the first golf course was Foxburg Golf Club, established in Western Pennsylvania by a man named Joseph Fox in 1887. This nine-hole course has ostensibly been in continuous play since that time.

For the next seventy years or so, golf seems to have faded into the background until another tantalizing story arose. It comes from White Sulphur Springs, West Virginia. There again is evidence that, in 1884, some New Englanders built a club called Oakhurst at a private estate. The club appears to have died out after a few years as there is no further reference to Oakhurst. However, support can be garnered to raise the possibility that Oakhurst was, in fact, the first golf club in the United States. This also is a matter of not insubstantial debate, given the aforementioned snippets evolving around Charleston and Savannah.

While each of these events can find its supporters to lay claim as the birthplace of American golf the popular sentiment finds its link between a linen merchant named Robert Lockhart and Old Tom Morris. Lockhart was a native of Dunfermline, Scotland, not far from St. Andrews. He immigrated to the United States but his job as a linen merchant found him traveling back home with some regularity. Lockhart was an avid golfer and learned to play the game on the Mussleburgh links. A man named John Reid, like Lockhart, was a transplanted Scotsman living in Yonkers, New York. He and Lockhart were schoolmates in Dunfermline. Reid was a top executive of the J. L. Mott Iron Works in Mott Haven, New York. As the story goes, by 1880, this success in his career allowed Reid to explore various forms of recreation. Lockhart frequently returned to the United States with gifts for his friends, including Reid. One time he returned with tennis racquets and balls for Reid. Reid even went so far as to construct a tennis court on his front lawn to play with his friends. To the good fortune of golf this interest in tennis never quite inspired Reid as golf would.

A few years later Reid and his friends decided to give golf a go since word had it that the game was capturing the hearts of Englishmen. Even better, it was a Scottish sport and—as time would prove true—Reid, with his loyalty to things Scottish, felt that there must be something to this game of golf. In the late summer of 1887, Lockhart made another visit to Scotland. Whether he purchased clubs on his own initiative or through the urgings of Reid, Lockhart stopped by the shop of Old Tom Morris at St. Andrews. There he purchased six clubs—a driver brassie (equivalent to today's 2-wood), a spoon (3-wood), a cleek (2 iron), a sand iron, and a putter, along with two dozen gutta percha balls. He arranged for these purchases to be shipped to his home in New York. Lockhart was not and did not become an avid player. He tested the clubs out at his home in New York City and then sent them to Reid at the latter's home in Yonkers. Thus did Lockhart drift into the background of the history of golf. His friend Reid subsequently assumed the role of, and became known as, "the Father of American Golf."

Reid had planned to wait until the spring of 1888 to try out the new clubs. However, a mid-winter thaw around George Washington's birthday in February 1888 presented Reid with the anticipated opportunity he had so eagerly awaited. On that 22nd of February, Reid could wait no longer. He invited six of his old sporting friends to his home in Yonkers. They laid out three rudimentary holes in the pasture across the street from Reid's home on Lake Avenue. Since they had but six clubs it was decided that two of them would play at a time. The two lucky lads were, of course, Reid and his friend John P. Upham. The four others present were Henry O. Tallmadge, who lived next door to the pasture, another neighbor, Kingman H. Putnam, Harry Holbrook and Alexander P. W. Kinnan. No scores were kept that day. All six became immediately enraptured with the game as played on February 22 in its ever- so rudimentary infancy on American soil.

The "Blizzard of '88" descended on Yonkers on March 12 and this precluded any more golf for a time. When warm spring weather returned, the golfers returned to the pasture for more of this enticing game. In the interim they had obtained enough clubs and balls from Scotland for all six of them to play. In April they decided that they needed a bigger course and built a six-hole course on a plot of land owned by their local butcher. This they used as their course throughout the summer and fall. The new course, despite its longer length, bore little resemblance to the Scottish links. The greens were circles of about twelve feet in diameter, and were only slightly less bumpy than the rest of the turf—hardly the look of fairways either. These pioneers of golf also established the first "nineteenth hole"—a table manned by one of Reid's servants who handled the beverages. On November 14, 1888 Reid and his friends played a round of golf and then four of Reid's guests retired to his home for dinner. Reid's guests were Holbrook, Putnam, Tallmadage, and Upham. After dinner the group established a club, drew up a proposed membership list and elected officers. John Reid was elected president and, at his suggestion, the club was named St. Andrew's (with an apostrophe) in the hopes that it would instill interest in the way that its namesake St. Andrews (no apostrophe) had done in Scotland.

There were good reasons to form the club before the next season presented itself in 1889. For one thing expenses were anticipated to be higher, and a club could handle this not-so mundane matter better than golfers acting as individuals. Also, the founding members anticipated that it wouldn't be long before other townspeople would want to join the play and the best way to handle this was through the formation of a club. Once the club was formed that evening it was resolved that Reid and Upham would devise a set of rules and regulations for St. Andrew's. Before adjourning for the evening the five men proposed a toast to Robert Lockhart, who had introduced them to the game. The club then honored Lockhart by electing him as the first member of the club. These incorporating resolutions were duly recorded in the minute book of the club. In a sense these represented the "Magna Carta" or Constitution of the club. Thus, it is this day, November 14, 1888, that is generally recognized as the birthday and official beginning of golf in the United States. And because he founded St. Andrew's, John Reid is almost unanimously recognized as the Father of American Golf. From that date of commencement of St. Andrew's, golf took off, slowly at first. Five years later, there would be a handful of clubs. Ten years later, clubs were appearing in abundance. By the turn of the century golf was spreading by leaps and bounds, and there were at least a thousand clubs in existence.

The next few seasons of St. Andrew's passed in relative tranquility. The membership rose to thirteen people and there was occasional discussion of expanding the course but no action was taken. Interestingly, Reid opposed the expansion of the club and the golf course. After a while the City of Yonkers began the process of expanding a street named Palisade Avenue farther north, right through the middle of St. Andrew's. So the club decided to head north to find a less confining site. St. Andrew's relocated four blocks to a thirty-four-acre apple orchard. The scenic property overlooked the Hudson River, and sloped severely to a valley below. Of course, apple trees were in abundant supply. Reid and his fellow members laid out the course in a single day. They did so without having to cut even one apple tree and threaded the course through the stands of trees. They constructed a six-hole layout of 1,500 yards, steeply banked with trees appearing ominously and challenging at every turn.

The golfers soon became known by the moniker the "Apple Tree Gang." This was because of one tree in particular, which loomed near the first tee and the last green, served the versatile purposes of locker room (the players slung their coats, lunches, and wicker containers of Scotch in the tree branches) and the nineteenth hole. Around the circumference of the tree was a circular bench large enough to seat all thirteen members and thus serve as the first lounge. The signature apple tree has long since disappeared but two branches remain. One hangs in the current clubhouse of St. Andrew's in Mt. Hope, New York. The other, a gift of the Yonkers club in 1923, rests in the Royal and Ancient Golf Club in St. Andrews, Scotland. As time progressed and other clubs began to sprout up across America, Reid and his fellow members moved to a new plot of land three miles away and built a nine-hole layout on Odell Farms at Grey Oaks. The course measured 2,382 yards and took only two days to construct.

With dozens of courses springing up across the country, many of them eighteen-hole layouts, St. Andrew's felt constrained to move and build again. Its membership roll also had expanded to well over one hundred people. This time, in 1897, and after three years at Odell Farms, the members approved a bond issue and purchased 160 acres of densely wooded land, a couple of miles up the valley. The price was $65,000. A clubhouse was built for another $65,000, the mortgage of $50,000 being personally signed by Andrew Carnegie, by then a member of the club. This move to Mt. Hope, New York proved to be the permanent home of St. Andrew's Golf Club, where it exists to this day. The original Mt. Hope course measured over

5,000 yards and played with nary a level hole as they were laid out sidehill, uphill, and downhill. Over one hundred years later the course has been lengthened by over 1,000 yards and has been redesigned by Jack Nicklaus. Yet it retains much of its original characteristics.

The Mt. Hope course was maintained in excellent shape for its day. The club hired a manger and golf professional, one Samuel Tucker, a young Scotsman who began offering lessons and repairing golf clubs. Of considerable importance in those days without lawnmowers and tractors were the durable horses. Showing their versatility they pulled the machinery that sculpted the new course and maintained it after construction. Additionally, horses were used for transportation by members of the club. As already noted the previous sites of St. Andrew's were relatively flat but the Mr. Hope location was five miles north of Yonkers and sat at the top of a long and steep hill. Thus horses became an indispensable part of the Mt. Hope site. An era ended in late 1897 when John Reid retired as president. By this time St. Andrew's was a decade old and American golf was flourishing. Within another decade there were roughly 2,000 golf courses in the United States —more than in the rest of the world combined.

In 1891, for the first time, the United States had a course that looked similar to a modern course. The course was built out on eastern Long Island at Southampton. The architect was Willie Dunn, a young Scottish professional who was both a golf pro and an architect. The course was backed by William K. Vanderbilt and some of his associates. To construct the course Dunn used a crew of 150 Indians from the nearby Shinnecock Reservation, and a number of horse-drawn roadscrapers. When Dunn was done with his work he had built a well-regarded seaside links named Shinnecock Hills Golf Club. It eventually became one of America's renowned courses, and enjoys a highly regarded reputation today, having hosted four U.S. Opens. A mere eighteen months after Dunn had surveyed the windswept and treeless acreage upon which he built the course, its reputation spread, and the officers of the club decided to limit the membership to those of a certain social elite. In addition to being the first golf course on Long Island, Shinnecock Hills was the first golf club to be incorporated, the first to have an architect-designed opulent clubhouse, and the first to have a waiting list!

Clubs began to spring up with each passing month on the East Coast and in the Midwest. In the Boston area a young woman by the name of Florence Boit returned to the United States, after a spell in Europe, to spend the summer of 1892 with her aunt and uncle. She had learned to play golf at

Pau, in the French Pyrenees. She introduced the game to several prominent Bostonians. One of the young men, Laurence Curtis, who learned the game of golf from Boit, was so enamored of the game, that he wrote a letter to the executives of The Country Club, in Brookline, Massachusetts, urging the club to give the game a trial. Not too long after golf took hold in Brookline —and The Country Club would play a prominent role in the popularity of golf after it held the historic U.S. Open of 1913.

Stepping back several years to 1890, golf was introduced to Newport, Rhode Island—at that time a prominent sailing venue. There is some support for the notion that the Brenton's Point course at Newport was the first nine-hole course in the country. The course stemmed from the impetus of a wealthy gentleman named Theodore A. Havemeyer. He fanned the interest of the moneyed set in this wealthy summer colony and became the president of the Newport Golf Club, which then became the Newport Country Club. Years later, the trophy for the winner of the U.S. Amateur Championship was named after Havemeyer. Cornelius Vanderbilt and John Jacob Astor, among other prominent Americans, belonged to the Brenton's Point Club.

New York City built the nation's first public golf course of nine holes at Van Cortlandt Park in the Bronx. A nine-hole course in Tuxedo, New York was formed in 1894. It enjoys the distinction of purportedly inviting the Shinnecock Hills Club to a seven-a-side team match in 1894 at Tuxedo. This appears to have been the first inter-club match played in the United States. Meanwhile, clubs were springing up in Philadelphia, Baltimore, and Washington, D.C. North of the border the Royal Montreal Golf Club was already flourishing, having been constructed back in 1873. It lays claim to being the first golf course in North America. The first eighteen-hole golf course was the Chicago Golf Club, built in 1893 by Charles Macdonald.

Other courses were being built throughout the 1890s and captured a list of firsts. The Lake Champlain Hotel in New York built the first hotel course. Van Cortland Park in New York was the first recognized public course. The Philadelphia Country Club was the first club to use the cylindrical holes that are used today. A team of golfers from The Country Club of Brookline played in the first international team matches against a squad from the Royal Montreal Golf Club.

8

Further Evolution of the Golf Ball

Up to the 1850s golf balls were made of a leather covering stuffed with feathers. When stuffed with feathers the balls, or "featheries" became quite hard. The balls were made by professional ball makers who usually had standing orders to provide them to various golfing societies.

Most of the golf balls dating from the nineteenth century were made in Scotland and were marked with the maker's name. Among the more prominent makers were Allan Robertson, Old Tom Morris, the Gourlays, Willie Dunn, and Jamie Dunn.

In the late 1840s other methods of constructing golf balls were attempted and, by 1850, balls molded out of gutta percha were becoming commonplace. The new balls were easier to produce and were much more economical. This relative inexpensive ball enabled many more people to take up the game.

Golfers soon discovered that gutta percha balls flew better after they had been used for a while. The nicked up balls had better aerodynamic qualities and in the 1850s ball makers began to purposely nick up the balls prior to sale. By the 1870s most smooth ball moulds had been replaced with ones that would place consistent markings in a regular pattern.

The golf ball was further improved during the 1870s when material such as ground-up cork, leather and other items began to be incorporated

Evolution of the golf ball

into the pure gutta percha. The composition ball was referred to as a "gutty" while the pure gutta percha ball continued to be called a "gutta." Although the rubber core ball was introduced in 1899 the gutty continued to be used until about 1910. By making the game of golf cheaper the gutta ball created a boom in the game in Scotland but the hard ball was not without defects of its own. It made the game distinctly hard work, for the player had to learn how to get the ball airborne and its unyielding hardness could give an unpleasant jolt to a player's arm if he mis-hit a shot with an iron club. While all the building of new golf clubs was underway in the 1890s the gutta percha ball was still the ball to use. And one of the most popular was the Vardon Flyer. But by the time that the Englishman Harry Vardon had returned from his 1900 tour of the United States, the Vardon Flyer was about to become obsolete but not without a tift.

The change came about with the advent of the rubber-cored ball late in the nineteenth century. Coburn Haskell was a wealthy sportsman originally from New England who migrated to Cleveland, Ohio. He combined forces with an associate, Bertram Work, and they developed an idea for a golf ball having a center of rubber thread wound under tension. They thought that their concept would produce a golf ball with liveliness not attainable with the hard gutta percha ball. Haskell was a talented individual. He was a bicycle maker, outdoorsman, horse racer, entrepreneur and, as it turned out, inventor. Haskell was also a successful businessman and "fair-to-middlin'" golfer at the Portage Golf Club near Cleveland, Ohio. Like golfers of that era he was not at all satisfied with the gutta percha ball's performance and he frequently thought about substances from which a superior ball could be fashioned. One day in 1898 he visited the office of Bertram Work, an engineer with the B.F. Goodrich Rubber Company in Akron, Ohio. Work invited Haskell to take a tour around the workplace. Haskell did just that and noticed a scrap basket full of elastic thread. He almost immediately hit upon an idea. He could wind those thin strands of rubber around a small rubber ball and wrap the assemblage with a gutta percha cover. While the idea was simplistic, wrapping several hundred feet of elastic proved to be harder than one could imagine.

Eventually Haskell was able to form a ball using this technique and he convinced Work's company to make the gutta percha cover for it. Together, he and Work perfected the mechanical means by which the strips could be wrapped around an elastic cover under tension. They submitted their patent application to the U. S. Patent Office on August 9, 1898. It was granted the following year. Just as the gutta percha ball did not enjoy instant success, the rubber-bound ball had a similar debut. It too had an early tendency to duck and dive in flight. This problem was addressed when the thin outside covering was changed from gutta percha to balata gum and the dimples on it were deepened and formed into patterns. With these changes the carry distance increased an average of twenty yards, and the Haskell ball would soon overtake the gutta percha ball as the ball preferred among golfers.

The Haskell balls were soon called the "Bounding Billies" because the new balls were harder to control around the green than the old gutties but a golfer did not have to strike them perfectly to achieve a reasonably straight shot. Moreover, the balls traveled farther, enhancing the popularity of golf among weekend players.

After short-hitting Walter Travis used the Haskell ball to win the 1901 U.S. Amateur the ball was embraced by American golfers. The invention was significantly improved when a man named John Gameter who, like Bertram Work, was an employee of the B.F. Goodrich Company, invented a machine to wind the cores which originally had been wound by hand. Soon the B.F. Goodrich Company was mass-producing Haskell balls on automatic winding machines. The Staughton Rubber Company then devised an improved cover made of balata. One Jack Jolly came up with the idea for a liquid center for the ball.

The pattern of choice on the Haskell ball became known as the "bramble" pattern. The story has been told that James Foulis, the golf professional at Chicago Golf Club, and winner of the 1896 U. S. Open, unwittingly put a Haskell ball into a ball press that produced a raised, bramble pattern. The ball was improved over other Haskell balls. It traveled farther and could be struck with greater accuracy. Thus, the bramble pattern was adopted as the ball-cover pattern of choice. A. G. Spalding bought the American rights, and by 1903 the dimple cover had become the standard. It soon became clear that indentations rather than bumps produced far better results. And so ingenuity prevailed again when an Englishman, William Taylor, patented the dimpled cover in 1905.

Other manufacturers became engrossed in increasing the distance of the early brands of golf balls. The secret was thought to be the makeup of the inner core. Various manufacturers experimented with different kinds of liquids and hard core centers. After the gutta percha Vardon Flyer fell out of favor Spalding introduced a rubber ball, the Wizard, in 1903. Spalding followed that with the introduction of a cover made of balata, a natural rubber that adhered to the rubber windings inside the ball far better than gutta percha strips did. This made the ball easier to control. Another advancement came in 1905, when Spalding introduced the first true white ball to replace the black material painted white.

The British were less willing to accept the Haskell ball, calling it, in the words of Old Tom Morris, as "nae gowf," [not golf] or referring to it as "the ball for the tired man." That negative view, however, was soon to change. After Travis's victory in the 1901 U.S. Amateur the Haskell ball made its way across the Atlantic to England. Among the most vocal opponents of the Haskell ball was Sandy Herd, a perennial contender for the British Open, who denounced the ball up to the advent of the 1902 British Open. During a practice round he was given a Haskell ball by the appropriately known amateur John Ball. Herd was so impressed with the ball that he put it in play, and won the Open by one stroke over Harry Vardon, who was still playing the ill-fated Vardon Flyer. Herd was the only player in the field to use the Haskell ball. The British adoption of the Haskell ball was soon complete. Shortly thereafter, an Englishman, Horace Hutchinson, wrote in 1903, "[w]e accept the American invention, as Britons will, of course, but with grumblings deep in our hearts."

The original wound rubber balls were light and large, about 1.55 ounces and 1.7 inches in diameter. Since there were no standards governing these measurements the improved performance suddenly threatened to make existing courses obsolete, much like the effect of new equipment on the modern era of courses. In 1920 the United States Golf Association

(U.S.G.A.) and the Royal and Ancient Golf Club of St. Andrews (the R & A), the two recognized governing bodies of golf, agreed on ball parameters. As of May 21, 1920, balls used in their competitions could not weigh any more than 1.62 ounces and could not measure less than 1.62 inches in diameter. Over the next decade the U.S.G.A. experimented with different limits. For a period of time, a lighter ball was standard, but it proved too light to stay in flight or hold the green. In 1932 the new U.S.G.A. rules were 1.62 ounces and 1.68 inches in diameter. These standards still apply today. The R & A held to the original 1.62/1.62 combination for a time. As America came to dominate the game and the equipment, the British gradually ceded to the larger ball in 1990.

Through the post-World War II era the ball's characteristics and performance did not change. There were improvements in the cover to minimize the cuts the balls endured, but the biggest changes came in 1972 when Spalding introduced the two-piece Top-Flite ball, constructed with a solid core inside a durable synthetic cover. At first it sacrificed control for greater distance and was an instant success. Today the modern ball is not a single ball with straightforward characteristics. Instead, there are two-piece and three-piece balls promoting different flight patterns, feel and distance and aligned with different levels of play. In short the golf ball has become a game of marketing in and of itself. And while the Titleist brand continues to reign supreme, it faces a constant barrage of new balls introduced by multiple manufacturers seeking to make their own inroads into the multimillion dollar golf ball market.

9

New Equipment

As with the featherie and the gutta percha balls that preceded it, the Haskell ball required alterations in clubs. The softer wound ball needed a harder wood, and persimmon was the new wood of choice. Woods were fitted with iron inserts. Irons were made larger to give the livelier ball more time on the clubface. The short scoring irons were manufactured with deeper grooves to impart more spin and improve control.

If there ever was an acorn from which a great tree grew it came in the impact of another smallish invention—the golf tee. It made its debut shortly after the Haskell ball did. For hundreds of years players "teed" their ball up by taking a pinch of sand and a cup of water to form a tiny mound on which they set the ball. One of the early jobs of caddies was to shape these little knobs of sand. By the turn of the century golfers were ready for some new device to get the golf ball airborne from the teeing box.

In 1899 George F. Grant patented the wooden tee (US Patent 638920) after decades in which every imaginable material and item was used for a tee—among them, rubber, cardboard and steel. Grant graduated from the Harvard Dental School and, while he was a student of golf, he allegedly had a distaste for dirtying his hands with every tee shot. As the story goes, his dental background influenced his desire to keep his hands clean. Grant had his tees made in Boston and never tried to sell them. Instead he handed

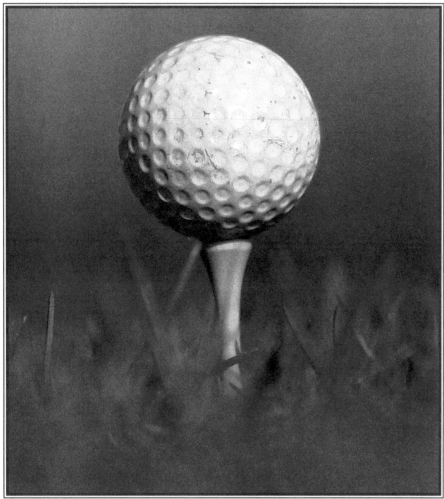

The golf tee

them out to his friends. Surprisingly, another dentist was to become the successful marketer of wooden golf tees. William Lowell, of Maplewood, New Jersey, patented and marketed the Reddy Tee in 1920. He eventually reached a deal with F. W. Woolworth to stock their stores with the new invention. Lowell enjoyed success until his patent expired in 1933 and other manufacturers entered the business.

10

The Founding of the
United States Golf Association
(U.S.G.A.)

After the founding of St. Andrew's in New York golf courses were springing up in other parts of the country. Among them were Shinnecock Hills Golf Club, Newport Golf Club, The Country Club and the Chicago Golf Club. On December 22, 1895, at the Calumet Club, on the corner of Fifth Avenue and Twenty-ninth Street in New York City, delegates of these five prominent clubs met to discuss the formation of an association of golf clubs. The delegates were John Reid and Henry Tallmadge from St. Andrew's, Theodore Havemeyer and Winthrop Rutherford from Newport Golf Club, Laurence Curtis and Samuel Sears from The Country Club, Charles Macdonald and Arthur Ryerson from the Chicago Golf Club and Samuel Parrish from Shinnecock Hills Golf Club.

Theodore Havemeyer was the driving force behind the meeting. He, Laurence Curtis and Henry Tallmadge had become increasingly concerned that a war of words between the Midwestern contingent led by Macdonald and the self-styled prominent clubs in the East would spiral down into a series of continuing controversies. Havemeyer felt that there was a real need for a governing body to settle controversies among clubs, to establish a set of laws in the United States that all golfers and clubs would be bound to follow, and to establish a uniform system of handicapping. And, of course, the governing body was to "decide on what links the Amateur and Open Championships shall be played," and to conduct such championships.

Theodore Havemeyer was one of the founders of the U.S.G.A. and served as its first president.

There followed the meeting at the Calumet Club and the Amateur Golf Association of the United States was formed. Havemeyer was elected its first president. In part, his election was due to his great wealth, which would be instrumental in convincing other clubs to join. His wealth also would be helpful in boosting the Association's start-up funding. Charles Macdonald had lobbied hard for the presidency but had to settle for being named second vice-president. Because the Association was going to conduct Amateur and Open Championships the members shortly thereafter changed the name to the American Golf Association. Not too long after that, the name was changed again to the eventual title of United States Golf Association (U.S.G.A.).

Havemeyer succeeded in bringing into the U.S.G.A. practically all the other prominent golf clubs, which was quite a feat given that many of them had been miffed at not being included among the original founders. Havemeyer also donated a striking trophy for the U. S. Amateur Championship.

Macdonald played a prominent role even though he was not in charge. As a long-time officer of the U.S.G.A. he was instrumental in drafting its constitution, and worked hard to see that the game in the United States conformed to the way that it was played in Scotland. In this regard, he advocated a single set of rules, convincing the U.S.G.A. and the R & A to create an almost unified set of rules. As it turned out over the decades the two entities have worked side-by-side to review the rules every two years, and thereby fulfill Macdonald's quest.

11

Charles B. Macdonald–
His Role in the Establishment
of American Golf

He has been called a sycophant and an egomaniac but there is no doubt that Charles Blair Macdonald played a prominent role in the development of the U.S.G.A, the birth of the Amateur and Open Championships, the standardization of the rules of golf and, perhaps most noteworthy, the architecture of golf courses at the turn of the century. In short, many have credited him with contributing more to the advancement of golf in America than any other person of his generation. While the leaders of the Eastern establishment were keenly aware that St. Andrews in Scotland had designated eighteen holes as comprising a round of golf, they were wary of expanding the game until they had become convinced that the game would meld into a permanent institution. Not so Charles Macdonald, who had migrated back to Chicago after being educated at the United Colleges of St. Salvador and St. Leonard's in St. Andrews. There he met up with Old Tom Morris and became an unabashed student of the game.

In Chicago the golfers under Macdonald's leadership were not about to wait for golf to take hold. Less than twelve months after the game was introduced in Chicago, Macdonald founded and designed the Chicago Golf Club, the first eighteen-hole course in the United States. The course opened in 1895, which also was the year that the first U.S. Amateur and Open Championships were conducted.

Macdonald was a very good golfer and considered himself to be the

*The National Golf Links of America–Charles Macdonald's
masterpiece in Southampton on Long Island.*

best player in the United States if not beyond. With his usual consummate zeal he set out to win the U.S. Amateur in the same way he approached other goals—with a spirit and an accompanying ego that would not allow anything to impede his aims. Macdonald first made a run at what was perceived to be the first U .S. Amateur Championship in September 1894 at the Newport Golf Club, a nine-hole course that bordered the Atlantic Ocean. The Club played host to twenty of the nation's best players in a stroke play competition of eighteen-hole rounds played over two days. Of course the strapping thirty-eight-year old Macdonald by force of physique and personality was the overwhelming favorite. Surprisingly, Macdonald did not win that initial event.

In the opening round over the Newport course he shot an 89 and led the field by four strokes. Inexplicably, on the second day, Macdonald's score rose to an even 100 strokes and he lost to a Newport member named W. G. Lawrence. Of note two of the strokes were for a ball lodged against a stone wall. Macdonald immediately began a protest. He challenged the manner in which Newport conducted the event and refused to recognize Lawrence as the champion. One of his complaints was that the stone wall did not constitute a true hazard and taking away the two-stroke penalty would have put him in a tie for the championship. Lastly Macdonald claimed that a true championship could not be conducted at stroke play, but only at match play.

Making a major concession to Macdonald, in part because they felt that he might be right, there was agreement to hold a match play event the following month. Macdonald won his first two matches to reach the semifinals. In a rash act of poor judgment, however, Macdonald engaged in a premature celebration by attending a party on the eve of his semi-final match against his nemesis, W. G. Lawrence. Nevertheless Macdonald prevailed in the match by 2 & 1 (Macdonald was up by two holes with only one hole left to play, and, thus, was the winner). Again, in an act of poor judgment, Macdonald consumed a bottle of champagne before his final round against Lawrence Stoddard, a member of Newport Golf Club. Macdonald played poorly but managed to find himself all even after eighteen holes. However, in the first play-off hole, a sliced tee shot spelled doom for him.

In keeping with his bluster and intimidating force of personality Macdonald dismissed Stoddard as he had Lawrence. At this point the U.S.G.A. concluded that something had to be done to avoid having American golf become the personal fiefdom of the mercurial Macdonald. Once again he refused to recognize the winner, Stoddard, as the national champion. He argued that Stoddard had won an invitation tournament sponsored by one club, and one club could not represent an entire nation. He said further that a national championship would have to have the approval of all clubs in the nation, and those clubs would have to be joined in an official organization. Thereupon, the U.S.G.A. held another "first" Amateur championship, returning to Newport for the tournament during the first three days of October 1895.

Macdonald was again the heavy favorite and this time he prevailed. With little opposition and his own good play he sailed through to the finals, where he defeated Charles E. Sands 12 & 11. Sands hardly posed much of a test since he was a young tennis buff who only three months previously had taken up golf.

Almost as an afterthought the U.S.G.A. also held its first U.S. Open Championship the very next day. The winner was twenty-one-year old Horace Rawlings, who shot a one-day score of 91-87-178 to defeat a field of nine other professionals and a lone amateur. He won $150. The runner-up was Willie Dunn who had been the architect for Shinnecock Golf Club.

The Women's U.S. Amateur Championship was played at Meadow Brook, on Long Island. A score of 69-63-132 over eighteen holes was good enough for Mrs. Charles S. Brown (Lucy Barnes) to defeat seventeen other players.

For a variety of reasons Macdonald's winning the U.S. Amateur Championship was held in higher esteem than Rawlins's U.S. Open Championship. For one thing the Amateur was played by sportsmen who played the game for fun. On the other hand the Open was primarily for professionals who, while generally the better golfers, belonged to a lower social stratum.

Although he tried many times Macdonald never won the U.S. Amateur again. However, the Championship stayed in the family for two more years as his son-in-law, H. J. Wigham, won in 1896 and 1897. These were the last two times that the U.S. Amateur and the U.S. Open were played together. Thereafter, the U.S. Open was expanded to seventy-two holes and held at a separate course.

Macdonald continued to have a lasting influence on the game of golf. Aside from his administrative prowess within the U.S.G.A., Macdonald made his mark as America's first great architect, even coining the title "golf architect."

In 1892 he was invited to lay out a few holes on an estate owned by Senator John B. Farwell. From that project his work progressed until he founded and built the Chicago Golf Club. The club was unique because it had a seaside links personality and was the first eighteen-hole course in the United States.

For the next thirty years he built a number of acclaimed course—Mid Ocean in Bermuda, the Yale University course in Connecticut, and the original course at the Greenbrier in West Virginia. Without doubt, however, his masterpiece was the National Golf Links of America out on Eastern Long Island, neighboring the Shinnecock Hills Golf Club. In developing the National Golf Links Macdonald used his substantial knowledge of St. Andrews. When National opened in 1911 it set a new standard for American golf architecture. Indeed, over one hundred years later, it still enjoys a pre-eminent position among the world's finest courses.

In his later years Macdonald moved from Chicago to New York. While he undoubtedly would like to have been known as Mr. American Golf this title eluded him throughout his long and storied golf career. It will have to be sufficient to acknowledge his major contributions to the advancement of golf in the United States—quite likely more than those of any other person of his generation.

CHAPTER

12

Harry Vardon's First Tour
of the United States

The formation of the U.S.G.A. put new life into golf in the United States. Golf made rapid progress even though most of the initial U.S. Open Championships were captured by immigrant Scots. Progress was swift and by 1900 there were over 1,000 courses in the United States.

Looking for ways to promote the game to the masses enterprising Americans turned to the Englishman, Harry Vardon, to fuel that growth. He was only too willing to assist.

As Vardon's fame was approaching its zenith he began searching out new challenges. He turned to the United States where the fledgling U. S. Open had originated in 1895. His visit to the United States took place in 1900, and came on the heels of his three British Open victories in the previous four years (1896-1899).

His American tour of 1900 had a momentous effect upon the development of golf in the United States. For starters it had a profound effect on golf commerce. Although his principal purpose in coming to the United States was to play in the U.S. Open, there was the promotion of a new golf ball and a lengthy string of exhibition matches.

Vardon's reputation received another substantial boost as a result of his endorsement contract with A. G. Spalding. Spalding paid Vardon 900 pounds to endorse a hot new gutta percha ball name the Vardon Flyer. This fee was remarkable for its time, especially considering that the prize for

Harry Vardon, winner of the 1900 U.S. Open and a record-setting six British Opens.

winning the British Open was only a modest 30 pounds. For his part Vardon embarked on a nine-month tour of the United States publicizing the new ball. During this tour he played more than seventy matches, winning all but about a dozen of them. This was an amazing record considering that he was playing unfamiliar courses, traveled considerable distances by train, and frequently matched his ball against the better ball of two local opponents. It should be noted that Vardon also accomplished his primary purpose by winning the 1900 U.S. Open over his old nemesis, J. H. Taylor, at the Chicago Golf Club in Wheaton, Illinois. This feat was remarkable in that Vardon interrupted his tour to return to St. Andrews for the British Open, where he finished second to J. H. Taylor. As noted he returned the favor in the U.S. Open.

Vardon's visit propelled the United States into a golf boom. Not long after his visit the U.S. counted a quarter-million players. This was more than all of the rest of the world combined.

Walter Travis dominated the U.S. Amateur at the turn of the twentieth century, winning three times in 1900, 1901, and 1903.

The Late 1800s
and Early 1900s

13

Golf For Women

N ot all of the quarter-million players in the United States at the turn of the century were men. Women played a role in golf, although not a prominent one, going back to the days of Catherine of Aragon, the first wife of Henry VIII. She is the earliest recorded female advocate of the sport. While Henry was rampaging about in France in 1513, Catherine commented on the game and noted that it was in good shape. Over half a century later Mary, Queen of Scots was roundly criticized for being spotted taking on a hole or two only a couple of days after the murder of her husband. This piece of "evidence" was brought up in her implication in the plot. Her political enemies felt that she showed a lack of decent feelings. It is not an exaggeration to conclude that she paid for this indiscretion with her head.

Several hundred years passed before women among the masses took any interest in the game. It is recorded that women in Musselburgh, Scotland, set about forming themselves into a golf society at their course near the city of Edinburgh.

In the early nineteenth century women also played at St. Andrews, but this was not well-received by their male counterparts. Fortunately the women of this time were tenacious and insisted on playing despite the trio of obstacles in the form of dress, male derision and alleged lack of decorum. The St. Andrews Ladies' Golf Club was formed in 1867, the first of its kind in the world. This was followed by the establishment of a ladies' society of golf at Westward Ho! in North Devon, located in southwest England.

A woman named Isette Parsons played an important role in the establishment of the Ladies Golf Union in 1893. That year the Ladies Golf Union sponsored the first British Ladies Amateur Championship. The winner was Lady Margaret Scott, whose father had laid out a course on his own property where the championship was played. Having this home-course advantage Lady Margaret also won the title in 1894 and 1895, before retiring from competition. It was believed that, having triumphed three times in a row, she retired so as to not appear too unlady-like.

In the United States women's golf was also beginning to take hold. In 1895, the same year as the men commenced competing in the U.S. Open and U.S. Amateur, the inaugural U.S.G.A. Women's Amateur Championship was held. It was played at the Meadow Brook Golf Club, Hempstead, New York, on November 9, 1895. The winner was Shinnecock Hills's Mrs. Charles S. Brown (Lucy Barnes). Eighteen contestants participated, and Mrs. Brown won with a score of 69-63-132. Subsequently the quality of play dramatically improved and matches were conducted at match play. The star was Beatrix Hoyt. Like Mrs. Brown, Hoyt was from Shinnecock Hills. She was sixteen when she won the first of three consecutive titles in 1896. Hoyt held the honor of being the youngest U.S.G.A. women's champion until 1971 when Laura Baugh displaced her. Hoyt retired from competitive golf in 1900 when she lost in the semi-finals on her home course. She was twenty years old. Inbee Park is now the youngest champion when she won the event at nineteen in 2010.

Golf positioned itself as a mainstay of women's activity, spurred on by commentary such as that recorded in the *New York Times*, which began one article during that time with "[t]he woman who wants to be good and beautiful—which is to say healthy—must play golf...the best game ever introduced in America."

The Shinnecock Hills Golf Club opened in 1891. By 1893 the wives of the members had convinced their husbands to build a separate nine-hole course for them. Other women golfers were not so fortunate and at least one group took matters into their own hands. In Morristown, New Jersey, a group of female golfers organized a club and built a nine-hole course. It opened in October 1894 and that month held its first tournament.

Meanwhile Florence Boit had returned from France to spend the summer with her aunt and uncle in Wellesley, Massachusetts. She had learned the rudiments of the game in France and she so interested her uncle in the game that he laid out a seven-hole course on property adjacent to his home. Among the visitors to the Boit home was Lawrence Curtis, a member of The Country Club in Brookline, Massachusetts. After a month or so of exposure to the game Curtis convinced The Country Club to add golf to the roster of its activities. In an early example of chauvinism, however, men began to regret their enthusiasm for inclusion of women. The Country Club had expanded to eighteen holes but it forbade women to play on Saturdays, holidays, and before 2:00 PM. on Sundays. Earlier, in 1895 the male financiers of the Morristown course, the first women's club, took the club back and voted in an all-male slate of officers. When they offered the winner of the first tournament, Annie Howland Ford, an honorary membership, she declined. This suggested that the women were not pleased with the change in emphasis at the club. At Shinnecock Hills the membership abandoned their ladies' course. Women at other courses suffered a similar fate.

In spite of this adversity the women persevered and, as previously noted, in 1895 they held their first U.S.Women's Amateur Championship at Meadow Brook Club in Hempstead, New York. The next year the U.S. Women's Amateur was held again. A visiting Scot, Robert Cox of Edinburgh, donated a silver cup as the trophy. This cup is still used today. In 1899 the championship was played for the first time in Philadelphia at the Bala Club of the Philadelphia Country Club. Women's golf grew and prospered in Philadelphia, and a Women's Golf Association was formed. The Merion Cricket Club in Haverford (later the Merion Golf Club in Ardmore) produced some of the finest women players in the early years of golf in America.

The Curtis sisters, Margaret and Harriot, of the Essex Country Club in Manchester, Massachusetts, began to dominate the women's golf scene in the first decade or so of the twentieth century. Between them they won the U.S. Women's Amateur four times from 1906 to 1912. In 1907 Margaret beat Harriot in an all-in-the-family U.S. Women's Amateur final. In 1905 the Curtis sisters traveled to Britain for the British Ladies Amateur Golf Championship, and they and other Americans played a match with a team of English, Scottish, and British players. The "English" team won 6-1 and the competition was such a success that the Curtis sisters were anxious to continue the matches. They got their wish and matches have continued to this day. In 1932 the competition was officially named the Curtis Cup.

*Margaret and Harriot Curtis, champion golfers who donated the trophy
for the Curtis Cup, a bi-annual competition between U.S. women
amateurs and British and Irish women amateurs.*

During the early days of women's golf women found themselves with
a further handicap. This was in the form of the fashions they were constrained to wear during those days. For the most part they wore wide-
brimmed hats, starched sleeves, corseted waistlines and ankle-length,
billowing skirts, which were attractive fashions but provided a significant ir-
ritant to playing golf. Amusingly the cardinal rule of "keep your eye on the

ball" proved to be a more challenging task and it became a "matter of extreme uncertainty." Emboldened over the early years the women eventually shortened their skirts and defrilled their blouses. After a while comfort and fashion united in the expediency and practicality of their dress. And so, down through the years, the demands of the sport eventually won out over the fashion of the day and there was a transformation toward abbreviation in feminine styles. The evolution in wear brought about the age of the sweater and a sensible skirt. Today shorts and an increasing trend toward "unisex" attire have become the standard wear of the day.

Looking back to the early Curtis-styled matches there were two early dominant women players—one on each side of the Atlantic. Competing in the first Curtis Cup matches were Glenna Collett (Mrs. E.H. Vare) of the United States and Joyce Wethered of England. The two dominated their contemporaries and were undoubtedly stars of the game. In the first singles Miss Wethered prevailed over Mrs. Vare by 6 & 4, signaling, early on, her dominance over the American. Earlier in their careers in a momentous final in the 1929 British Women's Amateur, Miss Wethered recovered from five down after eleven holes to defeat the then Miss Collett at the thirty-fifth hole. Bobby Jones, the greatest male amateur golfer of all time, described Miss Wethered as the best player, man or woman, he had ever seen. As his career established this was high praise indeed.

Glenna Collett Vare never was able to wrest away a British Amateur title, losing in the finals twice. On this side of the Atlantic, however, her superiority was unmatched, as she captured the U.S. Women's Amateur in 1922, and added five more wins to cement her title as the number one American woman player of her era. The six U.S. Amateur titles remain a record. Vare had taken over the mantle of best woman golfer from Alexa Stirling, a childhood golfing companion of Bobby Jones. Stirling was seventeen when she played in her first U.S. Women's Amateur in 1914 at the Nassau County Golf Club in Glen Cove, New York. That year, she lost in the first round of match play, but the following year, she survived through to the semi-finals. In 1916 she won her first title and followed that with consecutive titles in 1919 and 1920, with World War I intervening during 1917 and 1918.

Over the years the women's game garnered increasing popularity with champions such as Babe Didrikson, Mickey Wright, Patty Berg, Kathy Whitworth, Nancy Lopez, Julie Inkster, Annika Sörenstam, Karrie Webb, Se Ri Pak, Lorena Ochoa, Yani Tseng and Stacy Lewis among a long list of prominent women golfers. But more about these generations later.

14

Willie Anderson— Dominance in the U.S. Open at the Turn of the Century

After Harry Vardon's win in the 1900 U.S. Open during the midst of his first United States tour there appeared a Scottish immigrant by the name of Willie Anderson. This dour man from North Berwick, Scotland, shunned publicity but his rare talent put him in the public limelight. Anderson's record of four U.S. Open Championships has never been eclipsed and it has been equaled only by subsequent champions Bobby Jones, Ben Hogan and Jack Nicklaus. Anderson first appeared on the U.S. Open scene in 1897. Americans, anxious for a champion in the face of the Great Triumvirate (Vardon, Taylor, and Braid) and Vardon's 1900 U.S. Open Championship, adopted Anderson as their own. He nearly won the 1897 U.S. Open Championship three years before Vardon's victory. Only Joe Lloyd's superb three on the final hole at the Chicago Golf Club prevented Anderson from breaking through at the age of seventeen.

Anderson needed a few more years to triumph in the U.S. Open. When he did he dominated the game as no one had done previously in U.S. golf. From 1901 through 1905 he won the Open four times (1901, 1903-1905). From 1897 through 1910 he played in fourteen Opens. In addition to the four victories he finished lower than fifth only three times, second once, third once, fourth twice, fifth three times, eleventh twice and fifteenth once. His record of three straight victories from 1903 to 1905 is still a record. He was the only individual to win the U.S. Open with both the gutta percha

Willie Anderson won four U.S. Opens including a record-setting three in a row between 1903 and 1905.

and the Haskell ball. In comparison the Great Triumvirate of Harry Vardon, James Braid, and J.H. Taylor each also won the British Open using both types of balls. Willie Anderson was quite aptly called the first star of the American golf scene. Sadly, his stay at the apex was short-lived. He lived only thirty or thirty-two years (records are murky) and died of arteriosclerosis in 1910—at least that's what his death certificate read. That disease is often associated with alcoholism or old age and it is likely that the former corralled Anderson.

15

Walter J. Travis and Jerome D. Travers

Of all of America's early well-regarded golfers perhaps the most interesting personality was Walter J. Travis. Travis was born in Maldon, Victoria, Australia on January 10, 1862 and came to America when he was a small boy. While athletically inclined he spent his early years playing tennis and cycling. On a visit to England, however, he purchased a set of golf clubs because friends of his in Flushing, Long Island, had written to him about their desire to construct a golf course. When he returned from England in 1896 he started to play golf with his friends at the Oakland Club on Long Island. By golfing standards he was an old man of thirty-five. But he took to the game immediately and within two years he made it to the semi-finals of the U. S. Amateur. Two years later, in 1900, he won the U .S. Amateur Championship. This also marked the first of six times when Travis was the medalist. He went on to win the U. S. Amateur twice more, in 1901 and 1903. During his second win in 1901 Travis became the first player to win a Major Championship playing a Haskell-wound rubber ball.

In 1904 Travis traveled to England and became the first person from foreign soil to win the British Amateur. Disappointed with his performance when using his own putter in practice before the British Amateur, Travis borrowed a putter from an American friend with a shaft inserted in the middle of a mallet head.

The putter was named a "Schenectady" putter because a Mr. A. T. Knight

Jerry Travers won the 1907, 1908, 1912, and 1913 U.S. Amateurs, and the 1915 U.S. Open.

of that city (and an employee of General Electric) is credited with inventing it. With the Schenectady putter in hand Travis proved unbeatable on the greens. He tore through each ensuing round to the final against power-hitting Ted Blackwell. Travis's putting power more than offset Blackwell's length off the tee, and Travis prevailed 4 & 3. Several years later, under a ruling by the Royal and Ancient, the Schenectady putter was barred from British tournaments. Half a century later, in 1951, the ban was finally lifted. Travis had a few additional sparks of success after his British Amateur triumph. Three more times he was the medalist in the United States Amateur and in 1909 led all amateurs in the U.S. Open (won by George Sargent).

As time passed, however, Travis devoted more and more time to his other golfing interests. He immortalized his methods in a book entitled *Practical Golf* and became the founder and first editor of the highly influential and respected magazine *The American Golfer*. During this era he designed two of the finer courses in the New York metropolitan area—Garden City Golf Club and Westchester Country Club. Travis finally gave up tournament golf in 1915 when he was well into his fifties. He finished in style, winning the prestigious Metropolitan Amateur. Travis died in 1927. He was elected to the World Golf Hall of Fame in 1979.

In the course of his career Travis defeated a number of very capable young golfers. Among them was Jerry Travers. Their careers overlapped in an interesting saga—and not merely due to the similarities of their last names, for their games were also similar in style. Like many of the high-ranking golfers beginning to make their marks in the early decades of the twentieth century, Travers was the son of a well-to-do family, able to start the game young, develop under the watchful eye of top instructors and play and practice as he saw fit. Blessed with these advantages he had a much easier road to becoming a champion golfer than those who had to work for a living. Travers commenced playing golf on his father's estate at Oyster Bay on Long Island. When he was thirteen he began to play regularly at the Oyster Bay Golf Course. Two years later Jerry's father joined the Nassau County Club at Glen Cove, and Jerry became a junior member. He started taking lessons from the renowned professional Alex Smith (who had won the 1910 U.S. Open) and two years later he attracted national attention by defeating Walter Travis in the final of the Nassau Invitational tournament. This was the first of a long series of duels between Travers and Travis.

In 1906 Travers captured his first big championship—the Metropolitan Amateur. Travers was knocked out of the U.S. Amateur that year by Travis. The next season, 1907, a more experienced Travers climaxed his steady improvements by winning the first of his four U.S. Amateur Championships at the Euclid Golf Club, in Cleveland, Ohio. He defeated Archibald Graham in the final 6 & 5. He was all of twenty-one years old. Travers successfully defended his title in 1908 when the U.S. Amateur was played at Garden City Golf Club, in Garden City, New York. He marched relentlessly through to the final where he defeated Max Baer 8 & 7. In 1909 Travers made an unsuccessful attempt in the British Amateur. He lost in the first round and thus was not able to match Travis's British Amateur Championship.

Astonishingly, as the two-time defending champion, Travers elected in his eccentric way not to defend his U.S. Amateur Championship in 1909. Robert Gardner, the Yale pole vaulter, won it. Nor did Travers enter in 1910 when the winner was William Fownes, who, along with his father, had built Oakmont Country Club near Pittsburgh. The following year, 1911, Travers returned from his two lean years, learning that he could not be both a professional playboy and a world-class amateur golfer. He revisited his earlier triumphs by winning the Metropolitan and the New Jersey Amateurs. The 1911 U.S. Amateur was not as kind to him, however. He lost in the third round to the eventual champion, Harold Hilton.

The 1912 U.S. Amateur was held at the Chicago Golf Club. Travers played superb golf through to the final where his opponent was a young Chicagoan, Chick Evans, who would achieve his own glory several years later. The fact that Evans was also playing well, and would have the home advantage, made him the slight favorite. Travers finished the morning round one down. He had to make a thirty-five-foot putt on the eighteenth green to cut Evans's lead in half. The afternoon round decided the match. On the first hole Travers hit a wild drive that surely looked as though it was going to bounce into the tough, high rough on the left of the fairway. For-tuitously the ball bounded back onto the fairway and Travers won the hole. He went on to win six of the first nine holes in the afternoon to go five-up. He also won the tenth and finished with a 7 & 6 victory.

In 1913 the U.S. Amateur was played at the Garden City Golf Club, in Garden City, New York. Travers made it though to the semi-finals where his opponent was Francis Ouimet. Travers had a one-up lead after the morning round. He won the first hole of the afternoon and appeared headed to victory. But Ouimet won the second, third, and seventh holes to take a one-up lead. Travers landed a second shot on the eighth for a birdie, made the ten-inch putt and went on to victory. In the finals he had an easy time with John Anderson, winning 5 & 4. At the age of twenty-six Travers had won his fourth and last U.S. Amateur.

In the 1914 U.S. Amateur Ouimet gained revenge over Travers. This fol-lowed on the heels of Ouimet's stunning playoff victory over Harry Vardon and Ted Ray in the 1913 U.S. Open. In that 1914 U.S. Amateur, held at Ekwanok Country Club, Manchester, Vermont, Ouimet defeated Travers 6 & 5 in the finals. The U.S. Open in 1915 proved to be the culmination of Travers's career. The event was held at the famed Baltusrol Golf Course in Springfield, New Jersey. Travers's 297 was good enough to secure the victory.

In his career Travers won four U.S. Amateurs. Only Bobby Jones's five titles exceeded this feat. When Travers took the 1915 U.S. Open he became one of only five amateurs to win the U.S. Open, and one of ten golfers to win both the U.S. Open and the U.S. Amateur. He retired at the age of twenty-eight. Travers left the game with the legacy of being one of the fiercest match-play golfers with an amazing recovery ability along the lines of Walter Hagen. He also had the reputation of being a remarkable putter. Travers died in 1951 at the age of sixty-three. He was inducted into the World Golf Hall of Fame in 1976.

16

John McDermott—
A Native-Born American Breaks
Through at the 1911 U.S. Open

From the 1895 inception of the U.S. Open through the first decade of the twentieth century no native-born American had won the U.S. Open. Thus the scene was set in 1909 at a time when American professional golfers were beginning to close the gap between themselves and the foreign-born professionals.

In the 1909 U.S. Open Tommy McNamara of Boston shot a 69 to become the first American to break 70 in major competition in America. He finished second to Englishman George Sargent.

At the 1910 U.S. Open two Scottish brothers, Alex and Macdonald Smith, were dueling for the championship at the Philadelphia Cricket Club in Chestnut Hill, Pennsylvania. This was the second time in four years that the U.S. Open was held at the Cricket Club (Alex Ross was the earlier winner in 1907). The 1910 battle extended into a play-off where Alex Smith prevailed over Macdonald, his older brother, by six strokes. A third man was in that play-off. John McDermott, a native-born American, was a young professional at the Atlantic City Country Club and the eighteen-year old son of a Philadelphia mailman. He shot 75, losing to Alex by four strokes, but beating Macdonald by two. In defeat McDermott lost to a man twenty years his senior and vastly more experienced.

In 1911 the vastly improved McDermott took his game to the U.S. Open at the Chicago Golf Club where Harry Vardon had won in 1900. Here again

McDermott found himself in a three-man play-off, with Mike Brady and George Simpson. After taking a wretched six at the first McDermott played superbly thereafter and defeated Brady by two strokes and Simpson by five.

At the age of nineteen years, ten months, and twelve days McDermott was both the youngest player to win the U.S. Open and the first native-born American as well. He remains the youngest-ever winner of the U.S. Open. His breakthrough ended the domination by immigrant British (and the visiting Harry Vardon in 1900) and Scottish golfers. McDermott's victory showed that the Americans could outplay the best of the imports and heightened interest in the U.S. Open. By 1912 a field of 125 entered the U.S. Open at the Country Club of Buffalo, the first time that U.S. Open entries exceeded 100.

McDermott showed his worth as a champion by repeating his U.S. Open triumph at Buffalo. He had now won two U.S. Open titles before the age of twenty-one. By this time comparisons were being made to the great Willie Anderson, who had won three straight U.S. Open titles in 1903-1905. McDermott solidified this notion by defeating Harry Vardon in the Shawnee Open in 1913 at Shawnee Country Club, Shawnee-On-Delaware, Pennsylvania. He also won the 1913 Western Open which was, at that time, the second most prestigious tournament in the United States.

Then, almost as quickly as he had appeared on golf's stage, McDermott disappeared. He played in the 1913 Open in an effort to match Willie Anderson's record three consecutive U.S. Open triumphs, but failed to do so. He also made attempts at the British Open. After a dismal showing in the 1912 British Open at Muirfield, Scotland McDermott returned in 1913 and finished a respectable fifth at Hoylake, England, the best an American had ever done. Just as life was looking even brighter, when McDermott returned home, he got the bad news that he had lost heavily in some stock transactions. He was a bachelor who lived with his sisters and their parents and he kept the news from his family. They suspected that something was wrong and they were right. McDermott brooded so much that he entered into a serious depression.

Although he had won the 1913 Shawnee Open an incident there further deepened his depression. At the presentation ceremony he referred to the upcoming U.S. Open and cockily told the foreign golfers that they wouldn't win the U.S. Open. For this McDermott received a letter from the U.S.G.A. stating that due to his "extreme discourtesy," he might not be accepted into the field at the 1913 U.S. Open. Even though his entry was ac-

John J. McDermott, who was the first native-born American to win the U.S. Open, won this event in 1911 and 1912.

cepted his depression worsened before his arrival at The Country Club in Brookline, Massachusetts for the U.S. Open. Despite these troubles, however, McDermott showed his tenaciousness by finishing only four shots out of first place.

McDermott took the winter off but decided to enter the British Open in 1914. However, he did not make the tournament because of missed connections with a ferry and train. On his return home to the United States his boat collided with a grain carrier and sank in the English Channel. He was led to a lifeboat, returned to England and later made his way back to the United States. This event affected him more than was realized. It appears that his stock losses, the incident at Shawnee-On-Delaware and the shipwreck preyed heavily on his mind. He entered the 1914 U.S. Open but was never a factor. Later that season he blacked out at the Atlantic City pro shop where he was the head pro. At the age of twenty-three his tournament career was finished. He returned to his parents' home in Philadelphia and spent much of the rest of his life in and out of sanatoriums, undergoing a series of treatments. He lived the later part of his life in the suburbs of Philadelphia (Norristown State Hospital) and died in 1971 at the age of eighty.

17

Francis Ouimet
and the 1913 U.S. Open

arry Vardon's initial tour of the United States in 1900 had met with unparalleled success, capped off with his victory in the U.S. Open at the Chicago Golf Club. Vardon made his second tour of the United States in 1913 with the backing of Lord Northcliffe, the owner of the *Times* of London. Once again Lord Northcliffe suggested that it would advance the interest in sport between the United States and Great Britain if the latter was represented in the U.S. Open. Lord Northcliffe told Vardon to select a partner so that they could play a series of matches while touring the United States. Vardon asked Edward "Ted" Ray to accompany him. Ray was an ideal partner with his long-hitting prowess. The fact that he had won the 1912 British Open was also on his resumé.

Vardon and Ray decided to begin their tour right after the 1913 British Open won by J. H. Taylor. When Vardon and Ray departed for the United States in August it had been thirteen years since Vardon had made his initial trip to the United States in 1900. The highlight of their trip was to be the 1913 U.S. Open scheduled for The Country Club in Brookline, Massachusetts. But first there were numerous exhibition matches. The duo took part in forty-one matches against the leading American players and, by all accounts, they lost only one match. Wherever they played record or near-record crowds turned out. The spectators were curious to learn from Vardon how easy the game became in the hands of an expert and to gasp at Ray's thundering tee shots accompanied by his delicate touch around the greens.

Vardon and Ray interrupted their tour to play in the U.S. Open in September at The Country Club. The U.S.G.A. was so delighted to have them participate that they moved the date from June to September to accommodate the pair's exhibition schedule.

As events unfolded the 1913 U.S. Open's memory continues to live on while the accomplishment of John McDermott, in becoming the first native-born American to win the U.S. Open in 1911, is largely forgotten. Tension surrounding the 1913 U.S. Open was high. McDermott's victories in the 1911 and 1912 U.S. Opens and at the 1912 Shawnee Open boosted the Americans' confidence in a U.S. victory at the U.S. Open. The U.S.G.A. sought to load the field with Americans so as to improve their chances of victory. They practically pleaded with amateurs to enter the championship. Among those urged to enter was Jerry Travers and a young local player named Francis Ouimet, a salesman in a sporting-goods firm. Another entry in the field was a teenage upstart from New York named Walter Hagen.

Ouimet's home was near the Brookline course. At a young age he worked as a caddy at The Country Club and no doubt seized upon an occasional opportunity to play a few holes over the course himself. In 1913 Ouimet was all of twenty years old and not considered among the favorites, to say the least. Almost immediately after filing his entry Ouimet had second thoughts about his decision. He felt that he had taken too much time off from his job earlier that year to play in the U.S. Amateur (where he had given Jerry Travers a remarkable tussle in the semi-finals before losing), and to play in the Massachusetts State Amateur, which, surprisingly, he had won. After learning that Ouimet had entered and was considering withdrawing, his boss told him that he should play.

By padding the field the U.S.G.A. succeeded in achieving a record number of entries—165. To accommodate them two thirty-six-hole qualifiers were held, with half competing on one day and the other half on the following day. Vardon led the first-day qualifiers with a total of 151, a stroke ahead of Ouimet. Ray, with a total of 148, led the field on the second day in his qualifying section. With the qualifying rounds completed the favorites were set to settle matters with stroke play over seventy-two holes. Thirty-six holes would be played over each of two days.

Under fair skies and before a tremendous crowd of spectators Vardon shot an opening day two-round total of 147, and was tied with Wilfred Reid,

Harry Vardon, Francis Ouimet, and Ted Ray at the 1913 U.S. Open.

another British player. Ray shot 149. The American youngsters, Ouimet and Hagen, were stalking the leaders at 151. At this stage, Vardon thought things looked bright for a British victory. The second and last day opened with dreadful wet weather, which never let up. At the end of fifty-four holes in the morning round, Vardon, Ray, and Ouimet were tied for the lead at 225. Reid blew his chances with a lackluster third round.

Ouimet had caught the two favorites with a round of 74 but realistically most did not believe this inexperienced amateur could stand up to the pressures of the fourth round of the U.S. Open. By the fourth round the course was saturated with rain and little pools and rivulets marked every fairway. Ray was the first one of the leaders to finish his fourth round. He shot a 79 on the rain-soaked course and would have to wait to see if his 304 would stand up. Vardon, like Ray, was an early starter and also came in with an indifferent 79, which tied him with Ray. As the drama unfolded in the afternoon word came back to the clubhouse (there were no leader boards in those days) that Ouimet was the lone man left who could catch Ray and

Vardon. But Ouimet appeared to have squandered his chances when he made the turn in 43 and took a 5 on the short par four tenth hole.

To reach 304 Ouimet would have to play the water-logged course in one under par for the last eight holes. By the time he reached the fifteenth hole Vardon and Ray, having heard the rumor of Ouimet's play, decided to see for themselves what was happening. By this time Ouimet would have to play the final four holes in one under par to force a three-man play-off. He got his pars at the fifteenth and sixteenth holes. At the 360-yard par four seventeenth he hit his second shot on the dogleg left to within twenty feet of the hole. He then holed the putt. Ouimet had picked up the stroke he needed and, if he could par the eighteenth hole, he would be in a three-man play-off for the U.S. Open. He did just that. The crowd filled the air with a massive cheer. They mobbed their new-found hero and hoisted him on their shoulders. To settle matters there would be an eighteen-hole play-off the next day. This method of deciding the U.S. Open has carried over to today.

The next morning at a few moments before 10:00 Ouimet joined Vardon and Ray on the first tee for eighteen holes of stroke play. Adding to the mystique and lore was the youngster who served as Ouimet's caddy. He was pint-sized Eddie Lowery, half Ouimet's age.

In his adult years Lowery became active in amateur golf as a benefactor. He served on the Executive Committee of the U.S.G.A. Lowery was a mentor for, and employer of, two of the leading amateurs in the 1950's—Ken Venturi and E. Harvie Ward. But back to the play-off.

Vardon, Ray, and Ouimet teed off with Ouimet hitting first since he drew the longest straw. All three were out in 38. Over the inward nine each player landed his tee shot on the green of the 140-yard par three tenth hole. Vardon and Ray three-putted for bogeys. Ouimet made his par and, for the first time, led in the match. At the twelfth, a par four, Ouimet made par, and increased his lead to two strokes when Vardon and Ray made bogeys. On the short par four thirteenth Vardon's birdie put him within one stroke of Ouimet, and many thought the experienced Vardon would overtake Ouimet. This was not to be. At the long fourteenth Vardon managed to make his par five. So did Ouimet and Ray. On the fifteenth hole, a par four, Ray made a six after taking two shots to get out of a bunker. He was now four strokes behind Ouimet and three behind Vardon. With three holes to go Ray was finished.

On the short sixteenth Vardon and Ouimet made their par three's while the dispirited Ray made a careless four. Ouimet's lead remained at one. To the seventeenth, a 360-yard par four dogleg left, they went. Vardon still had the honor of hitting first. Vardon must have felt that this was the time to gamble so he tried to place his drive over the corner of the dogleg. The drive proved to be his undoing. He hooked his drive into a bunker at the angle of the dogleg. He was forced to lay up. From there he played his shot to the green and two-putted for a bogey five. Ouimet struck a perfect drive down the middle of the seventeenth fairway. His next shot was a mashie to within eighteen feet of the hole. Ouimet had hopes of getting down in two putts for that valuable insurance stroke against Vardon. Two putts would do this. Instead, Ouimet made the first putt for a birdie.

Ouimet now had a three-stroke lead on Vardon as they came to the home hole—a par four. Ouimet came through in fine fashion after landing his drive again down the middle of the fairway, and his second shot landed on the green. His approach putt left him with a four-footer for par. Ouimet made the putt. Vardon made six. Ouimet had done the unthinkable. He had won the U.S. Open, shooting 72 to Vardon's 77, and Ray's 78. It has been said that at least 10,000 hardy souls witnessed the achievement in the misty rain. While this is perhaps somewhat of an exaggeration the atten-dance was record-breaking, according to most who were there. Making his achievement even more remarkable was the fact that Ouimet had not only toppled the British duo but had done so by nearly beating their better-ball (the score on a hole being the lower of two scores made by a two-man team).

Even Vardon made something of a confession. He had begun the play-off with the pre-conceived notion that, if he could defeat his countryman, Ray, he would win the Championship. He hadn't intended to underesti-mate Ouimet's golf skills but he did not think that Ouimet could carry over his sterling regulation play into the play-off round. Vardon conceded that he had made a mistake. His prediction, however, that Ouimet's great victory would prove in the years to come to be a decisive factor in the advancement of golf in the United States proved ever so true. For his part Vardon re-turned to England and, at Prestwick the following year, in 1914, won his sixth British Open at the age of forty-four. Vardon and Ray returned to the United States in 1920. Ray redeemed himself by winning the U.S. Open that year at The Inverness Club in Toledo, Ohio, with Harry Vardon, Leo Diegel and Jack Burke as runners-up. At forty-three Ray became the oldest man to win the U.S. Open. In 1990, Hale Irwin became the oldest man to win the U.S. Open when he won his third Open (previously 1974, 1979) at the age of forty-five years and fifteen days.

In accepting the 1913 U.S. Open trophy from the U.S.G.A. Secretary, John Reid, Jr., Francis Ouimet remained his modest self. He told the enthusiastic crowd, "naturally it always was my hope to win out. I simply tried my best to keep this cup from going to our friends across the water. I am very glad to have been the agency for keeping the cup in America." Ouimet became a national hero. The effect of Ouimet's U.S. Open victory was enormous. Two of Britain's greatest golfers had been soundly beaten by a twenty-year-old amateur ex-caddy. As matters turned out this was a foreboding that the British were about to lose their dominance in the sport of golf, just as the Scots had. About 350,000 Americans were playing golf at the time of Ouimet's astonishing victory. Within the next decade an estimated two million had taken up this contagious game.

Ouimet never won another U.S. Open. The best he could do was a fifth-place finish in 1914, and he missed a play-off in 1925 by a single stroke. However, he won the U.S. Amateur in 1914 at Ekwanok Country Club in Manchester, Vermont, beating Jerry Travers in the final. In doing so Ouimet became the first golfer with career U.S. Open and U.S. Amateur titles. But then, within a few years, he was stripped of his amateur status, all for the shallow reason that he had worked for a sporting goods manufacturer that sold golf equipment. Justly he was reinstated as an amateur when he entered the U.S. Army during World War I. He played on or served as captain of the American team in eleven Walker Cup Matches, the competition played every other year between amateurs from the United States, and from the combined team of amateur golfers from Great Britain and Ireland.

The 1913 Open victory would have been a crowning achievement for any man. After capturing the U.S. Amateur in 1914 Ouimet was runner-up to Chick Evans in 1920. Ouimet made it to the semi-finals of the U.S. Amateur in 1924, 1926, 1927, and 1928. Then just when most were beginning to believe that he would not taste any more championship success, he staged a comeback by winning the U.S. Amateur in 1931 at the Beverly Country Club in Chicago, Illinois—eighteen years after his first Major victory in the U.S Open at The Country Club. Francis Ouimet was one of the most acclaimed figures of golf in the United States. He is often referred to as the Father of American Amateur golf. He never turned pro. In 1951, he was elected captain of the Royal and Ancient Golf Club—the first American to be so honored. Ouimet died in 1967. In 1974 he was in the inaugural class admitted to the World Golf Hall of Fame.

The 1914 U.S. Open was the first of eleven Majors won by "Sir" Walter Hagen.

SECTION 3

Walter Hagen, Gene Sarazen, and Others

18

Following Ouimet,
There Came Walter Hagen

With the strides fashioned by Walter Travis, Jerry Travers, John McDermott and then Francis Ouimet, America was ready for a new generation of golfing stars with the flair, personality, and skill to advance this Scottish-born game. Aside from winning the U.S. Amateur in 1914 Ouimet attempted to defend his U.S. Open title at Midlothian Country Club, near Chicago that summer. As in 1913 also in the U.S. Open field was Walter Hagen. Hagen came out on top. Not to take anything from Francis Ouimet, but at this time, America was looking for someone to step forward with a personality and star quality to accompany his golfing prowess. Walter Hagen fit that bill to a "tee". He was a street-wise kid from Rochester, New York, the son of a blacksmith. Remarkably, the 1913 U.S. Open was only the second tournament that Hagen had entered. He was twenty years old at the time—the same age as Ouimet. But there the similarities ended. While the 1913 Open had stimulated the game's expansion, it was small consolation to Hagen, who arrived at the U.S. Open with extreme confidence but came up short. He announced to the other Americans in the field that he'd come down from Rochester "to help you boys take care of Vardon and Ray."

The play proceeded to the fourth round and, at 227, Hagen was only two strokes behind the three leaders, Ouimet, Vardon and Ray. His afternoon round started off poorly but Hagen rallied and picked up the two strokes he needed to catch the leaders, Vardon and Ray. Hagen parred the tenth and the eleventh, but missed a ten-foot putt on the thirteenth that would have inched him ahead. On the fourteenth, a par five, Hagen hit his drive well enough to believe that he could reach the green in two. However, on his second shot he lashed into the ball with a brassie (two-wood) but the force of his swing caused him to top the ball. He hooked his next shot badly, finally holing out in seven and shooting an 80. His 307 left him three shots behind Vardon and Ray with only the enigmatic Ouimet left to confront the British stalwarts when he also came in with 304.

Hagen rued his misfortunate in coming so close only to be tripped up by one bad hole. Discouraged, Hagen returned to Rochester to pursue his dream of a baseball career. He even went to Florida to pitch with the Philadelphia Nationals and, when the team headed north, Hagen felt that he would be given a thorough tryout the next year. He returned to the Country Club of Rochester, resumed his duties as a teaching professional, and had every intention of pitching semi-pro baseball in Rochester. As Ouimet had originally done in 1913 Hagen decided not to enter the 1914 U.S. Open. Only when a local newspaper editor offered to pay his expenses did Hagen file his entry into the 1914 U.S. Open. The venue was the Midlothian Country Club, outside of Chicago.

After a comfortable qualifying score of 75-77-152 Hagen started his first of the four championship rounds with a rather uneven one under par 35 on the front nine. The back nine was a different story. Hagen birdied four of the last five holes and shot a five under par 68, breaking the course record by three strokes. Lurking right behind him was Ouimet, who had posted a first-round 69. In his second round that afternoon Hagen shot a 74 early and waited to see if anyone could match his 142. Tom McNamara nearly caught him with a 143, and, after his 76, Ouimet was well placed, three shots in arrears at 145 after the first day's play. The next day Hagen played two steady rounds of 75 and 73, and finished with 290, matching the U.S. Open record set by George Sargent, who had shot 290 in 1909 at Englewood Golf Club in Englewood, New Jersey.

Neither Ouimet nor McNamara could keep pace. Ouimet finished at 298 and McNamara's hopes evaporated with an 83 that left him at 302. But there was a new challenger who had surfaced. His name was Charles "Chick" Evans, Jr., a local boy from Chicago. With a score of 150 for the first two rounds Evans was eight strokes behind Hagen at the halfway point. In the third round, he shot a 71 and moved to within four shots of the lead.

When Hagen dropped three shots to par on the eighth and ninth holes of the fourth round Evans found himself within one shot of the lead. He missed a three-foot putt on the ninth that would have put him in a tie. Had Evans not missed several putts on the back nine he would have captured the lead from Hagen. As it was he reached the tee of the eighteenth hole two shots behind Hagen. Amazingly, he almost drove the green on the short eighteenth and left himself with about a 50-foot chip for the eagle he would need to tie Hagen. The crowd ringed the green and watched as Evans stroked his chip shot to within a foot left of the hole. His birdie left him one shot behind the victorious Hagen, who had led wire-to-wire.

Hagen promptly forgot about baseball when he realized that he could make far more money playing golf. Offers of exhibitions abounded and, as a natural showman, Hagen quickly became a fan favorite. In fact, except for the few times he was in the same field as the illustrious Bobby Jones, Hagen attracted the largest galleries. The 1914 U.S. Open was the first of eleven Major championship victories for Hagen. He repeated his U.S. Open triumph in 1919. In 1922, he became the first American to win the British Open, a feat that he repeated three more times before the end of the decade. However, it was in the Professional Golfers Association (P.G.A.) Championships that Hagen prospered the most.

Class-consciousness was still prevalent in golf during this period, particularly with regard to professionals. The early pros, most of them transplanted Scots, were looked upon as club repairmen and instructors, and nothing more. Led by the likes of Walter Hagen this was all about to change, albeit at a slower pace than Hagen would have liked. In January 1916, in New York City, the P.G.A. was formed. Its founding purposes were to set standards for golf professionals, match pros with the growing number of club jobs becoming available and give pros a voice in the selection of tournament sites. That fall the professionals teed up in the first P.G.A. Championship, a match play event held at Siwanoy Country Club, just north of New York City in Bronxville, New York. The trophy was donated by Rodman Wanamaker, an heir to a leading department store empire. The winner of the Wanamaker Trophy was an Englishman, Jim Barnes, who took home the first prize of $500. With this event the P.G.A. and professional golf began an astounding and lucrative path down to this day.

One thing Walter Hagen never forgot as he hobnobbed his way among the elite, and spent like the millionaire he became, was to look after his fellow professionals. He was on the cutting edge of emancipating his compatriots from their role as second-class citizens. Until the Hagen era professionals were barred from the clubhouses of country clubs where they worked and competed. Hagen, however, felt that this was an injustice and that he was just as good as the country club set. He lobbied hard for changes and got them. Clubs slowly began to relent and finally, at the 1920 U.S. Open at The Inverness Club in Toledo, Ohio, all competitors were welcomed to full use of the facilities.

In these early years of the P.G.A Championship the tournament was dominated by foreigners until Hagen came along. The "Haig," or "Sir Walter" as he came to be known, was the first American to win the P.G.A. Championship, in 1921. From 1921 to 1927 he won five P.G.A. Championships, including a still unprecedented four in a row (1924-1927). In 1923, one of the two he did not win during this stretch, he lost in the final to Gene Sarazen (thirty-eight holes, one up).

Hagen did not stop with the P.G.A. Championship. By the time his playing career concluded he had won eleven Major championships, adding two U.S. Opens (1914 and 1919) and four British Opens (1922, 1924, 1928, and 1929). This places him fourth behind Jack Nicklaus (eighteen), Tiger Woods (fourteen), and Bobby Jones (thirteen) for Major Championships won. There is some debate as to whether Hagen should be credited with more Majors. He also won five Western Opens (1916, 1921, 1926, 1927, and 1932) which was considered one of the premier golfing events on the schedule at that time. Including the Western Open victories Hagen would have tallied sixteen Majors. As for the Masters when it was inaugurated in 1934, Hagen was past his prime. His best finish was a tie for eleventh in 1936.

During his run of four straight P.G.A. Championships the Haig won twenty-two straight matches before Leo Diegel finally stopped him in 1928. In his only head-to-head match with Bobby Jones, an exhibition, Hagen dispatched Jones 12 & 11. Combining his prize money from tournaments and exhibitions Sir Walter became the first golfer to win one million dollars. On and off the course the ex-caddy and sandlot ball player conducted himself as a Hollywood star or a member of royalty. He loved the high life. He drank what would have been considered excessive for ordinary men. This is probably what caused him to lose his putting touch in the twilight of his career. Loving clothes as he did Hagen was known to change attire between morning and afternoon rounds in competition.

Hagen brought sartorial splendor to the golf course, passing up the traditional tweeds for expensive silk shirts, flannel pants, and white bucks. His love of stylish clothing, his flamboyant manner and his golfing skills endeared him to the golfing public. For twenty years Sir Walter ruled the world of professional golf. Only the spectacular career of Bobby Jones in the Roaring Twenties could compete with the star quality of the Haig. Walter Hagen died in 1969. He was inducted into the World Golf Hall of Fame in the inaugural class of 1974.

19

Chick Evans—
Among Amateur Golf's Best

At the time of the 1914 U.S. Open Charles "Chick" Evans, Jr. was known as the finest striker of the ball in American golf. Few elite golfers have it all and Chick's one flaw was his mediocrity on the greens. He often carried more than one putter and would even experiment during matches by switching putters. His battle with Walter Hagen in the 1914 U.S. Open, which Hagen narrowly won, propelled Evans into the limelight. Prior to this U.S. Open duel, however, Evans had suffered a number of defeats in national championships. By 1912 he had played in three U.S. Amateurs and been ousted in the semi-finals—each time by opponents most thought Evans had outplayed.

In the 1912 U.S. Amateur he suffered perhaps his most frustrating loss. It looked as if Evans had finally exorcised his shortcomings. For the first time he made it past the semi-finals and into the final of the U.S. Amateur. At the Chicago Golf Club, surrounded by his loyal hometown fans, he had opened a three-hole lead over Jerry Travers after the morning round. But, alas, Evans faltered in the afternoon round, and Travers prevailed 7 & 6. In 1913 his semi-final jinx at the U.S. Amateur betrayed him once again. He played wobbly golf through to the semi-finals where John G. Anderson ended his misery. Based on these performances many began to doubt whether Evans would ever break through all the way to a Major championship. But he showed signs of doing so when he almost caught Hagen at

Charles "Chick" Evans, Jr. won three Majors including both the U.S. Amateur and U.S.Open in 1916.

the 1914 U.S. Open. However, more of the same misfortune came his way in 1915. With the exception of Jerry Travers, the winner, Evans did better than any other amateur in the 1915 U.S. Open. In the 1915 U.S. Amateur Evans could not elevate his game. He was beaten in the first round by Ned Sawyer, a fellow Chicagoan whom Evans had defeated all summer.

Then, in 1916, success came in the blink of an eyelash. The U.S. Open was held at the Minikahada Country Club outside of Minneapolis, Minnesota. In the first round Evans shot nine-hole scores of 32-38 for a first round total of 70. In the afternoon Evans maintained his composure and shot an even better 36-33-69. These two-round scores gave him a three-shot lead over Wilfred Reid. The next day the oppressive heat got the better of many players but Evans hung on with a 74 in the morning round. He still retained a three-stroke lead with his closest pursuer being Jim Barnes, the long-hitting English professional who would capture the P.G.A. Championship later that year. Barnes had posted a morning round of 71. As the afternoon fourth round played out Evans learned that Barnes, who was playing three holes behind him, had caught him at the turn. This time, however, Evans dug in and made crucial three- and four-foot putts to secure the victory by four shots over Barnes and two over Jock Hutchinson, who had posted a masterful 68. Chick's four-round total of 286 stood up as a record for twenty years. As it turned out the 1916 U.S. Open was the last U.S. Open until after World War I.

Now, for the first time, instead of being close Evans could enjoy the comfort of having won a Major championship. Next was the 1916 U.S. Amateur at Merion Golf Club in Ardmore, Pennsylvania, outside of Philadelphia. With the 1916 U.S. Open under his belt Evans was the man to beat. He did not disappoint. The defending U.S. Amateur champion was Robert Gardner who had also captured the U.S. Amateur in 1909 at the age of nineteen. In addition to his golfing skills Gardner was a champion pole vaulter. In the third round of match play Gardner had defeated the fourteen-year old Bobby Jones who was making his debut at the national level.

Evans and Gardner hooked up in the final and Evans prevailed 4 & 3 over his fellow Chicagoan. A key to his victory was his steadiness with the putter on Merion's notoriously treacherous greens. Evans had accomplished the feat of becoming the first player to hold the U.S. Open and U.S. Amateur Championships in the same year. He would go on to secure a second U.S. Amateur title in 1920.

In much the fashion of Walter Hagen, Evans helped break golf's social barriers. As a former caddy he proved that it was not necessary to come out of a wealthy, country club background to be a success. Evans established the Evans Scholarship Fund to help Chicago-area caddies attend college. He was one of the original inductees into the P.G.A. Hall of Fame in 1940 and was elected to the World Golf Hall of Fame in 1975. He died in 1979.

20

The Hiatus of World War I–
Exhibition Matches

In April 1917 the United States entered World War I. Shortly after the declaration of war the U.S.G.A. cancelled the national championships. No official U. S. Open or U. S. Amateur was held during the war years of 1917 and 1918. However, the U.S.G.A., the P.G.A. and the Western Golf Association (W.G.A.) all sponsored informal tournaments and exhibitions to raise funds for the war effort. Fifteen-year-old Bobby Jones, from Atlanta, joined in the effort. Bobby played a full exhibition circuit with three other youngsters—Perry Adair, Alexa Stirling and Elaine Rosenthal. Elaine was then the best woman golfer in the Midwest, and the Atlanta-bred Alexa had captured the U.S. Women's Amateur in 1916 when she was only nineteen years old. She would repeat this performance after the war in 1919 and 1920. Perry was an Atlanta neighbor and boyhood rival of Bobby Jones. Together they raised $150,000. for the Red Cross.

While he was awaiting induction into the U.S. Army Francis Ouimet participated in many Red Cross exhibitions in New England. He was also engaged in a controversy with the U.S.G.A. before the war. In the winter of 1916 the U.S.G.A. barred Ouimet from amateur golf. At the time the U.S.G.A. definition of a professional golfer was a person engaged in any business connected with golf. Ouimet had been warned that, if he went into the business of opening a sporting-goods store, he would lose his amateur status. Ouimet persisted in the opening of the store and, under its

*"The Dixie Whiz Kids," Perry Adair, Alexa Stirling, Bobby Jones,
and Elaine Rosenthal.*

criteria, the U.S.G.A. had no choice but to consider him a professional. In the winter of 1918, when Ouimet was inducted into the U.S. Army, he was reinstated as an amateur by the U.S.G.A. The reported reason was that Ouimet had severed his connection with the sporting-goods company upon entering the military. The more plausible reason was that the U.S.G.A. seized upon an opportunity to right a wrong that was most unpopular with the golfing public.

Since so many golfers raised considerable sums during World War I golf achieved a new status with the public. People came to respect the star players even more and the professionals who had given so much for the war efforts. After World War I ended the U.S. Open, the U.S. Amateur, and the P.G.A. Championship resumed.

21

The Squire–Gene Sarazen

Eugene Saracini was born on February 27, 1902, a month before Bobby Jones. He spent his early years in Harrison, New York, twenty miles northeast of New York City. As a teenager showing some promise in golf matches Saracini did not much care for how his name appeared in newspaper articles covering his matches. So Eugene Saracini changed his name to Gene Sarazen. He got his start in golf as a ten-year old caddy at Larchmont Country Club, and then moved over to The Apawanis Club in Rye, New York–the site of the 1911 U.S. Amateur. During his teen years Sarazen's family moved to Bridgeport, Connecticut, where Sarazen found employment in a munitions factory. This job aided his family financially while supporting the U.S. war effort in World War I. It was while working in the factory that Sarazen contracted a severe case of pneumonia. When he regained his strength doctors recommended that he find employment outdoors. He took a job at Beardsley Park–a nine-hole municipal course not far from the heart of Bridgeport. Later he moved over to a course called Brooklawn. All the time he worked on sharpening his game.

Sarazen's game progressed to the point that, while still a teenager, he went to Florida to try his hand at making a living as a golf professional. This evolved into a job as an assistant pro at Fort Wayne Country Club in Indiana. Golfing comrades and members at Fort Wayne Country Club encouraged him to enter the 1920 U.S. Open, where he had an undistinguished performance at The Inverness Club in Toledo, Ohio. This was the U.S. Open won by Englishman, Ted Ray. Sarazen did not perform any better at the 1921 U.S. Open at Columbia Country Club in Chevy Chase, Maryland. He finished twenty-two strokes behind Jim Barnes. Thereafter Sarazen moved on to his next position as head professional at Highland Country Club, outside of Pittsburgh, Pennsylvania. By this time Sarazen had the confidence that he could play with the best golfers on the professional circuit and the leading amateurs of the day, the foremost of whom was Bobby Jones.

The 1922 U.S. Open was held at Skokie Country Club, outside of Chicago in Glendale, Illinois. For the first time an admission fee ($1) was charged for the U.S. Open. Sarazen's opening rounds of 72-73-145 placed him three shots off the lead. His third round 75 found him four shots behind the leaders, "Wild" Bill Melhorn and Bobby Jones. In his fourth round Sarazen caught fire with a 68 for 288, and a one-shot victory over Bobby Jones and John Black. Sarazen was twenty years old. Like Francis Ouimet he had won the U.S. Open as an ex-caddy. Back in Pittsburgh, where he continued to hold down his position at the Highland Country Club, Sarazen was greeted as a conquering hero. The high point was a victory dinner at the William Penn Hotel in Pittsburgh where Sarazen made a grand entrance inside a giant papier-mâché golf ball on the main ballroom stage. According to Sarazen's autobiography, *Thirty Years of Championship Golf*, he had even told those who asked that he was twenty-one, not twenty because he thought the U.S. Open champion should be a man, not a boy. Even still, Sarazen noted in his book that he was the youngest professional ever to win the U.S. Open.

Incredibly, within five weeks, Sarazen won the P.G.A. Championship at Oakmont Country Club in Oakmont, Pennsylvania, defeating the Scotsmen Jock Hutchinson and Bobby Cruickshank along the way. In the final he beat Emmet French 4 & 3. Later that year, he and Walter Hagen played a match called the "World Championship of Golf." It was played over thirty-six holes at the Oakmont course and Westchester Country Club in Rye, New York. Sarazen won 3 & 2. In 1923 Sarazen declined to defend his U.S. Open title at Inwood Country Club in Inwood, New York. This left the door open for Bobby Jones to capture his first Major Championship. Later that summer Sarazen resolved to hold onto his P.G.A. title by entering the 1923 P.G.A. Championship.

The match play 1923 P.G.A. Championship was held at Pelham Country Club in Rye, New York. Sarazen and Hagen marched through to the final in what was called one of the fiercest finals ever. In the final the two were all square after eighteen holes. After twenty-seven holes Hagen enjoyed a three-up lead but Sarazen mounted a comeback, and they were all square after thirty-six holes. On to extra holes they tied the thirty-seventhth hole. On the thirty-eighth hole Sarazen hit a niblick to within two feet, and when Hagen put his second shot into a bunker, Sarazen was victorious. This victory concluded the first half of Sarazen's illustrious career. Although he won many tournaments over the intervening nine years there were no Major victories.

Part of Sarazen's less-than-championship golf during these years was his poor sand play. Being an industrious sort and a real student of his game, Sarazen sought to improve by experimenting with different configurations on his wedge. He added a deep flange and bounce to a straight-faced niblick. Thus was born the sand wedge in 1930-1931 (although some dispute that he was the actual inventor). He called this new club a sand iron. It was not long before most professionals carried one in their bags. With respect to the invention of the sand wedge it must be pointed out that giving Sarazen credit for inventing the sand wedge might be more legend than fact. Some say that the sand wedge was actually invented and patented four years earlier in 1928 by one Edwin Kerr MacClain, a member at Houston Country Club in Texas. Once again the true story of the origins of the sand wedge is shrouded in the annals of time. A footnote to this bit of golf lore: there may be an answer to the dispute. McClain's "freak niblick" had a concave face, the result of which the game's ruling bodies outlawed it as of January 1, 1931. Sarazan's sand iron did not have a concave face and, thus, received acceptance.

In 1932, at the ripe old age of thirty, Sarazen decided to go after the third prestigious title (in addition to the U.S. Open and P.G.A. Championship) open to professionals at the time: the British Open. That summer he arrived at the Prince's Club in Sandwich, England, seeking the British Open Championship. At the halfway point Sarazen had a three-shot lead. After a third round 70 he had increased his lead to five shots. Sarazen shot a final round par 74, and captured the crown by a five-shot margin over Macdonald Smith.

Returning to the United States Sarazen played in the U.S. Open at Fresh Meadows in Flushing, New York. He started off poorly with his 74-76, leaving him five back of the lead. In the third round his 70 moved him to within one shot of the lead. It was the last round that propelled Sarazen to victory.

"The Squire," Gene Sarazen won seven Majors in the 1920s and 1930s.

Sarazen had caught fire over the last 10 holes of the third round in posting his 70. In the fourth round he shot a 66 for a three-shot victory over Phil Perkins and Bobby Cruickshank. How hot was Sarazen? He finished the last twenty-eight holes of the U.S. Open in 100 strokes! This elicited the comment from Bobby Jones that Sarazen's hot streak was "the finest competitive exhibition on record."

In 1933 Sarazen continued his run of Majors with a victory in the P.G.A. Championship at Blue Mound Country Club in Milwaukee, Wisconsin. In the final he had an easy time, defeating Willie Goggin 5 & 4. The year 1935 found Sarazen playing in the second edition of what would become known as the Masters at Augusta National Golf Club, Augusta, Georgia. The course was the product of the collaboration between Bobby Jones and architect Alister Mackenzie. Henry Picard held the halfway lead with rounds of 67-68-135. Craig Wood's 68 in the third round gave him a total of 209 and a one-shot lead over Picard. Wood was three shots clear of Sarazen. In the fourth round Wood played steady golf including a closing birdie on the eighteenth hole for a total of 282. Picard was in at 286. Sarazen came to the fifteenth hole trailing by three shots. He asked his caddy what he needed and the answer was birdies on three of the final four holes for a tie with Wood.

On the par-five fifteenth hole Sarazen hit a long drive with a tail-wind, hook and hard ground contributing. As he walked to his ball he heard the roar for Wood's birdie on eighteen. Sarazen's lie wasn't very good. He was 235 yards from the water-protected hole. He debated with his caddy whether to hit a three- or four-wood. Sarazen chose the four-wood. The second that Sarazen hit the ball he knew it would clear the pond in front of the green. On a low trajectory the ball landed on the green and hopped straight for the cup. The roaring crowd told Sarazen that it had gone in for a double-eagle two, and a tie with Wood, all in one stroke. Only about fifty people witnessed the shot, including Bobby Jones, who had wandered out to the hole to watch the action.

Sarazen almost birdied the par-three sixteenth and parred in for a 282 to tie Wood. The next day they played off over thirty-six holes of stroke play on a cold Augusta morning. For nine holes it was nip and tuck. On the tenth hole Sarazen took the lead and held a four-stroke advantage after the first eighteen holes. Sarazen added another stroke to his lead in the afternoon and won 144-149. With the victory Sarazen became the first man to win all four of the Majors open to professionals. This is an exclusive club. The only others to do so are Ben Hogan, Gary Player, Jack Nicklaus, and Tiger Woods.

Sarazen never won another Major. He came close in 1940, when he lost in a play-off to Lawson Little in the U.S. Open at Canterbury Golf Club near Cleveland, Ohio. And so he had, in effect, two careers of winning Major championships, separated by almost a decade. In all he won three Majors in the 1920s and four Majors in the 1930s for a total of seven career Majors. He captured thirty-nine P.G.A. tournaments over his distinguished career.

In 1973 the seventy-one-year old Sarazen returned to the British Open at Troon, Scotland, an honorary player under the new regulations. He had played at Troon fifty years earlier. Before the tournament Sarazen had made it clear that this would be the final Major championship in which he would compete. When Sarazen came to the eighth hole he had dropped a few shots to par. The eighth hole is called the "Postage Stamp" because of the small green. With a stiff wind blowing against the players Sarazen hit a five-iron that landed on the green and disappeared into the cup for a hole-in one. This was another amazing feat for "the Squire," as he had come to be known, and a memorable exit from competitive golf. During the 1960s Sarazen hosted the television series *Shell's Wonderful World of Golf*. He moved to Naples, Florida where he continued his life as a golf professional. For many years he was an honorary starter at the Masters.

Sarazen was an inaugural member of the P.G.A. Hall of Fame in 1940 and of the World Golf Hall of Fame in 1974. In 1992 he was awarded the highest honor of the U.S.G.A. when it named him the winner of the Bobby Jones Award in recognition of his distinguished sportsmanship. Although he could not match the flair of Hagen or the playing record of Jones, Sarazen earned his place alongside his two great contemporaries. And for all intents and purposes the three of them were the first of the great American triumvirates. Sarazen died at Marco Island, Florida, in 1999 at the age of ninety-eight.

Bobby Jones and Al Espinosa at the 1929 U.S. Open won by Jones in a play-off.

SECTION 4

Bobby Jones

22

Bobby Jones—
The Early Years

Robert Tyre Jones, Jr. was born on St. Patrick's Day, March 17, 1902, in Atlanta, Georgia. He would become the greatest amateur ever to play the game and among his peers was recognized as the best golfer there ever was. His feat of accomplishing the Grand Slam of golf (capturing in the same year the four Major golf tournaments open to amateurs—the U.S. and British Amateurs and Opens) is considered by many to be the greatest sporting accomplishment in the annals of American sports. Today the modern Grand Slam consists of the U.S. and British Opens, the Masters, and the P.G.A. Championship.

Jones grew up preferring to be called "Bob," but he became most affectionately known in the United States, as well as in Scotland, as "Bobby Jones."

Jones was named after his grandfather. He was a rather sickly, frail youth. Digestive problems plagued Jones and biographers have said that he did not eat solid food until he was five years old.

In 1907 Jones's family vacationed at East Lake on the eastern outskirts of Atlanta. Their house was adjacent to the second fairway of the East Lake Golf Club. It was there that Jones was formally introduced to the game of golf. At the age of five he and a friend mapped out a little two-hole course along the roadway and ditch outside the Jones home. His first club was a cut-down cleek (today's two iron). Jones would spend innumerable hours playing up and back on this hand-made "course."

Bobby Jones as a youth.

In 1908 the Jones family moved to East Lake, thus opening up Jones's prospects for a more formal introduction to the game. He met up with Stewart Maiden, a golf professional who had come from Carnoustie, Scotland, to work at East Lake Golf Club. Jones copied Maiden's swing but by all accounts did not take lessons from Maiden, although Maiden did give him advice. Maiden also had a hand in training other fine golfers at East Lake and vicinity. He advised Alexa Sterling, a childhood friend of Jones, who went on to capture three consecutive U.S. Women's Amateur titles. Maiden also mentored Watts Gunn who finished as the runner-up to Jones in the 1925 U.S. Amateur. Incidentally, the Jones-Gunn duel was the only time that two players from the same golf club met in a U.S. Amateur final.

As a youth Jones played with Stirling and another youth from the neighborhood, Perry Adair, who became a fine golfer in his own right. At the age of eleven Jones shot an 80 at East Lake. In 1915, as a thirteen-year-old, Jones captured the club championships at East Lake and Druid Hills.

The following year Jones burst onto the national scene. At the Georgia State Amateur he defeated Adair two-up to capture the title. His father, Robert "the Colonel" Jones, rewarded him by permitting him to enter the 1916 U.S. Amateur, which was being held at the Merion Golf Club, a four-year old club in Ardmore, just west of Philadelphia. Jones was only fourteen years old when he played in the 1916 U.S. Amateur. He stood five-four and was a chunky 165 pounds. When he arrived for the tournament Jones stayed at the Belleview-Strafford Hotel in Philadelphia, and took the suburban train out to Ardmore for the tournament.

There were two stroke-play qualifying rounds for match play, one at the West course and one at the East course. Jones shot 74 at the West course to lead the qualifying after one round. In the second round his nerves got the better of him as he shot an 89 on the East course, but qualified for match play with a 163.

In the first round of match play Jones was paired with Eben Byers, the 1906 U.S. Amateur champion, and twenty-two years Jones's senior. Jones won the match 3 & 2. The second round found Jones matched against Frank Dyer, the 1915 Pennsylvania State champion. Dyer started fast, winning five of the first six holes. Then Jones put on a furious rally. He played the next twenty-eight holes in a fraction over even four's and won 4 & 2. In the third round he came up against the defending champion, Bob Gardner. Jones's wildness off the tee and Gardner's superb putting in the afternoon spelled defeat for Jones. The final margin of victory for Gardner was 5 & 3.

Jones was the sensation of the tournament and everyone marveled at his smooth swing and length off the tee. In one respect he already had the shots and had only to learn how to manage his game around the course to become a golf champion. He worked on this aspect during World War I, when he toured the country playing Red Cross exhibitions. His playing partners were Perry Adair and Alexa Stirling from Atlanta and Elaine Rosenthal, a fine young player from Chicago. After the war Jones looked forward to playing in many renditions of the U.S. Amateur and the U.S. Open. He expected early success, but there would be a time before he would accomplish this dream.

23

Bobby Jones—
The Lean Years

After his initial appearance in the 1916 U.S. Amateur at Merion many predicted that Jones was on the verge of capturing the first of many Majors (the U.S. and British Amateurs and Opens). However, despite some near misses, he endured a period of seven years before he was finally able to break through at the 1923 U.S. Open. A large part of Jones's inability to win Major crowns in his lean years was his temper tantrums. The target of his tantrums was never his opponents, for he was otherwise always a gentleman and sportsman to his adversaries. In fact more than one of his rivals remarked that a chief reason that Bobby Jones had not won a Major Championship was that he went out of his way to console his opponents when they hit a bad shot.

Thus it could be said without exaggeration that during his lean years of 1916 through 1923 Jones's only weakness was a terrible temper. He was prone to fits of extreme anger, cussed a blue streak, and threw clubs with little or no provocation. The most glaring example of his fits came in the 1921 British Open at the Old Course at St. Andrews. This was Jones's first time playing at St. Andrews and he couldn't quite understand the subtleties of the course. After two rounds Jones was still in contention, six strokes back with a 151. In the third round the winds picked up and Jones shot a 46 on the front nine. On the tenth hole he made a double bogey six. On the short par three eleventh Jones again made a double bogey. So incensed was

Fourteen-year-old Bobby Jones at the 1916 U.S. Amateur held at Merion Golf Club.

the temperamental Jones with his play that he tore up his scorecard, picked up his ball and stormed off the course. It was an unforgettable display of unsportsmanlike conduct.

Back home at the 1921 U.S. Amateur Jones had another display of temper when, after a particularly poor shot, he flung his club and struck a woman in the leg. Jones was mortified by his bad temper and resolved to do something about it. He had no choice since the U.S.G.A. had written him, threatening to ban him from its events unless he could learn to control his temper.

Jones vowed to attack the problem and six months later he advised the U.S.G.A. that he was trying to control his temper. That turned out to be true. When it came to tournament golf, he set up the strictest code of sportsmanship. Never again would he lose his temper or throw a club in competition. In short he was beginning to learn that, before he could be a champion, he had to learn how to lose graciously. He had comprehended that golf, if played at the highest level, was a test of character and that in the game there was no place for boorish conduct.

The year 1919 could be called Jones's runner-up year. He lost in the semi-finals of the Southern Amateur, was runner-up in the Canadian Open and finished as the runner-up in the Southern Open. In 1919 the U.S. Amateur was conducted at Oakmont Country Club outside of Pittsburgh. Jones would later say that Oakmont "was, and is, a severe golf course, and the best test of championship golf in this country." After defeating his opponents in the first two rounds Jones met Bob Gardner in the third round.

He defeated Gardner 5 & 4, thus getting a measure of revenge for his defeat by Gardner in the 1916 U.S. Amateur. In the final he came up against David-son Herron, an Oakmont member. At the end of the morning round the match was all square. Herron made a number of long putts in the afternoon and won the championship 5 & 4. During the championship Jones lost eighteen pounds. This was common for him and resulted from his anxiety and the pressure he felt while playing competitive golf. Jones acknowledged that tournaments placed a tremendous strain on him. He remarked that "there are two kinds of golf: golf—and tournament golf. And they are not at all the same thing."

In 1920 Jones won the Southern Amateur and was runner-up in the Southern Open. It was also the year that Jones made his initial appearance in the U.S. Open, which was held at The Inverness Club in Toledo, Ohio.

In the U.S. Open Jones got going in the third round and shot a 70. This put him at 222. Fifty-year old Harry Vardon was leading with a 218. Jones thought he had a chance in the final round, and, in his own words, thought he needed a 70 to win. All the leaders played poorly and Jones's 77 took him out of the running. With nine holes to play Vardon was leading by four strokes but he lost six strokes on the last seven holes. Ted Ray took a 75 and won with a 295. Jones could have won with a 72 but it was not meant to be. It was another close call. His 299 placed him in a tie for eighth with Willie Macfarlane who five years later would beat Jones in a play-off for the U.S. Open at Worchester, Massachusetts.

The 1920 U.S. Amateur was held at the Engineers' Club in Roslyn, New York. Jones won his early matches by comfortable margins and faced Fran-cis Ouimet in the semi-finals. Jones was three down after the morning round. He could make no headway in the afternoon and lost 6 & 5. In the final, Chick Evans beat Ouimet 7 and 6.

As previously recounted 1921 was the year when Jones committed his egregious act of unsportsmanship, picking up his ball on the eleventh hole in the third round of the British Open at St. Andrews.

Jones lost to Allan Graham in the fourth round of the 1921 British Amateur at Royal Liverpool Golf Club, Hoylake, England. He then joined his American teammates in winning the informal match with Britain that presaged the Walker Cup. Jones won his singles and foursomes matches.

Jones returned to America to try his fortune in the 1921 U.S. Open, held at Columbia Country Club, Chevy Chase, Maryland. He opened with a 78 and a 71, five shots behind the leader and eventual champion, Jim

Barnes. Jones shot 77's in the final two rounds, finishing in a tie for fifth. He had moved up from eighth to fifth but didn't celebrate. Around that time Walter Hagen correctly predicted that Jones would win the U.S. Open before he won the U.S. Amateur.

Next came the 1921 U.S. Amateur at the St. Louis Country Club, Clayton, Missouri. Jones played well in the medal rounds and in the early match play rounds. He lost to Willie Hunter 2 & 1 in the quarter-finals.

Jones started 1922 with four operations on his left leg for varicose veins. The U.S. Open was held at Skokie Country Club in Glencoe, Illinois just outside of Chicago. Jones shot 74-72-70 in the first three rounds, and was tied for the lead. Jones then thought that a 68 would be enough to secure victory. He was on the course when word came that Gene Sarazen had shot a 68. Jones shot a 36 on the first nine, and realized that he needed a 36 coming in to tie with Sarazen. Jones came up just short and ended up tied for second. He had moved up a couple more notches with his second place finish, but a Major championship remained elusive. In August 1922 Jones headed north to the National Links at Southampton, Long Island, for the first international golf match for the Walker Cup. The American squad won the Walker Cup rather handily, 8-4. Jones did his part defeating Roger Wethered in his singles and pairing with Jess Sweetser to win their foursomes. A few days later Jones went to The Country Club in Brookline, Massachusetts for the 1922 U.S. Amateur. Jones's 145 placed him second in the medal rounds. In match play Jones made it the semi-finals where he was beaten by eventual champion Jess Sweetser, 8 & 7.

So by 1922 Jones was 20 years old, had now played in 11 national championships and was still looking for his first Major victory. The year 1923 would turn out to be that watershed year.

24

Bobby Jones—
The Run of Majors Leading Up
to the Grand Slam

fter the 1922 U.S. Amateur Jones went to Harvard to pursue a master's degree in literature. He played almost no golf until the following summer when he returned home to prepare for the 1923 U.S. Open at Inwood Country Club on Long Island.

At Inwood Jones opened with a 71, which was a stroke back of Jock Hutchison's 70. Jones was pleased with his position. In the afternoon round Jones shot a 73 to Hutchison's 72. So after two rounds Hutchison was at 142 and Jones was two back with 144. Bobby Cruickshank was in third place at 145. Only three other scores were under 150. Jones prepared himself to shoot a good third round but it was not to be. His score went a bit badly and he finished with a 76. His closest competitors, however, faired even worse. Cruickshank took a 78 and Hutchison staggered in with an 82. After the third round the scoring looked like this: Jones, 220; Cruickshank, 223; and Hutchison, 224.

Jones was wary of Cruickshank who was starting play after Jones did, as the leader did not always tee off last in those days. Jones started off poorly and was out in 39. After a reasonably good start to the back nine with a birdie on the tenth hole he felt that he had righted his wayward round. However, Jones finished feebly in his own mind with a 5-5-6, surrendering four strokes to par. He was worried that he had missed out on another

*Bobby Cruickshank, narrowly beaten by Bobby Jones at the 1923 U.S.
Open for Jones's first Major.*

chance for a Major Championship. In his own words *well, I didn't finish like
a champion. I finished like a yellow dog.*

Jones waited for Cruickshank to finish. Sure enough Cruickshank
caught him with a birdie three on the eighteenth. Jones felt that, if Cruick-

shank had faltered at the end, then he, Jones, would have backed into the championship. This was not how he wanted to win. He wished to prevail with his own good play, not due to the travails of his opponents. So it was on to an 18-hole play-off the next day.

Jones shot par for the first six holes and found himself two stokes behind. After nine holes the players were all square. The match went back and forth until they got to the eighteenth hole still all square. Jones sliced his drive into the short rough and found his ball on hard, clean ground. He decided to go for the green with a two-iron from about 200 yards. The miraculous shot he played to the green allowed him to make par with a four while Cruickshank made six. At last Jones had broken through and won the Major Championship he so desperately craved—the 1923 U.S. Open. Thus, after eleven attempts, Jones could cherish a national championship.

Jones was not finished in 1923 and he had high hopes for the U.S. Amateur at Flossmoor Country Club near Chicago, Illinois. He was the odds-on favorite to win but was eliminated in the second round by Max Martson, the eventual winner.

Following this early-round defeat Jones analyzed his continual spotty performance in match play competition. He concluded that he was putting himself at a disadvantage by playing his opponent when he should have been concerning himself with Old Man Par. If his opponent played better against par Bobby could accept this. What he wanted to eliminate was losing matches in which he had not been outplayed. After Flossmoor Jones adhered to an approach wherein he dueled exclusively with par. From that time on Jones was beaten only three times in championship match play—on each occasion by a foe that had sternly defeated Old Man Par.

In 1924 Jones was the runner-up to Cyril Walker in the U.S. Open at Oakland Hills, outside of Detroit. The 1924 U.S. Amateur was again held at Merion Golf Club, in Ardmore, Pennsylvania. This was eight years after Jones had made his debut in national championships there. Jones was not pressed hard after the second round. In the final he defeated George Von Elm 9 & 8. At last Jones had won the U.S. Amateur—a championship he had coveted since he first played in Major Championships. What made it so much better was that it happened at Merion, a course that would figure prominently in the year of his Grand Slam in 1930. In the Walker Cup that year, he won his singles at Garden City Golf Club on Long Island, as the Americans beat the British and Irish squad 9-3.

There was an interesting development on the equipment front in 1924. The U.S.G.A. permitted the use of steel-shafted clubs. However, Jones continued to play with hickory-shafted clubs throughout his career.

In 1925 Jones lost to Willie Macfarlane in a play-off for the U.S. Open at Worcester Country Club, Worcester, Massachusetts. The 1925 U.S. Amateur was held at Oakmont Country Club near Pittsburgh, Pennsylvania. In the final, Jones faced Watts Gunn, his boyhood rival from Atlanta, Georgia. Both had been captains of the golf team at Georgia Tech. Even more coincidental was the fact that both played out of East Lake Golf Club near Atlanta. This is the only time that the finalists at a U.S. Amateur have come from the same golf club.

Up until the final Gunn had been playing the best golf and was the young sensation of the tournament. After the eleventh hole of the first round of the thirty-six-hole finals Jones was one down to the inspired Gunn. Jones made a sensational bunker save on the twelfth for a half. This propelled him on a hot streak, and he was four-up as they headed to the afternoon round. Jones again started strong, and his 8 & 7 victory made him repeat champion of the U.S. Amateur. Unfortunately, later on in 1925 the Havemeyer Trophy, which goes to the U.S. Amateur champion, was destroyed in a fire at Bobby Jones's home club, East Lake Golf Club, outside of Atlanta.

The year 1926 was a busy year for Jones. First he played in a special match with Walter Hagen, who gave him a sound thrashing 12 & 11. Otherwise, Hagen never enjoyed much success in U.S. Open Championships in which he and Jones competed against each other.

Jones won his singles and foursomes in the 1926 Walker Cup at St. Andrews won by the Americans, 6½–5½ . He then proceeded to win the British Open with a score of 291 at Royal Lytham and St. Anne's Golf Club in Lancashire, England. Back in the United States Jones won the 1926 U.S. Open at Scioto Country Club in Columbus, Ohio. He became the first man to win the U.S. Open and British Open in the same year. In the final of the U.S. Amateur, where Jones was seeking his third straight win, he lost 2 & 1 to George Von Elm. Thus Von Elm had reversed the results of 1924. It was also the only time that the same two men met in the final of a U.S. Amateur, although it was not considered a "repeat" final, since there was an intervening year between their two meetings.

In 1927 Jones won his third U.S. Amateur in four years, beating Chick Evans 8 & 7 in the final. The tournament was held at Minikahada Club in

Minneapolis, Minnesota. In the 1927 U.S. Open Bobby finished in a tie for eleventh place at Oakmont Country Club.

At the 1928 U.S. Amateur, held at Brae Burn Country Club in West Newton, Massachusetts, Jones defeated T. Philip Perkins 10 & 9 in the final. This was his fourth U.S. Amateur crown in five years. The 1928 U.S. Open was played at Olympia Fields Country Club outside of Chicago. Going into the final round Jones led Walter Hagen by three shots and Johnny Farrell by five. Jones finished at 294 in a tie with Farrell. In the play-off Farrell defeated Jones by a single shot, 143-144. Two months later Jones played in the Walker Cup at the Chicago Golf Club. Jones won his singles match over the British Amateur champion, Thomas Perkins, 13 & 12. The U.S. team trounced the British and Irish squad, 11-1.

Jones had now been a national champion winner of either the U.S. Amateur or the U.S. Open for six consecutive years.

In 1929 the U.S. Open was played at Winged Foot Golf Club in Mamaroneck, New York. Jones opened with a 69 and ended up as the only player to break par in a round during the championship. He followed up with rounds of 75 and 71, and led going into the final round by four shots. By the time Jones reached the eighth hole of that final round he had a comfortable margin over the field. There he made a triple bogey, which brought him back to the field, especially to Al Espinosa. Espinosa was playing ahead of Jones and he came in with a 294 to lead the finishers. Jones struggled on the fifteenth hole, and again made a triple bogey. He therefore needed three four's to win. However, on the sixteenthth hole he missed a four-foot putt and made a bogey five. Now he would need two par four's to force a tie. He parred the seventeenth hole. On the eighteenth hole Jones pitched his third shot from a bunker and left himself with a menacing twelve -foot sidehill, downhill putt for a par. Jones stroked the putt with the deft touch of a diamond cutter. The putt held delicately on the edge of the cup and dropped for the par, which put Jones in a play-off with Espinosa.

The next morning Jones requested a one-hour delay so that Espinosa might attend mass. In the thirty-six-hole play-off Jones trounced Espinosa by 23 strokes.

Early in September 1929 the U.S. Amateur was played for the first time on the West Coast at Pebble Beach Golf Links, Monterey, California, then only ten years old and quickly acquiring a renowned reputation. Jones was co-medalist at one over par. In the first round Jones faced an unknown player from Omaha, Nebraska, named Johnny Goodman. To the surprise of the golfing world Goodman beat Jones one up. In 1933, Goodman would become the last amateur to win the U.S. Open. Instead of leaving Pebble Beach upset with his defeat Jones stayed around to watch the rest of the-tournament. This turned out to be fortuitous because Jones got to play Cypress Point, designed by Alister MacKenzie. Jones would later engage MacKenzie as co-designer of Augusta National Golf Club in Augusta, Georgia.

Next came 1930 and Jones's glorious run at the four Major Championships open to amateurs. This included the U.S. Amateur and Open Championships and the British Amateur and Open Championships.

25

Bobby Jones—
The Grand Slam
The "Impregnable Quadrilateral"

In January 1930 Jones laid out his plan for the 1930 campaign to win the four Major Championships to be held that year. Unlike in other years Jones undertook an exercise regimen to lose weight, increase his strength and improve his stamina. During this same period Jones told his friend, O.B. Keeler (a well-known Atlanta journalist who chronicled Jones's career), his wife, Mary, and his father that he planned to mount an assault on the four Major Championships open to amateurs.

With the 1930 Walker Cup Matches scheduled for England Jones felt that this would give him an excellent approach to playing in the British Amateur. The U.S. team prevailed 10-2 in the Matches, and Jones played superbly.

Soon the British bookmakers began to take odds on Jones capturing all four crowns. Bobby Cruickshank, who had been Jones's victim in his first national championship in 1923 the (U.S. Open), was a strong supporter of Jones's chances. Cruickshank wagered $500 at 120-1 odds that Jones would win all four Championships. He subsequently collected $60,000 for the wager as time would tell.

The 1930 British Amateur, the first of the four Majors, was held at St. Andrews, which by then had become one of Jones's favorite courses. Jones had his usual nervousness at playing the seven grueling matches that determined the British Amateur champion. In the first round Jones beat

Henry Roper 3 & 2 after a tough tussle. Jones prevailed rather easily, 5 & 3, over Cowan Shankland in the second round. The third round matched two golfers that the crowds viewed with much anticipation—Jones and Cyril Tolley.

Tolley was a large man, the defending British Amateur champion and one of the longest drivers in the United Kingdom. The winds were at a near-gale force. Jones won the first hole and Tolley the second. By the time they reached the seventeenth hole—the famous "Road Hole"—the match was tied. After both struck safe drives down the left side of the fairway Jones was first to hit his second shot. Fate intervened for Jones as his second shot carried the green and struck a spectator, the ball coming to rest on the back fringe of the green. Tolley, however, played short of the green and his third shot ended up two feet from the hole. Jones's chip came to rest eight feet from the hole. Jones holed his putt as did Tolley, thus maintaining the tie as they moved to the eighteenth hole. There, Jones rolled his twenty-five-foot putt close to the hole, then tapped in for a par. Now, all he could do was watch Tolley putt his twelve-footer for the match. Tolley missed. They went to the first hole of a sudden death play-off.

Both hit good drives. Jones's second shot came to rest ten feet from the hole. Tolley's second was over the green and his chip left him with a troublesome seven-footer for a par. Jones put his approach putt inches from the hole and, even better, he laid Tolley a stymie that he failed to negotiate.

A bit of explanation is in order. Prior to 1952 if a player's ball blocked another player's ball on the green and was more than six inches from it the offending player's ball was not lifted. Instead, the other player had to stroke his ball either around or over the offending player's ball. Incidentally, the scorecards back in those days were six inches in measurement, so that they could be used to measure the six inches governing stymies. After this close victory Jones believed he was destined to win the British Amateur crown, but there was much work to be done.

In his afternoon match Jones faced Harrison Johnston, his Walker Cup teammate and reigning U.S. Amateur champion. After a stiff battle, in which Jones lost three holes late in the match, Jones rolled in a tricky eight-foot putt at the last to win another close match, one-up.

He proceeded to beat another Englishman, G.O. Watt, and then Eric Fidden. In the semi-finals he went up against another Walker Cup team-mate, George Voigt. Voigt played superbly and, with five holes to play, found himself two-up. Jones won the fourteenth and sixteenth to square the

Bobby Jones with the four Grand Slam trophies in 1930.

match. Jones had to sink an eighteen-foot putt on the seventeenth to halve. He did. On the eighteenth Jones put his second shot eight feet from the pin. Voigt chipped his third to within six feet. Jones missed his putt but he got his par. Now, Voigt had to sink his six-footer for a par-saving half. He missed and Jones had secured another close victory. For the third time in three days Jones had won by the narrowest of margins—one-up.

In the thirty-six-hole final Jones faced Roger Wethered, a superb British player. After the morning round Jones found himself four-up. In the afternoon Jones played with a mixture of caution and aggressiveness. Wethered withered under Jones's play and began spraying his drives and missing short putts. When Jones rolled in a three-foot putt on the twelfth hole, the thirtieth hole of the match, he had defeated Wethered 7 & 6.

Virtually everyone acknowledged that the best player had won the 1930 British Amateur. The first leg of the Grand Slam was in the bag and Jones briefly basked in his triumph with a much-deserved respite in Paris, accompanied by his wife Mary and some friends.

The British Open came next at the Royal Liverpool Golf Club at Hoylake just outside of Liverpool, England. Jones qualified with rounds of 73 and 77 for a total of 150. This score tied him for twentieth place with six other players among the 196 entrants.

After the first round Jones led with a two-under par 70. Jones's second round was an even par 72, and he maintained his slim one-shot lead over English pro Fred Robson, three shots over Horton Smith and five over Archie Compston. Macdonald Smith and another American, Leo Diegel, were six shots to the rear. In the third round Compston played inspired golf while Jones's play was uneven. At the end of the morning third round Compston's 68 to Jones's 74 left Jones one behind Comptson. In the fourth round, at the long par five eighth, Jones played a wayward chip that failed to make the green. His second chip left him with a ten-foot putt for par. Jones putted two feet past the hole and missed the return putt. This gave him a double bogey. He finished the front nine with a 38.

Jones knew he needed to birdie the par five sixteenth for any chance for the championship. Jones got it by getting up and down from a greenside bunker. He parred the last two holes for a 75 and a total of 291. Compston faded with an 82. There were still Leo Diegel and Macdonald Smith to contend with. Diegel came to the sixteenth needing to par the last three holes to tie Jones. He bogeyed the sixteenth and that was it for Diegel. Smith had to play the last five holes in one-under par to tie. Coming to the eighteenth, he needed to hole his approach shot to tie Jones. His shot hit the green and ran past the pin. Jones had his second leg of the Grand Slam.

On July 2, 1930 Jones arrived back in the United States as the only American to win the British Amateur and British Open Championships in the same year. He was given a hero's welcome in the form of the traditional ticker-tape parade in New York City.

Shortly thereafter Jones headed to Interlachen Country Club in Edina, Minnesota. This was the site of the 1930 U.S. Open, and the weather was oppressively hot.

In the first round Jones shot a 71, which put him one shot behind Macdonald Smith and Tommy Armour. After a second round 73 Jones found himself two shots behind Horton Smith. Jones's third round was exceptional. He missed only three fairways. He also missed only three greens in regulation. He had nine one-putt greens. His third round total was 68 and

Plaque at Merion Golf Club honoring Bobby Jones's accomplishing the "Grand Slam" in 1930.

ON SEPTEMBER 27, 1930
AND ON THIS HOLE

ROBERT TYRE JONES. JR.

COMPLETED HIS "GRAND SLAM"
BY WINNING
THE U.S. AMATEUR CHAMPIONSHIP

it gave him a five-shot lead over "Lighthorse" Harry Cooper. It was the lowest round of the tournament.

Jones started off the fourth round slowly, shooting a 38, five shots worse than his morning round. After he played the thirteenth he found himself only one shot ahead of Macdonald Smith. Jones birdied the fourteenth and sixteenth with a par in between. After a lost ball on the seventeenth Jones made double bogey and felt the U.S. Open slipping away or at least into a tie. At the eighteenth Jones's approach landed 40 feet from the hole. Jones studied the putt for a long time. He rolled the putt in for a birdie. His final round had been erratic with three double bogeys and four birdies for a 75 and a total of 287, one shot off the U.S. Open record.

His victory had been sealed with the run of three birdies in the last five holes. The order of finish was the same as in the British Open—Jones first, Macdonald Smith second and Horton Smith third. Horton Smith would later, in 1934, become the winner of Jones's inaugural Invitational—now known as "the Masters." He would also win it in 1936.

Only one leg of the Grand Slam remained: the U.S. Amateur at Merion Golf Club, which began on September 22, 1930. Jones had started his appearances on the national scene at Merion in 1916. He won his first U.S. Amateur there, defeating George Von Elm 9 & 8 in 1924. So, Jones was familiar with the championship East Course nestled in Ardmore, Pennsylvania, a Philadelphia suburb, not ten miles west of the city.

Jones arrived in Philadelphia at the Broad Street Station on September 17th. He stayed at the Barclay Hotel on Rittenhouse Square. With the U.S. Amateur starting on September 22 Jones had several days to collect himself. Before the tournament started Jones was persuaded to play a practice round with Jess Sweetser at Pine Valley Golf Club across the Delaware River in

New Jersey. Today Pine Valley is generally regarded as the number-one ranked course in the United States.

In the two qualifying rounds at Merion Jones captured medalist honors when he shot rounds of 69-73-142. This equaled the lowest qualifying score in the U.S. Amateur.

In the first round Jones played Sandy Somerville, an accomplished golfer from Canada. Jones played the outgoing nine in four under par. Somerville played tenaciously and was one down after six holes. Jones proceeded to birdie seven, eight and nine to take a four-up lead at the turn. He won 5 & 4.

After defeating Somerville, Jones's afternoon eighteen-hole match was against Fred Hoblitzel, another Canadian. Jones could not maintain his sterling play from the morning round, and shot a wayward 42 on the outgoing nine. However, Hoblitzel did not have the game to stay with Jones and Jones won by the same 5 & 4 score by which he had won against Somerville.

The next day Jones won his quarter-final match (the first of the thirty-six-hole matches) against Fay Coleman from southern California. The score was 6 & 5.

On Friday, September 26 Jones played his semi-final match against his long-time foe, Jess Sweetser. Against Sweetser, Jones got off to a fast start, winning four of the first five holes. Over the next several holes he lapsed into some complacency so that, by the fourteenth hole, his lead had shrunk to two-up. Jones then won the fourteenth and eighteenth holes to break for lunch with a four-up lead. In the afternoon Jones continued with his solid play, extending his lead to six-up after six holes. He then won the seventh through the ninth holes and eventually prevailed 10 & 8.

The winner of the other semi-final was Eugene Homans, a twenty-two-year-old from Englewood, New Jersey. His opponent was Charlie Seaver who later became known as the father of Tom Seaver, the three-time Cy Young Award winner in Major League baseball.

Homans got off to a slow start against Seaver and was five down after the first eighteen holes. In the second eighteen-hole round Homans slowly pared Seaver's lead, and was one down with two holes to play. He won the last two holes and defeated Seaver one-up.

The final between Jones and Homans took place on Saturday, September 27, 1930—potentially the most important day in the history of golf. A crowd of 18,000 or so had gathered. Many of the interested spectators had come by trolley from Philadelphia or by the Pennsylvania Railroad on the

Paoli local, a commuter train that today continues to run up and down Philadelphia's Main Line. Those who drove paid 50 cents for parking in the vicinity of Ardmore Avenue and Haverford Road. By 10:00 AM, all the parking spaces were filled.

To protect Jones from the crush of the crowd a cadre of fifty U.S. Marines was in attendance to lead Jones and Homans around the course.

Jones appeared confident, as well he should have, but inside he was a bundle of nerves. His smallest margin of victory had been 5 & 4. Not since the final of the 1926 U.S. Amateur against George Von Elm had he been beaten at thirty-six holes. Homans was also nervous as he was well aware that he was the only obstacle between Jones and the unthinkable—the "Grand Slam" (coined by O.B. Keeler) or the "Impregnable Quadrilateral"— (credited to George Trevor, the sportswriter for the *New York Sun*) the acquisition of the four recognized Major Golf Championships an amateur could win in a single year.

Both players started off efficiently and Jones, while not playing his best golf, was two-up after seven holes. With Homans close on his heels Jones accelerated his game as he had done all week. At the end of the morning eighteen holes Jones suddenly had a seven-up lead. Jones had shot a 72. Homans was in with a 79. Now it was no longer a question of whether Jones would prevail but questions of when and by how much.

In the afternoon Jones quickly took the third and fourth holes, and his lead was now nine-up. Jones and Homans halved the next four holes. Jones lost the ninth hole and the two halved the tenth with double bogeys. It was only Jones's third double bogey in 151 holes of golf.

Going into the eleventh hole Jones was dormied, meaning that he had an eight-hole lead with but eight holes to play. He only had to win or tie one more hole to prevail. Merion's eleventh hole is a short 378 yards. One hundred yards from the tee the hole drops abruptly into a narrow valley. The pitch is to a small green with a stream called the Baffling Brook fronting the green and winding its way along the right side to the rear. Both players hit drives that landed in the fairway. Homans hit his pitch first and it landed eighteen feet above the pin. Jones pitched a high shot that landed twenty feet below the pin.

Jones's first putt was a thing of beauty under the circumstances, ending ten inches from the cup. Homans had to hole his putt to stay in the match. As his putt headed toward the hole it swerved to the right about half way there. He immediately conceded Jones's putt and strode over to shake

Jones's hand. Jones had won 8 & 7.

Jones, Homans, their caddies and the Marines marched in a corridor of spectators up the twelfth hole, across Ardmore Avenue, and on to the club-house. It was in every sense a triumphant journey. There by the first tee Jones received the Havemeyer Trophy, named after the first president of the United States Golf Association.

After the presentation Jones spoke briefly and the crowd waited in an-ticipation to hear what Jones would do next in his outstanding career now capped with the Grand Slam.

Jones gave a little hint. In words surrounded in ambiguity he said:

I expect to continue to play golf, but just when and
where I cannot say now. I have no definite plans
either to retire or as to when and where I may continue
in competition. I might play next year and lay off in 1932
I might stay out of the battle next season and
feel like another tournament the following year.
That's all I can say about it now.

The vague remarks puzzled the media. They had been led to believe that, after the U.S. Open, Jones had vowed to retire from Major Champi-onship golf if he won the U.S. Amateur. In truth there were no more worlds to conquer. For its part Merion Golf Club had been the beginning, the mid-dle and the end of Jones's career. Later he would gratefully accept an honorary membership in the Merion Golf Club. Another ticker-tape parade awaited Jones. Thus he became the only person ever to receive such honor on two occasions.

Jones gave his future some further thought over the next two months. In due course he penned a brief letter to the U.S.G.A. announcing that he was giving up his amateur status. The date was November 17, 1930.

A summary of his legendary accomplishments underscores his domi-nance: Jones won thirteen of the twenty-seven Major championships in which he competed. He did this playing with hickory shafts, and without a sand iron. From 1923 to 1930 Jones won or finished second in 80 percent of the Major championships in which he competed. During that period neither Walter Hagen nor Gene Sarazen, the premier professionals of the time, won a U.S. Open or a British Open in which Jones competed.

26

Bobby Jones—
The "Retirement Years"

A s Jones contemplated what endeavors he would pursue after he retired from Major Championship golf he understood that the opportunities were endless. Jones had only a couple of regrets when he retired. Had he retired too soon? Was he not a complete golfer? Only Bobby Jones, the consummate champion, deigned to ponder such questions. Once he retired, however, he realized that these questions would best be left unanswered, for it was time to get on with other pursuits.

Jones was not a rich man when he left champion golf's stage. As an example, in 1930, he was able to afford to make the trans-Atlantic trip for the first two legs of the Grand Slam, in part, because some of his expenses were covered through his participation in the Walker Cup. While many of his fans thought that he was well-to-do this was not the case. Only with the help of his family did he manage to purchase a large house in the Druid Hill section of Atlanta. Bobby Jones and his wife lived there for three years. In 1928, aided by his father's help with the financing, Jones and his family moved to a house in the northeast section of Atlanta known as Buckhead.

Once he chose to retire Jones was flooded with offers and opportunities. Many wanted to capitalize on the Jones mystique and popularity. However, they came face-to-face with a man of integrity and good taste who would not be exploited. Rather, the opportunities that Jones selected reflected his integrity, good sense, and sensibilities. There wasn't going to be

*Horton Smith, winner of the 1934 and 1936 tournament, which would
shortly thereafter become known as "The Masters."*

any passive endorsements or lending of Jones's name simply for the sake
of monetary reward. Jones wanted to earn his remuneration in all the projects and activities that he pursued.

Among his early ventures was the development of a series of instructional films he made for Warner Brothers. The first series was entitled *How
I Play Golf*. The cast of students included many well-known Hollywood stars
who worked without pay, for the privilege of appearing in these "shorts" as
they were called. Jones's next venture was to go on the radio at the same
time as his instructional short films were being released. His radio appearances were every Wednesday night and consisted of the highlights of
Jones's career with a little instruction added in.

In 1931 he was engaged by A.G. Spalding and Brothers to design a new
set of golf clubs. Jones set out to duplicate his hickory-shafted clubs though
with steel shafts. The set came out in 1932 and was a rousing success with
over two million sold in fifteen different models.

The lion's share of Jones's energy went into the pursuit of a dream to build a golf course with all the elements of the game to which he was partial. Jones founded and co-designed the course known as the Augusta National Golf Club. His co-designer was the architect Alister Mackenzie.

Mackenzie had shown his talents in the design of the spectacular course at Cypress Point in Monterey, California. Jones became acquainted with Mackenzie after Jones's first-round upset in the 1929 U.S. Amateur at the Pebble Beach Golf Links. He stayed at the tournament and played Cypress Point where he developed a friendship with Mackenzie.

In the fall of 1930 Clifford Roberts, a well-placed New York financier, took Jones to a 365-acre tract of land in Augusta called Fruitlands. It had been bought and run as a nursery by the family of a Belgian baron, Louis Edourard Matieu Berckmans.

It didn't take long for Jones to become convinced that this was the place to build his course. In due course he acquired the property. When the design and construction were almost finished Mackenzie called it his finest achievement. Alas, Mackenzie died in early 1932 just before the course was completed.

Augusta National's generous fairways, sparse bunkering and large greens gave the course an aura of accommodating play. Its looks were deceiving. The course was a masterpiece of strategic design and became the quintessential thinking-man's golf course.

In 1932 the course was completed and almost immediately the U.S.G.A., Jones, and Roberts conferred about bringing a U.S. Open to the venue. There was a timing problem, however. The U.S.G.A wanted to continue the Open in its usual June time slot but the bermuda and rye grasses of Augusta National could not withstand the summer heat. Jones and Roberts could not persuade the U.S.G.A. to yield on the timing. Accordingly, Jones and Roberts went in a different direction and there was born the springtime inaugural of Jones's invitational tournament which eventually became known as "the Masters."

The first Annual Invitation Tournament was held at Augusta National Golf Club, March 22 through March 25, 1934. While Roberts wanted to call the tournament "the Masters" from the outset, Jones vetoed the idea as being too presumptuous. And even though the sportswriters began calling it "the Masters," it wasn't until 1938 that "the Masters" became the tournament's official name.

Obviously Jones was the main attraction at the first Masters. He played well from tee to green. But his chipping and putting betrayed him and it became obvious that he no longer had the concentration and determination to play at the high level he expected of himself when he was an amateur. He opened with a 76 and finished the tournament at 294, in a tie for thirteenth place, ten shots behind the inaugural winner, Horton Smith. That was the best finish that Jones had in any of the dozen Masters in which he competed. He played in his last Masters in 1948, the last competitive golf he would play.

For 1935, the second year, the nines were reversed. Jones felt that the water on the new back nine would place a premium on strong play by the leaders and afford an opportunity for a player in the hunt to gamble and make up ground. It turned out that Jones was prophetic. At the 1935 Masters Craig Wood was in the clubhouse with a three-shot lead over Gene Sarazen when Sarazen stood in the fifteenth fairway. Sarazen made his famous double eagle with a four wood, caught Woods and beat him in the next day's play-off.

While golf was a continuing interest Jones also had a variety of other business ventures. He became a vice president for A.G. Spalding. In early 1939 he purchased a Coca-Cola franchise to bottle and distribute Coca-Cola in New England. He also founded the Peachtree Golf Club, another gem of a course, in Atlanta, Georgia. Along with these interests Jones also found some time to practice law.

In 1942 Jones enlisted in the army as a captain even though he had several exemptions available to him. He served in Europe during World War II and was discharged as a lieutenant colonel.

Jones continued to write occasional articles for the *American Golfer* and wrote regular columns for newspaper syndication. He wrote three books: the immensely popular *Down the Fairway* in 1927, followed by *Golf is My Game* in 1960, and *Bobby Jones on Golf* in 1966.

Disease finally got the better of Jones but not without an historic struggle. In July 1956 he underwent examination at the Columbia-Presbyterian Medical Center in New York. The diagnosis was syringomyelia, a disease of the spinal cord characterized as a degenerative muscular disease. This medical condition causes a gradual deterioration of the nerves. Most patients at that time died within five to seven years after being diagnosed. Representative of his fighting spirit Jones confounded the doctors by living with the disease for twenty-three years after first showing symptoms.

In 1958 Jones was invited back to St. Andrews to receive a very rare award. He was made a Freeman of the Royal Burgh of St. Andrews. This made him the first American so honored since Benjamin Franklin in 1757.

Jones continued to attend the Masters after his illness, and, when he could no longer walk the course, he could be found riding around the course in a golf cart. By 1967 he was too ill to go out on the course in a golf cart and would watch the play from his cabin off the tenth tee. In 1968 he made his last appearance at the Masters.

From April to December 1971 Jones was confined to bed. On December 4, 1971 he suffered a ruptured aneurysm which would have killed most people in a week. It took two and a half weeks for Jones to succumb.

On December 10, in a gesture to please his wife Mary, Jones converted to Catholicism. He said he would have done it sooner if he had known how happy it would have made her.

At 6:33 PM, on December 18th Bobby Jones died peacefully in his sleep at home. His grave at Oakland Cemetery in Atlanta sits near an old brick wall. His tombstone simply reads: Robert Tyre Jones, Jr. Born 1902, Died 1971. Eventually his wife and three children were buried at the same site.

The U.S.G.A. paid homage to Jones by naming its annual award for sportsmanship after him.

He left a legacy that was a legend like no other golfer. Grantland Rice, renowned sportswriter and longtime friend of Jones, said it with eloquence: "Whatever any future giant of the links does to par, no one will ever replace Bobby Jones in the hearts of those to whom golf means more than a game." While many great golfers have come along since including the likes of Ben Hogan, Sam Snead, Byron Nelson, Arnold Palmer, Jack Nicklaus, Gary Player, Tiger Woods,and Rory McIlroy, Rice's words for many have withstood the test of time.

Jones became an inaugural member of the World Golf Hall of Fame in 1974.

Byron Nelson won an unprecedented eleven tournaments in a row in 1945.

SECTION 5

The Era of Post-Bobby Jones
Through World War II

27

Glenna Collett Vare and Her Battles With Joyce Wethered

O n the cusp of the Roaring Twenties the undisputed champion golfer among women was Alexa Stirling. She had won three straight U.S. Amateur championships in 1916, 1919, and 1920 (war intervening from 1917 to 1918). After she retired a new generation of women stepped to the fore. Among the foremost of them were Glenna Collett Vare, of the United States, and Joyce Wethered, of England. Their spirited competition on both sides of the Atlantic reflected the boom in women's golf during the 1920s. The history of women's golf during this period would be incomplete without mention of another fine English golfer, Cecil Leitch. In 1914, she won the first of four British Ladies Amateurs. This ties a record she shares with Joyce Wethered.

Following Alexa Stirling's three successive U.S. Amateur titles Glenna Collett (later Mrs. E. H. Vare) took center stage in the United States.

As the best woman golfer in America in the 1920s Collett was a strong, graceful girl from Providence, Rhode Island, who eventually settled in Philadelphia. In 1917 when she was fourteen, her father encouraged her to hit golf balls, and she became hooked on the game. Her goal of becoming a champion golfer was enhanced when later that summer she watched Alexa Stirling play in a wartime exhibition with the other "Dixie Whiz Kids," Bobby Jones, Perry Adair, and Elaine Rosenthal. Over the next four years Collett honed her game and in 1921, at age eighteen, she won the Rhode

Island and Massachusetts amateur championships and was the medalist in the U.S. Women's Open qualifying.

In 1922, after capturing the prestigious North and South Amateur, the young Rhode Islander took the U.S. Women's Amateur at the Greenbrier in White Sulphur Springs, West Virginia. Collett was the medalist and sailed through to the championship. As had Bobby Jones, Collett had finally "broken though" and won a Major women's championship.

In 1923 Collett was poised to defend her U.S. Amateur title. Her defense ended in the quarter-finals when she was beaten 3 & 2 by Philadelphian Florence Vanderbeck.

The year 1924 turned out to be a sensational year for Collett. She competed in thirteen events and won twelve of them. Among her victories was her third consecutive Eastern Amateur, which was played at Whitemarsh Valley Country Club in Lafayette Hills, Pennsylvania. The runner-up, Alexa Stirling Fraser, was six strokes back.

Unfortunately, the only tournament that Collett did not win that year was the U.S. Women's Amateur. She lost in the semi-finals in her hometown of Providence to a nationally ranked tennis player and golfer, Mary K. Browne. The score was one-up. Perhaps the most amazing series of events to come out of this tournament were that in the same year Browne reached the semi-final round of the national golf championship and the final of the national tennis championship.

In 1925 Collett reclaimed the U.S. Women's Amateur at St. Louis Country Club, St. Louis, Missouri. She defeated Alexa Stirling Fraser in the final, 9 & 8. Her 78 average for the seven completed rounds was the best golf ever played in competition by an American woman.

It was not the best golf in all the world however, as, a few months earlier, Collett met her match in Joyce Wethered, England's women's champion. In the 1925 Ladies' British Amateur Championship at Troon, the two met in the third round. Wethered beat Collett 4 & 3, making six birdies over the extremely long par 79 course.

Compared to previous years 1926 was not a bright spot on Collett's golf résumé. She finished runner-up in the Eastern Amateur. At the U.S. Women's Amateur held at Merion Collett was the medalist in the qualifying rounds but yielded in the third round to Virginia Wilson. The following year Collett again won the North and South, and the Eastern Amateur. She came up short in the U.S. Women's Amateur losing to Alexa Stirling Fraser 2 & 1 in the second round.

In 1928 Collett won her third U.S. Women's Amateur at the Homestead in Hot Springs, Virginia. She won all of her matches easily, but none more so than in the final against Virginia Van Wie. The thrashing was an incredible 13 & 12, and was the most lopsided victory in the history of the championship. In winning her third championship Collett joined a celebrated group of four others who held the championship three times: Beatrix Hoyt, Margaret Curtis, Alexa Stirling Fraser and Dorothy Campbell Hurd. As time would tell this record would step by the wayside, done in by Collett herself (six) and much later by Joanne Gunderson Carner (five).

Collett also made another attempt in 1928 to win the British Ladies Amateur Championship at Hunstanton, Norfolk, England. In wretched weather she lost in the fourth round to Mabel Wragg. Joyce Wethered did not compete at Hunstanton, having withdrawn from tournament golf after her 1925 triumph at Troon.

While Collett represented the best golf American women could offer the title of the world's unrivaled best player belonged to Britain's Joyce Wethered. By 1929 she had already beaten Collett four & three in their only head-to-head competition at the British Ladies's Amateur Championship in 1925.

Wethered's record was incomparable even when matched against that of Collett. From 1920 through 1925 Wethered entered the English Ladies' Amateur Championship five times, and won it all five times. She entered the British Ladies' Amateur Championship five times and won it four times. Back before she won the Championship she was the runner-up in 1921.

Her first three wins in the British Ladies' Amateur Championship came in 1922, 1924, and 1925. Thereafter she did not enter the championship for three years. But the 1929 British Ladies' Amateur Championship was to be played over the Old Course at St. Andrews and this lured her back. Similarly, the prospect of playing at St. Andrews enticed Collett back, with the added incentive of another go against Wethered.

Neither of the two great champions had much difficulty gaining the final at St. Andrews. In the final Collett got off to a magnificent start, shooting a 34, two under men's par, on the front nine, and amassing a five-hole lead over Wethered after nine holes. But a combination of excellent play by Wethered and more mortal play on the part of Collett left the latter with only a two-hole lead after the first eighteen had been played. Halfway through the second round the American was four down. She had lost nine of the last fifteen holes and no one could recall such a reversal of fortunes.

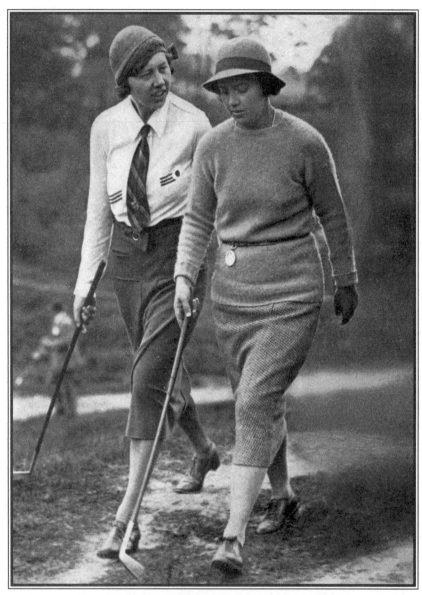

Joyce Wethered and Glenna Collett Vare, the English
and American rivals of the 1920s.

It wasn't that Collett was playing poorly but it was the brilliance of Wethered's play that turned the tide. Collett rallied and found herself two down with seven holes to play. She was dormie two at the 17th— the "Road Hole" (two down with two holes to play). Collett's rally ended at the Road

Hole as she carded a six and so Wethered won 3 & 1. This victory marked Wethered's fourth and last British Ladies' Amateur Championship. Down through the years the match is still generally regarded as one of the greatest matches in women's amateur golf. The win solidified Wethered's place as the world champion. For Collett it was to be the loss she regretted the most.

Back in the United States the 1929 U.S. Woman's Amateur was held at Oakland Hills in suburban Detroit. Here Collett won her second straight Amateur. It was the first time she had successfully defended her crown. Collett's victory was a milestone. She became the first women to win the Amateur four times, surpassing Beatrix Hoyt, Margaret Curtis, Alexa Stirling Fraser, and Dorothy Campbell Hurd. Yet it was the memory of St. Andrews and her loss to Joyce Wethered that left Collett with the feeling that she had let the world championship slip from her grasp.

In 1930, with Wethered not competing Collett went over to try again to win the British Ladies' Amateur Championship, this time as the favorite. She played unevenly and had some narrow escapes but made it to the final again against Diana Fishwick. The nineteen-year-old Fishwick stopped Collett on the thirty-third hole, 4 & 3.

Back Stateside the 1930 U.S. Women's Amateur was played for the first time on the West Coast at the Los Angeles Country Club. Now twenty-seven, Collett was the obvious favorite, and seeking her third straight U.S. Women's Amateur. She played Virginia Van Wie (who would win three straight U.S. Women's Amateurs herself from 1932 to 1934) in the thirty-six-hole final. Five-up after the morning round, Collett went on to win her third consecutive championship, 6 & 5. It was her fifth U.S. Women's Amateur overall.

In 1931 Collett went to the Country Club of Buffalo in late September to defend her U.S. Women's Amateur crown, now as Mrs. Edwin H. Vare, Jr. and a Philadelphia resident. Mrs. Vare met Virginia Van Wie again, this time in the semi-finals, and finally prevailed two-up.

In the final Mrs. Vare faced Helen Hicks of Long Island. Hicks played steady golf in the outward nine in the morning and held a two-up lead at the turn. By the end of the morning round, however, Mrs. Vare was on top by one hole.

Hicks won the fourteenth and fifteenth in the second round to go two-up. They halved the sixteenth, and Mrs. Vare needed a five-footer to win the seventeenth. She could not hole the putt and Hicks was the new champion, 2 & 1.

The Curtis Cup was first played in 1932 and was named for Harriet and Margaret Curtis who donated the Cup and who had been among the best of the American women players in the first dozen years of the twentieth century. The competition pitted the best women amateurs from the United States against their counterparts from Great Britain and Ireland.

Wethered was coaxed out of retirement to face Mrs. Vare in the number one foursomes (in foursomes, teams of two play alternate shots). The Americans won one- up. In the afternoon singles Mrs. Vare and Wethered again dueled head-to-head. History repeated itself and Wethered soundly beat Mrs. Vare 6 & 4. In the end, however, the Americans, with their strong play in the foursomes, won the first Curtis Cup. The final score was the United States 5½, Great Britain and Ireland 3½ .

The 1932 U.S. Women's Amateur was hosted by the Salem Country Club in Peabody, Massachusetts. The final was one of familiarity as Mrs. Vare faced her long-time rival, Virginia Van Wie. They had opposed each other in the 1928 final, the 1930 final and the 1931 semi-finals, Mrs. Vare being victorious all three times. This time the result was the other way around with Van Wie capturing a convincing win, 10 & 8.

With the birth of her first child, a daughter, Mrs. Vare did not compete in the 1933 U. S. Women's Amateur. In July 1934 Glenna gave birth to a son. That October, with Mrs. Vare serving as non-playing captain, the Americans retained the Curtis Cup, 6½ -5½ at the Chevy Chase Country Club in Chevy Chase, Maryland.

The 1934 U.S. Women's Amateur returned to the Philadelphia area with its playing at Whitemarsh Valley Country Club. Mrs. Vare shared medalist honors. In the semi-finals she faced Virginia Van Wie, by now the two-time defending champion. Mrs. Vare played creditably through the first twelve holes but Van Wie pulled away for a 3 & 2 victory.

Following her victory over Mrs. Vare, Van Wie captured her third and final national championship, 2 & 1 over a Californian, Dorothy Traung. Shortly thereafter Van Wie retired from competition. She declined to defend her title in 1935 and with little else to prove, her third consecutive U.S. Women's Amateur at Whitemarsh Valley brought down the curtain on her illustrious career.

The 1935 U.S. Women's Amateur was held at Interlachen Country Club in Edina, Minnesota. The course was well-known as the site of Bobby Jones's third leg of the Grand Slam (the U.S. Open) five years earlier.

Mrs. Vare shot an 85 in the medal round, six shots off the lead. Also shooting an 85 was a seventeen-year-old host club member named Patty Berg, who would later become a top professional in the women's game.

Mrs. Vare breezed through match play until the semi-finals when she was extended to the seventeenth hole before prevailing 2 & 1 over Beatrice Barrett. Mrs. Vare met Patty Berg in the final. It was a match-up of the best woman golfer in America against the long-hitting Berg from the home club.

After the morning round Mrs. Vare's superior iron play eased her into a four-up lead. By the thirty-third hole, however, Berg had cut the deficit in half. They both birdied this hole. On the thirty-fourth hole Berg rolled in a twenty-footer for a par. Mrs. Vare then made a birdie to win 3 & 2.

At the age of thirty-two Mrs. Vare had now won the U.S. Women's Amateur a total of six times, which was more than twice as many as anyone else had done to that date (in an eleven-year period beginning in 1957, Joanne Gunderson Carner won five titles before turning professional). Collett Vare's record is not likely to be broken.

With this 1935 championship win Mrs. Vare had no intention of retiring as had Bobby Jones, Virginia Van Wie and Joyce Wethered. Settling into her Philadelphia lifestyle she would simply play in a few competitions each year without the same sense of urgency with which she had previously filled her career.

In 1936 Mrs. Vare's golf consisted primarily of playing in the Curtis Cup. The American team traveled to Scotland to play the matches at Gleneagles. Mrs. Vare played with Patty Berg in the foursomes and they halved their match. Mrs. Vare won her singles match. The British and Irish squad, however, played to the level of the American team and the matches ended tied at 4½ points. This result allowed the Americans to retain the Cup, an apt result in which their opponents concurred as gracious competitors.

Mrs. Vare's health did not allow her to defend her U.S. Women's Amateur title in 1936. She also declined to play in 1937. Mrs. Vare returned to the U.S. Women's Amateur in 1938 at Westmoreland Country Club near Chicago, Illinois. She lost in the first round. Patty Berg was crowned champion.

The 1938 Curtis Cup was played at the Essex Country Club, the home club of Harriot and Margaret Curtis, in Manchester, Massachusetts. Mrs. Vare lost in the foursomes but won her singles match as the United States retained the Cup 5½–3½. It was Mrs. Vare's third appearance in the Curtis Cup. Because of the onset of World War II the event was not resumed until 1948.

Mrs. Vare last played in the Curtis Cup in 1948 at Southport's Royal

Birkdale course in England. She had not expected to play but placed herself in the foursomes where she and Dorothy Kirby prevailed 4 & 3. Mrs. Vare sat herself down in the singles, and the final tally was United States 6½, Great Britain & Ireland 2½. Mrs. Vare captained the American side in the 1950 Curtis Cup held at the Country Club of Buffalo. The American women prevailed, 7½-1½, the largest victory margin thus far. With this triumph Mrs. Vare concluded her Curtis Cup tenure. She had participated in the event since its inaugural in 1932, two times as a non-playing captain. She was forty-six.

Collett maintained her desire for competition albeit not at the national level. She played on Philadelphia Country Club's team in interclub matches until she was 70.

In 1962 the U.S.G.A. inaugurated the Senior Women's Amateur Championship. The first playing was at Manufacturers Golf and Country Club, Fort Washington, Pennsylvania—partly out of deference to Mrs. Vare. She finished second, seven strokes back of Maureen Orcutt. Mrs. Vare competed in the event several more times on into her sixties.

Despite being a lifelong amateur Mrs. Vare was inducted into the L.P.G.A. Hall of Fame in 1950. In 1953 that organization instituted the Vare Trophy for the lowest annual scoring average on the women's professional tour. Another honor bestowed on Mrs. Vare was the Bob Jones Award. She received this honor in 1965, which is given to a person who emulates Jones's sportsmanship, respect for the game and its rules, generosity of spirit, and sense of fair play.

Mrs. Vare's husband died in 1975 and for a number of years afterward she maintained her residence in Bryn Mawr, Pennsylvania. Later she divided her time between Narragansett, Rhode Island and Gulfstream, Florida, a resort village. Up until her last years Mrs. Vare regularly shot her age or better.

Mrs. Vare died at Gulfstream on February 3, 1989, at the age of eighty-five. She was remembered as the Great Glenna. She had come on the scene in the 1920s and changed the game for women. She hit the ball hard and far like a man, was fiercely competitive and had respected leadership skills, all while maintaining her attractive femininity. Perhaps the greatest tribute afforded Glenna Collett Vare was the acclamation of her admirers that she was "the female Bobby Jones."

28

After Bobby Jones,
Then Who?

Although Bobby Jones dominated his tenure on the world golf scene there were other great golfers who played in his time. Two, of course, who stood out were Walter Hagen and Gene Sarazen. Others also flourished in the Age of Bobby Jones.

The likes of Jock Hutchinson and Jim Barnes had had success in the early 1920s but were past their prime as the Age of Jones took center stage. Others like Craig Wood, Denny Shute and Johnny Goodman were only beginning to come into their own. And there were those who overlapped Jones and won before and after his time. This group included Hagen and Sarazen and the former youthful star, Francis Ouimet, who followed up his 1913 U.S. Open win and 1914 U.S. Amateur victory by taking his second U.S. Amateur in 1931.

There were other golfers who possessed championship qualities and would have captured a fair number of titles had they not played in the Jones era.

The British Open is a sound example of Jones's and Hagen's dominance. In only one year between 1924 and 1930 was another golfer able to break through their monopoly. That golfer was Jim Barnes, who won in 1925 at Prestwick Golf Club, near Glasgow, Scotland—a year in which neither Jones nor Hagen was entered.

Once Jones retired a highly respected group of golfers took over the British Open. Tommy Armour won in 1931. The year 1932 was Gene

Sarazen's to win the British Open. Denny Shute defeated Craig Wood in a playoff to capture the British Open in 1933. And Henry Cotton broke a string of ten years of American dominance by winning in 1934.

Of note, after Jones retired, was the 1931 U.S. Open. The champion turned out to be a rather unknown golfer named Billy Burke. He was a cigar-smoking former ironworker of Lithuanian lineage who had lost a finger in a mill accident. The U.S. Open was held in extremely oppressive July heat. The next year, the event was moved to June where it has remained ever since.

At The Inverness Club in Toledo, Ohio Burke and George Von Elm tied at 292. In the thirty-six-hole play-off, they tied at 149, thus requiring another thirty-six-hole play-off. In the second two rounds Burke shot 148 to Von Elm's 149 to win in a record play-off of four rounds—only one stroke separating them after eight rounds of golf—four rounds of regulation play and four play-off rounds.

Another champion in the early 1930s was Johnny Goodman. It should be recalled that he had traveled from Omaha, Nebraska, in a cattle car to the 1929 U.S. Amateur at Pebble Beach. There he knocked out Bobby Jones in a stunning first-round upset. In 1933 he staked his claim to fame when, as an amateur, he won the U.S. Open at North Shore Country Club in Glenview, Illinois. That in itself would bring fame to any golfer. In defeating Ralph Guldahl, Goodman still is the last amateur to win the U.S. Open. He is likely to remain so. Later on Goodman would capture another national championship. In 1937 he beat Ray Billows two-up to win the U.S. Amateur at Alderwood Country Club in Portland, Oregon.

In 1932 Gene Sarazen was in the second phase of his career. He captured the U.S. Open and the British Open, a rare double indeed, coming on the heels of Jones's same accomplishment in his Grand Slam year of 1930. The following year Sarazen would win the 1933 P.G.A Championship for the third time. In 1935 he would take the second rendition of the Masters, vastly aided by his double eagle on the fifteenth hole of the last round to tie Craig Wood, whom he would defeat in a play-off the next day.

In 1934 the U.S. Open came for the first time to the Merion Golf Club's East Course in Ardmore, Pennsylvania. Merion had already hosted the U.S. Amateur in 1916, 1924, and 1930. The club had also played host to the U.S. Women's Amateur in 1904 and 1909 (the Haverford Course) and in 1926 (the East Course).

Wiffy Cox and Bobby Cruickshank led the 1934 U.S. Open with one-

Johnny Goodman, the last amateur to win the U.S. Open,
which he accomplished in 1933.

over par 71's in the first round. Cruickshank fired another 71 in the second round to take a three-shot lead into Saturday's 36-hole finish. In the Saturday morning third round Gene Sarazen posted a 73 for a one-shot lead over Cruickshank, who had shot a pedestrian 77. Cox kept pace matching Sarazen's 73 for 220. Olin Dutra now surfaced as a contender, firing the morning's second-best round, a 71. This put him in a tie for fourth place with Ralph Guldahl, who had returned a par-70 round. He and Dutra were at 221, three behind the leader, Sarazen.

In the final round Guldahl fell out of contention with a 78. At the turn Cruickshank picked up a stroke to tie Sarazen. Cox was a stroke behind. Dutra remained three back. On the way in both Cruickshank's and Cox's game sagged and they each finished with 76's for a total of 295. Sarazen came to the famous eleventh (where Jones had captured the Grand Slam), and promptly hooked his drive into the Babbling Brook. He ended with a seven on the hole.

By the time Dutra reached the fifteenth he was one stroke up on Sarazen who was playing three holes in front of Dutra. Sarazen bogeyed the eighteenth and shot 76 for a total of 294. With three holes to play Dutra held a three-shot lead. As it turned out he needed all of this cushion. He parred the sixteenth, "the Quarry Hole." On the long par-three seventeenth he three-putted for a bogey and his lead was two. At the eighteenth Dutra was on the green in regulation two, forty feet from the pin. He left the putt five feet from the hole, putted to the lip and made a bogey five for a 72 and the championship by one stroke with a 273. So as the winner of the 1932 P.G.A. Championship, Dutra now had the U.S. Open as his second Major championship.

In 1935 the U.S. Open moved across Pennsylvania to Oakmont Country Club, outside of Pittsburgh. This time the winner was another long shot by the name of Sam Parks, a member of the host club. This victory enhanced the lore that the only golfers who could play Oakmont were its members. It was one of the top upsets in the championship, placing it alongside Ouimet's victory in 1913. Upset or not, Parks was the only player who broke 300 for the four rounds.

Over in Great Britain the ten-year dominance of the Americans in the British Open finally came to an end in 1934. The championship was won by an Englishman named T. Henry Cotton, a superb shotmaker. He proved this three years later by winning at Carnoustie Golf Links in Scotland and, had it not been for World War II, it seems likely that he would have won more British Opens other than the third title he captured at Muirfield Golf Course near Edinburgh, Scotland, in 1948.

Back in the United States, as the mid-1930s approached, no American had yet emerged as a successor to Bobby Jones.

It is not easy to fix an arbitrary date as to when the period of transition post-Jones was met with a new crop of consistent winners. Perhaps the first to do so was in the spring of 1934, when Lawson Little emerged as a superior amateur.

In 1934 he captured the U.S. Amateur at The Country Club in Brookline, Massachusetts, with a resounded eight & seven triumph over David Goldman. Little followed this up in 1935 with a repeat championship, beating Walter Emory 4 & 2 at the Cleveland Country Club in Cleveland, Ohio.

His legend was enhanced when he went over to Europe and repeated his American performance by winning the British Amateur the same two years in a row. The 1934 British Amateur was held at Prestwick, Scotland, where the first Open Championship had been held in 1860. Little was on the top of his game throughout the championship. In the final he faced James Wallace from Troon. Little overwhelmed him 14 & 13. In the spring of 1935, Little went back to Britain to defend his title at Royal Lytham & St. Annes. While he did not match his steamroller golf of the preceding year none of his opponents could raise their game enough to beat him. In the final Little faced Dr. William Tweddell who had won the 1927 British Amateur. Tweddell managed to catch Little at the thirtieth. Little proceeded to win the thirty-second and thirty-third holes to go two-up. Tweddell cut the margin in half when he won the thirty-fifth. He had an eighteen-footer at the thirty-sixth to force a play-off. When he missed Little had successfully defended his British Amateur crown.

After turning professional in 1936 (and thereby relinquishing a chance for three consecutive U.S. Amateurs and British Amateurs) Little would capture another Major championship when he took the 1940 U.S. Open at Canterbury Golf Club in Cleveland, Ohio. He defeated Gene Sarazen in a play-off.

Before Little's two-year reign of dual American and British amateur championships the biggest splash in the amateur ranks occurred in 1931. That year, seventeen years after his first U.S. Amateur win, and eighteen years after his famous play-off triumph in the U.S. Open, Francis Ouimet won his second U.S. Amateur. In the final he defeated Jack Westland 6 & 5 at Beverly Country Club in Chicago, Illinois.

The year 1934 was another crowning achievement for Bobby Jones as the first National Invitational (now the Masters) was conducted at his new club in Augusta, Georgia. The winner that inaugural year was Horton Smith. He was a Missouri native with superb putting skills that showcased him on the large and marvelous greens at Augusta. He took full advantage by winning that first year and capturing the title again in 1936.

In 1934 the relatively unknown Paul Runyan won the P.G.A. Championship at Park Country Club in Williamsville, New York. The following year the P.G.A. Championship at Twin Hills Country Club in Oklahoma City, Oklahoma, was won by Johnny Revolta, also considered a long shot.

In 1936 Tony Manero became the second straight dark horse (following Sam Parks) to win the U.S. Open. The event was played at Baltusrol Golf Club in Springfield, New Jersey. Manero set a U.S. Open scoring record with a total of 282. In the final round he shot a 33 on the front nine to inch within two shots of "Lighthorse" Harry Cooper. Cooper broke the scoring record with a 284 total but the record lasted only an hour until Manero finished.

The luckless Cooper never won a Major. In the 1936 Masters, he led by three shots going into the final round. Yet after a round of 76 he lost by a shot to Horton Smith.

Denny Shute followed his victory in the 1933 British Open with his second Major championship when he won the 1936 P.G.A. Championship on the No. 2 Course at Pinehurst, North Carolina.

The 1936 Walker Cup was played at Pine Valley in Clementon, New Jersey, the first of two championships ever to be held at Pine Valley (the other being the 1985 Walker Cup). In the 1936 matches the British-Irish team managed only three halves as the United States posted a 9-0 shutout (back then, ties were not awarded points). It has been the only shutout in Walker Cup history.

The 1936 U.S. Amateur champion was John Fisher, who defeated Jack McLean one-up (thirty-seven holes) at Garden City Golf Club, Garden City, New York. Fisher's victory was the last national championship where a player used hickory-shafted clubs.

Reckoning back to the Roaring Twenties Bobby Jones, Walter Hagen and Gene Sarazen loosely formed what could be called the first Great Triumvirate of American-born male golfers who stimulated interest among American golf fans. By 1937 the next trio was beginning to take shape. Byron Nelson won the Masters that year, only his third official P.G.A. Tour victory. Sam Snead made his debut at the start of the 1937 professional winter tour. Ben Hogan would appear in 1940.

In 1937 Johnny Goodman followed up on his 1933 U.S. Open triumph (where he was the last amateur to do so) by winning the U.S. Amateur with a one-up victory over Ray Billows at the Alderwood Country Club, Portland, Oregon.

Similarly, Henry Cotton captured a second British Open at Carnoustie. He would win again at Muirfield in 1948.

In the 1937 U.S. Open Ralph Guldahl set a new scoring record by winning with a seven-under par 281 at the Oakland Hills Country Club, in Birmingham, Michigan. It was the first time that a player completed all four rounds in even par or better. Playing in his first U.S. Open Sam Snead finished second, two shots behind Guldahl. He would never finish better than second in a U.S. Open.

Denny Shute won his second consecutive P.G.A. Championship with a one-up (thirty-seven holes) victory over Harold "Jugs" McSpaden at the Pittsburgh Field Club in Aspinwall, Pennsylvania.

The 1937 United States Ryder Cup team (American professionals) defeated the British professionals 8-4 at Southport and Ainsdale Golf Course in England. As the non-playing captain, Walter Hagen guided his team to its first victory on British soil. It was Hagen's last time as team captain, a position he had held for the first six matches, beginning in 1927. Because of World War II it would be the last Ryder Cup until 1947.

In the 1938 Masters Henry Picard won when he fired a final-round 70 to defeat Harry Cooper and Ralph Guldahl by two strokes. Picard won twenty-six tour events from 1925 to 1950.

In 1938 Ralph Guldahl completed a rare double when he repeated as U.S. Open champion at Cherry Hills Country Club in Denver, Colorado. Guldahl also won the 1939 Masters. He fashioned a comfortable six-shot victory over Dick Metz. Gudahl thus became only the fourth golfer up to that time to win back-to-back U.S. Opens. He joined Willie Anderson, Bobby Jones and John McDermott (later, Ben Hogan and Curtis Strange would also accomplish this feat). Willie Anderson surpassed them all when he won three straight US. Opens between 1903 and 1905.

Six of Guldahl's sixteen victories were arguably Major championships as he won the Western Open, then considered a Major, in 1936, 1937, and 1938. Even more impressive was the fact that all of these Major victories came within a four-year period from 1936 through 1939.

As quickly as he appeared on the national scene Guldahl left it at the age of twenty-nine. After serving in the military during World War II, he was never able to return to top form. He said years later that golf-related injuries ended his career.

At the 1938 P.G.A. Championship, held at Shawnee Country Club in Shawnee-on-Delaware, Pennsylvania, short-hitting Paul Runyan defeated Sam Snead 8 & 7. Snead outdrove Runyan by an average of forty yards per hole but Runyan's driving accuracy and short game led to victory. It was Runyan's second P.G.A. title following his 1934 victory at Park Country Club in Williamsville, New York.

The 1938 Walker Cup match was played at St. Andrews, and the combined team of Great Britain and Ireland finally won 7–4 with one match halved. This was on the heels of having lost every one of the first nine Cup matches, four of them by large margins.

The 1938 Curtis Cup was played at the Essex Country Club near Boston, Massachusetts. The United States squad won 5–3 with one match halved. After losing the foursomes in which Great Britain and Ireland dropped only ½ point the U.S. won five of the six singles matches.

The Curtis Cup players (including the visitors) next moved on to Illinois for the U.S. Women's Amateur at the Westmoreland Country Club, situated near Chicago, Illinois.

Patty Berg, runner-up in her first two U.S. Women's Amateurs, finally broke through, winning over Mrs. Julius Page six & five. Only one of the visiting Curtis Cuppers reached the third round.

On the rules front the U.S.G.A. instituted a new rule limiting players to fourteen clubs. Prior to this rule players such as Lawson Little and Harry Cooper were known to carry as many as twenty-six clubs in their bags.

CHAPTER

29

The New
American Great Triumvirate
Byron Nelson, Sam Snead, Ben Hogan

With Bobby Jones in retirement and Gene Sarazen and Walter Hagen past their prime the 1930s was in need of a new breed. The likes of Lawson Little, Denny Shute and Ralph Guldahl tried to fill the void but their efforts were not enough to lift the Americans out of the post-Jones doldrums. Herbert Warren Wind, the highly regarded golf writer, described this period as follows: "golf without Jones was like France without Paris—leaderless, lightless, and lonely." The sport of golf needed a new headliner to stir up the interest of golf fans, particularly with the onset of the Depression muting interest in all sports because of the economic calamity that had befallen the United States.

America was fortunate in that it got not one but three titans of golf—a new Great Triumvirate: Byron Nelson, Sam Snead, and Ben Hogan. All three ironically were born in 1912. The first of them to gain national prominence was Nelson, who promptly captured national attention when he won the 1937 Masters.

Byron Nelson
Byron Nelson lived as a youth in Fort Worth, Texas and caddied at the Glen Garden Country Club. Another caddy there was Ben Hogan and Nelson beat Hogan one year for the caddy championship.

Nelson spent 1937 into 1939 as the head pro at Reading Country Club in Reading, Pennsylvania. He secured the Reading position shortly before the 1937 Masters. Nelson hoped to play well in the Masters so that he could use the purse to stock the Reading pro shop in its English-styled clubhouse. Fortunately, this came about. At the 1937 Masters Nelson, then twenty-five, beat Ralph Guldahl. Nelson's climb to victory was highlighted by a birdie on the twelfth hole and an eagle on the par five thirteenth hole to erase Guldahl's lead.

While he was at Reading Country Club Nelson became acquainted with Glenna Collett. Also at nearby Hershey Country Club was his boyhood colleague, Ben Hogan. In 1939 both Nelson and Hogan were sought after for the position of head professional at The Inverness Club in Toledo, Ohio. Nelson ended up with the job.

The year 1939 was a prominent year for Nelson as he won the U.S. Open in stunning fashion at the Philadelphia Country Club's Spring Mill course in Gladwyne, Pennsylvania, near Philadelphia. In the final round Nelson shot a 68 and then was forced to watch as Sam Snead was out on the course with a chance for his first U.S. Open. Snead came to the eighteenth hole, a par five, thinking that he needed a birdie to win the tournament. He hooked his drive into the left rough, put his second shot into a bunker, took two shots to extricate himself and three-putted for an eight. This poor performance on the eighteenth hole doomed Snead's chances of victory.

In the meantime Craig Wood and Denny Shute both finished with the same 284 total as Nelson, leading to an eighteen-hole play-off.

In the play-off Nelson and Wood shot 68's. Shute shot a 76 and was eliminated. In the second play-off round of eighteen-holes between Nelson and Wood, Nelson shot a 70 to Wood's 73, giving the U.S. Open to Nelson. En route Nelson holed a one-iron shot at the fourth hole for an eagle to help seal the victory.

While it was Nelson's only U.S. Open victory, and further established his credentials, history has shown that it was Snead's collapse at the eighteenth hole that is most remembered about the 1939 U.S. Open.

Nelson won his third Major in the 1940 P.G.A. Championship at Hershey Country Club in Hershey, Pennsylvania. He won over Sam Snead one-up.

Part of Nelson's success could be attributed to his adaptability to steel-shafted clubs. He was able to get away from the handsy action of hickory-shafted clubs, which he realized could not work for steel. While most golfers continued to imitate the "Bobby Jones" style, with little leg movement and a pivot against a straight and braced left side, Nelson put action into his legs, letting his left knee bend and actually dipping downward through impact with the ball. However, he did replicate the Jones innovation of maintaining a straight left arm on the backswing and follow-through. Putting all these components of the swing together Nelson helped popularize the "modern" swing, similar to the one in use today.

In 1942 Nelson showed his prowess again against the two other members of the Great Triumvirate when he defeated Hogan by one stroke in a play-off for the Masters. Nelson shot 69 to Hogan's 70. Snead finished in a tie for seventh.

Shortly thereafter Hogan joined the Army Air Corps. Nelson was rejected for military service because of tendencies toward hemophilia. Snead served in the Navy during World War II.

Among the Majors Nelson was at his best in the P.G.A. Championship. Beginning in 1939 he was in the final of the then-match play P.G.A. Championship five of six times. He won the Championship in 1940 and 1945 and finished second in 1939, 1941, and 1944. The tournament was not held in 1943.

Nelson showed consistent success in tour events and the Majors leading up to 1945. It was that year, however, when he turned out to be totally dominant. He won nineteen of the thirty-one tour events that he entered. That statistic does not tell the whole story. As the winter circuit was winding down Nelson teamed with Harold "Jugs" McSpaden to take the Miami Four-Ball final. Then he really began to sizzle. He continued his winning streak through the Charlotte Open, the Greater Greensboro Open and the Durham Open, comprising the North Carolina swing. Then he took the Atlanta Open, the last stop on the winter circuit. At the Montreal Open Nelson won his sixth straight tournament.

Then came the Philadelphia Inquirer Invitation Tournament, played at Llanerch Country Club in Havertown, Pennsylvania. Although McSpaden finished with three impressive 66's, his play yielded only second place. This was because Nelson nosed him out by firing a final round of 63.

At the Chicago Victory Open Nelson won by seven shots. Now he had won eight tournaments in a row.

Next up was the 1945 P.G.A. Championship at the Moraine Country Club in Dayton, Ohio. Nelson tied with Johnny Revolta for the medal at six-under par. Nelson played a total of 204 holes and was thirty-seven under par. He beat Sam Byrd, the former Yankee baseball player, 4 & 3 in the final.

The next tournament that Nelson played in was George S. May's All-American Open. Nelson won it for the fourth time in five years. His total of 269, 19 under par, was eleven strokes better than the two players tied for second place, the aging Gene Sarazen and Army officer Ben Hogan. This was Nelson's tenth victory in a row.

Nelson's next test was the Canadian Open, played the first week of August. Nelson finished with a four-shot victory. He now had his eleventh triumph in a row.

Nelson's victory streak ended at the Memphis Open. Freddy Haas, an amateur, posted an eighteen-under par 270 for the win. Nelson's 276 placed him fourth. His unprecedented eleven consecutive victories had beaten the old mark of three consecutive wins by eight.

Nelson proved that his superiority in 1945 was no fluke. After the Memphis loss Nelson resumed his winning ways. He won at Knoxville, Spokane and Seattle. He then "allowed" some interloping when Hogan won at Nashville and Snead won at Dallas and Tulsa. Hogan also won at Portland. Thus, the Great Triumvirate's dominance became well-established.

Nelson's win at Seattle bordered on the sensational. His total of 259 broke Hogan's record for a four-round event by two shots. Then, Nelson took some time off until mid-December, when he played in the Fort Worth Open at Glen Garden Golf and Country Club, the course where he and Hogan had caddied as youths. Nelson shot a 273, eleven-under par, to finish seven shots in front of Jimmy Demaret.

The victory in the Fort Worth Open brought Nelson's 1945 win total to nineteen in P.G.A.-sponsored events. He collected $66,000 in War Bond prizes, the cash value being $52,511.32, which replaced his 1944 total of $25,005 as the all-time money winnings in a year.

Critics have said that Nelson's victories in 1945 did not come against the strongest of fields, in part, because Hogan and Snead spent part of the year still in the military. But they did appear mid-way through Nelson's march. And Nelson's average score for eighteen holes over his 120 tournament rounds was 68.33, without a doubt the most amazing feat by any golfer since Bobby Jones's Grand Slam. Also momentous was that not once did Nelson fail to finish under par in any tournament. Thus it can be argued with near certainty that the strength of the fields should not detract from his accomplishments.

On the strength of his record-setting performance in 1945 Nelson was voted Athlete of the Year by the *Associated Press* for the second year in a row.

In 1946, Nelson won five events and finished second in the U.S. Open.

At the end of that year, weary of the tournament grind in similar respects to Bobby Jones, Nelson retired and bought an 800-acre cattle ranch in Texas. He was thirty-four years old. He had won five Majors and a total of fifty-four tournaments.

Even in retirement, however, Nelson returned each year to play in a few tournaments until he retired for good. The AT&T Byron Nelson Championship is named in his honor. Today the annual award for low-scoring honor on the Senior P.G.A. Tour is called the Byron Nelson Trophy. Nelson was inducted into the P.G.A. Hall of Fame in 1953 and was a charter member of the World Golf Hall of Fame in 1974. Byron Nelson was the last of the Nelson-Snead-Hogan Great Triumvirate to pass away when he died on September 26, 2006 at the age of 94.

Sam Snead

Just as Nelson was retiring in 1946 there came out of the backwoods of the western parts of Virginia a player named Sam Snead with more raw talent than the game had ever seen before. His smooth swing and length off the tee earned him the nickname "Slammin' Sammy."

In 1933 this coordinated twenty-four-year old landed a job at the Homestead course in Hot Springs, Virginia. Shortly thereafter he took up employment at the nearby Cascades course. He returned to the Homestead course a year later, and stayed one season. The next two seasons found him at The Greenbrier, a rival resort in White Sulphur Springs, West Virginia.

When Snead tried the Hershey Open in 1936 he finished a respectable sixth. He felt that he was ready for the professional circuit in the winter of 1937. His first start was the Miami-Biltmore tournament where he finished in tenth place. Then he went to the West Coast to join the big-name professionals. There, as a total unknown, he finished sixth in the Los Angeles Open. His next start was the Oakland Open where he caught fire, shooting 69-65-67-69 for a winning total of 270. Following this breakthrough win at Oakland, Snead enhanced his reputation by winning the Rancho Santa Fe Open.

Snead's growing legion of fans came to recognize his prowess on two fronts. He was a prodigious hitter. In the driving contest at the P.G.A. Championship in 1937, Snead averaged 307 yards on three tries and won hand-

"Slammin'" Sam Snead won seven Majors and his 82 PGA Tour victories leads all male professionals.

ily. Even more of a marvel was his smooth, coordinated swing. For students of the game Snead was recognized as the most complete golfer when it came to the mechanics of the swing.

Another aspect of Snead was his engaging personality. Wherever he went he made a fan of virtually everyone in the gallery. His superb shot-making, combined with his backwoods mien and folksy way of talking, made him a crowd favorite. It also didn't hurt that he had a wonderful sense of humor and gave the media many worthwhile quotes for their articles on this slow-speaking young man from the mountains of western Virginia.

Snead's first big test was the 1937 U.S. Open at Oakland Hills Country Club in Birmingham, Michigan. A strong finish by Ralph Guldahl kept Snead from winning the title in his first attempt. Snead finished two shots behind in second place. This loss was a precursor to his frustrations throughout his career, where he came close but never won the U.S. Open. He made thirty-seven tries, had a dozen top ten finishes and was a runner-up four times.

In 1938 Snead, Henry Picard and a few others garnered all the publicity until it came to the U.S. Open. At Cherry Hills Country Club in Denver, Colorado Ralph Gudahl ran away with the title just as he had in 1937.

In 1939 Snead suffered his most painful loss in the U.S. Open at the Spring Mill course of the Philadelphia Country Club (the Bala course being the other one) in Gladwyne, Pennsylvania. Opening with 68, 71 and 73 Snead had gone into the final round a stroke behind Johnny Bulla and tied with three other golfers. In the meantime Byron Nelson was five shots off the lead. Nelson finished at 284 and all he could do was sit and hope.

Snead was playing behind him and, as he stood on the seventeenth tee, he needed two pars for 70 and 282. He bogeyed the seventeenth. There was little cause for concern as he could win with a par five on the eighteenth. While Nelson had finished Denny Shute and Craig Wood were playing behind Snead. Hearing occasional cheers Snead thought he needed birdie to win the U.S. Open. Snead hooked his drive into the rough, 275 yards from the green. His brassie landed him in a steep-faced bunker, 110 yards from the green. His third left him in the bunker. His fourth shot put him in another bunker, 40 yards from the green. His fifth landed on the green, 40 feet beyond the hole. From there he three-putted for an eight. Snead ended up with a 74 and a total of 286, two shots out of a play-off. Nelson won the play-off with Shute and Wood.

Snead's problems continued in the U.S. Open. A year later he opened with a 67 and was one stroke off the lead going into the last round at the Canterbury Golf Club in Cleveland, Ohio. However, he closed with an 81, his worst U.S. Open score ever, and dropped into a tie for sixteenth place.

After World War II intervened and Snead had been in the navy his next best opportunity to win the U.S. Open came in 1947 at the St. Louis Country Club. He holed an eighteen-foot putt to tie Lew Worsham and cause an eighteen-hole play-off. When the two came to the 18th hole the next day in the play-off, still even, both balls were about thirty inches from the cup. As Snead lined up to putt Worsham asked for a ruling as to who was away. Snead was indeed away and he missed his putt. Worsham made his for a one-stroke win. In 1949 Snead was the first winner to be awarded the Green Jacket at the Masters

In 1949 Snead needed pars on the last two holes to win the U.S. Open, held at Medinah Country Club in Medinah, Illinois. He took three strokes from the fringe at the seventeenth hole for a bogey. He lost by one stroke to Cary Middlecoff. Nevertheless, the year was good to Snead as he captured the first of his three Masters victories (the others were in 1952 and 1954). That year he also captured the middle of his three P.G.A. Championships at Hermitage Country Club in Richmond, Virginia. He also captured the P.G.A. in 1942 and 1952.

At Oakmont in 1953 Snead was one stroke back going into the final round of the U.S. Open. This was Ben Hogan's magical year and Snead shot a 76 in the last round to finish six strokes behind Hogan.

Snead also tackled the British Open at St. Andrews in 1946. In the fourth round he shot a 75 in high winds to finish first, four shots ahead of Johnny Bulla and Bobby Locke.

Despite his lack of success in the U.S. Open Snead had better fortune in the Masters. Following up on his 1949 victory in the Masters Snead repeated his wins in the 1952 and 1954 Masters.

As history records it Snead shrugged off his U.S. Open disappointments with a stellar career. Among his eighty-two P.G.A. Tour wins were three Masters, three P.G.A.'s and one British Open. Snead also won fourteen times on the Senior Tour. Including his eighty-two P.G.A. victories and his fourteen Senior Tour victories Snead won a record total of 165 times during his stellar career. The eighty-two P.G.A. Tour wins is a record for a male golfer (Kathy Whitworth owns the overall record with eighty-eight victories).

Age never seemed to slow Snead down. He won at least one tournament every year until 1962, more than a quarter-century after he began his career. In 1965 he won the Greater Greensboro Open for the sixth time, becoming, at the age of fifty-two years and ten months, the oldest player to win a P.G.A. tour event. His eight wins in the tournament are the most wins in any single event until Tiger Woods later won the Arnold Palmer Invitational eight times. In 1979 with rounds of 67 and 66 in the Quad Cities Open, Snead, at sixty-seven, shot and bettered his age—the first and only man to perform that feat in P.G.A. competition. Finally, in 1980 when he won the Commemorative, a Senior event, he became the first—and likely the last—to record P.G.A. victories in six consecutive decades.

Snead also had other accomplishments. He won four Vardon Trophies for low scoring average while leading the money list three times and he made eight Ryder Cup teams between 1937 and 1959. Snead was an honorary starter at the Masters from 1984 until 2002. He was elected to the P.G.A. Hall of Fame in 1953, and was a charter member of the World Golf Hall of Fame in 1974.

Snead died on May 23, 2002, in Hot Springs, Virginia.

Ben Hogan

The third member of this Great Triumverate was Ben Hogan. His and Byron Nelson's careers crossed when they both caddied at the Glen Garden Country Club near Fort Worth, Texas. Like Snead and Nelson, Hogan was born in 1912.

Unlike Nelson and Snead, Hogan did not burst onto the scene as a champion golfer. He fought a vicious hook during the early part of his career in the 1930s. As a result he played the P.G.A. circuit on and off during this time. All the while his legend at practice grew until he was able to master his untoward hook. He made three abortive attempts at the pro circuit before achieving modest success in 1937.

It was another three years—and several near-misses—before he finally broke through with his first victory at the Pinehurst North & South Open in 1940. By that time Nelson and Snead had won thirty tournaments between them. From that point Hogan began to make up for lost time. He won four tournaments in 1940 and finished the season as the leading money winner. In 1941 and 1942 he won another dozen tournaments and again led the money list in both years.

Then World War II came and Hogan served two years in the Army Air Corps. He was discharged in the late summer of 1945. He immediately got back to playing on the Tour and won five events during the rest of the year. He also played during the latter stages of Nelson's unparalleled run of eleven straight tourney wins.

The year 1946 was a banner year for Hogan. Of the 32 events that he entered he won thirteen and finished second in six others. He also finished

Ben Hogan, who won nine Majors.

third in three events, all the while competing against strong fields of play-ers returning from military service.

In 1946 Hogan won his first Major: the P.G.A. Championship. He de-feated Ed "Porky" Oliver of Wilmington, Delaware, 6 & 4 at the Portland Golf Club in Portland, Oregon. This marked the period after Nelson's retirement when Hogan and Snead took over from Nelson as the players to beat on the P.G.A. Tour.

That same year Hogan also nearly won the Masters and U.S. Open. He came in second in both events, to Herman Keiser and Lloyd Mangrum respectively. In each of these two Major tournaments Hogan missed eighteenth-hole putts that would have given him a shot at the titles.

Moving on to 1947 Hogan again led the tour in victories with seven, although he did not win any Major titles that year.

The year 1948 was an even better one for Hogan. He won ten more tournaments. These included his second P.G.A. Championship, where he defeated Mike Turnesa 7 & 6 at Norwood Hills Country Club in St. Louis, Missouri. That same year he won his first U.S. Open at Riviera Country Club in Los Angeles, California. He beat Jimmy Demaret at a course that would later be known as "Hogan's Alley" because of Hogan's success there.

In 1949 catastrophe struck Hogan and his wife Valerie. In February, after winning two of the first four events on the winter circuit of the P.G.A. Tour, they were looking forward to a brief respite from the tour grind before getting back to tournament golf during its Southern Swing. On the morning of February 2 the Hogans were driving east on a highway in western Texas when their car collided with a Greyhound bus that was trying to pass a truck on a foggy stretch of the highway. A split second before the crash Hogan flung himself across the seat in an effort to protect his wife. This was fortuitous because the steering wheel was driven through the driver's seat as a result of the impact of the two vehicles. Hogan broke his collarbone, fractured his pelvis, crushed his left ankle, sustained a broken right rib and suffered other internal injuries. There was considerable doubt whether he would ever sufficiently recover to be able to play competitive golf again.

After two months in the hospital, and having undergone an operation for blood clots, Hogan was brought home, weighing just ninety-eight-pounds. The indomitable Hogan willed his way back to competitive status by methodically drilling his body back into shape. By August 1949 he was swinging a club, and in November he was back at Colonial Country Club working his game into competitive shape.

In January 1950, less than a year after his nearly fatal accident, Hogan returned to competitive golf. The site was Riviera Country Club, the course where he won his first U.S. Open in 1948. Walking in bandaged legs he shot rounds of 73-69-69-69 and almost won the Los Angeles Open before Sam Snead tied him and won in a play-off.

Some seventeen months after the accident Hogan made his re-appearance in the 1950 U.S. Open, held at Merion Golf Club, in Ardmore, Pennsylvania. He was in visible pain on the thirty-six-hole final day. Nevertheless, he managed to tie Lloyd Mangrum and George Fazio at the end of regulation play. The next day he shot a 69 to beat Mangrum by four shots and Fazio by six. Truly this was one of the most compelling and inspirational performances in golf, if not in all of sports.

Hogan continued his remarkable comeback in 1951. He won his first Masters with Skee Riegel finishing second. In June Hogan won the U.S. Open at Oakland Hills in Birmingham, Michigan with a final round 67 over a course whose setup is still considered one of the most severe tests of golf. Hogan derived immeasurable satisfaction from the victory. Over the tough layout he had improved his score each day: 76-73-71-67.

The final round 67 was probably the best competitive round Hogan ever played, inspired by the challenge of the golf course. In later years he referred to it as the greatest round of his career. His oft-repeated quotation upon accepting the trophy says it succinctly: "[i]'m glad I brought the course, this monster, to its knees."

The year 1952 was not as rewarding for Hogan as he concentrated on the Major championships. He was in the thick of contention in the last round of the Masters, when he soared to a 79, his poorest performance in a Major championship since he started his comeback. Sam Snead claimed the victory—the second of his three Masters.

Two months later at the U.S. Open at Northwood Country Club in Dallas, Texas, Hogan seemed to be back on his game. He led off with a pair of 69's for a two-shot lead. However he wilted in the two-round final day in the 96-degree heat. He shot a pair of 74's to end up in third place behind Julius Boros and Porky Oliver, the latter being the perennial Wilmington, Delaware bridesmaid for whom a public course in Wilmington is named. Boros fashioned his victory with final rounds of 68 and 71.

Hogan gracefully accepted his failure to win his fourth U.S. Open but he was determined to make a better showing in 1953. He was not used to, nor did he like, going a full year without a Major victory.

During the ten months between the 1952 U.S. Open and the 1953 Masters Hogan did not play any competitive golf. This hiatus was not unusual since he harnessed his energy and focused on the Major championships.

When he arrived at the 1953 Masters many observers were of the mind that, at the age of forty, Hogan had lost something off his game and was not likely to regain it.

Hogan quickly used the Masters to dispel any notion that he could not regain top form. He shot rounds of 70, 69, 66, and 69. His 274, five strokes in front of runner-up Porky Oliver, was also five shots below the previous record for the Masters, set by Ralph Guldahl in 1939.

Usually quite reserved about his play Hogan referred to his four rounds at the Masters as "the best I've ever played for seventy-two holes." After the Masters Hogan played his way up to the U.S. Open in fine fashion. He won the Pan-American Open in Mexico City, and the Colonial Invitational in his hometown of Fort Worth, Texas.

The 1953 U.S. Open was set for Oakmont Country Club in Oakmont, Pennsylvania. Although the course had been softened by rain it still remained a sturdy test. Many still remembered that at the 1935 U.S. Open at Oakmont, only Sam Parks, Jr. had been able to break 300.

Hogan opened with a 67 and a 72 for a two-shot lead over Sam Snead going into the thirty-six-hole Saturday final. The two rounds on Saturday would be a duel between two familiar adversaries. In the morning round Snead shot a 72 to Hogan's 73 to close the gap to one stroke going into the last round.

In the afternoon both made the turn in 38. Hogan stepped up his game with a par on the long par three sixteenth hole, a birdie on the short seventeenth, and a birdie on the lengthy finishing hole. He finished with a 71 and a total of 283. As for Snead he could not get command of his game and struggled in with another 38 for a 76 and a 289 total, six shots behind Hogan.

With this victory Hogan joined Willie Anderson and Bobby Jones as the only winners of four U.S. Opens up to that time (Jack Nicklaus would later join them). Hogan's fourth U.S. Open was accomplished in only five attempts and also was his fourth in six years, having sat out 1949 because of his car accident.

Weeks before Hogan's triumph at Oakmont, when it became apparent that he was playing the finest golf of his life, the golfing public began encouraging him to go to Great Britain for the British Open scheduled for Carnoustie in early July. The golfing world clamored for a player of his caliber, and at the peak of his game, to take a crack at the British Open.

Many felt that it would be quite a feat if Hogan could make a strong showing and prove that he could adapt himself to the completely different conditions under which the British Open was played. Shortly before the U.S. Open Hogan filed his entry for the British Open. He went over ten days early and began his preparations in earnest, qualifying with plenty to spare.

The first day was windy and yet the scores were surprisingly low. Frank Stranahan shot the low round of 70. Hogan was three back at 73. In the second round, Hogan shot a 71 and his 144 was two shots off the lead.

The final two rounds were contested on the third day. Hogan shot a 70 and was tied with Roberto De Vincenzo for the lead after 54 holes. In the fourth round Hogan played superb golf and shot a 68 with a birdie at the last and his winning score of 282 placed him four shots ahead of the field.

Back in the United States Hogan's British Open victory was viewed as a national triumph. Hogan became only the third player to win the U.S. and British Opens in the same year (previously, Bobby Jones, 1926 and 1930; Gene Sarazen, 1932) and the first to combine them with a victory in the Masters. On his return to the United States Hogan became the first golfer since Bobby Jones to receive a ticker-tape parade in New York City. Unfortunately, Hogan could not take a run at the modern Grand Slam because, that year, the P.G.A. Championship conflicted with the British Open and his practice rounds.

In the following years Hogan cut back on his tournament play and focused on the Masters and the U.S. Open. In the 1954 Masters he finished second after losing a play-off to Snead by one stroke. The following year he finished runner-up to Cary Middlecoff. In 1956 a poor second round put Hogan out of the running and he finished eighth.

The 1954 U.S. Open was held at Baltusrol Golf Club, Springfield, New Jersey. Hogan made a rather disappointing defense of his U.S. Open title. He ended up in a tie for sixth behind the winner, Ed Furgol.

The next year, 1955, the U.S. Open produced one of the biggest surprises in U.S. Open history. The event was held at the Olympic Club in San Francisco, California. Hogan recorded rounds of 72, 73, 72, and a strong finishing 70 for a total of 287, a score that seemingly would bring him victory. But a little-known golfer named Jack Fleck caught him with two birdies and two pars on the last four holes. In the play-off the next day Fleck was the model of calmness and finished three shots ahead of Hogan, shooting 69 to Hogan's 72.

The 1956 U.S. Open was held at Oak Hill Country Club in Rochester,

New York. Again Hogan was the bridesmaid, finishing second by a stroke to Cary Middlecoff. The stroke by which he missed was a 2½ foot putt on the seventy-second hole. This was the beginning of the end of Hogan's run at Major championships.

In all Hogan won nine Major championships, six of them following his 1949 accident. His return to championship golf following his severe injuries has remained a story of courage, dedication, and spirit.

Hogan accumulated sixty-four Tour victories over his illustrious career. This puts him in fourth place behind Sam Snead (eighty-two), Jack Nicklaus (seventy-three), and Tiger Woods (seventy-nine).

In 1957 after his career wound down, Hogan wrote one of the top instruction books ever written, *Five Lessons: The Modern Fundamentals of Golf.* It remains one of the best-selling books on the modern golf swing.

Hogan was inducted into the P.G.A. Hall of Fame in 1953 and was an inaugural inductee into the World Golf Hall of Fame in 1974.

He spent much of his later years devoting himself to his equipment company. Hogan died on July 25, 1997.

30

The Years Following World War II

During the period of the American Triumvirate of Nelson, Snead, and Hogan other golfers staked claims to Major championships. Following up on his two U.S. Open championships in 1937 and 1938 Ralph Guldahl completed a superb run of Major championships by winning the 1939 Masters, his sixth Major in three years. One could argue that he won nine Majors if his three wins in the Western Open are included.

Henry Picard won the 1939 P.G.A. Championship by edging Byron Nelson in the final, one-up in thirty-seven holes at Pomonok Country Club in Flushing, New York. Picard won seven other tournaments in 1939.

The 1939 U.S. Amateur was won by Marvin "Bud" Ward at North Shore Country Club, Glenview, Illinois. It would be his first of two championships in three years.

In 1940, Texan Jimmy Demaret led the P.G.A. Tour with six victories, including the Masters and the Western Open.

Lawson Little won the 1940 U.S. Open at the Canterbury Country Club in Cleveland, Ohio. He won in an eighteen-hole play-off with Gene Sarazen (70-73), who had captured his first U.S. Open eighteen years earlier. This U.S. Open was marked by the disqualification of Porky Oliver, whose 287 tied for the play-off, but he and five others were disqualified for teeing off early in the fourth round to try and beat an oncoming storm.

Dick Chapman won the 1940 U.S. Amateur on his home course,

Denny Shute and Craig Wood, fierce rivals in the 1930s and 1940s.

Winged Foot, in Mamaroneck, New York. He earned medalist honors and won the final 11 & 9 over Duff McCullough.

The year 1940 also marked the year that Patty Berg turned professional after winning twenty-nine amateur events. In the U.S. Women's Amateur Betty Jameson won her second straight title. She later became one of the founders of the Ladies Professional Golf Association (L.P.G.A.).

With war in Europe the Royal & Ancient cancelled the British Open and British Amateur for the duration. These competitions would resume in 1946.

In 1941, after years of frustration, Craig Wood finally broke through and won the Masters and the U. S. Open. The 1941 U. S. Open was conducted at the Colonial Golf Club in Fort Worth, Texas. Wood defeated Denny Shute by three shots. It was Shute's second U.S. Open runner-up finish in three years. In 1939 he and Wood lost a play-off to Byron Nelson at the Philadelphia Country Club in Gladwyne, Pennsylvania.

In the 1941 U.S. Amateur Marvin "Bud" Ward won his second crown in three years at Omaha Field Club in Omaha, Nebraska, where he defeated Patrick Abbott four & three in the final.

At the 1941 P.G.A. Championship Vic Ghezzi defeated Byron Nelson one-up at Cherry Hills Country Club in Denver, Colorado. This would be the only Major title that Ghezzi would win in his career.

The 1941 U.S. Women's Amateur saw Philadelphian Helen Siegel make it to the final where she lost at The Country Club, in Brookline, Massachusetts to Betty Hicks Newell. Siegel would again finish runner-up in this event in 1948.

In 1942 the U.S. Open and the U.S. Amateur joined the British Open and British Amateur as cancelled tournaments for the duration of World War II. The Masters and the PGA were played one more time before a hiatus for the war.

Byron Nelson took the Masters and Sam Snead won the P.G.A. Championship in 1942. Then Snead reported for induction into the navy.

In 1943 the war effort put the brakes on competition. There were only three P.G.A. Tour events, and no official prize money was listed for the year. Byron Nelson, who was ineligible for military services because of a blood disorder, as mentioned before, played in numerous war-relief benefit matches.

In 1944, as the war was beginning to point to an Allied victory, the P.G.A. Tour began to regain its momentum. The P.G.A. Championship was re-started after a one-year hiatus. There was nearly a full schedule of events and Nelson won eight of them.

The lone Major event that was hosted in 1944 was the P.G.A. Championship at Manito Golf and Country Club in Spokane, Washington. Unknown Bob Hamilton from Indiana surprised the golf world by reaching the final, where he defeated Byron Nelson for the title one-up.

Likewise, the P.G.A. Championship was the only Major event held in 1945. In that Major, Nelson won for his ninth victory in a row at the Moraine Country Club in Dayton, Ohio. He defeated Sam Byrd 4 & 3.

The year 1946 was noted for the fact that the triumvirate of Nelson, Snead, and Hogan inspired each other to great play. Hogan came out on top that year. He played thirty-two tournaments, won thirteen and finished second six times.

While Hogan won the 1946 P.G.A. Championship over Porky Oliver his season was marred by two three-putt greens on the eighteenth hole which deprived him of victories in the Masters and the U.S. Open. He lost each by one stroke.

In the 1946 Masters, Hogan missed a 2½ foot putt that would have tied him with Herman Keiser. At the 1946 U.S. Open, Hogan missed a two-foot putt for a tie. Nelson, Lloyd Mangrum and Vic Ghezzi tied for the championship and Mangrum won the play-off by a stroke in a marathon thirty-six-hole play-off. After taking some time off Nelson officially retired from the P.G.A. Tour.

Sam Snead won the 1946 British Open, held for the first time since 1939.

In the U.S. Amateur Ted Bishop defeated Smiley Quick one-up at Baltusrol Golf Club in Springfield, New Jersey.

On the women's side Patty Berg captured the first of fifteen Majors when she won the inaugural U.S. Women's Open. It was the only time the event was held at match play. Babe Zaharias won the U.S. Women's Amateur at Southern Hills Country Club in Tulsa, Oklahoma.

The year 1947 was the year of South African Arthur D'Arcy Locke, known as Bobby Locke.He decided to give the P.G.A. Tour a try after defeating Sam Snead in twelve of sixteen matches played in South Africa.

Locke came to the United States in the spring of 1947 and proceeded to win six P.G.A. Tour events and finish runner-up twice. His strongest suit was his putting. Locke's unusual style of taking the club back inside and squaring up the blade, along with his uncanny ability to read greens, made him deadly on that surface. Locke continued his success on the P.G.A. Tour in 1948 and 1949. In 1949, he was not invited to the P.G.A. Championship because he was not a P.G.A. player or a "guest player." Some who followed the P.G.A. Tour felt that there was a tinge of envy in this ruling. Undeterred, Locke made the British Open his favorite tournament. He would go on to win the event in 1949, 1950, 1952, and 1957. Three years after his final

British Open victory Locke was seriously injured in an automobile accident and never again returned to his old form.

In April 1947 Jimmy Demaret, who led for all four rounds, became the third two-time winner of the Masters (he would win his third in 1950, his first coming in 1940), joining Horton Smith and Byron Nelson. Nelson and amateur Frank Stranahan tied for second.

The 1947 U.S. Open was held at St. Louis Country Club in Clayton, Missouri. Sam Snead made an eighteen-footer on the 72nd hole to tie Lew Worsham. But on the last hole of the eighteen-hole playoff, Snead was addressing a short putt when Worsham halted play to ask for a measurement as to who was away. Snead was indeed away but, rattled, he missed the putt and shot 70. Worsham won with a 69. Another close miss for Snead. The 1947 Open was the first U.S. Open to be televised—but only locally—on KSD-TV in St. Louis.

Plum Hollow Country Club, near Detroit, Michigan, was the site of the 1947 P.G.A. Championship. Australian Jim Ferrier defeated Chick Harbert two & one in the thirty-six-hole final.

Pebble Beach Golf Links hosted the 1947 U.S. Amateur. Robert "Skee" Riegel from suburban Philadelphia entered the event with a good measure of confidence, having been the medalist in the 1946 U.S. Amateur. In the 1947 final he defeated Johnny Dawson 2 & 1 to win the championship. Riegel became pro emeritus at three clubs in the Philadelphia and southern New Jersey area: Cape May National Golf Club, Edgemont Country Club and Commonwealth National Golf Club.

Louise Suggs won the 1947 U.S. Women's Amateur at Franklin Hills Country Club in suburban Detroit. She would win the British Ladies Amateur the following spring and go on to a stellar thirty-five-year professional career.

The U.S.G.A. was busy in 1947—revising and simplifying the Rules of Golf, going from sixty-one rules to twenty-one.

31

Mildred "Babe" Didrikson Zaharias

When she was single her name was Mildred "Babe" Didrikson. No one did more to ignite the growth of women's golf in the United States beginning in the 1930s. To examine her lineage Didrikson's entry on the American sports scene can be traced back to her track & field heroics in the 1932 Olympic Games held in Los Angeles, California. She was a lithe, muscled Texan and all of nineteen years old. Didrikson set two world records in the 1932 Summer Olympics. Babe set a new women's Olympic record in the javelin with a throw of 143 feet 4 inches. Next, she set a new world record in the high hurdles in winning her qualifying heat. Didrikson followed this by breaking the world record again in the final when she lowered the mark with a time of 11.7 seconds. In the high jump she was placed second for using a western-roll style that caused her head to clear the bar before her body. This was deemed "diving" and ruled illegal. Babe was, nonetheless, given a share of the world record at 5 feet ¾ inches. Her jumping style was legalized a short time afterwards.

With her success at the Olympics Babe Didrikson became an overnight celebrity. Before the end of 1932 she became a professional athlete and was barred from amateur competition because she had allowed a photograph of herself and an interview to be used in an automobile advertising campaign. In those days an athlete lost amateur status in all sports if the athlete was deemed to have engaged in a professional activity in any one sport.

Making a living as a professional athlete was difficult for women in the 1930s. For a time she toured as the only female member of the House of David baseball team.

In 1934 she turned her talents to golf. After practicing for a time Didrikson began to tour the country in exhibitions with the top professional men. In 1935, she went on an extensive tour of the country with Gene Sarazen. Although her golf was not all that impressive the public turned out to watch her hit prodigious drives. However, she realized that she would have to improve considerably if she wanted to compete with the complete women golfers of her day. This she did after settling down in southern California.

It was in Los Angeles in 1938 that she played in an exhibition with a professional wrestler named George Zaharias. A short time later they were married. Soon she developed superb iron and short games. In 1938 she qualified for the men's Los Angeles Open but did not make the cut.

As a professional she was not able to compete in the U. S. Women's Amateur and Women's British Amateur, the two championships in those days that determined the best women golfers. She continued to play in exhibitions and assorted minor tournaments through the war years.

During World War II Babe Didrikson Zaharias, as she was known by then, applied for reinstatement as an amateur. Her request was granted in 1944. Two years later, when the U.S. Women's Amateur was revived after the war, the Babe was set to make her mark on the national scene for women golfers.

By 1946 many of the top women amateurs during and after the reign of Glenna Collett Vare had retired from competition. Others, such as the 1938 U.S. Women's Amateur champion, Patty Berg, had turned professional. So had both Betty Jameson, the 1939 and 1940 Amateur champion, and Betty Hicks, the last pre-war Amateur champion in 1941.

However, there was plenty of amateur competition to be sure such as the 1937 U.S. Women's Amateur champion, Estelle Lawson Page, Helen Siegel of Philadelphia and 1947 U.S. Women's Amateur champion, Louise Suggs.

The 1946 U.S. Women's Amateur was conducted at Southern Hills Country Club in Tulsa, Oklahoma. Louise Suggs, who was thought to have the best chance to defeat Babe, was upset in the first round. Zaharias was hardly pressed as she advanced to the third round to face Helen Siegel. On the third hole Babe took a one-up lead. She held a three-up lead as they came to the ninth hole. Siegel won the ninth hole and made birdie at the

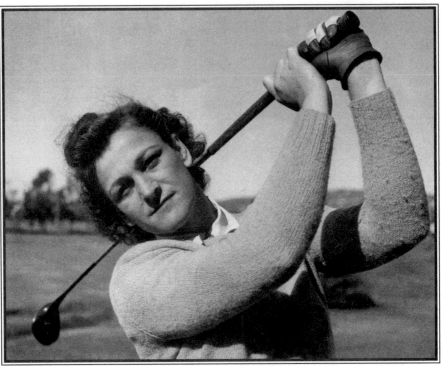

Mildred "Babe" Didrikson Zaharias, winner of three U.S. Women's Opens.

thirteenth to cut the deficit to one. Zaharias took the sixteenth hole to win the match 3 & 2.

The following day Babe met Clara Sherman of Pasadena, California, in the final. After the tenth hole it was a runaway for Babe. She needed only twenty-seven holes to win the thirty-six-hole final 11 & 9 and become the U.S. Women's Amateur Champion.

The following year, in May 1947, Zaharias traveled to Muirfield in Gullane, Scotland, to attempt what no American woman had yet to accomplish —win the British Ladies Amateur Golf Championship. Babe had no trouble reaching the thirty-six-hole final against Jacqueline Gordon.

After the first eighteen holes the match was all square. Babe launched a withering attack on the front nine of the afternoon round and by the twenty-ninth hole was five-up. Three halves later and the match was over. And so Babe had become the first American to win the British Ladies Amateur Golf Championship. These two Championships were part of a string of fifteen straight tournaments that Babe won in 1946-1947.

Two months after her return to the United States Babe turned pro again.

She had arguably become the best woman golfer in the world. It seemed to many, however, that there was one issue left unsettled: Who was the better golfer of all time: Babe or the British great, Joyce Wethered? This issue has left room for plenty of debate down through the years.

After Zaharias turned pro she signed a contract to represent Wilson Sporting Goods for $100,000. Along the way she engaged a well-known agent, Fred Corcoran, who, along with Babe, would be instrumental in the formation of the L.P.G.A. in 1948.

After the founding of the L.P.G.A. Babe won the U.S. Women's Open three times—in 1948, 1950, and 1954. She won four straight money titles and thirty-one tournaments.

In 1953 she was diagnosed with colon cancer. She vowed to return to the L.P.G.A. Tour. The following year she won five tournaments, including her third U.S. Women's Open. Winning the U.S. Women's Open while battling cancer is still considered one of the greatest feats in women's golf. In 1955 she had another three victories and then the cancer returned. She died of the disease on September 27, 1956 at the age of forty-two.

In 1957 Babe was posthumously awarded the Bob Jones Award for distinguished sportsmanship in golf. She was a charter member of the L.P.G.A. Hall of Fame (1967), and the World Golf Hall of Fame (1974). She was inducted into the P.G.A. Hall of Fame in 1976. In an *Associated Press* poll she was voted the greatest female athlete of the first half of the twentieth century.

32

Patty Berg

Patricia Jane "Patty" Berg was born in 1918 in Minneapolis, Minnesota. She took up golf at the age of thirteen and, three years later, won the 1934 Minneapolis City Championship. She won the Minnesota Championship at seventeen and that same year (1935) she advanced to the final of the U.S. Women's Amateur where she lost to Glenna Collett Vare.

Berg was U.S. Women's Amateur runner-up again in 1937, finishing second to Estelle Lawson Page. In 1938 she broke through and captured the U.S. Women's Amateur, a year in which she won ten of the thirteen amateur tournaments that she entered. She won 28 other amateur titles before turning pro in 1940. Like Babe Zaharias, she signed with the Wilson Sporting Goods Company.

Berg did not win her first professional event until 1941 when she captured her first Major, the Women's Western Open. A car crash in December 1941, in which she severely injured her knee, suspended her career for eighteen months.

In the fall of 1943 Berg returned to competition, recapturing the 1943 Women's Western Open before joining the Marine Corps Reserves. When World War II ended she resumed her golf career as a professional and participated in the few events conducted by the Women's Professional Golf Association, a predecessor to the L.P.G.A.

Berg won the first U.S. Women's Open in 1946, beating Betty Jameson 5 & 4 in the finals at the Spokane Country Club. It was the only U.S.

Patty Berg winning the 1938 U.S. Women's Open. She is the leading Majors winner among women with 15 Majors.

Women's Open ever conducted at match play. She won three other events in 1946.

Overall Patty Berg won twenty-nine amateur titles and fifty-seven professional tournaments.

In 1948 she teamed with Babe Zaharias and others to form the L.P.G.A., and served as its first president from 1949 to 1952.

Berg won a record fifteen Major titles, which included seven Women's Western Open titles, seven Titleholders Championships and the 1946 U.S. Women's Open. She won the L.P.G.A.'s Vare Trophy for the season's lowest scoring average in 1953, 1955, and 1956. She was the leading money winner three times (1954, 1956, and 1957).

Throughout her career Berg was plagued with health problems but she did not let this deter her. She had the severe knee injury in 1941. Over the years she endured cancer, back surgeries and a hip replacement. She continued her public appearances until she was diagnosed with Alzheimer's disease in 2005.

In 1963 she received the Bob Jones Award for "Distinguished Sportsmanship in Golf." Berg was among the first inductees to the L.P.G.A. Hall of Fame in 1951, and to the World Golf Hall of Fame in 1998.

She died on September 10, 2006 from complications caused by Alzheimer's disease. Berg was eighty-eight.

33

The Founding of the Ladies Professional Golf Association (L.P.G.A.)

The predecessor to the L.P.G.A. was the Women's Professional Golf Association (W.P.G.A.) founded in 1944. From the beginning it floundered for lack of funds, tournaments, and sponsorships. One bright spot, however, was that it initiated the U.S. Women's Open.

The women's pro tour was on shaky grounds almost from the start. In 1944 the circuit was founded by Hope Seignious, Betty Hicks and Ellen Griffin. The tour included the Western Open, the Tampa Open, George S. May's World and All-American Championships, the Titleholders Championship and several smaller events. It was mostly funded by Seignious but after a while she was nearly broke.

By January 1948 Babe Zaharias and Patty Berg decided that something had to be done. They met in Miami with George Zaharias and sports promoter Fred Corcoran, who was Babe's manager. Berg and Babe Zaharias decided to start a new organization that became the L.P.G.A. and they lobbied W.P.G.A. members to join them. A significant number of W.P.G.A. players did join them including Betty Jameson, Marlene Bauer, Louise Suggs and Marilyn Smith. Berg was elected the L.P.G.A.'s first president. Corcoran was named tournament manager. With the assistance of the Wilson Sporting Goods Company he began establishing tournaments and sponsors. The L.P.G.A. was chartered in 1950. With the foresight and planning of Corcoran, Zaharias and Berg, the L.P.G.A. began a period of early success.

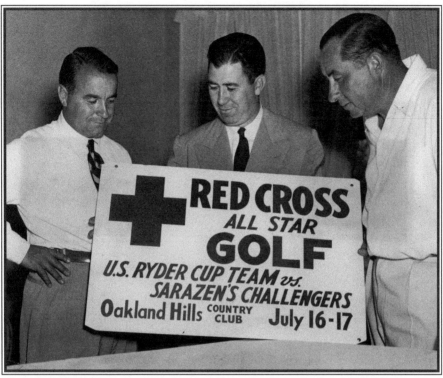

Gene Sarazen, Fred Corcoran, and Walter Hagen before a Red Cross Benefit Match in 1940.

By 1952 the L.P.G.A. had a twenty-one-event schedule which was three times the number of events in 1950. In 1951 Berg, Zaharias, Suggs and Jameson were elected to the L.P.G.A. Hall of Fame, in significant part for their work in getting the L.P.G.A. off the ground. Today it can be argued that the L.P.G.A. is the most accomplished women's sports organization in the world.

CHAPTER

34

Mickey Wright

M ary Kathryn "Mickey" Wright was born on February 18, 1935, in San Diego, California. She started playing golf at the age of eleven.

She won the U.S. Girls' Junior in 1952. After studying psychology for a year at Stanford she dropped out of college and turned professional in late 1954. Wright won sixty-five tournaments from 1957 through 1965. She won at least one tournament fourteen years in a row from 1956 through 1969. Over her career Wright won eighty-two tournaments, second only to Kathy Whitworth's eighty-eight victories.

Wright's Major victories included four U.S. Open titles and four L.P.G.A. victories. Besides Betsy Rawls she is the only woman golfer to capture four U.S. Women's Open titles (1958, 1959, 1961, and 1964). Her four L.P.G.A. Championship victories came in 1958, 1960, 1961, and 1963. Her total of thirteen Majors for a woman golfer is second only to the fifteen Majors won by Patty Berg.

Wright captured the Vare Trophy for low-scoring average five straight years between 1960 and 1964.

Churchill Valley Country Club outside of Pittsburgh, Pennsylvania, in Penn Hills, proved to be one of her favorite venues. She won the L.P.G.A. Championship there in 1958 and later that summer won the U.S. Women's Open at Forest Lake in Bloomfield Hills, Michigan. The following year, she

Mickey Wright won 13 Majors.

returned to Churchill Valley and repeated her U.S. Women's Open victory. Her feats thus included being the first woman to win two consecutive U.S. Women's Opens, and the first to win the L.P.G.A. Championship and the U.S. Women's Open in the same year.

The year 1961 was a banner one for Wright. She won ten events and again captured the U.S. Women's Open and the L.P.G.A. Championship. She followed up this feat with ten victories in 1962, thirteen (of thirty-two events) in 1963, and eleven in 1964—an amazing string of dominant years on the Ladies' Tour. To go along with these accomplishments she captured the money title from 1961 through 1964. Twice she won four tournaments in a row. Because of recurring foot problems Wright went into retirement at the age of thirty-four in 1969.

Wright is a member of the L.P.G.A. Hall of Fame (1964) and was inducted into the World Golf Hall of Fame in 1976.

Today, she makes her home in Port St. Lucie, Florida. In October 2006, she was diagnosed with breast cancer.

35

Three Women Who
Chased Patty Berg
Louise Suggs, Betsy Rawls, Betty Jameson

Louise Suggs

Mae Louise Suggs or, as she was known, "Louise Sluggs," was born in Atlanta, Georgia, on September 7, 1923. She took up the game of golf at age ten. This petite Georgian won the U.S. Women's Amateur in 1947 and the British Ladies Golf Championship in 1948. Then she turned pro.

Suggs promptly won the U.S. Women's Open in 1949. Her main rival was Babe Zaharias. Suggs won six tournaments in 1952, including a second U.S. Women's Open. In 1953 she won eight events and won at least one tournament every year until 1962 when she cut back on her career schedule.

In 1957 Suggs won her only L.P.G.A. Championship at the aforementioned Churchill Valley Country Club in Penn Hills, Pennsylvania. This was the first of three consecutive years that Churchill Valley hosted a major event (1958, the L.P.G.A. Championship; 1959, the U.S. Women's Open).

Over a thirty-five year career Suggs won a total of sixty-one professional tournaments, among which were eleven Majors. She ranks fourth in professional victories behind Kathy Whitworth (88), Mickey Wright (82), and Annika Sorenstam (72).

Suggs was a founder and charter member of the L.P.G.A. She helped Patty Berg, Babe Zaharias, Betty Jameson and Betsy Rawls move the L.P.G.A. ahead in its formative years. Suggs served as president from 1955 to 1957.

Louise Suggs, winner of fifty tournaments, among which were 11 Majors.

She was an inaugural member of the L.P.G.A. Hall of Fame in 1951. Suggs was inducted into the World Golf Hall of Fame in 1979.

In December 2006 the USGA announced that Suggs was named the 2007 Bob Jones winner in recognition of distinguished sportsmanship in golf.

Suggs died on August 7, 2015 in Sarasota, Florida.

Betsy Rawls

Elizabeth Earle "Betsy" Rawls was born in Spartanburg, South Carolina,

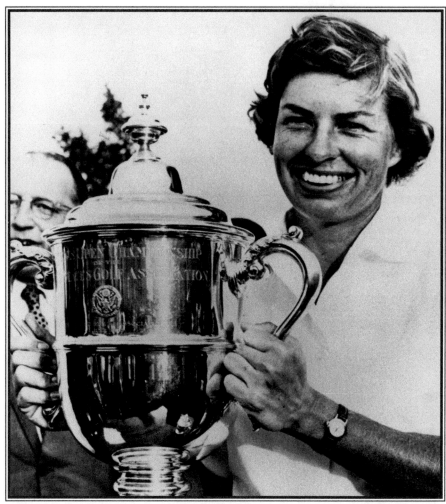

Betsy Rawls holding the trophy for her 1960 U.S. Women's Open victory.

on May 4, 1928. She started playing golf at age seventeen. She graduated Phi Beta Kappa from the University of Texas with degrees in mathematics and physics. After graduation in 1951 she joined the L.P.G.A. Tour. That year, she won the U.S. Women's Open.

Rawls won the U.S. Women's Open for a second time in 1953. She beat Jackie Pung in an eighteen-hole playoff. In 1957 she and Pung battled again for the title. This time Pung was disqualified for signing an incorrect scorecard. She signed for a score that was actually one shot higher. Rawls also won the U.S. Women's Open in 1957 and 1960. Her four U.S. Women's titles tied her with Mickey Wright for most U.S. Women's Open victories. Rawls's other Major victories were the 1959 and 1969 L.P.G.A. Championships. She was the leading money winner in 1952 and 1959. In 1959, she won ten times, and won the Vare Trophy for low-scoring average.Rawls won at least one tournament a year from 1951 to 1965. Her total of fifty-five L.P.G.A. victories places her fifth behind Kathy Whitworth (eighty-eight), Mickey Wright (eighty-two), Annika Sörenstam (seventy-two) and Patty Berg (fifty-seven) in total L.P.G.A. victories. In this mix it should be noted that Sam Snead has the most men's P.G.A. Tour victories (eighty-two).Rawls retired in 1975 and became the L.P.G.A. tournament director. In 1981 she took over as the long-time executive director of the L.P.G.A. MacDonald's Classic, a Major championship previously held at various venues in the Philadelphia, Pennsylvania, Wilmington, Delaware area, and Havre de Grace, Maryland. The 2015 L.P.G.A. Championship will be hosted by Westchester Country Club in Rye, New York. She is now retired from that position.

In 1996 Rawls was the winner of the Bob Jones Award for distinguished sportsmanship.

She was a 1960 inductee into the World Golf Hall of Fame and an inaugural member of the L.P.G.A. Hall of Fame in 1967.

Currently Rawls resides in Wilmington, Delaware.

Betty Jameson

Another of Patty Berg's strongest competitors was Elizabeth May "Betty" Jameson. She was born in Norman, Oklahoma on May 9, 1919.

Jameson won the U.S. Women's Amateur in 1939 and 1940. She was twenty years old when she won the first title. She attended the University of Texas and turned professional in 1945.

Jameson, along with Marlene Hagge, was considered one of the early "glamour girls" of the L.P.G.A.

In 1946 Jameson lost in the match-play final to Patty Berg in the inaugural U.S. Women's Open. The following year Jameson won the U.S. Women's Open when it switched to stroke play. Her 295 total was the first time a woman had shot under 300 in a seventy-two-hole event.

Jameson's other Majors were the 1942 Women's Western Open, which she won as an amateur, and the 1954 Women's Western Open.

Her best year was 1955 when she won four events. She won twelve individual events between 1947 and 1955.

*Betty Jameson, winner of the 1939 and 1940 U.S. Women's
Amateur Championship and the 1947 U.S. Women's Open*

Jameson helped Babe Zaharias and Patty Berg found the L.P.G.A. In 1952 Jameson donated the Glenna Collett Vare Trophy, awarded annually to the woman golfer with the lowest stroke average over a season.

Jameson retired from the L.P.G.A. Tour in 1970, having stepped away from a full-time role several years earlier.

Jameson was an inaugural member of the L.P.G.A. Hall of Fame in 1967, and is a 1951 member of the World Golf Hall of Fame.

She died on February 7, 2009.

36

The Late 1940s and Early 1950s: The Era Before Arnold Palmer

With Byron Nelson's retirement in 1946 the Great Triumvirate was down to two and Sam Snead and Ben Hogan were just beginning to hit their stride.

Claude Harmon took the 1948 Masters with a record-tying 279 total. He helped secure the victory on the final day when he hit his ball from the creek on the par-five thirteenth hole to secure his par.

In 1948 Hogan took his first U.S. Open title, at Riviera Country Club, Los Angeles, California. He would win four in six years. He made 1948 a monumental year when he received the Wanamaker Trophy for winning his second P.G.A. Championship at Norwood Hills Country Club in St. Louis, Missouri. It would be his second P.G.A. victory in three years.

Overseas, with a gap of eleven years between victories, Henry Cotton secured his third British Open in 1948. His first victory occurred back in 1934, and his second came in 1937.

At Birkdale, England the U.S. women defeated the Great Britain/Ireland squad 6 ½-2 ½, in the first post-war Curtis Cup Match.

Also in 1948 the first U.S. Junior was played. Dean Lind beat future U.S. Open champion Ken Venturi in the final.

The year 1949 was the year that Snead stepped to the forefront after Hogan had become the victim of a near-fatal automobile accident.

At the Masters Snead was one stroke behind beginning the final round.

*Jack Fleck and Ben Hogan at the 1955 U.S. Open won by Fleck
over Hogan in a play-off.*

He shot a 67 to win by three strokes. In May 1949 Snead won his second Major of the year when he captured the P.G.A. Championship at the Hermitage Club in Richmond, Virginia.

At the 1949 U.S. Open Snead had another near miss as he finished one stroke behind Cary Middlecoff at Medinah Country Club in Chicago, Illinois. It was one of four runners-up finishes in the U.S. Open for Snead.

Bobby Locke won the British Open at Royal St. George's in Sandwich, Kent, England in a play-off with Harry Bradshaw. Locke would win three more British Opens over the next eight years.

Charlie Coe won the 1949 U.S. Amateur at Oak Hill Country Club in Rochester, New York.

The precocious Marlene Bauer, at fifteen, won the inaugural U.S. Girls' Junior Championship in 1949 at the Philadelphia Country Club in Gladwyne, Pennsylvania. She, along with her sister Alice, would turn professional later in the year.

In 1950, less than a year after the near-fatal head-on car crash, Ben Hogan was back in competitive golf. He entered the Los Angeles Open at Riviera Country Club. After he had completed his four rounds Hogan amazingly led the tournament. When Sam Snead birdied the final two holes he and Hogan were tied. In the play-off Snead prevailed, 72-76. Nevertheless it was an astounding feat for Hogan, a man who was near death the previous year.

Hogan also challenged in the 1950 Masters before a final-round 76. Jimmy Demaret became the first three-time winner of the Masters when he won with a closing 69. He vaulted from four shots behind Jim Ferrier to take the title.

The 1950 U.S. Open in June at Merion Golf Club in Ardmore, Pennsylvania was a monumental achievement for Ben Hogan and secured his comeback from the accident. He opened with rounds of 72-69, for a tie for fifth going into the final two rounds. In the Saturday thirty-six-hole final, he shot 72 in the morning for a two-shot deficit. Hogan made four on the seventy-second hole for a three-way tie with Lloyd Mangrum and George Fazio. The following day he completed his triumph with a 69 to Mangrum's 73 and Fazio's 75. Hogan had his second U.S. Open.

South African Bobby Locke repeated as the 1950 British Open champion at Royal Troon Golf Club in Ayrshire, Scotland. His 279 beat Roberto De Vincenzo and broke the British Open record by four shots.

Chandler Harper won the P.G.A. Championship at Scioto Country Club in Columbus, Ohio. He beat Henry Williams, Jr. in the final, 4 & 3.

Sam Urzetta won the 1950 U.S. Amateur. He was a former caddy and beat Frank Stranahan, a wealthy two-time Walker Cup player, one-up in thirty-nine holes at Minneapolis Golf Club in Minneapolis, Minnesota. Earlier in the year Stranahan had captured the British Amateur.

This was also the year that Babe Zaharias won her second U.S. Women's Open at Rolling Hills Country Club in Wichita, Kansas. She won by nine strokes over Betsy Rawls, an amateur at the time. This was the first time that the L.P.G.A. took over administration of the U.S. Women's Open.

Hogan pursued his lofty goal of greatness in 1951, winning the Masters and the U.S. Open. In the 1951 Masters Hogan fired rounds of 70-72-70 to place him one stroke behind Skee Riegel. In the final round his masterful 68 garnered him the first of his two Masters by two strokes. The 1951 U.S. Open was held at Oakland Hills in Detroit, Michigan, which had been renovated into a terror by Robert Trent Jones. This was the U.S.

Open where Hogan's final round 67 was the lowest round of the tournament and gave him his third U.S. Open.

With no top Americans in the field Max Faulkner won the 1951 British Open at Royal Portrush, Portrush, Antrim, Northern Ireland.

Sam Snead took the 1951 P.G.A. Championship at Oakmont. He defeated Walter Burkemo 7 & 6 in the finals.

Also in 1951 Betsy Rawls won the first of her four U.S. Women's Opens at Atlanta's Druid Hills Golf Club.

Bill Maxwell cut through a record 1,416 entrants to win the 1951 U.S. Amateur. He beat Joseph Gagliardi 4 & 3 in the final at Saucon Valley Country Club in Bethlehem, Pennsylvania.

The year 1951 was also the year that the movie *Follow the Sun* debuted. It tracked Ben Hogan's recovery from the horrible road accident of 1949 and his return to golfing triumph. It opened in Hogan's hometown of Ft. Worth in March. Glenn Ford and Anne Baxter played the parts of Hogan and his wife.

The well-known golf magazine *Golf Digest* began publication in 1951.

In the 1951 Ryder Cup and the Walker Cup the U.S. squads triumphed rather handily over their opponents across the Atlantic.

The year 1951 found the U.S.G.A. and the R & A agreeing on a uniform Rules of Golf worldwide, effective the following year. The only remaining difference was the size of the ball (the R & A permitted a diameter of 1.62 inches compared with the U.S.G.A.'s 1.68 inches). The R & A would authorize the larger ball in 1990.

The stymie was abolished, center-shafted putters were legalized (in Britain, center-shafted putters had been illegal since 1909) and the out-of-bounds penalty was made stroke and distance.

Weather conditions at the 1952 Masters brought out the best in Sam Snead. Despite a 77 in windy third-round conditions Snead still led the field. His final round of 72 in similar conditions secured his victory by four shots over Jack Burke, Jr. Snead accomplished his victory despite hitting into the water on the par three twelfth hole.

Julius Boros claimed the spotlight in the 1952 U. S. Open at the Northwood Club in Dallas. His 281 was four strokes ahead of Porky Oliver. Ben Hogan led after two rounds, but faded in Saturday's double rounds and finished third.

The year 1952 witnessed another triumph for Bobby Locke in the British Open. This was his third victory in the Open in four years.

Jim Turnesa and Chick Harbert went the distance in the thirty-six-hole final of the P.G.A. Championship at Big Spring Golf Club in Louisville, Kentucky. Turnesa would prevail one-up.

After twenty years of trying Great Britain/Ireland won the 1952 Curtis Cup, beating the United States 5-4 at Muirfield.

There simply is not much more to say about 1953 except to acknowledge that Ben Hogan won all three Majors in which he entered. He won his second Masters in three years over Sam Snead with a record fourteen under par. He won the U.S. Open at Oakmont, leaving Snead again as the runner-up. Shortly thereafter Hogan traveled across the Atlantic to play in the British Open at Carnoustie, Scotland. He shot a lower round for each of the four rounds. His closing 68 secured his win by four strokes.

Hogan did not enter the P.G.A. Championship because it conflicted with the British Open and his practice rounds at Carnoustie. Walter Burkemo would claim the 1953 P.G.A. Championship at Birmingham Country Club in Birmingham, Michigan.

The United States defeated Great Britain-Ireland 9-3 in the 1953 Walker Cup at the Kittansett Club in Marion, Massachusetts. Victory also came to the United States 6 ½-5 ½ in the Ryder Cup Match at Wentworth, England.

In the 1953 U.S. Amateur the classic-swinging Gene Littler emerged as a player of national stature when he won the event at the Oklahoma City Golf and Country Club in Oklahoma City, Oklahoma.

Lew Worsham holed a shot to win the "World Championship" in Chicago, Illinois. What made the shot all the more dramatic was that it occurred in the first nationally televised golf tournament with two million viewers. Worsham sank a 135-yard wedge shot on the final hole to win the tournament by one shot. In a few seconds millions would be made aware of the excitement that golf could generate.

In April 1953 Babe Zaharias underwent cancer surgery. She announced that she would play a full schedule in 1954. That she did and starting slowly she earned victories in February and May. Next she set her sights on the U.S. Women's Open, which she had won in 1948 and 1950.

The 1954 U.S. Women's Open was played at hilly Salem Country Club in Peabody, Massachusetts. Zaharias soared to a six-stroke lead after the first two rounds. In Saturday's double round she shot a 73 to open up a 10-stroke lead. She extended this to a 12-stroke victory. She said that she wanted to show people that one could come back from a bout with cancer and return to a normal life. Two years later cancer took her life.

Sam Snead won the 1954 Masters but it wasn't easy. Both he and Hogan benefited from amateur Billy Joe Patton's final round double bogey on the thirteenth hole, which put him two strokes out of a play-off. Snead and Hogan tied for first with 289—the highest winning score in Masters history. Snead won the play-off, 70–71.

Despite a withered left arm (from a joint smashed in childhood) Ed Furgol claimed victory in the 1954 U.S. Open at Baltusrol Golf Club in Springfield, New Jersey. He edged Gene Littler by a stroke. It was the first U. S. Open to air on a national television network.

At the 1954 British Open Peter Thomson became the first Australian to win the tournament. It was the first of three consecutive British Opens that Thomson would win. He would win five overall.

In the 1954 P.G.A. Championship Chick Harbert beat Walter Burkemo, the defending champion, 4 & 3 in the thirty-six-hole final. It was a welcome victory for Harbert who had lost the 1952 P.G.A. Championship on the last hole.

Arnold Palmer made his debut on the national scene when he won the 1954 U .S. Amateur, thus beginning his reign as the most charismatic player in golf. He edged Robert Sweeney one-up at the Country Club of Detroit. For the first time in a national event the U.S.G.A. roped the fairways from tee to green to control the spectators.

In 1955 at the Masters Cary Middlecoff won, thanks to a second round 65. Ben Hogan finished seven strokes back in second place. Snead was third, one shot behind Hogan.

E. Harvie Ward won the 1955 U. S. Amateur after nine tries by beating Bill Hyndman III 9 & 8 at the Country Club of Virginia near Richmond. He duplicated the feat a year later to establish his place as the leading amateur of his time.

At the 1955 British Open Peter Thomson nailed down his second of three straight British Open titles.

Doug Ford won the 1955 P.G.A. Championship at Meadowbrook Country Club in Detroit, Michigan. He beat Cary Middlecoff in the thirty-six-hole final 4 & 3, and became P.G.A. champion in his first try.

The most exciting and surprising Major of the year was the 1955 U.S. Open held at the Olympic Club near San Francisco. Jack Fleck was a little-known pro from Davenport, Iowa. He was on his first full year on the P.G.A. Tour. His first round 76 did not portend any final-round heroics. The effect of Fleck's second round 69 was offset by his third round 75 over a typically demanding U. S. Open layout. In the meantime Hogan had finished with his best round of 70 for a total of 287. It seemed that no one could catch him for his fifth U.S. Open. Only Fleck had a chance to tie if could birdie the difficult final hole. Fleck made a great approach and sank the putt to force a play-off.

The next day Fleck took charge and went out to a lead of three strokes. Hogan fought back to cut the deficit to one stroke. His wayward drive on the eighteenth caused him to make a double bogey and Fleck's par gave him a three-shot victory, 69–72. There was a small consolation for Hogan in knowing that Fleck had been playing with a set of Ben Hogan golf clubs.

The United States squad prevailed in the 1955 Walker Cup with a 10–2 victory over Great Britain-Ireland at St. Andrews. Meanwhile, the U.S. team won the 1955 Ryder Cup 8–4 at the Thunderbird Ranch and Country Club in Palm Springs, California.

On the women's side Fay Crocker became the first foreign-born winner of the U. S. Women's Open. Crocker, of Montevideo, Uruguay, led after every round and won the 1955 event by four shots. Battling cancer, Babe Zaharias was unable to defend her title.

The year 1956 was Jackie Burke's year as he won both the Masters and the P.G.A. Championship.

In the Masters Burke found himself in the shadow of an amateur, Ken Venturi, who fired a 66 to take the first round lead. On Friday Venturi shot a 69 to tie the tournament record for thirty-six holes. Saturday's 75 was good enough for Venturi to hold a four-shot lead after three rounds. His lead over Burke was eight shots.

This vanished in no time as Venturi bogeyed every hole but the thirteenth, from the tenth to the fifteenth. In the meantime Burke had mounted his charge, culminating with a birdie on the seventeenth hole. This put him into a tie with Venturi. Venturi bogeyed the seventeenth, giving Burke a one-shot lead. Burke's par at the last and Venturi's missed 12-footer for a birdie there gave Burke the Green Jacket with a 71–289. Venturi shot a final round of 80.

The 1956 Masters was the first television broadcast of this Major. CBS did the broadcast, which has continued to this day with a minimum of commercial interruptions, as dictated by Masters officials.

The 1956 P.G.A. Championship brought Jackie Burke his second Major of the year. At Blue Hill Golf Club in Canton, Massachusetts, Burke came from behind to defeat Ted Kroll 3 & 2 in the thirty-six-hole final.

Cary Middlecoff took the 1956 U.S. Open at Oak Hill Country Club in Rochester, New York. Middlecoff shot a four-round total of 281 and then watched as Ben Hogan and Julius Boros tried to match him. Hogan's seventy-first-hole bogey proved to be his downfall. Boros needed a birdie over one of the last three holes for a tie, but settled for three pars. This was Middlecoff's second U.S. Open crown. His earlier victory came in 1949.

Australian Peter Thomson completed his hat trick at the British Open when he won at Royal Liverpool, Hoylake, England. A young, small and slight Gary Player finished fourth.

Harvie Ward won his second consecutive U.S. Amateur when he defeated Chuck Kocsis 5 & 4 in the 1956 final at Knollwood Club in Illinois. He is one of only nine golfers to win two U.S. Amateurs. Ward was not permitted to defend his title in 1957 because it was determined that he had violated the Rules of Amateur Status. It seems Ward's expenses at two tournaments in 1954 were paid for by his employer, Eddie Lowery, a San Francisco car dealer. Ward's punishment was a one-year suspension of his amateur status. The ruling drew even more notoriety because Lowery was on the U.S.G.A. Executive Committee. Lowery was also the 10-year old caddie for Francis Ouimet in 1913 at The Country Club where Ouimet defeated Harry Vardon and Ted Ray in a play-off for the U. S. Open.

Sadly, the golf world saw the passing of Babe Zaharias when she died of cancer at the age of forty-two on September 27th, 1956.

At the Masters in 1957 Doug Ford holed a bunker shot on the seventy-second hole to card a final round 66. That was good enough to beat Sam Snead by three shots.

Little-known Dick Mayer took the 1957 U.S. Open held at The Inverness Club in Toledo, Ohio. Mayer made a nine-foot putt on the 72nd hole to tie Cary Middlecoff at 282. The next day Mayer shot 72 to Middlecoff's 79 to win the Championship.

The 1957 British Open went to Bobby Locke. It was the South African's fourth British Open title.

Lionel Hebert won the 1957 P.G.A. Championship when he defeated Dow Finsterwald in the final 2 & 1 at Miami Valley Country Club in Dayton, Ohio. It was Hebert's first Tour victory and came in the last P.G.A. Championship conducted at match play.

Hillman Robbins, Jr. took the 1957 U.S. Amateur when he defeated Frank Taylor 5 & 4 at The Country Club in Brookline, Massachusetts.

Great Britain won the 1957 Ryder Cup 7½–4½ at Lundrick Golf Club in Yorkshire, England. It was Great Britain's first victory since 1933.

Signaling his ascension to the upper echelon of golfers was Arnold Palmer who led the P.G.A. Tour with four wins in 1957.

As 1958 dawned Arnold Palmer was on the verge of making his mark in Major championship golf. Palmer was a hot golfer when he arrived at Augusta for the Masters. After fifty-four holes, he and Sam Snead were tied at five-under 211.

In the final round Palmer made the turn in 36 to take a two-stroke lead. He bogeyed the tenth but reached the par five thirteenth in two, and made an eagle three from eighteen feet. His closing 73 gave him a one-stroke lead over Fred Hawkins and defending champion Doug Ford. Both failed to negotiate birdies at the last and Palmer had his first Green Jacket, and his first Major championship.

The 1958 U.S. Open Championship went to Tommy Bolt. He led after every round at Southern Hills Country Club in Tulsa, Oklahoma—his home state. He fended off the challenge of Gary Player.

Interrupted by Bobby Locke's triumph in 1957 Peter Thomson captured his fourth British Open in five years at Hoylake, Royal Liverpool. Thomson became the ninth golfer to win the British Open four times.

After thirty-nine years at match play the 1958 P.G.A. Championship converted to stroke play at Llanerch Country Club in Havertown, Pennsylvania. Dow Finsterwald produced the best card. In the final round he overtook third-round leader Sam Snead when he fired an outgoing 31, leading to a 67. Finsterwald finished with a 276, two strokes better than Billy Casper. Snead was two more shots to the rear.

At the 1958 U. S. Amateur Charles Coe of Oklahoma City won for the second time (previously, 1949) at the Olympic Country Club, in San Francisco, California. He defeated Tommy Aaron in the final, 5 & 4. Aaron would go on to win the 1973 Masters.

The year 1958 saw Patty Berg win her fifteenth and last Major (the Women's Western Open) and Mickey Wright take her first when she won the L.P.G.A. Championship at Churchill Valley Country Club in Penn Hills, Pennsylvania.

The Britain and Ireland team retained the 1958 Curtis Cup with a tie at Brae Burn Country Club in West Newton, Massachusetts.

Arnold Palmer, winner of seven Majors. His rivalries with Jack Nicklaus and Gary Player in the 1960s propelled the game of golf to new heights of popularity.

The Men's Modern "Big Four"

CHAPTER

37

Arnold Palmer
and the Dawn of a New Era

As the sun began to set on the career of Ben Hogan in the mid-1950s the public began searching for a worthy successor. The names of Ken Venturi, Dow Finsterwald and Billy Casper drew attention.

Venturi came agonizingly close to winning the 1956, 1958, and 1960 Masters but could not maintain the pace of a champion. In 1956 as an amateur he blew a four-shot lead on Sunday, shot an 80 and finished second to Jack Burke, Jr. In 1958 and 1960 Arnold Palmer proved his undoing.

To round out the picture Finsterwald and Casper were mentioned. Finsterwald finished fourth or better on the list of money-winners every year from 1956 to 1960. He had taken the 1958 P.G.A. Championship at Llanerch Country Club in Havertown, Pennsylvania when the tournament switched to stroke play. Yet, for most spectators he was not an exciting player to watch since he always played the percentage shot.

Casper was also one of the top money-winners. He was a sturdy, tee-to-green player but his strength was on the greens with his putter. He won the 1959 U. S. Open with a sensational exhibition of putting at Winged Foot in Mamaroneck, New York, taking only 114 putts over the four rounds. However, as a fast, disciplined player Casper did not exude the personality that the public was looking for. That void beckoned for a charismatic leader in the golf world. It wouldn't take long for the right golfer to make his presence felt—Arnold Palmer.

180

Arnold Palmer was born on September 10, 1929 in Latrobe, Pennsylvania, thirty miles east of Pittsburgh. His father, Deacon Palmer, was first the greens superintendent at Latrobe Country Club and subsequently became the golf professional there.

Palmer first began swinging golf clubs at the age of three. As a youngster he was allowed on the Latrobe course only in the early morning or late afternoon when the members weren't playing.

Palmer's friend Bud Worsham received a golf scholarship to Wake Forest University in North Carolina. He persuaded the golf coach to award one to Palmer also. When Worsham was killed in an automobile accident Palmer dropped out of Wake Forest and spent three years in the Coast Guard, based in Cleveland. When his hitch was up he briefly returned to Wake Forest in 1954.

He again dropped out of Wake Forest and took a job as a paint salesman in Cleveland. This gave him time to practice golf.

In 1954 he qualified for the U.S. Amateur, which was held at the Country Club of Detroit. Palmer made it into the final where he faced Bob Sweeney. After the morning round Sweeney was two-up. Palmer squared the match at the thirtieth hole. He won the thirty-second and thirty-third holes and went on to win one-up. His year was further highlighted by his marriage to Winifred Walzer whom he had met at a tournament at Shawnee Country Club, Shawnee-on-Delaware, Pennsylvania.

His first professional victory was the Canadian Open in 1955. He won twice more in 1956 and captured four victories in 1957.

Palmer solidified his position as a rising star at the 1958 Masters. After the third round his 211 left him tied with Sam Snead. Ken Venturi was settled in at 214. Palmer sealed his victory with an eagle on the par five thirteenth hole. It was at this tournament that the term Arnie's Army was born to describe his legion of fans. The phrase was coined in an article in the *Augusta Chronicle*.

Palmer came close to winning a second consecutive Masters in 1959 until he hit into the water at the par three twelfth hole in the final round. This paved the way for Art Wall to capture the Green Jacket and, although Palmer won three other tournaments in 1959, overall the season was somewhat of a letdown for him.

In 1960 and the subsequent two years Palmer more than made up for it as he had three fantastically successful seasons. First off was the 1960 Masters.

In the 1960 Masters Palmer found himself with a one-stroke lead going into the final round. With six holes to go Palmer was a stroke behind Venturi and Finsterwald. With only two holes to go he still trailed the sole leader, Venturi, by a single shot. On the seventeenth hole Palmer's second shot left him with a 27-foot putt for a birdie. His putt toppled in to tie Venturi.

On the eighteenth hole Palmer launched a second-shot six iron that settled five feet from the hole. Palmer made the putt and his birdie-birdie finish secured him his second Green Jacket. It was the first time that a player had finished birdie-birdie to win the Masters.

The 1960 U.S. Open was held at Cherry Hills Country Club in Denver, Colorado. In the thin air a mile above sea level the ball could be hit a long way and the course played short—especially the front nine.

During the first three rounds Palmer shot 72, 71 and 72. With scores very low he was not up among the leaders when the fourth round began on Saturday afternoon. He trailed the leader, Mike Souchak, by seven shots.

Before the round Palmer asked an old friend, Bob Drum, a sportswriter from the *Pittsburgh Press*, what a 65 would do for his chances. Drum told him that he was too far back. It's been reported that Palmer retorted that 65 would give him 280 and 280 wins the U.S. Open.

Palmer proceeded to birdie the par four first hole after driving the green. He then birdied six of the first seven holes for a 30 on the front nine. Palmer, now in a position to win, shot 35 on the incoming nine with a lone birdie and the rest pars. He outlasted Jack Nicklaus, Ben Hogan, Julius Boros and Jack Fleck, his nearest competitors, and finished with a two-stroke victory. His 65 was the lowest final round at the time in a U. S. Open. His record-breaking come-from-behind performance solidified his place as a legendary golfer, and hero to the masses comprising Arnie's Army.

Next up in 1960 was the British Open. Palmer's appearance was the beginning of a revitalization of the British Open, which had been losing some of its luster because of the lack of American stars making the trip over for the tournament. Palmer changed all of that.

Palmer played a very good tournament considering that this was his debut in the British Open. With a round to go he trailed Kel Nagle by four strokes. After a birdie-birdie start, Palmer cut the lead in half. Nagle regained his four-shoot cushion by birdieing the seventh and eighth holes. Palmer birdied the thirteenth, the fifteenth and the eighteenth to close within one shot. However Nagle closed with two pars for a one-stroke victory. Palmer's closing 68 was just not quite enough.

The rest of the year was somewhat of a wind-down for Palmer. He won two more tournaments and was in contention for the P.G.A. Championship at Firestone Country Club in Akron, Ohio until he made a triple bogey late in the third round. For the year Palmer won eight P.G.A. Tour events.

The year 1961 provided Palmer with a number of milestones although it was not as spectacular a year as 1960 had been. He took three victories in the first five tournaments of the year, and five victories for the year. His prize winnings of over $60,000 placed him second to Gary Player.

His play in the Majors was a lot more uneven. From start to finish the 1961 Masters was a duel between Palmer and Player. After the first day Palmer led by a stroke, 68-69. They reversed their scores in the second round so they shared the lead. In the third round Palmer, out first, shot a 73. Player shot a 69 to lead by four shots.

Sunday's rain pushed the fourth round to Monday. At one point Player widened his lead to six shots. On the back nine Player faltered and Palmer's consistent play left him with a one shot lead at the fourteenth. He made methodical pars on fourteen, fifteen, sixteen, and seventeen. Palmer needed a routine par on the eighteenth to win. His second shot found the right greenside bunker. His next hit flew over the green and he needed three shots to hole out. The double bogey cost him the tournament by one shot. There would not be a third Green Jacket for Palmer in 1961.

The venue for the 1961 British Open was Royal Birkdale, not far north of Liverpool, England. Palmer started off with a solid 70. The next day, in howling winds, Palmer had a marvelous 73. In the third round he shot a 69 for a one-shot lead. On the sixty-ninth hole Palmer hit the shot that won him the tournament. His six-iron from a very bad lie landed on the green where Palmer made his par. His closest competitor, Dai Rees, needed four birdies to tie. He made three of them and Palmer had won the British Open by a stroke.

The year 1962 was the third big year in a row for Palmer. Aside from the golf there was a budding business relationship with Mark McCormack. Mc-Cormack had been working on Palmer's business affairs since 1960. With ever-increasing business matters, in 1962 Palmer asked McCormack to take over as his manager. Thus was born the Palmer business empire and the start of McCormack's hugely successful International Management Group (IMG), which has gone on to represent hundreds of athletes from across the sports world.

With his affairs in order and some practice on his swing Palmer was ready to make his mark in 1962. After two runaway victories Palmer came to the Masters with his game in top form.

Going into the last round Palmer found himself with a two-stroke lead over Gary Player and Dow Finsterwald. Palmer ran into some sloppy play including a double-bogey on the tenth, to fall two back. At the sixteenth Palmer chipped in from 45 feet for a birdie and the lead was down to one. He ran in a twelve-footer on the seventeenth to forge a tie with Player and Finsterwald. After a saving par on the eighteenth there would be an eighteen-hole three-way play-off.

In the play-off Finsterwald was never a factor. Player bolted out to a three-stroke lead. Palmer then mounted a ferocious charge, canning birdies on ten, twelve, thirteen, and fourteen to give himself a four-shot lead. He finished with a 68 to Player's 71 and won by three shots. This was his third Masters—all in even-numbered years.

The next Major was the 1962 U.S. Open at Oakmont Country Club in Oakmont, Pennsylvania, a mere forty miles from Arnie's hometown of Latrobe, Pennsylvania. Palmer was the overwhelming favorite and his Army was out in full force.

The keyed-up gallery of Arnie's Army acted as if there was no one else on the course. For the first two rounds Palmer was paired with Jack Nicklaus from Columbus, Ohio, who had turned pro after winning the U.S. Amateur for the second time in 1961 at Pebble Beach Golf Links in Pebble Beach, California (previously, 1959).

Arnie shot a 71 in the first round and Nicklaus a 72. In the second round Palmer finished with a 68 while Nicklaus shot a 70. Palmer was three shots ahead of Nicklaus, and tied with Bob Rosburg at the halfway point.

In the third round on Saturday morning Palmer grabbed the lead with an eagle two on the par four seventeenth hole. He missed a short putt on the eighteenth, however, to drop into a tie with Bobby Nichols.

In the fourth round Palmer led Nicklaus by two shots at the turn. Nicklaus birdied the eleventh while Palmer bogeyed the thirteenth. Both parred in to set up an eighteen-hole play-off on Sunday.

The play-off brought out a large crowd, cheering overwhelmingly for Palmer, so much so that snippets of cheers when Nicklaus hit a wayward shot bordered on abuse and dampened the round.

Nicklaus raced off to a four-shot lead until Palmer mounted a rush with birdies on the ninth, eleventh, and twelfth holes. The thirteenth proved to be Palmer's undoing as he again bogeyed the hole. That just about wrapped up the U.S. Open for Nicklaus, who now had a two-shot lead. Palmer missed a meaningless short putt on the eighteenth to give Nicklaus the crown 71-74. It was Nicklaus's first professional victory and it signaled the advent of a rivalry that brought further new life to the P.G.A. Tour. Nicklaus's auspicious triumph would signal the run of a great champion, an intense rivalry with Palmer and Gary Player and the accolade as the greatest golfer of all time—at least until Tiger Woods arrived on the scene to make his own case.

What was next for Palmer after the disappointment on his home grounds of Oakmont? That proved to be the 1962 British Open at Troon, Scotland where Palmer was the defending champion. Palmer dominated play all week.

Over the burned out fairways Palmer was able to reach the par five's in two. After the first two rounds his lead was two shots over Kel Nagle. In the third round Palmer shot a course-record 67 and never looked back.

His lead grew to 10 shots before Nagle mounted a modest comeback. Palmer shot a final round of 69 to become a six-shot victor over Nagle. Many considered this the summit of Palmer's career.

The following week Palmer returned to the United States for a run at the 1962 P.G.A. Championship held at Aronomink Golf Club in Newton Square, Pennsylvania near Philadelphia. It was only a small exaggeration to say that the crowd worshipped Palmer's every move. However, he could do no more than tie for seventeenth as Gary Player took home the Wanamaker Trophy.

By now Palmer's legend had grown to such a point that his popularity transcended more than just golfing enthusiasts and spilled over into the general public. Much of his popularity was fueled by the coverage that television afforded. These new Palmer fans were enticed by the spirit that he brought to this reputedly stodgy game, and his unassuming, friendly and smiling personality had much to do with it. In short, Palmer had everything to do with the height to which the game became popularized in the early 1960s. It also didn't hurt that he was winning his share of Majors either, and that he faced serious rivals in Nicklaus and Player.

While 1963 was not quite up to Palmer's three previous years, neither was it a pedestrian year. Palmer led the money list thanks to seven tour wins including the Los Angeles and Western Opens.

Jack Nicklaus won his first Masters in 1963 and Palmer was not a factor. Tony Lema finished in second place.

The 1963 U.S. Open was played at The Country Club in Brookline, Massachusetts. It was being played there on the fiftieth anniversary of Francis Ouimet's 1913 play-off victory over Harry Vardon and Ted Ray. The course played exceedingly tough. At the end of regulation Julius Boros, Arnold Palmer and Jackie Cupit were tied at nine over par 293. Cupit had a two-stroke lead with two holes to play but double-bogeyed the seventy-first hole to open the door for a three-way playoff. In the play-off Boros won with a 70. Cupit came in with a 73 and Palmer finished with a 76. It was the second consecutive U.S. Open play-off loss for Palmer. For Boros it was his second U.S. Open title, having won in 1952.

In 1964 Palmer kept his record of winning the Masters in even years intact. His fourth victory in the Masters was a relatively easy six shots over Dave Marr and the defending champion Jack Nicklaus. Palmer became the first golfer to win four Green Jackets. Jimmy Demaret and Sam Snead had each won three apiece.

At the 1964 P.G.A. Championship held at Columbus Country Club in Columbus, Ohio Palmer shot four rounds under 70 (68-68-69-69) for a 274. But nobody would beat Bobby Nichols that week as he triumphed with a 271. Palmer and Nicklaus came in joint second.

Palmer's other highlights for the year were his finishing second to Nicklaus in the money race by a scant $81 and winning the inaugural Piccadilly World Match Play Championship at Wentworth, England.

In retrospect the years 1958-1964 were the prime years for Palmer. In that span he won four Masters, one U.S. Open and two British Opens. He won seven of the twenty-five majors contested and finished in the top ten on twelve other occasions. His only blemish, if one could call it that, was that he never won the P.G.A. Championship, just as Snead never could garner a U.S. Open championship, and Tom Watson never captured a P.G.A. Championship.

In 1966 Palmer manufactured another golden opportunity to win his second U.S. Open. The scene was the Olympic Country Club in San Francisco, California. After the first three rounds he had a three-shot lead at 207 over the newly-svelte Billy Casper who had gotten his weight down to 185 pounds thanks to an exotic diet that included avocado pears and buffalo meat.

The two were paired in the final round and Palmer charged out to a seven-shot lead after the outward nine. It seemed indubitable that the U.S. Open was Palmer's for the taking. He must have felt so too as by his own admission he began concentrating on breaking Ben Hogan's 1948 record of 276. Palmer began to fritter away strokes on the inward nine while Casper's steady play was punctuated by birdies. Palmer's lead was three shots with three to play. Palmer finished bogey-bogey, par to Casper's birdie-par-par.

That set up an eighteen-hole play-off. To the distress of Arnie's Army the play-off was a near repeat of the fourth round. Palmer surged to a two-stroke lead after nine, but the back nine proved his undoing again. Casper caught him on the eleventh hole with a birdie to Palmer's bogey. Then from holes thirteen to sixteen, Casper outplayed Palmer by four shots and that was the margin of victory for Casper, 69–73.

Moving ahead to 1968 Palmer had perhaps his best chance to win the P.G.A. Championship. The scene was Pecan Valley Country Club in San Antonio, Texas. Palmer had a chance to win but he missed several makeable birdie putts in the final round, to finish a shot back of Julius Boros. At age forty-eight Boros became the oldest player to win a Major championship. He still is, although in 2009, Tom Watson at fifty-nine, almost won the British Open, losing in a playoff to Stewart Cink.

In 1979 Palmer reached another milestone. He turned fifty on September 10, and became eligible for the senior tournaments that would soon arise. The Senior Tour would get a tremendous boost from Arnie's stellar drawing power. In 1980 the U.S.G.A. scheduled its first Senior Open for players age fifty-five and older. Argentinean Roberto De Vincenzo, took home the crown at Winged Foot Golf Club in Mamaroneck, New York.

However, it didn't take Palmer long to grab the spotlight on the Senior Tour. He won the second U. S. Senior Open in 1981 at Oakland Hills Country Club in Birmingham, Michigan. Palmer, Bob Stone and Billy Casper tied at 289. Palmer won the play-off with a 70 to Stone's 74 and Casper's 77. At age fifty-one Palmer was able to play in the Senior Open because the U.S.G.A. lowered the minimum age from fifty-five to fifty.

Overall, Palmer won ten events on the Senior Tour, including five senior Majors.

Palmer won the Vardon Trophy on the P.G.A. Tour for lowest scoring average four times: 1961, 1962, 1964, and 1967. He played on six Ryder Cup teams: 1961, 1963, 1965, 1967, 1971, and 1973. He was the last playing-captain in 1963 and captained the team again in 1975. Palmer won sixty-two times on the P.G.A., placing him fifth behind Sam Snead (eighty-two), Tiger Woods (seventy-nine), Jack Nicklaus (seventy-three), and Ben Hogan (sixty-four).

In 1986 Palmer was involved in a unique feat. In consecutive rounds in the pro-am of the Senior Tour's inaugural Chrysler Cup at the TPC at Avenel, Potomac, Maryland he made a hole-in-one at the par three, 187-yard, third hole on consecutive days.

In 2004 Palmer played in his fiftieth and last Masters. That was the record for most Masters played until 2008 when Gary Player was in the field for his fifty-first Masters. Palmer retired from competitive golf on October 13, 2006 at the Champions Tour Administaff Small Business Classic.

Palmer has accomplished much in his off-course activities. He was one of the founders of the Golf Channel. Palmer owns the Arnold Palmer Bay Hill Club and Lodge, the site of the Arnold Palmer Invitational, a popular tournament on the Southern Swing of the P.G.A. Tour. Since 1971 he has owned the Latrobe Country Club in Latrobe, Pennsylvania. He is also involved in the ownership of the Pebble Beach Golf Links.

The Arnold Palmer Hospital for Children in Orlando, Florida is a world-class medical facility. In 2006 a new campus was built, the Winnie Palmer Hospital for Women and Babies, named after Palmer's late wife. Its opening created a separate pediatrics and obstetrics hospital.

One of Palmer's favorite drinks, which he is credited with inventing, is a combination of half iced tea and half lemonade, a drink now popularly referred to as an "Arnold Palmer." Harkening back to an earlier era, Francis Ouimet, upon winning the 1913 U.S. Open, enjoyed a blend of ginger ale and lemonade called a "Horses's Neck."

Palmer was inducted as an inaugural member of the World Golf Hall of Fame in 1974. In 1980 he was made a member of the P.G.A. Hall of Fame.

Palmer spends his time in Orlando, Florida and Latrobe, Pennsylvania. He turned eighty on September 10, 2009.

38

The 1950s Turn Into the 1960s

Between Palmer's Masters triumph in 1958 and Nicklaus's stirring 1962 U.S. Open play-off victory two other golfers played themselves into prominence. During this time Gary Player and Billy Casper began to make their marks.

In the year 1959 (when Nicklaus won his first U.S. Amateur) Arnold Palmer had a six-shot lead going into the final round of the Masters. However, Art Wall closed with a record-tying 66 for a winning 284 total.

In the 1959 U.S. Open, held at Winged Foot Golf Club in Mamaroneck, New York, Billy Casper took home his first U.S. Open victory (also victorious in 1966) with a one-shot victory over Bob Rosburg. Palmer tied for fifth.

At the 1959 British Open at Muirfield, Gullane, Scotland, twenty-five-year old Gary Player opened with a poor 75, leaving him seven shots behind the leaders. He rallied to find himself in a position to win when he was out in 34 in the last round. He double-bogeyed the last to finish at 68 then had to wait to see if that was good enough to win. One after another rivals could not match Player's 284 and he became the youngest winner since Willie Auchterlonie in 1895.

The 1959 P.G.A. Championship was held at St. Louis Park in Minneapolis, Minnesota. Putting wizard Bob Rosburg's 277 edged Jerry Barber and Doug Sanders.

In 1960 Palmer took home his second Green Jacket at the Masters, and

Deane Beman won the U.S. Amateur in 1960 and 1963.

won his only U.S. Open at Cherry Hills Country Club in Denver, Colorado.

Jay Hebert won the 1960 P.G.A. Championship at Firestone Country Club in Akron, Ohio. Hebert's brother Lionel won the P.G.A. Championship in 1957, the last year it was conducted at match play. They are the only brothers to win the P.G.A. Championship.

The centenary British Open in 1960 was held at St. Andrews. Australian Kel Nagle beat Arnold Palmer by a stroke. Palmer's presence revitalized the Open.

Deane Beman won his first of two U. S. Amateurs at St. Louis Country Club when he defeated Robert Gardner in the final 6 & 4 (also won in 1963).

In 1961 Palmer, Nicklaus and Player all came through. Gary Player won the Masters for the first of his three Green Jackets. Palmer took the first of his two British Open titles. Nicklaus won his second U.S. Amateur.

Gene Littler held off Doug Sanders and Bob Goalby to win the 1961 U.S. Open by a stroke at Oakland Hills Country Club in Birmingham, Michigan.

Jerry Barber defeated Don January in a play-off for the 1961 P.G.A. Championship at Olympia Fields Country Club in Chicago, Illinois. Barber sank three monster putts on the last three holes to catch January, whom he beat 67-68 in the play-off.

In 1961 Charlie Sifford became first African-American golfer to receive a tour card after the P.G.A. reversed its notorious "Caucasians-only" clause. He was the first African-American to win a P.G.A. Tour event when he won the 1967 Greater Hartford Open.

39

Gary Player—
A World Class Player

H e was only five-foot-seven and 150 pounds but he made it to the pinnacle of golf and he did it on the world stage. Gary Player was a unique player in more ways than one. He maintained his physical skills with a strict diet and a strong work ethic. Allegedly, Player was the first golfer to maintain a regular and intensive physical regimen to make up for his small stature.

In order to keep up his phenomenal travel schedule he disdained alcohol and caffeine when flying, and always tried to get some sleep while traveling in air. With his full and still active career as a professional golfer throughout the world, those who keep loose track of these things have coined Player as the most frequent flyer of all time. Coming from South Africa during its years of apartheid he also had to have a thick skin to endure the course of racist taunts and death threats.

Gary Player was born on November 1, 1935 in Johannesburg, South Africa. He was the youngest of three children. His father bought him a set of clubs and the Virginia Park golf course in Johannesburg was where Player began to play golf. At age fourteen he played his first round of golf and at age seventeen he turned professional, urged on by his desire to emulate the great South African golfer, Bobby Locke. In addition to his excellent putting Player is also known for his skilled bunker play.

Player is one of the most successful golfers in the history of the sport. He ranks second to Sam Snead (165 victories) with 163 victories worldwide. He is tied with Ben Hogan for fourth in professional Major championships with nine (Nicklaus, eighteen; Woods, fourteen; Hagen, eleven). Along with Arnold Palmer and Jack Nicklaus he is recognized as one of "The Big Three" golfers of his era. This was the period from the late 1950s through the early 1970s and beyond when golf boomed in the United States and around the world, fueled by ever expanding television coverage and the rivalry among Player, Palmer, and Nicklaus.

With his 1965 play-off victory over Kel Nagle in the U. S. Open at Bellreive Country Club in St. Louis, Missouri he became, along with Gene Sarazen, Ben Hogan, Jack Nicklaus and, later, Tiger Woods, one of the only golfers to win the modern career "Grand Slam." Player was twenty-nine years old. It was also the first win in the U. S. Open by a foreigner since Ted Ray claimed victory in 1920.

Player played regularly on the P.G.A. Tour from the late 1950s until the 1980s. He led the money list in 1961, and took twenty-four career titles on that Tour. He also played all over the world and, at last count, had accumulated over fifteen million miles in air travel. He won the South African Open thirteen times and the Australian Open seven times.

Player's record in Major championships spanned three decades. In the British Open at Muirfield in 1959 he was in the lead after making up a four-shot deficit and felt that he had lost his chance at victory when he double-bogeyed the seventy-second hole. However, his pursuers faltered down the stretch too, and Player won by two shots.

At the 1961 Masters Player became the first foreign-born player to win the Green Jacket. He made a difficult par on the eighteenth hole and Palmer handed him the victory with a double bogey at the last. Afterward Palmer rued the fact that he had squandered away the Green Jacket which, as time would tell, would have given him three straight Masters, as he won in 1960 and 1962.

In 1962 Player won the P.G.A. Championship at Aronomink Golf Club in Newtown Square, Pennsylvania amid a crowd rooting for Palmer who was coming off victories in the Masters and British Open. After his 1965 win in the U.S. Open at Bellreive Player's next Major triumph was the 1968 British Open at Carnoustie, Scotland. He made up a two-shot deficit and won by one shot over Bob Charles and Jack Nicklaus.

For his next Major victory Player took the 1972 P.G.A. Championship

Gary Player, the "Black Knight," was part of the modern day Great Triumvirate with Jack Nicklaus and Arnold Palmer.

at Oakland Hills Country Club in Birmingham, Michigan. He won by two shots over Tommy Aaron and Jim Jamieson.

The year 1974 saw Player take his second Green Jacket when he came back from a one-shot deficit to defeat Dave Stockton and Tom Weiskopf by two shots.

That same year he won the British Open at Royal Lytham and St. Annes in Lancashire, England, shooting a final round 70 for a four-shot victory over Peter Oosterhuis.

Player won his ninth and last Major, and third Masters, in 1978. It came unexpectedly as he made up a seven-shot deficit to Hubert Green by shooting a final round 64 with six birdies on the back nine. Player's victory was by one shot over Green, Tom Watson and Rod Funseth.

Player was the only player in the twentieth century to win the British Open in three different decades. In the 1998 Masters, at the age of sixty-two, he became the oldest golfer to make the cut, breaking the twenty-five-year old record set by Sam Snead.

Player had a remarkable level of consistency in the Majors. He had over forty top ten finishes in these events.

Player also won the World Match Play Championship five times, sharing this record with Severiano Ballesteros until Ernie Els won the event for the sixth time in 2004.

Player's success continued into his fifties. He has won nineteen times on the Champions Tour with wins in six senior Majors. He also has thirteen other senior victories around the world, including three Senior British Opens (not recognized as Majors when Player won them). He and Jack Nicklaus are the only players to win career Grand Slams on the P.G.A. and Champions Tours. Overall, Player won 164 times worldwide including twenty-four P.G.A. Tour victories. This places him second behind Sam Snead's 165 worldwide victories.

In 2008 Player played in his fifty-first consecutive Masters, breaking the old record of fifty held by Arnold Palmer. Player's last Masters was the following year when he played in his fifty-second Masters.

In 1966 Player was awarded the Bob Jones Award for his distinguished sportsmanship in golf. He was inducted into the World Golf Hall of Fame in 1974.

A well-known quote from Player is: *the more I practice the luckier I get.*

A courageous style of play fired by a fiercely competitive nature, an always courteous demeanor and an inclination for black attire on the golf course has earned Player the nickname "the Black Knight."

CHAPTER

40

Through the Mid-1960s

Though the 1960s were dominated by the Big Three of Jack Nicklaus (of whom much will be said shortly), Arnold Palmer and Gary Player, other well-known players made their marks as well.

Nicklaus (the US Amateur), Palmer (the British Open) and Player (the Masters) each reached a golfing summit in 1961. The U.S. Open and P.G.A. Championship were captured by Gene Littler and Jerry Barber, respectively.

The year 1962 belonged to Palmer with his victories in the Masters and British Open and a runner-up finish to Nicklaus in the U.S. Open, losing in a play-off at Oakmont. Player took home the P.G.A. Championship.

On the women's side JoAnne Gunderson captured her third of five U.S. Women's Amateurs in 1962.

In 1963 Nicklaus won his first Masters and first P.G.A. Championship. He also finished one stroke out of a British Open play-off.

At the age of forty-three in 1963 Julius Boros became the oldest golfer to win the U. S. Open when he triumphed at The Country Club in Brookline, Massachusetts. Boros was 20 days older than Ted Ray who won in 1920. This record was later eclipsed by Raymond Floyd and then by Hale Irwin when he won the 1990 U.S. Open at the age of 45. Later, Boros would become the oldest player to win a Major when he won the 1968 P.G.A. Championship at the age of forty-eight.

There was a triple play-off in the 1963 U.S. Open, as in 1913 (when

Julius Boros, winner of the 1963 U.S. Open. He's the oldest to win a Major– the 1968 P.G.A. Championship at age 48.

Francis Ouimet won at The Country Club fifty years earlier) and Boros defeated Arnold Palmer and Jackie Cupit. Boros shot 70, Cupit a 73, and Palmer a 76. It was Palmer's second Open play-off loss in a row. He would endure a similar fate in 1966 against Billy Casper.

At the British Open at Royal Lytham & St. Annes, Lytham St. Annes, Lancashire, England Bob Charles became the first left-hander to win a Major championship. He defeated Phil Rodgers in a thirty-six-hole playoff 140-148. Subsequent lefthanders to win a Major were Mike Weir (2003 Masters) and Phil Mickelson (2004, 2006 and 2010 Masters; 2006 P.G.A. Championship; 2013 Open Championship).

Following up on his victory in 1960 Deane Beman won his second U.S. Amateur in 1963. He defeated Richard Sikes 2 & 1 at the Wakonda Club in Des Moines, Iowa.

Among the ladies in 1963 Mickey Wright won thirteen times on the L.P.G.A. Tour including Major victories at the L.P.G.A. Championship and the Women's Western Open.

In 1964, Palmer won his fourth Green Jacket at the Masters, continuing his even-year streak since 1958.

Bobby Nichols captured the 1964 P.G.A. Championship in Nicklaus's backyard at the Columbus Country Club in Columbus, Ohio. Nichols won by three strokes over runners-up Palmer and Nicklaus.

Tony Lema burst on the scene with his triumph in the 1964 British Open at St. Andrews. It was his first and only Major title. He garnered the nickname "Champagne Tony" after he promised to supply champagne to the media after he won a tournament. He won and served up the bubbly.

In 1966 Lema and his wife were killed in a plane crash when the small aircraft in which they were traveling from the P.G.A. Championship to a Chicago golf exhibition went down in Lansing, Michigan.

Among golfing enthusiasts the largest headline of 1964 was the U.S. Open held in the stifling heat at the Congressional Country Club in Bethesda, Maryland. Ken Venturi was in the spotlight.

In 1956 Venturi almost became the only amateur to win the Masters, but he finished with an 80 to lose by one shot to Jack Burke, Jr. The next year Venturi turned professional and proceeded to win ten tournaments in his first four years. In 1960 he came close again to a Green Jacket, only to be beaten out by Palmer who birdied the last two holes to snatch victory away from Venturi (a close fourth also occurred in 1958, two shots back).

In 1962 he suffered a pinched nerve in his right hand that caused his game to collapse. By the beginning of 1964 he was beginning to feel better and had some good performances in early tournaments.

In the U.S. Open qualifier he shot a 77-70 to barely make the field at Congressional. The weather was oppressively hot and humid throughout the tournament.

In the first round Venturi opened with a 72, which placed him four shots behind Arnold Palmer. A 70 in the second round left him six shots behind Tommy Jacobs. As was the custom in those days the final two rounds were played on Saturday. Saturday's temperature soared into the 100's.

Venturi started off the third round with good results. He birdied the first hole and had four more birdies on the front nine for a thirty. He was six-under par when he reached the seventh hole. There, he was obviously suffering from the heat. After bogeying the seventeenth and eighteenth he still shot a 66.

A doctor diagnosed him with heat prostration and accompanied him as he started out in the afternoon fourth round.

Despite his condition Venturi continued to play well while Jacobs made a string of bogeys. A key to Venturi's victory was an eighteen-foot birdie on the thirteenth hole. On the eighteenth hole he had a four stroke lead. He holed a 10-foot par putt for a winning 70. It was his first victory in four years.

The next year the U.S.G.A. decided to discontinue contesting the final two rounds on Saturday but to play the third and fourth rounds on Saturday and Sunday. That procedure remains in place today. As for Venturi he went on to win two more times in 1964 and was named P.G.A. Player of the Year.

Venturi never again achieved the heights of 1964 and in 2002 retired from broadcasting after a distinguished career as a long-time CBS golf analyst.

Bill Campbell won the 1964 U. S. Amateur at Canterbury Golf Club in Cleveland, Ohio. He later captured two U.S. Senior Amateurs and was named president of the U.S.G.A. in 1982.

As for the women Mickey Wright continued to dominate. She led the L.P.G.A. Tour in victories for the fifth straight year (eleven), led in earnings for the fourth straight year and won her fifth Vare Trophy, in the process, setting a scoring record of 72.46.

At the 1965 Masters Jack Nicklaus was in charge. Nicklaus shot 271 for his second Green Jacket (first, 1963). His score gave him a nine-shot victory over Arnold Palmer and Gary Player. Nicklaus broke the then Masters scoring record by three strokes. It was the first time that the Big Three had occupied the top three positions in a tournament.

At the 1965 U.S. Open at Bellerive Country Club in St. Louis, Missouri, Player became the third player, after Gene Sarazen and Ben Hogan, to win all four professional majors (a career Grand Slam) as he defeated Kel Nagle in an eighteen-hole play-off. It was the first one round a day U.S. Open. Later, Jack Nicklaus would win three career Grand Slams. Tiger Woods has also completed the career Grand Slam three times.

Arnold Palmer, like Jack Nicklaus at Columbus the preceding year, could not win the 1965 P.G.A. Championship in his own backyard at Laurel Valley Golf Club in Ligonier, Pennsylvania, not too far from Latrobe, Palmer's birthplace. The winner was Dave Marr, who stared down the charges of Jack Nicklaus and Billy Casper. Marr won by two shots thanks to a marvelous eight-iron at the last that landed within three feet of the cup. He tapped in for a par and 280.

Peter Thompson's victory in the 1965 British Open marked the fifth time he won the event. Only Harry Vardon with six victories could claim more. Later Tom Watson would also triumph five times. Like the changed format at the U. S. Open this was the last time that two rounds of the British Open were played on the third day.

The 1965 U. S. Amateur was held at Southern Hills Country Club, Tulsa, Oklahoma. Bob Murphy, a twenty-two-year old senior at the University of Florida, won the event by a stroke over Bob Dickson. This was the first time that the event was held at stroke play. Match play was re-instated in 1973.

41

Billy Casper—
The Fourth Member
(Almost) of the Big Three

William Earl "Billy" Casper was born on June 24, 1931 in San Diego, California. He was one of the top winners on the P.G.A. Tour from the mid-1950s to the mid-1970s.

Between 1956 and 1975 he won fifty-one P.G.A. Tour events. His success was often overshadowed, however, as he followed in the footsteps of Nelson, Hogan, and Snead, and was perennially in the shadow of Palmer, Nicklaus, and Player.

There was no denying that he was a top-flight player. Twice he was the leading money winner and he won the Vardon Trophy for low scoring average five times.

Casper was known for his excellence on the green with his unconventional wristy putting stroke. Many considered him the best putter of his era.

Casper was a member of eight Ryder Cup teams and was a non-playing captain in 1979.

Casper's greatest accomplishments were his victories in three Major championships.

In 1959 he won the U.S. Open at Winged Foot in Mamaroneck, New York. Exhibiting his putting prowess on the course's treacherous greens he took only 114 putts. At the halfway point Casper took over the lead with a 139, a stroke ahead of Hogan. By scoring a 69 in the third round Casper opened up a three-stroke lead.

A series of thunderstorms caused the fourth round to be played on Sunday. In the fourth round Hogan slid to a 76 and was out of it. Casper shot a 74 and won with a 282. In all, he averaged 29 putts a round and had only one three-putt green.

The 1966 U.S. Open was held at the Olympic Club in San Francisco, California. By now, Palmer was golf's new hero. Rather than being hailed as a comeback Casper victory the tournament became known as the one that Palmer threw away.

After the second round Casper and Palmer were tied with scores of 137. Palmer was facing a new Billy Casper.

He was no longer a roundish 220-pounder. Through an exotic diet that included buffalo and bear meat he got his weight down to 185 pounds. This diet also helped curtail his allergies.

The next day Casper fell three shots behind with a 73 to Palmer's 70. When Palmer shot a 32 on the more difficult front nine in the fourth round, he stood seven strokes ahead of Casper and nine ahead of Nicklaus.

It has been said that Palmer, having believed he had the Open won, began going after Hogan's record of 276. This turned out to be a fatal mistake. Palmer let four of the strokes go after the first six holes as he played them two over par while Casper registered a two under par.

Palmer bogeyed the sixteenth hole while Casper made birdie. Now the lead was a single stroke with two holes to play. Palmer's bogey to Casper's par at the seventeenth, drew the two of them even. At the eighteenth hole both made par for 278 with Palmer making a pressure putt from six feet. Palmer had shot 71 to Casper's 68.

The play-off resembled the fourth round. Palmer cruised to the turn with a 33 against Casper's 35. Casper picked up two shots on the eleventh and went ahead when he holed a fifty-footer for a birdie two at the thirteenth hole. Casper outplayed Palmer down the stretch and shot 69. Palmer finished with a 73.

As he had done seven years earlier Casper won the U.S. Open through his magnificent putting. He used only 117 putts and had no three-putt greens.

Despite Casper's wonderful golf—four of his five rounds were in the 60's—the 1966 Open will always be remembered less for Casper's winning than for Palmer's disheartening loss.

Casper won the Masters in 1970. It was sweet revenge after his final round collapse the previous year when he lost in a play-off to George Archer.

Billy Casper, winner of three Major championships.

The tables were turned in 1970 as Casper defeated Gene Littler in another play-off with Casper's hot putter spelling Littler's doom. Casper won 69-74. He was named P.G.A. Player of the Year.

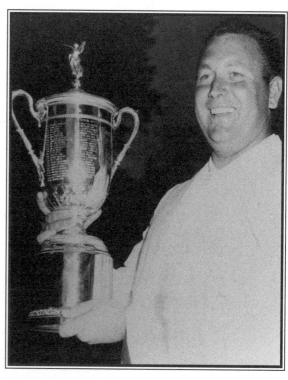

Casper joined the Senior Tour in 1981. He achieved only modest success but did win two senior Majors—the U.S. Senior Open in 1983 and the Mazda Senior Tournament Players Championship in 1988.

After his outstanding career Casper became an accomplished golf course designer.

He was elected to the World Golf Hall of Fame in 1978, and the P.G.A. Hall of Fame in 1982.

Casper, a Mormon, and his wife had eleven children. One of his sons, David, is serving a life sentence without parole in a Nevada prison for armed robberies and other felonies.

Casper died in February 2015 at 83.

CHAPTER
42

The Years 1966–1967

The year 1966 was the year of major accomplishments for Jack Nicklaus. By winning the British Open he joined Sarazen, Hogan and Player as players to win career modern Majors (career Grand Slams) (Tiger Woods would join them later). This was one year after Player had accomplished the feat with his win at the 1965 U.S. Open.

The British Open was conducted at Muirfield, Scotland. Nicklaus birdied the seventy-first hole to clinch the victory by one shot over Doug Sanders and Dave Thomas.

In winning the 1966 Masters Nicklaus became the first golfer to win the title back-to-back. Nicklaus was tied after three rounds with Tommy Jacobs. He finished tied after four rounds with Jacobs and Gay Brewer. Brewer lost the opportunity to win in regulation when he bogeyed the seventy-second hole. Nicklaus won the play-off shooting 70 to Jacob's 72 and Brewer's 78. Nick Faldo (1989–1990) and Tiger Woods (2001–2002) are the only other men to win consecutive Masters.

Al Geiberger captured his only Major title when he won the 1966 P.G.A. Championship at Firestone Country Club in Akron, Ohio. His even par 280 gave him a margin of four strokes over Dudley Wysong. The fifty-four-year-old Sam Snead led after two rounds.

Casper, of course, mounted his famous charge past Palmer to capture the 1966 U.S. Open at the Olympic Club in San Francisco, California.

At the U.S. Amateur Gary Cowan won his first of two titles, (the other being in 1971) defeating Deane Beman who was seeking a third title. Cowan, a twenty-seven-year old from Canada, caught Beman over the closing

The only amateur to win the U.S. Women's Open was Catherine Lacoste in 1967.

holes at Merion Golf Club in Ardmore, Pennsylvania and beat him by a stroke the next day in a play-off. Cowan was the first non-American to win the title since Ross Somerville, another native of Ontario, Canada, had done so in 1932.

Tragedy struck the P.G.A. Tour in 1966 when Tony Lema, his wife and two others were killed when their small aircraft crashed on the seventh green at a Lansing, Michigan golf course. Lema was traveling from the P.G.A. Championships to an exhibition near Chicago. Lema was the 1964 British Open champion.

Kathy Whitworth dominated the Women's Tour. She won nine times and led in earnings with a record of $33,517.

In 1967 Gay Brewer came back from his disappointment of a year earlier to capture the Masters. He closed with a final-round 67 to win by one shot over Bobby Nichols. Brewer shot 280.

Jack Nicklaus shot a tournament record 275 to win the 1967 U.S. Open at Baltusrol Golf Club in Springfield, New Jersey. Nicklaus needed a birdie on the seventy-second hole to break Hogan's U.S. Open record. Nicklaus drained a twenty-two-footer for the record.

Roberto De Vicenzo prevailed in the 1967 British Open at Hoylake in Liverpool, England. He shot a 278 and defeated defending champion Jack Nicklaus by two strokes. De Vicenzo, a native of Argentina, became the first golfer from South America to win a Major Championship.

The 1967 P.G.A. Championship was held at Columbine Country Club in Littleton, Colorado. Don Massengale finished with a blistering 66 to tie fellow Texan Don January, at 281. January won the playoff 69-71.

Bob Dickson won the 1967 U. S. Amateur at the Broadmoor Golf Club in Colorado Springs, Colorado. Dickson also won the 1967 British Amateur to accomplish the "Little Slam"—becoming the first golfer to accomplish the feat since Lawson Little in 1935.

Catherine Lacoste, daughter of tennis-great Rene Lacoste, became the first and only amateur to win the U.S. Women's Open when she won the 1967 rendition at the Hot Springs Golf and Tennis Club in Hot Springs, Virginia.

The first live color telecast of a golf tournament was the 1967 Bob Hope Desert classic.

43

The Golden Bear

J ack William Nicklaus was born on January 21, 1940 and eventually became known as "The Golden Bear" because of his blond hair and sturdy frame. He was a major force in amateur and professional golf from the late 1950s through the mid 1990s. His amateur success blended into his success on the P.G.A. Tour from the 1960s to the mid-to-late 1980s then on the Champions Tour from the early to mid-1990s.

Nicklaus is generally regarded as the greatest golfer of all time with his eighteen Major championships. A strong case can be made for Tiger Woods, even though Nicklaus has garnered more Major victories to date. To his credit, however, Woods, with his fourteen Majors as of 2015, has been more dominant during his ongoing playing career.

Together with Arnold Palmer, Nicklaus is credited with advancing golf as a major spectator sport. On the one hand Palmer brought television to the fore but it was the rising Nicklaus-Palmer rivalry that fueled the popularity that the game now enjoys.

Nicklaus was born in Columbus, Ohio in the suburbs of Upper Arlington, first earning his famous nickname there as an Upper Arlington Golden Bear. He overcame a mild case of polio as a youth. Nicklaus was encouraged by his dad, Charlie, a pharmacist, to take up the game of golf. At the age of ten Nicklaus proceeded to shoot 51 for his first nine holes. He played at Scioto Country Club where he came under the tutelage of Jack Grout, who would become his long-time instructor.

At the age of thirteen Nicklaus broke 70. He won the first of five straight Ohio State Junior titles at the age of twelve. Nicklaus won the Ohio State Open at age sixteen, competing against professionals.

He burst onto the national scene with a dramatic eighteenth hole victory in the finals of the 1959 U.S. Amateur at the Broadmoor Golf Club (East Course) in Colorado Springs, Colorado. He defeated Charlie Coe, the defending champion, one-up. Coe had also been the champion in 1949. In 1961 Nicklaus again won the U. S. Amateur at Pebble Beach Golf links, Pebble Beach, California. He coasted to an easy victory in the final, defeating Dudley Wysong, Jr. 8 & 6. Also in 1961 Nicklaus won the N.C.A.A. Championship while attending Ohio State University.

At the 1960 U.S. Open he shot a 282, finishing second to Arnold Palmer by two strokes. Nicklaus's score remains the lowest ever made by an amateur in the U. S. Open.

In the 1959 and 1961 Walker Cup matches Nicklaus enjoyed team victories while winning both of his singles matches in each competition.

In the 1960 World Amateur Team Championship for the Eisenhower Trophy Nicklaus shot a 269 in leading the United States to a 42-shot victory. Nicklaus's individual score was 18 strokes below Ben Hogan's 287 in 1950.

Nicklaus turned professional in 1962 after his second U.S. Amateur victory in 1961. Up until the U.S. Open that year, he had played well but had not yet come up with his first professional victory.

He broke through at the 1962 U.S. Open at Oakmont Country Club near Pittsburgh, Pennsylvania. The U.S. Open was virtually in the backyard of Latrobe, Arnold Palmer's hometown. Naturally, Arnie's Army was out in full force and most did not take kindly to the challenge mounted by the young, crew cut, full-figured, upstart Nicklaus.

Both played well through the first three rounds of the tournament. Nicklaus had to make up two strokes after the third round. Palmer opened the door with a bogey six on the par- five sixty-third hole. With five holes to play Nicklaus and Palmer were tied. On the seventy-first hole Palmer dropped his approach shot eight feet from the hole. A birdie would have given him the lead but he missed the putt.

On the seventy-second hole, a 462 yard bunker-laden hole, Palmer smashed his drive and hit an approach shot ten feet from the cup. Again, he missed the putt. He had shot a 71 to drop into a tie with Nicklaus.

The next day in the Sunday eighteen-hole play-off Palmer dropped behind early. After Nicklaus birdied the sixth Palmer was four strokes behind.

Jack Nicklaus, the "Golden Bear," leads the way with 18 Majors.

Palmer closed in on Nicklaus with birdies on the ninth, eleventh and twelfth holes. With six holes to play Nicklaus's lead looked shaky with Arnie's Army helping Palmer's charge.

But Palmer's hopes ended on the thirteenth where he three-putted and fell two shots behind. With the cushion Nicklaus eased to a three-shot victory, shooting a 71 to Palmer's 74. Nicklaus won on the greens. In the ninety holes, Nicklaus had only one three-putt green while Palmer had ten. It was Nicklaus's first win as a professional.

By the end of the year he had won twice more, completed his rookie year with over $60,000 in prize money, placed third on the P.G.A. Tour money list and was named Rookie of the Year.

In 1963 Nicklaus won two more Major championships. He won his first Masters and he captured the P.G.A. Championship at the Dallas Athletic Club in Dallas, Texas. He also won three other times that year.

In the 1964 British Open at St. Andrews Nicklaus set a new record for the lowest score in the final thirty-six holes with 66–68. This rally was not quite enough as he finished second behind Tony Lema.

Despite not winning a Major in 1964 Nicklaus placed first on the P.G.A. Tour money list for the first time in his career with a margin for the year of $81.13 over Arnold Palmer!

At the Masters in 1965 Nicklaus shot 271 to win by nine shots over Arnold Palmer and Gary Player. That score broke Ben Hogan's record of 274 set in 1953.

In 1966 Nicklaus became the first player to win back-to-back Masters. Gay Brewer's three-putt on the seventy-second hole opened the door for Nicklaus. This resulted in a three-way play-off among Nicklaus, Brewer and Tommy Jacobs. In the play-off Nicklaus shot a 70 to Jacob's 72 and Brewer's 78. This was Nicklaus's third Green Jacket and his third in four years.

Also in 1966 after five tries he won the British Open, giving him a modern career "Grand Slam" with a victory in each of the four Major professional championships. Nicklaus shot 282 to win by a stroke over Doug Sanders and Dave Thomas at Muirfield in Scotland. He birdied the seventy-first hole to secure the victory. This win enabled him to capture all four modern Major championships (the modern "Career Grand Slam"). Gene Sarazen, Ben Hogan and Gary Player preceded him in winning all four modern Majors. Tiger Woods has since achieved this feat as well.

The 1967 U.S. Open was held at Baltusrol Golf Club in Springfield, New Jersey. After the third round Nicklaus, Casper, and Palmer were tied at 210, one stroke behind amateur Marty Fleckman. In the fourth round Nicklaus shot a 65 for a 275 and the win.

On the eighteenth hole Nicklaus canned a twenty-foot putt for birdie.

This was the Golden Bear's second U.S. Open and seventh Major title in six years. Arnold Palmer finished in second place, four shots behind Nicklaus. The 275 was the lowest yet for the Championship, beating by one shot Ben Hogan's 276 in 1948.

Though the crowd was pro-Palmer the spectators burst into applause, hailing Nicklaus as a new hero. Jack had turned them around with his stellar play. No longer was he an anti-hero.

After Nicklaus won the 1967 U.S. Open he didn't win another Major championship until the 1970 British Open at St. Andrews. In addition his best showing on the Tour money list for the years 1968 to 1970 was second with a worst placing of fourth.

Nicklaus also had to deal with the death of his father, Charlie, in 1970. It was soon after this loss that Nicklaus won the 1970 British Open Championship, defeating Doug Sanders in a play-off in emotional fashion. Nicklaus threw his putter into the air after sinking the winning putt as he was thrilled to have won the British Open at the home of golf, St. Andrews. Doug Sanders could have won the tournament in regulation but he missed a three-foot putt on the seventy-second hole.

After winning the 1971 P.G.A. Championship Nicklaus became the first golfer to complete the "Double Grand Slam" (winning all four professional majors twice in a career). He later accomplished it a third time as has Tiger Woods. Nicklaus's money total of $244,490 was a record at the time and he won four other tournaments during the year.

In 1972 Nicklaus broke his money record again, winning over $300,000. He became the first player since Arnold Palmer in 1960 to win the first two legs of the Grand Slam.

At the Masters he was never in trouble after an opening round 68. Even though he shot a bad-weather 74 in the final round he won by three shots over Tom Weiskopf, Bruce Crampton, and Bobby Mitchell.

In the 1972 U.S. Open at Pebble Beach Golf Links Nicklaus struck a one-iron on the par three seventeenth hole into a stiff, gusty ocean breeze. His ball landed, hit the flagstick and ended up six inches from the cup. He shot 290 to win by three strokes over Crampton. The U. S. Open was Nicklaus's thirteenth career Major, and tied him with Bobby Jones for career Majors (although Jones's compilation of Majors was different—the U.S. Amateur and Open, and the British Amateur and Open).

The 1972 British Open was held at Muirfield, Scotland, one of Nicklaus's favorite venues. Lee Trevino won after a stirring duel with Tony Jacklin. Nicklaus was six shots back, beginning the final round. He fired a final round 66 to post a 279 score. Nicklaus could only wait for Trevino to finish. Trevino was in trouble on the par-five seventeenth but chipped in for par. That shot led to his successful defense of the British Open. Nicklaus finished a stroke behind and Jacklin was two strokes back.

With his second place showing at the 1972 British Open the Grand Slam pressure was off Nicklaus. At the P.G.A. Championship, held at Oakland Hills Country Club in Birmingham, Michigan he finished six shots behind Gary Player, who won by two shots over Tommy Aaron and Jim Jamieson.

Nicklaus won a total of seven tournaments in 1972 and was runner-up in three more.

The year 1973 was a milestone year for Nicklaus. By winning the P.G.A. Championship with a four-shot margin over Bruce Crampton he broke Jones's record for Majors won by capturing his fourteenth Major. He won six other events that year and led in earnings with $308,362. Nicklaus was named the P.G.A. Player of the Year for the third time and the second time in a row.

Nicklaus failed to win a Major in 1974. However, he won the first Tournament Players Championship (now known as the Players Championship). The year 1974 also marked the year that Nicklaus began his career in golf architecture. He started working with Pete Dye to design Harbour Town Golf Links at Hilton Head, South Carolina. Nicklaus was one of the originators of the "modern" style of golf course architecture. His masterpiece is Muirfield Village in Dublin, Ohio, home of Nicklaus's Memorial Tournament. To date Nicklaus has designed over 200 courses worldwide, and golf architecture is now his principal occupation.

Nicklaus's lack of a Major in 1974 was offset by his being one of the original inductees into the World Golf Hall of Fame.

Nicklaus's year in 1975 started off well. He won the Doral-Eastern Open, the Heritage Classic and the Masters in consecutive starts. The 1975 Masters is regarded as one of the greatest Masters of all time. It was a battle among Nicklaus, Tom Weiskopf and Johnny Miller. The Masters drama began in the third round. After starting with a 68 and a 67 Nicklaus seemed to have the tournament wrapped up. Coming from far back in the third round, however, Miller shot a 65. Weiskopf shot a 66. And when Nicklaus struggled in with a 73 Weiskopf took the lead.

The final round turned up the excitement. By the back nine Nicklaus and Weiskopf were tied for the lead with Miller right on their heels.

Weiskopf took a one-stroke lead with birdies on fourteen and fifteen. With Miller and Weiskopf standing on the sixteenth tee Nicklaus holed a dramatic 45-foot putt on the sixteenth hole to pull even with Weiskopf. Weiskopf bogeyed the sixteenth with a disappointing three-putt effort.

Miller caught Weiskopf with a seventeenth hole birdie, leaving each one shot behind Nicklaus going into the final hole. When Miller and Weiskopf failed to make birdie on the eighteenth hole Nicklaus had his fifth Green Jacket, eclipsing Palmer's record of four. For Weiskopf the loss was hard to take for he had now finished second four times.

In addition to his memorable Masters victory Nicklaus won four other tour events in 1975, including the P.G.A. Championship at Firestone Country Club in Akron, Ohio. Nicklaus claimed his fourth P.G.A. title by shooting 276, two strokes better than Bruce Crampton. It was the fourth time that he had won two Majors in the same year.

Boosted by these two Majors Nicklaus was named the 1975 P.G.A. Player of the Year for the fourth time, tying Ben Hogan for this accomplishment.

In 1976, Nicklaus topped the Tour money list despite competing in only sixteen events, winning only two events and capturing no Majors. Nicklaus won both the Tournament Players Championship and the World Series of Golf, as the World Series became an official event. He won a season-high $100,000 at the World Series and led the Tour in earnings ($266,438) for the eighth and final time.

He also won the 1976 P.G.A. Player of the Year award for a record fifth time. Between 1972 and 1976 the only time he failed to win this award was 1974.

The year 1977 was another year without a Major for Nicklaus but a runner-up finish to Tom Watson in the Open at Turnberry, Scotland turned out to be a classic duel.

In the calm weather at Turnberry both Nicklaus and Watson shot 68-70-65. This left them three shots ahead of the field entering the fourth round. It was more of a match play than stroke play final round.

With six holes remaining Nicklaus led by three shots. Then, Watson rolled in a 60-footer for a birdie on the fifteenth hole to tie. Nicklaus two-putted from four feet for a par at the par-five seventeenth hole and Watson made birdie for the lead. On the eighteenth, when it looked as if the title was Watson's, Nicklaus made a 32-footer for a birdie. Watson then made a two-foot birdie to secure the victory. Watson had shot 65 to Nicklaus's 66 in the dramatic duel. Watson's 268 was a British Open record by eight strokes.

The win was the second time in 1977 that Watson had beaten Nicklaus head-to-head. In the Masters, three months earlier, Watson's final round 67 gave him a two-stroke victory over Nicklaus, who had closed with a 66.

During 1977 Nicklaus captured his sixty-fifth career Tour win and passed Ben Hogan to take second place on this list, with only Sam Snead ahead of him, having compiled eighty-two victories.

Nicklaus won the 1978 British Open Championship to become the only player to have won each of the Major championships three times. He won by two strokes at St. Andrews. In 2008 Tiger Woods would accomplish this feat with his third win in the U.S. Open at Torrey Pines in San Diego, California.

In 1978 Nicklaus won three other tournaments on the P.G.A. Tour including the Tournament Players Championship and was named "Sportsman of the Year" by *Sports Illustrated*.

After this year Nicklaus suffered a lapse of form. He did not win another tournament until 1980. The year 1979 was Nicklaus's first professional year in which he failed to win a tournament. He dropped to seventy-first on the money list after finishing no lower than fourth on that list during his first seventeen seasons.

In 1980 Nicklaus stepped back into the spotlight. Although he recorded only three top-ten finishes two of them were in Majors: the U.S. Open and the P.G.A. Championship.

With whispers from his critics that he was over the hill Nicklaus silenced them by winning the U.S. Open at Baltusrol Golf Club in Springfield, New Jersey.

Nicklaus had won the 1967 U.S. Open at Baltusrol with a record total of 275. Thirteen years later he broke that mark with a 272. In the first round of his 1980 triumph he tied Johnny Miller's record 63 for a U.S. Open round (established in the final round of the 1973 U.S. Open at Oakmont Country Club, Oakmont, Pennsylvania). The victory did not come easily for Nicklaus who had to fend off Japan's Isao Aoki, who was paired with Nicklaus for all 72 holes. Nicklaus needed a birdie-birdie finish to win by two strokes.

He had now won his fourth U.S. Open, equaling the record of Willie Anderson, Ben Hogan and Bobby Jones.

Nicklaus provided even more emphasis that he was back in top form when he won the 1980 P.G.A. Championship at Oak Hill Country Club in Rochester, New York. With a six-under par 274 he cruised to a seven-stroke win over Andy Bean. He became the first player to sweep the U. S. Open and P.G.A. Championship in a single year since Ben Hogan in 1948. The P.G.A. Championship was his seventeenth Major.

During the next five years Nicklaus won only two times on the P.G.A. Tour including his own tournament, the Memorial, in 1984. But there was yet a third epic duel with Tom Watson.

At the U.S. Open at Pebble Beach Golf Links in 1982 Nicklaus had finished his final round knowing that Watson had to make two pars to force a play-off. Anything worse would give Nicklaus his fifth U.S. Open title. When Watson's tee shot on the par-three seventeenth missed the green long and left in heavy rough it looked as if Nicklaus would have his fifth U.S. Open. But then Watson pulled off a miraculous shot, holing the chip for a birdie and a one-shot lead. At the eighteenth hole Watson rolled in a twenty-foot birdie putt for a two-shot victory.

For Nicklaus this was his fourth runner-up finish in the U.S. Open, a record he now shared with Arnold Palmer, Bobby Jones and Sam Snead.

By 1986 most of the golf world had concluded that the forty-six-year old Nicklaus had finished his golf career with seventeen Majors. Nicklaus proved them otherwise with an incredible display of golf at the Masters.

Nicklaus played in his first Masters in 1959. Entering the 1986 Masters he had won the tournament a record five times.

It had been six years since Nicklaus had won a Major and two years since he had won a tournament.

The Golden Bear shot a 69 in the third round to go into Sunday's final round four shots off the lead held by Greg Norman. Through eight holes Nicklaus was even par for the day and had not made a move on the leaders.

Then, he began his charge. Nicklaus birdied the ninth hole. Then came birdies at the tenth and eleventh holes, when he holed long putts. Nicklaus bogeyed the short par-three twelfth, but came back with a birdie at the par-five thirteenth.

He still trailed Severiano Ballesteros by four shots. Nicklaus eagled the par-five fifteenth with a twelve-foot putt and made a three-footer for a birdie on the sixteenth. Ballesteros began to falter, perhaps affected by the roars for Nicklaus. He put his second in the water at the fifteenth and made bogey. Suddenly Nicklaus and Ballesteros were tied with Tom Kite at eight-under par after Kite birdied the fifteenth hole.

On the par-four seventeenth Nicklaus drove into the left rough and then pitched to within eleven feet. In dramatice fashion he struck the birdie putt dead center and grasped the lead by a stroke.

Minutes later a shaken Ballesteros three-putted the seventeenth for a bogey. For Kite a lengthy putt for par on the same hole kept him one back. Meanwhile, Norman continued his charge with birdies on fifteen and sixteen. He, too, was now only one back.

On the eighteenth Nicklaus did not let up. He drove to the front of the green, almost holed a forty-foot putt, and tapped in for his par.

Nicklaus had shot 65 with an unbelievable 30 on the back nine including five birdies and an eagle. Now he had to wait and watch Norman and Kite.

Needing a birdie to tie at the eighteenth Kite missed a twelve-footer as his putt drifted to the left of the hole.

Meanwhile, out at seventeen, Norman sank his twelve-foot putt for birdie and a tie with Nicklaus. Now, all he needed was a par on eighteen to force a play-off. A birdie would give Norman the win.

Norman hit a three-wood off the tee and launched a drive straight down the fairway. He decided to go for the pin and a birdie opportunity. Alas, he blocked his four-iron approach well to the right, pitched on and missed a fifteen-foot putt. His bogey gave Nicklaus a record sixth Green Jacket.

Nicklaus had his eighteenth Major championship as a professional and it was perhaps the most satisfying and memorable of all. At the age of 46, he became the oldest Masters champion in history.

This victory was to be his last on the P.G.A. Tour. At the age of 58 Nicklaus made another run for his seventh Green Jacket when he tied for sixth in the 1998 Masters.

Nicklaus became eligible to join the Champions Tour when he turned fifty on January 21, 1990. He started off quickly by winning in his first start on the Champions Tour. The tournament was the Tradition, which is a Champions Tour Major. Nicklaus would go on to win another three Traditions, more than any other player.

Later in 1990 Nicklaus won the Senior Players Championship. This was his second win of the year and second Senior Major.

In 1991 Nicklaus won three of the five events in which he played. All three were Majors: the U. S. Senior Open, the P.G.A. Senior Championship, and the Tradition for the second straight year.

Nicklaus did not win any events in 1992 but came back in 1993 to win the U. S. Senior Open for the second time. Also in 1993 he teamed up with Chi Chi Rodriguez and Raymond Floyd to win the Wendy's Three Tour Challenge for the Champions Tour team.

In 1994 Nicklaus won the Champions Tour's version of the Mercedes Championship (field of previous year's winners) for his only win of the year.

He won The Tradition again in 1995, a year where he made the top ten in all of the seven tournaments he entered. His 100th career win came in 1996 when he won the Tradition for the fourth time. This was to be his last win on the Champions Tour and the last official win of his career. Thereafter, he began to wind down his playing career and concentrate more on his business interests, the most prominent of which was his golf architecture business.

In April 2005 Nicklaus played at the Masters a month after the drowning death of his seventeen-month old grandson Jake (the child of his son Steve) on March 1, 2005. This was his forty-fifth and last appearance in the Masters.

The last competitive tournament in which Nicklaus played in the United States was the Bayer Advantage Classic in Overland Park, Kansas on June 13, 2005.

Nicklaus finished his professional career at the British Open at St. Andrews on July 15, 2005. He had turned sixty-five that year. On the eighteenth hole of the second round Nicklaus hit the final tee-shot of his career. He strolled over to the Swilcan Bridge and waved to an appreciative crowd. He concluded his competitive career with a birdie on his final hole. He missed making the thirty-six-hole cut with a three-over par 147.

Nicklaus now devotes much of his time to his thriving golf course design business. He is in partnership with his four sons and his son-in-law through Nicklaus Design. The company has over 300 courses open for play. Nicklaus is personally responsible for over 200 golf course designs. This includes his own Muirfield Village in Dublin, Ohio, along with Shoal Creek in Birmingham, Alabama and Castle Pines in Castle Rock, Colorado.

At Muirfield Village Nicklaus also continues to host the Memorial Golf Tournament that he created.

In a span of twenty-five years from 1962 to 1986 Nicklaus won eighteen Major championships. Tiger Woods holds down second place with fourteen Majors while Bobby Jones stands in third place with thirteen Majors.

Nicklaus and Tiger Woods are currently the only players to achieve a triple career "Grand Slam" by winning all four modern Major championships three times in a career. Nicklaus's six wins at the Masters is also a record, and he finished as runner-up a record-tying (with Tom Weiskopf) four times. Nicklaus won the U.S. Open four times, and this ties him with Ben Hogan, Bobby Jones, and Willie Anderson for most wins in the U.S. Open. He also had four runner-up finishes. Nicklaus won the British Open three times and was runner-up a record seven times. His five wins in the P.G.A. Championship ties him with Walter Hagen for most wins. He also finished second four times. He is third for most P.G.A. victories with seventy-three, behind Sam Snead who won eighty-two times and Tiger Woods who has won seventy-nine times.He was the leading money winner eight times. Nicklaus played on six Ryder Cup teams and was twice a non-playing captain. He and Gary Player are the only players to have won all four of the Major championships on both the P.G.A. Tour and the Champions Tour (the Senior British Open did not become the fifth Champions Tour Major until after Nicklaus retired from competitive golf).

From 1962-1978, Nicklaus finished in the top ten on the money list. Every year during that same period, he won at least one event a year.

Nicklaus was an original inductee into the World Golf Hall of Fame in 1974.

Nicklaus resides in North Palm Beach, Florida where his golf design company, Nicklaus Design, is located.

Tom Watson has won eight Majors. His seventeenth hole chip-in at the 1982 U.S. Open, which sealed his victory, is considered one of the all-time great golf shots.

Champions of the
1960s, 1970s, and 1980s

44

The Late 1960s and Early 1970s

In 1968 another prominent golfer arrived on the scene. His name was Lee Trevino. But first there was the tragedy at the Masters for Roberto De Vicenzo.

On Sunday at the 1968 Masters Bob Goalby and De Vicenzo were dueling on the back nine at Augusta National. Playing in front of Goalby, De Vicenzo made a birdie on the seventeenth hole, but his playing partner, Tommy Aaron, marked him down for a par four. Instead of giving De Vincenzo a rightful 65 Aaron had given him a 66. De Vicenzo did not notice the mistake, signed his scorecard in a rush and went off to talk to the media, which was anxious to interview him.

Minutes later Aaron and Masters officials noticed the mistake and, in accordance with U.S.G.A. Rule 6, Paragraph 6.6, Goalby was declared the winner and De Vicenzo the runner-up. The rule simply stated that, if a golfer incorrectly marked his card lower than what he shot, he would be disqualified and, that if the card was marked higher, then that score was considered official. Thus, since De Vicenzo had signed for the higher score that was official and his total of 278 was one shot behind Goalby. Consequently, there would be no play-off.

Beginning the next year Masters officials set up a scorecard-checking tent to alleviate the prospect that a golfer would make the same mistake that De Vicenzo had made.

Orville Moody was the surprise winner of the 1969 U.S. Open, his only official victory on the P.G.A. Tour.

The 1968 U.S. Open was held at Oak Hill Country Club in Rochester, New York. Lee Trevino's first three rounds were 69–68–69. He hit into the rough on the seventy-second hole but managed to hole a putt for a final round 69. He was the first golfer in U.S. Open history to break both par and 70 in all four rounds. Jack Nicklaus's final round 67 left him four shots behind Trevino in second place.

Julius Boros won the 1968 P.G.A. Championship at Pecan Valley, Country Club in San Antonio, Texas. At age forty-eight Boros became the oldest golfer to win a Major championship. Palmer had a chance to win his first P.G.A. Championship but missed several makeable birdie putts in the final round to finish a stroke back along with New Zealander Bob Charles.

Gary Player won the 1968 British Open at the demonic Carnoustie Golf Club in Carnoustie, Scotland. His winning total of 289 was the highest in twenty years. It was the second British Open (others in 1959 and 1974) victory for Player who had been in a drought since winning the 1965 U.S. Open.

Among the women Joanne Carner won her fifth U.S. Women's Amateur.

In the 1969 Masters George Archer escaped with a par from the water at the fifteenth hole at Augusta to hold off Tom Weiskopf, Billy Casper and George Knudson. Archer won by a stroke over the three runners-up with a 281.

The biggest shocker in any post-World War II U .S. Open occurred in 1969 when Orville Moody, just two years removed from the U.S. Army, won the event at the Champions Golf Club in Houston, Texas. The victory was Moody's only official win until he joined the Senior P.G.A. Tour in 1983.

Tony Jacklin claimed the British Open in 1969 at Royal Lytham & St.

Annes in Lancashire, England. Jacklin shot 280 to win by two strokes over Bob Charles. In the process, Jacklin became the first Englishman to win in eighteen years.

In the 1969 P.G.A. Championship Raymond Floyd shot a 276 to hold off Gary Player and win by a stroke at the NCR Country Club in Dayton, Ohio. Floyd's thirty-foot birdie putt on the seventieth hole was the difference.

On the women's side Catherine Lacoste won the U.S. Women's Amateur at Las Colinas Country Club in Irving, Texas. This occurred only two years after she became the first and only amateur to win the U.S. Women's Open at the Hot Springs Golf and Tennis Club in Hot Springs, Virginia.

In 1969 tensions between the P.G.A. and the American Tour players flared into the open. The Tour players felt that too much of the television and other money was going into the general P.G.A. fund. The Tour players had no difficulty in establishing a tour schedule of their own. In late summer the players announced the formation of the American Professional Golfers (A.P.G.).

Finally, the P.G.A. capitulated and a new division, the Tournament Players Division, was set up within the P.G.A. to run the Tour with a ten-man policy board at the top, made up of four players, three P.G.A. officials, and three businessmen. Joseph Dey became the commissioner of the Tournament Players Division—now known simply as the P.G.A. Tour. Dey did a commendable job of smoothing relations between the Tour players and the club professionals.

In his fourteenth attempt in 1970 Billy Casper became the Masters champion. It ended years of frustration including a final round collapse the previous year. In the final round Casper found himself tied with Gene Littler. They each had makeable birdie putts on the seventeenth, but both missed to end up tied at 279.

In the play-off the next day Casper's putting gave him the lead on the front nine. He and Littler played par golf on the back nine, and Casper had his Master's Green Jacket with a 69-74 victory. He had a very good year, winning three other events for which he was named P.G.A. Player of the Year. It would be the last great season for the aging Casper.

The 1970 U.S. Open was played at the difficult Hazeltine National Golf Club in Chaska, Minnesota, made even more challenging by high winds. Most of the pros struggled but not Englishman Tony Jacklin. He won by seven shots and became the first Englishman to win the U.S. Open since Ted Ray had won in 1920.

The 1970 British Open was held at St. Andrews and it is well-remembered for Doug Sanders's missed three-footer on the seventy-second hole, which would have given him the victory. Instead, he was forced into an eighteen-hole play-off with the indomitable Jack Nicklaus the next day. In the play-off Nicklaus was four strokes ahead after thirteen holes. Then Sanders made a late charge to get within one shot of Nicklaus.

At the eighteenth hole Sanders's run-up left him with a makeable birdie putt, which he made. Nicklaus's approach landed within three feet and he made the putt for the winning birdie. Nicklaus had held off Sanders 72–73.

At the 1970 U.S. Amateur two soon-to-be successful pros dueled at Waverly Country Club in Portland, Oregon. Both Lanny Wadkins and Tom Kite broke the stroke play championship record but Wadkins beat Kite by a stroke, 279–280.

Southern Hills Country Club in Tulsa, Oklahoma played host to the 1970 P.G.A. Championship. The weather was hot and so was Dave Stockton in the third round. Stockton shot a 66 on Saturday then closed with a 73 on Sunday to beat Arnold Palmer and Bob Murphy by two strokes.

The year 1971 was Lee Trevino's year as he won the U. S. Open, the Canadian Open and the British Open, all within the space of twenty-one days. Even though he won the U.S. Open in 1968, four other P.G.A. events and was the 1970s leading money winner, many golf purists didn't regard the "Merry Mex" too highly.

The 1971 Masters saw Charles Coody claim the Green Jacket. Two years earlier, he had lost the Masters by bogeying the last three holes. In 1971 he saved shots over the water at the fifteenth hole and another by the pond at the short sixteenth hole. He parred in to beat Jack Nicklaus and Johnny Miller. His winning margin was two shots.

In 1971 the P.G.A. Championship was held in February as part of an arrangement with the P.G.A. This decision was based on the fact that the event was being held at P.G.A. National Golf Club, Palm Beach Gardens, Florida and the P.G.A. opted not to play the Championship in Florida's hot and humid August weather.

Jack Nicklaus won the Championship with a fast start over the first thirty-six holes, shooting 138. He led from start to finish to beat Billy Casper by two shots. The win meant that Nicklaus became the first golfer to win the modern career "Grand Slam" twice.

In the 1971 U.S. Open at Merion Golf Club, Ardmore, Pennsylvania, Trevino and Nicklaus were tied after seventy-two holes. The play-off the next day sealed Trevino's reputation as a jokester. On the first tee Trevino tossed a rubber snake at Nicklaus. Trevino showed that he was relaxed and ready. Trevino led the play-off the whole way, shooting 68 to Nicklaus's 71, to win his second U.S. Open Championship.

The Canadian Open was next at Montreal's Richelieu Valley Country Club. The Merry Mex trailed Art Wall, Jr. by two shots going into the final round. Trevino forced another play-off with three birdies on the back nine. He won with a birdie on the first play-off hole.

Trevino wasn't done yet. The 1971 British Open was held at Royal Birkdale Golf Club in Southport, Lancashire, England. He was one of three first round leaders at 69. In the final round, Trevino broke clear of Tony Jacklin and Lu-Liang Huan from Formosa. On the seventy-first hole Trevino hit his drive on the 510-yard hole into one of Birkdale's devilish dunes. The double bogey seven left him only one shot ahead of Lu. Lu's failure to birdie the eighteenth led to a one-shot victory for Trevino. Trevino thus became the first person to capture the national titles of Britain, the United States, and Canada in the same year.

Gary Cowan, a Canadian, won the 1971 U.S. Amateur for the second time, the other being in 1966.

Bobby Jones, America's greatest and most beloved golfer prior to World War II, died on December 18, 1971 at the age of sixty-nine. For the past twenty years of his life Jones suffered from syringomyelia, a crippling spinal ailment that gradually paralyzed his arms and legs. He died at his home in Atlanta. He won thirteen Major championships, which places him third all-time behind Tiger Woods (fourteen) and Jack Nicklaus (eighteen).

In 1971 astronaut Alan Shepard took the game of golf to new frontiers by hitting a six iron shot during a walk on the moon.

Also in 1971 the number of golfers in the United States had doubled during the previous ten years—there were now ten million golfers.

CHAPTER

45

The Merry Mex—
Lee Trevino

L ee Buck Trevino was born on December 1, 1939 in Dallas, Texas. He is a beloved Mexican American and is often called "the Merry Mex."He was born into poverty to parents of Mexican descent. Trevino was raised by his mother and grandfather. He never knew his father. Trevino's childhood was spent occasionally attending school and working to help earn money for his family.

His start in golf came when his uncle gave him some golf balls and an old golf club. Trevino took it from there, sneaking onto country club courses to try his hand at this new game. At eight years old he began caddying at a local golf course. A few years later caddying became a full-time job, allowing Trevino to earn enough money to survive. For years after work Trevino hit balls at three short holes behind the caddy shack to improve his game.

When he was seventeen Trevino joined the United States Marine Corps and served for four years. He spent much of the final eighteen months of his hitch playing golf with Marine Corps officers.

After his discharge Trevino worked a number of golf jobs while improving his game. He became known for his gambling style and made a name by betting on himself in whatever golf challenges he could muster.

In 1967 Trevino began playing on the P.G.A. Tour. That year, he got some notice by playing in the U. S. Open and finishing fifth behind Jack

Lee Trevino, the "Merry Mex," won six Majors, two each of the U.S. Open, the British Open, and the P.G.A. Championship.

Nicklaus and runner-up Arnold Palmer at Baltusrol Golf Club in Springfield, New Jersey. He earned $6,000. As a rookie he won $26,472, which was forty-fifth on the P.G.A. Tour money list.

It was in 1968 that Trevino served notice to the golfing world that he was a player capable of challenging Jack Nicklaus. At Oak Hill Country Club in Rochester, New York he shot four rounds in the 60's to take the U.S. Open.

Over the course of his career Trevino won twenty-nine times on the P.G.A. Tour. This included six Majors: two U.S. Opens (1968 and 1971), two British Opens (1971 and 1972) and two P.G.A. Championships (1974 and 1984). He played sparingly at the Masters as he felt Augusta National did not suit his game.

In the early1970s he was Nicklaus's biggest rival, winning the money title in 1970 and winning ten tournaments between 1971 and 1972. Among his highlights during these two seasons were winning the 1971 U.S. Open in an eighteen-hole playoff at Merion Golf Club in Ardmore, Pennsylvania. Trevino roared home over the back nine of the final round to catch Nicklaus. Trevino won the play-off 68–71.

Jim Simons, an amateur from Pennsylvania, gave the pros a run for their money. He was the third round leader, then fell to 76 for joint fifth place.

Only two weeks later Trevino won the Canadian Open. He was a fan favorite of the Canadians. Trailing Art Wall, Jr. by two shots going into the final round the Merry Mex rallied with three birdies on the back nine to force another play-off. He holed an eighteen-foot putt for a birdie on the first play-off hole to become the first player since Tommy Armour in 1927 to win the U.S. and Canadian Opens in the same year.

Trevino's hot streak wasn't over. After three rounds in the 1971 British Open at Royal Birkdale in Southport, Lancashire, England he held a one-shot lead over Englishman Tony Jacklin and Taiwanese golfer, Lu-Laing Huan. After a front-nine 31 in the fourth round on Sunday Trevino appeared to be cruising with a five-shot lead over Lu. A woeful double bogey on the par-five seventeenth, however, cut his lead to one stroke. But a birdie on the final hole was good enough for Trevino to win his third national championship in twenty-one days.

The 1972 British Open was conducted at Muirfield in Scotland. Nicklaus was making a run at the Grand Slam after capturing the Masters and U.S. Open. Trevino was defending the title he had won at Royal Birkdale. In the final round Nicklaus shot a 32 on the front nine to catch both Trevino and Tony Jacklin. Nicklaus finished with a 66 but that score wasn't good enough to beat the Merry Mex.

Trevino found trouble on the par five seventeenth hole, and it looked as though either Jacklin or Nicklaus might catch him. However, the Merry Mex chipped in for a par to save his lead. He parred the last while another dropped shot by Jacklin at the eighteenth relegated him to third with 280, behind Trevino (278) and Nicklaus (279).

Trevino won the 1974 P.G.A. Championship at Tanglewood Golf Club in Winston-Salem, North Carolina. Leading by a stroke after fifty-four holes Trevino dueled with Nicklaus in the final round. Both finished with a 69, allowing that single stroke to hold up for Trevino's margin of victory.

In 1975 a not so pleasant thing happened to Trevino. During the second round of the Western Open on June 27 he, Bobby Nichols and Jerry Heard were hospitalized after being struck by lightning. Trevino suffered injuries to his spine and back. He later underwent surgery to remove a damaged spinal disk and back problems curtailed his play later in his career.

While Trevino did not quite return to his early 1970s form he remained one of the world's leading players for more than another decade. He proved this by winning his last Major, the 1984 P.G.A. Championship at the age of forty-four.

The tournament was held at Shoal Creek in Birmingham, Alabama. Trevino shot 69–68–67–69, four shots clear of Gary Player and Lanny Wadkins. In doing so he withstood a second-round 63 by the forty-eight-year old Player. This was Trevino's sixth and last Major title and twenty-seventh tour win.

Trevino also has won twenty-seven international and unofficial professional tournaments. In his fifties he was one of the charismatic stars who helped make the Senior P.G.A. Tour, now the Champions Tour, a commercial success. He won seven times in his first year on the Senior Tour in 1990. Overall, he won twenty-nine times on the Senior Tour, including four senior Majors. This matched the twenty-nine wins he had on the P.G.A. Tour.

Trevino played for the United States in the Ryder Cup six times and served as team captain in 1985. He won the Vardon Trophy for the lowest scoring average five times: 1970-1972, 1974 and 1980.

The Merry Mex was inducted into the World Golf Hall of Fame in 1981.

46

The Rest of the 1970s

The year 1972 mostly belonged to Nicklaus, who won the Masters and the U.S. Open, with Trevino defending his British Open title and Gary Player capturing the P.G.A. Championship. Despite shooting a final round of 74 Nicklaus hung on to win the Masters by three shots over Bruce Crampton, Tom Weiskopf and Bobby Mitchell. With the win Nicklaus caught up with Arnold Palmer on the roster of Masters Champions at four apiece.

Two months later at the U.S. Open at Pebble Beach Golf Links Nicklaus shot a seemingly high 290 but it was good enough to win by three shots over Bruce Crampton. Nicklaus obviously liked Pebble Beach since he had won the second of his two Amateur titles there and would finish runner-up to Tom Watson in the 1982 U.S. Open.

Oakland Hills Country Club in Bloomfield, Michigan was the site of the 1972 P.G.A. Championship. On Sunday Gary Player nearly relinquished the tournament in the final round when he bogeyed the fourteenth and fifteenth holes and sliced his drive on the sixteenth far to the right. However, he confounded his pursuers by lofting a nine iron over a tree and the lake guarding the green, leaving himself a putt within four feet of the hole. He tapped in for a birdie and won by two shots over Tommy Aaron and Jim Jamieson.

The 1972 U.S. Amateur was held at stroke play for the last time and

Marvin "Vinny" Giles took the title at Charlotte Country Club in Charlotte, North Carolina. Giles had been a three-time runner-up. Although Giles never turned professional he became a top agent for the likes of Tom Kite and Lanny Wadkins.

Also in 1972 the Colgate-Dinah Shore Winners Circle debuted on the L.P.G.A. Tour, offering the first six-figure purse in women's golf—$110,000.

Title IX legislation passed Congress in 1972. It forced colleges to provide more opportunities for female athletes. The expansion of women's college golf increased the talent pool of the L.P.G.A. Tour.

The 1973 Masters was won by Georgia native Tommy Aaron. After trailing by four strokes he shot a final round 68 to defeat J.C. Snead by a stroke.

The 1973 U.S. Open was one for the record books. After three rounds at the very penal Oakmont Country Club in Oakmont, Pennsylvania, four men shared the lead: Arnold Palmer, Julius Boros, Jerry Heard and John Schlee. Johnny Miller was six shots back. Overnight rains had softened the course for the final round. Miller birdied the first four holes. Five more birdies, a lone bogey on the eighth and eight pars later, Miller had shot a 63, still the lowest final round in the U.S. Open and equaled only three other times in the U. S. Open (but not in the final round). His 63 gave him a one-shot victory over John Schlee, 279-280.

The 1973 British Open was held at Troon, Scotland. After the first round Tom Weiskopf led by a stroke with a 68 then scored a 67 to stay ahead. After the third round Weiskopf led Johnny Miller by a single stroke. Weiskopf held off Miller for his only Major. In his career, Weiskopf wound up a four-time runner-up at the Masters and was runner-up at the 1976 U.S. Open.

Canterbury Golf Club in Cleveland, Ohio was the site of the 1973 P.G.A. Championship. Jack Nicklaus's victory marked his fourteenth career Major, breaking Bobby Jones's forty-three-year old record. Nicklaus captured the P.G.A. Championship by four shots over Bruce Crampton. He also won six other events, led in earnings and was named Player of the Year.

In 1973 the U.S. Amateur reverted to match play and twenty-year-old Craig Stadler emerged as the winner at The Inverness Club in Toledo, Ohio. In the process he defeated Vinny Giles, the defending champion, in the semi-finals.

In the equipment side of golf, graphite shafts were introduced in 1973.

While he didn't win any Majors in 1974 Johnny Miller proved that one could still win the Player of the Year Award. He won eight events, all non-

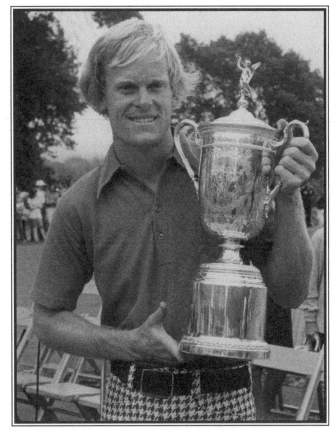

Johnny Miller shot the lowest final round in a U.S. Open with a 63 to capture the 1973 U.S. Open at Oakmont Country Club.

Majors, and set a record for most money won in a season. Miller won three times in January including the rain-shortened Bing Crosby National Pro-Am at Pebble Beach Golf Links. He rolled up twenty-four consecutive rounds under par.

Miller's fourth victory was the Sea Pines Heritage Classic at Hilton Head, South Carolina. He finished off his season by winning the Kaiser International at Silverado Country Club in Napa Valley, California, where he lived next to the eighth hole (Miller is now part-owner of Silverado). His season-ending total of $353,021.59 remained the Tour's highest until 1978 when the total P.G.A. Tour purse increased by $2 million.

Gary Player was another golfer who had a big year in 1974, winning the Masters and the British Open. At the Masters Player bounced back from kidney surgery. At the halfway point Dave Stockton led Player by five strokes. Player shot a 65 in round three to play himself back into contention. With two holes to go on Sunday Player led Tom Weiskopf and Dave Stockton by a stroke. Player's nine-iron approach on the seventeenth landed six inches from the hole, and he tapped in for a title-clinching birdie.

The 1974 British Open was played at Royal Lytham & St. Annes in England. Player shot 282, four shots better than Peter Oosterhuis, for his third British Open victory. Nicklaus finished five shots back.

The extremely difficult conditions for the 1974 U.S. Open, at Winged Foot Golf Club in Mamaroneck, New York had all the players making

concessions to par. Hale Irwin won his first of three U.S. Open Championships (also in 1979 and 1990) when he shot a 7-over-par 287 on the West
Course. He won by two shots over Forrest Fezler. Tom Watson, the third
round leader, fell away with a final-round 79.

Lee Trevino won the 1974 P.G.A. Championship by a shot over Jack
Nicklaus, protecting his one-shot lead after the third round. Both shot 69
in the final round at Tanglewood Golf Club in Winston-Salem, North
Carolina.

In the 1974 U.S. Amateur Jerry Pate defeated John Grace 2 & 1 in the
final at Ridgewood Country Club, Ridgewood, New Jersey.

In what some have called the greatest Masters ever Jack Nicklaus won
the 1975 rendition. He shot 68-67-73-68 to edge Johnny Miller and Tom
Weiskopf by a stroke. Nicklaus started with a 68, one ahead of Weiskopf.
Miller was seven back with a 75. Miller recovered somewhat with a 71 in the
second round. Nicklaus's 67 placed him six shots ahead of Weiskopf, who
shot a second-round 72. Weiskopf came roaring back in the third round
with a 66 to lead Nicklaus by a shot and was four ahead of Miller who had
recaptured his January form with a sparkling 65. Sunday's drama, naturally,
came on the back nine. Nicklaus was playing a hole ahead of Weiskopf and
Miller. Nicklaus and Weiskopf were even at the turn. Weiskopf's birdies on
fourteen and fifteen put him one ahead. He and Miller watched from the
short sixteenth tee as Nicklaus sank a putt of about 45 feet for a birdie two.
Weiskopf had a longer putt for a birdie, but he three-putted for a bogey,
putting Nicklaus one up on Weiskopf and two ahead of Miller. Miller
caught Weiskopf with a seventeenth hole birdie, so the pair of them were
one behind Nicklaus with one hole to play. Miller hit his approach on the
eighteenth hole to within twelve feet of the hole. Weiskopf followed with a
second shot eight feet from the cup and on the same line as Miller. If either
could make a birdie it would force a play-off with Nicklaus. However, neither could sink his birdie opportunity at the last and Nicklaus was Masters
Champion for the fifth time, overtaking Palmer's four Green Jackets.
Weiskopf found it all hard to take—this was his fourth second-place finish
at Augusta.

In 1975 Lee Elder became the first African American golfer to be
invited to the Masters. His play, however, was mediocre and he was never
in contention.

The 1975 U.S. Open was held at Medinah Country Club in Medinah,
Illinois. At the halfway point, Lou Graham was eleven shots behind Tom

Watson, who stood at 135. Watson stumbled in the final two rounds with a total of 155 and his undeserved reputation as a "choker" grew. Graham set up his victory with a 68 in the third round. John Mahaffey shot a 71 in the fourth round to tie Graham. In the play-off Graham shot a 71 to Mahaffey's 73 to win by two shots.

Three weeks after seeing the U.S. Open slip away Tom Watson went to Carnoustie, Scotland and captured the 1975 British Open. Watson holed a long birdie putt on the seventy-second hole to put himself in an eighteen-hole play-off with Australian Jack Newton. Newton had a birdie putt at the last but missed. In the play-off the eighteenth proved decisive. Newton made bogey while Watson made par to win, 71–72.

For the fourth time Jack Nicklaus achieved two Major championships in the same year when he added the 1975 P.G.A. Championship to his Masters victory. Nicklaus's 276 at the Firestone Country Club in Akron, Ohio was two shots better than runner-up Bruce Crampton.

Fred Ridley, who would later serve as U.S.G.A. president, took the 1975 U.S. Amateur when he defeated Keith Fergus, two-up in the final at the Country Club of Virginia in Richmond, Virginia.

In 1976 Raymond Floyd took the Masters. Following his win at the 1969 P.G.A. Championship Floyd entered a dry spell, and he did not enjoy as much success on the P.G.A. Tour as he would have liked.

Floyd eventually married and picked up his game. He won the 1975 Kemper Open in Charlotte, North Carolina. At the 1976 Masters he opened with a 65 to take the lead. His second and third rounds were 66 and 70 respectively, to give him an eight-shot lead over Jack Nicklaus. Floyd's Sunday round 70 was more than enough to win as he finished eight shots ahead of Ben Crenshaw and eleven in front of Nicklaus. Sunday's wind prevented Floyd from setting a new seventy-two-hole scoring record but his 271 tied Nicklaus's 1965 mark.

Like Jack Nicklaus, Jerry Pate made the 1976 U.S. Open his first victory. His was a dramatic victory as the tournament came down to the seventy-second hole. Four men including John Mahaffey, Tom Weiskopf, Al Geiberger and Pate had a chance to win.

Mahaffey hit into the water that fronts the eighteenth at the Atlantic Athletic Club, Duluth, Georgia. Weiskopf and Geiberger drove poorly and were forced to lay up in front of the water hazard. In the rough Pate rifled a five-iron over the lake to within two feet of the cup. His birdie gave him a one-shot victory over Weiskopf and Geiberger.

The 1976 British Open at Royal Birkdale in England was the year that a nineteen-year old Spaniard named Severiano Ballesteros made his debut on the world golf stage. After rounds of 69, 69 and 73 he led the British Open by two shots over Johnny Miller. Seve, as he became known, vaulted to a three-shot lead after the first hole in the final round. However, a seven at the eleventh and a Miller chip-in for an eagle on the thirteenth were conclusive. Miller ended up winning by six shots over Ballesteros and Jack Nicklaus. It was his second Major victory after the 1973 U.S. Open.

The Congressional Country Club, Bethesda, Maryland was the venue for the 1976 P.G.A. Championship. Dave Stockton holed a ten-foot par putt on the final green to win and thus avoid a play-off with Don January and Raymond Floyd.

Bill Sander defeated Parker Moore 8 & 6 in the final of the 1976 U.S. Amateur at Bel-Air Country Club in Los Angeles, California.

As for the ladies in 1976 Judy Rankin became the first L.P.G.A. player to earn $100,000 in a season. She totaled $150,734, thanks to six wins including the lucrative Colgate-Dinah Shore Winners Circle. Rankin also benefited from a Tour purse that jumped from $1.74 million in 1975 to $2.53 million in 1976.

The year 1977 was the year that Tom Watson became a serious challenger to Jack Nicklaus. He had already won the 1975 British Open and although he was winless in 1976, his rise to the top came in 1977.

Watson won two tournaments before the 1977 Masters. At the Masters Watson had a three-shot lead after fifty-four holes. On Sunday Nicklaus opened with six birdies in the first thirteen holes. Watson would not be overcome, however. Nicklaus finished with a 66 but Watson's 67 was good enough to defeat Nicklaus by two strokes, giving Watson his first of two Masters.

Neither Watson nor Nicklaus was in contention at the 1977 U.S. Open, which was played at Southern Hills Country Club in Tulsa, Oklahoma. Despite a death threat on the eve of the final round Hubert Green shot a 70 to defeat Lou Graham by a shot. It was the first tournament to receive eighteen-hole television coverage.

At the 1977 British Open Watson and Nicklaus renewed their head-to-head duel. They matched cards for the first three rounds (68-70-65) and the two of them entered the final round three shots ahead of the field. Nicklaus and Watson were paired together in the final round and it was more like match play than stroke play. Nicklaus was three strokes ahead with six holes remaining. Watson canned a 60-foot birdie putt on the fifteenth hole for a tie. He gained the lead on the seventeenth when he made birdie while Nicklaus was two-putting for a par from four feet. However the tournament wasn't over just yet. On the eighteenth Nicklaus drilled a shot from the rough to within 32 feet of the hole. He made the putt for a birdie. Watson knew he had to sink his two-foot birdie putt for the win. He did, shooting a 268, which was a British Open record by six strokes. Watson had defeated Nicklaus for the second time that year in a head-to-head duel.

Watson returned to the United States and won the Western Open to become the leading money winner for the year. He repeated in 1978-1980. He also led the P.G.A. Tour in wins with four, captured the Vardon Trophy and was named 1977 P.G.A. Player of the Year.

The P.G.A. Tour returned to the Pebble Beach Golf Links in Pebble Beach, California for the 1977 P.G.A. Championship. Lanny Wadkins and Gene Littler both shot 282 for a play-off. Wadkins won in sudden death (the first time in a Major that a play-off was sudden death) when he beat Littler with a par on the third extra hole. Littler had a chance to put away the Championship on the back nine of regulation, but he bogeyed five of six holes, allowing Wadkins to make up a five-stroke deficit.

A highlight of 1977 was Al Geiberger's record score of 59. He did it in the Danny Thomas Memphis Classic at Colonial Country Club in Memphis, Tennessee to become the first P.G.A. Tour golfer to break 60 in an official event. In one seven-hole stretch he made six birdies and an eagle. The only other male golfers to shoot 59's in competition are Chip Beck, David Duvall, Paul Goydos, Stuart Appelbey and Jim Furyk. Annika Sörenstam is the only female golfer to do so.

On September 5 at Aronomink Golf Club in Newtown Square, Pennsylvania John Fought defeated Doug Fischesser 9 & 8 for the 1977 U.S. Amateur title.

In 1978 at the age of forty-two, Gary Player became the oldest player to win the Masters—his third Green Jacket. Jack Nicklaus exceeded him at age forty-six in 1986. Player was seven strokes down after three rounds but he closed 34-30-64 to win by a stroke over three other golfers—Tom Watson, the defending champion, Hubert Green and Rod Funseth.

The venue for the 1978 U.S. Open was Cherry Hills Country Club in Denver, Colorado. Andy North built a two-stroke lead after three rounds and was four ahead with five holes to play. Then he began to lose strokes and needed a bogey five at the last hole to win. He put his third shot into a greenside bunker and lofted a sand shot to within four feet. He made the putt for a winning score of one over par. His margin was one stroke over Dave Stockton and J.C. Snead.

A victory in the 1978 British Open at St. Andrews was the highlight of Jack Nicklaus's year. With three holes remaining Simon Owen was a stroke ahead of Nicklaus after chipping in on the fifteenth hole. The sixteenth was Owen's undoing. He played through the green for a bogey while Nicklaus was recording a birdie. Nicklaus picked up another shot at the seventeenth —the "Road Hole." Owen had to share second place with Raymond Floyd, Ben Crenshaw and Tom Kite.

Oakmont Country Club, in Oakmont, Pennsylvania hosted the 1978 P.G.A. Championship. After three rounds John Mahaffey trailed leader Tom Watson by seven strokes. Mahaffey closed with a 66 to tie Watson and Jerry Pate at 276. Mahaffey made a twelve-foot birdie putt on the second play-off hole for the victory.

John Cook topped Scott Hoch 5 & 4 in the final of the 1978 U. S. Amateur at Plainfield Country Club in New Jersey. Cook was a three-time All-American at Ohio State.

The year 1979 was the year that the seeds of the Senior Tour were planted. Starting in the early 1970s Fred Raphael, who produced the television show *Shell's Wonderful World of Golf*, began trying to initiate a senior event called the Legends of Golf which would bring together the game's greats who were fifty and older. In 1978, with the help of NBC, the Legends of Golf with a two-man format, was born.

The first Legends was won by Sam Snead and Gardner Dickinson but it was the second year of the event in 1979 that catapulted senior golf into the limelight. The opponents were the pairing of Roberto De Vincenzo and Julius Boros against the team of Tommy Bolt and Art Wall.

They had tied in the better-ball format with scores of fifteen-under par at Onion Creek Country Club in Austin, Texas. The play-off started on the fifteenth hole. After a pair of pars on the fifteenth hole the teams matched birdies for four straight holes. Finally, on the fifth play-off hole De Vincenzo made his fifth straight birdie, a five-footer, for the win.

The dramatic play-off convinced Liberty Mutual to sponsor the event for many years to come. Soon, the Legends had company. The P.G.A. Tour sponsored two senior events in 1980 and the U.S.G.A. started the U.S. Senior Open that same year. Today the Champions Tour (as it is now called) is enjoying immense popularity as newly-minted fifty-year olds continue to stock the Tour.

The year 1979 saw The Masters won by Frank Urban "Fuzzy" Zoeller in a play-off with Ed Sneed and Tom Watson. Sneed had bogeyed the last three holes in regulation to fall into a tie with Zoeller and Watson. All three finished at 280. Zoeller cinched the win with a birdie on the second hole of the play-off. Earlier in the year Fuzzy claimed his first victory at the Wickes-Andy Williams San Diego Open.

The venue for the 1979 U.S. Open was The Inverness Club in Toledo, Ohio. After three rounds Hale Irwin led by three shots. In the fourth round he began backing up to the field with an untidy 40 on the back nine. Nevertheless, Irwin won his second of three U.S. Opens by two strokes over Gary Player and Jerry Pate. His other U.S. Open victories were in 1974 and 1990.

Severiano Ballesteros captured his first Major with a win at the 1979 British Open, hosted by Royal Lytham and St. Annes in England. He was twenty-two years old. Seve's 283 beat Jack Nicklaus and Ben Crenshaw by three shots. Ballesteros's victory included a wild drive that required a difficult recovery shot from a parking lot on the seventieth hole. He made a remarkable approach to fifteen feet and sank the putt for a birdie.

The 1979 P.G.A. Championship was held at Oakland Hills Country Club in Birmingham, Michigan. In the final round Australian David Graham shot a 65. This should have been enough to secure victory. However, he needed a par on the last hole for a 63 and a record total of 270. Instead, he made a double bogey to bring about a play-off for the third straight year.

Graham atoned with two long putts on the first and second holes of the play-off with Ben Crenshaw to stave off defeat. Graham won the Championship on the third play-off hole with a birdie.

Mark O'Meara trounced defending champion John Cook 8 & 7 in the final of the 1979 U. S. Amateur at Canterbury Golf Club in Cleveland, Ohio. O'Meara would become P.G.A. Rookie of the Year in 1981.

The year 1979 witnessed another remarkable event. In his forty-third and final year on the P.G.A. Tour, at age sixty-seven, Sam Snead shot his age in the second round of the Quad Cities Open. He was the first golfer to do so in a P.G.A. Tour event. Two days later he bested his age by a stroke when he shot a 66.

The 1979 Ryder Cup was conducted for the first time with Europeans eligible to join Great Britain and Ireland. Britain and Ireland had lost all but three of the biennial Matches since the inception of the Ryder Cup in 1927, Jack Nicklaus and British P.G.A. president Lord Derby were the prime movers to bring about the change. They feared that the Matches would die from lack of interest unless something could be done to make them more competitive. The 1979 Matches under this format were played at the Greenbrier in White Sulphur Springs, West Virginia. Before the twelve singles matches on the final day the United States, under Captain Billy Casper, were leading by a single point, 8½ to 7½. However, the United States pulled away in the singles matches for a winning score of 17-11.

On the equipment front TaylorMade introduced its first metal wood. In the next decade metal woods would become predominant.

Four Outstanding Women Golfers in the Modern Era
Nancy Lopez, Kathy Whitworth, Pat Bradley, Joanne Gunderson Carner

Nancy Lopez

Arguably the biggest golf story of 1978 did not involve the men. It was the electrifying emergence of twenty-one-year old Nancy Lopez on the L.P.G.A. Tour. Lopez was born on January 6, 1957, in Torrance, California. She won the U. S. Girls Junior Amateur Golf Championship in 1972 and again in 1974. In 1978 Lopez was a twenty-one-year old rookie on the L.P.G.A. Tour. That year she won an unbelievable nine L.P.G.A. Tour events including the L.P.G.A. Championship, which was part of five consecutive wins.

Her five consecutive wins started with the Baltimore Classic, then she won two more times before taking a week off to prepare for the L.P.G.A. Championship. A second round 66 led to a six-shot victory over Amy Alcott. Lopez won again the next week at the Bankers Trust Classic before she was stopped at the Lady Keystone Open at Hershey Country Club, Hershey, Pennsylvania.

The emergence of Lopez created a level of excitement for the L.P.G.A. Tour just when it was most needed. In addition to her golfing prowess Lopez had a smile that was to say, at the very least, a winning smile.

Lopez finished 1978 with two more victories to win $189,813 for the year, another L.P.G.A. record. She was named Player of the Year and Rookie of the Year in the same season. This feat has not been duplicated. Lopez

Nancy Lopez, the face of the L.P.G.A. in the late 1970s and 1980s. She won three Majors.

shrugged off any signs of a sophomore slump in 1979 by winning eight more times that year, giving her seventeen victories by the age of 22.

In 1983 she became the fifth woman—and the youngest player ever—male or female—to pass $1 million in career earnings.

In 1987, at the age of 30, she was inducted into the L.P.G.A. Hall of Fame and the World Golf Hall of Fame, by which time she had thirty-five career victories. During her career she won three Majors (the L.P.G.A. Championship in 1978, 1985, and 1989). She has forty-eight career wins.

About the only blemish on her otherwise stellar record is the absence of a U.S. Women's Open victory. She came closest in 1997 when she lost by a stroke to Englishwoman Allison Nicholas.

Lopez was a four-time L.P.G.A. Player of the Year (1978, 1979, 1985, and 1988). In 1998 she was voted the Bob Jones Award, the highest honor given by the United States Golf Association in recognition of distinguished sportsmanship in golf.

She resides in Auburn, Alabama after her 2009 divorce from former major league baseball player Ray Knight."

Lopez retired from the L.P.G.A. Tour in 2002. In 2007 she attempted a comeback but in six events failed to make the cut.

Kathy Whitworth

Kathy Whitworth was born on September 27, 1939, in Monahans, Texas. Growing up in Jal, New Mexico Whitworth began playing golf at age fifteen and won the 1957 and 1958 New Mexico State Amateur Championship. She turned professional at the age of nineteen and joined the L.P.G.A. Tour in December 1958.

In 1962 Whitworth won her first professional tournament. She was L.P.G.A. Player of the Year seven times between 1966 and 1973. Whitworth won the Vare Trophy for best scoring average by an L.P.G.A. Tour player a record seven times between 1965 and 1972.

Whitworth was the L.P.G.A. Tour leading money winner eight times between 1965 and 1973. In 1981 she became the first woman to reach career earnings of $1 million on the L.P.G.A. Tour.

She won ten tournaments in 1968, and eight each in 1963, 1965, 1966, and 1967.

And while she relinquished her throne to Nancy Lopez in the 1970s Whitworth continued to win at least once a year through 1978. After two winless years in 1979 and 1980 she had still accumulated eighty wins. But by 1981 she had re-discovered her game and won eight more times over the next five years.

She was the U.S. team captain at the inaugural Solheim Cup match in 1990, an event that matches U.S. professional women against a squad of women professionals from Europe in a Ryder Cup format.

In her career Whitworth won six Major championships including the L.P.G.A. Championship three times in 1967, 1971, and 1975. Her other Majors were the 1965 and 1966 Titleholders and the 1967 Women's Western Open. Her six Majors put her in ninth place as far as Majors won by a woman golfer. Patty Berg has the record with fifteen Majors.

The most outstanding feat on Whitworth's golf resume is tournaments won. Whitworth won eighty-eight L.P.G.A. Tour tournaments, more than anyone else has won on either the L.P.G.A. Tour or the P.G.A. Tour. Sam Snead won eighty-two times, as did Mickey Wright.

Whitworth was elected to the L.P.G.A. Hall of Fame in 1975 and to the World Golf Hall of Fame in 1982.

Pat Bradley

Pat Bradley was born on March 24, 1951, in Westford, Massachusetts. After attending Florida International University Bradley joined the L.P.G.A. Tour in 1974. She won thirty-one tournaments on the Tour including six Major championships. Bradley began a steady, if not spectacular, climb up the L.P.G.A. Tour ranks. She won her first professional event in 1976, her third year as a professional. Over the next ten years she never finished lower than eleventh on the money list.

Bradley's strength were her short game and her come-from-behind style. Her fellow pros acknowledged that her concentration was the most intense on the L.P.G.A. Tour.

Bradley had her best year in 1986. She won three of the four Majors (the Kraft Nabisco, the L.P.G.A. Championship, and the du Maurier Classic) and finished fifth in the U.S. Women's Open. That year she topped the money list. She also headed the money list in 1991.

In her stellar year of 1986 she added two more victories and the Vare Trophy for low scoring average. She also was named Player of the Year. Bradley's total of six Majors also included the 1980 and 1985 du Maurier Classic, and the 1981 U.S. Women's Open.

Bradley played for the United States in the Solheim Cup three times and served as the team captain in 2000.

She was inducted into the L.PG.A. Hall of Fame in 1991 and into the World Golf Hall of Fame in 1991.

Joanne Gunderson Carner

Joanne Gunderson Carner was born in Kirkland, Washington on April 4, 1939. Before getting married she picked up the nickname, the "Great Gundy." On the L.P.G.A. Tour she was affectionately known as "Big Mama."

She had an outstanding amateur career during which she accumulated five U.S. Amateur titles and the U.S. Girls' Junior Amateur Championship. Her five U.S. Amateurs ranks her second to Glenna Collett Vare who won six.

Carner turned professional in 1970 at the age of thirty after winning a professional event—the Burdine's Invitational—making her the last woman amateur to win a professional event. She earned Rookie-of-the-Year honors that year.

She won forty-three events on the L.P.G.A Tour including the Burdine's as an amateur and two Major championships—the 1971 and 1976 U.S. Women's Opens. Carner is the only golfer to have won the U.S. Girls' Junior, the U.S. Women's Amateur and the U.S. Women's Open. She played on four consecutive Curtis Cup Teams. Carner headed the L.P.G.A.'s money list in 1971, 1982 and 1983 and finished in the top ten on the money list twelve times between 1971 and 1984. She won the Vare Trophy for low stroke average five times. Carner's most productive years were in the early

1980s when she won three Vare Trophies, two money titles and two Player-of-the-Year awards. Carner's best year was 1982 when she won five tournaments for a total of $310,399. and she was inducted into the L.P.G.A. Hall of Fame. She eclipsed the $2 million career-earning mark in 1986.

Carner's last L.P.G.A. win was in 1985 but she continued playing the Tour. In 1999, at the age sixty, and playing in the du Maurier Classic, she became the oldest woman to make the cut at a Major. In 2004, at age sixty-four, she became the oldest player to make the cut at any L.P.G.A. event.

Carner was inducted into the World Golf Hall of Fame in 1985.

In 1981 she was voted the Bob Jones Award, the highest honor given by the U.S.G.A. in recognition of distinguished sportsmanship in golf.

Lopez–Whitworth–Bradley–and Carner, were the cornerstones of women's golf in the 1960s, 1970s, and 1980s.

48

1980–1984

T he 1980 Masters went to Severiano Ballesteros. Entering the back nine on Sunday Ballesteros had opened up a ten-shot lead. He immediately ran into trouble and saw his lead shrink to two but he righted matters with a birdie on the fifteenth and won by four over Gibby Gilbert and Jack Newton. Ballesteros became the youngest Masters winner ever, winning just four days after his twenty-third birthday and took Nicklaus's place in doing so. He also became the first European to win the Green Jacket. Tiger Woods has since become the youngest player to win the Masters when he won in 1997 at the age of twenty-one.

The "over-the-hill" Jack Nicklaus showed his opponents a thing or two at the 1980 U.S. Open. On January 21 Nicklaus turned forty and was coming off his worst year since joining the P.G.A. Tour. At the U.S. Open at Baltusrol Golf Club in Springfield, New Jersey he showed that he was still a major force.

Nicklaus had won the 1967 U.S. Open at Baltusrol with a record total of 275. Now, thirteen years later, he broke that record with a 272. He also tied Johnny Miller's U.S. Open eighteen-hole record with a 63 in the first round. He missed a three-footer on the eighteenth hole that would have given him a record 62.

Coincidentally, Tom Weiskopf also shot a 63 in his opening round. The first and only golfer to post a 63 in the final round of the U.S. Open was

Tom Weiskopf's only Major was the 1973 British Open. He was a four-time runner-up at the Masters.

Johnny Miller at Oakmont in 1973. Since then Vijay Singh shot the fourth 63, accomplishing it in the second round of the 2003 U.S. Open at Olympia Fields Country Club in Olympia Fields, Illinois..

Japanese golfer Isao Aoki was not awed by Nicklaus's 63. Nonetheless, Nicklaus's second-round lead gave him a record low thirty-six-hole total of 134, and so was his 204 for 54 holes. After three rounds Aoki's 68-68-68 matched Nicklaus's 63-71-70. Tom Watson was two back.

The final round turned into a Nicklaus-Aoki duel. After nine holes Nicklaus had a two-shot advantage. Nicklaus finished with a 68 but Aoki would not give up the chase. Both played the seventeenth and eighteenth brilliantly with birdies. Aoki turned in a 70 to finish two behind. And so Jack was back with his fourth U.S. Open Championship. Aoki got a bird's-eye view of Nicklaus's victory since he played all four rounds with him. Jack would turn back the clock even more at the P.G.A. Championship later that summer.

With good performances in the Masters and the U.S. Open Tom Watson was one of the favorites for the 1980 British Open at Muirfield, Scotland. Watson's 64 in the third round settled him at 202, four ahead of Lee Trevino and Ken Brown. On Sunday Watson cruised to a 69, leaving him with a four-shot margin of victory over Trevino. Ben Crenshaw and Nicklaus finished third and fourth, respectively.

This was one of the best seasons for Watson. In addition to his British Open victory (his third), he won six other P.G.A. Tour events including the World Series of Golf. Watson led in earnings for the fourth straight year.

The late summer 1980 P.G.A. Championship was Nicklaus's turn to shine again and refute his critics who considered him past his prime. The venue was Oak Hill Country Club in Rochester, New York. Nicklaus started off with rounds of 70, 69, and 66. With nine holes to go he led by five shots over Andy Bean and Lon Hinkle. He won going away by seven strokes. It was his seventeenth career Major championship.

The Country Club of North Carolina in Pinehurst, North Carolina was the site of the 1980 U.S. Amateur. Hal Sutton, another in a long line of "next Jack Nicklauses," won the championship 9 & 8, trouncing Bob Lewis, Jr. Sutton, the twenty-two-year-old from Shreveport, Louisiana, would qualify for the P.G.A. Tour in 1981, win a Tour event in 1982 and capture the P.G.A. Championship in 1983.

Perhaps the most popular of golf movies, *Caddyshack*, made its debut in 1980. This ultimate golf classic starred Bill Murray, Chevy Chase, Ted Knight and Rodney Dangerfield.

Tom Watson won the Masters in 1981—his second Green Jacket. Watson began the final round with a one-shot lead over Jack Nicklaus. He finished two shots to the good over Nicklaus and Johnny Miller with a 280 total.

Merion Golf Club in Ardmore, Pennsylvania, hosted the 1981 U.S. Open. Australian David Graham started the final round three shots behind George Burns. Burns's 205 was the best U.S. Open score for fifty-four holes. Graham shot 67 in an impeccable final round to finish three shots ahead of Burns and Bill Rogers. His 273 was one off the U.S. Open record held by Jack Nicklaus (Baltusrol, 1980). Graham became the first Australian to win the U.S. Open, and the first foreigner since Tony Jacklin in 1970.

The 1981 British Open was held at Royal St. George's Golf Club in Sandwich, England. Bill Rogers, who would turn out to have a career year with three P.G.A. Tour wins and three other victories worldwide, shot rounds of 72, 66 and 67 to take a five-shot lead after fifty-four holes. In the final round a double bogey on the seventh reduced his lead to one shot over Bernhard Langer. But birdies on the ninth and tenth righted his game and he went on to a four-stroke triumph. At four under 276 he was the only player to break par.

Larry Nelson, an Atlanta native, won a four-shot victory in the 1981 P.G.A. Championship at the Atlantic Athletic Club. A Vietnam veteran, Nelson shot 66-66 in the second and third rounds to give him a four-shot cushion going into the final round. His lead held up for the first of his three Majors (the others being the 1983 U.S. Open and the 1987 P.G.A. Championship). His performance earned him a late selection to the U.S. Ryder Cup team, which won the biennial competition 18½-9½ over the European squad. Nelson won all four of his matches.

Nathaniel Crosby, the son of Bing Crosby, won the 1981 U.S. Amateur in a thrilling finish at the Olympic Club in San Francisco, California. The course was less than twenty miles from his home. In the final he defeated Brian Lindley one-up in 37 holes. Crosby won it by holing a twenty-foot birdie putt on the first extra hole. It was the first U.S. Amateur to go to extra holes since 1950.

The U.S.G.A. added the U.S. Mid-Amateur Championship in 1981. It is for players twenty-five and older, an event in which career amateurs won't have to face college golfers, who had been dominating the U.S. Amateur. Today, the U.S.G.A. conducts thirteen national championships.

March 1982 saw the commencement of the Tournament Players Championship. The tournament is now known as The Players Championship and was moved to a more favorable date in 2007 when it was scheduled in May between the Masters (April) and the U.S. Open (June). Jack Nicklaus won the inaugural event and Phil Mickelson won the inaugural May event in 2007. With this new date and with traditionally one of the strongest fields in a P.G.A. Tour event The Players Championship is regarded by many as "the Fifth Major."

Craig Stadler won the 1982 Masters in what turned out to be his best year when he claimed three other tournaments and was the Tour's leading money winner. Known as "the Walrus" for his ample girth and large moustache the 1973 U.S. Amateur champion began with a 74 in the Masters' first round. Continued bad weather affected the scores. At the halfway point not a single player was under par and Stadler's even par 144 gave him the lead. His 67 on Saturday kept him atop the leader board. With six holes to play on Sunday, he had a seven-shot lead. Disaster then struck and he needed a par at the last for victory but three-putted for a bogey and a play-off with Dan Pohl. Pohl could not match Stadler's par on the first hole of sudden death and Stadler had his Green Jacket.

Next up was the 1982 U.S. Open, and what a memorable Open it turned out to be at the Pebble Beach Golf Links in Monterey, California. Tom Watson produced one of the most dramatic shots in a century of golf at the par-three seventeenth hole. Pebble Beach was one of Nicklaus's favorite venues as he had won the 1961 U.S. Amateur and 1972 U.S. Open at the course. But Watson also was familiar with the course from having played in the 1972 U.S. Open and frequently playing it in his college days at Stanford.

In the first two rounds Watson posted a rather indifferent 144 and found himself five shots off the lead. Tied with him was Nicklaus who had recovered from an opening 74 with a steady 70 in the second round. Beginning his move in the third round Watson shot a 68 for a 212, which put him atop the leader board with Bill Rogers. Meanwhile, Nicklaus shot 71 for a 215, leaving him three shots off the lead.

Nicklaus was in the fourth-from-last group on Sunday. After a slow start he made four consecutive birdies and found himself the co-leader with Rogers, while Watson was one stroke back. On the par-5 fourteenth Watson holed a 40-footer from the back of the green for birdie and a one-stroke lead.

The other players dropped out of the chase, leaving Nicklaus and Watson tied as Nicklaus walked off the fifteenth hole, playing in front of Watson. Nicklaus finished his round with three immaculate pars, and was in with 69 and 284. When Watson bogeyed the sixteenth, after hitting into a fairway bunker, they were tied.

In the clubhouse Nicklaus watched on the monitor as Watson played the par-three seventeenth hole. Nicklaus admitted afterwards that he was anticipating a fifth U. S. Open Championship which would have catapulted him past Willie Anderson, Bobby Jones, and Ben Hogan for the all-time record. It was not to be.

Watson's tee shot with a two-iron missed the seventeenth green long and was left in fluffy grass, eighteen feet from the hole. As he approached the ball he realized that, instead of being buried, the ball was sitting up enough for him to get his sand wedge under it. "Get it close," his caddy, Bruce Edwards said. Watson responded, "[i]'m not going to get it close; I'm going to make it."

Watson chopped at the ball. It hit the collar of the green, slammed against the flagstick and dropped from sight for a birdie two and an improbable one-shot lead. Watson leaped in the air and raced around the green, exalting in the four that miraculously had become a two. All that remained was the par-five eighteenth.

Taking no chances Watson hit three-wood and then a seven-iron to set up a full nine-iron to the green. Watson's approach stopped twenty feet above the hole. In a final tribute to the round Watson sunk the downhill left-to-right putt for a 70 and 282, two shots ahead of Nicklaus. Watson had his first and only U. S. Open.

Only four men had captured the U.S. and British Opens in the same year. Watson did it in 1982, winning the British Open by a stroke at Royal Troon in Troon, Scotland. He joined Bobby Jones (twice), Gene Sarazen, and Lee Trevino in accomplishing this feat. Nick Price and Peter Oosterhuis finished joint second.

The 1982 British Open seemed to be in Price's grasp as he held a three-shot lead in the final round. Price frittered away the three shots and found himself needing to par the last three holes to tie Watson who had finished with a 70 and 284. Price managed to par sixteen and seventeen and needed to make a twenty-five-foot par putt at the seventy-second hole, but he missed. For Watson it was his fourth British Open, all of them in Scotland.

Raymond Floyd won the 1982 P.G.A. Championship at Southern Hills Country Club in Tulsa, Oklahoma. Floyd opened with a 63, tying the P.G.A. Championship eighteen-hole record. His 63–69 for 132 gave him the halfway record and his fifty-four-hole total of 200 set a three-round record. Floyd shot a final round 72 for 272. He missed the seventy-two-hole record because he took two shots too many on the seventy-second hole. Floyd finished three clear of Lanny Wadkins, the 1977 champion who charged home in 67.

Jay Sigel, from Berwyn, Pennsylvania, captured the first of two consecutive U.S. Amateur crowns when he defeated David Tolley in the 1982 final, 8 & 7 at The Country Club in Brookline, Massachusetts. Sigel, age thirty-eight, never competed on the P.G.A. Tour, due in large part to a freak accident when he punched his left hand through a glass door, causing nerve damage. He has competed on the Champions Tour.

Julie Inkster won the 1982 U.S. Women's Amateur a third time in a row when she won at the Broadmoor Golf Club, in Colorado Springs, Colorado. She defeated Cathy Hanlon in the final 4 & 3 for her eighteenth straight match play victory in the U.S. Women's Amateur. No one since Virginia Van Wie (1932-1934) had any woman won three consecutive titles.

At the 1983 Masters Seve Ballesteros's rapid start in the final round left no doubt that he would capture his second Green Jacket in four years. Ballesteros started the final round (held Monday owing to inclement weather) at 212 with Tom Watson two shots behind. On the first four holes Ballesteros made birdie, eagle, par, birdie. He finished with a 69 for a four-shot victory over Ben Crenshaw and Tom Kite.

Oakmont Country Club, in Oakmont, Pennsylvania was the site of the 1983 U.S. Open. Like the Masters the Open came in for brutal weather and the title was not settled until Monday. The final round began with Seve

Ballesteros and the defending champion, Tom Watson, leading with 212, one ahead of Larry Nelson and Calvin Peete and two ahead of Raymond Floyd. Watson, with six birdies on the first nine on Sunday, looked like a good bet to retain his title but Nelson was out in 35 and caught Watson with a birdie on the fourteenth hole. One hole later a storm began, flooding the course. At the time play was suspended Watson was on the fourteenth green and Nelson was on the sixteenth tee. The next day Nelson's approach to the sixteenth left him with a sixty-foot putt. Nelson holed the putt for a birdie and the outright lead. Watson made par on the fourteenth. On the eighteenth Nelson three-putted for a bogey, dropping him back into a tie with Watson. However, at almost the same time, Watson missed his par putt on the seventy-first and this bogey was enough to give Nelson the title at four under par. His finish of 65–67 for 132 in the last two rounds was the best in U.S. Open history, beating by four shots the record set by Gene Sarazen in 1932.

Royal Birkdale Golf Club in Southport, England hosted the 1983 British Open. Tom Watson was gunning for his fifth British Open and got it. This placed him alongside J.H. Taylor, James Braid, and Peter Thompson as winners of five British Opens. The four of them remained a rung below Harry Vardon, six times a champion. Hale Irwin finished second by a stroke, tied with Andy Bean. This was a very untidy outcome for Irwin as he had made a careless flick at a two-inch putt on the fourteenth hole in the third round. His whiff cost him dearly. In the final round Graham Marsh shot a 64 to set a target of 277. Watson shot 275 with a final round 70. It was his fifth British Open in nine tries and all on different courses.

The 1983 P.G.A. Championship was held at Riviera Country Club in Pacific Palisades, California. Hal Sutton rode a first-round 65 to victory. Sutton shot 65-66-72-71 for 274 and led after every round of the tournament. Jack Nicklaus applied pressure with a final round 66, but the Golden Bear finished one stroke back.

For the second year in a row Jay Sigel captured the U. S. Amateur in 1983. At age thirty-nine, Siegel, the Pennsylvanian, became the eighth man to land consecutive titles. Harvie Ward was the last to successfully defend his crown in 1955-56. Sigel trounced Chris Perry, son of major-league pitcher Jim Perry, 8 & 7 in the final at North Shore Country Club in Glenview, Illinois. Sigel also won the 1983 U.S. Mid-Amateur, becoming the first man to win two U.S.G.A. events in the same year since Bobby Jones in 1930.

The 1984 Masters belonged to a soft-spoken Texan, Ben Crenshaw. He had been popular since he first joined the P.G.A. Tour in 1973 and shot a 65 in his first round as a professional at the Texas Open, which he won. He became only the second professional to win in his first tournament, Marty Fleckman having been the first in 1967. Crenshaw would go on to capture the 1994 Masters, the second of his two Majors. He would finish as runner-up five times in Major tournaments.

Known for his silky putting style envied by his fellow professionals Crenshaw's sixty-footer on the tenth hole of the final round was a key element in his 1984 Masters victory. He shot 68 in the final round and finished two strokes ahead of Tom Watson.

Crenshaw is also respected among his peers as a golf historian. He collects antique golf equipment and golf books. He once got himself in trouble by playing the Muirfield, Scotland course after the British Open of 1980, using old balls and equipment. His partner in crime was Tom Watson. Their "crime" was that they had played the course after it was closed.

The site for the 1984 U.S. Open was the venerable Winged Foot Golf Club in Mamaroneck, New York. Fuzzy Zoeller was a favorite with the galleries but Hale Irwin had been the early frontrunner with two 68's in the first two rounds. However, neither he nor other challengers, such as Curtis Strange, Johnny Miller or Fred Couples, could get within five shots of Zoeller or Greg Norman by the seventy-second hole. From the eighteenth fairway in the final round, Zoeller heard a roar back on seventeen and assumed that Norman had made birdie to capture the lead. In a humorous gesture, Zoeller waved a white towel in mock surrender. It turned out that Norman had only made par. Then Zoeller settled over his approach shot, landed it behind the pin and, by now aware of the situation, two-putted to force a tie. In the play-off the next day Zoeller easily outdueled Norman 67-75. The Australian was not short of humor either. On the final hole of the play-off, he waved his own white towel.

St. Andrews, Scotland, played host to the 1984 British Open. Ian Baker-Finch advanced to the front with rounds of 68-66-71. In the final round, however, he fell away to a 79. Seve Ballesteros at 207 was tied with Bernhard Langer. By the time Ballesteros and Watson reached the seventeenth—the Road Hole—they were tied for the lead.

After a miraculous approach shot Ballesteros found the green and two-putted for his par. Watson hit a two-iron through the green and was lucky to make five. Meanwhile, Ballesteros made birdie at the last for a two-shot lead. Watson needed an eagle two to tie but settled for a par and Ballesteros won by two shots over Watson and Langer. Thus, Watson's chance to move alongside Harry Vardon with a sixth British Open had fallen short.

Shoal Creek Country Club in Birmingham, Alabama (a Jack Nicklaus design), hosted the 1984 P.G.A. Championship. Lee Trevino's hot putter propelled him to victory. He shot rounds of 69-68-67-69 for 273. It was his first Major in ten years and last of his six Majors. Trevino started the last round with a birdie and finished with a birdie on the final hole. His 273 placed him four clear of Lanny Wadkins and Gary Player who, at the age of forty-eight, recorded a nine under par 63 in the second round.

At Oak Tree Golf Club in Edmond, Oklahoma, Scott Verplank defeated Sam Randolph 4 & 3 to win the 1984 U. S. Amateur. Randolph would come back to win the following year.

Hollis Stacy was making her mark on the women's side in 1984. After capturing three straight U.S. Girls' Juniors Stacy won her third U.S. Women's Open in 1984, at Salem Country Club in Peabody, Massachusetts (previously, 1977-1978; her other Major was the 1983 du Marier Classic).

49

Tom Watson—
Jack Nicklaus's Successor

Thomas Sturges "Tom" Watson was born on September 4, 1949, in Kansas City, Missouri. He was known as the Huckleberry Finn of golf because of his freckles, mop of auburn hair, and the boyish appearance he retains today. His father, who was a scratch golfer, introduced Tom to the game when he was six. Watson first gained local renown while on his high school golf team. He eventually became a four-time winner of the Missouri State Amateur.

Watson began his professional golf career in 1971, the same year that he graduated from Stanford University with a degree in psychology.

In the 1970s an entire crop of golfers, seven to thirteen years younger than Jack Nicklaus, were looking to supplant him as the number-one player. The group included Lanny Wadkins, Ben Crenshaw, Jerry Pate, John Mahaffey, Tom Kite and Tom Watson. As things turned out it was Watson, nearly ten years younger than Nicklaus, who would meet with the most success and succeed Nicklaus as the top player in the land.

Watson's early career was plagued with whispers of choking. This criticism was borne of his failures at the 1974 and 1975 U.S. Opens. In 1974, at the age of twenty-four, he had led the U.S. Open at ruggedly laid-out Winged Foot Golf Club in Mamaroneck, New York, by a shot with 213 after fifty-four holes. However, in the final round, he was out in 38 and in with 41 for a 79 and 292. His playing companion, Hale Irwin, shot a final round 73 and won with a seven-over par 287.

The next year at the 1975 U. S. Open held at Medinah Country Club in Medinah, Illinois, Watson started out marvelously with rounds of 67-68. Unfortunately, in the third round his putter deserted him and he shot 78. The next day he shot 77 when par would have won. Lou Graham and John Mahaffey tied in regulation and Graham won the play-off 71-74. Combined with his loss in 1974, talk about Watson's nerve surfaced.

Despite his shortcomings at the U. S. Opens Watson had begun to show promise earlier on the P.G.A. Tour. In 1972 he won $31,000. In 1973 he won $75,000 and in 1974 he went over $100,000, winning $135,474. By then he had come under the tutelage of Byron Nelson, who liked his aggressiveness and ability to concentrate.

Watson's failure to win a tournament ended in 1974 when he won the Western Open at Butler National Golf Club near Chicago and almost as tough a course as Winged Foot.

By 1975 (and despite the losses at the last two years of the U.S. Open) Watson had established himself as a quality player. He had won two P.G.A. events and the 1975 British Open held at Carnoustie, Scotland.

At Carnoustie the weather was placid for the first three days and the scores reflected the weather. After three rounds Bobby Cole of South Africa was at 204. Watson was in a group that included Jack Nicklaus and Hale Irwin. They were four strokes out of the lead

In the final round Watson shot an up-and-down round. He saved par at the sixteenth and seventeenth and birdied the eighteenth to finish tied with Jack Newton of Australia. Newton missed a putt on the eighteenth that would have given him the crown. In the eighteen-hole play-off the next day, the eighteenth again settled it as Watson's par trumped Newton's bogey, and Watson had his first British Open, 71-72.

Watson went winless in 1976 but one of his banner years (aside from 1982 when he won two more Majors) came in 1977, highlighted by the two duels with Jack Nicklaus. At the start of the 1977 season Watson had won the Bing Crosby National Pro-Am and the Andy Williams San Diego Open. When he went to Augusta for the Masters Nicklaus was waiting to challenge him face-to-face. It would be prophetic and masterful golf between the two of them. After fifty-four holes Watson was in a tie for the lead. Nicklaus was three back. In the final round Nicklaus began his charge early, birdieing six of the first thirteen holes. But Watson hung right there with him. However, Watson bogeyed the fourteenth to lose the outright lead. Then Nicklaus took over first place with a birdie on the fifteenth. Watson also birdied fifteen to forge a tie and re-took the lead with a birdie on the seventeenth, inciting a vigorous roar that Nicklaus could hear on the eighteenth. He subsequently went on to record a bogey on eighteen. Nicklaus finished with a 66 but Watson's courageous 67 allowed him to prevail by two shots. It gave Watson his first of two Masters (the other being in 1981).

Neither Watson nor Nicklaus was in contention in the 1977 U.S. Open and once again Watson failed in his attempt to capture a U.S. Open crown. The winner at Southern Hills Country Club in Tulsa, Oklahoma, was Hubert Green by a stroke over the 1975 winner, Lou Graham.

The 1977 British Open was held at Turnberry, Scotland. All eyes were again on Nicklaus and Watson. As both were playing well going into the British Open the public anticipated another battle between the two. History records that this was the case.

In the calm weather of the first three rounds Nicklaus and Watson matched scores, bringing in 68-70-65. It seemed as if the rest of the field had lost interest. Hubert Green, the U.S. Open champion, was the only other player to beat par for the 72 holes. His 279 left him eleven shots out of first place. Meanwhile, at 203 Nicklaus and Watson were three shots clear of the field, in effect making the last round one of match play instead of stroke play. With nine holes left Nicklaus led by a stroke. At the short par-three fifteenth Nicklaus was on the green and Watson was in the light fringe. Watson birdied with a sixty-foot effort. Nicklaus could not respond and the match was all square.

At the seventeenth Watson reached the green in two. Nicklaus's drive left him with a seven iron which he hit fat. His approach left him with a five-footer and he squandered the birdie opportunity when he missed the putt. Watson two-putted for a birdie and a one-shot lead.

On the eighteenth Nicklaus hit a poor tee shot into the rough while Watson found himself down the middle. Watson lofted an approach shot two feet from the cup. Nicklaus's approach was long but, with his never-say-die attitude, he rolled in a thirty-two-footer for a birdie. Watson kept his calm and sunk his putt for a matching birdie and a one-shot victory. Watson had shot 268, a British Open record by eight shots and defeated Nicklaus head-to-head for a second time that year. Incredibly, their weekend cards were Watson: 65-65, and Nicklaus: 65-66.

Watson did not win any Majors in 1978 and 1979 but he played superbly. He was Player of the Year both years and twice won the Vardon Trophy for low scoring average.

In 1980 Watson won his third British Open at Muirfield, Scotland with a 271 at the windswept course. In the third round he shot a round of 64 that included a 30 on the home half, and took a four-shot lead over Lee Trevino and Ken Brown. The widely held opinion on Saturday night was that no one could catch Watson. He vindicated that speculation by easing in with a 69, still four shots ahead of Trevino.

In addition to the two years in which Watson won two Majors (1977 and 1982) 1980 also was another superb season for Watson, as he won the British Open, six P.G.A. Tour events, including the World Series of Golf and led in earnings for the fourth straight year.

In 1981 Watson continued to rack up Majors by winning his second Masters. Once again Watson's primary nemesis was Jack Nicklaus. They began the Sunday round with Watson one shot ahead. The final round was not without its drama as Watson put his second shot into Rae's Creek on the par-five fifteenth hole. However, he played steadily over the final three holes, and held off Nicklaus and Johnny Miller by two strokes.

In 1982 Watson captured two Majors, the U. S. Open and his fourth British Open. The 1982 U. S. Open is best known for one of the most memorable shots in golf history and in the annals of the U. S. Open, where once again Watson stood down the challenge of Jack Nicklaus over the finishing holes of a final round.

In the final round Watson and Nicklaus were tied with Nicklaus in the clubhouse with 284, and Watson standing on the par-three seventeenth hole. As has been recounted Watson made a spectacular birdie by sinking an eighteen-foot sand wedge from the rough, long and left of the green. Watson finished with a birdie four at the last and his 282 gave him a two-stroke victory over Nicklaus. At last, Watson had his U. S. Open in hand.

The 1982 British Open was held at Royal Troon, Scotland. Watson won by one shot over Nick Price and Peter Oosterhuis.

The next year, 1983, Watson won another Major, his eighth and last. It was at the British Open at Royal Birkdale Golf Club, in Southport, England. He put himself beside J.H. Taylor, James Braid, and Peter Thompson as five-time winner of the British Open. This placed Watson only one rung below Harry Vardon, who had captured six British Opens. Craig Stadler took the opening round lead with a 64. Eight players, headed by Watson, Bill Rogers and Bernhard Langer, were within four shots of Stadler at the halfway point. Watson went ahead on the final day and with a steady 70, shot 275 to edge Andy Bean and Hale Irwin by a stroke.

Watson's superb play on the P.G.A. Tour faded in the late 1980s when he developed problems with his putting. However, he had a revival in the late 1990s, and the last of his thirty-nine wins on the P.G.A. Tour came at the 1998 MasterCard Colonial when he was forty-eight years old.

When he turned fifty in 1999 Watson joined the Champions Tour. He has fourteen wins on the Champions tour, including six senior Majors. He became the oldest winner of a Champions Tour Senior Major when he won the 2011 Senior P.G.A. Championship (Jock Hutchinson, 62 at the 1947 Senior P.G.A. Championship, when it was a 36-hole tournament, is the Championship's oldest winner).

Watson turned back the clock at the 2009 British Open held at Turnberry, Scotland, scene of his second British Open victory in 1977 when he out-dueled Jack Nicklaus in an epic weekend showdown. In 2009 Watson took a one-shot lead into the final round, just two months short of turning sixty years old. Needing only to par the seventy-second hole to tie Harry Vardon for six British Open victories and become the oldest golfer to win a Major, Watson made bogey that put him in a four-hole play-off with Stewart Cink. Cink handily won the play-off, thus depriving Watson of his ninth Major championship.

Watson was named P.G.A. Player of the Year six times (1977–1980, 1982, and 1984). He won the Vardon Trophy for lowest scoring average three straight years (1977–1979). He headed the P.G.A. Tour money list five times.He played on four Ryder Cup Teams (1977, 1981, 1983, and 1989) and captained the 1993 squad. Watson's eight Major championships are surpassed only by Nicklaus (eighteen), Tiger Woods (fourteen), Bobby Jones (thirteen), Walter Hagen (eleven), Ben Hogan (nine) and Gary Player (nine).

In 1987 Watson was voted the Bob Jones Award, the highest honor given by the U.S.G.A. in recognition of distinguished sportsmanship in golf. Watson was inducted into the World Golf Hall of Fame in 1988.

Watson continues to play the Champions Tour and occasionally the P.G.A. Tour. He played at the 2010 U.S. Open at Pebble Beach Golf Links on a special exemption. Watson currently resides in Stillwell, Kansas.

50

Seve Ballesteros—
The Spaniard Extraordinaire

Severiano "Seve" Ballesteros was born on April 9, 1957, in Pedrena, Cantabria, Spain. He learned the game on the beaches near his home, playing with a 3-iron given to him by his older brother, Manuel. At that time he was seven years old. His uncle, Ramon Sota, was the Spanish professional champion four times and finished sixth in the 1965 Masters.

Ballesteros turned professional in March 1974 at the age of sixteen. In 1976 he burst onto the international scene when he tied Jack Nicklaus for second place behind Johnny Miller at the British Open, held at Royal Birkdale, England. With his two-shot lead after three rounds, Ballesteros nearly had his first Major.

He won the European Tour Order of Merit (money title) in 1976 and repeated that win the following two years. He would go on to win the Order of Merit six times, a record at that time and since surpassed by Colin Montgomerie (eight times).

During his illustrious career Ballesteros won five Major championships.

In 1979, at the age of twenty-two, Seve captured his first Major championship by winning the British Open, at Royal Lythem & St. Annes in England. His 283 beat Jack Nicklaus and Ben Crenshaw by three strokes. On the seventieth hole Ballesteros hit a wild tee shot into a nearby car park, yet managed to reach the green in regulation and wound up birdieing the hole.

Ballesteros won the 1980 Masters with an impressive score of 275, four

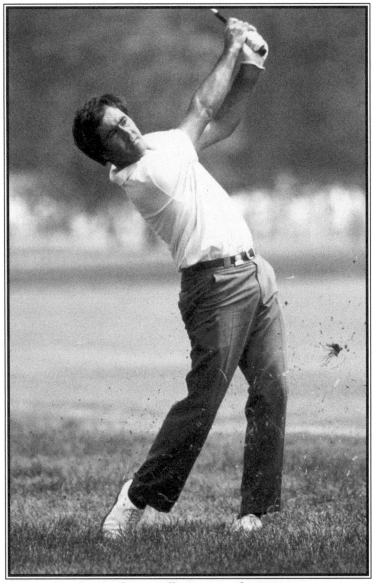

Spaniard Seve Ballesteros won five Majors.

shots better than runners-up Gibby Gilbert and Jack Newton. He became the youngest Masters winner ever, winning just four days after his twenty-third birthday. It was also the first win by a European. His youngest ever record was eventually broken by Tiger Woods in 1997.

Seve won the 1983 Masters at the age of twenty-six. He shot four-under-par on the first four holes on Sunday and finished at 280 to win by four shots over Tom Kite and Ben Crenshaw.

At the 1984 British Open Seve took his second British Open title on the Old Course at St. Andrews. He birdied the seventy-second while Watson bogeyed the seventy-first hole, thereby providing a two-stroke margin for Ballesteros.

Ballesteros again won the British Open in 1988 at Royal Lytham & St. Annes in England. In the final round he fired a 65 to surpass Nick Price and win this Major for the third time. Ballesteros's final round 65 equaled the lowest winning round in the 147-year history of the British Open.

Ballesteros also was great at match play. He won the World Match Play Championship five times and was a stalwart on the European Ryder Cup in the 1980s and 1990s. He had a successful partnership with fellow-Spaniard José Maria Olazábal in which they had eleven wins and two halved matches out of fifteen pairs matches. Ballesteros was a member of the European side that won the Ryder Cup in 1985, retained the Cup in 1987 (first victory on American soil at Muirfield Village in Dublin, Ohio), retained the Cup in 1989 and regained the Cup in 1995. The highlight of Ballesteros's career in the Ryder Cup was his captaincy of the winning 1997 European team at Valderrama Golf Club in Sotogrande, Spain. The score was 14½–13½. This was the first Ryder Cup ever held in continental Europe.

Among Ballesteros's more than ninety wins are forty-nine on the European Tour, and nine on the P.G.A. Tour. He also won thirty-six events around the world.

Ballesteros played sparingly in the first half of the 2000 decade because of back problems. He became eligible for the Champions Tour and the European Seniors Tour when he turned fifty on April 9, 2007. He retired from competitive golf on July 16, 2007.

Ballesteros had a business designing golf course. He was divorced with three children. In October 2008, it was announced that Ballesteros had a malignant brain tumor. In June 2009, he launched the Severiano Ballesteros Foundation, whose main purpose is to finance and promote brain cancer research. On May 7, 2011 he died in his hometown of Pedrena, Spain. He was 54.

Ballesteros was inducted into the World Golf Hall of Fame in 1997.

51

The Rest of the 1980s

T he 1985 Masters went to Germany's Bernhard Langer. Craig Stadler, the 1982 champion, shot a 67 in the second round, and, added to his first round 75, gave him a three-shot lead over Ballesteros and Sandy Lyle going into the weekend. Langer trailed by six shots. The tournament heated up on the back nine of the final round. At the turn Langer was four shots in arrears. He made up five shots in seven holes on leader Curtis Strange, who hit in the water at the par-five thirteenth and fifteenth. Strange needed a birdie at the last to forge a tie. He could not do so and Langer's final round 68 gave him his first of two Green Jackets, the other coming in 1993.

In 1985 Andy North won the second of his two U.S. Opens (winning also in 1978) at Oakland Hills in Birmingham, Michigan. Oddly, he won only three times on the P.G.A. Tour and two of them were U.S. Opens. North shot rounds of 70, 65, 70 and 74, highlighted by fine putting. North was the beneficiary of T.C. Chen's double hit of a chip, resulting in a quadruple bogey on the fifth hole of the final round. That erased Chen's four-shot lead and he lost by a stroke.

Scotsman Sandy Lyle became an international threat when he won his first Major championship, the 1985 British Open, at Royal St. George's in Sandwich, England. On day four Lyle had an uncomfortable wait after a bogey on the final hole for a 70 and a total of 282. He had to await

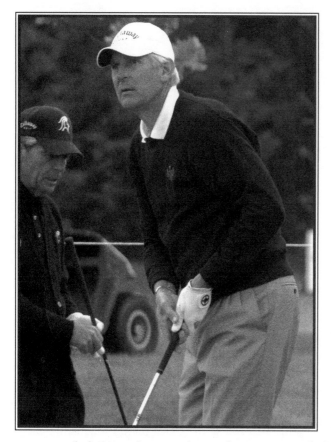

Andy North, winner of the 1978 and 1985 U.S. Open.

his closest pursuers, David Graham and Bernhard Langer, who were still out on the course. Both started with bogeys on the first hole and were never ever able to regain their form of the first three days. Graham and Langer finished in a five-way tie for third, two strokes behind Lyle. An up and coming American, Payne Stewart, with his plus-four clothing, slipped into second place with a 68, to finish a stroke back at 283.

Hubert Green won the 1985 P.G.A. Championship at Cherry Hills Country Club in Denver, Colorado. Lee Trevino led Green by two shots after two rounds but then Trevino closed 75-71 while Green rode a steady 70-72 to a two-stroke victory at 278. Trevino posted 280 and Andy Bean finished another stroke behind to finish solo third. For Green it was his second Major, having won the 1977 U.S. Open.

For the first time since 1957 the European Ryder Cup team wrestled the 1985 trophy away from the United States at the Belfry in West Midlands, England. It was also the first time that the Americans' opponent benefited by the expansion from British and Irish professionals to make all European professionals eligible in 1979. The Europeans had continued to lose in 1979, 1981, and 1983, until they broke through with the win in 1985. The European victory, 16½-11½, was only the fourth time in twenty-six matches that the United States had lost.

Sam Randolph, the runner-up in 1984, won the 1985 U.S. Amateur with a one-up victory over Peter Persons at Montclair Golf Club, West Orange, New Jersey.

Scott Verplank became the first amateur to win a Tour event since 1954, when he captured the 1985 Western Open. This put him in the company of Gene Littler, who had won the 1954 San Diego Open as an amateur. Verplank, a college star at Oklahoma State, won the N.C.A.A. golf championship in 1986 before turning pro. Including the 1985 Western Open, Verplank has won seven events on the P.G.A. Tour.

On the rules front the U.S.G.A. introduced the Slope System to adjust handicaps according to the difficulty of the course being played.

Jack Nicklaus played in his first Masters in 1959 while still an amateur. Through 1985 he had won the Masters five times and established the seventy-two-hole record of 271 in 1965 (Tiger Woods broke this record with a 270 in 1997 and in the 2015 Masters Jordan Spieth tied Tiger's record). Perhaps Nicklaus's finest hour came in 1986 when, at the age of forty-six, he captured his sixth and final Green Jacket. The Golden Bear shot a 69 in the third round to enter the final round four shots off the lead held by Australian Greg Norman. Through eight holes Nicklaus's even par was not gaining any ground. Then things began to happen. Nicklaus birdied the ninth, then played the back nine in 30. After birdies at ten, eleven and thirteen he still trailed Seve Ballesteros by four strokes. Nicklaus continued his surge with an eagle on fifteen, followed by a three-foot birdie on the par-three sixteenth. Meanwhile, Ballesteros put his ball in the water on fifteen and bogeyed the hole. They were both then tied.

The exclamation point on Nicklaus's round was a ten-foot putt on the seventeenth. Ballesteros bogeyed again and Nicklaus awaited the rest of the contenders out on the course after posting a nine-under 65.

Nick Price, who had set a Masters eighteen-hole record with a 63 the preceding day, fell three shots short with a 71. Tom Kite needed a birdie at the last for a tie. He missed from ten feet. All that was left was Greg Norman. He blocked his approach shot to the right on eighteen, chipped on and missed the fifteen-footer to finish with a bogey. Norman and Kite were joint second, one stroke behind Nicklaus. Nicklaus had his eighteenth and last Major Championship as a professional. He is the oldest player to win the Masters. What made the victory even more satisfying for Nicklaus was that his son, Jack Jr., was there, caddying for him.

Two months after the "venerable" Jack Nicklaus won the Masters, Raymond Floyd, all of forty-four years old, captured the 1986 U.S. Open at Shinnecock Hills Golf Club in Southampton, New York. He became the oldest U.S. Open champion at the time. (Hale Irwin is the oldest, winning at age forty-five in 1990). Floyd finished with a sparkling 66. His closest pursuers were Chip Beck and Lanny Wadkins (two strokes behind), the latter closing with a superb, but fruitless 65. Greg Norman, the third round leader, faded to twelfth.

Greg Norman had a bittersweet year in 1986. He led after fifty-four holes of all four Major championships but was able to take home only the British Open trophy. He won three times in Australia, three times in Europe, and twice in the United States.

At the 1986 British Open at Turnberry, Scotland the weather in the first and third rounds was atrocious. Norman's 65 on the second day will be remembered, not so much for his score, but for his three-putt at the last hole (missing a three-footer), which prevented him from breaking the British Open single round scoring record. In any event, after the second round Norman led Gordon Brand by two shots. After round three Norman led Tommy Nakajima 211 – 212. On the final day Nakajima faded to eighth. Gordon Brand held on for second place, two strokes behind Norman. Norman was the first Australian since Peter Thompson in 1965 to win the title.

Norman was again in fine position to win another Major at the 1986 P.G.A. Championship at The Inverness Club, Toledo, Ohio. His total after three rounds was 202, eleven under par, and four ahead of Bob Tway. After the front nine on the final day Norman led Tway by four shots. By the fourteenth the leader board found Norman and Tway tied at the top.

They still stood even at the eighteenth. Norman's approach was in rough around the green, while Tway's approach landed in a greenside bunker. Tway then proceeded to hole his sand shot for a two-shot victory, as he shot 70 to Norman's finishing 76. It would turn out not to be the first time that Norman was snakebitten.

Tway was only the first of four men to stun Norman with miraculous shots. The others were Larry Mize (the 1987 Masters), Robert Gamez (the 1990 Nestle Invitational), and David Frost (the 1990 U.S.F. & G. Classic).

Buddy Alexander won the 1986 U.S. Amateur, defeating Chris Kite 5 & 3 at Shoal Creek Golf and Country Club, Shoal Creek, Alabama.

By 1986, there were 20 million golfers and 12,384 courses in the United States.

The 1987 Masters showcased another miraculous shot, this one by Larry Mize. After the 1986 P.G.A. Championship, Greg Norman again was in the thick of a thriller. The final round featured multiple leaders, one of them being Mize, an Augusta, Georgia native, who regained a share of the lead with a five-foot birdie putt on the seventy-second hole. Seve Ballesteros got into sudden death with birdies on fifteen and seventeen and a saving par from a bunker at the last. Norman fell into the play-off after he failed to negotiate a twenty-five-foot birdie putt on the eighteenth hole. On the first play-off hole, the tenth, Mize had the best chance for a birdie but missed from ten feet. Ballesteros dropped out when he missed a five-foot par putt. So it was down to Mize and Norman. At the eleventh Norman hit his approach to the fringe and was in good position to make at least a par. Mize pushed his approach 45 feet to the right of the hole. Hoping to get up and down Mize used his sand wedge to pitch in for birdie and the Green Jacket, sending Norman down to another heart-breaking defeat.

Tom Watson entered the 1987 U.S. Open as the favorite at the Olympic Club in San Francisco, California. He was familiar with the course from his Stanford collegiate days. Watson dropped three shots over the first five holes of the final round, allowing relatively unknown, Scott Simpson, to catch him. The back nine proved crucial as Simpson made three birdies from the fourteenth to the sixteenth. Simpson finished at 277 to defeat Watson by one shot. Simpson made his way to victory with a stellar 32 on the back nine.

Muirfield, Scotland played host to the 1987 British Open. Paul Azinger shot 68-68 to grab a one-stroke lead over Nick Faldo, who had returned scores of 68-69. Faldo shot 71 in the third round to find himself one behind Azinger, who had also shot 71. In the final round Faldo was a model of consistency as he registered eighteen straight pars. In the meantime Azinger had forged a three-shot lead after nine holes. But he dropped shots at the tenth, the eleventh and the seventeenth to drop into a tie with Faldo. Azinger's approach on eighteen landed in a greenside bunker from where he could only manage a bogey. This paved the way for Faldo to win by one shot, 279-280. Rodger Davis joined Azinger in the runner-up position.

Larry Nelson beat Lanny Wadkins on the first hole of sudden-death to win the 1987 P.G.A. Championship at P.G.A. National Golf Club in Palm Beach Gardens, Florida. The hot and muggy weather, combined with the difficult course, produced the highest winning score (287) since the Championship was inaugurated in 1916.

The 1987 European Ryder Cup team repeated its 1985 victory by edging the U.S. squad 15–13. It was only the second time in thirty years that the United States had lost and it was the first loss ever for the United States on American soil. The match was held at Jack Nicklaus's Muirfield Village Golf Club in Dublin, Ohio.

Billy Mayfair won the 1987 U.S. Amateur with a 4 & 3 victory over Eric Rebmann at Jupiter Hills Golf Club in Jupiter Hills, Florida.

In a first for tournament golf, Craig Stadler was disqualified from the 1987 Andy Williams Open after viewers called in to complain of a rules violation after he placed a towel under his knees while playing from under a tree. Stadler forfeited a tie for second place and lost $37,333.

The year 1988 was the beginning of a four-year stretch in which the Masters was won by foreigners. The first was Sandy Lyle. He had been playing masterfully leading up to the Masters, having already won two P.G.A. events. Lyle overtook first-round leader Larry Nelson with a second-round 67. In the final round Lyle needed two birdies in the last three holes to capture the Green Jacket. On the par-three sixteenth hole his tee shot left him with a curling twelve-foot putt that he made. A par four at the seventeenth left him still in need of a birdie. His one iron off the eighteenth tee reached the fairway bunker 256 yards away. From there he made a career shot. With a seven iron he put the ball eight feet from the pin, leaving himself with a downhill putt. He sunk it to become the first Briton to win the Masters. His 281 defeated Mark Calcavecchia by a stroke.

Before the 1988 U.S. Open, held at The Country Club in Brookline, Massachusetts, Curtis Strange was on top of his game. He had won three times in both 1985 and 1987 and had already won twice in 1988. The U.S. Open turned out to be a duel with Nick Faldo. Strange found himself two ahead of Faldo after the first round. They both had 67's in the second round. Strange was still one shot ahead leading up to Sunday. In the final round Faldo shot 68 to Strange's 69. The key hole was the seventeenth, where Strange missed a six-footer and made bogey. This set up the second U.S.-Great Britain play-off in a U.S. Open at The Country Club. The first was seventy-three years earlier in 1913, when twenty-year old Francis Ouimet beat Englishmen Harry Vardon and Ted Ray. Strange made sure that it was another U.S. victory. He shot even par 71 to Faldo's 75, as Faldo shot 40 on the back nine. The critical hole was the seventeenth where Strange made an eighteen-footer for a birdie while Faldo made bogey, expanding Strange's one-shot lead to three shots.

Strange continued his fine 1988 play with another P.G.A. Tour victory.

He became the first P.G.A. Tour player to reach $1 million in official prize money during a year when he accumulated $1,147,844.

The venue for the 1988 British Open was Royal Lytham & St. Annes in Lytham St. Annes, Lancashire, England. Rain plagued the tournament and the fourth round carried over to Monday. A 69 by Nick Price in the third round increased his lead to two shots over Seve Ballesteros and defending champion Nick Faldo. In the final round Ballesteros fired a 65 to equal the lowest winning round in the 117-year history of the British Open. Tom Watson had set the mark in his historic duel with Jack Nicklaus in 1977. Price's 69 proved to be not enough as Ballesteros won by two shots over Price, and by six over Faldo.

The 1988 P.G.A. Championship was held at Oak Tree Golf Club in Edmond, Oklahoma. Jeff Sluman, who stood at five-seven, turned in one of the great finishing rounds in the Championship's history. He started the final round three shots behind Paul Azinger. Sluman shot 65 in that final round which included an eagle on the par-five fifth hole, where he holed a 100-yard wedge. His 272 total left Azinger in second place by a margin of three strokes.

In August Eric Meeks won the 1988 U.S. Amateur Championship when he defeated Danny Yates 7 & 6 at the Virginia Golf and Tennis Club in Hot Springs, Virginia.

In 1988 Nancy Lopez was named the L.P.G.A.'s Player of the Year for the fourth time. She won three tournaments, lost two others in play-offs and surpassed the $2 million mark in career earnings.

The year 1988 was the year that the groove war began. The U.S.G.A. ruled that Ping Eye-2 irons didn't conform to the Rules because the grooves were too close together. Karsten Manufacturing, maker of Ping, filed suit. A settlement was eventually reached in 1990 under which Ping irons were modified to conform and existing Pings were deemed acceptable.

The 1989 Masters saw the Europeans continue their winning ways with Nick Faldo claiming the Green Jacket. He was seemingly out of it with a 77 in the third round. However, he came back with a 65 in the final round to tie Scott Hoch. After Faldo bogeyed the first play-off hole, the tenth at Augusta National, Hoch had what appeared to be the winning par putt of about eighteen inches. Hoch spent a long time over the putt, picked a fragment from his line and then missed the putt. No one remembered a shorter missed putt to lose a Major. Faldo made the most of the miss. On the eleventh he hit a three-iron from 209 yards to within fifteen feet of the hole. He holed it for a birdie and his second Major title (the 1987 British Open being his first).

At the 1989 U.S. Open it was Tom Kite who failed to close the deal. Kite held a three-stroke lead after four holes of the final round at Oak Hill Country Club in Rochester, New York. He ran into trouble on the fifth hole and surrendered all of his lead with a triple bogey, three-putting from twelve feet. Kite made two double bogeys on the back nine and finished five shots out of first with a 78 that tied for ninth place. After an opening 71 the defending champion, Curtis Strange, scorched the par 70 layout with a 64 in the second round. While his 73 on Saturday left him three shots behind Kite, Strange's final round of even par was enough to secure his second straight U.S. Open. Strange thus became the sixth man to defend his title, and the first since Ben Hogan in 1950-1951.

Not since Tom Watson at Royal Birkdale six years back in 1983 had an American won the British Open. The 1989 venue was Royal Troon Golf Club in Troon, Scotland. Mark Calcavecchia followed an opening 71 with three consecutive 68's. His birdie on the seventy-second hole proved crucial. Greg Norman's final-round 64 (he birdied the first six holes) forced a playoff with Calcavecchia and Norman's fellow Aussie, Wayne Grady. The playoff was a four-hole format over the first, second, seventeenth, and eighteenth holes.

Norman started well with two birdies. Calcavecchia made a birdie at the second hole. Grady could not keep pace. Norman then misjudged a chip at the seventeenth, made bogey and was all square with the American. Norman then launched a prodigious drive on eighteen that reached a fairway bunker, thought to be unreachable. Norman's next shot found a greenside bunker from which he hit a shot over the green and out of bounds. He never finished the hole.

Calcavecchia, as he had scored on the seventy-second hole, fired a five-iron from the right rough and made birdie to seal the win. Thus ended the six-year drought for the Americans at the British Open. Seeking his sixth British Open Tom Watson's 277 left him two shots behind and kept him from making it a four-man playoff.

The fourth player that year to lose his hold on a Major was Mike Reid at the 1989 P.G.A. Championship hosted by Kemper Lakes Golf Club, near Chicago, Illinois. Despite a course-record first round of 64 by Craig Stadler, Reid led after two rounds as he added a 67 to a 66. On Sunday Reid held a three-shot lead over Payne Stewart with three holes to play. Reid pushed his drive into a lake at the sixteenth but was able to get up and down for a bogey. The par-three seventeenth was Reid's Waterloo. He overshot the green with his tee shot, stubbed a chip fifteen feet short and ran the ensuing putt two feet past. Reid rushed his two-footer, missed and settled for a double bogey. This placed Reid a shot behind Stewart, who had birdied the eighteenth up ahead. Reid missed an opportunity to tie Stewart at the eighteenth when his birdie try from six feet failed to fall. He finished a stroke back along with Curtis Strange and Andy Bean.

At the 1989 U.S. Amateur held at Merion Golf Club in Ardmore, Pennsylvania, Chris Patton defeated Danny Green 3 & 1.

Within the ladies' ranks Betsy King outdid her compatriots, winning six tournaments including the 1989 U.S. Women's Open. She was named Player of the Year, and set an L.P.G.A. record for earnings in a year with $654,132.

Payne Stewart won three Majors including the 1999 U.S. Open
before dying in an airplane accident.

The 1990s and Beyond

52

1990–1996

T he 1990 Masters showcased Nick Faldo's talent once again. He was three behind after 54 holes and four back on Sunday. On the back nine Faldo found a way to make up the four shots on Raymond Floyd whose birdie on the twelfth from the back fringe had given him the four-shot cushion. Floyd, at 47, trying to become the oldest Masters winner ever, felt that he could not lose if he parred in. He was wrong. Faldo shot 69 to catch Floyd who shot a 72. Faldo made a saving par from a bunker on twelve and birdied thirteen, fifteen and sixteen to forge a tie and he found himself in a play-off for the second consecutive year. The play-off started on the tenth hole. On the second play-off hole Floyd hit his approach in the water left of the green while Faldo two-putted for his second consecutive Green Jacket. This feat had been accomplished only once previously when Jack Nicklaus won in 1965 and 1966. Tiger Woods would accomplish the same with wins in 2001 and 2002.

Hale Irwin was the play-off winner of the 1990 U.S. Open held at Medinah Country Club in Medinah, Illinois. It was a victory every bit as tough as his U.S. Open triumph in 1974 where he shot seven-over-par and won by two shots. Irwin completed his round two hours before the last group came in. On the seventy-second hole he rolled in a putt of approximately sixty feet for a total of 280. Of all those who followed only Mike Donald could match Irwin. The eighteen-hole play-off on Monday was not enough to determine the winner as both shot 74. On the sudden-death nineteenth hole Irwin made an eight-footer for a birdie and took the crown. At the age of forty-five Irwin became the oldest U.S. Open winner. He also won in 1979.

Nick Faldo cruised to victory at the 1990 British Open, held at the Old Course at St. Andrews, Scotland. It was his second Major of the year, fourth overall and solidified his place as golf's dominant player. He finished five shots better than Payne Stewart and Mark McNulty. Faldo's total of 270 was six better than the previous Open best, set by Seve Ballesteros in 1984.

At the 1990 P.G.A. Championship held at Shoal Creek Country Club in Shoal Creek, Alabama Australian Wayne Grady shot a six-under par 282 to record a three-stroke victory. Fred Couples finished three back after bogeys on thirteen through sixteen in the final round. Gil Morgan made eighteen consecutive pars that Sunday to finish four strokes behind Grady.

The event made history for another reason, however. Shoal Creek openly discriminated against African-Americans, prohibiting their membership in the club. In the words of Shoal Creek founder Hall Thompson, "I think we've said that we don't discriminate in every area except the blacks." As a result of these remarks the major sponsors on ABC elected to drop out. The P.G.A., the P.G.A. Tour and the U.S.G.A. also reacted quickly. They pronounced that none of their events would henceforth be held at any club that discriminated in word or deed against minorities. Planned protests at the club were averted when, less than two weeks before the start of the Championship, Louis Willie, a local black businessman, was made an honorary member of Shoal Creek. The effects of Shoal Creek were felt after the Championship was finished. Over the next few months, nine clubs withdrew as tournament sites, including Merion, Aronomink, Cypress Point and Butler National. But many more, including Augusta National, admitted minorities and/or women to comply with the new guidelines.

Left-hander Phil Mickelson won the 1990 U.S. Amateur at Cherry Hills Country Club in Denver, Colorado. He defeated Manny Zerman 5 & 4 in the final.

Beth Daniel had a career year in 1990. She won seven events including the L.P.G.A. Championship. She became the first women to reach $700,000 in a season, easily captured Player of the Year honors and won the Vare Trophy.

Lee Trevino won seven times on the Senior Tour including the U.S. Senior Open at Ridgewood Country Club in Paramus, New Jersey. He became the first senior to win $1 million in a year.

The year 1991 saw the European dominance at the Masters continue. This time it was the diminutive Ian Woosnam. After day two, Woosnam, Mark Calcavecchia and Mark McCumber all trailed Tom Watson by two strokes. Watson had fashioned the lead by opening with a pair of 68's. He was trying to win a third Green Jacket and the first since he won his second a decade earlier. Woosnam shot a third round 67 to lead by one over Watson and three in front of José Maria Olazábal and Lanny Wadkins. In the final round Woosnam reached the turn three strokes ahead of Watson, Olazábal and Wadkins. Despite charges by Watson and Olazábal, Woosnam never faltered and his seventy-second hole birdie gave him a one-shot victory over Olazábal. For the first time European golfers finished first and second. Watson wound up a disappointing third, two shots behind.

The 1991 U.S. Open was conducted at Hazeltine National Golf Club in Chaska, Minnesota. Payne Stewart led after an opening round 67. Masters-winner Ian Woosnam was six shots behind with a 73. On day two Stewart's 70 kept him atop the leader board at the long and difficult course. In the final round Scott Simpson caught Stewart despite bogeying the seventieth and seventy-second holes. The high-scoring eighteen-hole play-off also was close. Stewart took the lead when he birdied the sixteenth. Simpson's chances ended with a water-bound tee shot at the short seventeenth. The final tally was Stewart 75 to Simpson's 77. It was Simpson's three bogeys on the last three holes that cost him the championship.

Royal Birkdale Golf Club in Southport, England hosted the 1991 British Open. Lanky Australian Ian Baker-Finch had the satisfaction of beating compatriot Mark Harwood. On the third day Baker-Finch made a big move with an impressive 64. This left him tied with Mark O'Meara. In the final round Baker-Finch demoralized the field with a front nine 29, making five birdies on the first seven holes. His 272 defeated Hayward by two and O'Meara by three.

The 1991 P.G.A. Championship was held at Crooked Stick Golf Club in Carmel, Indiana. A soon-to-be crowd favorite named John Daly rose out of the lore of obscurity to win the Championship as the ninth alternate awaiting a chance to enter the tournament if nine entrants dropped out. As luck would have it that's exactly what happened.

Fans hardly noticed his opening round 69. Daly began to draw attention when his 67 in the second round gave him the lead. By the weekend the crowds were flocking to see this swashbuckling blond kid rocket 300-plus yard drives. His third round 69 took him to a three-shot lead. Daly

John Daly, winner of the 1991 P.G.A. Championship
and the 1995 British Open.

never let anyone get closer than two strokes during the final round. He increased his lead to five shots midway through the back nine and a final round 71 enabled him to win by three shots over Bruce Lietzke. His win gave him a lifetime exemption into the Championship and a ten-year exemption on the P.G.A. Tour. Many hailed him as the next great player but his personal life was marred by marital troubles, bouts of alcoholism and gambling excesses. While long-time greatness proved elusive, there is no doubt that Crooked Stick was the key to Daly's becoming a fan favorite. He would go on to win the British Open in 1995.

Mitch Vogues won the 1991 U.S. Amateur at the Honors Course in Chattanooga, Tennessee, defeating Manny Zerman 7 & 5 in the final. For Zerman it was his second straight runner-up finish.

The 1991 Ryder Cup had one of its most exciting finishes ever under American captain Dave Stockton. The event was known as the "War by the Shore" at the Ocean Course, Kiawah Island, South Carolina. It was a roller-coaster of a competition from the start. The Europeans led off with its most potent pairing of Seve Ballesteros and José Maria Olazábal. This pairing worked well as they took three wins and a half in their four two-man matches (two foursomes and two four-balls).

Although the Europeans were down 3-1 after the first morning they cut the deficit to 4½-3½ in the afternoon. Back came Stockton's team, working up a three-point lead by lunch on the second day. In the afternoon, however, the Europeans won 3½ of 4 points so that going into Sunday's twelve singles matches, matters were all square. Because of an injury to American Steve Pate, there would turn out to be only eleven singles matches, and both squads started Sunday with ½ point. The climax was staggering in its tension. A major triumph was David Feherty's win over Payne Stewart, hard on the heels of Nick Faldo's victory over Raymond Floyd at the top. Paul Azinger, Corey Pavin and Chip Beck responded for the United States while Europe's Colin Montgomerie claimed a remarkable half from Mark Calcavecchia which he secured after being down by four holes with four to play. Europeans Paul Broadhurst and Seve Ballesteros won respectively against Wayne Levi and Mark O'Meara. However, Americans Fred Couples and Lanny Wadkins were victorious over Sam Torrance and Mark James. It all came down to Hale Irwin against Bernhard Langer. A win by Langer would tie the singles and the overall competition and allow the Europeans to retain the Cup because of their victory in 1989. Irwin was two up with four to play. Langer squared matters at the seventeenth. On the eighteenth, Langer had a makeable six-foot putt to beat Irwin, after Irwin bogeyed, but Langer missed on the right edge. The result was a half for Irwin and Langer. And so the Americans triumphed 14½-13½, giving the U.S. its first victory since 1983.

The 1990 U.S. Amateur Champion, Phil Mickelson, made history of sorts when he captured the 1991 Northern Telecom Open to become the first amateur to win a Tour event in six years (Scott Verplank, Western Open-1985). Mickelson would win his third N.C.A.A. championship in 1992.

The year 1991 also saw Chip Beck shoot a 59 during the Las Vegas Invitational to tie Al Geiberger's P.G.A. Tour record. Others who have recorded 59 are David Duval, Paul Goydos, Stuart Abbleby and Jim Furyk.

Entering the 1992 Masters Fred Couples was riding a hot streak. Two wins, two seconds, a third, and a sixth meant that he had already pocketed over $1 million. Still, at age thirty-two and regarded as one of the top players on the P.G.A. Tour, he had yet to win a Major.

In the second round Couples showed that his game was still sharp, carding a 67. In the third round he added a 69. This put him one shot behind Australian Craig Parry, with Raymond Floyd two shots off the lead.

Parry's balky putter took him out of contention on Sunday's front nine. This left a two-man duel between Couples and Floyd. Couples took the lead with birdies on numbers eight and nine. He stayed ahead on the back nine with eight pars and a birdie. But his big break came at the short par-three twelfth when his eight-iron barely cleared Rae's Creek, and stayed on the bank instead of rolling into the creek as most do. He managed to save par. Trying to become the oldest player to win the Masters, Floyd stumbled in the middle of the round and settled for his second runner-up finish in three years, two strokes behind Couples. And due to Couple's Masters triumph the four-year dominance of European golfers had ended.

The 1992 U.S. Open was held at Pebble Beach Golf Links in Monterey, California. Here, Tom Kite got a twenty-year old monkey off his back by winning his first and only Major. Dr. Gil Morgan, a certified optometrist, grabbed the lead with a 66-69 that put him at 135. Kite trailed by eight.

Morgan achieved the distinction of becoming the first golfer to reach ten-under par during a U.S. Open. He moved even further ahead in the third round and found his lead stretch to seven shots. Then he started to back up to the field. From his best position of twelve-under par Morgan fell to four under, only one stroke ahead of Kite, Mark Brooks and Ian Woosnam at the fifty-four-hole juncture.

Blustery winds kicked up on Sunday after three days of docile weather. Colin Montgomerie finished early before the winds took hold and his level par 288 seemed a secure number for the title. It was not to be. First, Jeff Sluman passed him with a 71 and 287. Then, Kite's 72 brought him the victory at 285. Kite's ability to handle the wind made the difference as did a little luck at the par-three seventh. Hitting dead into the wind at the 107-yard hole, Kite missed the green. But he chipped in for a two to propel him to the U.S. Open Championship. Only Kite and Sluman finished under par. Morgan faded to an 81 and a share of thirteenth place.

Nick Faldo won his third British Open in 1992 at Muirfield Golf Club in Gullane, Scotland, to go along with his victories in 1987 and 1990.

He opened with a 66 followed by a 64 and his halfway total of 130 placed him three ahead of Gordon Brand and John Cook. Faldo's third round of 69 made his fifty-four-hole score 199, four in front of Cook and Steve Pate. It equaled the fifty-four-hole record that Faldo had set at St. Andrews in 1990.

In the final round Faldo was three ahead with eight to play, then fell to two behind Cook with four to play. Faldo needed to right his game and then some to catch Cook. He did.

His second shot on the fifteenth led to a birdie. He chipped in to save par at the sixteenth hole. He had an eagle putt at the seventeenth, missed, but tapped in for a birdie. Meanwhile, Cook missed a two-foot birdie on seventeen and bogeyed eighteen. Faldo rolled a long putt close on eighteen and his tap-in gave him the victory by one shot over Cook.

Faldo was arguably the best player in the world in 1992, leading the European Tour in earnings and winning the Johnnie Walker World Cup. He closed out the year with a second-place finish at the P.G.A. Championship.

The thirty-five-year-old Nick Price won the final Major of 1992, the P.G.A. Championship at Bellerive Golf Course, St. Louis, Missouri. He was brought up in Rhodesia, which later became Zimbabwe upon earning its independence from Great Britain. In the first two rounds Price paced himself, starting with a pair of 70's, two under par and four behind the leader, Gene Sauers. Nick Faldo was two off the lead.

After round three Price was level with Jeff Maggert and two behind Sauers. Nick Faldo came back strong in the final round with a 67, finishing in second place, tied with a trio of other golfers, Gene Sauers, Jim Gallagher and his Muirfield rival, John Cook. A composed Price eased in with a 70 and a three-shot margin of victory. His was not a spectacular victory but his fourth-round play showed his nerve and course management. He did not birdie a hole until the eleventh but dropped only one shot with a hooked drive at the fifteenth. He got the shot back with a birdie on the sixteenth. Faldo had the satisfaction of again being the best finisher in Majors in 1992, averaging an impressive fifth.

The 1992 U.S. Amateur was held at Muirfield Village in Dublin, Ohio. Justin Leonard won the title with an 8 & 7 victory over North Carolinian Tom Scherrer. Leonard would eventually enter the pro ranks and win the British Open at Royal Troon in 1997.

The 1993 Masters was Bernhard Langer's time to capture his second Green Jacket. The devout Langer, who often led the players' prayer meetings, donned his second Green Jacket on Easter Sunday, eight years after his first in 1985. He became the twelfth man and third European to win two Masters. Jack Nicklaus opened with a 67 and Langer was one shot off the pace with a 68. Langer was still one behind the leader, Jeff Maggert, after thirty-six holes, which was completed on Saturday because of some inclement weather. The third round shone brightly on Langer who alone broke 70 and this propelled him to a four-shot lead heading into Sunday. On the final day Langer shot a 70 for a four-stroke margin over Chip Beck. John Daly was two strokes further back in the company of Steve Elkington, Tom Lehman, and Lanny Wadkins.

A bit of controversy arose in the final round involving Beck. He was playing with Langer, and got within two strokes after hitting a fine shot over the water at the thirteenth. Langer responded with an eagle. On the fifteenth Beck was criticized for laying up on the par five, just as Langer did, who was playing cautiously with the lead. Beck's lay-up gave him some unwanted notoriety as even Langer was surprised with Beck's conservative play.

Baltusrol Golf Club, in Springfield, New Jersey was the site of the 1993 U.S. Open. Payne Stewart, having won the U.S. Open in 1991, was in hot pursuit of a second title. Along came Lee Janzen to challenge. Janzen, a pro since 1990, had won twice on Tour. His first round 67 gave him a share of second place with Craig Stadler, one behind the trio of Scott Hoch, Joey Sindelar and Craig Parry. Janzen shot another sparkling 67 in the second round and no one else could keep pace. It gave him a two-shot lead over Tom Watson and equaled the thirty-six-hole U.S. Open record. Janzen also equaled the fifty-four-hole record Open record of 203 with a 69 in the third round but led by only one over Stewart. Despite Stewart's experience Janzen refused to fold. Janzen emulated Lee Trevino's 1971 record with his fourth sub-70 round, greatly aided by a thirty-yard chip-in on the sixteenth, for an eight-under par total of 272. This matched Nicklaus's score at Baltusrol in 1980. With a two-shot lead on the eighteenth Janzen smartly laid up on the par four, and made his par. Stewart, forced to go for it, found the sand and Janzen had the U.S. Open Championship.

In 1991 Greg Norman, the popular "Great White Shark," seriously considered giving up golf after seeing so many prizes slip from his grasp. Luckily for the 1993 British Open galleries at Royal St. George's, Sandwich, England he did not. His closing 64 was the lowest British Open winning final round. His 267 total, fifteen-under par, beat Tom Watson's record by one, set at Turnberry in 1977. Norman was the first British Open champion to break 70 in all four rounds. It was his second British Open Championship (previously, 1986). In shooting a 64 in the final round Norman's total was nine shots better than anyone had previously achieved at the Royal Saint George's course in eleven previous Opens.

In the fourth round birdies on the first, third, sixth, and ninth put Norman out in 31. He was, more or less, on his own from that point onward. Despite a missed two-footer at the seventeenth Norman played with equal brilliance on the way in to post the 64 for a two-shot margin over Nick Faldo, who made a run with a 67. Bernhard Langer was one further back.

A month later Norman was back to being snake-bitten again. This time it was at the 1993 P.G.A. Championship. He lost a play-off to Paul Azinger at The Inverness Club in Toledo, Ohio. Norman had now lost play-offs for all four Majors: to Fuzzy Zoeller (the 1984 U.S. Open), to Larry Mize (the 1987 Masters), and to Mark Calcavecchia (the 1989 British Open). A most distressing quadrilateral indeed. His "feat," if you could call it that, was also duplicated by Craig Wood who has been called the "Greg Norman of his era" (the 1930s and 1940s). These two are the only two men to have lost play-offs in all four Majors.

Vijay Singh from Fiji led after thirty-six holes by breaking the course record with a 63 in the second round. His halfway score of 131 put him two clear of Australian Steve Elkington and Lanny Wadkins. Norman's third round 67 gave him the lead by a stroke over Azinger, Bob Estes, Hale Irwin, Wadkins, Tom Watson and Singh. Norman shot a 69 in the final round to tie Azinger who had come in with a 68.

The first extra hole, the tenth was halved in fours. At the eleventh Norman three-putted while Azinger just missed his try for birdie. He made par and it was enough for Azinger to capture his first Major championship and leave Norman with another missed opportunity in a Major.

The 1993 U.S. Amateur was held at the Champions Golf Club in Houston, Texas. John Harris, a professional who had regained his amateur status, defeated Danny Ellis in the final 5 & 3. Harris later joined the Champions Tour.

In the U.S. Junior Championship young Tiger Woods made the world take notice when he won his third consecutive title in 1993. Little did anyone suspect that, after winning these three U.S. Juniors, the next three U.S. Amateurs would be the domain of Tiger Woods.

The year 1993 was a Ryder Cup year and was held at the Belfry in West Midlands, England. After the first two days of foursomes and four-balls the Europeans held an 8½-7½ lead. The United States came back to win 7½ of 12 points in the Sunday singles to eke out a 15-13 victory.

Among the women Sarah LeBrun Ingram became the first player to take the U.S. Women's Mid-Amateur Championship twice. She would go on to win a third in 1994. The event began in 1987.

At the 1994 Masters José Maria Olazábal extended the Europeans' dominance at the Masters. His was the ninth European victory in the previous fifteen Masters. Larry Mize had the halfway lead after posting a two-round total of 139. Tom Lehman, Dan Forsman and Greg Norman were a stroke behind. Olazábal got within two shots of Mize by adding a 67 to his first round 74. Olazábal finished 69-69 for a winning nine-under par total of 279. Lehman finished two shots behind and Mize was one shot further back.

The 1994 U.S. Open was held at venerable Oakmont Country Club near Pittsburgh, Pennsylvania. Approaching his forty-fifth birthday Tom Watson led Jack Nicklaus, Ernie Els, Frank Nobilo and Hale Irwin by a stroke with a 68 in round one. A half inch of rain helped slow up the lightning-fast Oakmont greens.

At the halfway mark Colin Montgomerie's 65 put him two shots in front of Irwin, John Cook, and David Edwards. Nicklaus loomed three shots back. In round three, Els's 66 placed him two shots ahead of Nobilo.

In the fourth round Montgomerie led at the turn with a 33. Loren Roberts closed on Montgomerie and Els with a lengthy chip-in at the 249-yard eighth, a long birdie at the ninth, and went ahead at the thirteenth. On the eighteenth Roberts pushed a six-foot putt that would have given him victory. In the meantime Montgomerie fell back with bogeys at the eleventh, twelfth, and thirteenth. Els made a four-foot bogey at the last to fall into a three-way play-off with Montgomerie and Roberts at 279.

In the eighteen-hole play-off Els and Roberts shot 74 while Montgomerie's 78 eliminated the Scotsman. Els and Roberts went back out to the tenth hole to continue the play-off in sudden death. Both made par fours on the tenth hole. Roberts hit into the rough on the eleventh, then into a bunker, and just barely missed his up-and-down par putt. Els, 15 feet from the hole, lagged his approach a little too harshly and left himself a four-footer for the title. He sank it and became the second South African after Gary Player and the fourth foreign-born player to win the U.S. Open since Tommy Armour in 1927, also at Oakmont. Oakmont would later host a record eighth U.S. Open in 2007.

Turnberry in Scotland hosted the 1994 British Open. Greg Turner led after day one with a 65. Tom Watson took over after thirty-six holes with a seven under par 135. Jesper Parnevik and Brad Faxon were one behind. The Saturday leader board became bunched up as Fuzzy Zoeller and Faxon were at 201, and stood one clear of Nick Price, Parnevik, Watson, and Ronan Rafferty.

In his pursuit of Harry Vardon's record of six British Open titles, Watson shared the lead with ten holes to play. Unfortunately, his double bogeys at the ninth and tenth led to a 74 and a tie for eleventh place.

Parnevik holed birdies at four holes from the eleventh to the seventeenth. He felt that he needed to make birdie on the eighteenth, and went for the pin. He came up short in the rough, and his par putt from almost nine feet missed. He finished at 269.

At almost the same time Price faced an eagle putt on the seventeenth. It dove into the cup as Price noticed that Parnevik had bogeyed the eighteenth. Price secured the victory at 268 when he two-putted the eighteenth. Like Greg Norman the year before, he had shot four rounds in the 60's.

The 1994 P.G.A. Championship was conducted at Southern Hills Country Club in Tulsa, Oklahoma. Not since Walter Hagen in 1924 had anyone won the British Open and P.G.A. Championship in the same year. Nick Price accomplished that feat at baking-hot Southern Hills. Never before in modern history had a year's four Majors gone to non-Americans.

Price and Colin Montgomerie were tied after first round 67's but Monty fell away in the second round. Price led by five at the halfway point and by three after fifty-four holes. In the end Price finished six shots ahead of Corey Pavin.

After winning three U.S. Juniors Tiger Woods was ready to step up to the 1994 U.S. Amateur. He beat Trip Kuehne by two holes and in the process, staged what is believed to be the biggest comeback in a U.S. Amateur final. Woods was six down at one point in the match. He took the lead for the first time with a thirty-fifth hole, twelve-foot birdie on the famous par three island green seventeenth at the TPC course at Sawgrass in Ponte Vedra Beach, Florida. His tee shot missed the lake at the back of the green by one foot.

Shortly before the 1995 Masters, Ben Crenshaw's longtime mentor, Harvey Pennick, died at the age of ninety. Crenshaw already was at Augusta, and he flew to Texas to serve as a pallbearer. How would this loss affect Crenshaw at the Masters? This Masters was always tight at the top. Defending champion José Maria Olazábal, David Frost, and Phil Mickelson led by one with 66's on the first day. Nicklaus was in second place. On day two Jay Haas was one ahead of Scott Hoch and John Huston. After the third round, Crenshaw was tied for the lead with Brian Henninger. Trailing by one was an impressive group that included Hoch, Haas, Steve Elkington, Mickelson and Fred Couples. On Sunday Crenshaw, one of the best putters on Tour, excelled with that club. He sank crucial birdies at the sixteenth and seventeenth. They were made more critical because of his bogey on eighteen—the only bogey he had made on the back nine all week.

He took his second Masters with a 274, one ahead of Davis Love III and two ahead of Haas and Greg Norman. Olazábal helped Crenshaw into his second Green Jacket, as Seve Ballesteros, Spain's other golfing hero, had done in 1984. It was a satisfying victory for American golfers who had been blanked in Majors in 1994.

Shinnecock Hills on eastern Long Island played host to the 1995 U.S. Open—its Centennial edition. Under sun and wind the course played increasingly more difficult each day. In fact, only the winner, five-foot-nine Corey Pavin, was able to equal the par of 280. The last round was everything a golf fan could hope for. Six players, led by Greg Norman and Tom

Lehman, initially struggled to keep the scores decent. Then Phil Mickelson and Bob Tway were closest. Finally Davis Love III and Pavin challenged as the wind rose.

On the eighteenth Pavin unleashed one of the finest shots under pressure in U.S. Open history. Standing 220 yards from the hole, Pavin struck a four wood to within four feet. It was truly one of the most decisive and magnificent single shots (shades of Tom Watson at the seventeenth in the 1982 U.S. Open) ever played at the climax of a Major championship.

Pavin had two putts for a 68 and the championship. He used both. Pavin's 68 gave him the even par 280. Norman's bogey at the seventeenth provided Pavin with a two-stroke margin of victory.

There were heavy winds at the 1995 British Open at St. Andrews—the 124th rendering of this Major, and the twenty-fifth at the world of golf's headquarters. The winner was John Daly in a four-hole play-off with Costantino Rocca, but it was how they got there that's at least half the story.

At the end of day one Daly, Tom Watson, Ben Crenshaw and Mark McNulty were tied at 67. Four others were a stroke away and nine more, including Corey Pavin, were two back. Daly, Brad Faxon and Katsuyoshi Tomori led after the second day, one shot clear of a group that included Pavin and Ernie Els. The young New Zealander Michael Campbell moved into position with a third round 65, but his game wavered on Sunday as Daly coped with the wind in fine fashion. After seventy-two holes, Daly had posted a six-under par 282, and appeared the certain winner. This seemed even more assured when Rocca flubbed his chip shot to the eighteenth green. Incredibly, he remained poised and holed a fifteen-foot birdie putt up the Valley of Sin in front of the eighteenth green. A four-hole play-off ensued.

Daly marched off to the play-off, seemingly unflustered. He got around the four holes in fifteen strokes, four better than Rocca. Daly had captured the British Open, which was his second Major (the other being the 1991 P.G.A. Championship at Crooked Stick).

After Corey Pavin's win at the 1995 U.S. Open Colin Montgomerie could ruefully claim the title of world's best golfer never to have won a Major. After his play-off loss in the 1994 U.S. Open he was on a mission to shed that unwanted title.

The 1995 P.G.A. Championship was the Major that Montgomerie was going after and it was being held at Riviera Country Club in Pacific Palisades, California. Going into the final round it was Steve Elkington who proved to be Monty's biggest menace.

Elkington finished first and recorded a 267, seventeen under par. This score equaled Greg Norman's lowest aggregate in a Major, established at the 1993 British Open held at Royal St. George's, Sandwich, Kent, England. Elkington's final round was a seven-under-par 64. Montgomerie needed birdies at each of the last three holes to catch the Australian, who watched as Montgomerie finished his three-hole hat trick of birdies by holing a twenty-footer at the last.

So, it was off to a sudden death play-off beginning at the eighteenth hole. On the green in two Elkington faced almost the same putt as Montgomerie had holed in regulation. In it went for the title and Monty was left with a play-off record of no wins and five losses. He could console himself only with the fact that he had not lost the championship but rather that Elkington had won it. Ernie Els and Jeff Maggert finished two back at 269.

Tiger Woods won his second U.S. Amateur in 1995 at Newport Golf Club in Newport, Rhode Island, with a two-up victory over George "Buddy" Marucci of Philadelphia. He gained it the same way as his first—at the last hole. Woods was three down after twelve and two down after nineteen but stayed ahead of Marucci from the thirtieth.

In the 1995 Ryder Cup at Oak Hills Country Club in Rochester, New York the Europeans, uncommonly, came from behind in the singles to win 14½-13½. In a losing cause Corey Pavin was the outstanding player in the Matches.

In 1995, the Golf Channel launched as a 24-hour cable television network devoted exclusively to covering the game. The channel originated in Birmingham, Alabama and is now headquartered in Orlando, Florida. Arnold Palmer was one of the original investor. Some of the more prominent shows are *Golf Central*, *Big Break*, and *Feherty*.

The 1996 Masters was yet another disappointment for Greg Norman. Once again he was second in a Major and this time it was as catastrophic as could be. The headlines on the Sunday morning of the final round in a local newspaper suggested that Norman was poised for the Green Jacket. Alas, it was not to be.

Norman held a six-stroke lead overnight on Saturday but ended up losing by five shots. Instead of donning the Green Jacket Norman was relegated to his third second-place finish in the Masters. He was also third twice.

Norman started the tourney with a 63 and led Phil Mickelson by two.

Norman followed that with rounds of 69 and 71 for his six-shot lead. Meanwhile, Faldo, after opening rounds of 69 and 67, shot a 73 and was seemingly going to have to settle for nothing more than runner-up status.

Norman began his fourth round with a hooked drive into the crowd. His next was into a bunker, and he took three more strokes to hole out. Norman made five at every hole from the eighth to the twelfth, and only at the eighth was it for a par. Faldo birdied the eighth. Just like that, the lead was gone.

Norman hit into Rae's Creek at the twelfth, and his double bogey gave Faldo a two-stroke lead. Both birdied the par five thirteenth and fifteenth. The short sixteenth settled matters. Norman's tee shot went into the water, and Faldo's par three put him ahead by four. A birdie three at the last by Faldo established the final margin of five strokes. Faldo had shot a 67, Norman a 78. The glaring difference was in greens hit in regulation. Faldo hit 16, Norman only half as many. It turned out to be Faldo's third and final Green Jacket (previously, 1989 and 1990).

It was on to Oakland Hills Country Club in Birmingham, Michigan for the 1996 U.S. Open. The winner was relatively unknown, Steve Jones of Artesia, New Mexico. He did have four Tour victories, but none since 1991 when he injured the ring finger on his left hand. This is a difficult injury for a P.G.A. Tour player, to say the least.

After opening with a 74 Jones shot 66-69-69 for a total of 278, besting Davis Love III and Tom Lehman. It all came down to the last hole. Love bogeyed the seventeenth and he came to the eighteenth eventually, as it turned out, needing to make par for a play-off with Jones who, like Lehman, was playing behind him.

From above the eighteenth hole, Love was too tentative with his downhill birdie putt and left it 24 inches short. He missed that tricky downhill par putt too, and could only wait and watch Jones and Lehman play the last.

Lehman drove into a bunker and lost a shot. Jones made a routine par (if it can be called that with the U.S. Open title on the line) for 278, winning by a shot over Love and Lehman who finished with 279. Unfortunately, their eighteenth hole bogeys sealed their fate.

For Love, his improved level of play on the P.G.A. Tour and in Majors got him only a share with Colin Montgomerie of the title of best player never to have won a Major. Love would shed his share of that label in 1997.

Royal Lytham in Lancaster, England served as the venue for the 1996 British Open. Atoning for letting the U.S. Open slip away, Tom Lehman

shot rounds of 67-67-64-73-271 to beat Mark McCumber and Ernie Els
by two shots and Nick Faldo by three.

Lehman's 73 on the final day did not give him much worry because on
the third day he shot a course record 64 and broke clear of his nearest rival,
Faldo, by six shots. This on top of his two opening 67's was enough to bring
the first British Open victory by a U.S. professional at Royal Lytham, although Bobby Jones had done so as an amateur in 1926. The leading amateur was Tiger Woods, as he was the only amateur to make the cut.

A month later, Woods won his third straight U.S. Amateur in the 1996
rendition at Pumpkin Ridge in Portland, Oregon. He faced Steve Scott in
the final, and once again had to play catch up. Scott led by two holes with
three to play. Thereupon, Woods birdied the thirty-fourth and thirty-fifth
holes to square the match. After pars at the thirty-sixth and thirty-seventh,
Scott made bogey at the thirty-eighth while Woods two-putted from ten feet
to seal his third straight U.S. Amateur victory.

Woods joined Jack Nicklaus, Bob Murphy, and Phil Mickleson in winning the U.S. Amateur and N.C.A.A. Championship in the same year.
Woods won the N.C.A.A. Championship as a student at Stanford University.

Woods had completed a six-year run of U.S.G.A. Championships—three
U.S. Junior titles and three U.S. Amateur crowns. During the week following his victory at Pumpkin Ridge Woods turned pro and signed endorsement contracts totaling more than $40 million. By that Thursday he had
accepted a sponsor's exemption into the Greater Milwaukee Open. Within
a month he began making his mark on Tour, winning events at Las Vegas
and Disney World.

Back in the professional ranks there was still to be played the 1996
P.G.A. Championship, held at Valhalla Golf Club, a new Jack Nicklaus
design, outside of Louisville, Kentucky. Twelve years later Valhalla would be
selected as the site for the 2008 Ryder Cup.

A different player led after each of the first three rounds—Kentuckian
Kenny Perry, Phil Mickelson, and another Kentuckian, Russ Cochran.
Cochran thrilled the locals with a course record 65, seven under par to lead
after the third round. On Sunday Cochran skied to a 77 and Mickelson
putted poorly in returning a mediocre par 72. The locals were still hopeful
that Perry would triumph but Texan Mark Brooks had other ideas. First,
Brooks forced a play-off with a birdie out of a bunker on the lengthy eighteenth hole. On the first play-off hole, the eighteenth, Brooks repeated his

birdie and the Wanamaker Trophy for winning the P.G.A. Championship was his.

U.S. Women's Amateur champion, Kelli Kuehne, had a very good 1996 She gained her second straight U.S. Women's Amateur crown. Then she completed that rare trans-Atlantic double, winning the British Women's Amateur. Combined with her 1994 U.S. Girls' Junior Championship, she had a hat-trick of U.S.G.A. Championships.

On the equipment front, Callaway wowed crowds at the 1991 P.G.A. Merchandise Show by introducing the Big Bertha. With a 190-cc steel head, Bertha paved the way for later models including today's 460-cc behemoths.

Developed in 1993 as part of an effort to limit the damage metal spikes inflicted on greens during the winter, turf-friendly plastic cleats would soon make the steel kind obsolete. However, professionals continued to be allowed to wear metal spikes.

53

One of Britain's Best—
Nick Faldo

Nicholas "Nick" Faldo was born on July 18, 1957, in Welwyn Garden City, Hertfordshire, England. From the late 1980s to the mid 1990s, he won six Major championships—three British Open Championships and three Masters.

At the age of fourteen, he borrowed some clubs from his neighbors after watching Jack Nicklaus play at the 1971 Masters. While working as a carpet fitter, Faldo won the British Amateur Championship and the British Youths' Championship in 1975.

He turned professional in 1976 and blossomed almost immediately. He finished eighth on the European Tour Order of Merit in 1977 and third in 1978. He won a European Tour event in each of those seasons. In the former year he became the youngest player, at the age of twenty-one, to appear in the Ryder Cup. Faldo was one of the leading players in Europe in the early 1980s and he won the Order of Merit in 1983.

In the mid-1980s Faldo's golf took a fairly dramatic turn. Feeling that he needed to improve his game in order to compete consistently in Major championships and eradicate the nickname "Nick Foldo" tagged by the British press (after collapses in the 1983 British Open and the 1984 Masters), Faldo spent time revamping his swing with coach David Leadbetter.

For a couple of years thereafter his play was mediocre at best. By 1987, however, he was playing at an even better level, capped off by his first Major title at the British Open.

Nick Faldo was a dominant player in the 1980s and 1990s, winning six Majors—three Masters and three British Opens.

From the late 1980s until the mid-1990s Faldo was considered the best golfer in the world. From 1987 to 1996, with his six Majors, he won more Majors than anyone else in that time frame.

He won the British Open again in 1990 at St. Andrews, Scotland and claimed it for a third time in 1992 at Muirfield, Scotland.

He also won the U.S. Masters two years running in 1989 and 1990. At the 1989 Masters he shot a 65, the low round of the tournament, to get into a play-off with Scott Hoch. This was the win where Hoch lost victory by missing an eighteen-inch putt on the first play-off hole. Faldo won by sinking a lengthy putt on the second play-off hole.

At the 1990 Masters he came from behind again to get into a play-off with Raymond Floyd. Faldo won on the second play-off hole when Floyd pulled his approach on the eleventh hole into the pond guarding the left side of the green.

Faldo claimed the European Tour Order of Merit a second time in 1992. He had worldwide earnings of 2,558,978 pounds, breaking the existing record. Throughout this time he played regularly on the European Tour, the P.G.A. Tour, and events around the world.

But in 1995 he elected to concentrate his play in the United States, as his priority became to win more Majors. He felt that his playing in the United States would enhance his chances for Majors as three of the four are contested in America.

His strategy seemed unproductive, as he had modest success in the 1995 season, and early in the 1996 season.

But then lightning struck at the unpredictable 1996 Masters, as he won his sixth and last Major championship.

He went into the final round trailing Greg Norman by six shots and seemingly out of it. However, Norman had his infamous collapse in stumbling to a 78 while Faldo shot a 67 to win by five shots. Though the 1996 Masters is frequently referred to as the Masters that Norman gave away, at the same time the steely-eyed Faldo displayed a memorable combination of concentration and consistency to capture the Green Jacket.

The P.G.A. Tour named Faldo Player of the Year in 1990 and he was named European Tour Player of the Year in 1989, 1990, and 1992. His professional wins include twenty-seven European Tour victories, nine on the P.G.A. Tour, and seven others.

Between the years 1987 to 1996 he made thirty-eight starts in the four Majors, winning six and finishing eighteen times in the top ten. He missed only one cut. In half of his ten attempts at the British Open in those years, he was third or better.

Discussion of Faldo's career would be incomplete without mention of his caddy during his preeminent years. That would be Fanny Sunesson, who carried Faldo's bag for ten years between 1990 and 2000. She became famous as a woman caddy among the male preserve of tour caddies.

As the late 1990s dawned and Faldo entered his forties, his form gradually declined and he began to devote more time to his off-course business activities.

The last season that he played regularly on the P.G.A. Tour was 2001. Afterward, he returned to the European Tour but did not play a full schedule. He returned to form somewhat with his tie for eighth place at the 2003 British Open. As of July 2005 his career European Tour earnings were just under eight million pounds, and his P.G.A. Tour earnings were over $5 million.

Faldo was also one of the most successful Ryder Cup players ever. He represented the European Team a record eleven times. He won twenty-three of his matches with nineteen losses and four halves. He also holds the record for having played in the most Ryder Cup matches. He captained the European Ryder Cup team in 2008 that lost to the U.S. at Valhalla Golf Club in Louisville, Kentucky.

Around the world, Faldo's record in preeminent events outside of the

Majors is first rate. He has had successes in high-profile tour events such as the French Open, Irish Open, Spanish Open, Swiss Open (now the European Masters), the European Open, the Johnnie Walker Classic and the Volvo Masters, as well as his Nissan Open, Doral Open and Heritage Classic successes in the United States. These wins are supplemented by his six Majors and his invitational wins in events such as the World Championship of Golf, the World Match Play, as well as team successes in the Dunhill Cup, the World Cup of Golf and the Ryder Cup.

As far as his business affairs and other activities Faldo keeps plenty busy. In 1991 he started his golf course design company, "Faldo Design," which has designed or remodeled dozens of courses spread across several continents. In 1996 he launched the "Faldo Series" to encourage young European girls and boys to take up the game of golf.

In conjunction with the Marriott hotel chain Faldo established the "Faldo Golf Institute" in 1997. Its purpose is to help golfers of every level to improve their skills and enjoyment of golf.

Faldo was inducted into the World Golf Hall of Fame in 1997. In November 2009, he was knighted by the Queen of England, becoming the second British golfer to be so honored (Sir Henry Cotton being the other).

When his playing schedule wound down Faldo signed on as an analyst for ABC's P.G.A. coverage. On October 3, 2006 it was announced that Faldo had signed a contract with CBS to replace Lanny Wadkins as the network's lead golf analyst. When the Golf Channel signed up with the P.G.A. Tour to be its lead golf network (especially for early round coverage), Faldo inked a contract to also be its lead analyst in an arrangement worked out with CBS.

During his playing days Faldo was notorious for his poor relationship with his fellow pros and the media. That reputation has mellowed since he wound down his career and became a golf analyst. Faldo's personal life could best be described as rocky. He has been married and divorced three times, all good fodder for the press in light of their frosty relationship. It is possible that his focus on golf cost him in terms of endearment with his fellow professionals, the press and the women in his life.

CHAPTER

54

The Rest of the 1990s

The 1997 Masters, to quote Jim Nantz of CBS, was "one for the ages." Tiger Woods won his first Major, becoming the youngest winner of the Masters at the age of twenty-one. He overtook Seve Ballesteros in the process. But more amazing was the margin of victory.

Woods shot a record score of eighteen-under par, winning by twelve strokes over Tom Kite. That was three better than Jack Nicklaus's record margin in 1965, when Nicklaus outplayed Arnold Palmer and Gary Player. This puts him in the company of seventeen-year-old Young Tom Morris, winner of the 1868 British Open.

As part of his record-breaking performance Woods's start was somewhat uninspiring. On the opening nine of the first day he made the turn in 40. He settled down on the back nine, shooting 30 for a first round total of 70. He followed that with rounds of 66–65 to drop the rest of the field from contention. On Sunday he shot 69 for 270 and the twelve-shot margin of victory. It seems unlikely that Augusta National will ever see such a dominant display again.

Congressional Country Club, Bethesda, Maryland hosted the 1997 U.S. Open. In a pressure cooker Ernie Els prevailed on Sunday's back nine for his second U.S. Open victory in four years (previously, 1994). Els, known as "The Big Easy" for his laid-back attitude, kept his focus in a four-way Sunday duel with Tom Lehman, Jeff Maggert and Colin Montgomerie. It should be recalled that Monty lost a play-off for the U.S. Open in 1994 at Oakmont, when Els beat him and Loren Roberts. On the tenth hole on Sunday, Els chipped in to draw level with the other three. He hit a majestic iron to the tough, long 480-yard seventeenth green, and he parred it for the fourth day in a row. Conversely, Montgomerie dropped a shot there every round, even during his opening 65.

On the seventeenth Montgomerie hit into the rough off the tee. After chipping to six feet he had to wait for five minutes until the approximately 20,000 fans could settle in the bowl-like greenside vantage points. His putt grazed the hole for a bogey.

Both Els and Montgomerie hit the short eighteenth and Els had a putt of five feet that he sank for a total of 276 and a one-shot victory over Montgomerie. Lehman was two back and Maggert finished five behind the champion.

The 1997 British Open was conducted at Royal Troon, Scotland. Justin Leonard was five shots back after round three but he turned that into a three-shot margin of victory over Sweden's Jesper Parnevik and Ireland's Darren Clarke. Leonard, a twenty-five-year-old from Dallas, Texas, became the third successive U.S. winner of the British Open, following John Daly and Tom Lehman.

Known as a short hitter, Leonard had a game that was strong around the greens, which included excellent putting, and which was suited to the windy conditions at most British Opens, with Royal Troon being no exception.

The title was first a duel between Clarke and American Jim Furyk. Then Leonard and Parnevik moved forward until Parnevik took the lead in round three with Clarke, Fred Couples and Leonard in close contact. On the final day Parnevik was playing behind Leonard. Parnevik seemingly became unnerved by what was going on up ahead of him, as Leonard was scoring birdies at two of the last three holes for a final round of 65. Meanwhile, Parnevik's undoing was his crucially pushed short birdie chance at the sixteenth. Leonard finished with a 272 while Parnevik and Clarke were three shots behind. Furyk finished seven shots back.

Winged Foot Golf Club, Mamaroneck, New York played host to the P.G.A. Championship in 1997. The results were going to play a large part in the selection of the U.S. Ryder Cup team, as captain Tom Kite was to finalize selection of the team after the event was concluded.

Davis Love III stood a nervous tenth in the Ryder Cup standings (the

Matt Kuchar, 1997 U.S. Amateur Champion.

top ten money winners automatically making the U.S. team), so he had more than pursuit of his first Major on his mind. He settled in with an opening 66. For the rest of the tournament he withstood pressure from others, especially Justin Leonard, to capture his first Major. In doing so he passed sole possession of the title of best-player-not-to-have-won-a -major to Colin Montgomerie. It also ensured his trip to Valderrama, Spain, the site of the 1997 Ryder Cup in September of that year.

Love finished with an eleven-under par 269 which included three 66's in the first, third and fourth rounds. With a closing 71 Leonard finished at 274.

Matt Kuchar, a sophomore-to-be at Georgia Tech, won the 1997 U.S. Amateur at Cog Hill Golf Club in Lemont, Illinois. He was the first U.S. Amateur winner of the post-Tiger Woods era. In the finals Kuchar defeated Joel Kribel 2 & 1.

Among the women Nancy Lopez had her best chance to win the U.S.

Women's Open at Pumpkin Ridge in Portland, Oregon. She became the only woman in Open history to record four rounds in the 60's and still fail to gain the one title she coveted the most. Five-foot tall Allison Nicholas, a resident of the English Midlands, played steadily against Lopez and the partisan American crowd. In the final round a 60-yard pitch for an eagle at the fourth when Lopez made birdie was a great boost to Nicholas. Despite a double bogey at the fourteenth Nicholas held on late to take the title by one stroke

Davis Love III, winner of the 1997 P.G.A. Championship.

over Lopez. Nicholas would later captain the European Solheim Cup team in a losing effort in 2009.

In the 1997 Ryder Cup the Europeans triumphed at Valderamma, Spain. Led by Colin Montgomerie and captain Seve Ballesteros the Europeans prevailed by the slim margin of 14½–13½.

Mark O'Meara took center stage in 1998, beginning with the Masters. Entering the final round he was at 212 and trailed Fred Couples by two shots. David Duval and Jim Furyk trailed by three. Couples shot a final round 70, but it was not enough to fend off the hard-charging O'Meara. O'Meara surged with a 67–279 and won by one stroke over Duval, who also finished with a 67, and over Couples, who shot a closing 70. Furyk ended up two shots back with a final round 68 and 281.

The 1998 U.S. Open was staged at the Olympic Club in San Francisco, California. From the outset the players complained about the brutal conditions of the course, especially the slippery greens and diabolical pin positions. Lee Janzen gained his second U.S. Open (previously, 1993), overcoming a five-shot deficit to win at level par over Payne Stewart. Janzen had dug himself a deep hole when he dropped strokes at two of the first three holes in the final round. This left Stewart with an excellent opportunity to repeat his Open victory at Hazeltine in 1991. On the other hand Janzen was faced with what Billy Casper achieved at Olympic in 1966 when he overcame Arnold Palmer from a deficit of seven strokes.

Janzen's good fortune began at the fifth on Sunday, where the wind dislodged his ball from a tree and he was able to chip in for a par after he overshot the green.

On the eleventh, he got a bounce from the rough to the green and made birdie. This was one of his four birdies in the last fifteen holes. Janzen caught Stewart after he dropped a stroke on the twelfth, when a divot filled with sand left him with a difficult lie. The eighteenth green completed Stewart's downfall when his attempt from eighteen feet slipped across the front of the hole. Janzen finished at 280 to Stewart's total of 281.

Mark O'Meara went to the 1998 British Open hoping to capture that rare double of a Masters and British Open title in the same year. The scene was Royal Birkdale, Southport, England. O'Meara shot steady rounds of 72-68-72-68 for 280. He had to withstand the heroics of three players on the last day. The first was Justin Rose, a seventeen-year old amateur from Hook in Hampshire, England. On the eighteenth, Rose finished with a pitch out of the rough from fifty yards or so over the bunkers for a birdie and a final 69 for joint fourth. The second was Tiger Woods whose closing 66 brought him into second place and, as it turned out, one stroke out of a play-off with a score of 281. The third was the relatively unknown Brian Watts, a native Montréaler who had played most of his golf, and quite successfully, in the Far East. He too had a miraculous shot at the seventy-second when he holed a bunker shot for a birdie and a tie with O'Meara at 280.

Watts lost the play-off by two strokes in the four-hole format that began at the fifteenth. O'Meara at once took the lead with a birdie four on the fifteenth and held off Watts. So, O'Meara had his two career Majors, and both in the same year.

Out to the Northwest went the 1998 P.G.A. Championship. The site was the relatively new Sahalee Golf Club near Seattle, Washington. Tiger Woods started round one by making a bogey from the right rough. He then went on to shoot a course record of 66. The record was broken with a 65 by Greg Kraft on day two. Nick Price tied the new record with a 65 on the final day.

Meanwhile Vijay Singh of Fiji was working his way through the tournament with a 70 or better round on four consecutive days, shooting 70-66-67-68 for a total of 271. This gave him a two-shot victory over Steve Stricker with Steve Elkington another shot back. In his four rounds O'Meara never exceeded par in his quest for a third Major. However, he wasn't able to overcome Singh and ended up five shots behind.

Hank Kuehne added to his family's trophy case with a 2 & 1 victory over Tom McKnight in the 1998 U.S. Amateur at Oak Hill Country Club, Rochester, New York. This added to his sister Kelli Kuehne's U.S. Girls Junior and two US Amateur Championships, in addition to her British Amateur crown. Adding to the family affair, Hank's brother, Trip, caddied for him. Trip, it will be recalled, lost to Tiger Woods, in Tiger's first of three straight U.S. Amateurs in 1994. Finally, Trip won the U.S. Mid-Amateur in 2007 at Bandon Dunes in Bandon, Oregon.

It had been five years since José Maria Olazábal had won his first Masters in 1994. With his experience, it was not a surprise when he won the 1999 Masters. Olazábal's tactics and good play on Friday sent him on the way to victory. On Friday his 66 put him at eight-under par and one stroke ahead of Greg Norman at the half-way point. He shot 73-71 on the weekend to beat Davis Love III by two shots and Norman by three. A windy, hot final day put a premium on good chipping and putting, which were

Olazábal's strengths. A key to his win was his par-saving bunker shot at the short par three twelfth hole over Rae's Creek. His sand shot landed within inches of the cup for his par.

Pinehurst's famed No. Two course, designed by Donald Ross, was the venue for the 1999 U.S. Open. Payne Stewart held off Phil Mickelson for the title.

There was not much rough at No. Two due to a drought, but the devilishly small crowned greens presented the players with a stiff challenge. Stewart wore a waterproof top with the sleeves cut off to free his swing on the damp final day. Putts of twenty-five, six, and eighteen feet at the last three holes were enough to beat Mickelson, who barely missed a birdie putt on the seventeenth just before Stewart holed his. Stewart's par at the last secured first place by one stroke. Stewart finished at 279 while Mickelson shot 280. Vijay Singh and Tiger Woods were joint third at 281.

In October Stewart would die in a plane crash when a malfunction in the oxygen system led to oxygen starvation. He was forty-two. Stewart was a striking figure in his plus fours, and had won over $11 million and three Majors. He left behind his wife Tracy, a son and a daughter.

When one thinks of the 1999 British Open at Carnoustie, Scotland the name that surfaces is usually not that of the winner, Paul Lawrie, of Aberdeen, Scotland. It is that of the Frenchman, Jean Van de Velde, who needed only a double bogey six to secure victory on the seventy-second hole. Instead, he stumbled to a seven and found himself in a three-way play-off with Lawrie, who closed with a 67, and Justin Leonard, who shot a final round 72.

Van de Velde's folly at the 1999 British Open deserves recounting, as he has entered golf lore as a name meaning unhinged, undone, and unbelievable.

In the final round, Van de Velde started five ahead and seemed destined to be the first Frenchman to win since Arnaud Massey in 1907. When he came to the last with a three-stroke lead, he merely needed a careful avoidance of the Barry Burn. If he had laid up, he would have been in a good position to make no worse than a bogey and garner a two-stroke victory.

His drive on the eighteenth went well right but into short grass near the seventeenth fairway. Incredibly, instead of laying up, he hit a two iron that hit a grandstand, and ricocheted back in front of the Burn into long grass. From there he hit into the Burn. Van de Velde was forced to take a drop, hit into a greenside bunker but got up and down from five feet. His triple bogey cost him the Claret Jug.

Thus began a three-man, four-hole playoff, beginning on the fifteenth hole. On the fifteenth hole the Frenchman made six while his opponents made five's. All bogeyed the short sixteenth. Lawrie seized the lead with his second birdie of the day on the seventeenth hole. Van de Velde also birdied the hole.

At the eighteenth Lawrie hit a 220-yard four iron to within three feet. He made the birdie and won the play-off by three shots. At last the difficult "Carnasty" had yielded a champion, and Van de Velde was left to ponder what could have been.

The 1999 P.G.A. Championship was held at Medinah Country Club in Medinah, Illinois. It came down to a shoot-out between Tiger Woods and the young phenom Sergio Garcia of Spain. Woods was five ahead of the Spaniard with seven holes to play but bogeyed the twelfth hole. Up ahead Garcia holed a long putt for a birdie on the thirteenth . Woods was less fotunate on thirteen and made double bogey. The lead was down to one shot.

Garcia fell two shots off the pace when he bogeyed the fifteenth. On the sixteenth he pulled off a miracle shot around a tree from 200 yards and onto the green where he made par. Coming up behind him Woods bogeyed the hole to again reduce his lead to one shot. Garcia parred the last two holes, but it was not enough and Woods had his victory by one, posting a total of 277. Stewart Cink finished third with a 280 total. Woods had shed the title of a one Major (1997 Masters) wonder with his second Major. There would be plenty more.

The captain of the 1999 Ryder Cup was Ben Crenshaw. The site was The Country Club in Brookline, Massachusetts. The U.S. team was looking for revenge after losing a closely-contested Ryder Cup in 1997 at Valderrama, Spain, 14½–13½. The U.S. team was also feeling the pain of a rout in the Presidents Cup in Australia in 1998, its first and only loss in that competition.

The results of the 1999 Ryder Cup, as usual, rested on a U.S. comeback in the Sunday singles when twelve matches were to be decided. Europe had built a commanding lead, 10-6 after the first two days in foursomes and four-balls, and needed only four of twelve points in the Sunday singles to retain the Cup.

The U.S. started off powerfully in the singles, and its smallest margin of victory in the first six matches was 3 & 2. The key match was that of Justin Leonard and José Maria Olazábal. Down the stretch, Olazábal held a four-hole lead, but Leonard began making putts until they reached the seventeenth. Here Leonard holed a monster putt which set off an American celebration that was not looked upon too kindly by the Europeans, since Olazábal had a putt for a half. After the celebration died down Olazábal missed his putt and the worst Leonard could do was half the match for the key ½ point needed by the U.S. to regain the Cup. This turned out to be the case as Olazábal holed a sizeable putt on the eighteenth for the half. Fueled by its 8½–3½ dominance in the singles the U.S. won back the Cup, 14½–13½. The victory set off a long and raucous celebration by the Americans as they saluted their never-say-die captain, Ben Crenshaw.

The 1999 U.S. Amateur was staged at the Pebble Beach Golf Links in Pebble Beach, California. Tennessee native, David Gossett, a University of Texas product, won the title. After some rough early patches in his game (he qualified for match play by a stroke), he cruised to a 9 & 8 victory in the final over seventeen-year old Sung Yoon Kim.

Thirteen-year-old Aree Wongluekiet became the youngest winner in U.S.G.A. championship history when she captured the U.S. Girls Junior championship at Green Spring Valley Hunt Club in Owings Mills, Maryland.

CHAPTER

55

2000–2006

A ugusta National usually produces a victor who is a good putter. Vijay Singh is considered a fine ball striker and steady from tee to green. His weakness, allegedly, has always been with the putter. He confounded the experts with excellent green play at the 2000 Masters.

Singh built a three-shot lead going into Sunday's final round. He was steady on the front nine but was shaky early in the inward nine, as many Sunday back nine leaders in the past have found themselves. Singh put his ball in the water on the difficult eleventh hole and carded a bogey. He got a lucky bounce from back of the short par three twelfth and managed a par. At that point his nearest challenger was David Duval, three shots back. Duval's biggest chance to catch Singh came at the short par-five thirteenth. He fluffed his second shot into Rae's Creek. Singh, on the other hand, found the green in two, two-putted for a birdie and re-established his three-shot lead. He also birdied the par-five fifteenth. Singh finished with a winning 278, while Ernie Els moved up to finish second with a 281 total. Duval was one shot further back.

Pebble Beach Golf Links in Pebble Beach, California hosted the 2000 U.S. Open and it showcased the enormity of Tiger Woods's talents, most especially in Majors. For a good while before the U.S. Open, Woods had been working on swing changes with his coach, Butch Harmon. This typified Woods's seemingly never-ending quest to improve his swing and his game.

The South African, Retief Goosen, won the 2001 and 2004 U.S. Open

While he had won a record-setting Masters (1997), and the 1999 P.G.A. Championship, Woods hadn't won his country's national championship. His critics suggested that he didn't drive the ball straight enough to win a U.S. Open.

At Pebble Beach Woods added the national title to his résumé, and he did it in a record-setting way too. He won by fifteen strokes, shooting 65-69-71-67, 272. He finished at twelve-under par. Among the records that Woods broke was Old Tom Morris's winning margin in a Major. Old Tom had won the 1862 British Open by thirteen shots and Woods bettered that by two.

Even considering that it was a U.S. Open, a number of Europeans ended up on the leader board, vying for runner-up honors. Miguel Ángel Jiménez and Ernie Els tied for second, while Lee Westwood and Padraig Harrington shared fifth. The American, John Huston, slipped in-between to capture fourth place.

Woods continued his quest for Majors at the 2000 British Open, hosted by the Old Course at St. Andrews. At the event, Jack Nicklaus said goodbye to the tournament that he had won twice there.

From his opening tee shot Woods seemed pre-ordained to win and he did. His was another dominant performance just as that at Pebble Beach. He made only three bogeys and never put his ball in any of the Old Course's numerous bunkers.

In the first two rounds Woods shot 67-66 to race clear of the pack chasing him. He finished 67-69 for a 269 total. Ernie Els finished joint second with the Dane, Thomas Bjørn, at 277. Tom Lehman and David Toms were a stroke further back. For Els it was the third straight Major where he finished as runner-up. Woods's victory was historic in that his eighteen-under par total was the lowest British Open score ever recorded at St. Andrews. And, at age twenty-four, he joined Gene Sarazen, Ben Hogan, Jack Nicklaus and Gary Player in the elite group who had won all four modern Majors, and thus a "Career Slam."

The next Major that Woods set his sights on was the 2000 P.G.A. Championship at Valhalla Golf Club, Louisville, Kentucky. Woods was attempting to become only the second man in history, after Ben Hogan in 1953, to win three modern Majors in a calendar year.

Woods started the final round with a one-shot lead over Bob May, a journeyman pro who had preceded Woods as the leading amateur in California. At the tenth tee they were tied at the top. May inched ahead with a birdie at the eleventh. A crucial moment occurred at the sixteenth. Woods faced a twelve-footer for par while May had a four-footer for birdie. It seemed that May would move to a three-shot lead. However, Woods made his putt while May missed and so the lead remained at one.

Woods birdied the seventeenth to tie May. The eighteenth was a 542-yard par five that seemed to suit Woods's strength against the shorter-hitting May. Sure enough, Woods had a six-footer for birdie while May faced a fifteen-footer for a birdie. May made his birdie putt but Woods was up to the task as he converted his shorter birdie putt. They went to a four-hole play-off.

Woods birdied the first play-off hole and went on to win the epic duel. Commentators compared the finish to the duel between Tom Watson and Jack Nicklaus at Turnberry in the 1977 British Open. The quality of the Woods-May battle was evidenced by the fact that both shot back-nine 31's that Sunday at Valhalla.

Baltusrol Golf Club in Springfield, New Jersey played host to the 2000 U.S. Amateur. This was the 100th edition of the championship. Jeff Quinney of Eugene, Oregon faced off against James Driscoll in the final. With three holes to play Quinney was dormie three (ahead by three holes). He proceeded to lose the next three holes to allow the match to go to extra holes.

The first extra hole was halved with pars. On the second extra hole both had short putts for par. With a storm approaching they conceded each other's putt. At that point play was suspended for the day.

The next morning the players faced a par three on the third hole of the play-off. Driscoll hit his drive over the green. He chipped fifteen feet past the pin. Quinney's tee shot landed thirty feet from the hole. To his relief, after squandering the lead, Quinney sank the birdie putt and was the 2000 U.S. Amateur champion.

Going into the 2001 Masters Tiger Woods had won the preceding three Majors in 2000. If he won the 2001 Masters he would hold all four professional trophies at the same time. However, it would not be considered the professional Grand Slam since it would not have been accomplished in the same calendar year. So, what to call it? The media called it the "Tiger Slam" and golf aficionados could not wait to see if he could accomplish this unique feat.

They were not disappointed as Woods kept his date with destiny. His statistics spoke for themselves. At Augusta he averaged 305.5 yards off the tee, hit 82 percent of greens in regulation and made twenty-three birdies in four rounds of golf. Yet he did not play the kind of stunning golf that he had played while lapping the field at St. Andrews and at Pebble Beach. But, he did enough to accomplish the Tiger Slam. With three holes left in the final round Woods had only a one-stroke lead over the hard-charging David Duval. On the seventeenth, Woods faced a testing up-and-down putt to save par. True to his grit, he made it. Meanwhile, on the eighteenth, Duval had a four-footer for birdie, and a tie for the lead. Duval missed, pulling his putt to the left. Woods went to the eighteenth knowing that a par would secure victory. His birdie three put an exclamation point on the victory and the Tiger Slam.

The 2001 U.S. Open was played at Southern Hills Country Club in Tulsa, Oklahoma. It ended in an improbable play-off between South African Retief Goosen and America's Mark Brooks. Going into the final round it looked as though Phil Mickelson and Sergio Garcia would play central roles. However, both faltered with Mickelson limping in with a 75 and Garcia even more down the line with a 77.

All the drama was packed into the eighteenth hole, involving Goosen, Brooks and Stewart Cink. After the seventeenth, Goosen and Brooks were tied at five-under par with Cink one stroke behind.

Brooks, the 1996 P.G.A.champion, was up first. He had a fifty-foot putt for a birdie but ended up over-judging the pace, and missed the one coming back for a three-putt bogey.

Next it was Goosen's turn. He had hit a six-iron to twelve feet and putted his birdie effort to within two feet. He marked his ball and watched as Cink attempted a ten-foot birdie putt. It slid past the left edge and the disappointed Cink lost concentration and missed his eighteen-inch second

putt to fall out of a tie with Brooks and ultimately miss out on a play-off after
what happened next to Goosen.

All Goosen needed to win was to make his two-foot second putt for a
par. Nerves got the better of him and his putt never even hit the hole. He
and Brooks finished at 276 and Cink came in at 277. So it was on to an
eighteen-hole play-off the next day between Goosen and Brooks.

In the play-off, after a tight beginning, Goosen took command with
birdies at the ninth and the tenth. He leaped to a five-shot lead, and eased
home with a par 70 and a two-shot win over Brooks.

Royal Lytham and St. Annes in Lancashire, England was the venue for
the 2001 British Open. Americans had won five out of the last six British
Opens and were aiming to make it six out of seven in a run of dominance.

Colin Montgomerie led early with an opening round of 65 to jump to
the top of the leader board. He continued to lead the field at the halfway
point, but as was often his case, sadly, he slid out of contention on the weekend. Picking up the mantle for the Europeans were Darren Clarke and Ian
Woosnam.

Clarke played well deep into the weekend and was one shot off the lead
before he came to the seventy-first hole, where he ended up in two bunkers
on the way to a double bogey. He had to settle for a tie for third. Woosnam's
downfall was a bit more tragic. On the second hole of the final round his
caddie told him that he had the two drivers in his bag that he had been
warming up with. This put him one club over the limit of fourteen and he
incurred a two-stroke penalty. The penalty turned Woosnam's opening
birdie into a bogey and dashed his hopes of victory, as he could not recover
from this mental error.

On that Sunday it was all about David Duval, tagged with the then current moniker of best player never to have won a Major. He ended that on
Sunday. In calm conditions, he began the final day with birdies at the third,
sixth, and seventh which took him to nine-under par and into sole possession of the lead. He lengthened his lead with birdies at the eleventh and the
thirteenth and cruised home to victory with a total of 274 despite some
wayward driving on the finishing holes. Sweden's Niclas Fasth finished second, three shots back. A grouping finished tied for third at 278, four off the
pace. They included Clarke, Ernie Els, Manuel Ángel Jiménez, Bernhard
Langer, Billy Mayfair and the star-crossed Woosnam.

The Atlanta Athletic Club in Atlanta, Georgia hosted the 2001 P.G.A.

Championship. It came down to a duel between the veteran left-hander, Phil Mickelson and a relative unknown, thirty-four-year old Louisianan David Toms. The seeds for Toms's Sunday heroics were planted on the 243-yard par three fifteenth hole on Saturday. Going into the hole, Mickelson held a two-shot lead over Toms. Mickelson made a sloppy bogey. Lightning struck quickly as Toms followed immediately with a five-wood shot for a hole-in-one. Thus Mickelson's two-shot lead evaporated into a one-stroke deficit. Toms would go on to lead by two after fifty-four holes.

On Sunday Mickelson clawed himself back into a tie with Toms on the back nine. But on the sixteenth Lefty three-putted to drop back by one once again.

They came to the eighteenth with Toms clinging to the one-shot lead. Toms's drive found the rough. Mickelson's drive was in the middle of the fairway. Upon reflection, and after surveying the 200-plus yards over water, Toms elected to lay up. He hit an iron to 88 yards short of the water.

He pitched over the water to about ten feet and holed the putt for a par. Mickelson could only match him and Toms held the Wanamaker Trophy. In doing so he shot a record-low total of 265. Mickelson finished at 266. Steve Lowery finished third, two shots further back.

The 2001 U.S. Amateur was held at East Lake Golf Club in Atlanta, Georgia, the course where Bobby Jones had learned the game as a youth. Bubba Dickerson, from the University of Florida, played Robert Hamilton in the final. Hamilton built an early five-hole lead through fourteen holes. By lunch Dickerson had reduced the gap to one hole. At the thirty-fifth hole Dickerson was still one down. He won the hole to square the match. Dickerson then took the U.S. Amateur with a ten-foot birdie putt on the par three thirty-sixth hole.

On September 11, 2001 the world changed forever when terrorists hijacked planes and crashed them into the World Trade Center and the Pentagon. It was the Tuesday before the WGC-NEC Invitational Tournament and the event was cancelled. Also cancelled was the Ryder Cup which was to take place the following week at the Belfry. The teams that had been selected would play the matches twelve months later, putting the Cup on an even-numbered year rotation. The Presidents Cup was then assigned to be played during odd-numbered years.

Up until the 2002 Masters only two players, Jack Nicklaus (1965-66) and Nick Faldo (1989-90), had successfully defended their Masters titles. With his 2001 victory Tiger Woods was looking to join them and earn his third Green Jacket overall. When the final round began on Sunday Woods was tied for the lead with reigning U.S. Open champion Retief Goosen. Right on their heels came Ernie Els, Vijay Singh, Phil Mickelson, Sergio Garcia and José Maria Olazábal. Goosen bogeyed the first hole and did not mount much pressure on Woods during the round, despite a couple of late birdies. However, Singh and Els did threaten. Both got to within two shots of Woods, only to see things slip away on the two par-fives at thirteen and fifteen. Singh made nine on the fifteenth after a couple of shots in the water and Els found Rae's Creek on the way to a triple bogey eight on the thirteenth. In the meantime Woods seized control with early birdies on the second and third holes. In the end, his 71-276 gave him a margin of three shots over Goosen, with the late-charging Mickelson a stroke further back, after matching Woods with a closing 71.

Thus, Tiger joined Nicklaus and Faldo as the third player to successfully defend his Masters title.

At the 2002 Masters, coverage was extended to eighteen holes.

Bethpage State Park's Black Course in Farmingdale, New York hosted the 2002 U.S. Open. At 7,214 yards it was the longest course ever used for a U.S. Open. It was also the first public course to host the event. Coming off his Masters victory, Woods, the world's number-one player, was the favorite and he did not disappoint. He shot a 67 in the opening round and, after adding rounds of 68 and 70 to it, he cruised into Sunday with a four-shot lead over Sergio Garcia and Phil Mickelson. He went on to a three-shot victory and became only the seventeenth man in history to go wire-to-wire in victory at a Major.

Muirfield, Scotland was the site of the 2002 British Open and it did not lack for excitement. As he had proved adept at doing Tiger Woods maneuvered himself into contention after two rounds, just behind the leaders. The weather turned treacherous on Saturday and Woods struggled from the outset. He made bogey on the first hole and could not get on track. He shot 81, his highest score as a professional golfer. He came back with a sharp 65 on Sunday but was not a contender during the final round. The wind abated on the back nine on Saturday and overnight leaders Padraig Harrington, Shigeki Maruyama and Ernie Els were now introduced to some birdie opportunities. Els took the most advantage, carded a 72 and found himself with a two-shot lead.

Sunday's weather turned out to be calm and dry. As the field came down the stretch, it was Els who held a one-shot lead with three holes to play. He missed the green on the sixteenth and made a double bogey. Suddenly he needed a birdie at the seventeenth to join a play-off.

He got the birdie and entered a four-hole play-off with Australian Steve Elkington and Frenchman Thomas Levet. With Elkington failing to keep pace after the four holes, Els and Levet were still tied. On they went to sudden death. Levet faltered on the first sudden death hole, driving into a bunker, from where he made bogey. Els also drove into a bunker but made a great up-and-down for par, and his third Major (previously, 1994 and 1997 U.S. Opens).

The 2002 P.G.A. Championship was conducted at Hazeltine National Golf Club in Minneapolis, Minnesota. The P.G.A. Championship had become known for producing first-time winners of a Major, the most unlikely of whom had been John Daly in 1991 at Crooked Stick Golf Club in Carmel, Indiana. The year 2002 would produce another first time Major winner, but not without a brilliant charge from Tiger Woods.

After three rounds of play Justin Leonard held a three-shot lead over unknown Rich Beem. The tournament was Leonard's to win but he relinquished his lead with a double-bogey at the eighth hole in the final round and tailed off to a 77. The back nine turned into a duel between Beem and Woods. At the par five eleventh, Beem held a one-shot lead. Playing aggressively, he hit two lengthy shots to reach the 597-yard par-five hole in two. His second shot left him with a five-footer for an eagle and he sank it. Now his lead was three over Woods.

Woods fell five shots back with bogeys on the thirteenth and fourteenth. Being the champion that he was, Woods then birdied the final four holes. Beem's lead shrank to one shot with three holes left. Continuing his aggressive play, Beem hit driver on the water-guarded sixteenth, and holed a fifty-footer for birdie. His lead was now two. He parred seventeen, and his three-putt bogey at the last secured him the Championship by one shot. Once again, an unknown had won the P.G.A. Championship. For Woods it was his first runner-up finish in a Major.

The 2002 U.S. Amateur was hosted by Oakland Hills Country Club in Bloomfield Hills, Michigan. Ricky Barnes, a native of Stockton, California, made it to the final, where he met Hunter Mahan. Both played excellent golf in the final, and with Barnes leading in the afternoon, Mahan made a small charge to cut Barnes's lead to two-up after the thirty-third hole. However, Barnes closed Mahan out on the thirty-fifth hole, winning 2 & 1.

Postponed from 2001, the Ryder Cup was held at the Belfry in Sutton

Coldfield, Warwickshire, England. Led by Colin Montgomerie's four and a half points, the Europeans prevailed 15½–12½. While the Americans are typically strong in the Sunday singles, this time it was the Europeans who outdueled the Americans in the singles, 7½–4½ to provide the margin of victory.

Carol Semple Thompson, playing in her record twelfth Curtis Cup Match, sank a twenty-seven-foot birdie putt from the fringe at the eighteenth hole to secure the U.S.'s 11–7 victory over Great Britain and Ireland. The dramatic putt came in Thompson's hometown of Pittsburgh, Pennsylvania, at the Fox Chapel Golf Club. It was also Thompson's eighteenth victory in Curtis Cup play, another record.

Phil Mickelson had never won a Major and it was time for the 2003 Masters. The last and only time that a left-hander had won a Major was when Bob Charles won the 1963 British Open at Royal Lytham and St. Annes, England. The popular Mickelson was widely assumed to have the best chance of being number two. As it was, he stood as the then best player never to have won a Major.

Tiger Woods was trying to become the first man to win three Masters in a row. He struggled to make the cut and even a Saturday 66 could not boost him into contention on Sunday.

The leader by four strokes going into Sunday was Jeff Maggert. He succumbed to the pressure, however, and shot himself out of contention with a closing 75, finishing in fifth place. Sunday afternoon found Canadian left-hander Mike Weir and American Len Mattiace battling for the lead with Mickelson looming right behind.

Mattice made an eagle at the eighth to mount his charge, and he followed with eight birdies. A par four at the last would have given him a 64, and—as it would have turned out—the victory. Alas, his drive found the trees and he subsequently made bogey.

Weir needed to finish the final four holes in one-under for a tie. He got the birdie at the par-five fifteenth and came to the eighteenth needing par to force a play-off. He faced a testing seven-footer, and made the pressure putt. So it was off to sudden death for Weir and Mattice. The play-off was anti-climactic. Mattice hooked his second shot on the first play-off hole (the tenth), chipped to thirty feet, and three-putted for a six. This gave Weir three putts for the title, and he took all three to become the first Canadian and second left-hander ever to win a Major. Mickelson closed with a four-under

68, but it was not enough. He finished third, two strokes from joining Weir and Mattice in the play-off.

Olympia Fields Country Club in Olympia Fields, Illinois played host to the 2003 U.S. Open. At that time, Jim Furyk was running neck-and-neck with Phil Mickelson for the title of best player never to have won a Major. At Olympia Fields, Furyk played himself out of the running by winning.

Furyk was born in West Chester, Pennsylvania and graduated from high school in Lancaster County. His unorthodox swing has long been criticized for its looping motion, but it has produced results. He was tutored in the game by his father and coach. His father was also a golf professional.

Olympia Fields was a controversial choice because it allegedly did not measure up to the test of being tough enough for the U.S. Open. This belief seemed ratified when Vijay Singh equaled the lowest round in a Major with a 63. Added to this was Furyk's performance, where his 272 equaled the record low score in U.S. Open history. Furyk shot 67–66 on days one and two and followed this up with a 67 on day three for a three-shot lead going into the final round. Stephen Leaney was in the runner-up position. No one mounted any charge at Furyk and his closing 72 gave him his 272, and a three-shot victory over Leaney. Kenny Perry and Mike Weir were another four shots back at 279.

Royal St. George, Kent, England was the venue for the 2003 British Open. As usual, Tiger Woods was the betting favorite.

However, Woods did not get off to a good start. He lost his ball off the first tee in round one and carded a double-bogey. This would eventually cost him as he finished two shots out of first place.

The unlikely winner was American Ben Curtis who was making his first appearance in a Major. Thus, he became the first person to win a Major in his first appearance since Francis Ouimet in the 1913 U.S. Open. The victory did not come easily.

Curtis battled down the stretch with Woods, Vijay Singh, and Davis Love III. And despite being only two shots off the lead after fifty-four holes, little was expected of Curtis. He got everyone's attention, however, with a run of birdies at the first, fourth, seventh, ninth, and eleventh holes in the final round. This string of birdies gave him a two-shot lead as he played the twelfth hole. His play then deteriorated with bogeys at the twelfth, fourteenth, fifteenth and seventeenth. At the last, he made a tricky eight-footer to save par.

In the meantime, the new leader, Denmark's Thomas Bjørn, left two shots in the bunker at the sixteenth and carded a double-bogey. The Dane made a bogey at the seventeenth and this left Curtis atop the leader board with a one-shot lead. When Bjørn's birdie attempt failed to drop at 18, Curtis was the surprising winner at 283. Bjørn's collapse left him in a tie for second at 284 with Singh. Love and Woods were another stroke back.

The 2003 P.G.A. Championship was played at Oak Hill Country Club in Rochester, New York. As happens frequently in this event, another long shot emerged victorious. The P.G.A. champion turned out to be the unlikely Shaun Micheel.

After an opening round of 69 Micheel was tied for the lead with Chad Campbell. Micheel took the outright lead with a second-day 68. He maintained that lead after fifty-four holes with another 69. Now, all that was left was a pressure-packed final round.

Micheel managed his final round so that, even after a seventeenth hole bogey, he stood on the seventy-second hole with a one-stroke lead over Campbell, his playing partner in the last group. From the fairway, Micheel had 174 yards and played a seven-iron. He hit a career shot (and likely the shot of the year) when his ball landed two inches from the hole. That gave him a two-stroke victory, and a total of four-under par 276. Campbell had to settle for second place with a 278. Tiger Woods finished thirty-ninth at twelve-over-par.

For the first time since 1969, each of the 2003 Major winners had won a Major for the first time.

Fabled Oakmont Country Club, outside of Pittsburgh, Pennsylvania hosted the 2003 U.S. Amateur. A nineteen-year old Australian named Nick Flanagan became the first golfer from outside North America to win the U.S. Amateur since Englishman Harold Hilton in 1911. Flanagan defeated American Casey Wittenberg with a par on the first extra hole.

The year 2004 started off once again with lefthander Phil Mickelson atop the leader board, still holding the tag of best player never to have won a Major. With so many close finishes (e.g., second, 1999 U.S. Open; second, 2002 U.S. Open; third 2003 Masters), it seemed only a matter of time before he would break through with a victory. Mickelson approached this Masters with a different strategy from his go-for-broke game. He hit three-woods off the tee, aimed for the center of the greens and lagged difficult putts up to the hole. Judiciously, he elected to attack only when it was a safe course of action. Mickelson opened with a par 72, which put him five shots behind Britain's Justin Rose. Mickelson elevated his play with a pair of 69's on Friday and Saturday. This boosted him into a tie for the lead with Chris DiMarco.

When Mickelson finished the front nine in two-over-par on Sunday, it appeared that another Major might slip from his grasp. This seemed even more likely, given the play of Ernie Els, another player who had several near misses in Majors (in addition to the three he had won). Els leaped up the leader board to first place with a pair of eagles and a birdie four at the fourteenth.

At this point Mickelson shook off his mediocre play with a series of back nine birdies. He birdied the twelfth, thirteenth, fifteenth and sixteenth to forge a tie with Els. At the eighteenth he made two quality shots to give himself an eighteen-footer for birdie and his first Major. He made it and secured the Green Jacket. To do so, he had come home in 31. Mickelson had fired three consecutive 69's for a total of nine-under-par 279, with Els a shot back at 280.

Shinnecock Hills Golf Club in Shinnecock Hills, New York was the venue for the 2004 U.S. Open. Carrying forward his momentum from the Masters and buoyed by the partisan crowd, Phil Mickelson made a run at winning two Majors in a row after his long drought. But once again, he finished a close second. The winner was South African Retief Goosen, making it two U.S. Opens to his credit (previously, 2001 at Southern Hills). Goosen held off the pro-Mickelson crowd and the brutally tough Shinnecock, set-up in his usual unflappable fashion. The conditions were so tough on the greens that the U.S.G.A. was forced to water them between groups. It did little to save some of golf's big names from shooting high scores. Sergio Garcia faded to an 80, and Ernie Els did the same.

On Sunday Mickelson was playing even with Goosen until he came to the sixteenth, which he double bogeyed to leave the door open for Goosen. Goosen fired a closing 71 to match Mickelson and secure a two-shot victory at 276. The decisive statistic on the last day was Goosen needing only twenty-four putts on Shinnecock's devilish greens.

Royal Troon Golf Club in Troon, Scotland hosted the 2004 British Open. For the second year in a row an unknown American took home the trophy as a 500-1 outsider. Todd Hamilton, who had spent most of his professional career on the Asian Tour, was that golfer.

Colin Montgomerie, the hometown favorite, started off impressively. After this start, however, he predictably faded over the weekend.

Going into the final round there were ten players within five shots of the lead, including stalwarts Phil Mickelson and Ernie Els, along with Hamilton. At the start of play on Sunday, it seemed only a matter of time before Hamilton would succumb to the pressure. Following a birdie at the sixteenth hole Hamilton had a two-stroke lead over Els and Mickelson. Els made a birdie at the seventeenth and a bogey by Hamilton left Els with an eight-footer for birdie at the last to take the title. He missed, and the Open went to a four-hole play-off for the second time in three years. Els bogeyed the third hole, giving Hamilton the advantage. He secured victory with a forty-yard chip and run that settled close to the flag on the fourth extra hole. Mickelson once again came up just short, as his 275 left him one shot out of the play-off. Lee Westwood was another three shots off the pace.

Whistling Straits in Kohler, Wisconsin was the venue for the 2004 P.G.A. Championship. A three-way play-off decided matters. Justin Leonard appeared to have the Wanamaker Trophy in hand when he took a two-shot lead with five holes to play on Sunday. However, he missed four putts within twelve feet down the stretch, producing two bogeys to fall into a play-off with Vijay Singh and Chris DiMarco. DiMarco also had a chance to win, but he left short his eighteenth hole birdie putt. For his part, after three successive rounds in the 60's, Singh, the 1998 champion, found himself with a one-shot lead over Leonard as Sunday's play began. His closing 76, devoid of birdies, was the worst final round of any Major winner since Reg Whitcomb shot 78 in the British Open at Royal St. George's in 1938. Singh, Leonard, and DiMarco finished at 280. In the three-hole play-off, Singh nearly drove the par four first hole. He made birdie from six feet, and that was the decisive shot to give him his third Major overall (previously, P.G.A., in 1998; Masters, in, 2000).

For the fourth Major in a row Ernie Els and Phil Mickelson found themselves in contention going into the final round. Els three-putted the eighteenth to fall one shot out of the play-off while Mickelson finished a further stroke behind. Tiger Woods finished without a Major victory for the second consecutive year that left his Major victory total at eight.

In addition to his P.G.A. Championship victory Singh won eight other times in 2004. He earned over $10 million and dethroned Woods from the top of the world's rankings. This occurred in September and ended a record 264 weeks at number one for Woods.

The 2004 U.S. Amateur was played at Winged Foot Golf Club in Mamaroneck, New York. The winner was Ryan Moore of Seattle, Washington.

He became only the fourth person to win the U.S. Amateur and the N.C.A.A. individual title in the same year. The other three were Jack Nicklaus, Phil Mickelson, and Tiger Woods. Moore's victim in the U.S. Amateur was Luke List, two-up. Moore's victory was even more impressive as he was down by two holes with four to play. Completing his sensational summer, Moore became the first player to sweep the U.S. Amateur and the U.S. Public Links in a single summer. With this feat he joined Chick Evans (1916 U.S. Open and U.S. Amateur), Bobby Jones (1930 U.S. Open and Amateur), and Jay Sigel (1983 U.S. Amateur and Mid-Amateur) as the only men to win two U.S.G.A. Championships in the same year. Later, joining this elite group would be Colt Knost, who became the second player after Moore to win the U.S. Amateur and the U.S. Public Links in the same year when he captured both titles in 2007.

Following a two-year victory drought in Majors Tiger Woods rectified matters by winning the 2005 Masters. After Saturday's play was punctuated by inclement weather, the field had to play twenty-seven holes on Sunday. Chris DiMarco arrived at the course on Sunday with a four-shot cushion.

It wasn't long before he was chasing Woods. Having finished Saturday with three birdies, Woods picked up right where he had left off by birdieing the tenth, eleventh, twelfth and thirteenth holes to equal Steve Pate's Augusta record of seven birdies in a row.

This run turned a four-shot deficit for Woods into a three-shot lead. Statistically, he now had to be the odds-on favorite based on history, to wit: Woods had won every Major that he had either led or co-led after fifty-four holes. He would do so again, but not without a serious threat from DiMarco. Woods continued his superb play in the final round with two opening birdies. DiMarco would not back down, however, and with three holes to play, Woods's lead was down to one shot.

At the par three sixteenth DiMarco had the honors and he hit his tee shot to within fifteen feet. Woods followed, and left himself with a treacherous chip. He pulled off a magnificent shot by chipping his ball away from the flag, then watching as it rolled slowly back down the slope and dropped in for a birdie and a two-shot lead.

Woods quickly let the lead slip away with sloppy bogeys at the seventeenth and eighteenth. DiMarco parred the two holes and a play-off ensued. Woods hit two great shots on the first play-off hole (the eighteenth), then made birdie for his fourth Masters victory. Luke Donald and Retief Goosen finished in a tie for third.

The 2005 U.S. Open was held at the Donald Ross gem, the fabled Pinehurst No. 2 Course in Pinehurst, North Carolina. Off his Masters victory, Woods had the momentum to try to capture his tenth Major. He gave it a heroic try but fell two shots shy. After the third round, three men were atop the leader board. They were Retief Goosen, Jason Gore, and Olin Browne. All three succumbed to the Open pressure on Sunday, and shot a combined 35 over par. Browne shot an 80. Goosen carded an 81. Gore staggered in with an 84. At one point in the final round, Goosen had a three-shot lead which he promptly gave up in a three-hole stretch.

As is usual in Majors Woods shot himself into contention on Sunday and was trying for the first time to win a Major in which he did not lead or co-lead after fifty-four holes. On the back nine his challenger was thirty-six-year-old New Zealander, Michael Campbell. Woods's attempt to overtake Campbell came up short as he bogeyed the seventeenth and eighteenth, missing eight-foot and six-foot putts, respectively. Playing behind Woods, Campbell made a birdie on the seventeenth for a three-shot cushion. This gave him breathing room so that he could bogey the eighteenth for a two-shot victory, and an even par 280. Campbell became the first New Zealander to win the U.S. Open and the first to win a Major since Bob Charles won the British Open in 1963.

Sergio Garcia, Tim Clark, and Mark Hensby tied for third at five over par 285.

The Old Course at St. Andrews, Scotland, was the venue for the 2005 British Open. In search of his tenth Major, Tiger Woods garnered it with a wire-to-wire victory. This left him eight Majors behind Jack Nicklaus and one behind Walter Hagen for the all-time most Majors record.

Woods opened the first day with a six-under par 66, and a one-shot lead over Mark Hensby. His five-under par 67 on the second day kept him in the lead. On Saturday Woods holed a fifty-foot putt at the last for a two-shot lead. His Saturday round was a one-under par 71. In the final round Colin Montgomerie and José Maria Olazábal both crept up the leader board until they were only one shot behind Woods. The unflappable Woods simply would not let go of his record of winning every Major where he held or was tied for the fifty-four-hole lead. Paired with Olazábal in the final group on Sunday, Woods stood on the twelfth green with a two-shot lead. Montgomerie was in the group ahead. In a matter of minutes, the tournament was over. Olazábal missed a short par putt. Montgomerie did the same at the thirteenth. Woods's birdie at the twelfth resulted in a two-shot swing, and he cruised to a 274, fourteen-under par for a five-shot victory over Montgomerie, who finished with a nine-under par 279. Olazábal ended up joint third with Fred Couples at eight-under par 280. So, in the first three Majors of the year, Woods had finished 1-2-1.

Baltusrol Golf Club in Springfield, New Jersey was the venue for the 2005 P.G.A. Championship. It produced a wire-to-wire victor in Phil Mickelson who won his second Major in two years. In round one, Mickelson shot a three-under 67 for a share of the lead with five other golfers. On Friday, Mickelson's 65 gave him a three-shot lead. Mickelson struggled to a two-over 72 on Saturday and dropped into a tie for the lead with Davis Love, III.

Rain plagued the final round, forcing play over into Monday when twelve players were still on the course. At that time Mickelson held a one-shot lead over Steve Elkington and Thomas Bjørn. At the seventy-second hole, Elkington and Bjørn both missed birdie putts on the par-five hole, which would have broken a tie with Mickelson. Playing behind Elkington and Bjørn, Mickelson needed a birdie on the seventy-second hole to capture the Championship. His second shot landed in greenside rough about 50 feet from the hole. Mickelson then hit a flop shot to within three feet. He made the putt to win the 87th P.G.A. Championship. His birdie at the last duplicated his feat at the 2004 Masters.

For the tournament Mickelson came in at four-under par 276. Elkington and Bjørn tied for second at 277, with Tiger Woods another stroke back, tied for joint fourth with Love.

The East course at Merion Golf Club in Ardmore, Pennsylvania, hosted the 2005 U.S. Amateur. The final featured Edoardo Molinari from Italy and Dillon Dougherty, who played collegiate golf at Northwestern University, and was from Woodland, California. After the morning round in the finals, Dougherty had built a three-up lead. However, the afternoon round was a different story. Molinari's hot putter propelled him to a 4 & 3 triumph. In winning, Molinari became the first Italian to capture the U.S. Amateur.

At the 2006 Masters Phil Mickelson was gunning for his second consecutive Major, a feat last accomplished when Tiger Woods won the 2002 Masters and U.S. Open. In the first round, Vijay Singh shot a five-under par to take the lead. Mickelson's 70 put him three shots off the lead. After two rounds, Chad Campbell led by three shots. By the time the third round was complete, Mickelson had caught Campbell and led by one shot.

In the final round Mickelson pulled away with birdies on the seventh, eighth, thirteenth and fifteenth holes. Coming to the last, his lead was three.

His bogey on the eighteenth left him with a two-shot margin of victory. Mickelson's closing 69 resulted in a seven-under par 281, and his second Green Jacket (first, 2004).

South African Tim Clark holed out at eighteen for 69 and sole possession of second place. Tiger Woods birdied four of the last six holes for a share of third at 284, with José Maria Olazábal, Retief Goosen, Fred Couples, and Campbell.

For the previous best golfer never to have won a Major, Mickelson had now won three of the past nine Majors.

The 2006 U.S. Open was played at Winged Foot Golf Club in Mamaroneck, New York. Phil Mickelson was seeking his third consecutive Major, and he almost got it, but for his collapse on the seventy-second hole. By the time they got to the third round, Mickelson was tied at the top at two-over par 212, with Englishman Kenneth Ferrie. One shot back was Australian Geoff Ogilvy. With four holes to play Mickelson had a two-shot lead. In hot pursuit were Ogilvy, Jim Furyk, and Colin Montgomerie.

Ogilvy played solidly over the last two holes but with Furyk, Montgomerie, and Mickelson ahead, he did not believe he had a very realistic chance to win. He did par the last two holes including a chip-in on seventeen and a six-footer on eighteen. Now all he could do was wait.

Furyk and Montgomerie were the first to stumble. They relinquished the chance to win with bogeys at the eighteenth. They were followed by Mickelson, who had a one-shot lead over Ogilvy, needing only to par the eighteenth to capture the U.S. Open.

Despite the fact that he had hit only two fairways until the eighteenth, the aggressive Mickelson hit driver off the eighteenth tee. It resulted in a drive to the left that landed in a trampled-down area near a hospitality tent. From there, instead of chipping out and going for par, Mickelson tried a fade shot that struck a tree and advanced the ball only twenty-five yards. His third shot was a buried lie in a bunker to the left of the green. From the bunker, he was not able to stop the ball with the green sloping away from him and his fourth shot landed in the rough to the right of the green. He subsequently made a double bogey six, and Ogilvy was the winner by a stroke at five-over par 285. It was the highest winning score in the U.S. Open since Hale Irwin's seven-over par thirty-two years earlier, also at Winged Foot. Ogilvy became the second Australian to win the Open. David Graham had done so in 1981.

Mickelson could only ask himself, "what was I thinking," and declared himself "an idiot" for his reckless play at the seventy-second hole when the trophy was within his grasp.

Royal Liverpool in Hoylake, England, hosted the 2006 British Open. After missing the cut at the U.S. Open, following the death of his father, Earl, Tiger Woods was looking for his second straight British Open. He successfully defended his crown, winning his third Claret Jug and eleventh Major. Woods opened with a 67 in the first round, leaving him one shot behind the leader, Graeme McDowell of Northern Ireland. Phil Mickelson, seeking to overcome the shock of his U.S. Open collapse, opened with a 69, but was not in contention the rest of the way. Woods's second round was punctuated by an eagle at the fourteenth hole, which led to a seven-under-par 65 and a one-shot lead over Ernie Els. This was his best score ever in a Major round. At the halfway point, Woods's total was a twelve-under-par 132. In the third round, Woods faltered a bit on the greens and had three three-putt holes. Without the three-putts he would have broken away from the field. As it was, he shot 71 and led Ernie Els, Sergio Garcia, and Chris DiMarco by one shot, thanks to a birdie at the eighteenth. His total was a thirteen-under 203. In the final round, Woods was on the thirteenth hole with a precarious one-shot lead over DiMarco. Woods promptly birdied the fourteenth, fifteenth, and sixteenth holes to leave no doubt he would repeat.

His final round 67 gave him an eighteen-under 270, two shots ahead of DiMarco, and five shots clear of Els. Woods's victory left intact his remarkable record of winning all eleven of his Majors from the lead or co-lead after fifty-four holes.

The venue for the 2006 P.G.A. Championship was Medinah Country Club in Medinah, Illinois. Tiger Woods had fond memories of Medinah, as this was the course where he fended off the challenge of nineteen-year-old Sergio Garcia to win the 1999 P.G.A. Championship. The damp weather allowed Medinah to play soft for the entire tournament and the course yielded a record number of rounds under par. In the first round, Lucas Glover and Chris Riley shot six-under par 66's for the lead. A quality triumvirate of Tiger Woods, Phil Mickelson and Geoff Ogilvy was two shots back at 69. In the second round Englishman Luke Donald and Swede Henrik Stenson carded four-under par 68's to put themselves in a four-way tie with Tim Herron (67) and Billy Andrade (69). Woods's 68 left him one shot back. The third round saw Woods fire a seven-under-par 65 to tie him with Donald after fifty-four holes at fourteen-under par 202.

The fourth round was all Woods. He had a four-shot lead at the turn and carded a 68 for an eighteen-under-par 270, and a five-shot margin of victory. Shaun Micheel (the 2003 P.G.A. Championship winner) turned in a closing 69 for solo second place. Adam Scott, Sergio Garcia and Donald finished one shot further back at 276.

In winning at Medinah for his twelfth Major Woods became the first person to win two P.G.A. Championships at the same course. He also became the first player in history to win at least two Majors in consecutive years. His twelfth Major overtook Walter Hagen and vaulted Woods into third place behind Bobby Jones's Thirteen Majors and Jack Nicklaus's eighteen Majors. Lastly, Woods continued his amazing streak of winning after being in the fifty-four-hole lead or co-lead. He was a perfect 12-0 in winning that twelfth Major.

The 2006 U.S. Amateur was conducted at Hazeltine National Golf Club in Chaska, Minnesota. Rickey Ramsey, a twenty-three-year-old Scotsman, won 4 & 2 over University of Missouri senior John Kelly. Ramsey became the first Scotsman since Findlay Douglas in 1898 to take home the U.S. Amateur.

On the equipment front, in 2004 the U.S.G.A. set maximum driver volume at 460 cubic centimeters, more than twice the size of the original Big Bertha.

CHAPTER

56

International Icons
Ernie Els, Vijay Singh, Padraig Harrington

With Tiger Woods on the P.G.A. scene beginning in 1996, and capturing fourteen Majors through 2008 in the process, the going could not have been easy for any other player with designs on multiple Major victories. However, there were three who managed to win multiple Majors with four victories for Ernie Els and three apiece for Vijay Singh, and Padraig Harrington.

Ernie Els

Born on October 17, 1969, Theodore Ernest "Ernie" Els is a native of South Africa. He is known as "The Big Easy" for his imposing stature (6-foot-3) and his seemingly effortless and fluid golf swing. As a youth he played rugby, cricket, tennis, and, starting at the age of eight, golf. He was a skilled junior tennis player. By the age of fourteen he was a scratch golfer and decided to concentrate exclusively on golf.

His entrance on the world golf scene occurred in 1984 when he won the Junior World Golf Championship in the boys 13-14 category, beating out Phil Mickelson. Els turned professional in 1989 and won his first professional tournament on the Southern Africa Tour in 1991.

Els has played all over the world and owns twenty-eight European Tour wins to go along with his nineteen P.G.A. Tour victories. Playing in South Africa he also has won sixteen times on the Southern Africa Tour (now the Sunshine Tour). He also has thirteen other wins around the world.

317

Els's most prestigious accomplishments are his four Majors. He has won two U.S. Opens and two British Opens. In 1994 at Oakmont Country Club in Oakmont, Pennsylvania he won his first U.S. Open for which he was named P.G.A. Tour Rookie of the Year. Els defeated Colin Montgomerie and Loren Roberts in a play-off. He dispatched Montgomerie in the eighteen-hole play-off. In the sudden death play-off with Roberts, Els prevailed when he made par to Roberts's bogey on the first sudden death hole.

In 1997, at Congressional Country Club in Bethesda, Maryland, he won the U.S. Open by one shot over Colin Montgomerie.

His third Major came at the 2002 British Open that he won in a play-off over Stuart Appleby, Steve Elkington, and Thomas Levet. Appleby and Elkington were out after the initial four-hole play-off. On the first sudden death hole Els made par to Levet's bogey.

Els' won his fourth Major and second British Open in 2012 at Royal Lytham and St. Annes when he defeated Adam Scott by one shot. Scott bogeyed the last four holes to hand the Open to Els.

Els has also distinguished himself by winning the World Match Play Championship a record seven times.

In July 2005 Els injured his left knee while sailing with his family in the Mediterranean. His recovery was slow but he resurrected his game after two years with his third-place finish at the 2006 British Open. Further progress was evidenced by his fourth-place finish at the 2007 British Open and a third at the 2007 P.G.A. Championship. His comeback was complete when he won the Honda Classic in March 2008. In 2010 he won two consecutive tournaments leading up to the Masters. Els captured his fourth Major in 2012, winning the Claret Jug at Royal Lytham & St. Annes.

In addition to his globe-trotting golf Els has a golf course design business, a charitable foundation which supports golf among underprivileged youngsters in South Africa and a highly-regarded wine-making business. With a son who has autism, he is a spokesman in the fight against this handicap.

In September 2010 Els was elected to the World Golf Hall of Fame. The Big Easy maintains residences in George, South Africa and in Jupiter, Florida.

Vijay Singh

Vijay Singh was born in Lautoka, Fiji on February 22, 1963. He is an Indo-Fijian of Hindu ancestry. His father, Mohan Singh, taught him how to play golf. Singh grew up playing many sports including snooker, cricket,

Vijay Singh

soccer and rugby, in addition to golf.

As he began to focus on improving his golf Singh used the swing of Tom Weiskopf as a model for his own swing. Among Tour players he is known as one of the hardest working and most meticulous players, hitting an enormous number of practice balls to improve his game.

Singh turned professional in 1982. Two years later, he won the Malaysian P.G.A. Championship. However, in 1985 he became the subject of a major controversy over allegations that he had altered his scorecard at a tournament.

It was alleged that he lowered his score from one-over par to one-under par in order to make the cut. Singh denied this and also contended that, regardless, it should only have resulted in disqualification from the event rather than a suspension from the Asian Tour. He also felt that his treatment had been harsher because the marker was the son of a VIP in the Indonesian P.G.A.

Because of the ban, Singh was forced to take a job at a club in Malaysia. While this resulted in a hardship for him, he used the time well, improving his game and gaining experience. After a time he began to re-enter tournaments and resurrected his career. This was culminated when he won the Nigerian Open in 1988.

Singh obtained his European Tour card at the end of 1988. In 1989 he won his first title on the European Tour at the Volvo Open Championship in Italy and he finished twenty-fourth on the European Tour Order of Merit. Singh continued his ascent on the European Tour by winning again in 1990 and twice in 1992. He also achieved victories at tournaments in Asia and Africa during this period. In 1993, Singh made his debut on the P.G.A. Tour. That year, he won the Buick Classic in a play-off. As a result, Singh was named the 1993 Tour Rookie of the Year. Hampered by injuries in 1994, he came back in 1995 to win the Buick Classic again, as well as the Phoenix

Open. Singh had a successful year in 1996, although he had no victories. The year 1997 saw Singh win both the Memorial Tournament and the Buick Open.

In 1998 he captured his first Major, the P.G.A. Championship at Sahalle in Sammamish, Washington. Singh's second-round 66 tied the course record. He finished at nine under par 271. Steve Stricker was runner-up, two strokes behind. Singh won his second Major in 2000 when he captured the Masters, with a three-stroke victory over Ernie Els. Singh's winning score was 10-under par 278.

Although he did not win on the P.G.A. Tour in 2001 Singh had a very successful year. He concluded the year with a Tour-best fourteen top ten finishes and ended up fourth on the money list. In 2002, he won the Shell Houston Open and the Tour Championship.

Singh had another accomplished year in 2003. He won four tournaments and had eighteen top-ten finishes. He also finished the year as the Tour's leading money winner. His victories came at the Phoenix Open, the EDS Byron Nelson Championship, the John Deere Classic, and the FUNAI Classic at the Walt Disney World Resort.

In 2004 Singh picked up where he left off in 2003, winning the A.T.&T. Pebble Beach National Pro-Am. He captured his third Major in 2004 when he won his second P.G.A. Championship at Whistling Straits, Kohler, Wisconsin. Singh won in a three-hole play-off with Justin Leonard and Chris DiMarco. Singh led by a stroke over Leonard, entering the final round, but shot a 76. This final round 76 was the highest winning final round in a Major championship since 1938. Singh's birdie on the first hole of the play-off, his first of the day, proved to be the difference.

On September 6, 2004 Singh won the Deutsche Bank Championship. With this win he overtook Tiger Woods at the top of the Official World Golf Rankings, ending Woods's streak of 264 weeks at number one. Singh stayed on top for thirty-two weeks.

Singh won a career-best nine victories in 2004, a record $10,905,166 in earnings, and was named the P.G.A. Tour's Player of the Year. He also won the money title and the Vardon Trophy for low-stroke average.

In 2005 Singh became the youngest living player elected to the World Golf Hall of Fame. Because of a scheduling conflict, he deferred his induction for a year and it took place in October 2006.

In 2007 Singh joined Tiger Woods, Phil Mickelson, and Zach Johnson as the only multiple winners during the 2007 P.G.A. Tour season.

In 2008, he won the season-ending FedEx Cup.

Singh has won twenty-two events since turning forty, beating Sam Snead's record by three. His record-setting nineteenth win came at the first event of the 2007 P.G.A. Tour season, the Mercedes-Benz Championship. As a result of his Mercedes-Benz win Singh also became the second man, after Tiger Woods, to reach $50 million in P.G.A. Tour career earnings.

To date, Singh has sixty-five victories. These include thirty-four on the PGA Tour and thirteen on the European Tour (including three co-sanctioned with the P.G.A. Tour). His thirty-second P.G.A. Tour victory came at the WGC-Bridgestone Invitational in August 2008. With this victory he became the international player with the most victories on the P.G.A. Tour. This broke the tie he had with "Lighthorse" Harry Cooper.

The year 2009 marked the eighth time he had been selected to play in the Presidents Cup. Currently Singh plays on both the P.G.A. Tour and the European Tour. Singh resides in Ponte Vedra Beach, Florida with his wife and son.

Padraig Harrington

Padraig Harrington is an Irish golfer born on August 31, 1971 in Ballyroan, Dublin, Ireland. He burst onto the Majors scene with victories in the 2007 and 2008 British Opens and the 2008 P.G.A. Championship.

After a successful amateur career, including winning the Walker Cup with the Great Britain & Ireland team in 1995, Harrington turned professional. His first victory on the European Tour came quickly, in the 1996 Peugeot Spanish Open, but for the next several years he found himself in the runner-up position on a number of occasions. However, beginning in 2000 he had at least one win on the European Tour up to 2004. He has finished in the top ten on the European Tour's Order of Merit seven times, including second places in 2001 and 2002 and third places in 2003 and 2004 and eventually won the Order of Merit in 2006.

Coming over to the P.G.A. Tour Harrington was the runner-up in the Players Championship in 2003 and 2004. In 2005 he became a member of the P.G.A. Tour and garnered his first P.G.A. Tour victory at the Honda Classic.

At the 2007 British Open Harrington defeated Sergio Garcia in a four-hole play-off at Carnoustie, becoming the first Irishman to win the British Open in sixty years.

A year later at the 2008 British Open he successfully defended his title when he overcame a two-shot deficit to Greg Norman with a final round

69. He shot a four-under-par 32 on the back nine, highlighted by an eagle on the par-five seventeenth. In capturing his second straight British Open Harrington became the first European since James Braid in 1906 to retain the Claret Jug.

Just three weeks after winning his second British Open, Harrington won the P.G.A. Championship. He shot eight-under par on the weekend to finish two strokes ahead of Sergio Garcia and Ben Curtis. Harrington became the first European to win the P.G.A. Championship in seventy-eight years (the last was Tommy Armour in 1930) and is the first winner from Ireland.

This latest Major win secured Harrington's position as the number one player in Europe, and earned him the number one spot on the 2008 European Ryder Cup team.

Harrington and his wife Caroline were married in 1997 and they have two sons, Patrick and Ciarán. The Harringtons reside in Dublin, Ireland.

57

Phil Mickelson

Phil Mickelson was born in San Diego, California, on June 16, 1970. He is nicknamed "Lefty" for his left-handed swing, although he is otherwise right-handed.

Mickelson graduated from Arizona State University in 1992. While there he captured three N.C.A.A. individual championships and three Haskins Awards (1990, 1991 and 1992) as the outstanding collegiate golfer. In 1990 he became the first left-hander to win the U.S. Amateur when he defeated Manny Zerman 5 & 4 at Cherry Hills Country Club in Denver, Colorado. Mickelson achieved another rare milestone in 1991. He won his first P.G.A. Tour event as an amateur when he captured the Northern Telecom Open. He became only the fourth amateur in P.G.A. history to accomplish this feat and was the first since Scott Verplank won the 1985 Western Open. Mickelson turned pro in 1992.

Mickelson is known for his powerful full swing but even more so for his superlative short game around the green. His patented shot is the "Phil flop shot," where he takes a big swing with a lob wedge against a tight lie so that the ball flies high in the air for a short distance and lands softly on the green.

Through the 1990s and the early 2000s Mickelson continued on a steady pace of winning golf tournaments. Among his wins were the Byron Nelson Golf Classic in 1996, the World Series of Golf in 1996 and the

A.T.&T. Pebble Beach National Pro-Am in 1998. He won the Colonial Invitational in 2000, the Greater Hartford Open in 2001 and again in 2002.

Despite these accomplishments Mickelson's résumé was devoid of Major championships. He seemed always to come up just short. Thus, he held the title for a long while as the best golfer never to have won a Major. It wasn't that he didn't have his chances. Indeed, in the five-year span between 1999 and 2003, he had six second-place or third-place finishes in Major championships.

His critics laid the blame on his taking too many risky shots, missing too many short putts, and a general lack of being able to close out a Major. For his part Mickelson continued to assert that by putting himself in a position to win, he would eventually come out on top in a Major. He proved to be prophetic in 2004.

His first Major came at the 2004 Masters, where he won with an eighteen-foot putt on the last hole to defeat Ernie Els by a stroke. In addition to getting the monkey off his back as the best player never to have won a Major, Mickelson made news for left-handers. He became only the third left-hander to win a Major. The others were New Zealander Bob Charles at the 1963 British Open and Canadian Mike Weir who won the 2003 Masters.

The following year at the 2005 P.G.A. Championship at Baltusrol Golf Club in Springfield, New Jersey, Mickelson captured his second Major. It occurred in a Monday final round. On the seventy-second hole, he hit one of his trademark flop shots from heavy greenside rough to within three feet of the hole. His birdie allowed him to finish at four-under par 276, one shot ahead of Steve Elkington and Thomas Bjørn.

The following spring Lefty went on to capture the 2006 Masters for his third Major. He shot a three-under-par final round to win by two strokes over Tim Clark. This win vaulted him into second place in the Official World Golf Rankings (his career best) behind Tiger Woods.

Next Mickelson set his sights on a fourth Major and third in a row at the 2006 U.S. Open, which was being held at Winged Foot Golf Club in Mamaroneck, New York. Alas, it was not to be as he came close to equaling Jean Van de Velde's collapse at the 1999 British Open at Carnoustie.

Leading by a stroke with one hole to play, all Lefty needed to win was to par the seventy-second hole. Throwing caution to the wind, however, Mickelson chose to hit driver. He hit his drive well to the left. This decision was widely criticized since he had hit only two of thirteen fairways in the round.

The ball settled in trampled down grass near a hospitality tent. Rather

Phil Mickelson

than pitch out safely Mickelson's second shot hit a tree. He followed that with a shot into a greenside bunker, from which he was unable to get up and down. This left him with a double bogey and a one-shot loss to Australian Geoff Ogilvy. It also ended his bid to join Ben Hogan and Tiger Woods as the only players to win three consecutive professional Majors.

Afterward, Phil admitted "[I] still am in shock that I did that. I just can't believe I did that. I'm such an idiot."

In the spring of 2007, frustrated with his driving accuracy, Mickelson made the decision to leave his long-time swing coach Rick Smith. He turned to Butch Harmon, who was a former coach of Tiger Woods. The change produced almost immediate results.

At the 2007 Players Championship in May, Mickelson came from a stroke back on the final round to shoot a three-under par 69 to win with an eleven-under par 277. It was a nice Mother's Day present for his wife, Amy, and their three children—Amanda, Sophia and Evan.

In the 2007 U.S. Open at Oakmont Country Club in Oakmont, Pennsylvania, after shooting eleven-over par for the first two rounds, Mickelson missed the cut by a stroke for the first time in thirty-one Majors. The last time he had missed the cut at a Major was at the 1999 British Open at Carnoustie. No doubt he was hampered by a wrist injury that he had incurred while practicing in the thick rough at Oakmont a few weeks before the tournament.

The lingering effects of the wrist injury prevented him from being a factor in the 2007 British Open at Carnoustie, Scotland, and at the 2007 P.G.A. Championship at Southern Hills Country Club, in Tulsa, Oklahoma. However, Mickelson showed that he had returned to form at the Deutsche Bank Championship held over the 2007 Labor Day weekend at the Tournament

Players Club of Boston in Norton, Massachusetts. He beat Tiger Woods, who tied for second, two strokes behind Lefty. It was the first time that Mickelson was able to beat Woods while paired together on the final day of a tournament.

The win secured Mickelson's place in the final event (the Tour Championship) of the FedEx Cup to be held at the East Lake Golf Club in Atlanta, Georgia. In that event he finished twentieth.

In 2008 Mickelson won two times—at the Northern Trust Open and the Crowne Plaza Invitational at Colonial.

Mickelson had a good 2009 although he did not win a Major. He defended his title at the Northern Trust Open for his thirty-fifth tour win. He won his his first world championship tournament when he won the WGC-CA Championship. Among the Majors, Mickelson finished runner-up for the fifth time at the U.S. Open. He won his thirty-seventh P.G.A. title by winning at the season-ending FedEx Tour Championship, although Tiger Woods won the overall FedEx Cup and the $10 million check that goes along with it.

To close out the 2009 season Mickelson won the HSBC Championship in Shanghai, China, beating a strong field that included Tiger Woods and Ernie Els. He earned $1.2 million for his fourth victory of the year, matching his career best, although the Shanghai event is not counted as a P.G.A. tour event.

The year 2010 started off slowly for Mickelson who no doubt was distracted by medical issues in his private life since his wife and mother were battling breast cancer. As the 2010 Masters approached, Mickelson admitted that he was not playing his best golf. However, after three rounds he found himself only one shot behind Englishman Lee Westwood. On Sunday Mickelson took over on the back nine, birdieing four of the last seven holes to capture his third Green Jacket and fourth Major overall (2004 and 2006 Masters; 2005 P.G.A. Championship). Westwood finished second, three shots behind, followed by Anthony Kim and Tiger Woods.

Mickelson, who was one of the favorites for the U.S. Open at Pebble Beach shot a 74 and 66 on Thursday and Friday to sit a shot off the lead. However, two weekend scores of 73 gave him a T-4 finish. During the rest of the 2010 season Mickelson had multiple opportunities to become the number one player in the Official World Golf Ranking following the travails of Tiger Woods. However, a string of disappointing finishes by Mickelson saw the number one spot eventually go to Englishman Lee Westwood.

In the days leading up to the 2010 P.G.A. Championship at Whistleing Straits, Mickelson announced he had been diagnosed with psoriatic arthritis. It appears that this will have no long-term effect on his golf career. He went on to finish T-12 five shots back of victor Martin Kaymer. On April 3, 2011, Mickelson won the Shell Houston Open over Scott Verplank. Mickelson rose to no.3 in the world ranking. At the 2011 British Open Championship, Mickelson tied for second with Dustin Johnson.

2012
Mickelson finished tied for third at the 1912 Masters Tournament. He ended up with a score of eight-under over all.

He fought to make the cut in the U.S. Open and finished T-65. He missed the cut at the Open Championship shooting 73-78 (11 over par)

He then finished T-36 at the P.G.A. Championship.

2013
At the 2013 U.S. Open Mickelson entered the final round leading by one stroke, but he finished the final round poorly to fall out of the lead. He re-gained the lead with an eagle on the 10th hole. However, he bogeyed the 17th hole to fall one stroke behind the leader Justin Rose. Mickelson finishing tied for second with Jason Day. It was the sixth runner-up finish of Mickelson career at the U.S. Open, second behind Jack Nicklaus's seven runner-up finishes at the Open Championship.

The week before the British Open Championship, Mickelson won the Scottish Open. A week later, he won his fifth professional Major title at the 2013 British Open Championship shooting a final round 66 at Muirfield, Gullane, Scotland. He was five shots off the lead held by Lee Westwood entering the final round, but birdied four of the last six holes to beat Sweden's Henrik Stenson by three strokes.Tiger Woods tied for sixth..

2014
Mickelson had a down year in 2014 not winning any Major championships, or regular titles for that matter.

Mickelson has 42 career victories on the P.G.A. Tour and eight wins on the European Tour. He has been named to seven Ryder Cup teams, and has been a member of eight Presidents Cup squads.

In 2011, Mickelson, with his four Major victories, was inducted into the World Golf Hall of Fame.

Currently Mickelson and his family reside in Rancho Santa Fe, California.

58

2007–2008

T he 2007 Masters was played in unsettled weather with the winds affecting the scoring. It was thirty-one-year-old Iowan, Zack Johnson, who captured the Green Jacket. It was his first Major and only his second P.G.A. victory. Shortly thereafter he would capture his third victory at the A.T.&T. Classic.

In the final round of the Masters Johnson stood on the par-five thirteenth, needing a birdie on the reachable par five to claim the lead. As he had done all four rounds Johnson stuck to his game plan and laid up short of Rae's Creek. His approach landed ten feet from the pin. He sank the putt for the birdie that gave him the outright lead. For the week, Johnson's strategy led him to a eleven-under-par on the four par fives. Hot on his heels were Tiger Woods, Retief Goosen and Rory Sabbatini. The unflappable Johnson responded with a birdie on the fourteenth for a two-shot lead.

He birdied the seventeenth to extend his lead to three shots and the cautious bogey he made on eighteen secured a two-shot victory at one-over par 289 over the aforementioned Woods, Goosen, and Sabbatini, who all finished at 291.

Johnson's 289 total was the highest winning score at the Masters since Jackie Burke, Jr.'s total fifty-one years previously and matched by Sam Snead's score fifty-three years ago. For his part Woods felt he was in position to capture his fourth Green Jacket and thirteenth Major, but he blamed his bogey-bogey finishes on both Thursday and Saturday for his failure to do so.

Oakmont Country Club, near Pittsburgh, Pennsylvania, hosted the 2007 U.S. Open. It was the 107th U.S. Open and a record eighth for Oakmont.

The winner of his first Major was thirty-six-year-old Argentinean Ángel Cabrera. Reflecting the difficulty of Oakmont, Cabrera's winning score was five-over par 285. After opening with 69-71 he took a two-shot lead into Saturday, but a third-round 76 left him four shots behind Australian Aaron Baddeley. Baddeley took himself out of contention on Sunday with a triple bogey at the first and an 80 for the day. That left Woods with the lead as he tried to win his first Major coming from behind. However, he let the field back into the tournament with a double bogey on the third hole. Meanwhile, Cabrera took command on the back nine, playing in the fourth group from the last. He bogeyed the short par-four seventeenth but made a pressure lag putt on eighteen for a one-under par 69. Then all he could do was wait.

Pennsylvania native Jim Furyk's three straight birdies on the back nine put him in a tie going to the drivable seventeenth. He drove into greenside rough, took two to get out and missed an eight-foot putt to card a bogey. He was able to manage only a par at the last hole and finished one behind Cabrerea. Woods also came to the eighteenth hole, needing a birdie to force a play-off. His 30-foot putt for birdie was too strong, and Cabrerea had his first Major.

Carnoustie, Scotland was the venue for the 2007 British Open. The tournament was there for the taking by the young Spaniard, Sergio Garcia, but he let a three-shot lead slip away on Sunday and lost in a four-hole play-off with Irishman Padraig Harrington. Garcia opened with 65-71, and, after a Saturday 68, found himself with a three-shot advantage going into the final round. Also of note on Saturday was Steve Stricker's course record 64.

On Sunday Garcia relinquished the lead and came to the seventeenth, one shot behind Harrington, who was playing ahead of Garcia. Harrington could close the deal, but the pressure got to him. He hit into the Barry Burn twice, and managed a double-bogey six only by making a gut-wrenching five footer.

Then, it was Garcia's turn to win with the one-shot lead. He, too, felt the pressure at the eighteenth hole, and bunkered his second shot. His third left him a ten-foot putt for par and victory. The putt skimmed the hole, and both players went back to the fifteenth hole for a four-hole play-off. They had both shot seven-under par 277's.

Harrington took immediate advantage. On the first hole of the play-off

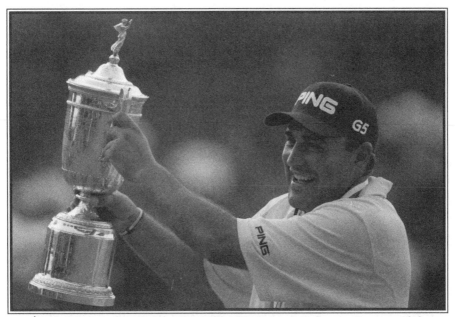

Ángel Cabrera after winning the 2007 U.S. Open at Oakmont Country Club.
He later won the 2009 Masters.

he sank an eight-footer for birdie while Garcia failed to get up and down from a bunker. Harrington jumped into a two-shot lead.

They matched shots on the sixteenth and seventeenth. At the eighteenth Harrington laid up in two. Garcia hit to the center of the green. Harrington pulled his third shot outside of Garcia's ball. Harrington's lag putt went by three feet. Garcia just missed a birdie and Harrington sank his bogey putt to claim victory by one stroke. With this victory Harrington became the first Irishman to win the British Open since Fred Daly in 1947.

Tiger Woods was trying to become the first player in fifty-one years to capture three straight British Opens (Peter Thomson had done so in 1954-1956). After an opening 69 Tiger could not stay in contention and a closing 70 left him five behind in a tie for twelfth place.

The 2007 P.G.A. Championship was played at sultry Southern Hills Country Club in Tulsa, Oklahoma, where the 100 degrees plus temperature and high humidity made it the hottest weather ever for a Major championship. The tournament appeared to be over after thirty-six holes when Woods shot a seven-under par 63 to tie the all-time eighteen-hole scoring mark at a Major. Woods's Saturday 63 increased his lead from two shots to three over Stephen Ames. Woods stood in good position for Sunday, as he had never lost a Major the twelve times that he led or tied after fifty-four holes.

Ames started Sunday with two bogeys and skied to a 76, slipping to twelfth place.

Uncharacteristically, Woods left himself with a challenge on the back nine on Sunday. He missed a four-foot par putt on the fourteenth, and saw his lead shrink to one shot over Woody Austin and Ernie Els. Austin had started Sunday four strokes back and Els had been six shots in arrears at the beginning of Sunday's play.

After the fourteenth hole bogey, Woods quickly made amends with a fifteen-footer for birdie on the fifteenth hole. His one-under par 69 gave him a two-shot victory over Austin, with Els three back. Woods finished at eight-under 272. He now had his thirteenth Major and fourth P.G.A. Championship—his second in a row. He was now one behind Walter Hagen and Jack Nicklaus for P.G.A. Championships won. His thirteen Majors left him only five Majors behind Jack Nicklaus, and in second place, for most Majors won. Lastly, he extended his record of never losing a Major when leading or tied for the lead after fifty-four holes.

The Olympic Club in Daly City, California played host to the 2007 U.S. Amateur. One of the favorites was Colt Knost of Dallas, who had already won the U.S. Public Links in June.

Knost prevailed in the finals by holding off the University of Alabama's Michael Thompson of Tucson, Arizona, 2 & 1. In winning, Knost became only the second player to capture both the U.S. Amateur and the U.S. Public Links titles in the same year. Ryan Moore had pulled off the feat in 2004.

The year 2007 marked the debut of the FedEx Cup. It is the year ending championship trophy for the PGA Tour. Four playoff tournaments make up the FedEx Cup with the winner determined after the Tour Championship in which the top thirty points leaders participate. The 2007 winner was Tiger Woods. Vijay Singh won in 2008. Woods won again in 2009.

At the 2008 Masters Trevor Immelman of South Africa won with a three-shot victory over Tiger Woods. Immelman's four-round total was 280. He became the first player since Severiano Ballesteros in 1980 to go wire-to-wire. Once again Woods preserved his dubious record of never clawing back at a Major without having a fifty-four-hole lead or a share of the lead. Brandt Snedeker (the P.G.A. Tour's 2007 Rookie of the Year) and veteran Stewart Cink finished joint third, a stroke behind Woods.

The 2008 U.S. Open was held at Torrey Pines in San Diego, California. Playing with a sore knee occasioned by April surgery, Tiger Woods won with a par to Rocco Mediate's bogey on the first sudden-death hole after each shot par 71 in the eighteen-hole Monday play-off. Getting into the play-off was not easy for Woods, but when he had to, he came up with the shots. On Saturday, he made two eagles on the back nine, the second of which was a forty-footer at eighteen to get to three-under for the outright lead. That was important considering that he was 13-0 in Majors when leading or tied for the lead after fifty-four holes. In between the two eagles he birdied seventeen on a fast moving pitch shot that dove into the hole after one bounce. After fifty-four holes Tiger Woods was one ahead of Lee Westwood and two ahead of Rocco Mediate. In the fourth round, Woods had to make a twelve-foot birdie putt on the seventy-second hole to tie Rocco Mediate and force the eighteen-hole play-off. The two were still tied after the eighteen holes, but on the first sudden death hole Woods's par to Mediate's bogey gave Woods his fourteenth Major and third U.S. Open. It also preserved his streak of never losing a Major when he held at least a share of the lead after fifty-four holes. With his third U.S. Open Woods tied Nicklaus with three career Grand Slams.

The next day it was announced that Woods had a torn anterior cruciate ligament and two stress fractures. Surgery and rehabilitation would keep him from playing for the rest of the 2008 season. As a consequence Woods would miss the first two Majors of his professional career (the British Open and the P.G.A. Championship), and would not be able to participate in the 2008 Ryder Cup.

At the 2008 U.S. Women's Open nineteen-year old Inbee Park became the youngest winner ever when she won the event held at Interlachen Country Club in Edina, Minnesota. Previously, Se Ri Pak was the youngest at the age of twenty years, nine months.

The 2008 British Open was held at Royal Birkdale in Southport, England. The weather was unsettling to say the least with the players battling rain and heavy winds for significant parts of the tournament. Going into the final round, the surprise leader was Greg Norman, who held a two-shot lead over defending champion Padraig Harrington. He was attempting to become the oldest winner of a Major since Julius Boros won the 1968 P.G.A. Championship at age forty-eight. After starting with three straight bogeys Norman settled down and held a one-shot lead with nine holes to play. Harrington was up to the challenge, first birdieing the par five fifteenth, then hitting a five-wood second shot to within four feet of the pin on the par five seventeenth. He would eagle the hole and take a four-shot victory over the late-charging Ian Poulter. Harrington's four-round total was a three-over-par 283. He became the first European since James Braid in 1905-1906 to win back-to-back British Opens. Norman would end up joint third with Henrik Stenson, six shots behind. The loss for Norman was the seventh time he had lost out on a Major when he held the fifty-four-hole lead.

The final Major of 2008, the P.G.A. Championship, was played at Oakland Hills Country Club in Bloomfield Hills, Michigan. Padraig Harrington rallied from three shots behind in the final round to capture his second Major of the year and third in the last six Majors. As he did in the 2007 British Open, Harrington outdueled Sergio Garcia down the stretch by holing three lengthy putts for a two-shot victory. Garcia had a one-shot lead in the middle of the sixteenth fairway but gave it away when he hit into the water. Ben Curtis lost a chance to validate his shocking victory at the 2003 British Open, but he bogeyed two of the final four holes to end up in a tie with Garcia.

South Korea native Danny Lee won the 2008 U.S. Amateur when he defeated Drew Kittleson 5 & 4 at Pinehurst Resort's famed Donald Ross-designed No. 2 course in Pinehurst, North Carolina. In addition to becoming the first Asian native to win the U.S. Amateur, Lee became the youngest champion. At eighteen years, one month, Lee was six months younger than Tiger Woods was in 1994 when he won the first of three consecutive U.S. Amateurs. This record would last only one year until seventeen-year old South Korean Byeong Hun-An won the 2009 U.S. Amateur.

Duke University standout, Amanda Blumenherst, won the 2008 U.S. Women's Amateur a year after finishing as the runner-up. She defeated Spain's Azahara Munoz 2 & 1 at Eugene Country Club in Eugene, Oregon.

According to the National Golf Foundation, as of the end of 2008 there were 28.7 million golfers in the United States. There were 15,990 golf facilities, of which 11,608 are open to the public. A facility is a location that has at least one golf course.

The U.S. won the 2008 Ryder Cup 16½–11½ at Valhalla Club in Louisville, Kentucky.

59

2009-2011

The 2009 Masters turned out to be a riveting affair. Kentuckian Kenny Perry, a hero of the 2008 Ryder Cup, was trying to become the oldest winner of a Major championship at forty-eight years, eight months (Julius Boros is the oldest golfer to win a Major when he won the 1968 P.G.A. Championship at the age of forty-eight years, four months and eighteen days). Going into the final round, Perry was tied with Argentinian Angel Cabrera at eleven under par with Texan Chad Campbell two shots back. Tiger Woods and Phil Mickelson made valiant charges on Sunday, getting to ten under par, but then fell back.

After birdieing the sixteenth hole, Perry held a two shot lead. However, his closing bogeys on the seventeenth and eighteenth holes forced him into a playoff with Cabrera and Campbell. They played the eighteenth hole and Cabrera made a miraculous par after hitting his drive into the woods. Perry also parred, but Campbell missed a short par putt to drop out. On the next hole, the tenth, Perry pulled his approach and Cabrera's par gave him the Green Jacket. He became the first Argentinian to win it and it was his second Major, following up on his U.S. Open victory at Oakmont in 2007. Cabrera also became the first player to have his first two P.G.A. victories come in Major championships. At number sixty-nine in the world, Cabrera became the lowest-ranked player to win the Masters since the world rankings began in 1986. It was the eighth sudden death playoff in Masters history.

For the second time Bethpage State Park (Black) in Farmingdale, New

Lucas Glover hoisting the trophy for winning the 2009 U.S. Open.

York hosted the U.S. Open. The 2009 version followed the 2002 rendition won by Tiger Woods. Rain plagued the tournament, which did not end until Monday. This was only the third time that the event ended on a Monday and did not involve a play-off.

The winner was twenty-nine-year old Clemson graduate, Lucas Glover. Glover shot a four under par 276 and overtook Ricky Barnes, the 2002 U.S. Amateur champion, who at one time in the third round held a six shot lead. Glover's margin of victory was two strokes over Barnes, Phil Mickelson and David Duval, making a comeback from his days in the early part of the decade as the number one player in the world. For Mickelson, a non-winner of the tournament, it was a record-setting sixth time that he finished as the runner-up.

The 2009 British Open returned to Turnberry, Scotland. It was at Turnberry in 1977 that a twenty-eight-year old Tom Watson defeated Jack Nicklaus in the famous "Duel in the Sun" for the second of his five British Open victories. Watson, by 2009 just two months shy of sixty years old, reverted to his 1977 form and showed his comfort with links-style courses by leading after three rounds. Incredibly, he found himself within reach of Harry Vardon's six British Open crowns. On Sunday Watson came to the seventy-second hole, needing a par four to claim victory. His eight-iron second shot just ran through the green. He putted back up the slope and left himself an eight-footer for victory. Alas, his putt came up short and he found himself in a four-hole playoff with fellow American, thirty-six-year old Stewart Cink, who had made a twelve-foot birdie putt on the eighteenth. Cink overwhelmed Watson in the play-off by six shots to capture his first Major. Watson's near miss meant that the oldest player to win a Major remained a forty-eight-year old Julius Boros, who captured the P.G.A. Championship in 1968.

Hazeltine National Golf Course in Chaska, Minnesota hosted the 2009 P.G.A. Championship. The surprise winner was Y.E. Yang from South Korea. He became the first Asian-born player to win a Major men's tournament. Aside from this accomplishment was the man he beat—the 54 hole leader, Tiger Woods. It was the first time in fifteen Majors that Woods lost a Major when he was ahead or tied for the lead after fifty-four holes. His two-shot lead was not enough as he shot a final round 75 to Yang's 70. Yang finished with a three-shot margin of victory. Another of Woods's records also fell. It was the first time that he lost a tournament when leading by two shots or more after fifty-four holes. It was the second time that Woods finished runner-up at Hazeltine, both times to a surprise winner. Seven years prior he came up one shot short to Rich Beem.

The season-ending FedEx Cup was won by Tiger Woods for the second time (previously 2007).

The United States stayed unbeaten at home in the eighth Presidents Cup, winning 19½–14½ over the International team at Harding Park Golf Course in San Francisco, California. The win pushed the U.S. record to 6-1-1. Tiger Woods and Phil Mickelson led the U.S. with strong support from Steve Stricker and Anthony Kim.

Seventeen-year old Byeong Hun-An of South Korean won the 2009 U.S. Amateur when he defeated Clemson senior Ben Martin 7 and 5 at Southern Hills Country Club in Tulsa, Oklahoma. In doing so An became the youngest winner of the prestigious event. He was a month and a half younger than Danny Lee, last year's winner who had been the youngest winner.

Among the amateur women Jennifer Song won the U.S. Women's Amateur and Women's Public Links.

In October 2009 the International Olympic Committee announced that golf had been added to the list of Olympic sports for the 2016 Olympics to be held in Rio de Janeiro, Brazil. It is the first time since 1904 that golf will be an Olympic sport.

There was an equipment change promulgated by the U.S.G.A. and the Royal & Ancient in 2009. For twenty years wide U-grooves have been comonplace on irons and wedges. This allowed elite players to impart considerable backspin on their shots, particularly from the rough. The result was a lessened importance of accurate tee shots. To address this concern, the two governing bodies mandated that new smaller U-grooves be used on clubs after December 31, 2009. As a result, balls hit from thick grass will not spin as much or as predictably as they did when hit from similar lies with the old-style grooves. This will make it more difficult for elite players to control their approach shots. The rule will not affect average players until at least 2024.

The 2010 Masters had as its biggest storyline the return of Tiger Woods to competition since his five months self-imposed exile following the revelation of his marital infidelities. Woods finished fourth behind Phil Mickelson who won his third Green Jacket (2004 and 2006 were his previous victories). Mickelson joined Jimmy Demaret, Sam Snead, Gary Player and Nick Faldo as three-time winners. They are exceeded by Arnold Palmer (four), Woods (four) and Jack Nicklaus (six) as Masters winners. Lee Westwood and Anthony Kim finished second and third respectively.

On May 2, 2010, Ryo Ishikawa shot a twelve-under-par 58 in Togo, Japan—the lowest score ever on a major tour—to win The Crowns for his seventh Japan Tour title. The 18-year old had twelve birdies in his bogey-free round.

The 2010 U.S. Open returned to the Pebble Beach Golf Links, Pebble Beach, California for the fifth time. Graeme McDowell from Northern Ireland became the first from his country and the first European since Tony Jacklin in 1970 to capture the crown.

The 150th rendition of the British Open was held in 2010 at St. Andrews. The winner by seven strokes was South African Louis Oosthuizen. No doubt a pep talk from Gary Player on Sunday morning aided Oosthuizen's steady march to his comfortable victory. The win also occurred on Nelson Mandela's 92nd birthday.

German Martin Kaymer won the 2010 P.G.A. Championship at Whistling Straits, Kohler, Wisconsin. He won by a stroke in a three-hole play-off over Bubba Watson. Dustin Johnson missed the play-off when he inadvertently grounded his club in a sand bunker on the seventy-second hole, incurring a two-shot penalty. Jim Furyk won the 2010 FedEx Cup and the Tour Championship. Furyk was also named 2010 Player of the Year.

The Europeans won the 2010 Ryder Cup in inclement weather at Celtic Manor in Wales by the score of 14 ½–13 ½.

In late 2010, the L.P.G.A. voted to allow transgender women the chance to compete on the Tour in response to a lawsuit filed by a California woman. Players voted to remove a constitutional clause that competitors must be "female at birth."

Kevin Na set a dubious mark of highest score on a par 4 when he recorded a 16 on the par 4 ninth hole at the Texas Valero Open in April 2011.

Tiger Woods at the 2005 PGA Championship at Baltusrol

SECTION 9

Tiger Woods

60

Tiger Woods

There is so much that can be written about Tiger Woods the golfer that he could be the subject of a book, and, indeed, he has been the subject of several books. Just as the mist of time has obscured the origins of the game, so too the mist of the future will determine if he is the greatest golfer ever to play the game. So far, he has done everything to suggest that he will turn out to be so. But, like most things, only time will tell if he surpasses Jack Nicklaus for the honor of being the greatest golfer of all time.

Tiger Woods was born Eldrick "Tiger" Woods on December 30, 1975, in Cypress, California to Earl and Kultida Woods. He is the only child of their marriage but has two half-brothers and a half-sister from his father's first marriage. Woods is multi-racial, being one-quarter Chinese, one-quarter Thai, one-quarter African American, one-eighth Native American, and one-eighth Dutch.

Earl Woods nicknamed him "Tiger" after a Vietnamese soldier friend of Earl's. Tiger Woods became generally known by that name as he achieved prominence in junior and amateur golf. On his twenty-first birthday, Woods legally changed his name from Eldrick to Tiger.

Woods was married to Swedish model Elin Nordegren. They were married on October 5, 2004, on the island of Barbados, and prior to their divorce in August 2010, resided at Isleworth, a community in Windermere, a suburb of Orlando, Florida. In January 2006 Woods purchased a

$29 million residential property on Jupiter Island, Florida where he now lives..

Tiger and his wife became parents on June 18, 2007, when their first child, a daughter named Sam Alexis Woods, was born in Orlando, Florida. The birth occurred just one day after Woods finished tied for second at the U.S. Open. Tiger and Elin became parents for a second time when a boy, Charlie Axel, was born on February 8, 2009.

In November 2009 Woods publicly admitted that he had engaged in "transgressions" and confessed to marital infidelity. In December 2009 Woods stated that he was taking a hiatus from golf to work on his marriage and his relationship with his wife. In February 2010 he told a public gathering of friends and business associates that he was "truly sorry" for his marital infidelity. At the time he was in rehabilitation therapy for "sexual addiction." In March 2010 Woods announced that he was returning to golf at the 2010 Masters. He finished fourth. In August 2010 the Woods finalized their divorce. While no monetary, alimony, or child support terms were reported at the time, the couple did agree to joint parenting responsibility for their two children. At a press conference after the divorce, Tiger said he was looking forward to being the best parent he could be.

Woods was a child golf prodigy who began to play the game when he was just two years old. As a three-year-old in 1978, he putted against comedian Bob Hope in a television appearance on *The Mike Douglas Show*. In 1984, at the age of eight, he won the 9–10- year-old boys' event at the Junior World Golf Championships. He would go on to win the event six times.

As the 1990s unfolded Woods began to make his mark in amateur golf. In 1991, when he was fifteen, he became the youngest ever U.S. Junior Amateur Champion. (Jim Liu, at age fourteen years, eleven months, and fifteen days, eclipsed Tiger's mark by more than seven months when he won the 2010 U.S. Junior Amateur Championship).

In 1992 he became the first multiple winner of the U.S. Junior when he successfully defended his title. That year he also competed in his first P.G.A. Tour event, the Nissan Los Angeles Open. The following year, 1993, he won his third consecutive U.S. Junior Amateur Championship, and remains the event's only multiple winner.

Woods became the youngest winner of the U.S. Amateur when he won the event in 1994. That mark was eventually surpassed by Danny Lee in 2008 and by Byeong-Hun An in 2009.

In 1995 he played on the Walker Cup team. Later that year, he matriculated at Stanford University, majoring in economics. Also in 1995 he won his second consecutive U.S. Amateur title and was voted Pac-10 Player of the Year, and N.C.A.A. First Team All-American. He accomplished another milestone in 1995 when he participated in his first P.G.A. Tour Major, the Masters, and tied for forty-first as the only amateur to make the cut.

In 1996, at the age of twenty, he became the first player to win three consecutive U.S. Amateur titles, and also won the N.C.A.A. individual golf championship. After two years at Stanford, he turned professional in August 1996. Immediately upon doing so Woods signed endorsement deals worth $40 million with Nike and $20 million with Titleist. He also signed a long-term pact with Buick.

Tiger played his first Tour event as a professional at the 1996 Greater Milwaukee Open, and tied for sixtieth place. He went on to win two events in the next three months to qualify for the Tour Championship. For his performances, Woods was named *Sports Illustrated*'s 1996 Sportsman of the Year and P.G.A. Rookie of the Year.

The following April Woods won his first Major at the 1997 Masters. He won by a record margin of twelve strokes, becoming the youngest Masters winner. He won another three P.G.A. Tour events that year. On June 15, 1997, in only his forty-second week as a professional, Woods captured the number-one ranking in the Official World Golf Rankings, the fastest ascent to world number one. At the end of the year he was named P.G.A. Player of the Year.

While Woods enjoyed a successful 1997, his performance wavered during the second half of the year and he won only one P.G.A. Tour event the following year. Woods answered critics of his play by explaining that he was undergoing extensive swing changes with his coach, Butch Harmon.

Woods's refinement of his swing paid off during the 1999 season. In June 1999 Woods won the Memorial Tournament and this marked the beginning of one of the greatest sustained periods of dominance in the history of men's golf. He won his last four starts of 1999, including the P.G.A. Championship, and finished the season with eight wins. He also was a member of the Ryder Cup team that mounted the heroic comeback against the Europeans at The Country Club in Brookline, Massachusetts. He was voted P.G.A. Tour Player of the Year and Associated Press Male Athlete of the Year for the second time in three years.

Tiger began the 2000 campaign by earning his fifth consecutive victory. This was a precursor to the rest of the year. He won three consecutive Majors (the U.S. Open, the British Open, and the P.G.A. Championship). All told, Woods won nine P.G.A. Tour events. He won his sixth consecutive Tour event at the 2000 A.T.&T. Pebble Beach National Pro-Am with a sterling comeback. Trailing by seven strokes with seven holes to play, Woods finished eagle-birdie-par-birdie for a 64 and a two-shot victory. These six consecutive victories were the most since Ben Hogan in 1948 and only five behind Byron Nelson's record of eleven in a row, set in 1945.

In the 2000 U.S. Open at Pebble Beach, Woods broke or tied nine U.S. Open records with his fifteen-shot win, including Old Tom Morris's record for the largest margin of victory ever in a Major championship. Woods led by a record ten shots going into the final round.

Tiger won the 2000 British Open at St. Andrews by eight strokes. He set the record for lowest score (nineteen-under par) in any Major and he held at least a share of that record in all four Majors until Jason Day won the 2015 P.G.A. Championship at 20 under par. At twenty-four he became the youngest golfer to achieve the career Grand Slam, joining Gene Sarazen, Ben Hogan, Gary Player and Jack Nicklaus in that achievement. He also matched Ben Hogan (1953) as the only other player to win three professional Majors in one season.

The 2000 P.G.A. Championship was held at Valhalla Golf Club in Louisville, Kentucky. Woods and an unknown, Bob May, hooked up in a classic duel. Woods made a testing six-footer at the eighteenth hole of the final round to force a three-hole play-off. A birdie at the first play-off hole gave Woods a narrow advantage, and two holes later he was holding the Wanamaker trophy.

Of the twenty events he entered in 2000, Woods finished in the top three fourteen times. His actual scoring average of 68.17 was the lowest in P.G.A. Tour history, bettering his own record of 68.43 set in 1999, and Byron Nelson's average of 68.33 set in 1945. He was named the 2000 *Sports Illustrated* Sportsman of the Year.

The year 2001 found Woods continuing to dominate. With his win at The Masters he held all four modern-day Majors at the same time—a first-time achievement by any golfer. This feat is now known as the "Tiger Slam." However, it is not viewed as a true Grand Slam in the sense that Bobby Jones had achieved it, because it was not accomplished in a single calendar year.

Tiger was not a factor in the three remaining Majors in 2001. However, he finished the year with the most P.G.A. Tour victories in the season with five.

Woods started 2002 on a strong note by repeating as Masters champion. In doing so he joined Jack Nicklaus (1965-66) and Nick Faldo (1989-90) as the only players to have repeated as Masters champions.

Two months later Woods was the only golfer under par in winning the 2002 U.S. Open at Bethpage Black in Farmingdale, New York. There was mounting speculation of a calendar year Grand Slam. At the 2002 British Open at Muirfield in Gullane, Scotland, however, his third round 81 dashed his chances for the Grand Slam. At the 2002 P.G.A. Championship at Hazeltine National Golf Club in Chaska, Minnesota, Woods nearly repeated his 2000 feat of winning three professional Majors in the same year, but back nine bogeys in the final round cost him the Championship by one stroke to Rich Beem. Further accolades were bestowed on Tiger in 2002, however, as he took home the money title, the Vardon Trophy, and Player of the Year honors.

The next two years, 2003-2004, could be referred to as the rebuilding phase of Woods's career. He remained among the top players on the Tour but was not quite so dominant. For the first time in his professional career, Woods went two consecutive years without winning a Major. He fell to second in the P.G.A. Tour money list in 2003 and fourth in 2004. In September 2004 Woods's record streak of 264 consecutive weeks as the world's number-one player came to an end at the Deutsche Bank Championship, when Vijay Singh won and replaced Woods at the top of the Official World Golf Rankings.

Many commentators were puzzled by Tiger's fall from dominance. In response Woods emphasized that he again was working on swing changes in the hopes of reducing the stress on his surgically-repaired left knee. The ever-optimistic Tiger was confident that once the adjustments were complete he would return to top form.

In 2005 Woods proved prophetic when he quickly returned to his winning ways. He won the Buick Invitational in January and in March he beat Phil Mickelson to win the Ford Championship. He temporarily regained the top spot on the Official World Golf Rankings until Singh displaced him two weeks later.

In April 2005 Woods broke his drought in the Majors when he won the 2005 Masters and ninth Major in a play-off with Chris DiMarco. This regained him the number-one spot in the World Rankings and he and Singh would swap positions several times over the next several months until the British Open at St. Andrews. There Woods captured his tenth Major. He finished the year with wins in six official money events on the P.G.A. Tour and topped the money list for the sixth time in his career.

Woods began the year 2006 with victories in his first two starts. Although he was in contention at the Masters, Woods fell short on Sunday and failed in his attempt to become the first two-time back-to-back winner.

On May 3, 2006, Woods's father, Earl, died after a long bout with prostate cancer. Tiger took a nine-week hiatus from golf to be with his family. He returned for the U.S. Open and his inactivity was apparent. He missed the cut at Winged Foot in Mamaroneck, New York—the first time that he had missed the cut in a Major as a professional and ended his record-tying streak of thirty-nine consecutive cuts made at Majors.

Woods overcame the missed cut when he played at the 2006 British Open. The site was Royal Liverpool, Hoylake, England. He was at his best. Using almost exclusively long irons, he missed only four fairways all week and his score of eighteen-under par was just one off of his Major championship record of nineteen-under par, set at St. Andrews in 2000. The victory was an emotional one that he dedicated to his father.

Four weeks later at the 2006 P.G.A. Championship at Medinah Country Club in Medinah, Illinois, Woods was again dominant. He made only three bogeys, tying the record for fewest bogeys in a Major. Tiger and Bob May finished at eighteen-under-par, equaling the relation-to-par record in the Championship. A record that stood until the 2015 P.G.A. Championship.

In August 2006 he won his fiftieth professional tournament at the Buick Open and at age 30 years and seven months became the youngest to do so. Tiger ended the year on another tear by winning six consecutive P.G.A. Tour events. For his efforts Woods was named the Associated Press Male Athlete of the Year for a record-tying fourth time.

In 2007 Woods began the year with a victory at the Buick Invitational for his seventh consecutive win on the P.G.A. Tour. His streak ended at the Accenture Match Play Championship when he lost in twenty holes to Australian Nick O'Hern.

For the record book, Byron Nelson set the record of eleven consecutive Tour victories in 1945. Woods's streak of seven straight was the second longest. Commentators noted that, while Tiger had won seven in a row, the "purity" of his streak was questionable because he failed to win four times during the streak while competing on other worldwide tours.

At the 2007 Masters Woods was in the final group on the last day of a

Major for the thirteenth time in his career but, unlike the previous twelve occasions, he failed to win. He finished tied for second, two strokes behind Iowan Zack Johnson.

In winning at the 2007 Wachovia Championship (to go along with his Buick Invitational and WGC-CA Championship victories), Woods had collected at least three wins in a season nine times.

At the 2007 U.S. Open at Oakmont Country Club in Oakmont, Pennsylvania, Tiger was in the final group for the fourth consecutive Major but began the day two strokes back and finished in a tie for second place. Thus, his streak of never having come from behind to win a Major continued.

At the 2007 British Open held at Carnoustie in Carnoustie, Scotland, Woods was seeking his third consecutive victory. He fell behind with a second round 74 and never was able to mount a charge. He finished tied for twelfth, five shots behind winner Padraig Harrington.

In early August 2007 Woods won the WGC-Bridgestone Invitational by eight shots for his third consecutive, and sixth victory overall, at the event. In doing so he became the first golfer to win the same event three straight times on two separate occasions (1999-2001, 2005-2007).

The following week, Woods won his second straight P.G.A. Championship when he beat Woody Austin by two strokes at Southern Hills Country Club in Tulsa, Oklahoma. He became the first golfer to win the P.G.A. Championship in back-to-back seasons on two different occasions (1999-2000; 2006-2007).

Tiger won his sixtieth P.G.A. Tour victory at the 2007 BMW Championship by shooting a course record 63 in the final round to win by two strokes.

Woods concluded 2007 with a runaway victory at the Tour Championship at East Lake Golf Club, Atlanta, Georgia. He became the only two-time winner of the event and also the champion of the inaugural FedEx Cup. He finished the year with four victories in his last five starts. As of the end of 2007 Tiger had won sixty-one official P.G.A. Tour events, had twenty other individual professional titles, owned two team titles in the two-man WGC-World Cup and had won the inaugural FedEx Cup despite sitting out one of the four play-off tournaments.

He won his first event of 2008, the Buick Invitational, to lift his career P.G.A. Tour total to sixty-two wins, tying him with Arnold Palmer. In February 2008 he captured the Accenture Match Play Championship for victory number sixty-three. This moved him past Arnold Palmer and into third place for career wins. Next he won the Arnold Palmer Invitational, his fifth P.G.A. title in a row, to tie Ben Hogan at sixty-four victories. His sixty-four victories placed him behind only Sam Snead (eighty-two) and Jack Nicklaus (seventy-three). Amazingly, it took Woods only eleven years to accomplish his sixty-four wins. His sixty-fifth victory came at the 2008 U.S. Open in a play-off with Rocco Mediate. Now he was all alone in third place for career P.G.A. Tour victories.

He won his sixty-sixth victory at the 2009 Arnold Palmer Invitational. His sixty-seventh victory was Jack Nicklaus's Memorial Tournament in Dublin, Ohio. It was his record fourth time that he won Nicklaus's tournament. Woods added to his total when he won his sixty-eighth victory by capturing his own tournament, the A T&T National in July 2009. Woods won his fourth tournament of 2009 when he won the Buick Open for the third time, raising his career record to sixty-nine victories. He followed that up with his seventieth victory the very next week at the Bridgestone Invitational at the Firestone Country Club in Akron, Ohio. He became the first person in PGA Tour history to win seven times on the same golf course. In September 2009 Woods won the BMW Championship for his seventy-first career victory, leaving him two short of Jack Nicklaus for second on the PGA Tour's career list.

To finish off 2009 Woods won the Australian Masters for his seventh victory of the year. It was the eighty-second time worldwide in his career. Woods now has a win from every continent where golf is played (no golf is played in Antarctia).

Woods has successfully defended a title twenty times on the P.G.A. Tour, has finished runner-up twenty-three times, has placed third seventeen times, and has won 28 percent (61 out of 216) of his professional starts on the P.G.A. Tour.

He has a 31-6 record when leading after thirty-six holes in Tour events, and a 42-4 record when leading after fifty-four holes. Up until the 2009 P.G.A. Championship Woods was 14-0 when going into the final round of a Major with at least a share of the lead. He lost that perfect record when he finished second by three shots to Y.E. Yang in the P.G.A. Championship after holding a two-shot lead at the fifty-four-hole mark. Until the 2010 Chevron World Challenge, he had never lost any tournament when leading by at least three shots going into the final round. This record of accomplishments has earned him the accolade of "the greatest closer in golf history." It goes without saying that Tiger owns the lowest career scoring average and the most career earnings of any P.G.A. professional, topping $100 million in that category.

Woods has amassed an ever-growing list of further accomplishments. He has been the PGA Tour money winner nine times (breaking the record he shared with Jack Nicklaus), the P.G.A. Player of the Year a record nine times, the Vardon Trophy winner a record seven times, and the Byron Nelson Trophy winner a record eight times.

Tiger is one of five players (along with Gene Sarazen, Ben Hogan, Jack Nicklaus, and Gary Player) to have won all four professional Majors in his career, known as the "Career Grand Slam," and is the youngest to do so. He and Jack Nicklaus have accomplished this feat three times. Bobby Jones won all four of what in his era were considered Major championships (U.S. and British Amateurs and Opens)—winning all four in 1930 to become and remain the only golfer to capture the Grand Slam.

Woods holds at least a share of the scoring record in relation to par in all four Majors and also holds the margin of victory record in The Masters and the U.S. Open.

At the 2003 Tour Championship Tiger set the all-time record for most consecutive cuts made, starting in 1998 with 114. Byron Nelson held the previous record of 113. Woods extended this mark to 142 before it ended in May 2005, at the EDS Byron Nelson Championship. This is considered one of his most remarkable accomplishments, given the margin by which he broke the old record, given that he was playing against stronger fields than in Nelson's day, and given that, during his streak, the next longest streak by any other player was usually only in the 10's or 20's.

It also cannot go without mention that Woods won the first and third playings of the FedEx Cup in 2007 and 2009—now the Tour-ending Championship.

With his usual modesty Woods attributes much of his success to his longtime caddy and friend, New Zealander Steve Williams, who had caddied for him until 2011. Before that his caddy was veteran Mike "Fluff" Cowan.

On April 15, 2008 Woods underwent arthroscopic surgery on his left knee to repair cartilage damage. He had previously had procedures on the same knee in 1994 and 2002. Woods returned to the Tour at the U.S. Open held at Torrey Pines in San Diego, California. Despite soreness in his knee, he managed to force an eighteen-hole playoff with Rocco Mediate when he sank a twelve-foot birdie on the seventy-second hole. The next day the two were still tied after eighteen holes. On the first sudden death hole Woods's par gave him his third U.S. Open and his fourteenth Major overall. By winning his third U.S. Open Woods had now accomplished the career Grand Slam three times.

Immediately after the U.S. Open it was announced that Woods was finished playing golf for the rest of 2008 because of a torn anterior cruciate ligament in his left knee. He had also sustained two recent stress fractures to his left tibia. This meant that he would miss the British Open and the P.G.A. Championship and that he would not be available for the 2008 Ryder Cup. On June 24, 2008, Woods underwent surgery to repair the ligament.

He returned to action in late February 2009 at the Accenture Match Play Championships and was beaten in the second round. After playing in one more event his comeback was complete when he won the Arnold Palmer Invitational in late March 2009 with a seventy-second hole birdie.

At the 2010 Masters Tournament, he finished in a tie for fourth place. He followed the Master with a poor showing at the Quail Hollow Championship and the Players Championship, where he withdrew in the fourth round citing injury. Shortly afterward, Hank Haney, Wood's coach since 2003, resigned the position; he was replaced in August by Sean Foley. The rest of the season went badly for Woods, who failed to win a single event for the first time since turning professional while nevertheless finishing the season ranked No. 2 in the world.

Woods' performance continued to suffer in 2011, taking a toll in his ranking. After falling to No. 7 in March, he rebounded to No. 5 with a strong showing at the 2011 Masters where he tield for fourth place. Due to injuries incurred at the Masters he missed several summer events; in July he fired his longtime caddy Steve Williams, replacing him temporarily with friend Byron Bell. After returning to tournament play in August, Woods continued to falter and his ranking gradually fell to as low of No. 58. He rose to No. 50 in mid-November after a third-place finish at the Emirates Australian Open, and broke his winless finish streak with a victory in Decembers Chevron World Challenge

Woods began his 2012 western swing season with two tournaments. At the first, the AT&T Pebble National Pro Am, Woods started off well but struggled on the final round. Following the WGC-Accenture Match Play championship where he was knocked out in the second round by missing a 5-foot putt, putting technique proving his undoing and he tied for second place at the Honda Classic. After a short time off due to another leg injury,

Woods won the Arnold Palmer Invitational, his first win on the P.G.A. Tour since the BMW Championship in September 2009. Woods notched his 73rd P.G.A. win at the Memorial Tournament in June, tying Jack Nicklaus' record for most P.G.A. Tour victories. A month later, Woods surpassed Nicklaus's record with a win at the AT&T National.

2013 would bring a return to Woods' dominating play. He won the Farmers Insurance in January 2013 by four shots for his 75th P.G.A. Tour win. In March, he won the WGC-Cadillac Championship, giving him his 17th WGC title and first since 2009. Two weeks later, he won the Arnold Palmer Invitational, winning the event for a record-tying 8th time (tying Sam Snead, who accomplished his feat at the Greater Geensboro Open). The win moved him back on top of the world rankings.

In the 2013 Masters Tournament, Woods tied for fourth in the event. In May 2013, Woods won the Players Championship, his second ccareer win in the event, notching his fourth win of the 2013 season. It was the quickest he had ever gotten to four wins in any season in his professional career.

At the 2103 U.S. U.S. Open he finished 12 strokes behind winner, Justin Rose. After a prolonged break because of injury, he missed the Greenbrier Classic and his own AT&T National, but returned at the British Open Championship. He finished in sixth place, five shots behind winner, Phil Mickelson. Two weeks later Woods returned to form at the WGC-Bridgestone Invitational. Recording his fifth victory of the season. Woods would never contend at the P.G.A. Championship and would come up short of winning a Major for the fifth full season, only contending in two of the four Majors in 2013.

After a slow start in 2014, Woods injured himself during the Honda Classic and was unable to finish. He subsequently competed in the WGC Cadillac championship but was visibly in pain during the final round, citing back pain. On April 2 he announced that he would miss the Masters Tournament for the first time after undergoing a microdisectomy. Woods competed in the Open Championship and finished 69th. Despite his back pain, Woods played at the 2014 P.G.A. Championship where he failed to make the cut. He cut ties with his swing coach, Sean Foley and his new coach is Chris Como.

Outside of golf Woods has established several youth and charitable projects. The Tiger Woods Foundation was established in 1996. It focuses on projects for children. These projects include golf clinics and a grant program. Now these projects also include the Tiger Woods Learning Center and the Start Something character-development program. Most recently the Foundation has linked up with the P.G.A. Tour to create a new invitational P.G.A. Tour event involving AT&T in the Washington D.C. area, with a significant portion of the revenues going to charity.

Since 1997 the Tiger Woods Foundation has conducted junior golf clinics across the country. The Foundation began the "In the City" golf program in 2003, targeting youth ages 7-17 and their families. These tournaments for youth are three-day events that feature golf lessons on Thursdays and Fridays, with a community festival on Saturdays.

The Tiger Woods Learning Center is a 35,000-square-foot educational facility in Anaheim, California, which opened in February 2006. It is being used by several thousand students each year, with a day program for grades four to six, and an after-school program for grades seven to twelve. The Center features extensive multi-media facilities and an outdoor golf teaching area.

The Tiger Jam is an annual fundraising concert that has raised over $10 million for the Tiger Woods Foundation. The 2009 Tiger Jam featured the group No Doubt. And there was no doubt that in 2009 Woods had recovered from his 2008 knee surgery. Other past performers include Sting, Bon Jovi, and Stevie Wonder.

Other charitable activities include the Target World Challenge (a charity golf event) and the Tiger Woods Foundation National Junior Golf Team (an eighteen-member team that competes in the annual World Golf Championships).

Woods made a major announcement relating to his off-course activities when he announced the commencement of his golf course design career in December 2006. He is developing his first golf course in the United Arab Emirates. The Tiger Woods Dubai will feature a 7700-yard par-72 course named Al Ruwaya (meaning "serenity"). Also included will be a golf academy, homes and a hotel with eighty suites. In August 2007 Woods announced his first course design in the United States, The Cliffs at High Carolina, which is located in the Blue Ridge Mountains near Asheville, North Carolina. In 2008 Woods began work on his third golf course called Punta Brava, an oceanfront course in Ensenada, Mexico. In November 2010, construction of the Cliffs was put on hold until 2013 at the earliest. In February 2011, it was announced that work on the Tiger Woods Dubai has been suspended because of a drop in demand for luxury properties.

Aside from his winnings on the golf course, Woods has been called the world's most marketable athlete. Shortly after he turned professional Tiger signed numerous endorsement deals with companies that included Nike, Titleist, General Motors, American Express, Accenture and General Mills. Later, he added AT&T, EA Sports, Gatorade, Gillette, Net Jets, TAG Heuer, TLC Laser Eye and Upper Deck. Because of his admission of marital infidelity, however, many of these sponsors have either severed their relationship with Woods or cut back on their use of Woods in their promotions and advertisements. No doubt, these actions have had a significant negative impact on the value of Woods's endorsement pacts. Only time will tell the long-range implications of this fall-out.

In 2000 Woods renewed his contract with Nike for another five years at around $105 million dollars. In February 2004 he renewed his endorsement contract with Buick for another five years at a reported $40 million. Due to financial difficulties, however, Buick announced in November 2008 that it would not be renewing its contract with Woods. However, as of 2010 Nike has stood behind Woods despite his personal problems.

The ultimate impact Woods will have on the game of golf is not yet in the books. However, there is every reason to believe that he is on the cusp of going down as the greatest golfer who ever played the game. The one "Major" goal he is still in pursuit of is the number of Majors won in a career. Since he has fourteen Majors as of the 2015 Open Championship and is 39 years old, the odds are decreasing that he will ever catch Jack Nicklaus, who ended his career with eighteen Majors.

With his ability to drive up television ratings and attract crowds to events, there has been an unprecedented surge in tournament prize money for which the other players must owe Tiger a debt of gratitude. Also his endorsement deals have had a positive impact on the deals that the other players can attract.

For now golf enthusiasts can enjoy and marvel at the talents that the incredible Tiger Woods brings to all aspects of the game of golf. Only his personal issues mar the image of Tiger Woods.

The year 2011 showed some indication of Woods's comeback. At the Presidents Cup, he clinched the U.S. victory with the winning point in singles. At the December 2011 Chevron World Challenge which he hosts, Woods defeated Zack Johnson by a stroke to capture his first win in over two and a half years.

Woods ended a thirty-month victory drought when he won the Arnold Palmer Invitation for the seventh time in March 2012. It was his seventy-second career P.G.A. title, leaving him one behind Jack Nicklaus. After winning the 2012 Memorial, he tied Jack Nicklaus with seventy-three Tour victories, both behind Sam Snead who won eighty-two times. Two months later, he won the AT & T National which was his 74th P.G.A. Tour victory. This moved him past Jack Nicklaus into second place on the P.G.A. Tour, eight short of Sam Snead's record eighty-two victory. In 2013, Woods won his seventy-fifth P.G.A. Tour title when he won the Farmers Insurance Open.

Tiger showed he has regained his top form when he won the Arnold Palmer Invitational in March 2013 and regained his world's number one ranking. In August 2013, Woods won the World Golf Championship Bridgestone Invitational, matching his eight at the Arnold Palmer Invitational, and tying Sam Snead for the most victories at a single event (Greater Greensboro Open). He also tied the record for most times (eight) winning the same tournament. He is now tied with Sam Snead who won the Greater Greensboro Open eight times. This was Woods' 79th P.G.A. Tour win, second only to Sam Snead (82).

Stepping forward to 2015, Woods got off to inaspicious start, missing the cut at the Waste Management Phoenix Open and withdrawing from the Farmers Insurance Open with a bad back. He returned to the P.G.A. tour for the Masters where he tied for seventeenth. At the 2015 U.S. Open and 2015 P.G.A. Championship he failed to make the cut.

Annika Sörenstam

Women of the 1980s, 1990s, and 2000s

61

Three Generations of Women During the 1980s, 1990s, and 2000s
Betsy King, Amy Alcott, Patty Sheehan,
Beth Daniel, Julie Inkster, Laura Davies

The 1980s, 1990s and the first years of the twenty-first century have seen a cavalcade of women golfers make their mark on the game. Due to their talents, the L.P.G.A. and the women's game are enjoying success. Some women who have made significant contributions during those years have already been noted: Kathy Whitworth, Nancy Lopez, Pat Bradley, and Joanne Gunderson Carner. A brief look at some of the other important women golfers who have made, or are continuing to make, a significant contribution to the game is in order.

Betsy King
Betsy King was born on August 13, 1955 in Reading, Pennsylvania.

King was the leading money winner on the L.P.G.A. Tour in 1984, 1989, and 1993. She finished in the top ten on the money list every year from 1984 to 1995, and again in 1997.

She won thirty-four titles in her career, including six Major championships: the 1987 Nabisco Dinah Shore, the 1989 U.S. Women's Open, the 1990 Nabisco Dinah Shore, the 1990 U.S. Women's Open, the 1992 L.P.G.A. Championship, and the 1997 Nabisco Dinah Shore. King also won the British Women's Open in 1985 before it became a Major championship in 2001.

Betsy King

King played for the United States in the Solheim Cup five times and was the captain of the 2007 team. She led the 2007 team to a 16-12 win at the Solheim Cup over Europe held in Halmstad, Sweden, in September 2007.

King was inducted into the World Golf Hall of Fame in 1995.

Amy Alcott

Amy Alcott was born on February 22, 1956 in Kansas City, Missouri. She first became known on the national scene when she won the U.S. Junior Girls' Amateur in 1973. At the age of nineteen she turned professional and won the Orange Blossom Classic in her third start. That year she was named Rookie of the Year.

Alcott counts five Majors among her twenty-nine titles. Her Majors were the 1979 du Maurier Classic, the 1980 U.S. Open, and the Kraft Nabisco Championships in 1983, 1988, and 1991. Alcott finished in the top ten on the money list eleven times between 1976 and 1988. She was inducted into the World Golf Hall of Fame in 1999.

Patty Sheehan

Patty Sheehan was born on October 27, 1956 in Middlebury, Vermont. She attended the University of Nevada and San Jose State University. She joined the L.P.G.A. Tour in 1980. Over the course of her career, Sheehan won thirty-five tournaments, including six Major championships. Her Majors were the 1983 and 1984 L.P.G.A. Championships, the 1992 U.S. Women's Open, the 1993 L.P.G.A. Championship, the 1994 U.S. Women's Open and the 1996 Kraft Nabisco Championship.

Sheehan finished in the top ten on the money list every year from 1982 to 1993. She played for the U.S. team in four Solheim Cups, and captained the 2002 and 2003 U.S. Solheim teams. Sheehan was inducted into the World Golf Hall of Fame in 1993.

Beth Daniel

Beth Daniel

Beth Daniel was born on October 14, 1956, in Charleston, South Carolina. Among her amateur accomplishments, Daniel won the 1975 and 1977 U.S. Women's Amateur. After turning professional she was the leading money winner on the L.P.G.A. Tour in 1980, 1981 and 1990 and finished in the top ten on the money list twelve times between 1980 and 2003.

Daniel won thirty-three titles on the L.P.G.A. Tour including one Major at the 1990 L.P.G.A. McDonald's Championship. She played on eight Solheim Cup teams: 1990, 1992, 1994, 1996, 2000, 2002, 2003, and 2005. She was assistant captain of the 2007 Solheim Cup team that beat the Europeans 16-12. She was the captain of the victorious U.S. team in the 2009 Solheim Cup. In 1990 Daniel was named the Associated Press Female Athlete of the Year. She was inducted into the World Golf Hall of Fame in 2000.

Currently, Daniel works part-time as an analyst for the Golf Channel.

Julie Inkster

Julie Inkster (born Julie Simpson) was born on June 24, 1960, in Santa Cruz, California. She attended San Jose State University, where she was an all-American in 1979, 1981 and 1982. Inkster won three consecutive U.S. Women's Amateurs from 1980 to 1982, and was a member of the winning U.S. Curtis Cup team in 1982.

Inkster has won thirty-one L.P.G.A. Tour events including seven Major championships. Her Majors victories are the 1984 Kraft Nabisco Championship, the 1984 du Marier Classic, the 1989 Kraft Nabisco Championship, the 1999 L.P.G.A. McDonald's Championship, the 1999 U.S. Women's Open, the

Julie Inkster

Laura Davies

2000 L.P.G.A. McDonald's Championship and the 2002 U.S. Women's Open. Inkster is currently third on the career money list. She won a tournament in sixteen out of twenty-four seasons from 1983 to 2006.

Inkster played on the United States Solheim team in 1992, 1998, 2000, 2002, 2003, 2005, 2007, and 2009. She was inducted into the World Golf Hall of Fame in 2000.

Laura Davies

Laura Davies was born on October 5, 1963 in Coventry, England. She is acclaimed as the most accomplished English female golfer in the modern era. She currently has eighty-four professional wins worldwide with twenty of them coming on the L.P.G.A. Tour including four Majors: the 1987 U.S. Women's Open, the 1994 L.P.G.A. McDonald's Championship, the 1996 L.P.G.A. Championship and the 1996 du Marier Classic.

As an amateur Davies was a notable international player for England. She was a member of the Great Britain and Ireland Curtis Cup team in 1984. She turned professional in 1985 when she won both Rookie of the Year and Order of Merit titles on the WPGET (now L.E.T.) tour. She repeated the Order of Merit win in 1986, having won four titles, with one of them being the British Women's Open before it became a Major in 2001. Since 1988, Davies has played on both the L.P.G.A. and L.E.T. Tours.

In 1990 she was a member of the inaugural European Solheim Cup Team. She was also a member of the victorious European squad in 1992. Davies is the only player to have participated in twelve of the thirteen Solheim Cup teams to date (1990–2011).

In 1994 she was the first golfer, male or female, to win on five different golf tours in one calendar year: U.S., Europe, Asia, Japan, and Australia.

Davies was elected to the World Golf Hall of Fame in October 2014.

In 2001 she joined the BBC Sport commentary team at the British Open and has appeared regularly as a commentator for major golf events on the BBC.

A Modern Women's
Great Triumvirate
Annika Sörenstam, Karrie Webb, Se Ri Pak

Annika Sörenstam

Annika Sörenstam was born on October 9, 1970, in Bro, near Stockholm, Sweden. She is one of the most successful female golfers in history.

Interestingly, her younger sister, Charlotta, is also a professional golfer. Annika and Charlotta are the only two sisters to have each won $1 million on the L.P.G.A. Tour.

In her youth Annika Sörenstam played competitive tennis, becoming a nationally ranked junior tennis player. At the age of twelve she switched to golf and shared her first set of golf clubs with her sister. Sörenstam had a successful junior career and, while awaiting college in Sweden, she worked as a personal assistant at the Swedish P.G.A. After a coach spotted Sörenstam playing in a collegiate event in Tokyo, she moved to the United States to attend college at the University of Arizona. Sörenstam won seven collegiate titles and in 1991 became the first non-American and the first freshman to win the individual N.C.A.A. Championship. At the 1992 U.S. Women's Amateur Championship she was the runner-up to Vicki Goetze. Sörenstam turned professional in 1992 but missed obtaining her L.P.G.A. Tour card at the L.P.G.A. Final Qualifying Tournament by one shot. So she began her professional career on the LET.

In 1993, Sörenstam finished second four times on the LET and was the Ladies European Tour Rookie of the Year. After tying for twenty-eighth at the L.P.G.A. Final Qualifying Tournament she earned non-exempt status for the 1994 L.P.G.A. season.

Sörenstam captured her first professional victory at the 1994 Holden Australian Open Championship. In the United States she was the 1994 L.P.G.A. Rookie of the Year, had three top-10 finishes, and made her Solheim Cup debut.

In 1995 Sörenstam had her breakout year when she won her first L.P.G.A. Tour title and her first Major. Both milestones came at the U.S. Women's Open. Sörenstam also finished at the top of the money list, was the first non-American winner of the Vare Trophy and was also named Player of the Year. Because of her win at the 1995 Australian Ladies Masters and two other wins on the LET Sörenstam finished atop the LET Order of Merit and became the first player to lead both the European and L.P.G.A. Tour money lists in the same season.

In 1996 Sörenstam won three L.P.G.A. tournaments, one of which was the U.S. Women's Open, her second Major. She became the first non-American to win back-to-back U.S. Women's Open titles. Sörenstam also passed the $1 million mark in L.P.G.A. career earnings and won her second consecutive Vare Trophy.

She won six L.P.G.A. titles in 1997. Sörenstam also won the money list title and was Player of the Year.

In 1998 she won her third Major at the du Marier Classic. Sörenstam retained the Player of the Year and money list titles, and became the first player in L.P.G.A. history to finish a season with a sub-70 scoring average (69.99).

In 1999 Sörenstam's play backed off somewhat and Australian Karrie Webb rose to become the best woman player that year. Nevertheless, Sörenstam had won more L.P.G.A. tournaments than any other Tour player during the 1990s.

Sörenstam qualified for the World Golf Hall of Fame when she won the 2000 Welch's Circle K Championship but was not eligible for induction until finishing her tenth year on the L.P.G.A. Tour in October 2003. She became the first international player to be inducted into the Hall of Fame through the L.P.G.A. point-system criteria.

The L.P.G.A. awards one point for every victory and major award, and two points for a Major victory. Players are eligible for the Hall of Fame when they reach 27 points which has since been modified to account for stellar play even though falling short of the numerical requirements.

Sörenstam re-energized her career in 2001 when she had eight L.P.G.A. wins and also became the only female golfer to shoot 59 in competition, which she accomplished at the Standard Register Ping tournament. Sörenstam won her fourth Major at the Kraft Nabisco Championship. She achieved another milestone when she became the first L.P.G.A. player to cross the $2 million mark in single-season earnings. She regained the Vare Trophy and won her fourth Player of the Year and money list titles. In a made-for-TV alternate shot competition, she and Tiger Woods beat the team of Karrie Webb and David Duval.

The year 2002 was another sensational year for Sörenstam. She matched Mickey Wright's record by winning eleven L.P.G.A. tournaments in a season and earned her fifth Player of the Year title and fifth Vare Trophy. Sörenstam successfully defended her Kraft Nabisco Championship, her fifth Major victory. For the year, Sörenstam won thirteen times in twenty-five starts worldwide.

In May 2003 she played in the men's Bank of America Colonial Golf Tournament, becoming the first woman to play in a P.G.A. Tour event since Babe Zaharias, who qualified for the 1945 Los Angeles Open. After shooting a one-over par 71 on the first day, Sörenstam missed the cut. Later in 2003 she won the McDonald's L.P.G.A. Championship (sixth Major) and the Women's British Open (seventh Major), becoming only the sixth player to complete the L.P.G.A. Career Grand Slam. Sörenstam earned her sixth Player of the Year award in 2003.

She continued her dominance in 2004 with her seventh L.P.G.A. Player of the Year award, tying Kathy Whitworth for the most Player of the Year awards in L.P.G.A. history. Sörenstam had sixteen top-ten finishes in eighteen L.P.G.A. starts, including eight wins, and in addition had two international wins. In 2004 Sörenstam became the first player to reach $15 million in L.P.G.A. career earnings and lowered her own L.P.G.A. single-season scoring average record to 68.69. However, she had played too few rounds that year to win the Vare Trophy. Sörenstam also won the L.P.G.A. McDonald's Championship for the second year in a row (eighth Major). She found time to write a combination autobiography and golf instructional book, *Golf Annika's Way*.

In 2005 Sörenstam won the Kraft Nabisco Championship for her ninth Major. She became the first player in L.P.G.A. history to win the same Major three years in succession, when she won the L.P.G.A. McDonald's Championship (tenth Major). Sörenstam also became the first player, male or female, to win the same event five consecutive years. She accomplished this at the Mizuno Classic. In 2005 Sörenstam also took home her eighth money list title (tying the L.P.G.A. record), a record eighth Player of the Year award and a sixth Vare Trophy. She is the only L.P.G.A. player ever to win the Money List, Player of the Year and Vare Trophy in the same year in five different years.

The year 2005 saw Sörenstam make her seventh consecutive Solheim Cup appearance. Her four points gave her a career total of 21 and made her the event's all-time leading points earner. For the third consecutive year, Sörenstam was voted the Associated Press Female Athlete of the Year.

When the first-ever official Women's World Golf Rankings were released in February 2006 she was confirmed as the number-one player in women's golf, a position she held until Lorena Ochoa succeeded her in April 2007.

At the 2006 U.S. Women's Open Sörenstam won an eighteen-hole play-off over Pat Hurst for her eleventh Major championship, placing her third in most Major championships all-time (Mickey Wright, thirteen; Patty Berg, fifteen).

At the 2007 Kraft Nabisco Championship Sörenstam shot the highest seventy-two-hole score in a Major in nine years, a result explained by her subsequent diagnosis with ruptured and bulging discs in her neck. After a two-month break for rehabilitation Sörenstam returned to the L.P.G.A. Tour. Her efforts to return to form came slowly. At the 2007 L.P.G.A. McDonald's Championship, she finished tied for fifteenth place, and at the U.S. Women's Open she finished tied for thirty-second as the defending champion.

Sörenstam did not win any events in 2007. This was the first time that she had failed to do so since her rookie season in 1994. Sörenstam made sure this would not be the case in 2008. She won the season-opening SBS Open in Kahuku, Hawaii, for her seventieth L.P.G.A. Tour title, and first since September 2006. She won again at the Stanford International Pro-Am. In early May she won the Michelob Ultra Open, defeating Paula Creamer in a play-off.

On May 14, 2008 Sörenstam announced that at the end of the 2008 season she would "step away" from professional golf to spend more time on her off-course activities and to start a family with her second marriage on the horizon. At the time of the announcement she had won eighty-eight tournaments around the world, including seventy-two on the L.P.G.A. Tour. Her last tournament was the ADT Championship in November 2008 where she failed to make the cut.

Sörenstam's off-course activities center on her passions for golf, fitness, and cooking, with various businesses under the ANNIKA brand. Her first golf course design project was the Annika Course at Mission Hills Golf Club in Hong Kong, which was completed in 2003. Sörenstam's second design project, launched in 2006 was at the Euphoria Golf Estate & Hydro in South Africa. In conjunction with her business partnership with Ginn Resorts, Sörenstam got involved in designing Patriots Point Links Course near Charleston, South Carolina, her first course design in the United States.

Sörenstam opened the ANNIKA Academy at Ginn Reunion Resort near Orlando, Florida in April 2007. In addition to golf instruction, there is an emphasis on overall fitness training, geared toward improving students' golf skills.

Currently, Sörenstam resides in Orlando, Florida. She married Mike McGee (her second marriage), managing director for the ANNIKA brand businesses, in January 2009. In March 2009 they announced that they were expecting their first child. Ava Madelyn McGee was born on September 1, 2009.

In November 2011, it was announced that Sörenstam will receive the U.S.G.A.'s 2012 Bob Jones Award presented in recognition of distinguished sportsmanship in golf.

Karrie Webb

Karrie Webb was born on December 21, 1974 in Ayr, Queensland, Australia. She turned professional in 1994, playing on the LET. Webb finished second at the Australian Ladies Open and won one tournament on the Futures Tour in the United States. In 1995 she became the youngest winner of the Women's British Open in her rookie season in Europe, before the event was classified as a Major. Webb was named European Rookie of the Year and qualified for the L.P.G.A. Tour when she finished second at the L.P.G.A. Final Qualifying Tournament.

In 1996 Webb won her first L.P.G.A. tournament in her second L.P.G.A. start. It was at the HealthSouth Inaugural on the fourth hole of a sudden-death play-off. That year she also won three other times and became the first L.P.G.A. player to win $1 million in a single season. She was also named the 1996 L.P.G.A. Tour Rookie of the Year.

Webb won three tournaments in 1997 on the L.P.G.A. Tour, including the Women's British Open, again before it was declared a Major. That year she also won her first Vare Trophy.

In 1998 she won twice, at the ANZ Australian Masters and the MBNA America Classic.

Webb won her first of seven Majors in 1999 when she captured the du

Karrie Webb

Maurier Classic. She capped off the year by winning her first L.P.G.A. Tour Player of the Year award.

The year 2000 was another great year, as Webb won two more Major championships. She followed her win at the Kraft Nabisco Championship with a victory at the U.S. Women's Open. This propelled her to her second consecutive Player of the Year title and the Vare Trophy.

Webb successfully defended her U.S. Women's Open title in 2001 and won the L.P.G.A. McDonald's Championship to become, at the age of twenty-five, the youngest winner of the L.P.G.A. Career Grand Slam.

The following year she won the 2002 Women's British Open, which had become a Major in 2001.

Webb then endured a three-year slump. She earned just two L.P.G.A. wins in the next two years. In 2005 she had a best L.P.G.A. Tour finish of tied for sixth. However, she did win her fifth ANZ Ladies Masters back home in Australia.

In 2000, at the age of twenty-five, Webb qualified to enter the World Golf Hall of Fame but was not eligible for induction until she had played ten L.P.G.A. Tour events in each of ten seasons. She met this criterion in June 2005. At the age of thirty-one she became the youngest living person to enter the World Golf Hall of Fame. She retained that distinction until 2007, when Hall of Famer Se Ri Pak completed her tenth year on the L.P.G.A. Tour at the age of twenty-nine.

Webb made a comeback in the 2006 season in spectacular fashion at the Kraft Nabisco Championship. She holed a 116-yard shot to eagle the eighteenth hole, and then birdied the same hole in a sudden-death play-off to beat Mexican star Lorena Ochoa. It was Webb's second Kraft Nabisco Championship and her seventh career Major.

She won four other tournaments in 2006 including the Evian Championship and Mizuno Classic. Her 2006 Kraft Nabisco win landed her in the top ten of the Women's World Golf Rankings for the first time since

Se Ri Pak

the rankings were introduced in February 2006. Webb has completed the L.P.G.A. career Grand Slam, joining a list that includes Mickey Wright, Louise Suggs, Pat Bradley, Julie Inkster, and Annika Sörenstam.

Webb's forty-one L.P.G.A. Tour victories places her tenth on the list of women golfers with the most career L.P.G.A. Tour victories. She adds to this list thirteen wins on the Australian Ladies Professional Golf Tour. She had her second child named Will, on March 21, 2011.

Se Ri Pak

Se Ri Pak was born on September 2, 1977, in Daejon, Korea. She turned professional in 1996. In her first two years as a professional, Pak won six tournaments on the Korean L.P.G.A. She joined the L.P.G.A. Tour full-time for the 1998 season and immediately made her mark with victories in two Majors, the L.P.G.A. McDonald's Classic and the U.S. Women's Open. She was a shoo-in for Rookie of the Year honors.

Pak has gone on to win twenty-five L.P.G.A. Tour events including three more Majors: the Women's British Open in 2001 and the L.P.G.A. McDonald's Classic in 2002 and 2006. She also won the Vare Trophy in 2003.

In June 2007 she qualified for the World Golf Hall of Fame, surpassing Karrie Webb for the honor of being the youngest living entrant ever.

Pak went through a dry spell in 2004-2005, but regained her form when she won the 2006 L.P.G.A. McDonald's Classic for the third time, reaching her current mark of five Majors.

In 2007 she won the Jamie Farr Owens Corning Classic for the fifth time. This accomplishment made her only the third player in L.P.G.A. history to win the same tournament five or more times.

Pak currently resides in Orlando, Florida.

Sörenstam, Webb and Pak are on a list that includes other women who have performed well in Major championships. Sörenstam and Webb join Pat Bradley, Julie Inkster, Mickey Wright and Louise Suggs as female golfers who have accomplished a career Grand Slam. Pak needs only to win the Kraft Nabisco to join this group.

63

The Ladies' New Blood
of the New Millennium

Lorena Ochoa, Cristie Kerr, Natalie Gulbis,
Paula Creamer, Morgan Pressel, Michelle Wie

The new millennium saw a group of young American female golfers appear on the scene to challenge the "old" guard of Sörenstam–Webb–Pak. There is also a star player from Mexico who, turned out to be the world's best in the 2000s. Her name is Lorena Ochoa.

Lorena Ochoa

Lorena Ochoa was born on November 15, 1981, in Guadalajara, Jalisco, Mexico. In 2007 she rose to be the number-one ranked woman player in the world. As one of the L.P.G.A.'s elite players, she was the first Mexican golfer of either gender to be ranked number one in the world.

Ochoa grew up next door to the Guadalajara Country Club and began playing golf at the age of five. As a junior golfer, she captured twenty-two state events in Guadalajara and forty-four national titles in Mexico. She won five consecutive titles at the Junior World Golf Championships. In 2000 she enrolled at the University of Arizona and was very successful for the next two years. She won the N.C.A.A. Player of the Year Awards for 2001 and 2002, finishing runner-up at both the 2001 and 2002 N.C.A.A. National Championships. In her sophomore year she won eight times in ten events and set an N.C.A.A. record with seven consecutive victories in her first seven events. She set the single-season N.C.A.A. scoring average as a

Lorena Ochoa

freshman at 71.33 and broke her own record as a sophomore with a 70.13 average.

After her sophomore year in 2002 Ochoa turned professional. She qualified for the L.P.G.A. Tour in 2003. In her rookie season she had eight top-ten finishes and was named Rookie of the Year. In 2004 she won her first two L.P.G.A. Tour titles: the Franklin American Mortgage Championship (where she became the first Mexican-born player to win on the L.P.G.A. Tour) and the Wachovia L.P.G.A. Classic. In 2005 she won the Wegman's Rochester L.P.G.A. In 2006 she carded a 62 in the Kraft Nabisco Championship, tying the record for lowest score by a golfer, male or female, in any Major tournament. She lost in a play-off to Karrie Webb, but it was her best finish in a Major until 2007. She won six tournaments in 2006, topped the money list and claimed her first L.P.G.A. Player of the Year award. She also won the Vare Trophy for lowest scoring average. She was named the 2006 Associated Press Female Athlete of the Year.

In April 2007 Ochoa passed Annika Sörenstam as the World's number-one ranked woman golfer.

In August 2007 Ochoa won her first Major, the Women's British Open at the Old Course at St. Andrews. She followed that with victories in the next two events, the CN Canadian Women's Open and the Safeway Classic, to become the first woman to win three consecutive events since Annika Sörenstam in 2005. The year 2007 also saw her become the first woman golfer to earn more than $4,000,000 in a single season when she won $4,364,994. This total easily broke Sörenstam's previous record of $2,863,904. Ochoa won eight times in 2007 and has twenty-seven career L.P.G.A. victories. Her eighteenth career victory was a Major —the 2008 Kraft Nabisco Championship in which she defeated Annika Sörenstam by five shots. In 2008 she won six other times including a streak of four straight. In 2009 she won three times.

Ochoa qualified for the L.P.G.A. Hall of Fame in April 2008 by winning the Corona Championship in Morella, Mexico. The Mexican star became the second-youngest to qualify for the Hall of Fame, although she had to be

Christie Kerr

a tour member for ten years—in her case, until 2012—to be eligible for induction. Ochoa qualified at twenty-six years, four months, twenty-nine days. Previously the youngest to qualify was Se Ri Pak.

On April 10, 2010 Ochoa announced that she would retire from professional golf. In October 2010 she won the 2010 Bob Jones Award for distinguished sportsmanship. She married Andrés Conesa Labastida, CEO of Aeroméxico in December 2009.

Ochoa had her first child, Pedro, on December 8. 2011

Cristie Kerr

Cristie Kerr was born on October 12, 1977, in Miami, Florida. Kerr started playing golf when she was eight years old. She had a successful amateur career, capped off in 1996 when she played in the Curtis Cup and was low amateur at the U.S. Women's Open. Kerr turned professional in 1996.

Late that year she tied for sixth place at the L.P.G.A. Final Qualifying Tournament to gain exempt status for 1997. Kerr won her first tournament, the Longs Drugs Challenge, in 2002. By 2004, she was one of the leading players on the L.P.G.A. Tour with three victories and a fifth place on the money list. Kerr won two tournaments in 2005. On the Majors front she tied for second at the 2000 U.S. Women's Open and at the 2006 Women's British Open.

Kerr's first win in 2006 came at the Franklin American Mortgage Championship. She went on to win two more times that year.

Kerr has won two Majors. Her first was the 2007 U.S. Women's Open. Her second came at the 2010 L.P.G.A. Championship, which she won by a lopsided twelve strokes. This victory resulted in her becoming the first American to attain the status of number one woman golfer in the world since the current system was instiued in 2006. Kerr now has seventeen L.P.G.A. victories.

She was also a member of the U.S. Solheim Cup team in 2002, 2003, 2005, 2007, 2009 and 2013.

Kerr is actively involved in fundraising for breast cancer research. In

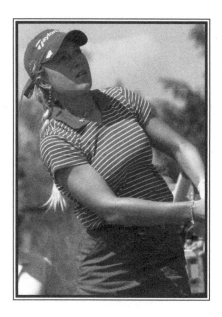

Natalie Gulbis

2006, she was awarded the L.P.G.A. Komen Award for her dedication to find a cure for breast cancer through her foundation called Birdies for Breast Cancer.

Kerr maintains residences in Scottsdale, Arizona, and New York City, New York.

Natalie Gulbis

Natalie Gulbis was born on January 7, 1983, in Sacramento, California.

She played in her first L.P.G.A. Tour event as an amateur at the age of fourteen. Gulbis turned professional in 2001 when she was eighteen years old after playing for one season on the women's golf team at the University of Arizona.

During her first five years on the L.P.G.A. Tour she did not win a tournament. However, her consistent level of play led to her finishing sixth on the L.P.G.A. money list in 2005 with over $1 million in prize money. That year she also played on the winning U.S. Solheim Cup team.

Her superb play continued in the Majors. She placed in the top-ten in four consecutive Majors from the 2005 L.P.G.A. McDonald's Championship to the 2006 Kraft Nabisco Championship. Gulbis broke through for her first professional win at the 2007 Evian Masters in France (an L.P.G.A.-sanctioned event), where she defeated Jeong Jang in a play-off to take home $3,000,000. With its lucrative purse the Evian Championship annually attracts a strong field. It is now a Womens Major

Gulbis has been a member of the winning U.S. Solheim Cup teams in 2005, 2007, and 2009.

With her comely looks and engaging personality, Natalie is considered a lovely ambassador for the L.P.G.A. Tour. However, when a calendar featured Gulbis in different pictures playing golf and in striking poses in swimwear, the U.S.G.A. barred the calandar from being sold at the 2004 U.S. Women's Open. Many criticized the U.S.G.A. for overreacting. Gulbis has not been shy about expressing her delight at the attention she gets. Others applaud her as being an ambassador who has brought only positive publicity for the L.P.G.A. Tour.

Paula Creamer

Based on her beauty, her win at the Evian Masters and her off-course business interests, Gulbis is certainly a marquee player on the L.P.G.A. Tour. She currently resides in Las Vegas, Nevada.

Paula Creamer

Paula Creamer was born on August 5, 1986, in Mountain View, California. She won nineteen amateur national titles and was a semi-finalist in the 2003 U.S. Women's Amateur Championship at the age of sixteen. She reached the semi-finals of the Amateur again in 2004. Also in 2004, she tied for thirteenth in the U.S. Women's Open, represented the United States in the Curtis Cup and placed second in the ShopRite L.P.G.A. Classic.

Creamer won the 2004 L.P.G.A. Tour Qualifying School by five shots and turned professional in 2005.

In May 2005 she won the Sybase Classic at the age of eighteen years, nine months, seventeen days. This made her the second-youngest first-time winner of an L.P.G.A. tournament after Marlene Bauer-Hagge, whose first victory was in 1952 at the age of eighteen years, fourteen days. However, Creamer was the youngest winner of a 72-hole event until sixteen-year Lexi Thompson won the 2011 Navistar Classic at the age of sixteen in September 2011. Thompson's record was then broken by fifteen-old amateur Lydia Ko, who won the Canadian Women's Open in August 2012.

In July 2005 she added a win in the Evian Masters tournament in France and became the youngest and quickest player to reach $1 million in L.P.G.A. career earnings. She also had two victories on the L.P.G.A. of Japan Tour in 2005. Creamer was named the 2005 L.P.G.A. Rookie of the Year.

Creamer's third L.P.G.A. victory came in February 2007, when she won at the SBS Open. Creamer won three times in 2008.

She reached the pinnacle of her career to date when she won the 2010 U.S. Women's Open at Oakmont Country Club outside of Pittsburgh. This triumph was even more remarkable since she was coming off major surgery to her right thumb earlier in 2010. Including her U.S. Women's Open

Morgan Pressell

victory, Creamer has ten L.P.G.A. victories.

She was a member of the 2005, 2007, and 2009 Solheim Cup teams.

Because of her fondness for wearing the color pink, Creamer has earned the nickname "the Pink Panther." Her golf clubs have pink grips, her golf bag is pink with a Pink Panther head cover for her driver, and she has been known to use a pink golf ball during the last round of a tournament. With her colorful and excellent play, Creamer has been in the forefront of the of U.S. stars on the L.P.G.A. Tour. She currently resides in Orlando, Florida.

Morgan Pressel

Morgan Pressel was born on May 23, 1988, in Tampa, Florida. After her mother died of breast cancer in September 2003, she moved in with her grandparents, Shirley and Dr. Herb Krickstein. They are the parents of former top-ten tennis player Aaron Krickstein, Pressel's uncle.

As a twelve-year-old in 2001, she became the youngest player to qualify for the U.S. Women's Open. This record stood until 2007 when Alexis Thompson, another twelve-year-old, beat Pressel's record by several months.

In 2005, at the age of seventeen, Pressel was tied for the U.S. Women's Open lead as she stood in the eighteenth fairway in the final round. Up ahead, Birdie Kim holed out from the bunker to win the U.S. Women's Open. Pressel's second-place finish gave her a share of the low amateur honors with Brittany Lang.

Pressel'a one crowning achievement in 2005 was her win at the U.S. Women's Amateur.

Pressel turned professional in January 2006 after successfully appealing to the L.P.G.A. to become a member as a seventeen-year-old. An appeal was necessary because L.P.G.A. rules state that members must be at least eighteen years old. Until her graduation from high school in May 2006, Pressel played part-time on the L.P.G.A. Tour.

Michelle Wie

The year 2007 was a memorable one for Pressel as she earned her first professional victory and it was in a Major, the Kraft Nabisco Championship. She became the youngest winner of an L.P.G.A. Major at eighteen years, ten months, eight days.

Pressel played on the victorious U.S. Solheim Cup teams in 2007 and 2009.

Her second L.P.G.A. victory came at the Kapalua L.P.G.A. Classic in October 2008.

She resides in Boca Raton, Florida.

Michelle Wie

Michelle Wie was born in Honolulu, Hawaii, on October 11, 1989. Until 2009 she had been the product of mostly unfulfilled promise since, at the age of eleven in 2000, she qualified for the U.S. Women's Amateur Public Links Championship and advanced to match play. She became the youngest player to compete in a U.S.G.A. women's amateur competition.

In 2002 Wie became the youngest player to qualify for an L.P.G.A. event, the Takefuji Classic, where she missed the cut. The record stood until 2007 when it was broken by eleven-year old Ariya Jutanugarn.

In 2003 Wie became the youngest player to make a cut in an L.P.G.A. event at the Kraft Nabisco Championship. A few months later, she earned an historic victory at the U.S. Women's Amateur Public Links, becoming the youngest person, male or female, to win a U.S.G.A. adult event.

In 2004 Wie became the youngest female to play in a P.G.A. Tour event at the Sony Open. She missed the cut by one stroke. That year she became the youngest woman to play on a U.S. Curtis Cup team.

In 2005 Wie again played in the P.G.A. Tour Sony Open, where she also missed the cut. That June she placed second at the L.P.G.A. McDonald's Championship. Later that year she played in the P.G.A. John Deere Classic in her third attempt to make the cut at a P.G.A. Tour event. She missed the cut by two strokes.

In October 2005, a week before her sixteenth birthday, Wie turned

professional. Her first professional event was the Samsung World Championship. She was disqualified for signing an incorrect scorecard after she
had inadvertenly dropped a ball closer to a hole than its original lie during
the third round.

In 2006 Wie played at the P.G.A. Tour Sony Open and missed the cut
by four strokes. On the L.P.G.A. Tour she finished in a tie for third in the
Kraft Nabisco Championship. In May Wie was the first female medalist in
a local qualifier for the Men's U.S. Open but did not advance to the final
stage. In June Wie tied for fifth in the L.P.G.A. McDonald's Championship
and tied for third in the U.S. Women's Open.

By the end of 2006, her first full year as a professional, Wie had missed
the cut in eleven out of twelve tries against men, and remained winless in
all thirty-three professional women's tournament she had entered.

In 2007 Wie reportedly incurred injuries to both of her wrists and undertook a four-month absence from competition. Her return was marked by
controversy.

Playing in the 2007 Ginn Tribute hosted by Annika Sörenstam, Wie
shot a 14-over par through sixteen holes in the first round before withdrawing. At that time she was in danger of running afoul of the Rule of 88,
which states that a non-L.P.G.A. member (which Wie was at the time), who
shoots a score of 88 or worse is forced to withdraw and is subsequently
banned from L.P.G.A. events for the remainder of the year. There was some
controversy as to whether Wie withdrew because of the possible infraction
of the Rule of 88 or because of her wrist ailments.

The next week at the 2007 L.P.G.A. McDonald's Championship Wie
made the cut but finished last of those who did so. In June at the 2007 U.S.
Women's Open Wie withdrew midway through the second round while at
seventeen-over par.

At the 2007 Women's British Open, she missed the cut by two strokes.
It was her first missed cut in a Major. She also missed the cut at the Canadian Women's Open and the Safeway Classic, and she finished nineteenth
out of twenty players in the Samsung World Championship. Three weeks
later she began her freshman year at Stanford University.

Wie's difficulties continued in 2008. After playing poorly for the first
half of the year, she had another sloppy incident at L.P.G.A. State Farm Classic. She was playing her best golf of the year and was one stroke off the lead
going into the final round. When she finished her third round, rules offi-

cials informed her that she was being disqualified for failing to sign her scorecard after the second round.

Up until 2009 Wie's professional career was marked by criticism. She was criticized for playing in P.G.A. Tour events when she has not won on the L.P.G.A. Tour. Her penchant for withdrawing from events had also been looked upon disapprovingly. Finally, her ever-present, and some would say overbearing, parents had not endeared her to players and the public.

While Wie had shown sparks of excellence during her amateur and professional careers, she continued to remain a controversial subject until 2009.

On November 15, 2009 Wie won her first professional individual tournament, the Orena Ochoa Invitational in Guadalajara, Mexico, a limited field on the L.P.G.A. Tour, posting a score of thirteen under par 275 for a two-stroke margin over Paula Creamer.

On April 19, 2014, Wie won her third L.P.G.A., the L.P.G.A. Lotte Championship. She won by two strokes over Angela Standford,

She graduated from Stanford University in 2012, and makes her home in Jupiter, Florida. Significantly, Wie earned her first Major in 2014, at the U.S. Women's Open at Pinehurst. She finished at two-under for a two-shot victory, but she had to earn it. Indeed, Wie held a three-shot lead over Stacy Lewis with only three holes left, but made a sloppy double-bogey on No. 16. With only a one-stroke lead, Wie sank a fast, tricky 25-foot birdie putt on No. 17 to provide a cushion for the last hole.

Bubba Watson winner of the 2012 and 2014 Masters.

SECTION 11

2011 and Beyond

64

The Rise of the Asian Women

The Decades of the 1990's and 2000's have seen the phenomenal growth of talent and results of and by women golfers from Asian Countries. They were inspired by none other than South Korean Si Re Pak. Pak joined the L.P.G.A. Tour in 1998, and in her rookie year won the McDonald's L.P.G.A. Championship and the U.S. Womens' Open. She later won the McDonald's two other times. She won the Women's British Open in 2001. These five Major victories propelled her into the World Golf Hall of Fame in 2007 at the age of 29, making her the youngest living entrant voted into that Hall.

Yani Tseng

Yani Tseng was the top-ranked amateur in Taiwan from 2004 to 2006 Her amateur highlight was beating Michelle Wie in the final one up in the 2004 U.S. Women's Amateur Public Links.

She turned professional in January 2007. In 2008 she claimed her first L.P.G.A. Tour victory at the L.P.G.A. Championship to become the first player from Taiwan to win an L.P.G.A. Major championship. In 2010, Tseng won the Kraft Nabisco (and third overall) Championship, her second Major. She went on to win her third Major of the year in August 2010 by winning the Women's British Open, and became the youngest woman in the modern era to win three Major championships.

In 2011 she assumed the number one position in the Women's World Golf Ranking. That year she won the L.P.G.A. Championship for the second time. That same year she defended her title in the Women's British Open, giving her five Major championships.

In 2012 she won three tournaments, but did not win any events in 2013 as she entered a dry spell, if you can call it that. She did win the Taifong Ladies Open (The L.P.G.A. of Taiwan) in January 2014 to break the dry spell.

Inbee Park

Off of winning the first three Majors of the year, Inbee Park became the number one ranked player in the Women's World Golf Rankings.

In winning the first three Majors of 2013, she became only the fourth L.P.G.A. Tour player to win three Majors in a calendar year. She is the youngest player to win the U.S. Women's Open.

Park turned professional in 2006 and joined the L.P.G.A. Tour in 2007. She has 16 professional wins including ten on the L.P.G.A. Tour. She has seven majors completing the women's Grand Slam by winning the 2015 Women's British Open.

Na Yeon Choi

Na Yeon Choi is a South Korean golfer who began playing on the L.P.G..A. Tour in 2008. She gained fully exempt status for 2009 by reason of her high conditional status and consistent good play put her in nearly every tournament. She won over $1 million and finished eleventh on the 2008 money list with nine top-ten finishes. She finished second in the 2008 L.P.G.A. Rookie of the Year, just behind winner Yani Tang.

In 2009 Choi won twice on the L.P.G.A. Tour. She also won two other world-wide events, The Samsung World Championship and the Hana Bank-KOLON Championship.

Her third L.P.G.A. Tour win came in July 2010 at the Jamie Farr Owens Corning Classic in which she beat three other golfers on the second hole of a sudden-death playoff.

Choi has won 13 times on the L.P.G.A. Tour. The highlight of her career came in 2012 when she won the U.S. Women's Open. In 2015 Choi won the North West Arkansas Championship.

With her initials of NYC, she is affectionally called "the Big Apple" as the initials coincide with the initials for New York City which, of course, has the same nickname.

Ai Miyazato

Ai Miyazato is the leading Japanese female golfer. She competes on the L.P.G.A. Tour and the L.P.G.A. of Japan Tour.

She was the top-ranked golfer in the Women's World Golf Rankings on three occasions in 2010.

As an amateur in 2003, she won a professional event on the L.P.G.A. of Japan Tour while she was attending high school at the time.

In her 2004 rookie season on the L.P.G.A. of Japan Tour, she won five tournaments.

In 2005 she won six events on the L.P.G.A. of Japan Tour. In winning the Japan Open Championship at age 20 in 2005, Miyazato became the youngest player on the L.P.G.A. of Japan to Tour win a

Japanese Major.

Miyazato easily secured her L.P.G.A. Tour card for the 2006 season. In her fourth season on the L.P.G.A. Tour in 2009, Miayzato earned her first win at the Evian Masters (now a Women's Major as of 2013), defeating Sophie Gustafson on the first hole of a sudden-death playoff.

In 2010 she won four of the first nine official tournaments on the L.P.G.A. Tour and rose to number 1 in the Women's World Golf Rankings on June 21. She held the top spot for only one week and was replaced by Christie

Kerr. Miyazato regained the top spot again on July 19. Kerr briefly took over the top spot, but again Miyazato regained the number one position in August, but then gave it up to Kerr in October.

In April 2012, Miyazato won her eighth L.P.G.A. event. In July 2012 she won her ninth L.P.G.A. title

She has placed in the top fifteen in the five Women's Majors, with her best finish being a tie for third at the Women's British Open (2009) and twice a third place finisher at the 2006 and 2010 L.P.G.A. Championship.

Lydia Ko

Lydia Ko is not technically an Asian golfer. She is a New Zealand golfer, but born in South Korea. She had been the top-ranked woman golfer in the world for over two years when she announced she was turning professional on October 23, 2013. She became the youngest person ever to win a professional golf tour event, and the youngest player to win an L.P.G.A. tour event. In August, 2013 she became the youngest amateur ever to win two L.P.G.A. tour events. As an amateur she never missed a cut in 25 professional tournaments, and by Sepember, Ko had risen to fifth in the Women's World Golf Ranking in only a few professional tournaments.

In April, 2014, Ko was named as one of *Time* magazine's 100 Most Influential People. That same month she advanced to No. 2 womans professional golfer in the world.

On August 26, 2012, at the age of 15 and four months, Ko became the youngest-ever winner of an L.P.G.A. tour event, winning the CN Canadian Women's Open. Her win also made her only the fifth amateur to have an L.P.G.A. victory and the first in over 43 years. Ko successfully defended her title at the 2013 CN Canadian Open shooting 265 for a five-stroke victory.

After finishing runner-up to Suzann Pettersen in The Evian Championship in France, Ko announced that she would turn pro in 2014. However, she turned pro immediately and tied for 21st at the 2013 CME Group Titleholders.

In October, the L.P.G.A. granted Ko's request to join the L.P.G.A., waiving the Tour's requirement of members being at least 18 years old

On April 27, 2014, Lydia earned her first L.P.G.A. win as a professional and her first win in the U.S., by winning the Swinging Skirts L.P.G. Classic. She won her second tournament of the year, the Marathon Classic. She won the L.P.G.A. Rookie of the Year.

Ko has seven victories on the L.P.G.A. tour through 2014.

On November 23, 2014 she won the CME Group Tour Championship in a playoff with Carlota Ciganda and Julieta Granada.

She is one of the brightest, if not the brightest rising star on the L.P.G.A. tour. She is competing with Americans Lexi Thompson and Stacy Lewis for that honor,

65

Two Rising American Stars:
Stacy Lewis and Lexi Thompson

Stacy Lewis

Stacy Lewis has been the best U.S. Woman golfer for the past half dozen years. She plays on the L.P.G.A. tour and has won two Major championships, the Kraft Nabisco Championship in 2011 and the Women's British Open in 2013.

She was ranked number one in the Women's World Golf Rankings for four weeks in 2013 and reclaimed the position in June 2014 with a victory at the ShopRite L.P.G.A. Classic.

Born in Toledo, Ohio, Lewis grew up in Texas at The Woodlands outside of Houston from The Woodlands High School in 2001. Suffering from scoliosis, Lewis underwent a spinal fusion when she was in high school and in her first collegiate golf season.

Lewis was a decorated amateur and four-time All-American at the University of Arkansas. She redshirted her first year while recovering from back surgery. As a member of the U.S. Curtis Cup team in 2008, Lewis became the first player ever to go 5-0 in a single Curtis Cup. The U.S. won 13-7 for a sixth consecutive victory over Great Britain & Ireland.

Lewis's first official professional victory came at the 2011 Kraft Nabisco Championship, a Major, where held off the then current number 1 and defending champion Yani Tseng to win by three strokes.

Stacy Lewis

In 2012 Lewis won four tournaments, and became the first American to win the L.P.G.A. Player of the Year since Beth Daniel in 1994. She won three times in 2013 and unseated Yani Tseng as the No. 1 ranked woman golfer in the world. She held this position for four weeks until she was replaced by Inbee Park on April 15. Lewis won her second Major at the Women's British Open in August 2013 two strokes ahead of runners-up Na Yeon Choi and Hee Young Park.

In 2014, Lewis won the North Texas L.P.G.A. Shootout on May 4 for her ninth official victory on tour, six strokes ahead of runner-up Meena Lee. Four weeks later, she won the ShopRite L.P.G.A. Classic and reclaimed the top position in the world rankings. A week after a runner-up finish in the U.S. Women's Open at Pinehurst, North Carolina, Lewis won the Walmart NW Arkansas Championship on June 29. Lewis would go on to win her second L.P.G.A. Player of the Year award, her second in a three-year span. She would also win her second consecutive Vare Trophy for the season's lowest scoring average.

Lewis has 11 L.P.G.A. victories

Lexi Thompson

Alexis "Lexi" Thompson is an American professional golfer who plays on the L.P.G.A. Tour. She was born on February 10, 1995.

In 2007 at age 12, she was the youngest golfer ever to qualify to play in the U.S. Women's Open. She turned professional in June 2010 at age 15. On September 18, 2012, Thompson set a new record as the youngest ever winner of an L.P.G.A. tournament at age 16 years, seven months, and, eight days, when she won the Navistar L.P.G.A. Three months late she became the second youngest winner of a Ladies European Tour event, capturing the Dubai Ladies Masters on December 17, 2011. She won her first Major championship at the 2014 Kraft Nabisco Championship.

The record of yougest player to quaify for the U.S. Open was surpassed in 2014 by Lucy Li.

Lexi Thompson

As a 14-year old in 2009 she qualifed again for the U.S. Women's Open. As a 15-year old in 2010, she qualifed a third time for the U.S. Women's Open and made the cut, finshing tied for 34th.

In 2009, she represented the winning United States team in the Curtis Cup competition and went undefeated, winning four matches and tying in a fifth.

In December 2010, Thompson petitioned the L.P.G.A. to allow her to play in up to 12 L.P.G.A. tournaments in 2011 using sponsor exemptions instead of the six allowed to non-members by L.P.G.A. rules. In January 2011, Commissioner Mike Whan denied Thompson's petition, but announced that the L.P.G.A. rules would be changed to all non-members to participate in Monday qualifying. In effect this gave Thompson the opportunity to play in more than 12 tournaments in 2011.

As mentioned Thompson won her first L.P.G.A. event, the Navistart L.P.G.A. Classic by a five-stroke margin over L.P.G.A. Tour rookie Tiffany John. At age sixteen, she became the youngest winner ever on the L.P.G.A. Tour, breaking the previous record set by Marlene Hagge at age 18 in 1952. Her record stood for 11 months until 15-year old Lydia Ko won the 2012 CN Canadian Women's Open on August 26, 2012.

On December 17, 2011, Thompson won the Dubai Ladies Masters, an event on the Ladies European Tour (LET), with a four-stroke margin. This made her the youngst professional winner on the LET at age 16 years, 10 months, 7 days. The youngest–ever winner on the LET is Amy Yang, who was four months younger when she won the 2006 ANZ Ladies Masters as an amateur at 16 years, 6 months, 8 days.

Thompson earned her fourth career L.P.G. win and first Major win at the 2014 Kraft Nabisco Championship. The victory made her the second-youngest women's Major winner to date. She has four wins on the L.P.G.A. Tour.

CHAPTER
66

The Changing of the Guard–
The 20 Somethings

The 2015 Masters had 21-year old Jordan Spieth winning with a dominating performance. Rory McIlory of Northern Ireland at 25 was the world's number one player until August 2015. They lead a generation of 20 something golfers who represent the changing of the guard.

Rory McIlroy

McIlroy is the number two ranked golfer in the world. He is a four-time Major champion having won the 2011 U.S. Open, the 2012 P.G.A. Championship, the 2014 Open Championship, and the 2014 P.G.A. Championship. He finished fourth in the 2015 Masters, which he needs to become only the 6th player to win a career Grand Slam.

Jordan Spieth

Spieth tied for second in the 2014 Masters in his debut at that Tournament. In 2015 he had a first and two seconds going into the Masters where he stood at No. 4 in the world rankings. As chronicled elsewhere, he blew away the field, finishing at 270 for a four-shot victory over Phil Mickelson and Justin Rose. His 270 tied him with Tiger Woods for low 72 hole score. He also became the youngest golfer to lead after the first round. He set the 36-hole scoring mark as well as the 54-hole score. He also made the most birdies in the event at 28. And he became only the fifth player to win wire-to-wire. As a result of his 2015 Masters victory and his runnerup finish in the 2015 P.G.A. Championship he moved up to No.1 in the world.

Spieth showed he was more than a flash in the pan when he won the 2015 U.S. Open at Chambers Bay in University Place, Washington. He became only the sixth player to win the Masters and U.S. Open in the same year. Spieth became the youngest player to win the U.S. Open since Bobby Jones in 1923. Spieth missed a playoff for the 2015 British Open Championship by one stroke..

Jordan Spieth also won the 2015 John Deere Classic for a second time when he beat Tom Gillis in a playoff.

Patrick Reed

Patrick Reed is a 24-year old who is most noted for his victory in the 2014 WGC-Cadillac Championship. He has 4 P.G.A. Tour wins. He finished 47th at the 2015 Masters.

Rickie Fowler

This 22-year-old player had a stellar amateur career, after which he turned pro in 2009. He finished in the top five in each of the 2014 Majors. He finished 12th at the 2015 Masters and won the 2015 Players Championship on Mother's Day, winning a three-man playoff. Fowler now has two P.G.A. Tour victories.

Dustin Johnson

Long-hitting Dustin Johnson is 31. He has won 9 P.G.A. Tour wins. He played well at the 2015 Masters, finishing seventh, seven shots behind winner Jordan Spieth. His three putt on the 18th hole cost him a tie and a playoff with Jordan Spieth at the 2015 U.S. Open.

Webb Simpson

Webb Simpson is 29 years old and is most noted for winning the 2012 U.S. Open. He has 4 P.G.A. Victories. He finished 31st at the 2015 Masters.

Jason Day

Jason Day is a 27-year old Australian who has played very well in the Majors. He has been runner-up on three occasions with two of these coming consecutively at the 2011 Masters and the 2011 U.S. Open. In 2014, Day won his first WGC title, the WGC Accenture-Match Play Championship. In 2015 he won the P.G.A. Championship at Whistling Straits, Koelher, WI.

Keegan Bradley

Keegan Bradley, a 29-year old has won three P.G.A. Tour events, most notably the 2011 P.G.A. Championship. He is one of four golfers to win in their Major debut, along with Ben Curtis, Willie Park, Sr. and Francis Ouimet. He was the 2011 P.G.A. Tour Rookie of the year. At the 2015 Masters, he finished 22nd.

There are a number of other 20 somethings who contribute to the deep bench of this group. It is appropriate to mention them here:

Russel Henley—This 26-year American won the 2013 Sony Open and the 2014 Honda Classic.

Seung Yuh Noh—won the 2014 Zurich Classic of New Orleans one month shy of his 23 rd birthday. Noh is South Korean.

Chris Kirk—this 30-year old American Golfer won the 2011 Victory Classic, the 2013 McGladrey Classic, the 2014 Deutsche Bank Championship and the 2015 Colonial Invitational.

Hideki Matsuyama—A 23-year Japanese golfer, Matsuyama won the 2013 Memorial Tournament. He finished fifth at the 2015 Masters.

Sang-Moon Bae—A 26-year old South Korean, Bae won the 2013 HP Byron Nelson Classic and the 2014 Frys.com tournament.

Brian Harmon—this 28-year old American golfer won the 2014 John Deere Classic.

Robert Streb—Streb, who is a 28 years old American golfer won the McGladrey Classic in 2015.

Harris English—This 25-year old American won the 2013 St. Jude FedEx Classic, and later in the year won the OHL Classic at Mayakoba.

CHAPTER

67

Rory McIlory
Sucessor to Tiger Woods?

In the year 2011, there arose a spectacular young golfer who took charge of the golfing world. His name was Rory McIlroy from Northern Ireland.

McIlroy won his first Major at age 22 at the U.S. Open in 2011, setting a record score of 16-under par on his way to an eight-stroke victory.

The following year he won the 2012 P.G.A. Championship at Kiawah Island by a second eight strokes for his second Major title. Two years later he won the final two Majors in 2014. With his victory at the British Open Championship in July McIlroy became the first European to win three different Majors, and joined Jack Nicklaus and Tiger Woods as one of three to win three Majors by the age of 25. Three weeks later he won his second P.G.A. Championship for his fourth Major title.

He had a successful amateur career, topping the World Amateur Ranking for one week as a 17-year old in 2007. Later that year he turned professional and soon established himself on the European Tour. He had his first win on the European Tour in 2009, and on the P.G.A. Tour in 2010. In 2011 at the age of 22, he became the youngest player ever to reach 10 million pounds in career earnings on the European Tour. In 2012, he became the youngest player to reach $10 million in career earnings in the P.G.A. Tour.

McIlroy has represented Europe, Great Britain & Ireland, and Ireland as both an amateur and a professional. At the Ryder Cup he played for Europe

Rory McIlory has Four Major titles.

against the United States in2010, 2012, and 2014, Europe, winning all three matches.

McIlroy has been cited as the most exciting young prospect in golf and as having the potential to become one of the highest earners in sports in terms of endorsements. In January 2014, he signed a large endorsement deal with Nike with wide speculation on its terms. The speculated terms are likely $100 million for a deal of undetermined length.

In addition to his wins in The U.S. Open, the Open Championship, and the P.G.A. Championship, McIlroy has a best finish of 4th in the 2015 Masters Tournament.

McIlroy has been the P.G.A. Tour leading money winner in 2012 and 2014. He was P.G.A. Player of the Year in those two years. He won the Vardon Trophy in the same years as well. He also won the Byron Nelson Trophy those same two years. On the European Tour he won the Order of Merit in 2012 and 2014. He was European Tour golfer of the year in 2012.

2007

McIlroy turned professional on September 18, 2007, the day before the Quinn Direct Master Masters. He signed with International Sports Management. At the tournament McIlroy shot 2 over par which put him in a tie for 42nd place. He finished in 3rd place at the Alfred Dunhill Links Championship. The next week he secured his card for 2008 by finishing in a tie for 4th place in 95th place in the Order of Merit list.

2008

Before his season started, Tiger Woods invited McIlroy to play in the 2007 Target World Challenge, held in December. McIlroy declined the invitation, preferring to play in the European Open

McIlroy started his 2008 Tour season at the UBS Hong Kong Open. He did not make the one-under cut. He entered the top 200 of the Official World Golf Rankings for the first time on January 27, 2008. On January 7, 2008, McIlroy, took a four-stroke lead into the final round of the Omega European Masters and lost in a play-off.

McIlroy finished the European Tour season in November 2008 with sixth top-10 placements and ranked 79th in the World Golf Rankings

2009

After finishing second in the UBS Hong Kong Open in November 2008, McIlroy attained his highest world ranking position of 50. He finished the 2008 calendar year at 39th in the world rankings after finishing joint 3rd in the South African Open. This earned him an invitation to the 2009 Masters Tournament. His first professional win came at age 19 when he won the Dubai Desert Classic on February 1, 2009, this win took him to 16th place in the world rankings,

In the WGC-Accenture Match Play Championship, McIlroy reached the quarterfinals. In the first round he defeated Louis Ooshuizen 2&1, in the second round he beat Hunter Mahan one-up, and in the third round he beat Tim Clark 4 &3. He lost to Geoff Ogilvy who won the tournament in the quarterfinals 2&1. McIlroy continued to play on the P.G.A. Tour until May. He finished tied for 11th at the Honda Classic, tield for 20th at the WGC-CA Championship and tield for 19th at the Shell Houston Open.

In April, McIlroy made his Masters Tournament appearance, his first Major championship as a professional. He finished the tournament tied for 20th place, two strokes under par for the tournament. Of the players to make the cut, McIlroy achieved his higest average driving distance, beaten only by Dustin Johnson and Andrês Romero. McIlroy played in two more events in the P.G.A. events on the P.G.A. Tour after the Master Tounament including his first appearance at The Players Championship, where he missed the cut.

McIlroy then returned to Europe and recorded two top- 25 finished leading up to his first U.S. Open. He finished fifth at the BMW P.G.A. Championship and twelfth at the European Open. He played in his second major as a professional at the BMW after the 2009 U.S. Open. His final round of 69 (-2) helped him finish in a tie for 10th, his first top-ten finish in a Major.

McIlroy finished the 2009 season ranked second on the Race to Dubai, behind Lee Westwood and in November he entered the top ten of the world rankings for the first time. McIlroy finished 2009 ranked 9th in the world. In November 2009, McIlroy announced that he would join the American-based P.G.A. tour for the 2010 season.

McIlroy accepted an invitation from Gary Player to participate in the 2009 Nedbank Golf Challenge at the Gary Player Country Club at Sun City, South Africa in December, but withdrew after not feeling well.

2010

McIlroy finished 3rd at the 2010 Abu Dhabi Golf Championship. As defending champion at the 2010 Dubai Desert Classic, McIlroy shot a final round 73 to finish in a tie for fifth place. In the 2010-Accenture Match Play Championship he beat Kevin Na 1-up in the first round and then lost on a play-off hole to Oliver Wilson. After the Accenture-Play Championship, McIlroy took time off from golf with a sore back. After a two-week break McIlroy returned in the Honda Classic and finished in a tie for 40th.

On May 2, McIlroy recorded his first P.G.A. tour win after shooting 62 in the final round of the Quail Hollow Championship. The round set a new course record and concluded with six consecutive scores of three. He became the first player since Tiger Woods to win a P.G.A. event prior to his

21st birthday. The win earned him a two-year tour exemption. On June 2, McIlroy played in the Memorial Skins Game at Muified Village Golf Club in Dublin, Ohio. McIlroy finished tied for 10th place at that same week's Memorial Tournament.

On July2010, McIlroy confirmed his status as a favorite for the Open title on the Old Course at St. Andrews by shooting a 9-under par 63 on the opening day, the lowest-ever first round score in the 150-year history of the Open Championship and tying the course record. He missed a 5-foot birdie putt on the 17th, The Road Hole which would have given him the outright record. His finished tied third in the 2010 Open Championship which raised him to a career high world ranking of seventh. His final–hole birdie putt narrowly missed the hole to leave him one stroke out of a play-off with Bubba Watson and eventual winner Martin Kaymer. McIlroy finished tied for third. On October 4 McIlroy won a crucial half point to help Europe regain the Ryder Cup. Following the Ryder Cup he announced that he would return to play full-term on the European Tour, although he also stated that he would continue to play 11 or 12 tournaments in the U.S. per year. He attributed the decision to having closer friends on the European Tour, his part in the Ryder Cup, and his wanting to be nearer his girl friend and family.

McIlroy later stated that he regretted his 2010 decision to give up his P.G.A. tour card, and his skipping the 2010 Player Championship at TPC Sawgrass.

2011

On April 3, McIlroy shot a bogey-free 7 under par 65 in the first round of the Masters Tournament in Augusta, Georgia to take the lead after the first day of the competition. He was the youngest player to date to lead the Masters at the close of the first day. This has since been eclispsed by Jordan Spieth in 2015. On Friday, he shot a 69 to lead by two strokes over Jason Day with a 10-under par score. On Saturday, he shot a 70 to finish 23 under-par, four shots ahead of four other challengers. However, on the fourth and final day, he shot the worst round in history by any professional leading after the third round of the Masters Tournament. McIlroy scored a one-over par on the first nine and still had a lead, but shot a round of 80, finishing T15 at 4-under for the Tournament,

McIlroy failed to make the cut in his title defense at Quail Hollow in early May, and was well off the pace at the BMW P.G.A. Championship. He held the 18-hole lead at the Memorial Tournament but finished in 5th place.

Rest of 2011

McIlroy took a month off from competitive golf. At the Open Championship, he struggled in tough weather over a difficult layout at Royal S. George Golf Club, failing to contend with the conditions. He was again a non-factor at the P.G.A. championship at Atlantic Athletic Club after injuring his wrist on the 3rd hole of the third around after playing a stroke from behind a tree root. McIlroy went on the win the Lake Malaren Shanghai Masters in a playoff against Anthony Kim. In November he finished tied for 4th in the WGC-HSBC Championship to move to a then career high of number two in the Official World Golf Ranking. In December 2011, he won the UBS Kong Open by two strokes.

2012 U.S. Open Win

McIlroy won the U.S. Open held at Congressional in Bethesda, Maryland on June 19, winning by eight strokes over Jason Day. McIlroy set several records in his victory, most notably his 72-aggregate score of 268 (16 under) was a new U.S. Open record. The 268 aggregate beat the previous record of 273 held by Jack Nicklaus (Balustrol, 1980, Lee Janzen, 1993), Tiger Woods (Pebble Beach, 2000), and Jim Furyk (Olympia Fields, 2003. The 16-under in relation to par beat Tiger Woods" 12 under at Pebble Golf Links in 20001. He became the youngest winner since Bobby Jones in 1923. The victory lifted McIlroy position in the official World Golf Rankings to a then career high of number four.

On June 17, during the second round McIlroy became the first player in the history of the tournament to reach a score of 13-under par at any point in the tournament. He achieved this feat by making birdie at the 17th hole in the second round. Despite a double bogey on the final hole, his two-day total of 131 set a record lowest 36-hole total in U.S. Open history (11-under par). He was also the fastest golfer to reach double digits under par in U.S. Open history, reaching 10-under par in 26 holes.

On June 18, during the U.S. Open's third round, he became the first player to reach14-under par at the tournament by making a birdie at the 15th hole, on his way to a 54-hole U.S. Open record of 1999. A final round of 69 allowed him to claim of his first Major championship setting a 72-hole record.

2012

McIlroy's first tournament of the year was at the Abu Dhabi HSBC Golf

Championship during the desert swing of the European Tour at the end of January. The Tournament was in the spotlight due to its high profile field including Tiger Woods, Luke Donald and Lee Westwood. McIlroy played alongside Woods and Donald in the marquee group during the first two days. McIlroy shot rounds of 67-72-69 to start round 4 in joint 3rd place behind joint leaders Robert Rook and Tiger Woods. He shot a 3-under par 69 on Sunday to finish lone second one stroke behind Robert Rook.

At the Omega Desert Classic McIlroy finished 5th on 14-under par, four strokes behind winner Rafael Cabrera-Bello. He continued to play well at the WGC-Accenture Match Play Championship in Arizona where he won matches against Georg Coetzze, Anders Hanson, Miguel Ángel Jiménez, Sang-Moon Bae and Lee Westwood before losing to Hunter Mahan in the final. After ten holes in the final match McIlroy was four down to Mahan, but cut the deficit to two down through 16 holes. The 17th hole was halved with pars, securing the win for Mahan. There was anticipation surrounding the semi-final match between McIlroy and Westwood as the winner would become the number one golfer in the world if they also won the final. McIlroy's runner-up finish moved him up to number two in the world while also putting him at the top of the Race to Dubai leaderboard.

In his next tournament, McIlroy claimed the Number 1 spot in the world rankings. He started the fourth round in first place at 11-under par after rounds of 66-67-66, ahead of a chasing pack including Tiger Woods, LeeWestwood and Keegan Bradley. McIlroy shot a final found on 69 to claim his third P.G.A. Tour title and finished two strokes ahead of Tiger Woods and Tom Gillis. McIlroy became the second youngest Number 1 and moved up to fourth place in the FedEx Cup standings.

McIlroy played the following week at the WGC-Cadillac Championship in Miami, Florida. His recent good form began to dwindle slightly on Thursday, when he shot a 1-over part 73. However, he shot 69 and 65 the next two days to begin the fourth round tied for 8th place. Going into the back nine on Sunday, he had a chance of winning his second title of 2012 in as many weeks due to the leaders faltering. However, two late bogeys halted his chance and he settled for 3rd place, two strokes behind winner Justin Rose.

McIlroy lost his number one ranking on March 18 to Luke Donald after Donald won the Transitions Championship. McIlroy was one stroke off the lead going into the weekend at the Masters but struggled in his last two rounds and finished in a tie for the 40 position. He regained the top spot in the world rankings in April 15, but lost it to Donald again on April 29. On

May 6, McIlroy was in contention at the Wells Fargo Championship and went to a playoff with Rickie Fowler and D.A. Points. Fowler won the tournament on the first playoff hole with a birdie. The runner-up finish put McIlroy back at the top of the Official World golf Rankings. After the runner-up finish, McIlroy would later miss the cut in his next three events and fell from the number one rankings.

P.G.A. Championship
McIlroy won the 2012 P.G.A. Championship by a record eight strokes, which was done with a birdie on the final hole. The record stood since Jack Nicklaus won the 1980 P.G.A. Championship by seven strokes. McIlroy started the final round with a three stroke lead and shot a bogey free 66 to run away from the field. With this win, McIlroy became the youngest multiple Major champion since Seve Ballesteros won the 1980 Masters Tournament, and the sixth youngest number one ranking.

2013
McIlroy began 2013 with high aspirations, but mostly did not fare well in early tournaments. Struggling with equipment change having signed a large endorsement deal with Nike, he withdrew from the Honda Classic in February, and finished at two over par and in a tie for 25th place at the 2013 Masters Tournament. McIlroy won the 2013 Emirates Australian Open on the 72nd hole. He beat Australian Adam Scott by one stroke.

2014
In March, McIlroy lost in a four-man sudden-death playoff at the Honda Classic on the P.G.A. Tour despite leading the tournament through four rounds until the back nine on Sunday. He shot a final round 74 (+4) and had a superb shot to the par-five 18th in regulation play to qualify for the playoff, after missing the eagle putt for the win. He lost on the first extra hole, when Russell Henley was the only one of the four to birdie the hole.

In May in England, McIlroy won the BMW P.G.A. Championship at Wentworth by one stroke. He carded a six-under par 66 final round to beat Thomas Bjorn who started the day seven strokes clear of McIlroy. The win was McIroy's first on either of the two Major tours in 18 months.

Open Championship
On July 20, McIlroy won the 2014 Championship at Royal Liverpool by

two strokes over Rickie Fowler and Sergio Garcia to capture the third Major championship of his career, having led the field throughout the tournament. McIlroy and Tiger Woods are the only golfers to win the Silver Medal and The Gold Medal at the Open Championship. It was his third Major title having won the 2011 U.S. Open and 2012 P.G.A. Championship. McIlroy became the first European to win three different Majors and joined Jack Nicklaus and Tiger Woods as one of three golfers to win three Majors by the age of 25.

Rest of 2014

McIlroy won the WGC-Bridgestone Invitational at Firestone and returned to world number one. Starting the final day three strokes behind Sergio Garcia, McIlroy shot a 66 to finish at 15 under par and two strokes clear. The following week he won the P.G.A. Championship at Valhalla for his fourth Major, one stroke ahead of runner-up Plil Mickelson. After his victory, Jack Nicklaus said "Rory is an unbelievable talent. I think Rory has an opportunity to win 15 or 20 Majors or whatever he wants to do if he wants to keep playing. I love his swing. I love his rhythm. I love his moxie. He's got a little swagger there, it's a bit cocky but not offensive."

2015

McIlroy finished 4th in the Masters tournament and won the Wells Fargo Championship, and the WEC Cadillac Match Play Championship. He finished ninth at the U.S. Open.

Awards

In 2012, besides leading the P.G.A. money list, McIlroy won the P.G.A. Player of the Year, P.G.A. Tour Player of the year, the Vardon Trophy, and Byron Nelson Trophy. In addition the winning the Race to Dubai, he was voted the European Tour Golfer of the Year. He also won the Mark H. Mc-Cormack Award for leading the official Golf Ranking for the most weeks in the year (28 of 52 weeks) Also in 2012 he won a Laureus World Sports Award in the category Breakthrough of the year.

In 2014, McIlroy again swept the P.G.A. Tour awards: Arnold Palmer Award (leading money winner), P.G.A. Player of the year, P.G.A. Tour Player of the Year, Vardon Trophy, and Byron Nelson Award.

In short, his future looks extremely bright!

68

The World of Golf
2011-2015

South African Charl Schwartzel birdied the last four hole to win the 75th Masters. He shot 274. Runners-up were Jason Day and Adam Scott. The two Aussies shot 276. They came up short in trying to become the first Australian to win the Masters. Fifty-four hole leader Rory McIlroy couldn't hold on to a four-shot lead, shot an 80 and finished tied for fifteenth.

At the 2011 U.S. Open, Northern Ireland youngster 22-year old Rory McIlroy blew away the field at Congressional Country Club, Bethesda, Maryland with a record-setting sixteen-under par 268. This was the lowest score for a U.S. Open and was the lowest in relation to par in U.S. Open history, beating Tiger Woods's 2000 mark by four. The Congressional Country Club Blue Course was the longest U.S. Open course to date at 7,574 yards, par 71, .

At 22 years, 1 month, 15 days, McIlroy was the youngest winner of the U.S. Open since Bobby Jones in 1923 until Jordan Speith claimed that distinction by winning the 2015 U.S. Open. McIlroy shot four rounds in the 60s to finish eight strokes ahead of Jason Day who was eight shots back at eight-under par. Woods still holds the record for widest margin on victory with his fifteen-stroke romp in 2000).

At Royal St. George's, forty-two year old Irishman Darren Clarke fended off Sunday charges by Phil Mickelson and Dustin Johnson to capture his first Major the 2011 British Open Championship. The victory came five years after he lost his wife, Heather, to breast cancer. Clarke became the third golfer from Northern Ireland to win a Major in the last six renditions. Graeme McDowell won the 2010 U.S. Open and Rory McIlroy won the 2011 U.S. Open. Phil Mickelson and Dustin Johnson finished tied for second at 278.

Beginning in 2013, the Evian Masters became the L.P.G.A.'s fifth Major. The event moved from July to September and was renamed the Evian Championship. The move will separates it from the Women's British Open.

P.G.A. Tour rookie Keegan Bradley is the nephew of six-time Ladies Major Champion Pat Bradley, won the 2011 P.G.A. Championship at the Atlantic Athletic Club. Bradley overcame a five-shot deficit after triple bogeying the fifteenth hole, and birdied sixteen and seventeen to earn a three-hole aggregate score play-off with Jason Dufner whom he beat by one shot. Bradley became the first player to win a Major with a long putter. He became only the third player in over 100 years to win a Major in his first try.

Former Southern Methodist standout Kerry Kraft defeated favored UCLA sophomore Patrick Cantley two-up at Erin Hills Golf, Erin, Wisconsin to win the 2011 U.S. Amateur.

In the 2011 Walker Cup the British/Irish team upset the favored American 14-12 at Aberdeen, Scotland.

In the Solheim Cup the Europeans defeated the U.S. Team 15-13. At Klileen Castle, Ireland. Norway's Suzann Pettersen led a Sunday charge for the Europeans.

Bill Hass won the Tour Championship and thus clinched the FedEx Cup in 2011.

At the 2011 Presidents Cup, held for the second time, at Royal Melbourne in Melbourne, Australia, the Americans's strong showing in foursomes (alternate shot) resulted in a 19-15 victory. Jim Furyk led the U.S. with a 5-0 record. The U.S. now leads the series 7-1-1.

Lydia Ko, a fourteen-year old amateur from New Zealand, won the New South Wales Open on the Australian Ladies Professional Golf Tour, becoming the youngest player to win an event on a sanctioned tour. In 2012, she won the U.S. Woman's Amateur. Ryo Ishikawa, at fifteen, was the previous youngest winner on a sanctioned tour.

The 2012 Masters got underway with honorary tee shots by Jack Nicklaus, Arnold Palmer, and Gary Player. What followed was another classic. South African Louis Oosthuizen (winner of the 2010 British Open) made a two (an albatross) on the par five second hole in the fourth round. This means that all four par five's have produced an albatross.

This shot was not enough, however, to carry Oosthuizen to victory as Bubba Watson carded four straight birdies on the back nine (thirteen-sixteen) to force a playoff with the South African. Watson won on the second playoff hole (the tenth) with a miraculous gap wedge from the right trees over a distance of 155 yards to within twelve feet of the pin. When Oosthuizen couldn't reach the green from 231 yards in two due to a poor tee shot and carded a bogey, Watson two-putted for par and the victory.

At the 2012 L.P.G.A. Championship, Shanshan Feng became the first Chinese player to win an L.P.G.A. Tour title and a Major. She beat Stacy Lewis, Suzann Pettersen, Mika Miyazato, and Eun-Hee Ji by two strokes.

The 2012 U.S. Open returned to The Olympic Club near San Francisco for the fifth time and the first time since 1998 when Lee Janzen was the winner. The tough par 70 course refused to allow the winner to shoot under par. That winner turned out to be Webb Simpson who shot one over par while shooting 68-68 on the weekend. His total of 281 outlasted Tour rookie Michael Thompson and Northern Ireland's Graeme McDowell (winner of the 2010 U.S. Open) by one stroke.

Royal Lytham and Saint Annes hosted the 2012 British Open Championship. Adam Scott of Australia held the lead from the outset through the fourth round. However, he bogeyed the final four holes on Sunday's fourth round to lose the Championship by one stroke to South Africa's Ernie Els. Scott missed a seven-foot putt on the last hole, which would have forced a four-hole play-off. For Els, it was his second British Open Championship (first in 2002) and fourth Major overall (1994 and 1997 U.S. Opens).

The 2012 P.G.A. Championship was held at the Ocean Course at Kiawah Island Golf Resort designed by Pete Dye. It was the venue for the 1991 "War by the Shore" Ryder Cup won by the United States. Rory McIlroy took the P.G.A. title with a 275, besting Englishman David Lynn by eight shots. This margin of victory was the largest since the P.G.A. switched from match play to stroke play fifty-five years previously.

Steven Fox, a twenty-one year old from Hendersonville, Tennessee, was two down with two holes to play in the thirty-six hole final of the 2012 U.S. Amateur at Cherry Hills Country Club, Denver, Colorado. He rallied to force a play-off and made an eighteen-foot birdie on the first extra hole to defeat Michael Weaver of Fresno, California.

On August 20, 2012, The Augusta National Golf Club announced that it was accepting its first two women in the eighty-year history of the Club. They were former Secretary of State Condoleeza Rice and South Carolina finance executive Darla Moore.

Later on in August 2012 (the 26th to be exact), fifteen-year old amateur Lydia Ko became the youngest winner of an L.P.G.A. event when she won the Canadian Women's Open. She broke the record of Lexi Thompson who was sixteen when she won the Navistar L.P.G.A. Classic in September 2011. Ko became only the fifth amateur to win an L.P.G.A. event, and the first amateur winner since JoAnne Carner at the 1969 Burdine's Invitational.

At the Tour Championship in Atlanta, Georgia, Brandt Snedeker rode a hot putter to victory and also captured the FedEx Cup. His winnings for the two events totaled $11,4 million.

In the 39th rendition of the Ryder Cup held at Medinah Country Club in 2012, the U.S. team could not hold onto an 8-4 lead going into the last day of twelve singles matches. It could only garner 3 ½ points and the collapse gave the Euros a 14 ½-13 1/2 victory to allow them to retain the Cup.

In November 2012, the U.S.G.A. and Royal & Ancient announced that, beginning in January 2016, the use of anchoring would be banned. This primarily affects the putting stroke. Both governing bodies noted that the decision was not impacted by the fact that recent Majors had been won by players using the anchored putting stroke (Keegan Bradley, 2011 P.G.A.; Webb Simpson , 2012 U.S. Open; and Ernie Els, 2012 Open Championship; Adam Scott, 2012 Masters—thus, completing a grand slam of the four Majors). Instead, they emphasized that anchored strokes threaten to supplant traditional strokes, which, with all their frailties, are integral to the long-standing character of the sport. They further stated that the objective is to preserve the skill and challenge, which is such a key element of the game of golf. After taking months of comments, including opposition from the P.G.A., the banning on using anchoring was confirmed, effective January 1, 2016. The P.G.A. also adopted the ban.

The number of rounds played in the United States increased 5.7 percent in 2012. The gain of 26 million rounds, which raised the national total to approximately 490 million was attributable mostly to improved weather.

In March 2013, Tiger Woods won his record-tying eighth Arnold Palmer Invitational, becoming only the second golfer to win the same event that many times. Sam Snead won the Greater Greensboro Open eight times. As an added bonus, Woods re-gained the world's number one ranking.

At the Masters, another riveting finish took place. Australian Adam Scott made a 25-foot birdie on the 72nd hole to give himself a one-shot lead on Ángel Cabrera (2009 winner of the Masters) who was in the last group out in the 18th fairway. Cabrerra proceeded to hit a seven iron within two feet of the flag and tapped in to force a play-off.

Both players then hit their approaches short on the first play-off hole (the 18th) They matched pars and went to the second play-off hole (the 10th). After Cabrera's birdie putt just missed, Scott rolled in a 15-foot birdie to capture the 77th Master. In doing so, Scott became the first Australian to capture the Green Jacket.

Scott also became the fourth player in the past six Majors to use a long putter. The other three were Keenan Bradley (2011 P.G.A.), Webb Simpson (2012 U.S. Open), and Ernie Els (2012 British Open).

Guan Tianiang of China, at age 14 became the youngest player to compete in the Masters, and the same could be said for making the cut. He finished 58th.

The 2013 U.S. Open was held at Merion Golf Club in Ardmore, PA. The club was hosting a record eighteenth U.S.G.A. event and its fifth U.S. Open. There was much concern that its 6996 yard length (shortest length since Shinnecock Hills in 2004) was too susceptible to low scoring. However, the heavy rough, the pin placement, difficult fescue grass, absence of any first cut of rough, numerous sand bunkers, fast and undulating greens etc. proved more than adequate in making the tournament a severe test for the players.

There were no even or under par scores. The winner was Justin Rose from England who shot a one-over-par 281. His even par 70 in the last round was enough to hold off Phil Mickelson who had a one-shot lead after 54 holes. However, two front nine double bogeys was too much to offset his second nine comeback (including an eagle two at the par four tenth hole when he holed out from the fairway). He shot a final round 73. This was Mickelson's sixth runner-up finish in the U.S. Open, breaking his own dubious record of five. The Australian, Jason Day, also finished runner-up at 283.

Inbee Park won the 2013 U.S. Women's Open, making her only the second woman to win the first three Majors of the year, and matching Babe Didrikson Zaharias' feat in 1950. She had already won the first two Majors of 2013, the Kraft Nabisco Championship and the L.P.G.A. Championship.

Park added to another historic U.S. Women's Open victory in 2008 when she became the event's youngest champion at age nineteen.

Nineteen-year old Jordan Spieth won the 2013 John Deere Classic in a five-hole playoff with defending champion Zack Johnson and Canadian David Hearn. In doing so, Spieth became the first teenager in 82 years to win on the P.G.A. Tour. The last teenager to win was Ralph Guldahl who, at nineteen, won the Santa Monica Open in 1931.

At the 2013 British Open (or "The Open Campionship"), 43-year old Phil Mickelson won his fifth Major, leaving only the U.S. Open to complete the career Grand Slam (he's finished second a record six times at that championship). Mickelson was five shots out of the lead going into the final round at Muirfield in Gullane, but shot a brilliant round of sixty-six to defeat Henrik Stenson by three shots. Mickelson's 72-hole score of 281 made him the only golfer under par for the tournament. His victory came one-week after he won the Scottish Open. Tiger Woods finished tied for sixth, making it nineteen Majors in a row that he played, and did not win. He remains at fourteen Major victories, leaving him still four Majors behind Jack Nicklaus's eighteen Majors.

At the 113th U.S. Amateur held at The Country Club in Brookline, Massachusetts, Englishman Matt Fitzpatrick beat Australian Oliver Goss 4 and 3 to become the first English champion since Harold Hilton in 1911. The event came on the 100th anniversary of local caddie Francis Ouimet's landmark U.S. Open victory over British professionals Harry Vardon and Ted Ray at The Country Club.

In 2013, the 95th P.G.A. Championship at Oak Hill Country Club, Rochester, NY was won by Jason Dufner. Dufner shot a course-record 63 (also tying the low round in a Major) in the second round. After fifty-four holes he found himself one shot behind Jim Furyk. In the final round, Dufner marched out to a two-shot lead, and when both bogeyed the first and second toughest two finishing holes, Dufner had his Major victory and raised the Wanamaker Trophy.

In the 2013 Tour Championship, Henrik Stenson of Sweden held off rookie Jordan Spieth by 3 shots to win the $1.44 million first prize. Better yet for Stenson, he won the season-long FedEx Cup and the $10 million that goes along with that.

At the 2013 Presidents Cup, held at Muirfield Village in Dublin, Ohio, the U.S.A. prevailed over the International team 18-1/2-15-1/2. Tiger

Woods captured the deciding point in the Sunday singles matches. It was the third straight Presidents Cup in which Woods won the cup-clinching match—all three with Fred Couples as the captain.

Lefty Bubba Watson outplayed 20 year old Jordan Spieth and Swede Jonas Blixt to win his second Green Jacket at the 2014 Masters. It was his second victory in three years, having won in 2012. The keys were a four shot swing on hole 8 and 9 on Sunday, and Spieth hitting into the water on the short par three twelfth. Spieth was trying to overcome Tiger Woods and become the youngest Masters winner in his first try.

In February 2013, the U.S.G.A. announced that it is cancelling the men's and women's U.S. Amateur Public Links tournaments in favor of U.S. Amateur Four-Ball Championships starting in 2015 to meet what it says is a trend at state and regional levels.

The 2014 U.S. Open winner was Martin Kaymer of Germany. He won wire-to-wire by eight strokes over Americans Rickie Fowler and Eric Compton at Pinhurst No. 2, Pinhurst, NC. In the course of winning, Kaymer set the 36 hole mark of 130 by opening with two 65's. He also set the 36-hole mark of largest margin of a lead with a six stroke lead. He became the first German to win the United States Championship. Kaymer also won the 2010 P.G.A. Championship.

Rory McIlroy from Northern Ireland went wire-to-wire in winning the 2014 Open Championship at Royal Liverpool, Holylake, England. After shooting 68's (four under par per round) the first two days, McIlory held off late charges on Sunday by Sergio Garcia and Rickie Fowler to win by two strokes. In doing so, McIlroy at 25 joins only Jack Nicklaus and Tiger Woods as players who have won three Majors since 1934 who were 25 years old or younger. McIlroy's other Majors were the U.S. Open and the P.G.A. Championship, leaving him short only of the Masters for the career Grand Slam.

The year 2015 welcomed the playing of the 79th Masters. The record-setting winner was 21-year old Jordan Spieth of Dallas Texas. Spieth led wire-to-wire, becoming only the fifth player to do so, and the first since Raymond Floyd in 1976. His 270 total tied the low total set by Tiger Woods. Spieth set the 36-hole record of 130, as well as the 54-hole record of 200. He was the youngest player at 21 years 8 months to lead after the first round. Spieth carded 28 birdies for a new record, supplanting Phil Mickelson's previous record of 25 birdies. Spieth had entered the tournament with a first and two seconds in his previous three tournaments, climbing to number 4 in the world. Spieth moved to number 2 in the world after the Masters win.

The Masters co-runners up were Phil Mickelson and Justin Rose who shot 14 under par 274's. The worlds number one player. Rory McIlroy, finished strongly on the weekend, but had to settle for fourth place. Tiger Woods, making his appearance after a two-month hiatus, carded 5 under par 283, good for a tie for17th place.

Jordan Spieth followed his 2015 Masters win with a hard fought victory over Dustin Johnson and Louis Oosthuizen in the U.S. Open at Chambers Bay in University Place, Washington. Spieth won by one stroke at 275. Johnson missed forcing a playoff when he 3 putted the 72nd-hole. Spieth became only the sixth player to win the Masters and the U.S. Open in the same year. He also became the youngest winner of the U.S. Open since Bobby Jones in 1923. Spieth became the yougest winner of two Majors in the same year since Gene Sarazen in 1922.

The 2015 Open Championship was played at St. Andrews. Jordan Spieth saw his chances for a third straight major end when he fell one shot short of a four hole aggregate playoff among Zack Johnson, Louis Oosthuizen, and Marc Leishman. Zack Johnson won the playoff and captured the Claret Jug.

Spieth attained the number one ranking after winning the 2015 U.S. Open and finishing as runnerup in the 2015 P.G.A. Championship in August 2015.

Carol Semple Thompson holding the Curtis Cup for the victorious
U.S. team in 2006.

Professional and Amateur
Team Competitions

69

The Competitions

The Ryder Cup, The Presidents Cup, The Walker Cup, The Solheim Cup, The Curtis Cup

The United States participates in five major team "Cup" competitions on a bi-annual basis. The men compete in three events: the Ryder Cup, the Presidents Cup, and the Walker Cup. The women participate in two events: the Solheim Cup and the Curtis Cup.

The Ryder Cup

The "Ryder Cup" is a golf trophy contested bi-annually in an event called the "Ryder Cup Matches." It is contested between twelve male professional golfers from the United States against twelve men professionals from Europe. The teams are selected after the P.G.A. Championship. For the U.S., eight of the slots are awarded under a complicated money winnings system while the remaining four positions are captain's picks by the U.S. captain. The European team consists of ten players under a system that looks to the European tour list and world golf rankings with captain's picks for the other two positions. The formal competition began following an exhibition in 1926 of a team representing American professionals against a similar one representing the British P.G.A. on the East Course, Wentworth Club, Virginia Water, Surrey, England. The early Matches were fairly even (the first four Matches were split), but after the Second World War the Americans began to dominate the Matches. The British team was expanded to include Irish players in 1973. Still the results were one-sided in favor of the Americans. This led to a decision to extend representation of the British and Irish to include all of Europe in 1979. Jack Nicklaus was instrumental in this broadening of representation.

This change was successful in part because of the fine play of Spanish golfers Severiano Ballesteros and Antonio Garrido. They were the first Spaniards to play in the event in 1979. Since then, Europe also has been represented by golfers from Denmark, Sweden, Germany, France, and Italy.

The expansion of the British and Irish team to include players from Europe has resulted in more even competition. Since the change, Europe has won ten times, retained the Cup once with a tie, while the Americans have won seven times.

The Matches involve three different forms of match play. They consist of eight foursome matches, eight four-ball matches, and twelve single matches. One point is awarded for a victory and a ½ point is awarded when a match ends in a tie (there is no play-off when a match ends tied).

A foursome match is a competition between two teams of two golfers. It is also referred to as "alternate shot." The golfers on each team play with one ball per side and take alternate shots on each hole. Each hole is won by the team that finishes the hole in the fewest strokes.

A four-ball match is also a competition between two teams consisting of two players each. It is also referred to as "best ball" or "better ball." Every player plays his own ball, and a hole is won by the team whose individual golfer has the lowest score.

A singles match is a standard match-play competition between two golfers.

The matches take place over three days, Friday through Sunday. In the Friday matches there are four foursome matches and four four-ball matches. There is a morning session and an afternoon session. The home team captain determines which format is played in each session. On the Saturday, the same schedule repeats. In the Sunday matches there are twelve singles matches.

The name "Ryder Cup" dates to the 1926 exhibition. Present at the 1926 Matches was Samuel Ryder, a seed merchant from England. He thought it would be worthwhile to make the matches official by donating a trophy for the start of the Ryder Cup Matches.

The first official match was held at Worcester Country Club in Worcester, Massachusetts. The United States under captain Walter Hagen defeated the Great Britain team captained by Ted Ray, 9½–2½. The Ryder Cup has been held on a two-year cycle since, apart from 1939 to 1945 when it was cancelled because of World War II. The only other exception occurred in 2001.

The 2001 match was delayed for a year, as it was due to take place shortly after the September 11 attacks by terrorists in the United States. It was subsequently decided to hold the Ryder Cup in even-numbered years instead of odd-numbered years. The 2002 matches were held at the Belfry, Wishaw, Warwickshire, England, and were referred to as "the 2001 Ryder Cup."

The United States leads the Matches 24-10-2 after thirty-six competitions.

Seven of the more memorable Ryder Cup Matches were those held in 1969, 1983, 1987, 1989, 1991, 1999, 2008, and 2012.

1969 Ryder Cup
The 1969 Ryder Cup was held at Royal Birkdale, Southport, England. It was one of the most competitive Matches with eighteen of thirty-two matches going to the eighteenth hole. In a magnanimous show of sportsmanship, Jack Nicklaus conceded a two-foot putt by Englishman Tony Jacklin after Nicklaus made a four-footer for par on the last green. Although the putt was far from a sure thing, Nicklaus said he didn't want to give Jacklin the opportunity to miss in front of his home fans. As a result, this was the first tie in the Matches with the U.S. retaining the Cup because of its victory in 1967 at the Champions Golf Club in Houston, Texas.

1983 Ryder Cup
With never more than a point separating the two sides, the U.S. retained the Ryder Cup, 14½-13½ at P.G.A. National in Palm Beach Gardens, Florida. After the two-man competitions of the first two days, the teams were level at 8-8. In the twelve singles matches, the U.S. did not dominate as was its custom, but did eke out a 6½-5½ margin in the singles for the victory.

After ten singles matches, the competition was still tied at 13-13. In one match it was José-Maria Cañizares against Lanny Wadkins. Cañizares had lost a three-hole lead and at the last under-hit his pitch while Wadkins hit a marvelous shot to 18 inches of the hole for a tie and a half point for each team.

With the Matches still tied, it came down to Bernard Gallacher versus

Tom Watson. Gallacher was one down on the seventeenth. Gallacher's three-iron to this 191-yard hole bounced through the green. Watson then missed the green on the right. Both flubbed their chips, but Watson's second effort was close. Gallacher missed from four feet, and lost 2 & 1, thereby giving the U.S. its one-point margin of victory.

1987 Ryder Cup

In 1985 the U.S. was parted from the Ryder Cup for the first time since the British team did the trick in 1957. The venue was the Belfry in Sutton Coldfield, West Midlands, England. So the U.S. was looking to re-capture the Cup on home soil in 1987. It was not to be.

The 1987 Matches were held at Jack Nicklaus's Muirfield Village, Dublin, Ohio. The Europeans retained the Cup and registered their first victory on American soil. When the third day dawned, the Europeans reflected their four-ball/foursomes superiority by leading 10½-5½. Nicklaus's team needed nine points out of twelve in the singles to win, and they made a great run at it. The U.S. won the singles 7½-4½, but it was not enough to overcome the Europeans. As usual, Seve Ballesteros was in the thick of things with a key victory, 2 & 1, over Curtis Strange. The final tally was 15-13 in Europe's favor.

1989 Ryder Cup

The 1989 Ryder Cup returned to the Belfry and the Europeans were looking to make it three in a row. After sweeping the afternoon four-balls on the first day, the Europeans led 5-3. The teams split the eight points on the second day of foursomes/four-ball, so the Europeans held a 9-7 lead going into Sunday's twelve singles matches. The Europeans needed five points for a 14-14 draw, which would allow them to retain the Cup. And that's exactly what happened. The Europeans captured their five points through the first eight singles matches, and they needed every one of them, as the U.S. swept the final four singles matches.

1991 Ryder Cup

The 1991 Matches were held at the Kiawah Island Golf Resort in Kiawah, South Carolina. The Matches were known as the "War by the Shore." The U.S. was intent on winning back the Cup following the European victory on the U.S. home turf in 1987. (The Europeans had retained the Cup in 1989 with a tie at the Belfry.).

The outcome of the Matches came down to the singles match between Hale Irwin and Germany's Bernhard Langer. On the eighteenth green Langer had an opportunity to win the match and allow the Europeans to retain the Cup with a 14–14 tie. His six-foot putt slid by the hole and gave Irwin a half, resulting in a 14½–13½ victory for the Americans under Captain Dave Stockton.

1999 Ryder Cup

The Europeans had won the 1995 and 1997 Matches by the thinnest of margins (14½ - 13½) and were seeking their third victory in a row at The Country Club in Brookline, Massachusetts. The U.S. staged a remarkable comeback on the last day. After trailing 10-6 going into the singles on Sunday, the U.S. went 8-3-1 in singles to seal the American victory.

Controversy erupted in the match between Justin Leonard and Spaniard José Maria Olazábal. The match being all square at the seventeenth hole, Leonard needed to earn at least a half-point. He would earn a full point if he defeated Olazábal in what, in effect, was a two-hole match. He would earn the necessary half point if they finished the match all square.

Olazábal's approach left him with a twenty-two-footer for birdie, while Leonard was forty-five feet away for his birdie. Incredibly, Leonard holed the putt that set off a wild celebration among the American players, their wives, and fans running onto the green. Olazábal still had an opportunity to extend the match if he could make his putt. When things quieted down after the American celebration, he settled over the difficult putt, but missed. The miss assured Leonard of a half-point and the U.S. a victory by the margin of 14½-13½.

Although the celebration broke no official rules of golf, some of the Europeans complained that the actions broke the unwritten rules and codes of conduct for golf. In response, many of the Americans believed the European response was hypocritical since European players, in particular Seve Ballesteros, had allegedly been guilty of excessive celebration as far back as the 1985 Ryder Cup Matches.

Following these Matches a number of the members of the U.S. squad apologized and there was a new aura of friendliness that came about. As a result, subsequent Matches have been played more in the spirit of the game.

Since the 1999 Matches the Europeans became dominant again, winning the following three Matches.

2008 Ryder Cup

The U.S. was facing a fourth consecutive defeat at the 2008 Matches held at Valhalla Golf Club in Louisville, Kentucky. There were whispers that another defeat would cause a lessening of interest in the Ryder Cup on the part of American fans. The Americans under captain Paul Azinger faced off against the European squad headed by Nick Faldo.

In both the Friday and Saturday play, Azinger elected to start off the morning sessions with foursomes, the weakest of the three formats for the Americans during the last half dozen renditions of the Ryder Cup. Surprisingly, the U.S. took the Friday-morning foursomes 3-1. In the afternoon fourballs, the U.S. prevailed 2½-1½ to lead 5½-2½ after Friday's play. On Saturday, the Europeans battled back to capture the morning foursomes 2½-1½ to reduce the U.S. lead to 7-5. The squads tied the Saturday-afternoon fourballs 2-2, and thus the U.S. took a 9-7 lead going into Sunday's twelve singles matches.

Azinger sent out Anthony Kim in the number-one singles against European stalwart Sergio Garcia. Playing brilliantly, Kim walloped Garcia 5 & 4. This set the tone for the rest of the singles as the U.S. won them 7½-4½. Fittingly, the deciding match was captured by Kentuckian J.B. Homes who defeated Soren Hansen 2 & 1. Another Kentuckian who contributed to the victory was forty-eight-year old Kenny Perry who posted a 2½-1 record. The final score was U.S. 16½-Europe 11½.

2012 Ryder Cup

The 39th Ryder Cup was held in September 2912 at the Medinah Country Club in Medinah, Illinois. At the start of the final day's play, the U.S. led 10-6 and required 4 ½ points to win. Europe required 8 points to retain the cup and 8½ to win it outright. Europe achieved one of the greatest comebacks in Ryder cup history by winning 8 and tying one of the 12 singles matches. Martin Kaymer's five-foot putt on the 18th hole to defeat Steve Stricker took the score to 14-13, allowing Europe to retain the cup. Tiger Woods halved the final match which secured Europe's victory 14½-13½. The victory was Europe's fifth in the last six contests. Europe would go on to win in 2014.The United States leads the Matches 25-12-2.

The Presidents Cup

The Presidents Cup is a golf match between a team of U.S. professional golfers against a team of professional golfers representing the rest of the world except for Europe. The Presidents Cup is held bi-annually. Initially it was held in even-numbered years. However, the cancellation of the 2001 Ryder Cup because of the attacks of September 11 pushed both tournaments back a year. Thus, the Presidents Cup is now held in odd-numbered years. It is hosted alternately in the United States and elsewhere in the world.

The scoring system of the event is match play. The format is drawn from the Ryder Cup, consisting of twelve players per side and a non-playing captain. The doubles events are both the foursomes and four-ball formats. With eleven foursomes matches, eleven four-ball matches, and twelve singles matches, the Presidents Cup is played for a total of 34 points (The Ryder Cup has only eight foursome matches and eight four-ball matches, and, along with the 12 singles matches, represents a total of 28 points.). Thus, in the Presidents Cup, a team must win a total of 17½ points to capture the Cup.

The format of the Presidents Cup is different from that of the Ryder Cup mainly in that the Presidents Cup includes six additional matches. Thus, depth is critical in the Presidents Cup because, according to the rules of play, a team cannot hide its weaker players by having them sit out the two-man matches, as can be done in the Ryder Cup.

The Presidents Cup had its inaugural playing in 1994 when the U.S. won 20-12 at the Robert Trent Jones Golf Club in Gainesville, Virginia (up until 2003, the competition was for 32 points instead of the current 34 points). This course has hosted the Matches on four occasions.

The U.S. has won eight times, lost once (at Royal Melbourne Golf Club in Melbourne, Australia in 1998), and tied in 2003 when the Match was halted because of darkness after three sudden-death play-off holes. The 2003 Presidents Cup was deemed a tie with both teams sharing the Cup until 2005.

The teams are announced one day after completion of the year's final Major, the P.G.A. Championship held in August. The U.S. team consists of ten players selected on the basis of money winnings with two captain's picks. The international squad is based on world golf rankings for ten of the players with two captain's picks. In 2003, 2005 and 2007 Jack Nicklaus captained the U.S. team and Gary Player captained the International team.

The 2009 Presidents Cup was played at Harding Park Golf Club, San Francisco, California. Fred Couples captained the U.S. team while Greg Norman was chosen to head the international squad. Led by Tiger Woods,

Phil Mickelson, Steve Stricker and Anthony Kim, the United States won by a comfortable 19½-14½ score. Overall, the U.S. team leads the Internationals 8-1-1.

The U.S. won in 2011 at Royal Melbourne Golf Club in 2011, 19-15. They also prevailed at Muirfield Village in Dublin, Ohio by the score of 18 ½-15½

The Walker Cup

The Walker Cup Match is a competition conducted bi-annually in odd-numbered years between amateur golfers of the U.S., and Great Britain and Ireland. It is co-organized by the R & A (Royal & Ancient) and the U.S.G.A., and is named in honor of George Herbert Walker Bush who was president of the U.S.G.A. when the Match was begun in 1920. Bush is the grandfather of George H. W. Bush, the forty-first president of the United States and the great- grandfather of George W. Bush, the forty-third president of the United States. The U.S. leads the series 39-8-1.

The Match was an unofficial event in 1921 and was conducted annually up to 1924. From there it became the bi-annual event that it is today. After World War II, it was switched to odd-numbered years. It is played alternately on either side of the Atlantic.

The Match employs a combination of foursomes (alternate shot) and singles competition. There are two ten-man teams in eighteen singles competitions and eight foursomes matches.Unlike the Ryder Cup, the Walker Cup has never been expanded to make all European amateur golfers eligible to compete. Even though the U.S. leads the series 38-8-1 through 2009, there is little current impetus for expansion. This is because over the last eleven Matches, the United States leads 6-5, and the 2003-2007 matches have been decided by one point.

Francis Ouimet, who won the 1913 U.S. Open, 1914 U.S. Amateur, and 1931 U.S. Amateur, captained the U.S. team a record six times. His captaincies occurred in 1932, 1934, 1936, 1938, 1947, and 1949. The current U.S. practice for naming captains is to award the post to an outstanding U.S. amateur golfer for two Walker Cup competitions. This way the captain has the opportunity to lead the U.S. team at home and across the Atlantic.

The 2007 captain of the U.S. team at Royal County Down Golf Club, Newcastle, Ireland was Buddy Marucci of Berwyn, Pennsylvania. The score in the Match was 12½-11½ in favor of the Americans. Marucci also captained the Americans when the Match was next played in 2009 at Merion

Golf Club in Ardmore, Pennsylvania. Marucci is a member at Merion. Led by Oklahoma State players Rickie Fowler (also a member of the 2007 squad), Peter Uihlein, Morgan Hoffman and Alabama's Bud Cauley, all of whom were undefeated, the United States won the 2009 Match 16½–9½. In September 2008 Marucchi won the U.S. Men's Senior Amateur.

Great Britain & Ireland prevailed in 2011 at Royal Aberdeen Golf Club by the score of 14-12. In 2013, the U.S. won at the National Golf Links by a stellar score of 17-9.

The Solheim Cup

The Solheim Cup is a bi-annual golf match for professional women golfers contested by teams representing Europe and the United States. It is named for the late Norwegian-American golf club manufacturer Karsten Solheim, who was the driving force behind the inauguration of the event.

The first rendition of the Cup was held in 1990 and the matches were held in even-numbered years until 2002. As a result of the September 11 attacks in 2001, the Solheim Cup was switched to odd-numbered years beginning in 2003. This means that the Cup does not clash with the Ryder Cup, which is the equivalent men's event between the U.S. and Europe.

The U.S. team is primarily selected on the basis of a points system with American players on the L.P.G.A. Tour receiving points based on their performances in L.P.G.A. Tour events. For the European team, up to 2005, seven of the twelve players were selected on a points system, based on results on the L.E.T. This allows for top European players to be selected who compete mainly on the L.P.G.A. Tour and ensures that the European team is competitive.

Since 2007 only the top five players from the L.E.T. qualify for the European squad, and another four are selected on the basis of the Women's World Golf Rankings. This reflects the increasing dominance of the L.P.G.A. Tour, where almost all of the top European golfers play most of their time. In addition, to round out the twelve-women squads, each team has a number of "captain's picks"—players chosen at the discretion of the team captains, regardless of their point standings. However, generally speaking, captain's picks are usually the next highest ranked players.

The Cup is contested over three days and since 2002 has consisted of eight foursomes matches, eight four-ball matches, and twelve singles matches for a total of 28 points. Thus, it duplicates the Ryder Cup format.

Team captains are usually recently retired professional golfers who have played in previous Solheim Cup competitions.

The inaugural Cup in 1990 was played at Lake Nona Golf & Country Club in Orlando, Florida. Under captain Kathy Whitworth, the U.S. won easily over the Europeans by the score of 11½-4½.

In 2007 the matches were played at Halmstad Golf Club, Halmstad, Sweden. Betsy King and Helen Alfredsson captained the U.S. and European teams respectively. The Americans prevailed, 16-12.

In 2009 the Americans hosted the matches at Rich Harvest Farms, Sugar Grove, Illinois. Beth Daniel captained the U.S. team while the Europeans were led by Englishwoman Alison Nicholas. After two days of foursomes and fourball, the matches stood all square at 8-8. In the twelve Sunday singles, the Americans showed their strength in this format by prevailing 8-4, making the final tally 16-12 in favor of the U.S. The Americans were led by Michelle Wie who finished with a 3-0-1 record.

In the 2011 rendition, Europe won 15-13 by winning the singles 7-5. The matches were held at Killeen Castlein County Meith, Ireland.

The year 2013 saw the matches being held at Colorado Golf Club in Parker, Colorado. The Europeans made history by winning for the first time on American soil, 18-10, to retain the Cup. Swede Caroline Hedwall became the first player in Solheim Cup history to win all five of her matches.

In the thirteen renditions of the Cup, the U.S. now holds an 8-5 advantage.

The Curtis Cup

The Curtis Cup is awarded to the winner of the Curtis Cup Match, a biannual competition for women amateur golfers representing the U.S. against women amateurs from Great Britain and Ireland. It is co-organized by the U.S.G.A. and the Ladies Golf Union (L.G.U.). Unlike the Ryder Cup and the Solheim Cup, neither the Curtis Cup nor its companion Walker Cup for men has expanded the Great Britain and Ireland team to include all of Europe. The trophy was donated by the outstanding American amateur golfing sisters, Margaret and Harriot Curtis. Margaret won the U.S. Women's Amateur in 1907, 1911, and 1912, while her sister Harriot was the winner in 1906.

The Curtis sisters had competed in the 1905 British Ladies Amateur Golf Championship, where an informal match took place between teams of

U.S. and British women amateur golfers. Over the years, the sisters promoted the idea of an international competition to promote international friendships in the world of women's golf. In fact the Cup is inscribed *"[t]o stimulate friendly rivalry among the women golfers of many lands."*

Through the 1920s discussions about a competition took place among various golf associations, and the Curtis sisters donated the trophy in 1927 to help advance an agreed-upon competition. Finally, in 1931, the U.S.G.A. and the LGU agreed to co-sponsor the event and it began the following year. The inaugural Match was played at the Wentworth Club in England and was won by the U.S.

The Curtis Cup Match is played every two years in even-numbered years, alternating between the two sides of the Atlantic. Each team consists of eight golfers.

Eighteen points are contested in foursomes and singles match play formats. Thus, 9½ points are needed to capture the Cup. Since 1964 the competition was expanded from a single day of competition to two days. Each day there are three foursomes and six singles matches. Starting in 2008 the format changed to a three-day competition with three foursomes and three four-ball matches on each of the first two days and eight singles matches on the final day.

The 2006 Match was played at Bandon Dunes Golf Resort in Bandon, Oregon. With captain Carole Semple Thompson leading the U.S., the Americans won 11½–6½. In 2008 the U.S. squad prevailed 13–7 at St. Andrews. It was the sixth consecutive victory for the Americans. Consecutive victory number seven came in 2010 at the Essex Country Club in Manchester-by-the-Sea, Massachusetts, the home course of the Curtis sisters. Powered by a 6–0 sweep in the middle day of the competition, the U.S. team won easily 12½–7½. The European squad triumphed at Nairn Golf Club, Nairn, Scotland in 2012, winning by the score of 10½-9½. The U.S. won at St. Lous Country Club Ladue, Missouri in 2014 by the score of 13-7.

Overall, the U.S. leads in the competition, 28-7-3.

Epilogue

So, there you have it. A good walk (I hope) through the history of golf. Another thought occurred to me as to why golf is a good walk. The *Scandinavian Journal of Medicine and Science in Sports* did a study in 2008 of golfers who walk when playing golf and their longevity. The study of about 300,000 Swedish people concluded that such golfers lived an average of five years longer than non-golfers!

"And Then Some" is what, you might ask. Well, may I suggest reading more about the history of golf, playing the game, practicing golf, taking a golf lesson or two, or doing what I have been doing for almost fifty years—thinking what a great game golf is and the incomparable satisfaction it brings to you (I hope this too)!

Winners of Major Championships and Team Competitions

United States Open Championship

YEAR	WINNER	SCORE	RUNNER-UP	COURSE
1895	Horace Rawlins	173–36 holes	Willie Dunn (175)	Newport Golf Club, Newport, RI
1896	James Foulis	152–36 holes	Horace Rawlins (155)	Shinnecock Hills Golf Club, Southhampton, NY
1897	Joe Lloyd	162–36 holes	Willie Anderson (163)	Chicago Golf Club, Wheaton, IL
1898	Fred Herd	328	Alex Smith (335)	Myopia Hunt Club, Hamilton, MA
1899	Willie Smith	315	George Low, W.H. Way & Val Fitzjohn (326)	Baltimore Country Club, Baltimore, MD
1900	Harry Vardon	313	J.H. Taylor (315)	Chicago Golf Club, Wheaton, IL
1901	Willie Anderson	331	Alex Smith (331)	Myopia Hunt Club, Hamilton, MA
1902	Laurie Auchterlonie	307	Stewart Gardner (313)	Garden City Golf Club, Garden City, NY
1903	Willie Anderson	307	David Brown (307)	Baltusrol Golf Club, Springfield, NJ
1904	Willie Anderson	308	Gil Nicholls (308)	Glen View Golf Club, Golf, IL
1905	Willie Anderson	314	Alex Smith (316)	Myopia Hunt Club, Hamilton, MA
1906	Alex Smith	295	Willie Smith (308)	Onwentsia Club, Lake Forest, IL
1907	Alec Ross	302	Gil Nicholls (304)	Philadelphia Cricket Club, Chestnut Hill, PA
1908	Fred McLeod	322	Willie Smith (322)	Myopia Hunt Club, Hamilton, MA
1909	George Sargent	290	Tom McNamara (294)	Englewood Golf Club, Englewood, NJ
1910	Alex Smith	298	Macdonald Smith & John McDermott (298)	Philadelphia Cricket Club, Chestnut Hill, PA
1911	John McDermott	307	George Simpson & Mike Brady (307)	Chicago Golf Club, Wheaton, IL
1912	John McDermott	294	Tom McNamara (296)	Country Club of Buffalo, Buffalo, NY
1913	a-Francis Ouimet	304	Harry Vardon & Ted Ray (304)	The Country Club, Brookline, MA
1914	Walter Hagen	290	a-Chick Evans (291)	Midlothian Country Club, Blue Island, IL
1915	a-Jerome Travers	297	Tom McNamara (298)	Baltusrol Golf Club, Springfield, NJ
1916	a-Chick Evans	286	Jock Hutchison (288)	Minikahda Club, Minneapolis, MN

YEAR	WINNER	SCORE	RUNNER-UP	COURSE
1917	Not held – World War I			
1918	Not held – World War I			
1919	Walter Hagen	301	Mike Brady (301)	Brae Burn Country Club, West Newton, MA
1920	Ted Ray	295	Jock Hutchison, Jack Burke, Leo Diegel & Harry Vardon (296)	Inverness Club, Toledo, OH
1921	Jim Barnes	289	Walter Hagen & Fred McLeod (298)	Columbia Country Club, Chevy Chase, MD
1922	Gene Sarazen	288	a-Bobby Jones & John Black (289)	Skokie Country Club, Glencoe, IL
1923	a-Bobby Jones	296	Bobby Cruickshank (296)	Inwood Country Club, Inwood, NY
1924	Cyril Walker	297	a-Bobby Jones (300)	Oakland Hills Country Club, Birmingham, MI
1925	Willie Macfarlane	291	a-Bobby Jones (291)	Worcester Country Club, Worcester, MA
1926	a-Bobby Jones	293	Joe Turnesa (294)	Scioto Country Club, Columbus, OH
1927	Tommy Armour	301	Harry Cooper (301)	Oakmont Country Club, Oakmont, PA
1928	Johnny Farrell	294	a-Bobby Jones ((294)	Olympia Fields Country Club, Matteson, IL
1929	a-Bobby Jones	294	Al Espinosa (294)	Winged Foot Country Club, Mamaroneck, NY
1930	a-Bobby Jones	287	Macdonald Smith (289)	Interlachen Country Club, Hopkins, MN
1931	Billy Burke	292	George Von Elm (292)	Inverness Club, Toledo, Ohio
1932	Gene Sarazen	286	Bobby Cruickshank & Phil Perkins (289)	Fresh Meadow Country Club, Flushing, NY
1933	a-Johnny Goodman	287	Ralph Guldahl (288)	North Shore Golf Club, Glenview, IL
1934	Olin Dutra	293	Gene Sarazen (294)	Merion Cricket Club, Ardmore, PA
1935	Sam Parks, Jr.	299	Jimmy Thomson (301)	Oakmont Country Club, Oakmont, PA
1936	Tony Manero	282	Harry E. Cooper (284)	Baltusrol Golf Club, Springfield, NJ
1937	Ralph Guldahl	281	Sam Snead (283)	Oakland Hills Country Club, Birmingham, MI
1938	Ralph Guldahl	284	Dick Metz (290)	Cherry Hills Country Club, Denver, CO
1939	Byron Nelson	284	Craig Wood & Denny Shute (284)	Philadelphia Country Club, Gladwyne, PA
1940	Lawson Little	287	Gene Sarazen (287)	Canterbury, Golf Club, Cleveland, OH
1941	Craig Wood	284	Denny Shute (287)	Colonial Club, Ft. Worth, TX
1942	Not held – World War II			
1943	Not held – World War II			
1944	Not held – World War II			
1945	Not held – World War II			
1946	Lloyd Mangrum	284	Byron Nelson & Vic Ghezzi (284)	Canterbury Golf Club, Cleveland, OH
1947	Lew Worsham	282	Sam Snead (282)	St. Louis Country Club, Clayton, MO
1948	Ben Hogan	276	Jimmy Demaret (278)	Riviera Country Club, Pacific Palisades, CA
1949	Cary Middlecoff	286	Clayton Heafner & Sam Snead (287)	Medinah Country Club, Medinah, IL
1950	Ben Hogan	287	Lloyd Mangrum & George Fazio (287)	Merion Golf Club, Ardmore, PA
1951	Ben Hogan	287	Clayton Heafner (289)	Oakland Hills Country Club, Birmingham, MI

YEAR	WINNER	SCORE	RUNNER-UP	COURSE
1952	Julius Boros	281	Porky Oliver (285)	Northwood Club, Dallas, TX
1953	Ben Hogan	283	Sam Snead (289)	Oakmont Country Club, Oakmont, PA
1954	Ed Furgol	284	Gene Littler (285)	Baltusrol Golf Club, Springfield, NJ
1955	Jack Fleck	287	Ben Hogan (287)	Olympic Country Club, San Francisco, CA
1956	Cary Middlecoff	281	Ben Hogan & Julius Boros (282)	Oak Hill Country Club, Rochester, NY
1957	Dick Mayer	282	Cary Middlecoff (282)	Inverness Club, Toledo, OH
1958	Tommy Bolt	283	Gary Player (287)	Southern Hills Country Club, Tulsa, OK
1959	Billy Casper	282	Bob Rosburg (283)	Winged Foot Country Club, Mamaroneck, NY
1960	Arnold Palmer	280	a-Jack Nicklaus (282)	Cherry Hills Country Club, Denver, CO
1961	Gene Littler	281	Doug Sanders & Bob Goalby (282)	Oakland Hills Country Club, Birmingham, MI
1962	Jack Nicklaus	283	Arnold Palmer (283)	Oakmont Country Club, Oakmont, PA
1963	Julius Boros	293	Arnold Palmer & Jacky Cupit (293)	The Country Club, Brookline, MA
1964	Ken Venturi	278	Tommy Jacobs (282)	Congressional Country Club, Bethesda, MD
1965	Gary Player	282	Kel Nagle (282)	Bellerive Country Club, St. Louis, MO
1966	Billy Casper	278	Arnold Palmer (278)	Olympic Country Club, San Francisco, CA
1967	Jack Nicklaus	275	Arnold Palmer (279)	Baltusrol Golf Club, Springfield, NJ
1968	Lee Trevino	275	Jack Nicklaus (279)	Oak Hill Country Club, Rochester, NY
1969	Orville Moody	281	Al Geiberger, Deane Beman & Bob Rosburg (282)	Champions Golf Club, Houston, TX
1970	Tony Jacklin	281	Dave Hill (288)	Hazeltine National Golf Club, Chaska, MN
1971	Lee Trevino	280	Jack Nicklaus (280)	Merion Golf Club, Ardmore, PA
1972	Jack Nicklaus	290	Bruce Crampton (293)	Pebble Beach Golf Links, Pebble Beach, CA
1973	Johnny Miller	279	John Schlee (280)	Oakmont Country Club, Oakmont, PA
1974	Hale Irwin	287	Forest Fezler (289)	Winged Foot Country Club, Mamaroneck, NY
1975	Lou Graham	287	John Mahaffey (287)	Medinah Country Club, Medinah, IL
1976	Jerry Pate	277	Al Geiberger & Tom Weiskopf (279)	Atlanta Athletic Club, Duluth, GA
1977	Hubert Green	278	Lou Graham (279)	Southern Hills Country Club, Tulsa, OK
1978	Andy North	285	Dave Stockton & J.C. Snead (286)	Cherry Hills Country Club, Denver, CO
1979	Hale Irwin	284	Gary Player & Jerry Pate (286)	Inverness Club, Toledo, Ohio
1980	Jack Nicklaus	272	Isao Aoki (274)	Baltusrol Golf Club, Springfield, NJ
1981	David Graham	273	George Burns & Bill Rogers (276)	Merion Golf Club, Ardmore, PA
1982	Tom Watson	282	Jack Nicklaus (284)	Pebble Beach Golf Links, Pebble Beach, CA
1983	Larry Nelson	280	Tom Watson (281)	Oakmont Country Club, Oakmont, PA
1984	Fuzzy Zoeller	276	Greg Norman (276)	Winged Foot Country Club, Mamaroneck, NY
1985	Andy North	279	Dave Barr, T.C. Chen & Denis Watson (280)	Oakland Hills Country Club, Birmingham, MI

YEAR	WINNER	SCORE	RUNNER-UP	COURSE
1986	Raymond Floyd	279	Lanny Wadkins & Chip Beck (281)	Shinnecock Hills Golf Club, Southhampton, NY
1987	Scott Simpson	277	Tom Watson (278)	Olympic Club, San Francisco, CA
1988	Curtis Strange	278	Nick Faldo (278)	The Country Club, Brookline, MA
1989	Curtis Strange	278	Chip Beck, Ian Woosnam & Mark McCumber (279)	Oak Hill Country Club, Rochester, NY
1990	Hale Irwin	280	Mike Donald (280)	Medinah Country Club, Medinah, IL
1991	Payne Stewart	282	Scott Simpson (282)	Hazeltine National Golf Club, Chaska, MN
1992	Tom Kite.	285	Jeff Sluman (287)	Pebble Beach Golf Links, Pebble Beach, CA
1993	Lee Janzen	272	Payne Stewart (274)	Baltusrol Golf Club, Springfield, NJ
1994	Ernie Els	279	Colin Mongomerie & Loren Roberts (279)	Oakmont Country Club, Oakmont, PA
1995	Corey Pavin	280	Greg Norman (282)	Shinnecock Hills Golf Club, Southhampton, NY
1996	Steve Jones	278	Davis Love III & Tom Lehman (279)	Oakland Hills Country Club, Birmingham, MI
1997	Ernie Els	276	Colin Montgomerie (277)	Congressional Country Club, Bethesda, MD
1998	Lee Janzen	280	Payne Stewart (281)	Olympic Club, San Francisco, CA
1999	Payne Stewart	279	Phil Mickelson (280)	Pinehurst Country Club, Pinehurst, NC
2000	Tiger Woods	272	Miguel Angel Jimenez & Ernie Els (287)	Pebble Beach Golf Links, Pebble Beach, CA
2001	Retief Goosen	276	Mark Brooks (276)	Southern Hills Country Club, Tulsa, OK
2002	Tiger Woods	277	Phil Mickelson (280)	Bethpage State Park (Black), Farmingdale, NY
2003	Jim Furyk	272	Stephen Leaney (275)	Olympia Fields Country Club, Matteson, IL
2004	Retief Goosen	276	Phil Mickelson (278)	Shinnecock Hills Golf Club, Southhampton, NY
2005	Michael Campbell	280	Tiger Woods (282)	Pinehurst Country Club, Pinehurst, NC
2006	Geoff Ogilvy	285	Jim Furyk, Colin Montgomerie & Phil Mickelson (286)	Winged Foot Country Club, Mamaroneck, NY
2007	Angel Cabrera	285	Jim Furyk & Tiger Woods (286)	Oakmont Country Club, Oakmont, PA
2008	Tiger Woods	283	Rocco Mediate (283)	Torrey Pines Golf Club (South), San Diego, CA
2009	Lucas Glover	276	Phil Mickelson, David Duval, & Ricky Barnes (278)	Bethpage State Park (Black), Farmingdale, NY
2010	Graeme McDowell	284	Gregory Havret (285)	Pebble Beach Golf Links, Pebble Beach, CA
2011	Rory McIlory	268	Jason Day (276)	Congressional Country Club, Bethesda, MD.
2012	Webb Simpson	281	Michael Thompson and Graeme McDowell (282)	Olympic Club, San Francisco, CA
2013	Justin Rose	281	Jason Day (283)	Merion Golf Club, Ardmore, PA
2014	Martin Kaymer	271	Rickie Fowler (279) Eric Compton (279)	Pinhurst No. 2, Pinhurst, NC
2015	Jordan Spieth	275	Dustin Johnson & Louis Oosthuizen (276)	Chambers Bay, University Place, WA

The Masters

YEAR	WINNER	SCORE	RUNNER-UP
1934	Horton Smith	284	Craig Wood (285)
1935	Gene Sarazen	282	Craig Wood (282)
1936	Horton Smith	285	Harry Cooper (286)
1937	Byron Nelson	283	Ralph Guldahl (285)
1938	Henry Picard	285	Ralph Gudahl & Harry Cooper (287)
1939	Ralph Gudahl	279	Sam Snead (280)
1940	Jimmy Demaret	280	Lloyd Mangrum (284)
1941	Craig Wood	280	Byron Nelson (283)
1942	Byron Nelson	280	Ben Hogan (280)
1943	Not Held-World War II		
1944	Not Held-World War II		
1945	Not Held-World War II		
1946	Herman Keiser	282	Ben Hogan (283)
1947	Jimmy Demaret	281	Frank Stranahan & Byron Nelson (283)
1948	Claude Harmon	279	Cary Middlecoff (284)
1949	Sam Snead	282	Lloyd Mangrum & Johnny Bulla (285)
1950	Jimmy Demaret	283	Jim Ferrier (285)
1951	Ben Hogan	280	Skee Riegel (282)
1952	Sam Snead	286	Jack Burke, Jr (290)
1953	Ben Hogan	274	Porky Oliver (279)
1954	Sam Snead	289	Ben Hogan (289)
1955	Cary Middlecoff	279	Ben Hogan (286)
1956	Jack Burke, Jr.	289	Ken Venturi (290)
1957	Doug Ford	283	Sam Snead (286)
1958	Arnold Palmer	284	Doug Ford & Fred Hawkins (285)
1959	Art Wall, Jr.	284	Cary Middlecoff (285)
1960	Arnold Palmer	282	Ken Venturi (283)
1961	Gary Player	280	Arnold Palmer & Charles R. Coe (281)
1962	Arnold Palmer	280	Dow Finsterwald & Gary Player (280)
1963	Jack Nicklaus	286	Tony Lema (287)
1964	Arnold Palmer	276	Jack Nicklaus & Dave Marr (282)
1965	Jack Nicklaus	271	Arnold Palmer & Gary Player (280)
1966	Jack Nicklaus	288	Gay Brewer, Jr. & Tommy Jacobs (288)
1967	Gay Brewer, Jr.	280	Bobby Nichols (281)
1968	Bob Goalby	277	Roberto De Vicenzo (278)
1969	George Archer	281	Billy Casper, George Knudson & Tom Weiskopf (282)
1970	Billy Casper	279	Gene Littler (279)
1971	Charles Coody	279	Jack Nicklaus & Johnny Miller (281)
1972	Jack Nicklaus	286	Bruce Crampton, Bobby Mitchell & Tom Weiskopf (289)
1973	Tommy Aaron	283	J.C. Snead (284)
1974	Gary Player	278	Tom Weiskopf & Dave Stockton (280)

YEAR	WINNER	SCORE	RUNNER-UP
1975	Jack Nicklaus	276	Johnny Miller & Tom Weiskopf (277)
1976	Raymond Floyd	271	Ben Crenshaw (279)
1977	Tom Watson	276	Jack Nicklaus (278)
1978	Gary Player	277	Hubert Green, Rod Funseth & Tom Watson (278)
1979	Fuzzy Zoeller	280	Ed Sneed & Tom Watson (280)
1980	Seve Ballesteros	275	Gibby Gilbert & Jack Newton (279)
1981	Tom Watson	280	Jack Nicklaus & Johnny Miller (282)
1982	Craig Stadler	284	Dan Pohl (284)
1983	Seve Ballesteros	280	Ben Crenshaw & Tom Kite (284)
1984	Ben Crenshaw	277	Tom Watson (279)
1985	Bernhard Langer	282	Curtis Strange, Seve Ballesteros & Raymond Floyd (284)
1986	Jack Nicklaus	279	Greg Norman & Tom Kite (280)
1987	Larry Mize	285	Seve Ballesteros & Greg Norman (285)
1988	Sandy Lyle	281	Mark Calcavecchia (282)
1989	Nick Faldo	283	Scott Hoch (283)
1990	Nick Faldo	278	Raymond Floyd (278)
1991	Ian Woosnam	277	José Maria Olazábal (278)
1992	Fred Couples	275	Raymond Floyd (277)
1993	Bernhard Langer	277	Chip Beck (281)
1994	José Maria Olazábal	279	Tom Lehman (281)
1995	Ben Crenshaw	274	Davis Love III (275)
1996	Nick Faldo	276	Greg Norman (281)
1997	Tiger Woods	270	Tom Kite (282)
1998	Mark O'Meara	279	Fred Couples & David Duval (280)
1999	José Maria Olazábal	280	Davis Love III (282)
2000	Vijay Singh	278	Ernie Els (281)
2001	Tiger Woods	272	David Duval (274)
2002	Tiger Woods	276	Retief Goosen (279)
2003	Mike Weir	281	Len Mattiace (281)
2004	Phil Mickelson	279	Ernie Els (280)
2005	Tiger Woods	276	Chris DiMarco (276)
2006	Phil Mickelson	281	Tim Clark (283)
2007	Zach Johnson	289	Tiger Woods, Retief Goosen & Rory Sabbatini (291)
2008	Trevor Immelman	280	Tiger Woods (283)
2009	Angel Cabrera	276	Kenny Perry & Chad Campbell (276)
2010	Phil Mickelson	272	Lee Westwood (275)
2011	Charles Scwartzel	274	Adam Scott, Jason Day (276)
2012	Bubba Watson	278	Louis Oosthuizen (278)
2013	Adam Scott	279	Angel Cabrerra (279)
2014	Bubba Watson	280	Jonas Blixt, Jordon Spieth (283)
2015	Jordan Spieth	270	Phil Mickelson, Justin Rose (274)

The P.G.A. Championship

YEAR	WINNER	SCORE	RUNNER-UP	COURSE
1916	Jim Barnes 1-up		Jock Hutchson	Siwanoy Country Club, Bronxville, NY
1917	Not Held World War I			
1918	Not Held-World War I			
1919	Jim Barnes 6 & 5		Fred McLeod	Engineers Country Club, Roslyn, NY
1920	Jock Hutchison 1-up		J. Douglas Edgar	Flossmoor Country Club, Flossmoor, IL
1921	Walter Hagen 3 & 2		Jim Barnes	Inwood Country Club, Inwood, NY
1922	Gene Sarazen 4 & 3		Emmet French	Oakmont Country Club, Oakmont, PA
1923	Gene Sarazen 1-up/ 38 holes		Walter Hagen	Pelham Country Club, Pellam, NY
1924	Walter Hagen 2-up		Jim Barnes	French Lick Country Club, French Lick, IN
1925	Walter Hagen 6 & 5		Bill Mehlhorn	Olympia Fields Country Club, Matteson, IL
1926	Walter Hagen 5 & 3		Leo Diegel	Salisbury Golf Club, Westbury, NY
1927	Walter Hagen 1-up		Joe Turnesa	Cedar Crest Country Club, Dallas, TX
1928	Leo Diegel 6 & 5		Al Espinosa	Five Farms Country Club, Baltimore, MD
1929	Leo Diegel 6 & 4		John Farrell	Hillcrest Country Club, Los Angeles, CA
1930	Tommy Armour 1-up		Gene Sarazen	Fresh Meadow Country Club, Flushing, NY
1931	Tom Creavy 2 & 1		Denny Shute	Wannamoisett Country Club, Rumford, RI
1932	Olin Dutra 4 & 3		Frank Walsh	Keller Golf Club, St. Paul, MN
1933	Gene Sarazen 5 & 4		Willie Goggin	Blue Mound Country Club, Milwaukee, WI
1934	Paul Runyan 1-up/ 38 holes		Craig Wood	Park Country Club, Williamsville, NY
1935	Johnny Revolta 5 & 4		Tommy Armour	Twin Hills Country Club, Oklahoma City, OK
1936	Denny Shute 3 & 2		Jimmy Thomson	Pinehurst Country Club, Pinehurst, NC
1937	Denny Shute 1-up/ 37 holes		Harold McSpaden	Pittsburgh Field Club, Aspinwall, PA
1938	Paul Runyan 8 & 7		Sam Snead	Shawnee Country Club, Shawnee-on-Delaware, PA
1939	Henry Picard 1-up/ 37 holes		Byron Nelson	Pomonok Country Club, Flushing, NY
1940	Byron Nelson 1-up		Sam Snead	Hershey Country Club, Hershey, PA
1941	Vic Ghezzi 1-up/ 38 holes		Byron Nelson	Cherry Hills Country Club, Denver, CO
1942	Sam Snead 2 &1		Jim Turnesa	Seaview Country Club, Atlantic City, NJ
1943	Not Held-World War II			
1944	Bob Hamilton 1-up		Byron Nelson	Manito Golf & Country Club, Spokane, WA
1945	Byron Nelson 4 & 3		Sam Byrd	Morraine Country Club, Dayton, OH
1946	Ben Hogan 6 & 4		Porky Oliver	Portland Golf Club, Portland, OR
1947	Jim Ferrier 2 & 1		Chick Harbert	Plum Hollow Country Club, Detroit, MI
1948	Ben Hogan 7 & 6		Mike Turnesa	Norwood Hills Country Club, St. Louis, MO
1949	Sam Snead 3 & 2		John Palmer	Hermitage Country Club, Richmond, VA
1950	Chandler Harper 4 & 3		Henry Williams, Jr.	Scioto Country Club, Columbus, OH
1951	Sam Snead 7 & 6		Walter Burkemo	Oakmont Country Club, Oakmont, PA
1952	Jim Turnesa 1-up		Chick Harbert	Big Spring Country Club, Louisville, KY

YEAR	WINNER	SCORE	RUNNER-UP	COURSE
1953	Walter Burkemo 2 & 1		Felice Torza	Birmingham Country Club, Birmingham, MI
1954	Chick Harbert 4 & 3		Walter Burkemo	Keller Golf Club, St. Paul, MN
1955	Doug Ford 4 & 3		Cary Middlecoff	Meadowbrook Country Club, Detroit, MI
1956	Jack Burke, Jr. 3 & 2		Ted Kroll	Blue Hill Country Club, Boston, MA
1957	Lionel Hebert 2 & 1		Dow Finsterwald	Miami Valley Golf Club, Dayton, OH
1958	Dow Finsterwald	276	Billy Casper (278)	Llanerch Country Club, Havertown, PA
1959	Bob Rosburg	277	Jerry Barber &	
			Doug Sanders	Minneapolis Golf Club, St Louis Park, MN
1960	Jay Hebert	281	Jim Ferrier (282)	Firestone Country Club, Akron, OH
1961	Jerry Barber	277	Don January (277)	Olympia Fields Country Club, Matteson, IL
1962	Gary Player	278	Bob Goalby (279)	Aronimink Golf Club, Newtown Square, PA
1963	Jack Nicklaus	279	Dave Ragan, Jr. (281)	Dallas Athletic Club, Dallas, TX
1964	Bobby Nichols	271	Jack Nicklaus &	
			Arnold Palmer (274)	Columbus Country Club, Columbus, OH
1965	Dave Marr	280	Jack Nicklaus &	
			Billy Casper (282)	Laurel Valley Golf Club, Ligonier, PA
1966	Al Geiberger	280	Dudley Wysong (284)	Firestone Country Club, Akron, OH
1967	Don January	281	Don Massengale (281)	Columbine Country Club, Littleton, CO
1968	Julius Boros	281	Arnold Palmer &	
			Bob Charles (282)	Pecan Valley Country Club, San Antonio, TX
1969	Raymond Floyd	276	Gary Player (277)	NCR Golf Club, Dayton, OH
1970	Dave Stockton	279	Arnold Palmer &	
			Bob Murphy (281)	Southern Hills Country Club, Tulsa, OK
1971	Jack Nicklaus	281	Billy Casper (283)	PGA National Golf Club, Palm Beach Gardens, FL
1972	Gary Player	281	Jim Jamieson &	
			Tommy Aaron (283)	Oakland Hills Golf Club, Birmingham, MI
1973	Jack Nicklaus	277	Bruce Crampton (281)	Canterbury Golf Club, Cleveland, OH
1974	Lee Trevino	276	Jack Nicklaus (277)	Tanglewood Golf Club, Winston-Salem, NC
1975	Jack Nicklaus	276	Bruce Crampton (278)	Firestone Country Club, Akron, OH
1976	Dave Stockton	281	Don January &	
			Raymond Floyd (282)	Congressional Country Club, Bethesda, MD
1977	Lanny Wadkins	282	Gene Littler (282)	Pebble Beach Golf Links, Pebble Beach, CA
1978	John Mahaffey	276	Jerry Pate &	
			Tom Watson (276)	Oakmont Country Club, Oakmont, PA
1979	David Graham	272	Ben Crenshaw (272)	Oakland Hills Country Club, Birmingham, MI
1980	Jack Nicklaus	274	Andy Bean (281)	Oak Hill Country Club, Rochester, NY
1981	Larry Nelson	273	Fuzzy Zoeller (277)	Atlanta Athletic Club, Duluth, GA
1982	Raymond Floyd	272	Lanny Wadkins (275)	Southern Hills Country Club, Tulsa, OK
1983	Hal Sutton	274	Jack Nicklaus (275)	Riviera Country Club, Pacific Palisades, CA
1984	Lee Trevino	273	Lanny Wadkins &	
			Gary Player (277)	Shoal Creek, Birmingham, AL
1985	Hubert Green	278	Lee Trevino (280)	Cherry Hills Country Club, Denver, CO
1986	Bob Tway	276	Greg Norman (278)	Inverness Club, Toledo, OH

YEAR	WINNER	SCORE	RUNNER-UP	COURSE
1987	Larry Nelson	287	Lanny Wadkins (287)	PGA National Golf Club, Palm Beach Gardens, FL
1988	Jeff Sluman	272	Paul Azinger (275)	Oak Tree Golf Club, Edmond, OK
1989	Payne Stewart	276	Andy Bean, Mike Reid & Curtis Strange (277)	Kemper Lakes Golf Club, Hawthorn Woods, IL
1990	Wayne Grady	282	Fred Couples (285)	Shoal Creek, Birmingham, AL
1991	John Daly	276	Bruce Lietzke (279)	Crooked Stick Golf Club, Carmel, IN
1992	Nick Price	278	Nick Faldo, John Cook, Jim Gallagher & Gene Sauers (281)	Bellerive Country Club, St. Louis, MO
1993	Paul Azinger	272	Greg Norman (272)	Inverness Club, Toledo, OH
1994	Nick Price	269	Corey Pavin (275)	Southern Hills Country Club, Tulsa, OK
1995	Steve Elkington	267	Colin Montgomerie (267)	Riviera Country Club, Pacific Palisades, CA
1996	Mark Brooks	277	Kenny Perry (277)	Valhalla Golf Club, Louisville, KY
1997	Davis Love III	269	Justin Leonard (274)	Winged Foot Golf Club, Mamaroneck, NY
1998	Vijay Singh	271	Steve Stricker (273)	Sahalee Country Club, Redmond, WA
1999	Tiger Woods	277	Sergio Garcia (278)	Medinah Country Club, Medinah, IL
2000	Tiger Woods	270	Bob May (270)	Valhalla Golf Club, Louisville, KY
2001	David Toms	265	Phil Mickelson (266)	Atlanta Athletic Club, Duluth, GA
2002	Rich Beem	278	Tiger Woods (279)	Hazeltine National Golf Club, Chaska, MN
2003	Shaun Micheel	276	Chad Campbell (278)	Oak Hill Country Club, Rochester, NY
2004	Vijah Singh	280	Chris DiMarco & Justin Leonard (280)	Whistling Straits, Kohler, WI
2005	Phil Mickelson	276	Steve Elkington & Thomas Bjorn (277)	Baltusrol Golf Club, Springfield, NJ
2006	Tiger Woods	270	Shaun Micheel (275)	Medinah Country Club, Medinah, IL
2007	Tiger Woods	272	Woody Austin (274)	Southern Hills Country Club, Tulsa, OK
2008	Padraig Harrington	277	Ben Curtis & Sergio Garcia (279)	Oakland Hills Country Club, Birmingham, MI
2009	Y.E. Yang	280	Tiger Woods (283)	Hazeltine National Golf Course, Chaska, MN
2010	Martin Kaymer	277	Bubba Watson (277	Whistling Straits, Kohler, WI
2011	Keegan Bradley	272	Jason Dufner (272)	Atlanta Athletic Club, Duluth, GA
2012	Rory McIlroy	275	David (283)	Kiawah Island, SC
2013	Jason Dufner	270	Jim Furyk (272)	Oak Hill Country Club, Rochester, NY
2014	Rory McIlory	268	Phil Mickelson (269)	Valhalla Golf Club, Louisville, KY
2015	Jason Day	268	Jordan Spieth (271)	Whistling Straits, Kohler, WI

The Open Championship (British)

YEAR	WINNER	SCORE	RUNNER-UP	COURSE
1860	Willie Park	174	Tom Morris, Sr. (176)	Prestwick Club, Ayrshire, Scotland
1861	Tom Morris, Sr.	163	Willie Park (167)	Prestwick Club, Ayrshire, Scotland
1862	Tom Morris, Sr.	163	Willie Park (176)	Prestwick Club, Ayrshire, Scotland
1863	Willie Park	168	Tom Morris, Sr. (170)	Prestwick Club, Ayrshire, Scotland

YEAR	WINNER	SCORE	RUNNER-UP	COURSE
1864	Tom Morris, Sr.	167	Andrew Strath (169)	Prestwick Club, Ayrshire, Scotland
1865	Andrew Strath	162	Willie Park (164)	Prestwick Club, Ayrshire, Scotland
1866	Willie Park, Sr.	169	David Park (171)	Prestwick Club, Ayrshire, Scotland
1867	Tom Morris, Sr.	170	Willie Park (172)	Prestwick Club, Ayrshire, Scotland
1868	Tom Morris, Jr.	157	Robert Andrew (159)	Prestwick Club, Ayrshire, Scotland
1869	Tom Morris, Jr.	154	Tom Morris, Sr. (157)	Prestwick Club, Ayrshire, Scotland
1870	Tom Morris, Jr.	149	Bob Kirk (161)	Prestwick Club, Ayrshire, Scotland
1871	Not Held			
1872	Tom Morris, Jr.	166	David Strath (169)	Prestwick Club, Ayrshire, Scotland
1873	Tom Kidd	179	Jamie Anderson (180)	St. Andrews, St. Andrews, Scotland
1874	Mungo Park	159	Tom Morris, Jr. (161)	Musselburgh, Musselburgh, Scotland
1875	Willie Park	166	Bob Martin (168)	Prestwick Club, Ayrshire, Scotland
1876	Bob Martin	176	David Strath (176)	St. Andrews, St. Andrews, Scotland
1877	Jamie Anderson	160	Bob Pringle (162)	Musselburgh, Musselburgh, Scotland
1878	Jamie Anderson	157	Bob Kirk (159)	Prestwick Club, Ayrshire, Scotland
1879	Jamie Anderson	169	Andrew Kirkaldy & James Allan (172)	St. Andrews, St. Andrews, Scotland
1880	Bob Feurguson	162	Peter Paxton (167)	Musselburgh, Musselburgh, Scotland
1881	Bob Feurguson	170	Jamie Anderson (173)	Prestwick Club, Ayrshire, Scotland
1882	Bob Feurguson	171	Willie Fernie (174)	St. Andrews, St. Andrews, Scotland
1883	Willie Fernie	159	Bob Ferguson (159)	Musselburgh, Musselburgh, Scotland
1884	Jack Simpson	160	Douglas Rolland & Willie Fernie (164)	Prestwick Club, Ayrshire, Scotland
1885	Bob Martin	171	Archie Simpson (172)	St. Andrews, St. Andrews, Scotland
1886	David Brown	157	Willie Campbell (159)	Musselburgh, Musselburgh, Scotland
1887	Willie Park, Jr.	161	Bob Martin (162)	Prestwick Club, Ayrshire, Scotland
1888	Jack Burns	171	David Anderson & Ben Sayers (172)	St. Andrews, St. Andrews, Scotland
1889	Willie Park, Jr.	155	Andrew Kirkaldy (155)	Musselburgh, Musselburgh, Scotland
1890	a-John Ball	164	Willie Fernie & Archie Simpson (167)	Prestwick Club, Ayrshire, Scotland
1891	Hugh Kirkaldy	166	Andrew Kirkaldy & Willie Fernie (168)	St. Andrews, St. Andrews, Scotland
1892	a-Harold Hilton	305	a-John Ball, Sandy Herd, & Hugh Kirkaldy (308)	Muirfield, Gullane, Scotland
1893	Willie Auchterlonie	322	Johnny Laidley (324)	Prestwick Club, Ayrshire, Scotland
1894	J.H. Taylor	326	Douglas Rolland (331)	Royal St. George's, Sandwich, England
1895	J.H. Taylor	322	Sandy Herd (326)	St. Andrews, St. Andrews, Scotland
1896	Harry Vardon	316	J.H. Taylor (316)	Muirfield, Gullane, Scotland
1897	a-Harold Hilton	314	James Braid (315)	Hoylake, Hoylake, England
1898	Harry Vardon	307	Willie Park, Jr. (308)	Prestwick Club, Ayrshire, Scotland
1899	Harry Vardon	310	Jack White (315)	Royal St. George's, Sandwich, England
1900	J.H. Taylor	309	Harry Vardon (317)	St. Andrews, St. Andrews, Scotland
1901	James Braid	309	Harry Vardon (312)	Muirfield, Gullane, Scotland

YEAR	WINNER	SCORE	RUNNER-UP	COURSE
1902	Sandy Herd	307	Harry Vardon (308)	Hoylake, Hoylake, England
1903	Harry Vardon	300	Tom Vardon (306)	Prestwick Club, Ayrshire, Scotland
1904	Jack White	296	James Braid (297)	Royal St. George's, Sandwich, England
1905	James Braid	318	J.H. Taylor & Rowland Jones (323)	St. Andrews, St. Andrews, Scotland
1906	James Braid	300	J.H. Taylor (304)	Muirfield, Gullane, Scotland
1907	Arnaud Massy	312	J.H. Taylor (314)	Hoylake, Hoylake, England
1908	James Braid	291	Tom Ball (299)	Prestwick Club, Ayrshire, Scotland
1909	J.H. Taylor	295	James Braid (299)	Deal, Deal, England
1910	James Braid	299	Sandy Herd (303)	St. Andrews, St. Andrews, Scotland
1911	Harry Vardon	303	Arnaud Massy (303)	Royal St. George's, Sandwich, England
1912	Ted Ray	295	Harry Vardon (299)	Muirfield, Gullane, Scotland
1913	J.H. Taylor	304	Ted Ray (312)	Hoylake, Hoylake, England
1914	Harry Vardon	306	J.H. Taylor (309)	Prestwick Club, Ayrshire, Scotland
1915	Not Held – World War I			
1916	Not Held – World War I			
1917	Not Held – World War I			
1918	Not Held – World War I			
1919	Not Held – World War I			
1920	George Duncan	303	Sandy Herd (305)	Deal, Deal, England
1921	Jock Hutchison	296	Roger Wethered (296)	St. Andrews, St. Andrews, Scotland
1922	Walter Hagen	300	George Duncan & Jim Barnes (301)	Royal St. George's, Sandwich, England
1923	Arthur Havers	295	Walter Hagen (296)	Royal Troon, Troon, Scotland
1924	Walter Hagen	301	Ernest Whitcombe (302)	Hoylake, Hoylake, England
1925	Jim Barnes	300	Archie Compston & Ted Ray (301)	Prestwick Club, Ayrshire, Scotland
1926	a-Bobby Jones	291	Al Watrous (293)	Royal Lytham, Lytham, England
1927	a-Bobby Jones	285	Aubrey Boomer (291)	St. Andrews, St. Andrews, Scotland
1928	Walter Hagen	292	Gene Sarazen (294)	Royal St. George's, Sandwich, England
1929	Walter Hagen	292	Johnny Farrell (298)	Muirfield, Gullane, Scotland
1930	a-Bobby Jones	291	Macdonald Smith & Leo Diegel (293)	Hoylake, Hoylake, England
1931	Tommy Armour	296	José Jurado (297)	Carnoustie, Carnoustie, Scotland
1932	Gene Sarazen	283	Macdonald Smith (288)	Prince's, Prince's, England
1933	Denny Shute	292	Craig Wood (292)	St. Andrews, St. Andrews, Scotland
1934	Henry Cotton	283	Sid Brews (288)	Royal St. George's, Sandwich, England
1935	Alf Perry	283	Alf Padgham (287)	Muirfield, Gullane, Scotland
1936	Alf Padgham	287	Jimmy Adams (288)	Hoylake, Hoylake, England
1937	Henry Cotton	290	Reg Whitcombe (292)	Carnoustie, Carnoustie, Scotland
1938	Reg Whitcombe	295	Jimmy Adams (297)	Royal St. George's, Sandwich, England
1939	Dick Burton	290	Johnny Bulla (292)	St. Andrews, St. Andrews, Scotland
1940	Not Held – World War II			
1941	Not Held – World War II			

YEAR	WINNER	SCORE	RUNNER-UP	COURSE
1942	Not Held – World War II			
1943	Not Held – World War II			
1944	Not Held – World War II			
1945	Not Held – World War II			
1946	Sam Snead	290	Bobby Locke & Johnny Bulla (294)	St. Andrews, St. Andrews, Scotland
1947	Fred Daly	293	Frank Stranahan & Reg Horne (294)	Hoylake, Hoylake, England
1948	Henry Cotton	284	Fred Daly (289)	Muirfield, Gullane, Scotland
1949	Bobby Locke	283	Harry Bradshaw (283)	Royal St. George's, Sandwich, England
1950	Bobby Locke	279	Roberto De Vicenzo (281)	Royal Troon, Troon, Scotland
1951	Max Faulkner	285	Tony Cerda (287)	Royal Portrush, Portrush, Ireland
1952	Bobby Locke	287	Peter Thomson (288)	Royal Lytham, Lytham, England
1953	Ben Hogan	282	Frank Stranahan, Dai Reese, Tony Cerda & Peter Thomson (286)	Carnoustie, Carnoustie, Scotland
1954	Peter Thompson	283	Sid Scott, Dai Rees & Bobby Locke (284)	Royal Birkdale, Southport, England
1955	Peter Thomson	281	Johnny Fallon (283)	St. Andrews, St. Andrews, Scotland
1956	Peter Thomson	286	Flory Van Donck (289)	Hoylake, Hoylake, England
1957	Bobby Locke	279	Peter Thomson (282)	St. Andrews, St. Andrews, Scotland
1958	Peter Thompson	278	Dave Thomas (278)	Royal Lytham, Lytham, England
1959	Gary Player	284	Flory Van Donck & Fred Bullock (286)	Muirfield, Gullane, Scotland
1960	Kel Nagle	278	Arnold Palmer (279)	St. Andrews, St. Andrews, Scotland
1961	Arnold Palmer	284	Dai Rees (285)	Royal Birkdale, Southport, England
1962	Arnold Palmer	276	Kel Nagle (282)	Royal Troon, Troon, Scotland
1963	Bob Charles	277	Phil Rodgers (277)	Royal Lytham, Lytham, England
1964	Tony Lema	279	Jack Nicklaus (284)	St. Andrews, St. Andrews, Scotland
1965	Peter Thomson	285	Christy O'Connor & Brian Huggett (287)	Royal Birkdale, Southport, England
1966	Jack Nicklaus	282	Doug Sanders & Dave Thomas (283)	Muirfield, Gullane, Scotland
1967	Roberto De Vicenzo	278	Jack Nicklaus (280)	Hoylake, Hoylake, England
1968	Gary Player	289	Jack Nicklaus & Bob Charles (291)	Carnoustie, Carnoustie, Scotland
1969	Tony Jacklin	280	Bob Charles (282)	Royal Lytham, Lytham, England
1970	Jack Nicklaus	283	Doug Sanders (283)	St. Andrews, St. Andrews, Scotland
1971	Lee Trevino	278	Lu Liang Huan (279)	Royal Birkdale, Southport, England
1972	Lee Trevino	278	Jack Nicklaus (279)	Muirfield, Gullane, Scotland
1973	Tom Weiskopf	276	Johnny Miller & Neil Coles (279)	Royal Troon, Troon, Scotland
1974	Gary Player	282	Peter Oosterhuis (286)	Royal Lytham, Lytham, England
1975	Tom Watson	279	Jack Newton (279)	Carnoustie, Carnoustie, Scotland

YEAR	WINNER	SCORE	RUNNER-UP	COURSE
1976	Johnny Miller	279	Seve Ballesteros & Jack Nicklaus (285)	Royal Birkdale, Southport, England
1977	Tom Watson	268	Jack Nicklaus (269)	Turnberry, Turnberry, Scotland
1978	Jack Nicklaus	281	Tom Kite, Raymond Floyd, Ben Crenshaw & Simon Owen (283)	St. Andrews, St. Andrews, Scotla
1979	Seve Ballesteros	283	Jack Nicklaus & Ben Crenshaw (286)	Royal Lytham, Lytham, England
1980	Tom Watson	271	Lee Trevino (275)	Muirfield, Gullane, Scotland
1981	Bill Rogers	276	Bernhard Langer (280)	Royal St. George's, Sandwich, England
1982	Tom Watson	284	Peter Oosterhuis & Nick Price (285)	Royal Troon, Troon, Scotland
1983	Tom Watson	275	Hale Irwin & Andy Bean (276)	Royal Birkdale, Southport, England
1984	Seve Ballesteros	276	Bernhard Langer & Tom Watson (278)	St. Andrews, St. Andrews, Scotland
1985	Sandy Lyle	282	Payne Stewart (283)	Royal St. George's, Sandwich, England
1986	Greg Norman	280	Gordon Brand (285)	Turnberry, Turnberry, Scotland
1987	Nick Faldo	279	Paul Azinger & Rodger Davis (280)	Muirfield, Gullane, Scotland
1988	Seve Ballesteros	273	Nick Price (275)	Royal Lytham, Lytham, England
1989	Mark Calcavecchia	275	Greg Norman & Wayne Grady (275)	Royal Troon, Troon, Scotland
1990	Nick Faldo	270	Payne Stewart & Mark McNulty (275)	St. Andrews, St. Andrews, Scotland
1991	Ian Baker-Finch	272	Mike Harwood (274)	Royal Birkdale, Suothport, England
1992	Nick Faldo	272	John Cook (273)	Muirfield, Gullane, Scotland
1993	Greg Norman	267	Nick Faldo (269)	Royal St. George's, Sandwich, England
1994	Nick Price	268	Jesper Parnevik (269)	Turnberry, Turnberry, Scotland
1995	John Daly	282	Constantino Rocca (282)	St. Andrews, St. Andrews, Scotland
1996	Tom Lehman	271	Mark McCumber & Ernie Els (273)	Royal Lytham, Lytham, England
1997	Justin Leonard	272	Jesper Parnevik & Darren Clarke (275)	Royal Troon, Troon, Scotland
1998	Mark O'Meara	280	Brian Watts (280)	Royal Birkdale, Southport, England
1999	Paul Lawrie	290	Justin Leonard & Jean Van de Velde (290)	Carnoustie, Carnoustie, Scotland
2000	Tiger Woods	269	Thomas Bjørn & Ernie Els (277)	St. Andrews, St. Andrews, Scotland
2001	David Duval	274	Niclas Fasth (277)	Royal Lytham, Lytham, England
2002	Ernie Els	278	Thomas Levet, Stuart Appleby & Steve Elkington (278)	Muirfield, Gullane, Scotland

YEAR	WINNER	SCORE	RUNNER-UP	COURSE
2003	Ben Curtis	283	Vijay Singh & Thomas Bjørn (284)	Royal St. George's, Sandwich, England
2004	Todd Hamilton	274	Ernie Els (274)	Royal Troon, Troon, Scotland
2005	Tiger Woods	274	Colin Montgomerie (279)	St. Andrews, St. Andrews, Scotland
2006	Tiger Woods	270	Chris DiMarco (272)	Royal Liverpool, Hoylake, England
2007	Padraig Harrington	277	Sergio Garcia (277)	Carnoustie, Carnoustie, Scotland
2008	Padraig Harrington	283	Ian Poulter (287)	Royal Birkdale, Southport, England
2009	Stewart Cink	278	Tom Watson (278)	Turnberry, Turnberry, Scotland
2010	Louis Oosthuizen	272	Lee Westwood (279)	St. Andrews, St. Andrews, Scotland
2011	Darren Clarke	275	Phil Mickelson and Dustin Johnson (278)	Royal St. George's England
2012	Ernie Els	273	Adam Scott (274)	Royal Lytham, Laytham, England
2013	Phil Mickleson	281	Henrick Stenson (284)	Muirfield, Gullane, Scotland
2014	Rory McIlory	271	Rickie Flower, and Sergio Garcia (273)	Hoylake, Hoylake, England
2015	Zach Johnson	273	Marc Leishman and Louis Oosthuizen (273)	St. Andrews, St Andrews, Scotland

United States Amateur

YEAR	WINNER	YEAR	WINNER	YEAR	WINNER
1895	Charles Macdonald	1919	Davidson Herron	1943	Not Held-World War II
1896	H.J. Whigham	1920	Chick Evans	1944	Not-Held World War II
1897	H.J. Whigham	1921	Jesse Guilford	1945	Not Held-World War II
1898	Findlay Douglas	1922	Jess Sweetser	1946	Ted Bishop
1899	H.M. Harriman	1923	Max Martson	1947	Skee Riegel
1900	Walter Travis	1924	Bobby Jones	1948	William Turnesa
1901	Walter Travis	1925	Bobby Jones	1949	Charles Coe
1902	Louis James	1926	George Von Elm	1950	Sam Urzetta
1903	Walter Travis	1927	Bobby Jones	1951	Billy Maxwell
1904	H. Chandler Egan	1928	Bobby Jones	1952	Jack Westland
1905	H. Chandler Egan	1929	Harrison Johnston	1953	Gene Littler
1906	Eben Byers	1930	Bobby Jones	1954	Arnold Palmer
1907	Jerry Travers	1931	Francis Ouimet	1955	E. Harvie Ward
1908	Jerry Travers	1932	Ross Somerville	1956	E. Harvie Ward
1909	Robert Gardner	1933	George Dunlap	1957	Hillman Robbins
1910	W.C. Fownes, Jr.	1934	Lawson Little	1958	Charles Coe
1911	Harold Hilton	1935	Lawson Little	1959	Jack Nicklaus
1912	Jerry Travers	1936	John Fischer	1960	Deane Beman
1913	Jerry Travers	1937	John Goodman	1961	Jack Nicklaus
1914	Francis Ouimet	1938	William Turnesa	1962	Labron Harris
1915	Robert Gardner	1939	Bud Ward	1963	Deane Beman
1916	Chick Evans	1940	Richard Chapman	1964	Bill Campbell
1917	Not Held-World War I	1941	Bud Ward	1965	Bob Murphy
1918	Not Held-World War I	1942	Not Held-World War II	1966	Gary Cowan

YEAR	WINNER	YEAR	WINNER	YEAR	WINNER
1967	Bob Dickson	1984	Scott Verplank	2000	Jeff Quinney
1968	Bruce Fleisher	1985	Sam Randolph	2001	Bubba Dickerson
1969	Steve Melnyk	1986	Buddy Alexander	2002	Ricky Barnes
1970	Lanny Wadkins	1987	Billy Mayfair	2003	Nick Flanagan
1971	Gary Cowan	1988	Eric Meeks	2004	Ryan Moor
1972	Vinny Giles	1989	Chris Patton	2005	Edoardo Molinari
1973	Craig Stadler	1990	Phil Mickelson	2006	Richie Ramsay
1974	Jerry Pate	1991	Mitch Voges	2007	Colt Knost
1975	Fred Ridley	1992	Justin Leonard	2008	Danny Lee
1976	Bill Sander	1993	John Harris	2009	Byeong Hun-An
1977	John Fought	1994	Tiger Woods	2010	Peter Uihlein
1978	John Cook	1995	Tiger Woods	2011	Kerry Kraft
1979	Mark O'Meara	1996	Tiger Woods	2012	Steven Fox
1980	Hal Sutton	1997	Matt Kuchar	2013	Matt Fitzpatrick
1981	Nathaniel Crosby	1998	Hank Kuehne	2014	Gunn Yang
1982	Jay Sigel	1999	David Gossett	2015	
1983	Jay Sigel				

British Amateur

YEAR	WINNER	YEAR	WINNER	YEAR	WINNER
1885	Allan MacFie	1903	Robert Maxwell	1926	Jess Sweetser
1886	Horace Hutchinson	1904	Walter Travis	1927	William Tweddell
1887	Horace Hutchinson	1905	Arthur Barry	1928	Thomas Perkins
1888	John Ball	1906	James Robb	1929	Cyril Tolley
1889	Johnny Laidley	1907	John Ball	1930	Bobby Jones
1885	Allan MacFie	1908	E.A. Lassen	1931	Eric Smith
1886	Horace Hutchinson	1909	Robert Maxwell	1932	John deForest
1887	Horace Hutchinson	1910	John Ball	1933	Michael Scott
1888	John Ball	1911	Harold Hilton	1934	Lawson Little
1889	Johnny Laidley	1912	John Ball	1935	Lawson Little
1890	John Ball	1913	Harold Hilton	1936	Hector Thomson
1891	Johnny Laidley	1914	J.L.C. Jenkins	1937	Robert Sweeny, Jr.
1892	John Ball	1915	Not Held-World War I	1938	Charles Yates
1893	Peter Anderson	1916	Not Held-World War I	1939	Alexander Kyle
1894	John Ball	1917	Not Held-World War I	1940	Not Held-World War II
1895	Leslie Balfour-Melville	1918	Not Held-World War I	1941	Not Held-World War II
1896	Freddie Tait	1919	Not Held-World War I	1942	Not Held-World War II
1897	Jack Allan	1920	Cyril Tolley	1943	Not Held-World War II
1898	Freddie Tait	1921	William Hunter	1944	Not Held-World War II
1899	John Ball	1922	Ernest Holderness	1945	Not Held-World War II
1900	Harold Hilton	1923	Roger Wethered	1946	James Bruen
1901	Harold Hilton	1924	Ernest Holderness	1947	William Turnesa
1902	Charles Hutchings	1925	Robert Harris	1948	Frank Stranahan

YEAR	WINNER	YEAR	WINNER	YEAR	WINNER
1949	Samuel McCready	1972	Trevor Homer	1994	Lee James
1950	Frank Stranahan	1973	Dick Siderowf	1995	Gordon Sherry
1951	Richard Chapman	1974	Trevor Homer	1996	Warren Bledon
1952	E. Harvie Ward	1975	Vinny Giles	1997	Craig Watson
1953	Joe Carr	1976	Dick Siderowf	1998	Sergio Garcia
1954	Douglas Bachli	1977	Peter McEvoy	1999	Graeme Storm
1955	Joe Conrad	1978	Peter McEvoy	2000	Mikko Ilonen
1956	John Beharrell	1979	Jay Sigel	2001	Michael Hoey
1957	Reid Jack	1980	Duncan Evans	2002	Alejandro Larrazabal
1958	Joe Carr	1981	Phillipe Ploujoux	2003	Gary Wolstenholme
1959	Deane Beman	1982	Martin Thompson	2004	Stuart Wilson
1960	Joe Carr	1983	Philip Parkin	2005	Brian McElhinney
1961	Michael Bonallack	1984	José Maria Olazábal	2006	Julien Guerrier
1962	Richard Davies	1985	Garth McGimpsey	2007	Drew Weaver
1963	Michael Lunt	1986	David Curry	2008	Reinier Saxton
1964	Gordon Clark	1987	Paul Mayo	2009	Matteo Manassero
1965	Michael Bonallack	1988	Christian Hardin	2010	Jin Jeong
1966	Bobby Cole	1989	Stephen Dodd	2011	Bryden Macpherson
1967	Bob Dickson	1990	Rolf Muntz	2012	Alan Dunbar
1968	Michael Bonallack	1991	Gary Wolstenholme	2013	Garrick Porteous
1969	Michael Bonallack	1992	Stephen Dundas	2014	Bradley Neil
1970	Michael Bonallack	1993	Ian Pyman	2015	Romain Langasque
1971	Steve Melnyk				

United States Women's Open

YEAR	WINNER	SCORE	RUNNER-UP	COURSE
1946	Patty Berg	5 & 4	Betty Jameson	Spokane Country Club, Spokane, WA
1947	Betty Jameson	295	a-Sally Sessions & a-Polly Riley (301)	Starmount Forest Country Club, Greensboro, NC
1948	Babe Zaharias	300	Betty Hicks (308)	Atlantic City Country Club, Northfield, NJ
1949	Louise Suggs	291	Babe Zaharias (305)	Prince Georges Country Club, Landover, MD
1950	Babe Zaharias	291	a-Betsy Rawls (300)	Rolling Hills Country Club, Wichita, KA
1951	Betsy Rawls	293	Louse Suggs (298)	Druid Hills Golf Club, Atlanta, GA
1952	Louise Suggs	284	Marlene Hagge (291)	Bala Golf Club, Philadelphia, PA
1953	Betsy Rawls	302	Jackie Pung (302)	Country Club of Rochester, Rochester, NY
1954	Babe Zaharias	291	Betty Hicks (303)	Salem Country Club, Peabody, MA
1955	Fay Crocker	299	Mary Lena Faulk (303)	Wichita Country Club, Wichita, KA
1956	Kathy Cornelius	302	Barbara McIntire (302)	Northland Country Club, Duluth, MN
1957	Betsy Rawls	299	Patty Berg (305)	Winged Foot Golf Club, Mamaroneck, NY
1958	Mickey Wright	290	Louise Suggs (295)	Forest Lake Country Club, Detroit, MI
1959	Mickey Wright	287	Louise Suggs (289)	Churchill Valley Country Club, Penn Hills, PA
1960	Betsy Rawls	292	Joyce Ziske (293)	Worcester Country Club, Worcester, MA
1961	Mickey Wright	293	Betsy Rawls (299)	Baltusrol Golf Club, Springfield, NJ

YEAR	WINNER	SCORE	RUNNER-UP	COURSE
1962	Murle Breer	301	Jo Anne Prentice & Ruth Jessen (303)	Dunes Golf Club, Myrtle Beach, SC
1963	Mary Mills	289	Sandra Haynie & Louise Suggs (292)	Kenwood Country Club, Cincinnati, OH
1964	Mickey Wright	290	Ruth Jessen (290)	San Diego Country Club, Chula Vista, CA
1965	Carol Mann	290	Kathy Cornelius (292)	Atlantic City Country Club, Northfield, NJ
1966	Sandra Spuzich	297	Carol Mann (298)	Hazeltine National Golf Club, Chaska, MN
1967	a-Catherine LaCoste	294	Susie Berning & Beth Stone (296)	Hot Springs Golf Club, Hot Springs, VA
1968	Susie Berning	289	Mickey Wright (292)	Moselem Springs Golf Club, Fleetwood, PA
1969	Donna Caponi	294	Peggy Wilson (295)	Scenic Hills Country Club, Pensacola, FL
1970	Donna Caponi	287	Sandra Haynie (288)	Muskogee Country Club, Muskogee, OK
1971	JoAnne Carner	288	Kathy Whitworth (295)	Kahkwa Country Club, Erie, PA
1972	Susie Berning	299	Kathy Ahern, Pam Barnett & Judy Rankin (300)	Winged Foot Golf Club, Mamaroneck, NY
1973	Susie Berning	290	Gloria Ehret (295)	Country Club of Rochester, Rochester, NY
1974	Sandra Haynie	295	Carol Mann & Beth Stone (296)	La Grange Country Club, La Grange, IL
1975	Sandra Palmer	295	JoAnne Carner, a-Nancy Lopez & Sandra Post (299)	Atlantic City Country Club, Northfield, NJ
1976	JoAnne Carner	292	Sandra Palmer (292)	Rolling Green Country Club, Springfield, PA
1977	Hollis Stacy	292	Nancy Lopez (294)	Hazeltine National Golf Club, Chaska, MN
1978	Hollis Stacy	289	Joanne Carner & Sally Little (290)	Country Club of Indianapolis, Indianapolis, IN
1979	Jerilyn Britz	284	Debbie Massey & Sandra Palmer (286)	Brooklawn Country Club, Fairfield, CN
1980	Amy Alcott	280	Hollis Stacy (289)	Richland Country Club, Nashville, TN
1981	Pat Bradley	279	Beth Daniel (280)	La Grange Country Club, La Grange, IL
1982	Janet Anderson	283	Beth Daniel, Sandra Haynie & Donna White (289)	Del Paso Country Club, Sacramento, CA
1983	Jan Stephenson	290	JoAnne Carner (291)	Cedar Ridge Country Club, Tulsa, OK
1984	Hollis Stacy	290	Rosie Jones (291)	Salem Country Club, Peabody, MA
1985	Kathy Baker	280	Judy Dickenson (283)	Baltusrol Golf Club, Springfield, NJ
1986	Jane Geddes	287	Sally Little (287)	NCR Golf Club, Dayton, OH
1987	Laura Davies	285	Ayako Okamoto & JoAnne Carner (285)	Plainfield Country Club, Plainfield, NJ
1988	Lisolette Neumann	277	Patty Sheehan (280)	Baltimore Country Club, Baltimore, MD
1989	Betsy King	278	Nancy Lopez (282)	Indianwood Golf & Country Club, Lake Orion, MI
1990	Betsy King	284	Patty Sheehan (285)	Atlanta Athletic Club, Duluth, GA
1991	Meg Mallon	283	Pat Bradley (285)	Colonial Country Club, Ft. Worth, TX
1992	Patty Sheehan	280	Juli Inkster (280)	Oakmont Country Club, Oakmont, PA

YEAR	WINNER	SCORE	RUNNER-UP	COURSE
1993	Lauri Merten	280	Donna Andrews &	
			Helen Alfredsson (281)	Crooked Stick Golf Club, Carmel, IN
1994	Patty Sheehan	277	Tammie Green (278)	Indianwood Golf & Country Club, Lake Orion, MI
1995	Annika Sörenstam	278	Meg Mallon (279)	The Broadmoor, Colorado Springs, CO
1996	Annika Sörenstam	272	Kris Tschetter (278)	Pine Needles Lodge & Golf Club, Southern Pines, NC
1997	Alison Nicholas	274	Nancy Lopez (275)	Pumpkin Ridge Golf Club, North Plains, OR
1998	Se Ri Pak	290	a-Jenny Chuasiriporn	
			(290)	Blackwolf Run Golf Club, Kohler, WI
1999	Juli Inkster	272	Sherri Turner (277)	Old Waverly Golf Club, West Point, MS
2000	Karrie Webb	282	Cristie Kerr &	
			Meg Mallon (287)	Merit Club, Libertyville, IL
2001	Karrie Webb	273	Se Ri Pak (281)	Pine Needles Lodge & Golf Club, Southern Pines, NC
2002	Juli Inkster	276	Annika Sörenstam (278)	Praire Dunes Country Club, Hutchinson, KS
2003	Hilary Lunke	283	Angela Stanford &	
			Kelly Robbins (283)	Pumpkin Ridge Golf Club, North Plains, OR
2004	Meg Mallon	274	Annika Sörenstam (276)	Orchards Golf Club, South Hadley, MA
2005	Birdie Kim	287	a-Brittany Lang &	
			a-Morgan Pressel (289)	Cherry Hills Country Club, Denver, CO
2006	Annika Sörenstam	284	Pat Hurst (284)	Newport Country Club, Newport, RI
2007	Cristie Kerr	279	Angela Park &	
			Lorena Ochoa (281)	Pine Needles Lodge & Golf Club, Southern Pines, NC
2008	Inbee Park	283	Helen Alfredsson (287)	Interlachen Country Club, Edina, MN
2009	Eun-Hee Ji	284	Candie Kung (285)	Saucon Valley Country Club, Bethlehem, PA
2010	Paula Creamer	281	Suzann Pettersen &	
			Na Yeon Choi (285)	Oakmont Country Club, Oakmont, PA
2011	So Yeon Ryu	281	Hee Kyung Seo (281)	Broadmoor (East Course), Colorado Springs, CO
2012	Na Yeon Choi	281	Amy Yang (285)	Blackwolf Run Golf Club, Kohler, WI
2013	Inbee Park	280	K. Kim (284)	Sebonack Golf Club, Southhampton, NY
2014	Michelle Wie	278	Stacy Lewis (280)	Pinehurst No. 2, Pinhurst, NC
2015	Inn Gee Chun	272	Amy Yang (273)	Lancaster Country Club, Lancaster, PA

ANA Inspiration

(Replaced Kraft Nabisco Championship in 2015 which had become the L.P.G.A.'s Fourth Major Championship in1983)

YEAR	WINNER	SCORE	RUNNER-UP	COURSE
1972	Jane Blalock	213	Carol Mann & Judy Rankin (216)	Played at Mission Hills Country Club,
1973	Mickey Wright	284	Joyce Kazmierski (286)	Rancho Mirage, CA since it began
1974	Jo Anne Prentice	289	Jane Blalock & Sandra Haynie (289)	
1975	Sandra Palmer	283	Kathy McMullen (284)	
1976	Judy Rankin	285	Betty Burfeindt (288)	
1977	Kathy Whitworth	289	JoAnne Carner & Sally Little (290)	
1978	Sandra Post	283	Penny Pulz (283)	
1979	Sandra Post	276	Nancy Lopez (277)	
1980	Donna Caponi	275	Amy Alcott (277)	

YEAR	WINNER	SCORE	RUNNER-UP
1981	Nancy Lopez	277	Carolyn Hill (279)
1982	Sally Little	278	Hollis Stacy & Sandra Haynie (281)
1983	Amy Alcott	282	Beth Daniel & Kathy Whitworth (284)
1984	Juli Inkster	280	Pat Bradley (280)
1985	Alice Miller	275	Jan Stephenson (278)
1986	Pat Bradley	280	Val Skinner (282)
1987	Betsy King	283	Patty Sheehan (283)
1988	Amy Alcott	274	Colleen Walker (276)
1989	Julie Inkster	279	Tammie Green & JoAnne Carner (284)
1990	Betsy King	283	Kathy Postlewait & Shirley Furlong (285)
1991	Amy Alcott	273	Dottie Pepper (281)
1992	Dottie Pepper	279	Juli Inkster (279)
1993	Helen Alfredsson	284	Amy Benz & Tina Barrett (286)
1994	Donna Andrews	276	Laura Davies (277)
1995	Nanci Bowen	285	Susie Redman (286)
1996	Patty Sheehan	281	Kelly Robbins, Meg Mallon, & Annika Sörenstam (286)
1997	Betsy King	276	Kris Tschetter (278
1998	Pat Hurst	281	Helen Dobson (282)
1999	Dottie Pepper	269	Meg Mallon (275)
2000	Karrie Webb	274	Dottie Pepper (284)
2001	Annika Sörenstam	281	Akiko Fukushima, Janice Moodie, Dottie Pepper, Rachel Teske & Karrie Webb (284)
2002	Annika Sörenstam	280	Liselotte Neumann (281)
2003	P. Meunier-Lebouc	281	Annika Sörenstam (282)
2004	Grace Park	277	Aree Song (278)
2005	Annika Sörenstam	273	Rosie Jones (281)
2006	Karrie Webb	279	Lorena Ochoa (279)
2007	Morgan Pressel	285	Catriona Matthew, Brittany Lincicome & Suzann Pettersen (286)
2008	Lorena Ochoa	277	Suzann Pettersen & Annika Sörenstam (282)
2009	Brittany Lincicome	279	Cristie Kerr & Kristy McPherson (280)
2010	Yani Tseng	275	Suzann Pettersen (276)
2011	Stacy Lewis	275	Yani Tseng (278)
2012	Lexi Thompson	274	Michelle Wie (277)
2013	Inbee Clark	273	So Yeon Ryu (277)
2014	Lexi Thompson	274	Michelle Wie (277)
2015	Brittany Lincicome	279	Stacy Lewis (279)

L.P.G.A. Championship

YEAR	WINNER	SCORE	RUNNER-UP	COURSE
1955	Beverly Hanson	220	Louise Suggs (223)	The tournament began in 1955 and
1956	Marlene Hagge	291	Patty Berg (291)	has had stays at Stardust Country
1957	Louise Suggs	285	Wiffi Smith (288)	Club, Las Vegas, NV (1961–66),
1958	Mickey Wright	288	Fay Crocker (294)	Pleasant Valley Country Club, Sutton,

YEAR	WINNER	SCORE	RUNNER-UP
1959	Betsy Rawls	288	Patty Berg (289)
1960	Mickey Wright	292	Louise Suggs (295)
1961	Mickey Wright	287	Louise Suggs (296)
1962	Judy Kimball	282	Shirley Spork (286)
1963	Mickey Wright	294	Mary Lena Faulk & Mary Mills (296)
1964	Mary Mills	278	Mickey Wright (280)
1965	Sandra Haynie	279	Clifford A. Creed (280)
1966	Gloria Ehret	282	Mickey Wright (285)
1967	Kathy Whitworth	284	Shirley Englehorn (285)
1968	Sandra Post	294	Kathy Whitworth (294)
1969	Betsy Rawls	293	Susie Berning & Carol Mann (297)
1970	Shirley Englehorn	285	Kathy Whitworth (285)
1971	Kathy Whitworth	288	Kathy Ahern (292)
1972	Kathy Ahern	293	Jane Blalock (299)
1973	Mary Mills	288	Betty Burfeindt (289)
1974	Sandra Haynie	288	JoAnne Carner (290)
1975	Kathy Whitworth	288	Sandra Haynie (289)
1976	Betty Burfeindt	287	Judy Rankin (288)
1977	Chako Higuchi	279	Pat Bradley, Sandra Post & Judy Rankin (282)
1978	Nancy Lopez	275	Amy Alcott (281)
1979	Donna Caponi	279	Jerilyn Britz (282)
1980	Sally Little	285	Jane Blalock (288)
1981	Donna Caponi	280	Jerilyn Britz & Pat Meyers (281)
1982	Jan Stephenson	279	JoAnne Carner (281)
1983	Patty Sheehan	279	Sandra Haynie (281)
1984	Patty Sheehan	272	Beth Daniel & Pat Bradley (282)
1985	Nancy Lopez	273	Alice Miller (281)
1986	Pat Bradley	277	Patty Sheehan (278)
1987	Jane Geddes	275	Betsy King (275)
1988	Sherri Turner	281	Amy Alcott (282)
1989	Nancy Lopez	274	Ayoko Okamoto (277)
1990	Beth Daniel	280	Rosie Jones (281)
1991	Meg Mallon	274	Pat Bradley & Ayako Okamoto (275)
1992	Betsy King	267	JoAnne Carner, Karen Noble & Liselotte Neumann (278)
1993	Patty Sheehan	275	Lauri Merten (276)
1994	Laura Davies	279	Alice Ritzman (280)
1995	Kelly Robbins	274	Laura Davies (275)
1996	Laura Davies	213	Julie Piers (214)
1997	Chris Johnson	281	Leta Lindley (281)
1998	Se Ri Pak	273	Donna Andrews & Lisa Hackney (276)
1999	Juli Inkster	268	Liselotte Neumann (272)
2000	Juli Inkster	281	Stefania Croce (281)
2001	Karrie Webb	270	Laura Diaz (272)
2002	Se Ri Pak	279	Beth Daniel (282)

MA (1967-68, 1970-74), the Jack Nicklaus Sports Center, Kings Island, OH (1978-89), Bethesda Country Club, Bethesda, MD (1990–93), DuPont Country Club, Wilmington, DE (1994-2004), Bulle Rock Golf Club, Havre de Grace, MD (2005-2009), and Locust Hill Country Club, Rochester, NY (2010-2013). Weschester Country Club, Rye, NY (2015)

2003	Annika Sörenstam	278	Grace Park (278)
2004	Annika Sörenstam	271	Shi Hyun Ahn (274)
2005	Annika Sörenstam	277	a-Michelle Wie (280)
2006	Se Ri Pak	280	Karrie Webb (280)
2007	Suzann Pettersen	274	Karrie Webb (275)
2008	Yani Tseng	276	Maria Hjorth (276)
2009	Anna Nordquist	273	Lindsey Wright (277)
2010	Christie Kerr	269	Song-Hee Kim (281)
2011	Yani Tseng	272	Brittany Lang (276)
2012	Shanshan Feng	282	Stacy Lewis, Suzann, Pettersen, Mika Miyazato & Eun-Hee Ji (284
2013	Inbee Park	285	Catriana Mathews (285)
2014	Inbee Park	277	Brittany Lincicome (277)
2015	Inbee Park	273	Sei-Young Kim (278)

Women's British Open

(Became the Fourth Major Championship in 2001 when it Replaced the du Maurier Classic)

YEAR	WINNER	SCORE	RUNNER-UP	COURSE
1994	Liselotte Neumann	280	Dottie Mochrie &	
			Annika Sörenstam (283)	Woburn Golf & Country Club, Milton Keynes, England
1995	Karrie Webb	278	Annika Sörenstam &	
			Jill McGill (284)	Woburn Golf & Country Club, Milton Keynes, England
1996	Emilee Klein	277	Penny Hammel &	
			Amy Alcott (284)	Woburn Golf & Country Club, Milton Keynes, England
1997	Karrie Webb	269	Rosie Jones (277)	Sunningdale Golf Club, Berkshire, England
1998	Sherri Steinhauer	292	Sophie Gustafson &	
			Brandie Burton (293)	Royal Lytham, Lytham, England
1999	Sherri Steinhauer	283	Annika Sörenstam (284)	Woburn Golf & Country Club, Milton Keynes, England
2000	Sophie Gustafson	282	Kristy Taylor,	
			Liselotte Neumann,	
			Becky Iverson &	
			Meg Mallon (284)	Royal Birkdale, Southport, England
2001	Se Ri Pak	277	Mi Hyun Kim (279)	Sunningdale Golf Club, Berkshire, England
2002	Karrie Webb	273	Michelle Ellis &	
			Paula Marti (275)	Turnberry Golf Club, Turnberry, Scotland
2003	Annika Sörenstam	278	Se Ri Pak (279)	Royal Lytham, Lytham, England
2004	Karen Stupples	269	Rachel Teske (274)	Sunningdale Golf Club, Berkshire, England
2005	Jeong Jang	272	Sophie Gustafson (276)	Royal Birkdale Golf Club, Southport, England
2006	Sherri Steinhauer	281	Cristie Kerr &	
			Sophie Gustafson (284)	Royal Lytham, Lytham, England
2007	Lorena Ochoa	287	Jee Young Lee &	
			Maria Hjorth (291)	St. Andrews, St. Andrews, Scotland
2008	Ji-Yai Shin	270	Yani Tseng (273)	Sunningdale Golf Club, Berkshire, England
2009	Catriona Matthew	285	Karrie Webb (288)	Royal Lytham, Lytham, England
2010	Yani Tseng	277	Katherine Hull (278)	Royal Birkdale Golf Club, Southport, England

YEAR	WINNER	SCORE	RUNNER-UP	COURSE
2011	Yani Tseng	272	Brittany Lang (276)	Carnoustie, Carnoustie, Scotland
2012	SJiiyai Shin	279	No Yeon Choi (282)	St. Andrews, St. Andrews, Scotland
2013	Stacy Lewis	280	Inbee Park (288)	Royal Liverpool Golf Club, Hoylake, England
2014	Melissa Martin	287	Shanshan Feng	
			Suzann Pettersen (288)	Turnberry, Scotland
2015	Inbee Park	276	Jin Young Ko (279)	Turnberry, Scotland

Western Open (1930-1967)
(Was Considered a Major Title on the Women's Tour Until it was Discontinued After the 1967 Tournament)

YEAR	WINNER	YEAR	WINNER	YEAR	WINNER
1930	Mrs. Lee Mida	1943	Patty Berg	1956	Beverley Hanson
1931	June Beebe	1944	Babe Zaharias	1957	Patty Berg
1932	Jane Weiller	1945	Babe Zaharias	1958	Patty Berg
1933	June Beebe	1946	Louise Suggs	1959	Betsy Rawls
1934	Marian McDougall	1947	Louise Suggs	1960	Joyce Ziske
1935	Opal Hill	1948	Patty Berg	1961	Mary Lena Faulk
1936	Opal Hill	1949	Louise Suggs	1962	Mickey Wright
1937	Betty Hicks	1950	Babe Zaharias	1963	Mickey Wright
1938	Bea Barrett	1951	Patty Berg	1964	Carol Mann
1939	Helen Detweiler	1952	Betsy Rawls	1965	Susie Maxwell
1940	Babe Zaharias	1953	Louise Suggs	1966	Mickey Wright
1941	Patty Berg	1954	Betty Jameson	1967	Kathy Whitworth
1942	Betty Jameson	1955	Patty Berg		

Titleholders Championship (1937–1972)
(Was Considered a Major Title on the Women's Tour Until it was Discontinued After the 1972 Tournament)

YEAR	WINNER	YEAR	WINNER	YEAR	WINNER
1937	Patty Berg	1949	Peggy Kirk	1961	Mickey Wright
1938	Patty Berg	1950	Babe Zaharias	1962	Mickey Wright
1939	Patty Berg	1951	Pat O'Sullivan	1963	Marilynn Smith
1940	Betty Hicks	1952	Babe Zaharias	1964	Marilynn Smith
1941	Dorothy Kirby	1953	Patty Berg	1965	Kathy Whitworth
1942	Dorothy Kirby	1954	Louise Suggs	1966	Kathy Whitworth
1943	Not held – World WarII	1955	Patty Berg	1967	Not held
1944	Not held – World War II	1956	Louise Suggs	1968	Not held
1945	Not held – World War II	1957	Patty Berg	1969	Not held
1945	Not held – World War II	1958	Beverly Hanson	1970	Not held
1946	Louise Suggs	1959	Louise Suggs	1971	Not held
1947	Babe Zaharias	1960	Fay Crocker	1972	Sandra Palmer
1948	Patty Berg				

du Maurier Classic (1979–2000)

(added as Women's Fifth Major) (Was Considered a Major Title on the L.P.G.A. Tour From 1979
Until it was Discontinued After the 2000 Tournament)

YEAR	WINNER	YEAR	WINNER	YEAR	WINNER
1973	Jocelyne Bourassa	1983	Hollis Stacy	1992	Sherri Steinhauer
1974	Carole Jo Skal	1984	Juli Inkster	1993	Brandi Burton
1975	JoAnne Carner	1985	Pat Bradley	1994	Martha Nause
1976	Donna Caponi	1986	Pat Bradley	1995	Jenny Lidback
1977	Judy Rankin	1987	Jody Rosenthal	1996	Laura Davies
1978	JoAnne Carner	1988	Sally Little	1997	Colleen Walker
1979	Amy Alcott	1989	Tammie Green	1998	Brandie Burton
1980	Pat Bradley	1990	Cathy Johnston	1999	Karrie Webb
1981	Jan Stephenson	1991	Nancy Scranton	2000	Meg Mallon
1982	Sandra Hayniz				

The Evian Championship

(added as Women's Fifth Major) Played at Evian Resort Golf Club

YEAR	WINNER	YEAR	WINNER	YEAR	WINNER
2013	Suzann Peterden	2014	Kim Hyo-joo	2015	

United States Women's Amateur

YEAR	WINNER	YEAR	WINNER	YEAR	WINNER
1895	Mrs. C.S. Brown (Lucy Barnes)	1915	Florence Vanderbeck	1935	Glenna Collett Vare
1896	Beatrix Hoyt	1916	Alexa Stirling	1936	Pamela Barton
1897	Beatrix Hoyt	1917	Not held – World War I	1937	Estelle Lawson
1898	Beatrix Hoyt	1918	Not held – World War I	1938	Patty Berg
1899	Ruth Underhill	1919	Alexa Stirling	1939	Betty Jameson
1900	Frances Griscom	1920	Alexa Stirling	1940	Betty Jameson
1901	Genevieve Hecker	1921	Marion Hollins	1941	Elizabeth Hicks
1902	Genevieve Hecker	1922	Glenna Collett	1942	Not held – World War II
1903	Bessie Anthony	1923	Edith Cummings	1943	Not held – World War II
1904	Georgianna Bishop	1924	Dorothy C. Hurd	1944	Not held – World War II
1905	Pauline Mackay	1925	Glenna Collett	1945	Not held – World War II
1906	Harriot Curtis	1926	Helen Stetson	1946	Babe Zaharias
1907	Margaret Curtis	1927	Miriam Burns Horn	1947	Louise Suggs
1908	Katherine Harley	1928	Glenna Collett	1948	Grace Lenczyk
1909	Dorothy Campbell	1929	Glenna Collett	1949	Dorothy Porter
1910	Dorothy Campbell	1930	Glenna Collett	1950	Beverley Hanson
1911	Margaret Curtis	1931	Helen Hicks	1951	Dorothy Kirby
1912	Margaret Curtis	1932	Virginia Van Wie	1952	Jacqueline Pung
1913	Gladys Ravenscroft	1933	Virginia Van Wie	1953	Mary Lena Faulk
1914	Katherine Harley	1934	Virginia Van Wie	1954	Barbara Romack

YEAR	WINNER	YEAR	WINNER	YEAR	WINNER
1955	Patricia Lesser	1975	Beth Daniel	1995	Kelli Kuehne
1956	Marlene Stewart	1976	Donna Horton	1996	Kelli Kuehne
1957	JoAnne Gunderson	1977	Beth Daniel	1997	Silvia Cavalleri
1958	Anne Quast	1978	Cathy Sherk	1998	Grace Park
1959	Barbara McIntire	1979	Carolyn Hill	1999	Dorothy Delasin
1960	JoAnne Gunderson	1980	Juli Inkster	2000	Marcy Newton
1961	Anne Quast Decker	1981	Juli Inkster	2001	Meredith Duncan
1962	JoAnne Gunderson	1982	Juli Inkster	2002	Becky Lucidi
1963	Anne Quast Welts	1983	Joanne Pacillo	2003	V. Nirapathpongporn
1964	Barbara McIntire	1984	Deb Richard	2004	Jane Park
1965	Jean Ashley	1985	Michiko Hattori	2005	Morgan Pressel
1966	JoAnne Gunderson Carner	1986	Kay Cockerill	2006	Kimberly Kim
1967	Mary Lou Dill	1987	Kay Cockerill	2007	Maria Jose Uribe
1968	JoAnne Gunderson Carner	1988	Pearl Sinn	2008	Amanda Blumenherst
1969	Catherine Lacoste	1989	Vicki Goetze	2009	Jennifer Song
1970	Martha Wilkinson	1990	Pat Hurst	2010	Danielle Kang
1971	Laura Baugh	1991	Amy Fruhwirth	2011	Danielle Kang
1972	Mary Budke	1992	Vicki Goetze	2012	Lydai Ko
1973	Carol Semple	1993	Jill McGill	2013	Emma Talley
1974	Cynthia Hill	1994	Wendy Ward	2014	Kristen Gillman
				2015	

British Women's (Ladies) Amateur

YEAR	WINNER	YEAR	WINNER	YEAR	WINNER
1893	Lady Margaret Scott	1912	Gladys Ravenscroft	1931	Enid Wilson
1894	Lady Margaret Scott	1913	Muriel Dodd	1932	Enid Wilson
1895	Lady Margaret Scott	1914	Cecil Leitch	1933	Enid Wilson
1896	Amy Pascoe	1915	Not held – World War I	1934	Helen Holm
1897	Edith Orr	1916	Not held – World War I	1935	Wanda Morgan
1898	Lena Thomson	1917	Not held – World War I	1936	Pam Barton
1899	May Hezlet	1918	Not held – World War I	1937	Jessie Anderson
1900	Rhona Adair	1919	Not held – World War I	1938	Helen Holm
1901	Mary Graham	1920	Cecil Leitch	1939	Pam Barton
1902	May Hezlet	1921	Cecil Leitch	1940	Not held – World War II
1903	Rhona Adair	1922	Joyce Wethered	1941	Not held – World War II
1904	Lottie Dod	1923	Doris Chambers	1942	Not held – World War II
1905	Bertha Thompson	1924	Joyce Wethered	1943	Not held – World War II
1906	Mrs. W. Kennion	1925	Joyce Wethered	1944	Not held – World War II
1907	Mary Hezlet	1926	Cecil Leith	1945	Not held – World War II
1908	Maud Titterton	1927	Simone de la Chaume	1946	Jean Hetherington
1909	Dorothy Campbell	1928	Nanette le Blan	1947	Babe Zaharias
1910	Elsie Grant-Suttie	1929	Joyce Wethered	1948	Louise Suggs
1911	Dorothy Campbell	1930	Diana Fishwick	1949	Frances Stephens

YEAR	WINNER	YEAR	WINNER	YEAR	WINNER
1950	Lally de St. Sauveur	1972	Michelle Walker	1994	Emma Duggleby
1951	Catherine MacCann	1973	Ann Irvin	1995	Julie Wade Hall
1952	Moira Paterson	1974	Carol Semple	1996	Kelli Kuehne
1953	Marlene Stewart	1975	Nancy Roth Syms	1997	Alison Rose
2002	Stewart Ginn	1976	Cathy Panton	1998	Kim Rostron
1955	Jessie Valentine	1977	Angela Uzielli	1999	Marine Monnet
1956	Wiffi Smith	1978	Edwina Kennedy	2000	Rebecca Hudson
1957	Philomena Garvey	1979	Maureen Madill	2001	Marta Prieto
1958	Jessie Valentine	1980	Anne Quast Sander	2002	Rebecca Hudson
1959	Elizabeth Price	1981	Belle Robertson	2003	Elisa Serramia
1960	Barbara McIntire	1982	Kitrina Douglas	2004	Louise Stahle
1961	Marley Spearman	1983	Jill Thornhill	2005	Louise Stahle
1962	Marley Spearman	1984	Jody Rosenthal	2006	Belen Mozo
1963	Brigitte Varangot	1985	Lillian Behan	2007	Carlota Ciganda
1964	Carol Sorenson	1986	Marnie McGuire	2008	Anna Nordqvist
1965	Brigitte Varangot	1987	Janet Collingham	2009	Alahana Muñoz
1966	Elizabeth Chadwick	1988	Joanne Furby	2010	Kelly Tidy
1967	Elizabeth Chadwick	1989	Helen Dodson	2011	Lauren Taylor
1968	Brigitte Varangot	1990	Julie Wade Hall	2012	Stephanie Meadow
1969	Catherine Lacoste	1991	Valerie Michaud	2013	Gorgia Hall
1970	Dinah Oxley	1992	Bernille Pedersen	2014	Emily Pedesen
1971	Michelle Walker	1993	Catriona Lambert	2015	

Senior P.G.A. Championship

YEAR	WINNER	YEAR	WINNER	YEAR	WINNER
1937	Jock Hutchison	1954	Gene Sarazen	1971	Julius Boros
1938	Fred McLeod	1955	Mortie Dutra	1972	Sam Snead
1939	Not held	1956	Pete Burke	1973	Sam Snead
1940	Otto Hackbarth	1957	Al Watrous	1974	Roberto De Vicenzo
1941	Jack Burke	1958	Gene Sarazen	1975	Charlie Sifford
1942	Eddie Williams	1959	Willie Goggin	1976	Pete Cooper
1943	Not held – World War II	1960	Dick Metz	1977	Julius Boros
1944	Not held – World War II	1961	Paul Runyan	1978	Joe Jiminez
1945	Eddie Williams	1962	Paul Runyan	1979	Jack Fleck
1946	Eddie Williams	1963	Herman Barron	1979	Don January
1947	Jock Hutchison	1964	Sam Snead	1980	Arnold Palmer
1948	Charles McKenna	1965	Sam Snead	1981	Miller Barber
1949	Marshall Crichton	1966	Fred Haas	1982	Don January
1950	Al Watrous	1967	Sam Snead	1983	Not held
1951	Al Watrous	1968	Chandler Harper	1984	Arnold Palmer
1952	Ernest Newnham	1969	Tommy Bolt	1984	Peter Thomson
1953	Harry Schwab	1970	Sam Snead	1985	Not Held

YEAR	WINNER	YEAR	WINNER	YEAR	WINNER
1986	Gary Player	1996	Hale Irwin	2006	Jay Haas
1987	Chi Chi Rodriguez	1997	Hale Irwin	2007	Denis Watson
1988	Gary Player	1998	Hale Irwin	2008	Jay Haas
1989	Larry Mowry	1999	Allen Doyle	2009	Michael Allen
1990	Gary Player	2000	Doug Tewell	2010	Tom Lehman
1991	Jack Nicklaus	2001	Tom Watson	2011	Tom Watson
1992	Lee Trevino	2002	Fuzzy Zoeller	2012	Roger Chapman
1993	Tom Wargo	2003	John Jacobs	2013	Kōki Idoki
1994	Lee Trevino	2004	Hale Irwin	2014	Colin Montgomerie
1995	Raymond Floyd	2005	Mike Reid	2015	Colin Montgomerie

U.S. Senior Open

YEAR	WINNER	YEAR	WINNER	YEAR	WINNER
1980	Roberto DeVicenzo	1992	Larry Laoretti	2004	Peter Jacobsen
1981	Arnold Palmer	1993	Jack Nicklaus	2005	Allen Doyle
1982	Miller Barber	1994	Simon Hobday	2006	Allen Doyle
1983	Billy Casper	1995	Tom Weiskopf	2007	Brad Bryant
1984	Miller Barber	1996	Dave Stockton	2008	Eduardo Romero
1985	Miller Barber	1997	Graham Marsh	2009	Fred Funk
1986	Dale Douglass	1998	Hale Irwin	2010	Bernhard Langher
1987	Gary Player	1999	Dave Eichelberger	2011	Olin Brown
1988	Gary Player	2000	Hale Irwin	2012	Roger Chapman
1989	Orville Moody	2001	Bruce Fleisher	2013	Kenny Perry
1990	Lee Trevino	2002	Dan Pooley	2014	Colin Montgomerie
1991	Jack Nicklaus	2003	Bruce Lietzke	2015	Jeff Maggert

Senior Players Championship

YEAR	WINNER	YEAR	WINNER	YEAR	WINNER
1983	Miller Barber	1995	J.C. Snead	2005	Peter Jacobsen
1984	Arnold Palmer	1996	Raymond Floyd	2006	Bobby Wadkins
1985	Arnold Palmer	1997	Larry Gilbert	2007	Loren Roberts
1986	Chi Chi Rodriguez	1998	Gil Morgan	2008	D.A. Weibring
1987	Gary Player	1999	Hale Irwin	2009	Jay Haas
1988	Billy Casper	2000	Raymond Floyd	2010	Mark O'Meara
1989	Orville Moody	2001	Allen Doyle	2011	Red Couples
1990	Jack Nicklaus	2002	Stewart Ginn	2012	Joe Daley
1991	Jim Albus	2002	Stewart Ginn	2013	Kenny Perry
1992	Dave Stockton	2003	Craig Stadler	2014	Bernhard Langher
1993	Jim Colbert	2004	Mark James	2015	Bernhard Langher
1994	Dave Stockton				

The Tradition

YEAR	WINNER	YEAR	WINNER	YEAR	WINNER
1989	Don Bies	1998	Gil Morgan	2007	Mark McNulty
1990	Jack Nicklaus	1999	Graham Marsh	2008	Fred Funk
1991	Jack Nicklaus	2000	Tom Kite	2009	Mike Reid
1992	Lee Trevino	2001	Doug Tewell	2010	Fred Funk
1993	Tom Shaw	2002	Jim Thorpe	2011	Tom Lehman
1994	Raymond Floyd	2003	Tom Watson	2012	Tom Lehman
1995	Jack Nicklaus	2004	Craig Stadler	2013	David Frost
1996	Jack Nicklaus	2005	Loren Roberts	2014	Kenny Perry
1997	Gil Morgan	2006	Eduardo Romero	2015	Jeff Maggert

Senior British Open

YEAR	WINNER	YEAR	WINNER	YEAR	WINNER
1987	Neil Coles	1997	Gary Player	2007	Tom Watson
1988	Gary Player	1998	Brian Huggett	2008	Bruce Vaughan
1989	Bob Charles	1999	Christy O'Connor, Jr.	2009	Loren Roberts
1990	Gary Player	2000	Christy O'Connor, Jr.	2010	Bernhard Langher
1991	Bobby Verwey	2001	Ian Stanley	2011	Rus Cochran
1992	John Fourie	2002	Noboru Sugai	2012	Fred Couples
1993	Bob Charles	2003	Tom Watson	2013	Mark Wiebe
1994	Tom Wargo	2004	Pete Oakley	2014	Bernhard Langher
1995	Brian Barnes	2005	Tom Watson	2015	
1996	Brian Barnes	2006	Loren Roberts		

Ryder Cup

YEAR	RESULTS	COURSE
1927	U.S.A. 9 1/2–2 1/2	Worcester C.C. (MA)
1929	Britain-Ireland 7–5	Moortown, England
1931	U.S.A. 9–3	Scioto C.C. (OH)
1933	Great Britain 6 1/2–5 1/2	Southport & Ainsdale, England
1935	U.S.A. 9–3	Ridgewood C.C. (NJ)
1937	U.S.A. 8–4	Southport & Ainsdale, England
1939	Not held – World War II	
1941	Not held – World War II	
1943	Not held – World War II	
1945	Not held – World War II	
1947	U.S.A. 11–1	Portland C.C. (OR)
1949	U.S.A. 7–5	Ganton G.C., England
1951	U.S.A. 9 1/2–2 1/2	Pinehurst C.C. (NC)
1953	U.S.A. 6 1/2–5 1/2	Wentworth, England

YEAR	RESULTS	COURSE
1955	U.S.A. 8–4	Thunderbird Ranch & C.C. (CA)
1957	Britain-Ireland 7 1/2–4 1/2	Lindrick G.C. (England)
1959	U.S.A. 8 1/2–3 1/2	Eldorado C.C. (CA)
1961	U.S.A. 14 1/2–9 1/2	Royal Lytham & St. Annes, England
1963	U.S.A. 23–9	East Lake C.C. (GA)
1965	U.S.A. 19 1/2–12 1/2	Royal Birkdale, England
1967	U.S.A. 23 1/2–8 1/2	Champions G.C. (TX)
1969	Draw 16–16	Royal Birkdale, England
1971	U.S.A. 18 1/2–13 1/2	Old Warson C.C. (MO)
1973	U.S.A. 19–13	Muirfield, Scotland
1975	U.S.A. 21–11	Laurel Valley G.C. (PA)
1977	U.S.A. 12 1/2–7 1/2	Royal Lytham & St. Annes, England
1979	U.S.A. 17–11	The Greenbrier (WV)
1981	U.S.A. 18 1/2–9 1/2	Walton Heath G.C., England
1983	U.S.A. 14 1/2–13 1/2	P.G.A. National G.C. (FL)
1985	Europe 16 1/2–11 1/2	The Belfry, England
1987	Europe 15–13	Muirfield Village G.C. (OH)
1989	Draw 14–14	The Belfry, England
1991	U.S.A. 14 1/2–13 1/2	Kiawah Island's Ocean Course (SC)
1993	U.S.A. 15–13	The Belfry, England
1995	Europe 14 1/2–13 1/2	Oak Hill C.C. (NY)
1997	Europe 14 1/2–13 1/2	Valderrama, Costa del Sol, Spain
1999	U.S.A. 14 1/2–13 1/2	The Country Club (MA)
2002	Europe 15 1/2–12 1/2	The Belfry, England
2004	Europe 18 1/2–9 1/2	Oakland Hills C.C. (MI)
2006	Europe 18 1/2–9 1/2	The K Club, Ireland
2008	U.S.A. 16 1/2–11 1/2	Valhalla Golf Club (KY)
2010	Europe 14 1/2-13 1/2	Celtic Manor, Wales
2012	Europe 14 1/2–13 1/2	Medinah Country Club (IL)
2014	Europe 16 1/2–11 1/2	Gleneagles, Scotland

Presidents Cup

YEAR	RESULTS	YEAR	RESULTS	YEAR	RESULTS
1994	U.S.A. 20–12	2003	Draw 17–17	2011	U.S.A. 19–15
1996	U.S.A. 16 1/2–15 1/2	2005	U.S.A. 18 1/2–15 1/2	2013	U.S.A. 18 1/2-15 1/2
1998	International 20 1/2–11 1/2	2007	U.S.A. 19 1/2–14 1/2		
2000	U.S.A. 21 1/2–10 1/2	2009	U.S.A. 19 1/2–14 1/2		

Walker Cup

YEAR	RESULTS	YEAR	RESULTS	YEAR	RESULTS
1922	U.S.A. 8–4	1924	U.S.A. 9–3	1928	U.S.A. 11–1
1923	U.S.A. 6 1/2–5 1/2	1926	U.S.A. 6 1/2–5 1/2	1930	U.S.A. 10–2

YEAR	RESULTS	YEAR	RESULTS	YEAR	RESULTS
1932	U.S.A. 9 1/2–2 1/2	1959	U.S.A. 9–3	1989	Britain-Ireland 12 1/2–11 1/2
1934	U.S.A. 9 1/2–2 1/2	1961	U.S.A. 11–1	1991	U.S.A. 14–10
1936	U.S.A. 10 1/2–1 1/2	1963	U.S.A. 14–10	1993	U.S.A. 19–5
1938	Britain-Ireland 7 1/2–4 1/2	1965	Draw 12–12	1995	Britain-Ireland 14–10
1940	Not held – World War II	1967	U.S.A. 15–9	1997	U.S.A. 18–6
1942	Not held – World War II	1969	U.S.A. 13–11	1999	Britain-Ireland 15–9
1944	Not held – World War II	1971	Britain-Ireland 13–11	2001	Britain-Ireland 15–9
1946	Not held – World War II	1973	U.S.A. 14–10	2003	Britain-Ireland 12 1/2–11 1/2
1947	U.S.A. 8–4	1975	U.S.A. 15 1/2–8 1/2	2005	U.S.A. 12 1/2–11 1/2
1949	U.S.A. 10–2	1977	U.S.A. 16–8	2007	U.S.A. 12 1/2–11 1/2
1951	U.S.A. 7 1/2–4 1/2	1979	U.S.A. 15 1/2–8 1/2	2009	U.S.A. 16 1/2–9 1/2
1953	U.S.A. 9–3	1981	U.S.A. 15–9	2011	Britian-Ireland 14-12
1955	U.S.A. 10–2	1983	U.S.A. 13 1/2–10 1/2	2013	U.S.A. 17-9
1957	U.S.A. 8 1/2–3 1/2	1985	U.S.A. 13–11	2015	
		1987	U.S.A. 16 1/2–7 1/2		

Solheim Cup

YEAR	RESULTS	YEAR	RESULTS	YEAR	RESULTS
1990	U.S.A. 11 1/2–4 1/2	2000	Europe 14 1/2–11 1/2	2009	U.S.A. 16–12
1992	Europe 11 1/2–6 1/2	2002	U.S.A. 15 1/2–12 1/2	2011	Europe 15-13
1994	U.S.A. 13–7	2003	Europe 17 1/2–10 1/2	2013	Europe 18-10
1996	U.S.A. 17–11	2005	U.S.A. 15 1/2–12 1/2	2015	
1998	U.S.A. 16–12	2007	U.S.A. 16–12		

Curtis Cup

YEAR	RESULTS	YEAR	RESULTS	YEAR	RESULTS
1932	U.S.A. 5 1/2–3 1/2	1960	U.S.A. 6 1/2–2 1/2	1988	British Isles 11–7
1934	U.S.A. 6 1/2–2 1/2	1962	U.S.A. 8–1	1990	U.S.A. 14–4
1936	Draw 4 1/2–4 1/2	1964	U.S.A. 10 1/2–7 1/2	1992	British Isles 10–8
1938	U.S.A. 5 1/2–3 1/2	1966	U.S.A. 13–5	1994	Draw 9–9
1940	Not held – World War II	1968	U.S.A. 10 1/2–7 1/2	1996	British Isles 11 1/2–6 1/2
1942	Not held – World War II	1970	U.S.A. 11 1/2–6 1/2	1998	U.S.A. 10–8
1944	Not held – World War II	1972	U.S.A. 10–8	2000	U.S.A. 10–8
1946	Not held – World War II	1974	U.S.A. 13–5	2002	U.S.A. 11–7
1948	U.S.A. 6 1/2–2 1/2	1976	U.S.A. 11 1/2–6 1/2	2004	U.S.A. 10–8
1950	U.S.A. 7 1/2–1 1/2	1978	U.S.A. 12–6	2006	U.S.A. 11 1/2–6 1/2
1952	British Isles 5–4	1980	U.S.A. 13–5	2008	U.S.A. 13–7
1954	U.S.A. 6–3	1982	U.S.A. 14 1/2–3 1/2	2010	U.S.A. 12 1/2–7 1/2
1956	British Isles 5–4	1984	U.S.A. 9 1/2–8 1/2	2012	British Isles 10 1/2-9 1/2
1958	Draw 4 1/2–4 1/2	1986	British Isles 13–5	2014	U.S.A. 13-7

Bibliography

Books

Alliss, Peter, *The Who's Who of Golf*, Englewood Cliffs, NJ: Prentice Hall, 1983.

Atha, Anthony, Foston, Paul, Newell, Steve, *Better Golf*, London, England: Hermes House, 2006.

Barkow, Al, *Golf's Golden Grind, The History of the Tour*, NY: Harcourt Brace Jovanovich, 1974.

Barkow, Al, *The History of the PGA Tour*, New York: Doubleday, 1989.

Barkow, Al, David Barrett, David Earl, Rhonda Glenn, and Pat Seelig, *20th Century Golf Chronicle*, Lincolnwood, IL: Publications International, Ltd., 1993.

Barrett, Ted, *The Complete Encyclopedia of Golf*, second edition, New York: Sterling Publishing Co., Inc., 2010.

Brown, Gene, *The Complete Book of Golf*, NY: Ames Press, 1980.

Brown, Gerry and Michael Morison, *2008 ESPN Sports Almanac*, New York: ESPN Books, 2007.

Browning, Robert, *A History of Golf*, Stamford, CT: Reprint, Classics of Golf, Robert Macdonald, first published 1955, Great Britain.

Cook, Kevin, *Tommy's Honor,*, NY: Penguin Group (USA), Inc. 2007.

Cook, Kevin, editor, *The Golf Book*, NY: Sports Illustrated Books, 2009.

Cotton, Henry, *The Game of Golf*, London, England: Charles Scribner's Sons, 1948.

Darwin, Bernard, *Golf Between Two Wars*, Stamford, CT: Reprint, Classics of Golf, Robert Macdonald.

Darwin, Bernard, *Mostly Golf*, Stamford, CT: Reprint, Classics of Golf, Robert Macdonald, 1986.

Davidson, John, *Hockey for Dummies*, 2nd Edition, NY: Wiley Publishing Inc, 2000.

Davis, Martin, *The Greatest of Them All: The Legend of Bobby Jones*, Greenwich, CT: The American Golfer, Inc., 1996.

Dobereiner, Peter, *The Glorious World of Golf*, NY: McGraw Hill, 1973.

Editors of *Golf Magazine*, *Golf Magazine's Encyclopedia of Golf (Second Edition)*, New York: Harper-Collins, 1993.

Finegan, James W., *A Centennial Tribute to Golf in Philadelphia The Champions and the Championships The Clubs and the Courses*, State College, PA: Jostens Printing & Publishing, Inc., 1996.

Finegan, James W., *Pine Valley Golf Club: A Unique Haven of the Game*, State College, PA: Pine Valley Golf Club, 2000.

Frost, Mark, *The Grand Slam: Bobby Jones, America, and the Story of Golf*, New York: Hyperion, 2004.

Frost, Mark, *The Greatest Game Ever Played: Harry Vardon, Francis Ouimet, and the Birth of Modern Golf*, New York: Hyperion, 2002.

Frost, Mark, *The Match*, NY: Hyperion, 2007.

Glenn, Rhonda, *The Illustrated History of Women's Golf*, Dallas, TX: Taylor Publishing Company, 1991.

Green, Robert, *An Illustrated History of Golf*, London, England: HarperCollinsWillow, 1987.

Grimsley, Will, *Golf: Its History, People & Events*, Englewood Cliffs, NJ: Prentice Hall, 1966.

Henderson, Ian and David Stirk, *Golf In the Making (Revised Edition)*, London, England: Sean Arnold, 1994.

Jenkins, Dan, *The Dogged Victims of Inexorable Fate*, Stamford, CT: Reprints, Classics of Golf, Robert Macdonald, 1985.

Jones, Jr., Robert T., *Bobby Jones on Golf*, NY: Doubleday & Company, Inc., 1966.

Jones, Jr., Robert T., and O.B. Keeler, *Down the Fairway*, NY: Minton Balch & Company, 1927.

Jones, Jr., Robert T., *Golf Is My Game*, Garden City, NY: Doubleday & Company, Inc., 1960.

Kirsch, George B., *Golf in America*, Urbana, IL: University of Illinois Press, 2009.

Lane, James M., *The Complete Golfer's Almanac 1995*, NY: The Berkeley Publishing Group, 1995.

Lazarus, Adam and Schlossman, *Chasing Greatness, Johnny Miller, Arnold Palmer, and the Miracle at Oakmont*, NY: New American Library, a divison of Penguin Group (USA) Inc., 2010

Lee, James P., *Golf in America: A Practical Manual*, NY: Dodd, Mead & Company, 1995.

Lowe, Stephen, *Sir Walter and Mr. Jones*, Chelsea, MI, Sleeping Bear Press, 2000

Macdonald, Charles B., *Scotland's Gift–Golf*, Stamford, CT: Reprint, Classics of Golf, Robert Macdonald, 1985

March, Ray A., *A Paradise Called Pebble Beach*, Trumbull, CT: Golf Digest/Tennis, Inc., 1992.

McCord, Robert, *Golf–An Album of Its History*, Short Hills, NJ: Burford Books, 1998.

Martin, H.B., *Fifty Years of American Golf*, NY: Dodd, Mead & Company, 1936.

Matthew, Sidney L., *Bobby Jones Extra*, Tallahassee, FL: I.Q. Press, 2004.

Matthew, Sidney L., *Life & Times of Bobby Jones*, Chelsea, MI: Sleeping Bear Press, 1995.

Mayo, James, *The American Country Club*, New Brunswick, NJ: Rutgers University Press, 1998.

Miller, Dick, *Triumphant Journey*, NY: Holt, Rinehart and Winston, 1980.

Mintzer, Rick and Peter Grossman, *The Everything Golf Book*, Holbrook, MA: Adams Media Corporation, 1997.

Murdock, Joseph, *The Library of Golf*, Detroit, MI: Gale Research Co., 1968 Supplement, privately printed, 1978.

Nelson, Bryon, *How I Played the Game*, NY: Dell Publishing, a division of Bantam Double Dell Publishing Group, Inc., 1993.

Nickerson, Elinor, *Golf: A Women's History*, Jefferson, NC: McFarland, 1987.

Nicklaus, Jack, with Herbert Warren Wind, *The Greatest Game of All, My Life in Golf*, NY: Simon & Schuster, 1969.

Olman, John M. and Morton W. Olman, *The Encyclopedia of Golf Collectibles*, Florence, AL: Books Americana, 1985.

Ouimet, Francis, *A Game of Golf*, Boston, MA: Houghton, Mifflin, 1932.

Pace, Lee, *Pinehurst Stories: A Celebration of Great Golf and Good Times*, Pinehurst, NC: Resorts of Pinehurst Inc., 1991.

Pedrali, Hubert and Mary Tiegereen, *A Passion for The Game of Golf*, Kansas City, MO, Andrews & McMeel, 2015

Peper, George, *Golf In America: The First One Hundred Years*, NY: Abradale Press, 1994.

Peper, George, *The Story of Golf*, NY: Cramer Productions, 1999.

Platts, Mitchell, *Illustrated History of Golf*, NY: Portland House, 1988.

Platts, Mitchell, *The Illustrated History of Golf*, NY: Gramercy Books, 2000.

Player, Gary, *The Golfer's Guide to the Meaning of Life: Lessons I've Learned From My Life on the Links*, NY: Skyhorse Publishing, 2008.

Player, Gary, *Don't Choke*, NY: Skyhorse Publishing, Inc., 2010.

Price, Charles, *A Golf Story: Bobby Jones, Augusta National, and the Masters Tournament*, NY: Atheneum Macmilan Publishing Company, 1986.

Price, Charles, *The American Golfer*, NY: Random House, 1964.

Price, Charles, *The World of Golf*, NY: Random House, Inc., 1962.

Rapoport, Ron, *The Immortal Bobby*, Hobokem, NJ: John Wiley & Sons, Inc., 2005

Sampson, Curt, *Hogan*, Nashville, TN: Rutledge Hill Press, 1996.

Sampson, Curt, *The Masters*, NY: Villard, 1998.

Sarazen, Gene, with Herbert Warren Wind, *Thirty Years of Championship Golf*, Stamford, CT:

Reprint, Classics of Golf, Robert Macdonald, 1987.

Sheehan, Colin, *The United States Amateur*, Pearl River, NY: Classics of Golf, 2006.

Sidorsky, Robert, *Golf's Greatest Moments*, NY: Harry N. Abrams, Inc., 2003.

Sidorsky, Robert, *Golf 365 Days*, NY: Harry N. Abrams, Inc., 2008.

Sommers, Robert, *The U.S. Open: Golf's Ultimate Challenge*, Stamford, CT: Reprint, Classics of Golf, Robert Macdonald, 1989

Sounes, Howard, *The Wicked Game*, NY: HarperCollins Publishers, 2004

Stanley, Louis, *St. Andrews—The Home of Golf*, Topfield, MA: Salem House, 1986.

Steel, Donald and Peter Ryders, editors, *The Encylopedia of Golf*, NY: Viking Press, 1975.

Stirk, David, *Carry Your Bag, Sir?*, London: H.F. & G. Witherby LTD, 1989.

Stirk, David, *Golf History & Tradition 1500–1945*, Shropshire, England: Excellent Press, 1998.

The United States Golf Association, *Golf: The Greatest Game*, NY: Jones & Janello, 1994.

The United States Golf Association, *The 2006 United States Golf Association Championship Annual*, Far Hills, NJ: The United States Golf Association, 2006.

The United States Golf Association, *The 2007 USGA The Championship Year,* Far Hills, NJ: The United States Golf Association, 2007.

Tolhurst, Desmond, *Golf at Merion* Ardmore, PA: Merion Golf Club, 1989.

Trostel, Michael and Robert Williams, *Great Moments of the U.S. Open*, Buffalo, NY: Firefly Books, Ltd., 2013

Tufts, Richard, The Scottish Invasion, Pinehurst, NC: Pinhurst Publishers, 1962

Vardon, Harry, *Vardon on Golf*, Stamford, CN: Reprint, Classics of Golf, Robert Macdonald, 1989.

Wallechinsky, David, *The Complete Book of the Summer Olympics*, Woodstock, NY: The Overlook Press, Peter Mayer Publishers, Inc., 2000.

Wind, Herbert Warren, editor, *The Complete Golfer*, NY: Simon & Schuster, 1954.

Wind, Herbert W., *The Story of American Golf*, Third Edition, NY: Alfred A. Knopf, Inc., 1975.

Wind, Herbert Warren, *Following Through*, NY: Ticknor & Fields, 1985

Magazines

Achenbach, James, *Cold Reality*, GOLFWEEK, 6 August 2010: 39.

Achenbach, James, *Good for the Game*, GOLFWEEK, 7-14 December: 18.

Babineau, Jeff, *Red Hot*, GOLFWEEK, 18 August 2007: 8-13.

Babineau, Jeff, *Dream Nearly Becomes Reality*, GOLFWEEK, 25 July 2009, 22-23.

Baldry, Beth Ann, *Pak's Success Spurs Burgeoning Pack*, GOLFWEEK, 10 November 2007: 17.

Baldry, Beth Ann, *Sörenstam Soaks Michelob Field*, GOLFWEEK, 17 May 2008: 20.

Baldry, Beth Ann, *Another Weird Chapter in Wie's Tale*, GOLFWEEK, 26 July 2008:31.

Baldry, Beth Ann, *Coming of Age*, GOLFWEEK, 29 August 2009: 16-18.

Baldry, Beth Ann, *The Start of Something Big*, GOLFWEEK, 28 November 2009: 26-27.

Baldry, Beth Ann, *The Next Chapter,* GOLFWEEK, 30 April 2010: 14-20.

Baldry, Beth Ann, *The Team Effort*, GOLFWEEK, 18 June 2010: 17-20.

Baldry, Beth Ann, *Untouchable*, GOLFWEEK, 2 July 2010: 14-15.

Baldry, Beth Ann, *Tough Enough*, GOLFWEEK, 16 July 2010:12-18.

Baldry, Beth Ann, *My Year*, GOLFWEEK, 17 June 2011:23.

Balicki, Ron, *Head of the Class*, GOLFWEEK, 30 August 2008: 18-23.

Balicki, Ron, *Buddy System*, GOLFWEEK, 19 September 2009: 25-26.

Blue Monday, GOLFWORLD, 11 October 2010: 22-28.

Call Him Johnny Quest, GOLFWEEK, 29 October 2010: 3.

Diaz, Jaime, *Adaption Agents*, GOLFWEEK, 28 December 2009: 45-49.

Diaz, Jaime, *JACK'S KCAB*, Golf Digest, October 2010: 111-117.

Fields, Bill, *Checks and Balances*, GOLFWORLD, 28 December 2009: 62-66.

Fields, Bill, *Party Pooper*, GOLFWORLD, 9 August 2010: 21-23.

Fields, Bill, *Cashing In On Borrowed Time* , GOLFWORLD, 6 June 2011: 24

GOLFWEEK, 18 January 2010: 8.

GOLFWEEK, 30 July 2010: 29.

Hoggard, Rex, *Ride of His Life*, GOLFWEEK, 19 April 2008: 14-20.
Hoggard, Rex, *Monster Mash*, GOLFWEEK, 16 August 2008: 13-15.
Klein, Bradley S., *Macdonald a Visionary of Course Architecture*, GOLFWEEK, 10 November 2007: 15.
Klein, Bradley S., *Wind Wrote The Book on Golf Writing*, GOLFWEEK, 26 October 2008:
Klein, Bradley S., *Star Power*, GOLFWEEK, 26 October 2008: 32
Lavner, Ryan, *Take That, Tiger*, GOLFWEEK, 24 June 2011 16.
Martin, Sean, *Strait & Steady*, GOLFWEEK, 20 August 2010: 19-20, 37-38.
McCabe, Jim, *Head of His Class*, GOLFWEEK, 20 April 2015: 18-26.
McCabe, Jim, *That Old Green Magic*, GOLFWEEK, 16 April 2009: 21.
McCabe, Jim, *U.S. in Trouble? Not for Long*, GOLFWEEK, 29 August 2009: 20.
McCabe, Jim, *Creamer Leads by Example*, GOLFWEEK, 29 August 2009: 21.
McCabe, Jim, *Punching Back*, GOLFWEEK, 3 October 2009: 14-16.
McCabe, Jim, *A Real-Life Drama*, GOLFWEEK, 16 April 2010: 23-28.
McCabe, Jim, *Cliff Hanger*, GOLFWEEK, 25 June 2010: 19-24.
McCabe, Jim, *Mystery Solved*, GOLFWEEK, 1 October 2010: 13-14.
McCabe, Jim, *'An Underdog All His Life*, GOLFWEEK, 19 August 2011: 18.
McCabe, Jim, *Great Escape*, GOLFWEEK, 30 April 2012: 19
McCabe, Jim, *Its Brookline, Euro-style*, GOLFWEEK, 5 October 2012: 12-17.
Moriarty, Jim, *Attack Mode*, GOLFWORLD, 19 April 2010: 34-40.
Moriarty, Jim, *Staggering Results*, GOLFWORLD, 28 June 2010: 29-35.
Moriarty, Jim, *He Was Something Els(e)*, GOLFWORLD, 26 July 2010: 20-24.
Moriarty, Jim, *Strangeness at the Straits*, GOLFWORLD, 23 August 2010: 25-30.
Moriarty, Jim, *Gale Force*, GOLFWORLD, 25 July 2011: 24
Moriarty, Jim, *Demolition Derby*, GOLFWORLD, 25 June 2012: 40-46z
Moriarty, Jim, *Destiny's Child*, GOLFWORLD, 17 August 2012: 10-17
Moriarty, Jim, *Red, White, & Very Blue*, GOLFWORLD, 8 October 2012: 28-33.
Ochoa Wins U.S.G.A.'s Bob Jones Award, GOLFWORLD, 1 November 2010: 8
Rude, Jeff, *Welcome to the Club*, GOLFWEEK, 23 June 2007: 8-12.
Rude, Jeff, *It Hurts so Good*, GOLFWEEK, 21 June 2008: 12-16.
Rude, Jeff, *History Illuminates, 'The No. 2 Wood'*, GOLFWEEK, 25 October 2008: 33.
Rude, Jeff, *Cruel in the Sun*, GOLFWEEK, 25 July 2009: 17-20.
Rude, Jeff, *One-Man Show*, GOLFWEEK, 23 July 2010: 16-18, 35-36.
Rude, Jeff, *Els' 'comfortable ride' leads to Hall of Fame*, GOLFWEEK, 1 October 2010: 8.
Sirak, Ron, *What's Next?*, GOLFWORLD, 21 December 2009: 15-19.
Sirak, Ron, *I Am Ready to Start a New Life*, GOLFWORLD, 3 May 2010: 33-36.
Sirak, Ron, *Tickled Pink*, GOLFWORLD, 19 July 2010: 20-24.
Sirak, Ron, *The Wizard of Oz*, GOLFWORLD, 28 November 2011: 34-43.
Tait, Alistair, *Twice as Nice*, GOLFWEEK, 26 July 2008:12-15.
Tait, Alistair, *Crazy*, GOLFWEEK, 27 July 2012:15-19.
Tait, Alistair, *Ground Control*, GOLFWEEK, 26 July 2013:14-18.
U.S.G.A.to Honor Ochoa with Bob Jones Award, GOLFWEEK, 29 October 2010: 12
Whiten, Ron, *Congressional Acts*, GOLF DIGEST, June 2011: 133

Newspapers
Ecenbarger, William. "History's Familiar Turf Is Out For More." *The Philadelphia Inquirer* 21 Dec. 2008, city & suburbs edition: pages A1+.
Ferguson, Doug. "Woods, Wife Elin Divorce Finalized." *The Philadelphia Inquirer* 24 August 2010, pages D1, D4.
Juliano, Joe. "An Unlikely Champ Beats the Field and the Weather." *The Philadelphia Inquirer* 23 June 2009, pages D1+.
Newport, John Paul. "A Most Gracious Throwback." *The Wall Street Journal* 11 Sept. 2009, page W5.

Newport, John Paul. "All Hail the Sacred Texts of Golf." *The Wall Street Journal* 24-25 Oct. 2009, page W4.

Newport, John Paul, "Looking Back: Year of the Tiger." *The Wall Street Journal* 19-20 Dec. 2009, page W4.

Newport, John Paul, "Getting Into Your Groove." *The Wall Street Journal* 16-17 Jan. 2010, page W4.

Newport, John Paul, "A Tough Little Gal' Grows Up." *The Wall Street Journal* 3-4 July 2010, page W6.

The Wall Street Journal, 13 Oct. 2009, page D8.

The Wall Street Journal, 2 Dec. 2010, page D7.

The Philadelphia Inquirer, 2 Aug. 2010, page D2.

The Philadelphia Inquirer 30 Aug. 2010, page D3

The Philadelphia Inquirer, 11 October 2010, page D11.

The Philadelphia Inquirer 6 Dec. 2010, page D8.

Video

The Complete History of Golf, Videocassette, MPI Home Video, 1992.

Golf And All Its Glory, Videocassette, Bridge Television Productions, 1992.

The Spirit of the Game, Videocassette, Cowen Media, Inc., 1999.

The Story of Golf, Videocassette ans DVD, Cramer Productions and Public Television Documentary, 1999.

Golf Digest's 50 Greatest Players of All Time, Videocassette, CBS Sports, 2000.

Internet

1986 Masters, Everything2.com, 12 April 2004, 3 January 2008.

Amy Alcott, Wikipedia, 6 October 2007, 16 October 2007.

Annika Sörenstam, Wikipedia, 15 October 2007, 16 October 2007.

Arnold Palmer, Wikipedia, 2 January 2007.

Babe Zaharias, Wikipedia, 10 November 2007, 17 November 2007.

Ben Hogan, Wikipedia, 6 November 2007, 17 November 2007.

Beth Daniel, Wikipedia, 12 October 2007, 16 October 2007.

Betsy King, Wikipedia, 10 October 2007, 16 October 2007.

Billy Casper, Wikipedia, 8 January 2006, 14 January 2007.

Byron Nelson, Wikipedia, 14 November 2007, 17 November 2007.

Christie Kerr, Wikipedia, 18 September 2007, 24 October 2007.

Ernie Els, Wikipedia, 6 September 2007, 7 September 2007.

Gary Player, Wikipedia, 25 December 2006, 9 January 2007.

George F. Grant, Wikepedia, 14 November 2010, 24 November 2010.

History of Golf, Maps of World.com, September 26, 2009.

Jack Nicklaus, Wikipedia, 3 February 2007.

Joanne Carner, Wikipedia, 15 May 2007, 20 May 2007.

Julie Inkster, Wikipedia, 26 September 2007, 14 October 2007.

Karrie Webb, Wikipedia, 1 October 2007, 16 October 2007.

Kathy Whitworth, Wikipedia, 10 May 2007, 20 May 2007.

Laura Davies, Wikipedia, 7 October 2007, 16 October 2007.

Laura Davies, Wikepedia, 15 November 2010, 24 November 2010.

Lee Trevino, Wikipedia, 23 April 2007, 27 April 2007.

Lorena Ochoa, Wikipedia, 10 October 2007, 24 October 2007.

Michelle Wie, Wikipedia, 23 October 2007, 24 October 2007.

Mickey Wright, Wikipedia, 15 September 2007, 17 November 2007.

Morgan Pressel, Wikipedia, 15 October 2007, 24 October 2007.

Nancy Lopez, Wikipedia, 7 March 2007, 20 May 2007.

NGF, National Golf Foundation, 2 February 2008, 2 February 2008.

Padraig Harrington, Wikipedia, 19 August 2008, 28 August 2008.

Pat Bradley, Wikipedia, 3 May 2007, 20 May 2007.

Patty Sheehan, Wikipedia, 6 October 2007, 14 October 2007.

Paula Creamer, Wikipedia, 19 October 2007, 24 October 2007.

Phil Mickelson, Wikipedia, 10 September 2007, 11 September 2007.

Presidents Cup, Wikipedia, 15 October 2007, 24 October 2007.

Ryder Cup, Wikipedia, 11 October 2007, 24 October 2007.

Sam Snead, Wikipedia, 13 November 2007, 17 November 2007.

Se Ri Pak, Wikipedia, 2 October 2007, 16 October 2007.

Severiano Ballesteros, Wikipedia, 6 June 2007, 7 June 2007.

Solheim Cup, Wikipedia, 24 October 2007.

Tiger Woods, Wikipedia, 23 September 2007.

Tiger Woods, *Tiger Woods's Full Apology,* YouTube, www.youtube.com, 19 February 2010.

Tom Watson, Wikipedia, 29 May 2007, 2 June 2007.

USGA History, United States Golf Association, 29 January 2008, 30 January 2008.

Vijay Singh, Wikipedia, 10 September 2007.

Walker Cup, Wikipedia, 4 October 2007, 24 October 2007.

Index

NOTE: Page numbers in *italics* indicate photographs.

A

Aaron, Tommy, 177, 193, 209, 218, 227, 228
Abbott, Patrick, 151
Abu Dhabi Golf Championship, 394, 396-97
Accenture Match Play Championship, 347, 348, 351
Adair, Perry, 80, *81*, 91, 118
Administaff Small Business Classic, 188
ADT Championship, 365
A.G. Spalding and Brothers, 36, 37, 46-47, 112, 114
Albany, New York, 26
Alcott, Amy, 237, 359
Alexander, Buddy, 262
Alfred Dunhill Links Championship, 393
Alfredsson, Helen, 419
American Tour players, 220
Ames, Stephen, 332
ANA Inspiration, 439-40. *See also* Kraft Nabisco Championship
An, Byeong Hun-, 334, 337
anchoring ban, 403
Anderson, Jamie, 20
Anderson, John, 59-60
Anderson, John G., 77
Anderson, Willie, 55-56, *56*, 62, 132, 146
Andrade, Billy, 315
Andy Williams Open, 264
ANNIKA Academy, 366
ANNIKA brand, 365-66
ANZ Australian Masters, 366
ANZ Ladies Masters, 367, 387
Aoki, Isao, 211, 243
Appleby, Stuart, 318
Archer, George, 200-201, 219
Armour, Tommy, 106, 126
"Arnie's Army," 181
Arnie's Army, 181, 184, 187, 205, 206
Arnold Palmer Award, McIlroy, 399
Arnold Palmer International, 352
Arnold Palmer Invitational: **2008**, 349; **2009**, 349, 351; **2012**, 354-55; **2013**, 352, 355, 403; Woods (eight times), 141-42
Asian Tour, 319
Associated Press Athlete of the Year

Daniel, 360
Nelson, 138
Ochoa, 370
Sörenstam, 365
Woods, 344, 347
Associated Press poll, 157
Atlanta Open, 136
AT&T Byron Nelson Championship, 138
AT&T Classic, 329
AT&T National, 349, 355
AT&T Pebble Beach National Pro-Am, 320, 324, 345, 351
attire for women, 53-54
attire, Hagen's, 75-76
Augusta National Golf Club, 113-14, 403
Austin, Woody, 332, 348
Australian Ladies Masters, 363
Australian Ladies Open, 366
Australian Ladies Professional Golf Tour, 368, 401
Australian Masters, 349
Australian Open, 192
Azinger, Paul, 263, 265, 273, 277, 415

B

Badderley, Aaron, 330
Baer, Max, 59
Bae, Sang-Moon, 390, 397
Baker-Finch, Ian, 249, 272
Ballesteros, Severiano "Seve," 257
  British Open, 232, 235, 249-50, 256, 265
  career summary, 256
  The Masters, 212-13, 242, 247, 256-58, 259, 261, 263, 290
  Ryder Cup, 273-74, 293, 411, 413
  U.S. Open, 247-48
  World Match Play Championship, 194
Ball, John, 20
balls. *See* golf balls
Baltimore Classic, 237
Bankers Trust Classic, 237
Bank of America Colonial Golf Tournament, 364
Barber, Jerry, 189, 190, 195
Barnes Brown, Lucy, 44, 51
Barnes, Jim, 74, 78, 83, 126

Barnes, Ricky, 305, 336
Barrett, Beatrice, 124
Bauer-Hagge, Marlene, 167, 170, 373
Baugh, Laura, 51
Bayer Advantage Classic, 214
Bean, Andy, 244, 248, 260, 267
Beck, Chip, 262, 273, 274, 276
Beem, Rich, 305, 337, 346
Belgium and history of golf, 3-4
Beman, Deane, 190, *190*, 196, 202-3
Berg, Patty
  biographical information, 158, 159, *159*
  career stats, 159, 162, 167
  career summary, 150, 158-59
  Curtis Cup, 124
  endorsement, 158
  and L.P.G.A., 168
  Minneapolis City Championship, 158
  Minnesota Championship, 158
  Titleholders Championship, 159
  U.S. Women's Amateur, 124, 133, 158
  U.S. Women's Open, 152, 158-59, 167
  Women's Western Open, 158, 159
B. F. Goodrich Company, 35
Billows, Ray, 127, 132
Bing Crosby National Pro-Am, 229
Birdies for Breast Cancer Foundation, 372
Bishop, Ted, 152
Bjorn, Thomas, 398
Bjørn, Thomas, 299, 308, 313, 324
Blackheath golf club, 14
Black, John, 83
Blackwell, Ted, 58
Blixt, Jonas, 406
Blumenherst, Amanda, 334
BMW Championship: **2007**, 348; **2009**, 349,
  352, 394; **2011**, 395; **2014**, 398
Bob Jones Award
Berg, 159
  Carner, 241
  Lopez, 238
  Ochoa, 371
  Player, 194
  Rawls, 167
  Sarazen, 87
  Suggs, 165
  Vare, 125
  Watson, 255
  Zaharias, 157
Boit, Florence, 31-32, 51-52
Bolt, Tommy, 177, 234
Boros, Julius, *196*
  Legends of Golf, 234
  P.G.A. Championship, 187, 219, 333, 335, 336
  U.S. Open, 145, 172, 176, 182, 186, 195, *196*,
  196, 228
Bradley, Keegan, 390, 397, 401
Bradley, Pat, 239-40
Bradshaw, Harry, 170

Braid, James, 22, *23*, *24*, 56, 248, 322, 334
Brand, Gordon, 262, 275
Brenton's Point, Newport, Rhode Island, 32
Brewer, Gay, 207
Bridgestone Invitational, 349, 355
British Amateur Championship: winners list,
  436-37; **1890**, 20; **1892**, 20; **1904**, 57-58;
  1909, 59; **1911**, 21, 22; **1921**, 95; **1930**, 103-5;
  1934, 130; **1935**, 130; **1950**, 171; **1967**, 203
British Ladies Amateur Golf Championship: winners list, 445-46; **1893-1895**, 51; **1905**, 52,
  419-20; **1922**, 120; **1924**, 120; **1925**, 119, 120;
  1928, 120; **1929**, 54, 120-22; **1930**, 122; **1947**,
  156-57; **1948**, 153; **1996**, 285
British Ladies Golf Championship, 164
British Open Championship: about, 19-21; winners list, 430-35; 1860, 19; **1862**, 299; **1867**,
  19; **1868**, 19-20; **1869**, 20; **1870**, 20; **1872**, 20;
  1877-1883, 20; **1890**, 20; **1892**, 20; **1894**, 21,
  22; **1895**, 22; **1896**, 21, 22, 46; **1897**, 20; **1898**,
  22, 46; **1899**, 22, 46; **1900**, 22, 47; **1901**, 22;
  1902, 36; **1903**, 22; **1905**, 22, 334; **1906**, 22,
  322, 334; **1907**, 295; **1908**-1911, 22; **1912**, 64;
  1913, 22, 62; **1914**, 22, 63; **1921**, 93-94; **1922**,
  73, 75; **1924**, 75; **1925**, 126; **1926**, 100; **1928**,
  75; **1929**, 75; **1930**, 106; **1931**, 126; **1932**, 84,
  126-27; **1933**, 127; **1934**, 129, 169; **1936**, 129;
  1937, 132, 169; **1938**, 310; **1946**, 141, 152;
  1947, 331; **1948**, 129, 132, 169; **1949**, 152, 170;
  1950, 152, 171; **1951**, 172; **1952**, 152, 172;
  1953, 146-47, 173; **1954-1955**, 174; **1956**, 174,
  176; **1957**, 152, 176; **1958**, 177; **1959**, 189, 192;
  1960, 182, 190; **1961**, 183, 190; **1962**, 185, 195;
  1963, 195, 196, 312, 324; **1964**, 196, 207; **1965**,
  198; **1966**, 202, 207; **1967**, 203; **1968**, 192,
  219; **1969**, 219-20; **1970**, 208, 221; **1971**, 221,
  222, 224, 225; **1972**, 208-9, 224, 225, 227;
  1973, 87, 228; **1974**, 194, 229; **1975**, 231, 232;
  1976, 232, 256; **1977**, 210-11, 232-33, 265,
  336; **1978**, 211, 234; **1979**, 235, 256; **1980**,
  243; **1981**, 244; **1982**, 247; **1983**, 248; **1984**,
  249-50, 258; **1985**, 259-60; **1986**, 262; **1987**,
  263, 266, 286; **1988**, 258, 265; **1989**, 266;
  1990, 271, 287; **1991**, 272; **1992**, 275, 287;
  1993, 277, 282; **1994**, 279; **1995**, 273, 281;
  1996, 283-84; **1997**, 291; **1998**, 293-94; **1999**,
  295-96; **2000**, 299-300, 345; **2001**, 302; **2002**,
  304-5, 318, 346; **2003**, 288, 307-8; **2004**,
  309-10; **2005**, 214, 312-13, 346-47; **2006**,
  315, 318, 347; **2007**, 318, 321, 325, 330-31,
  348; **2008**, 321-22, 333-34; **2009**, 187, 336;
  2010, 338, 395; **2011**, 327, 396; **2012**, 327, 402;
  2013, 327-28, 352, 405; **2014**, 352, 391, 398-
  99; **2015**, 389, 407
British Women's Open, 358, 361
British Youths Championship, 286
Broadhurst, Paul, 273-74
Brooks, Mark, 275, 284-85, 301-2
Browne, Mary K., 119

Browne, Olin, 312
Brown, Lucy Barnes, 44, 51
Buick Classic, 319
Buick endorsement of Woods, 344
Buick Invitational, 346, 347, 348
Buick Open, 320, 347, 349
Bulla, Johnny, 140, 141
Burdine's Invitational, 1970, 240
Burke, Billy, 127
Burke, Jackie, 175
Burke, Jack, Jr., 172, 180, 197
Burkemo, Walter, 172, 173, 174
Burns, George, 244
Bush, George Herbert Walker, 417
Byers, Eben, 92
Byrd, Sam, 137, 152
Byron Nelson Golf Classic, 323, 390
Byron Nelson Trophy, 138, 350, 393, 399

C

Cabrera, Ángel, 330, *331*, 335, 404
Cabrera-Bello, Rafael, 397
Calcavecchia, Mark, 264, 266, 272, 273, 277
Campbell, Bill, 198, 314
Campbell, Chad, 308, 313-14, 335
Campbell, Michael, 281, 312
Canadian Open: **1919**, 94; **1945**, 137; **1955**, 181; **1956**, 181; **1957**, 181; **1971**, 221, 222, 224-25
Canadian Women's Open, 373, 403
Cañizares, José-Maria, 412
Cantley, Patrick, 401
  career Grand Slams
  Nicklaus, 202, 207
  Player, 198
  Sarazen, 127
  Woods, 198, 215, 300, 301, 333, 345, 350-51
Carnegie, Andrew, 30
Carner, Joanne Gunderson, 120, 195, 219, 240-41, 403
Casper, William Earl "Billy"
  biographical information, 199, 201, *201*
  career summary, 199-201
  The Masters, 200-201, 219, 220
  P.G.A. Championship, 177, 198, 221
  putting prowess, 180, 200
  Ryder Cup, 199, 236
  U.S. Open, 186-87, 189, 199-200, 202, 207
U.S. Senior Open, 187
Catherine of Aragon, 50
Cauley, Bud, 418
Champions Tour
  about, 234
  Harris, 278
  Nicklaus, 204, 213
  Palmer, 188
  Player, 194
  Watson, 255
  Wendy's Three Tour Challenge, 214
Chapman, Dick, 149-50

Charles, Bob, 192, 196, 220, 312
Charleston, South Carolina, 26
Charlotte Open, 136
Chen, T.C., 259
Chevron World Challenge, 349, 351, 354
Chicago Victory Open, 136
China, 3
Choi, Na Yeon "The Big Apple," *381*, 381-82, 386
chole, 3-4, 6
Chrysler Cup, 188
Ciganda, Carlota, 384
Cink, Stewart, 296, 301, 332, 336
Clarke, Darren, 291, 302, 400-401
Clark, Tim, 312, 314, 324, 393
class consciousness, 74-75, 79
clubs. *See* golf clubs
CME Group Titleholders, 383
CME Group Tour Championship, 384
CN Canadian Women's Open, 370, 383
Cochran, Russ, 284
Coe, Charles, 177
Coe, Charlie, 170, 205
Coetzze, George, 397
Coleman, Fay, 108
colf, 5
Colgate-Dinah Shore Winners Circle, 228, 232
Collett, Glenna, 54, 118-25, *121. See also* Vare Trophy
Colonial Invitational, 146, 324, 390
Como, Chris, 352
Complete Golfer, The (Vardon), 25
Compston, Archie, 106
Compton, Eric, 406
Coody, Charles, 221
Cook, John, 234, 235, 275, 279
Cooper, "Lighthorse" Harry, 107, 131, 132, 321
Corcoran, Fred, 157, 160-61, *161*
Corona Championship, 370-71
Cotton, T. Henry, 127, 129, 132, 169
Couples, Fred
  British Open, 291, 313
  The Masters, 274, 280, 293, 314
  P.G.A. Championship, 271
  Presidents Cup, 406, 416
  Ryder Cup, 274
  U.S. Open, 249
Cowan, Gary, 202-3, 222
Cowan, Mike "Fluff," 350
Cox, Robert, 52
Cox, Wiffy, 127-29
Crampton, Bruce, 208, 209, 210, 227, 228, 231
Creamer, Paula "the Pink Panther," 365, *373*, 373-74, 377
Crecy window in Gloucester Cathedral, 3, *6*
Crenshaw, Ben
  biographical information, 249, 280
  British Open, 234, 235, 243, 256, 281
  The Masters, 231, 247, 248-49, 258, 280
  P.G.A. Championship, 235

Ryder Cup caption, 296-97
Crocker, Fay, 175
Crosby, Nathaniel, 245
Crowne Plaza Invitational, 326
The Crowns (Japan Tour), 338
Cruickshank, Bobby, *98*
 and Jones, 97-99, 103
 P.G.A. Championship, 83
 U.S. Amateur, 97-99
 U.S. Open, 85-86, *98*, 127-29
cup competitions, 410. *See also* Curtis Cup;
 FedEx Cup; Presidents Cup; Ryder Cup; Sol-
 heim Cup; Walker Cup
Cupit, Jackie, 186, 195-96
Curtis, Ben, 307-8, 322, 334
Curtis Cup: about, 52, 53, 419-20; **1932**, 54,
 123, 420; **1934**, 123; **1936**, 124; 1938, 124,
 133; **1948**, 124-25, 169; **1950**, 125; **1952**, 173;
 1958, 177; **1982**, 360; **1984**, 361; **1996**, 371;
 2002, 306; **2004**, 373, 375; **2006**, *408*, 420;
 2008, 385, 420; **2009**, 387; **2010**, 420; **2012**,
 420; **2014**, 420
Curtis, Harriet, 52, *53*, 123, 419
Curtis, Laurence, 32, 40, 52
Curtis, Margaret, 52, *53*, 120, 123, 419

D

Daly, John, 272-73, 276, 281
Daniel, Beth, 271, 360, *360*, 419
Danny Thomas Memphis Classic, 233
Davies, Laura, 361, *361*
Davis, Rodger, 263
Dawson, Johnny, 153
Day, Jason
 career summary, 389-90
 The Masters, 395, 400
 U.S. Open, 327, 396, 404
Demaret, Jimmy, 137, 144, 149, 153
Deutsche Bank Championship, 320, 325-26,
 346, 390
DeVicenzo, Roberto, 171, 187, 203, 218, 234
Dey, Joseph, 220
Dickerson, Bubba, 303
Dickinson, Gardner, 234
Dickson, Bob, 198, 203
Didrikson Zaharias, Mildred "Babe," 154-57, *156*,
 164, 171, 173
Diegel, Leo, 75, 106
DiMarco, Chris
 British Open, 315
 The Masters, 309, 311, 346
 P.G.A. Championship, 310, 320
discrimination against African-Americans, 271
Dixie Whiz Kids, 80, *81*, 92, 118
Donald, Luke, 311, 315-16, 397
Donald, Mike, 270-71
Doral-Eastern Open, 209
Double Grand Slam, Nicklaus, 208, 221
Dougherty, Dillon, 313

Driscoll, James, 300-301
Drum, Bob, 182
Dubai Desert Classic, 393, 394
Dubai Ladies Masters, 386, 387
Dufner, Jason, 401, 405
du Maurier Classic: winners list, 444; **1979**, 359;
 1980, 240; **1984**, 360; **1985**, 240; **1986**, 240;
 1996, 361; **1998**, 363; **1999**, 241, 366-67. *See
 also* Women's British Open
Dunn, Willie, 17, 31, 44
Durham Open, 136
Dutch and history of golf, 3, 3-5, *4*
Dutch golf clubs, *3*
Dutch Kolf (Neer), *4*
Dutra, Olin, 129
Duval, David, 293, 298, 301, 302, 336, 364
Dye, Pete, 209
Dyer, Frank, 92

E

Eastern Amateur, 119
Edinburgh Golfers, Honourable Company of,
 9-13
EDS Byron Nelson Championship, 138, 320, 350
Edwards, David, 279
Elder, Lee, 230
Elkington, Steve
 British Open, 305, 318
 The Masters, 276, 280
 P.G.A. Championship, 278, 281-82, 294, 313,
 324
Ellis, Danny, 278
Els, Ernie "The Big Easy"
 biographical information, 317, 318
 British Open, 281, 284, 302, 304-5, 310, 315,
 318, 402
 career stats, 402
 career summary, 317-18
 Honda Classic, 318
 The Masters, 298, 304-5, 309, 320, 324
 P.G.A. Championship, 282, 332
 U.S. Open, 278-79, 290-91, 299, 309, 318
 World Match Play Championship, 194, 318
Emirates Australian Open, 351, 398
Emory, Walter, 130
English Amateur Championship, 286
English, Harris, 390
English Ladies Amateur Championship, 1920-
 1924, 120
Espinosa, Al, *88*, 101
European Open, 394
European Rookie of the Year, 366
European Tour
 Ballesteros, 256, 258
 Els, 317
 Faldo, 275, 287, 288
 Harrington, 321
 McIlroy, 391, 393, 395
 Mickelson, 330

Singh, 319, 321
European Tour Golfer of the Year, McIlroy, 399
European Tour Order of Merit
Ballesteros, 256
Davies, 361
Faldo, 286, 287
Harrington, 321
McIlroy, 393
Montgomerie, 256
Singh, 319
Sörenstam, 363
European Tour Player of the Year, Faldo (three times), 288
Evans, Charles, Jr. "Chick"
biographical information, 78, 79
career summary, 77-79, 311
U.S. Amateur, 59-60, 69, 77, 78, 79, 95, 100-101
U.S. Open, 73-74, 77-78
Evans Scholarship Fund, 79
Evian Championship: about, 401; winners list, 444; **2005**, 373; **2006**, 367; **2007**, 372; **2009**, 382; **2013**, 383
Evian Masters, L.P.G.A., 372, 373, 382, 401
exhibition circuit during W.W.I., 80-81

F

"Faldo Golf Institute," 289
Faldo, Nicholas "Nick"
biographical information, 286, 287, 289
British Open, 263, 265, 271, 275, 277, 284, 286, 287, 288
British Youths Championship, 286
career stats, 288
career summary, 286-89
English Amateur Championship, 286
European Tour Order of Merit, 286
The Masters, 202, 265-66, 270, 283, 287, 288, 338
P.G.A. Championship, 276
Ryder Cup, 273, 286, 288, 415
U.S. Open, 264
Farmers Insurance Open, 352, 355
Farrell, Johnny, 101
Farwell, John B., 45
Fasth, Niclas, 302
Faulkner, Max, 172
Faxon, Brad, 279, 281
Fazio, George, 171
featheries, 15-16, 16, 33
FedEx Cup: about, 332; **2007**, 326, 332, 348, 350; **2008**, 321, 332; **2009**, 326, 332, 337, 350; **2010**, 338; **2011**, 401; **2012**, 403; **2013**, 405
FedEx Tour Championship. *See* Tour Championship
Feherty, David, 273
Feng, Shanshan, 402
Ferguson, Robert, 20
Fernie, Willie, 20

Ferrie, Kenneth, 314
Ferrier, Jim, 153, 171
Fezler, Forrest, 230
Fidden, Eric, 104
Finsterwald, Dow, 176, 177, 180, 182, 184
Fischesser, Doug, 233
Fisher, John, 131
Fishwick, Diana, 122
Fitzpatrick, Matt, 405
Five Lessons (Hogan), 148
Flanagan, Nick, 308
Fleck, Jack, 147, 170, 174-75, 182
Fleckman, Marty, 207, 249
Floyd, Raymond
British Open, 234
The Masters, 231, 270, 274, 287
P.G.A. Championship, 220, 232, 247
Ryder Cup, 273
U.S. Open, 248, 261-62
Wendy's Three Tour Challenge, 214
Foley, Sean, 351
Ford, Annie Howland, 52
Ford Championship, 346
Ford, Doug, 174, 176, 177
Forsman, Dan, 278
Fort Worth Open, 137
Fought, John, 233
Foulis, James, 35-36
Fowler, Rickie, 389, 398, 399, 406, 418
Fownes, William, 59
Foxburg Golf Club, Pennsylvania, 27
Fox, Steven, 402
France and history of golf, 3, 6, 51-52
Franklin American Mortgage Championship, 370, 371
Fraser, Alexa Stirling, 54, 80, 81, 91, 118, 119, 120
Freeman of the Royal Burgh of St. Andrews Award, 114-15
French, Emmett, 83
Frost, David, 262, 280
Frys.com tournament, 390
FUNAI Classic, 320
Funseth, Rod, 194, 233
Furgol, Ed, 147, 174
Furyk, Jim
biographical information, 307
British Open, 291
career stats, 233, 274
FedEx Cup, 338
The Masters, 293
P.G.A. Championship, 405
President's Cup, 401
Tour Championship, 338
U.S. Open, 307, 314, 330, 396
Futures Tour, 366

G

Gagliardi, Joseph, 172

Gallacher, Bernard, 412-13
Gameter, John, 35
Gamez, Robert, 262
Garcia, Sergio
  British Open, 315, 321, 330-31, 399, 406
  The Masters, 304, 312
  P.G.A. Championship, 296, 315-16, 322, 334
  Ryder Cup, 415
  U.S. Open, 301, 304, 309, 312
  WGC-Bridgestone Invitational, 399
Gardner, Robert "Bob," 59, 79, 92, 94-95, 190
Garrido, Antonio, 411
Geiberger, Al, 202, 231, 233
Gentlemen Golfers of Leith, 9-11
George S. May's All-American Open, 137
Georgia State Amateur, 91
Ghezzi, Vic, 151, 152
Gilbert, Gibby, 242, 257
Giles, Marvin "Vinny," 227-28
Gillis, Tom, 389
Ginn Tribute, 376
Glasgow Club, 14
Glenna Collett Vare Trophy. *See* Vare
  Trophy
Gloucester Cathedral Crecy window, 3, 6
Glover, Lucas, 315, 336, *336*
Goalby, Bob, 190, 218
Goetze, Vicki, 362
Goggin, Willie, 86
Goldman, David, 130
golf
  birth of golf in the United States, 26-30
  evolution of stance, grip, and swing, 24-25
  growth of golf in the United States, 30-32, 40-43, 46-47, 403
  health generated by, 421
  as Olympic sport, 337
  origins of, 2-6, *3, 4, 5, 6*
  Scotland's golf clubs, 9-14, *10, 11*
  Scotland's influence, 7-8, *8*, 28, 31, 50-51
  See also rules of golf
golf balls, 33-37, *34*
  Bounding Billies, 35
  bramble pattern, 35-36
  featheries, 15-16, *16*, 33
  gutties, 16-18, *17*, 33-34, 36, 56
  jeu de mail, 5
  parameters, 36-37, 172
  rubber-cored, 34-37
  solid core with synthetic cover, 37
  Top-Flite, 37
  Vardon Flyer guttie, 34, 36, 46-47
Golf Channel, 188, 282, 289, 360
golf clubs, 9-14, 26-32, 50-54. *See also specific
  groups*
golf clubs (equipment)
  Callaway's Big Bertha, 285
  Dutch golf clubs, *3*
  fourteen club limit, 133

graphite shafts, 228
grooves on, 38, 265, 337-38
gutties and, 18
for Haskell ball, 38
jeu de mail, 5
metal woods, 236
Ping Eye-2 irons dispute, 265
putters, 57-58, 172, 404
sand wedge, 84
steel shafts, 100, 112, 135-36
in United States, 26-27, 40-41
U.S.G.A. maximum driver volume
  increase, 316
golf equipment
  attire for women, 53-54
golf tee, 38-39, *39*
grass mower, 18
  horse-drawn machinery, 31
  plastic cleats, 285
  See also golf balls; golf clubs (equipment)
golf tee, 38-39, *39*
Goodman, Johnny, 101-2, 127, *128*, 132
Goosen, Retief, *299*
  The Masters, 304, 311, 314, 329
  U.S. Open, 301-2, 309, 312
Gordon, Jacqueline, 156-57
Gore, Jason, 312
Gossett, David, 297
Goss, Oliver, 405
Grace, John, 230
Grady, Wayne, 266, 271
Graham, Allan, 95
Graham, Archibald, 59
Graham, David, 235, 244, 260, 314
Graham, Lou, 230-31, 232
Granada, Julieta, 384
Grand Slam/career Grand Slam winners
  Jones, 90, 103-10, *105, 107*, 350
  Mickelson, 405
  Nicklaus (three), 198, 202, 207, 208, 215, 221
  Player, 192, 198, 202
  Tiger Slam, 301, 345, 350
  Woods (three), 198, 215, 333, 345, 350-51
Grand Slam winners, L.P.G.A.
  Bradley, 368
  Inkster, 368
  Sörenstam, 364, 368
  Suggs, 368
  Webb, 367-68
  Wright, 368
Grant, George F., 38-39
Greater Greensboro Open, 136, 141, 355, 403
Greater Hartford Open, 324
Greater Milwaukee Open, 284, 344
Green, Danny, 267
Green, Hubert, 194, 232, 233, 260
Griffin, Helen, 160
  grip, evolution of, 24-25
Grout, Jack, 204

Gulbis, Natalie, *372*, 372-73
Guldahl, Ralph
　biographical information, 132-33
　career summary, 132, 149
　The Masters, 132, 135, 146, 149
　Santa Monica Open, 405
　U.S. Amateur, 127
　U.S. Open, 129, 132, 140, 149
Gunderson Carner, Joanne, 120, 195, 219, 240-41, 403
Gunn, Watts, 91, 100
Gustafson, Sophie, 382
gutta percha golf ball "gutties," 16-18, *17*, 33-34, 36, 46-47, 56

H

Haas, Freddy, 137
Haas, Jay, 280
Hagen, Walter "Sir Walter"
　biographical information, *70*, 72, 73, 74, *161*
　British Open, 74, 126
　career stats, 75
　career summary, 72-74, 75
　and class consciousness attitude, 74-75
　and Jones, 100
　P.G.A. Championship, 74, 75, 83-84
　Ryder Cup, 132
　U.S. Open, 65, 66, 72-74, 77-78, 101
　Western Open, 75
　World Championship of Golf, 83
Hagge, Marlene, 167, 170, 373
Hamilton, Bob, 151
Hamilton, Robert, 303
Hamilton, Todd, 309-10
Hana Bank-KOLON Championship, 382
Haney, Hank, 351
Hanlon, Cathy, 247
Hansen, Soren, 415
Hanson, Anders, 397
Harbert, Chick, 153, 173, 174
Harmon, Brian, 390
Harmon, Butch, 298, 325, 344
Harmon, Claude, 169
Harper, Chandler, 171
Harrington, Padraig
　biographical information, 321, 322
　British Open, 304, 321-22, 330-31, 333-34, 348
　career summary, 321-22
　Honda Classic, 321
　P.G.A. Championship, 322, 334
　Players Championship, 321
　Ryder Cup, 322
　U.S. Open, 299
　Walker Cup, 321
Harris, John, 278
Harwood, Mark, 272
Haskell, Coburn, 34-37
Haskins Awards, 323

Hass, Bill, 401
Havemeyer, Theodor A., 32, 40-41, *41*
Havemeyer Trophy, 100
Hawkins, Fred, 177
HealthSouth Inaugural tournament, 366
Heard, Jerry, 225, 228
Hearn, David, 405
Hebert, Jay, 190
Hebert, Lionel, 176, 190
Hedwall, Caroline, 419
Henley, Russell, 390, 398
Henninger, Brian, 280
Henry VIII, king of France, 50
Hensby, Mark, 312
Herd, Sandy, 36
Heritage Classic, 209
Herron, Davidson, 95
Herron, Tim, 315
Hershey Open, 138
Hicks, Betty, 151, 155, 160
Hicks, Helen, 122
Hilton, Harold, 20, 59
Hinkle, Lon, 244
Hoblitzel, Fred, 108
Hoch, Scott, 234, 265, 277, 280, 287
Hoffman, Morgan, 418
Hogan, Ben
　biographical information, 142, *143*, 144-45, 148, 172
　All American Open, 137
　British Open, 146-47, 173
　car accident and recovery, 144-45, 172
　career stats, 146, 147
　career summaries, 142-43, 145-48, 152, 169, 173, 345
　Colonial Invitational, 146
　Los Angeles Open, 144-45, 171
　The Masters, 136, 144, 145, 146, 147, 152, 171, 173, 174
　and Nelson, 134, 135, 137, 142
　Nelson-Snead-Hogan triumvirate, 131, 134, 138
　North & South Open, 142
　Pan-American Open, 146
　P.G.A. Championship, 143, 144, 169
　U.S. Open, 141, 144, 145, 146, 147-48, 169, *170*, 171-72, 173, 175, 176, 182, 199-200
Holbrook, Harry, 28-29
Holden Australian Open Championship, 363
Homans, Eugene, 108-9
Homes, J.B., 415
Honda Classic: **2005**, 321; **2008**, 318; **2009**, 394; **2010**, 394; **2011**, 351; *2013*, 398; **2014**, 352, 390, 398
Honourable Company of Edinburgh Golfers, 9-13
How I Play Golf (instructional film), 112
Hoyt, Beatrix, 51, 120
HP Byron Nelson Classic, 390

HSBC Championship, Shanghai, China, 326
Hun-An, Byeong, 334, 337
Hunter, Willie, 96
Hurd, Dorothy Campbell, 120
Huston, John, 280, 299
Hutchinson, Horace, 36
Hutchinson, Jock, 78, 83, 97
Hyndman, Bill, III, 174

I
Immelman, Trevor, 332
Ingram, Sarah LeBrun, 278
Inkster, Julie, 247, 360, *360*
International Management Group (IMG), 183
Irwin, Hale
  British Open, 248, 252, 254
  P.G.A. Championship, 278
  Ryder Cup, 274, 414
  U.S. Open, 68, 195, 230, 235, 249, 251, 261-62,
    270-71, 278-79
Ishikawa, Ryo, 338, 401

J
Jacklin, Tony, 208-9, 219-20, 222, 225, 244, 412
Jack Nicklaus Memorial Tournament.
  See Memorial Tournament
Jacobs, Tommy, 197, 202, 207
James IV, king of Scotland, 7, *8*
James, Mark, 274
Jameson, Elizabeth May "Betty," 150, 155, 158-
  59, 167-68, *168*
Jamie Farr Owens Corning Classic, 368, 382
Jamieson, Jim, 193, 209, 227
Jang, Jeong, 372
January, Don, 190, 203, 232
Janzen, Lee, 276-77, 293
  Japan Open Championship, 382
  Japan Tour, 338
  jeu de mail, 3, 5
Ji, Eun-Hee, 402
Jiménez, Miguel Ángel, 299, 302, 397
  John Deere Classic, 320, 375, 389, 390, 405
  Johnnie Walker World Cup, 275
Johnson, Dustin, 327, 338, 389, 394, 400-401,
  407
Johnson, Zack, 329, 348, 405, 407
Johnston, Harrison, 104
John, Tiffany, 387
Jones, Robert Trent, 171
Jones, Robert Tyre, Jr. "Bobby"
  biographical information, 90-91, *91, 94*, 97, 222
  and Augusta National Golf Club, 113-14
  British Amateur, 95, 103-5
  British Open, 93-94, 100, 106
  career stats, 110, 214
  career summary, 126, 311
  as Dixie Whiz Kid, 118
  exhibition circuit during W.W.I., 80, *81*
  Freeman of the Royal Burgh of St. Andrews

award, 114-15
  Grand Slam win (1930), 90, 103-10, *105, 107*,
    350
  on Joyce Wethered, 54
  Merion Golf Club plaque in honor of, *107*
  retirement years, 111-15, 134
  temper tantrums, 93-94
  U.S. Amateur, 79, 91-92, 94-95, 96, 99, 100-
    101, 101-2, 107-10
  U.S. Open, 83, *88*, 95-96, 97-99, 100, 101,
    106-7, 146
  Walker Cup, 95, 96, 99, 100, 101, 103
Jones, Steve, 283
Junior World Golf Championship, 343, 369
Junior World Golf Championships, 317
Jutanugarn, Ariya, 375

K
Kaiser International, 229
Kapalua L.P.G.A. Classic, 375
Kaymer, Martin, 338, 395, 406, 415
Keeler, O.B., 103
Keiser, Herman, 144, 152
Kelly, John, 316
Kemper Open, 231
Kerr, Christie, *371*, 371-72
Kim, Anthony
  The Masters, 326, 338, 396
  Presidents Cup, 337
  Ryder Cup, 415, 417
Kim, Birdie, 374
Kim, Sung Yoon, 297
King, Betsy, 267, 358-59, *359*, 419
Kinnan, Alexander P.W., 28-29
Kirby, Dorothy, 125
Kirk, Chris, 390
Kite, Chris, 262
Kite, Tom
  British Open, 234
  The Masters, 212-13, 247, 258, 261, 290
  U.S. Amateur, 221
  U.S. Open, 266, 274-75
Kittleson, Drew, 334
Knight, A. T., 57-58
Knost, Colt, 311, 332
Knudson, George, 219
Kocsis, Chuck, 176
Ko, Lydia, 373, *383*, 383-84, 387, 401, 403
Korean L.P.G.A., 368
Kraft, Greg, 294
Kraft, Kerry, 401
Kraft Nabisco Championship: winners list, 439-
  40; **1983**, 359; **1984**, 360; **1986**, 240; **1988**,
  359; **1989**, 360; **1991**, 359; **1996**, 359; **2000**,
  367; **2001**, 364; **2002**, 364; **2003**, 375; **2005**,
  364; **2006**, 367, 370, 372, 376; **2007**, 365, 375;
  2008, 370; **2010**, 380; **2011**, 385; **2013**, 404;
  2014, 386, 387
Kribel, Joel, 292

Krickstein, Aaron, 374
Kroll, Ted, 175
Kuchar, Matt, 292, 292
Kuehne, Hank, 294
Kuehne, Trip, 280, 294

L

Lacoste, Catherine, 203, *203*, 220
Ladies Amateur, 120. *See also* British Ladies
  Amateur
Ladies Professional Golfers Association.
  See L.P.G.A.
Lady Keystone Open, 237
Lang, Brittany, 374
Langer, Bernhard
British Open, 244, 249-50, 254, 260, 277, 302
The Masters, 259, 276
Ryder Cup, 274, 414
Las Vegas Invitational, 274
Laureus World Sports Award, 399
Lawrence, W. G., 43, 44
Lawrie, Paul, 295-96
Leadbetter, David, 286
Leaney, Stephen, 307
Lee, Danny, 334
Lee, Meena, 386
left-handed Majors winners, 196, 306, 324. *See*
  also Mickelson, Phil
Legends of Golf, 234
Lehman, Tom
British Open, 283-84, 291, 299
The Masters, 276, 278
U.S. Open, 280-81, 283, 290-91
Leishman, Marc, 407
Lema, Tony, 185, 196-97, 203, 207
Leonard, Justin
British Open, 291, 295
P.G.A. Championship, 292, 305, 310, 320
Ryder Cup, 296-97, 414
U.S. Amateur, 276
L.E.T. (Ladies European Tour)
Order of Merit winners, 361, 363
Rookie of the Year, 361, 362
and Solheim Cup, 418
and Sörenstam, 362-63
and Thompson, 386, 387
and Webb, 366
and Yang, 387
Levet, Thomas, 305, 318
Levi, Wayne, 274
Lewis, Bob, Jr., 244
Lewis, Stacy, 377, 385-86, *386*, 402
L.G.U. (Ladies Golf Union), 419, 420. *See also*
  Curtis Cup
Lietzke, Bruce, 273
Lind, Dean, 169
Lindley, Brian, 245
Links of Leith, 9-10
List, Luke, 311

Little, Lawson, 87, 130, 149
Littler, Gene
The Masters, 201, 220
P.G.A. Championship, 233
San Diego Open, 261
U.S. Amateur, 173
U.S. Open, 174, 190, 195
Lloyd, Joe, 55
Locke, Arthur D'Arcy "Bobby," 141, 152-53, 170,
  171, 172, 176
Lockhart, Robert, 27, 28-29
Longs Drugs Challenge, 371
Lopez, Nancy, 237-38, 238, 265, 292-93
Los Angeles Open, 138, 144-45, 155, 171, 185,
  343
Love, Davis, III, 292
British Open, 307-8
The Masters, 280, 294
P.G.A. Championship, 291-92, 313
U.S. Open, 281, 283
Lowell, William, 38-39
Lowery, Eddie, 67
Lowery, Steve, 303
L.P.G.A. (Ladies Professional Golfers
  Association)
age restrictions for membership, 374
and Berg, 159
founding of, 157, 159, 160-61, 168
and Jameson, 168
point system for Hall of Fame, 363
Rawls and, 167
and Suggs, 164-65
Thompson's petition for 12 sponsor
  exemptions, 387
on transgender women, 338
WPGA as predecessor, 158, 160
See also Grand Slam winners, L.P.G.A.
L.P.G.A. Career Grand Slam, 364, 367, 368
L.P.G.A. Championship: winners list, 440-42;
  1957, 164; **1958**, 162; **1959**, 167; **1960**, 162;
  1961, 162, 163; **1963**, 162, 196; **1967**, 239;
  1969, 167; **1971**, 239; **1975**, 239; **1978**, 237,
  238; **1983**, 359; **1984**, 359; **1985**, 238; **1986**,
  240; **1989**, 238; **1992**, 358; **1993**, 359; **1996**,
  361; **2006**, 383; **2010**, 371, 383; **2011**, 381;
  2012, 402; **2013**, 404
L.P.G.A. Final Qualifying Tournament, 371
L.P.G.A. Hall of Fame
about, 363
Berg, 159, 161
Bradley, 240
Carner, 241
Jameson, 161, 168
Lopez, 238
Ochoa, 370
Rawls, 167
Suggs, 161, 165
Vare, 125
Whitworth, 239

Wright, 163
Zaharias, 157, 161
L.P.G.A. Japan Tour, 373, 382
L.P.G.A. Komen Award, Kerr, 372
L.P.G.A. Lotte Championship, 377
L.P.G.A. McDonald's Championship: **1990**, 360;
  1994, 361; **1998**, 368, 380; **1999**, 360; **2000**,
  361; **2001**, 367; **2002**, 368; **2003-2005**, 364;
  2005, 372, 375; **2006**, 368, 376; **2007**, 365, 376
L.P.G.A. of Japan, 373
L.P.G.A. Player of the Year
  1986, Bradley, 240
  1989, King, 267
  1990, Daniel, 271
  1999, Webb, 367
  2000, Webb, 367
  Lewis, 386
  Lopez (4 times), 237, 238, 265
  Ochoa, 370
  Sörenstam (8 times), 363, 364, 365
  Whitworth (7 times), 239
L.P.G.A. Rookie of the Year: 1975, Alcott, 359;
  1978, Nancy Lopez, 237; **1994**, Sörenstam, 363;
  1996, Webb, 366; **1998**, Pak, 368; **2003**,
  Ochoa, 370; **2008**, Tang, 381; **2014**, Ko, 384
L.P.G.A. State Farm Classic, 376-77
L.P.G.A. Tour and Solheim Cup, 418
L.P.G.A. Tour Qualifying School, 373
Lu Liang Huan, 222, 225
Lyle, Sandy, 259-60, 264
Lynn, David, 402

M

MacClain, Edwin Kerr, 84
Macdonald, Charles B., 32, 40, 41, 42-45
Macfarlane, Willie, 95, 100
Mackenzie, Alister, 102, 113
Maggert, Jeff, 282, 290-91, 306
Mahaffey, John, 231, 234
Mahan, Hunter, 305, 393, 397
Maiden, Stewart, 91
Malaysian P.G.A. Championship, 319
Manero, Tony, 131
Mangrum, Lloyd, 144, 152, 171
Marathon Classic, 384
Mark H. McCormack Award, McIlroy, 399
Marr, Dave, 186, 198
Marsh, Graham, 248
Martin, Ben, 337
Marucci, George "Buddy," 282, 417-18
Maruyama, Shigeki, 304
Mary Queen of Scots, 8, 8, 50
Massachusetts Amateur, 65, 119
Massengale, Don, 203
Massey, Arnaud, 295
The Masters Annual Invitational: winners list,
  426-27; **1934**, 113-14, 130-31; **1935**, 86, 114,
  127; **1936**, 75, 131; **1937**, 131, 135; **1938**, 132;
  1939, 146, 149; **1940**, 149; **1941**, 151; **1942**,

136, 151; **1946**, 144, 152; **1948**, 169; **1949**, 141,
169-70; **1950**, 171; **1951**, 171; **1952**, 141, 172;
1953, 145, 173, 207; **1954**, 141, 147, 174; **1955**,
147, 174; 1956, 147, 175, 180, 197; **1957**, 176;
1958, 177, 180, 181; **1959**, 181, 189; **1960**, 180,
181-82, 189-90, 197; **1961**, 183, 190, 192;
1962, 184, 195; **1963**, 185, 195, 207; **1964**,
186, 196; **1965**, 198, 207; **1966**, 202, 207; 1967,
203; **1969**, 219; **1970**, 200-201, 220; **1971**,
221; **1972**, 208, 227; **1973**, 228; **1974**, 193, 229;
1975, 209-10, 230; 1976, 231; **1977**, 211, 232;
1978, 194, 233; **1979**, 235; **1980**, 242, 256-57;
1981, 244; **1982**, 245; **1983**, 247, 257-58;
1984, 248-49; **1985**, 259; **1986**, 212, 261;
1987, 262-63; **1988**, 264; **1989**, 202, 265-66,
287; **1990**, 202, 270, 287; **1991**, 272; **1992**, 274;
1993, 276; **1994**, 249, 278; **1995**, 280, 344;
1996, 282-83, 288; **1997**, 242, 290, 344; **1998**,
194, 213, 293; **1999**, 294-95; **2000**, 298, 320;
2001, 202, 301, 345; **2002**, 202, 303-4, 313,
345-46; **2003**, 196, 306-7, 324; **2004**, 196,
308, 324; **2005**, 311, 346; **2006**, 196, 313-14,
324, 346-47; **2007**, 329, 347-48; **2008**, 194,
332; **2009**, 194, 335, 394; **2010**, 326, 338, 343,
351; **2011**, 351, 389, 395, 396, 400; **2012**, 327,
401-2; **2013**, 352, 398, 404, 406; **2014**, 388;
2015, 388, 389, 390, 392, 399, 406-7
Matsuyama, Hideki, 390
Mattice, Len, 306-7
Maxwell, Bill, 172
May, Bob, 300, 345
Mayer, Dick, 176
Mayfair, Billy, 264, 302
Mazda Senior Tournament Players
  Championship, 201
MBNA America Classic, 366
McCormack, Mark, 183
McCumber, Mark, 272, 284
McDermott, John, 61-63, 63
McDowell, Graeme, 315, 338, 401, 402
McGladrey Classic, 390
McIlroy, Rory, 392
  Abu Dhabi Golf Championship, 396-97
  BMW Championship, 394, 398
  British Open, 395, 396, 398-99, 406
  career stats, 388, 391, 397-98, 399
  career summary, 391-99
  Dubai Desert Classic, 393, 394
  endorsements, 392, 398
  European Tour, 391, 393, 395
  Honda Classic, 394, 398
  The Masters, 392, 394, 396, 398, 399, 400, 407
  Memorial Skins Game, 395
  Omega Desert Classic, 397
  Omega European Masters, 393
  P.G.A. Championship, 391, 396, 397, 399, 402
  Quail Hollow Championship, 394-95
  Race to Dubai, 394
  South African Open, 393

UBS Hong Kong Open, 396
U.S. Open, 391, 396, 400
WEC Cadillac Match Play Championship, 399
Wells Fargo Championship, 398, 399
WGC-Accenture Match Play
  Championship, 393-94
WGC-Bridgestone Invitational, 399
WGC-Cadillac Championship, 397
WGC-HSBC Championship, 396
McLean, Jack, 131
McNamara, Tom, 73
McNulty, Mark, 271, 281
McSpaden, Harold "Jugs," 132, 136
media, 289
Mediate, Rocco, 333, 349
Meeks, Eric, 265
Melhorn, "Wild" Bill, 83
Memorial Skins Game, 395
Memorial Tournament: **1997**, 320; **1999**, 344;
  2009, 349; **2010**, 395; **2011**, 352, 395; **2012**,
  355; **2013**, 390
Memphis Open, 137
Mercedes-Benz Championship, 321
Merion Golf Club, Ardmore, Pennsylvania, 404
Metropolitan Amateur, 58, 59
Metz, Dick, 132
Miami-Biltmore tournament, 138
Miami Four-Ball final, 136
Micheel, Shaun, 308, 316
Michelob Ultra Open, 365
Mickelson, Phil
  biographical information, 323, *325*, 326, 328
  British Open, 310, 315, 327-28, 400-401, 405
  Byron Nelson Golf Classic, 323
  career summary, 196, 284, 308, 323-28
  Deutsche Bank Championship, 325-26
  FedEx Cup, 326
  Grand Slam win, 405
  health challenges, 325, 327
  HSBC Championship, Shanghai, China, 326
  The Masters, 280, 282, 304, 306-7, 308-9,
    313-14, 324, 326, 327, 335, 338, 388, 407
  Northern Telecom Open and N.C.A.A., 274, 323
  P.G.A. Championship, 284, 303, 313, 315, 324,
    327, 399
  Players Championship, 245
  Presidents Cup, 337, 417
  Shell Houston Open, 327
  Tour Championship, 326
  U.S. Amateur, 271
  U.S. Open, 281, 295, 301, 304, 307, 309, 314-
    15, 324-25, 326, 327, 336, 404
  WGC-CA Championship, 326
  World Series of Golf, 323
Middlecoff, Cary, 141, 147, 148, 170, 174, 176
Miller, Johnny
  Bing Crosby National Pro-Am, 229
  British Open, 228, 232
  career stats, 243, 244

  career summary, 228-29
  Kaiser International, 229
  The Masters, 209-10, 221, 230
  Sea Pines Heritage Classic, 229
  U.S. Open, 228, *229*, 249
Ming Dynasty, China, 3
Minneapolis City Championship, 158
Minnesota Championship, 158
Mitchell, Bobby, 208
Miyazato, Ai, *382*, 382-83
Miyazato, Mika, 402
Mize, Larry, 262-63, 277, 278
Mizuno Classic, 364-65, 367
modern Grand Slam, 90. *See also* career Grand
  Slam winners
Molinari, Edoardo, 313
Montgomerie, Colin "Monty"
  British Open, 302, 309, 312-13
  career summary, 283
  P.G.A. Championship, 280, 281-82
  Ryder Cup, 273, 293, 306
  U.S. Open, 275, 278-79, 281, 290-91, 314, 318
Montreal Open, 136
Moody, Orville, 219, *219*
Moore, Darla, 403
Moore, Parker, 232
Moore, Ryan, 310-11, 332
Morgan, Gil, 271, 274-75
Morris, "Old" Tom, xx, 17-18, 28, 36, 42, 299
Morris, "Young" Tom, 19-20, 290
Mt. Hope, New York, 30-31
Munoz, Azahara, 334
Murphy, Bob, 198, 221, 284

N
Nabisco Dina Shore Championship, 358
Nagle, Kel, 182, 185, 190, 192, 198
Nakajima, Tommy, 262
Na, Kevin, 339, 394
National Golf Foundation, 334
National Golf Links of America, Southhampton,
  43, 45
National Invitational. *See* The Masters Annual
  Invitational
Navistar L.P.G.A. Classic, 373, 386, 387, 403
N.C.A.A. Championship: **1961**, 205; **1990**, 323;
  1991, 323, 362; **1992**, 274, 323; **1996**, 284,
  344; **2001**, 369; **2002**, 369
N.C.A.A. First Team All-American, 344
N.C.A.A. Player of the Year, Ochoa, 369
Neer, Aert van der, *4*
Nelson, Byron
  biographical information, *116*, 134-35, 136,
    138
  Canadian Open, 137
  career stats, 137, 347
  career summy, 134-38
  Chicago Victory Open, 136
  Fort Worth Open, 137

George S. May's All-American Open, 137
and Hogan, 142
The Masters, 131, 135, 136, 151, 152-53
Memphis Open, 137
Nelson-Snead-Hogan triumvirate, 134, 138
P.G.A. Championship, 135, 136-37, 149, 151-52
Philadelphia Inquirer Invitation Tournament, 136
retirement of, 143-44
Seattle Open, 137
U.S. Open, 135, 138, 140, 151
Nelson, Larry, 244-45, 248, 263, 264
Netherlands and history of golf, 3, 3-5, *4*
Newell, Betty Hicks, 151, 155, 160
New Jersey Amateur, 59
Newport, Rhode Island, 32
New South Wales Open, 401
Newton, Jack, 231, 242, 257
Nicholas, Alison, 238, 292-93, 419
Nichols, Bobby, 184, 186, 196, 203, 225
Nicklaus, Charlie, 208
Nicklaus, Jack, Jr., 261
Nicklaus, Jack "the Golden Bear," *206*
 British Open, 192, 203, 207, 208-9, 210-11, 214, 221, 225, 229, 232-33, 234, 235, 256, 258, 265, 336
 career Grand Slam, 207, 350
 career stats, 212, 399, 406
 career summary, 195, 202, 204-15, 284
 Champions Tour, 213
 Doral-Eastern Open, 209-10
 and golf course design, 209, 214, 284
 Grand Slam wins, 198, 202, 207, 208, 215, 221
 Heritage Classic, 209-10
 The Masters, 185, 186, 195, 198, 202, 207, 208, 209-10, 211, 221, 230, 231, 232, 244, 261, 276, 280, 338
 Palmer-Nicklaus-Player triumvirate, 192, 195
 P.G.A. Championship, 186, 195, 196, 198, 207, 209, 210, 211, 212, 221, 225, 228, 230, 231, 243-44, 248
 Players Championship, 209, 210, 211, 245
 Ryder Cup, 412, 413
 Senior Players Championship, 213
 U.S. Amateur, 190, 205
 U.S. Open, 182, 184-85, 195, 203, 205-9, 208, 211, 212, 219, 221-22, 223-24, 227, 242-43, 246, 278-79, 396
 U.S. Senior Open, 213, 214
Nigerian Open, 319
Nike and Woods, 344
Nissan Los Angeles Open, 343
Nobilo, Frank, 278-79
Noh, Seung Yuh, 390
Nordegren, Elin, 342
Norman, Greg "Great White Shark"
 British Open, 266, 277, 321-22, 333-34
 The Masters, 212-13, 261, 262-63, 278, 280,

282-83, 288, 294-95
 P.G.A. Championship, 262, 277-78
 U.S. Open, 249, 262, 280-81
North, Andy, 233-34, 259, *260*
Northcliffe, Lord, 64
Northern Telecom Open, 274, 323
Northern Trust Open, 326
North & South Amateur, 119
North & South Open, 142
North Texas L.P.G.A. Shootout, 386
North West Arkansas Championship, 382

O

Oakhurst, New England, United States, 27
Oakland Open, 138
Ochoa, Lorena, 361, 367, 369-71, *370*
Ogilvy, Geoff, 314, 315, 325, 393-94
O'Hern, Nick, 347
Ohio State Junior and Open, 205
OHL Classic, 390
Olazábal, José Maria
 and Ballesteros, 258
 British Open, 312-13
 The Masters, 272, 278, 280, 294-95, 304, 314
 Ryder Cup, 273, 296-97, 414
Oliver, Ed "Porky," 143, 145, 146, 149, 152, 172
Olympic Games, 154, 337
O'Meara, Mark, 235, 272, 274, 293-94
Omega Desert Classic, 397
Omega European Masters, 393
Oosterhuis, Peter, 229
Oosthuizen, Louis, 338, 393, 402, 407
Open Championship. *See* British Open
Orange Blossom Classic, 359
Orcutt, Maureen, 125
Order of Merit. See European Tour Order of Merit
Orena Ochoa Invitational, 377
Ouimet, Francis
 biographical information, 65, *66*, 69, 80-81
 career summary, 65, 417
 U.S. Amateur, 60, 65, 69, 95, 130
 U.S. Open, 65-69, 72-73, 264, 307
Owen, Simon, 234

P

Pac-10 Player of the Year, 344
Page, Estelle Lawson, 155, 158
Page, Mrs. Julius, 133
Pak, Se Ri, 333, 367, 368, *368*, 380
Palmer, Arnold
 biographical information, *178*, 181, 183-84, 188
 Arnie's Army, 181, 184, 187, 205, *206*
 British Open, 182, 183, 185, 190, 195
 Canadian Open, 181
 career stats, 183, 186, 187
 career summary, 177, *178*, 188, 195
 consecutive holes-in-one, 188
 Los Angeles Open, 185

The Masters, 177, 180, 181-82, 183, 184, 186, 188, 189, 192, 195, 196, 198, 207, 338
and Nicklaus, 204
Palmer-Nicklaus-Player triumvirate, 192, 195
P.G.A. Championship, 183, 185, 186, 187, 196, 198, 219, 221
Piccadilly World Match Play Championship, 186
retirement years, 188
U.S. Amateur, 174, 181
U.S. Open, 182, 184-85, 186-87, 190, 196, 197, 200, 205-7, 207-8, 223-24, 228
U.S. Senior Open, 187
Western Open, 185
Pan-American Open, 146
Park, Hee Young, 386
Park, Inbee, 333, 381, *381*, 386, 404, 405
Parks, Sam, 129
Park, Willie, 19
Parnevik, Jesper, 279, 291, 342
Parrish, Samuel, 40
Parry, Craig, 274, 277
Parsons, Isette, 51
Pate, Jerry, 230, 231, 234, 235, 245
Paterson, Robert, 16-17
Pate, Steve, 273, 275
Patton, Billy Joe, 174
Patton, Chris, 267
Pavin, Corey, 273, 280-81, 282
Peete, Calvin, 248
Pennick, Harvey, 280
Perkins, Thomas, 101
Perkins, T. Philip "Phil," 85-86, 101
Perry, Chris, 248
Perry, Kenny, 284, 307, 335, 415
Persons, Peter, 260
Pettersen, Suzann, 383, 401, 402
Peugeot Spanish Open, 321
P.G.A. (Professional Golfers Association), 74, 271, 403
P.G.A. Championship: winners list, 428-30;
1916, 74; **1921**, 75; **1922**, 83; **1923**, 83-84; **1924-1927**, 75; **1933**, 86, 127; **1934**, 131, 133; **1935**, 131; **1936**, 131; **1937**, 132; **1937** driving contest, 138-39; **1938**, 133; **1939**, 136, 149; **1940**, 135, 136; **1941**, 136, 151; **1942**, 141, 151; **1944**, 136, 151; **1945**, 136-37, 152; **1946**, 143, 152; **1947**, 153; **1948**, 144; **1949**, 141, 152, 169-70; **1950**, 171; 1951, 172; **1952**, 141, 173, 174; **1953**, 173; **1954-1955**, 174; **1956**, 175; **1957**, 176, 177, 190; **1957** conversion to stroke play, 177; **1958**, 180; **1959**, 189; **1960**, 183, 190; **1961**, 190, 195; **1962**, 185, 192, 195; **1963**, 195, 207; **1964**, 186, 196; **1965**, 198; **1966**, 202; **1967**, 203; **1968**, 187, 195, 196, 219, 333, 336; **1969**, 220, 231; **1970**, 221; **1971**, 208, 221; **1972**, 192-93, 209, 227; **1973**, 209, 228; **1974**, 224, 225, 230; **1975**, 210, 231; **1976**, 232; **1977**, 233; **1978**, 234; **1979**, 235; **1980**, 211,
212, 243-44; **1981**, 244; **1982**, 247; **1983**, 248; **1984**, 224, 225, 250; **1985**, 260; **1986**, 262; **1987**, 244-45, 263; **1988**, 265; **1989**, 266-67; **1990**, 271; **1991**, 272-73; **1992**, 275-76; **1993**, 277; **1994**, 279-80; **1995**, 281-82; **1996**, 284-85; **1997**, 291-92; **1998**, 294, 320; **1999**, 296, 315, 344; **2000**, 300, 345; **2001**, 302-3; **2002**, 305, 346; **2003**, 308; **2004**, 310, 320; **2005**, 313, 324; **2006**, 196, 315-16, 347; **2007**, 318, 331-32, 348; **2008**, 321, 322, 334; **2009**, 337, 349; **2010**, 327, 338, 406; **2011**, 390, 396, 401; **2012**, 398; **2012**, 327, 391, 402; **2013**, 352, 405; **2014**, 352, 391, 399
P.G.A. Hall of Fame
Casper, 201
Evans, 79
Hogan, 148
Nelson, 138
Palmer, 188
Sarazen, 87
Snead, 142
Zaharias, 157
P.G.A. Player of the Year
1964, Venturi, 197
1970, Casper, 201, 220
1974, Miller, 228-29
1990, Faldo, 288
2010, Furyk, 338
McIlroy, 393, 399
Nicklaus (5 times), 197, 209, 210, 228
Watson (6 times), 233, 253, 255
Woods (9 times), 344, 346, 350
P.G.A. Rookie of the Year
1962, Nicklaus, 207
1979, O'Meara, 235
1994, Els, 318
1996, Woods, 344
Nicklaus, 207
P.G.A. Senior Championship, 213
P.G.A. Tour Player of the Year, 320, 399
P.G.A. Tour Rookie, Bradley, 390
Philadelphia Inquirer Invitation Tournament, 136
"Phil flop shot," 323
Phoenix Open, 319-20, 355
Picard, Henry, 86, 132, 140, 149
Piccadilly World Match Play Championship, 186
Player, Gary "the Black Knight"
biographical information, 191, *193*
British Open, 176, 189, 192, 194, 219, 229
career Grand Slam, 192
career stats, 192, 194
career summary, 192-94, 195, 215
Grand Slam winner, 192, 198, 202
The Masters, 183, 184, 188, 189, 192, *193*, 194, 198, 207, 229, 233, 338
and McIlroy, 394
Palmer-Nicklaus-Player triumvirate, 192, 195
P.G.A. Championship, 185, 192-93, 209, 220,

225, 227, 250
U.S. Open, 177, 192, 235
Players Championship: about, 245; **1974**, 209; **1976**, 210; **1978**, 211; **1982**, 245; **2003-2004**, 321; **2007**, 245, 325; **2009**, 394; **2010**, 351; **2013**, 352; **2015**, 389
Pohl, Dan, 245
Points, D.A., 398
Poulter, Ian, 334
Presidents Cup: about, 303, 415-16; winners list, 449; **1998**, 296; **2003**, 416; **2005**, 416; **2007**, 416, 417; **2009**, 321, 337, 416-17, 417-18; **2011**, 354, 401, 417, 418; **2013**, 405-6; Mickelson (8 times), 327
Pressel, Morgan, *374*, 374-75
Price, Nick
    British Open, 247, 254, 258, 265, 279
    career summary, 247
    The Masters, 261
    P.G.A. Championship, 275-76, 280, 294
Professional Golfers Association. *See* P.G.A.
Pung, Jackie, 166
Putnam, Kingman H., 28-29
putters, 57-58, 172
putting style, 152, 199

Q

Quad Cities Open, 235
Quail Hollow Championship, 351, 394-95
Quick, Smiley, 152
Quinn Direct Master Masters, 393
Quinney, Jeff, 300-301

R

Race to Dubai, 394, 397, 399
Rafferty, Ronan, 279
Ramsey, Rickey, 316
Rancho Santa Fe Open, 138
Randolph, Sam, 250, 260
Rankin, Judy, 232
Raphael, Fred, 234
Rattray, John, 10-11
Rawlings, Horace, 44
Rawls, Elizabeth Earle "Betsy," 165-67, *166*, 171, 172
Ray, Edward "Ted," *24*, 60, 65-69, *66*, 83, 95
Rebmann, Eric, 264
Red Cross exhibitions, 80-81, 92, *161*
Reed, Patrick, 389
Rees, Dai, 183
Reid, John, 27, 27-28, 27-29, 31, 40
Reid, John, Jr., 69
Reid, Mike, 266-67
Reid, Wilfred, 65-66, 78
Revolta, Johnny, 131, 136-37
Rhode Island Amateur, 118-19
Rice, Condoleeza, 403
Rice, Grandland, 115
Ridley, Fred, 231

Riegel, Robert "Skee," 153
Riley, Chris, 315
Rivington, James, 26
Robbins, Hillman, Jr., 176
Roberts, Clifford, 113
Roberts, Loren, 279, 291, 318
Robertson, Allan, 17-18
Robson, Fred, 106
Rocca, Costantino, 281
Rodgers, Phil, 196
Rodriguez, Chi Chi, 214
Rogers, Bill, 244, 246
Romero, Andrês, 394
Rook, Robert, 397
Roper, Henry, 104
Rosburg, Bob, 184, 189
Rose, Justin
    British Open, 293-94
    The Masters, 309, 388, 407
    U.S. Open, 327, 352, 404
    WGC-Cadillac Championship, 397
Rosenthal, Elaine, 80, *81*, 118
Ross, Alex, 61
Royal & Ancient Golf Club, 10-13, 36-37, 69. *See also* rules of golf
Royal Montreal Golf Club, Montreal, Canada, 32
rules of golf
    agreement between U.S.G.A. and R & A, 172
    on amateur status, 176
    anchoring ban, 403
    ball parameters, 36-37, 172
    and celebrations before end of game, 414
    Leith and St. Andrews, 10-13
    limit of fourteen clubs, 133
    pre-1952 rules on stymies, 104
    Slope System to adjust handicaps, 261
    sudden-death playoffs, 233
    Title IX legislation, 228
Runyan, Paul, 131, 133
Rutherford, Winthrop, 40
Ryder Cup: about, 410-11, 412, 415; winners list, 448-49; **1927**, 411; **1937**, 132; **1951**, 172; **1953**, 173; **1955**, 175; **1957**, 177; **1961**, 187; **1963**, 187; **1965**, 187; **1967**, 187, 412; **1969**, 412; **1971**, 187; **1973**, 187; **1975**, 187; **1979**, 235-36; **1981**, 245; **1983**, 412-13; **1985**, 258, 260, 413; **1987**, 258, 263-64, 413; **1989**, 258, 413; **1991**, 273-74, 402, 413-14; **1993**, 278; **1995**, 258, 282, 414; **1997**, 291-92, 293, 414; **1999**, 296-97, 344, 414; **2001**, 412; **2002**, 305-6, 412; **2008**, 288, 322, 334, 335, 415; **2010**, 338, 391-92, 395; **2012**, 391-92, 403, 415; **2014**, 391-92, 415
    McIlroy (3 times), 391-92, 395
    Mickelson (7 times), 327
    Nicklaus (6 times), 215
    Snead (eight teams), 142
Ryder, Samuel, 411
Ryerson, Arthur, 40

S

Sabbatini, Rory, 329
Safeway Classic, 370
Samsung World Championship, 376, 382
Sander, Bill, 232
Sanders, Doug, 189, 190, 207, 208, 221
San Diego Open, 261
Sands, Charles E., 44
Santa Monica Open, 405
Sarazen, Gene "The Squire"
  biographical information, 82, *85, 161*
  All American Open, 137
  British Open, 84, 87, 126–27
  career summary, 82–87
  The Masters, 86, 114
  P.G.A. Championship, 75, 83–84, 86
  U.S. Open, 82–83, 84–86, 96, 127–29, 130, 149
Sargent, George, 61, 73
Sauers, Gene, 276
Savannah Golf Club, Savannah, Georgia, 26–27
Sawyer, Ned, 78
SBS Open, 365, 373
Scandinavian Journal of Medicine and Science in Sports, 421
Schenectady putter, 57–58
Scherrer, Tom, 276
Schlee, John, 228
Schwartzel, Charl, 400
Scotland's golf clubs, 9–14, *10, 11*
Scotland's influence on golf, 7–8, 8, 28, 31
Scott, Adam, 316, 398, 400, 404
Scottish Open, 327, 405
Scott, Lady Margaret, 51
Scott, Steve, 284
Sea Pines Heritage Classic, 229
Sears, Samuel, 40
Seattle Open, 137
Seaver, Charlie, 108
Seignious, Hope, 160
Semple Thompson, Carol, 306, *408*
Senior British Open, 194, 448
Senior P.G.A. Championship winners list, 446–47
Senior P.G.A. Tour, 138, 141, 187, 188, 194, 201, 234. *See also* Champions Tour
Senior Players Championship, 201, 213, 447
Senior Women's Amateur Championship, 125
September 11, 2001, terrorist attacks, 303, 412, 418
Severiano Ballesteros Foundation, 258
Shankland, Cowan, 104
Shawnee Open, 62, 65
Shell Houston Open, 320, 327, 394
Shepard, Alan, 222
Shinnecock Hills Golf Club, 31
Shoal Creek Country Club discrimination issues, 271
ShopRite L.P.G.A. Classic, 373, 385, 386
Shute, Denny, 127, 131, 132, 135, *150*, 151

Siegel, Helen, 151, 155–56
Siegel, Jay, 247
Sigel, Jay, 248, 311
Sikes, Richard, 196
Simons, Jim, 224
Simpson, Scott, 263, 272
Simpson, Webb, 389, 402
Sindelar, Joey, 277
Singh, Mohan, 318
Singh, Vijay
  biographical information, 318–19, *319*
  AT&T Pebble Beach National Pro-Am, 320
  British Open, 308
  Buick Classic, 319
  career stats, 321, 346
  career summary, 310, 319–21
  Deutsche Bank Championship, 320
  EDS Byron Nelson Championship, 320
  European Tour, 319, 321
  FedEx Cup, 321, 332
  FUNAI Classic, 320
  John Deere Classic, 320
  Malaysian P.G.A. Championship, 319
  The Masters, 298, 304, 313, 320
  Memorial Tournament, 320
  P.G.A. Championship, 277–78, 294, 310, 320
  Shell Houston Open, 320
  Tour Championship, 320
  U.S. Open, 243, 295, 307
  Volvo Open Championship, 319
Slope System to adjust handicaps, 261
Sluman, Jeff, 265, 275
Smith, Alex, 59, 61
Smith, Horton, 106, 107, 112, 114, 131
Smith, Macdonald, 61, 84, 106–7
Smith, Rick, 325
Snead, J.C., 228, 234
Snead, Sam "Slammin' Sammy"
  biographical information, 138, *139*, 142
  British Open, 141, 152
  career summary, 138–42, *139*, 141–42, 167
  Greater Greensboro Open (eight times), 141, 355, 403
  hitting prowess and personality, 138–40
  Legends, 234
  Los Angeles Open, 171
  The Masters, 136, 141, 146, 147, 169–70, 172, 174, 176, 177, 181, 338
  Nelson-Snead-Hogan triumvirate, 131, 134, 138
  P.G.A. Championship, 133, 151, 172, 177, 202
  Quad Cities Open, 235
  U.S. Open, 132, 135, 140–41, 153, 234
Snedeker, Brandt, 332, 403
Sneed, Ed, 235
snobbery, 74–75, 79
Society of St. Andrews Golfers, 12–14
Solheim Cup
  about, 239, 418–19

2007, 419
2009, 293, 419
2011, 401, 419
2013, 419
Bradley (4 times), 240
Creamer (3 times), 374
Daniel (10 times), 360
Gulbis (3 times), 372
Inkster (8 times), 361
Kerr (6 times), 371
King (six times), 359
Pressel (2 times), 375
Sheehan (6 times), 359
Sörenstam (7 times), 363, 365
Solheim, Karsten, 418
Somerville, Ross, 203
Somerville, Sandy, 108
Song, Jennifer, 337
Sony Open, 375, 376, 390
Sörenstam, Annika, 356, 362–66
Sörenstam, Charlotta, 362
Souchak, Mike, 182
South African Open, 192, 393
Southern Africa Tour, 317
Southern Amateur, 94, 95
Southern Open, 94, 95
Spalding, A. G., 36, 37, 46–47
Spieth, Jordan, 388–89, 395, 400, 405, 406–7
Sportsman of the Year (*Sports Illustrated*), 344, 345
Stacy, Hollis, 250
Stadler, Craig "the Walrus," 228, 245, 259, 264, 277
stance, evolution of, 24–25
Standard Register Ping tournament, 364
St. Andrew's Golf Club, Mt. Hope, New York, 30–31
St. Andrew's Golf Club, Yonkers, New York, 28–29, 30
St. Andrews Ladies' Golf Club, Scotland, 50–51
St. Andrews, Scotland, 10, 11–14, 20
Stanford International Pro-Am, 365
Start Something character-development program, 353
Staughton Rubber Company, 35
St. Clair, William, 9–13
Stenson, Henrik, 315, 334, 405
Stewart, Payne, 268
　British Open, 260, 271
　P.G.A. Championship, 266–67
　Ryder Cup, 273
　U.S. Open, 272, 276–77, 293, 295
Stirling, Alexa, 54, 80, 81, 91, 118, 119, 120
St. Jude FedEx Classic, 390
Stockton, Dave, 193, 221, 229, 232, 234, 273, 414
Stoddard, Lawrence, 44
Stone, Bob, 187
Stranahan, Frank, 147, 171

Strange, Curtis
　The Masters, 259
　P.G.A. Championship, 267
　Ryder Cup, 413
　U.S. Open, 249, 264, 266
Streb, Robert, 390
Stricker, Steve, 294, 320, 330, 337, 415, 417
stymies, rules on, 104, 172
sudden-death playoffs, 233
Suggs, May Louise "Louise Sluggs," 153, 155, 164–65, 165
Sunesson, Fanny, 288
Sutton, Hal, 244, 248
Swedish P.G.A., 362
Sweeney, Robert "Bob," 174, 181
Sweetser, Jess, 96, 108
swing, evolution of, 25, 135–36
Swinging Skirts L.P.G. Classic, 383–84
Sybase Classic, 373

T
Taifong Ladies Open, 381
Takefuji Classic, 375
Tallmadge, Henry O., 28–29, 40
Target World Challenge, 353
Taylor, John Henry "J.H.", 21, 22–24, 23, 24, 47, 56, 248
Taylor, William, 36
television
　1947 U.S. Open, 153
　1953 World Championship, 173
　1954 U.S. Open, 174
　1956 Masters, 175
　1977 U.S. Open, 232
　Faldo as golf analyst, 289
　Golf Channel, 188, 289, 360
　Palmer and, 185
Texas Open, 249
Texas Valero Open, 339
Thirty Years of Championship Golf (Sarazen), 83
Thomas, Dave, 207
Thompson, Alexis "Lexi," 373, 374, 386–87, 387, 403
Thompson, Carol Semple, 306, 408, 420
Thompson, Hall, 271
Thompson, Michael, 332, 402
Thompson, Peter, 174, 176, 177, 198, 248
Tianiang, Guan, 404
ticker-tape parade in NYC, 106, 110
Tiger Jam, 353
Tiger Slam, 301, 345, 350
Tiger Woods Foundation, 352–53
Tiger Woods Learning Center, 352, 353
Time magazine, 383
Titleholders Championship, 159, 160, 239, 443
Titleist and Woods, 344
Tolley, Cyril, 104
Tomori, Katsuyoshi, 281
Toms, David, 299, 303

Torrance, Sam, 274
Tour Championship: **2002**, 320; **2003**, 350; **2007**, 326, 332, 348; **2010**, 338; **2011**, 401; **2012**, 403; **2013**, 405. *See also* FedEx Cup
Tournament Players Championship. *See* Players Championship; Senior Players Championship
Tournament Players Division of P.G.A. *See* P.G.A. Tour
The Tradition, 213, 214, 448
transgender women, 338
Traung, Dorothy, 123
Travers, Jerome D. "Jerry," 58, 58-60, 65, 69, 77
Travis, Walter J., 35, 36, 48, 57-58
Trevino, Lee Buck "Merry Mex"
  biographical information, 223, *224*
  British Open, 208-9, 225
  Canadian Open, 224-25
  career summary, 223-26
  P.G.A. Championship, 225-26, 230, 250, 260
  Senior Tour, 271
  struck by lightening, 225
  U.S. Open, 219, 221-22, 223-24
  Western Open, 225
Tseng, Yani, 380-81, *381*, 385
Tucker, Samuel, 31
Turner, Greg, 279
Turnesa, Jim, 173
Turnesa, Mike, 144
Tuxedo, New York, 32
Tway, Bob, 262, 281
Tweddell, William, 130

U

UBS Hong Kong Open, 393, 396
Uihlein, Peter, 418
Upham, John P., 28-29
Urzetta, Sam, 171
U.S. Amateur: about, 198; winners list, 435-36; **1894**, 43-44; **1895**, 44, 45; **1896-1897**, 45; **1898**, 57, 316; **1900**, 57; **1901**, 35, 36, 57; **1903**, 57; **1906-1910**, 59; **1911**, 20-21, 22, 59, 308; **1912**, 59-60, 77; **1913**, 60, 65, 77; **1914**, 60, 69; **1915**, 78; **1916**, 79, 91-92, 94; **1919**, 94-95; **1920**, 69, 79, 95; **1921**, 94, 96; **1922**, 96; **1923**, 83, 99; **1924**, 69, 99; **1925**, 91, 100; **1926**, 69, 100; **1927**, 69, 100-101; **1928**, 69, 101; **1929**, 101-2, 127; **1930**, 107-10; 1931, 130; **1932**, 203; **1934-1935**, 130; **1936**, 131; **1937**, 127, 132; **1939**, 149; **1940**, 149-50; **1941**, 151; **1946**, 152; **1947**, 153; **1949**, 170, 205; **1950**, 171; **1951**, 172; **1953**, 173; **1954**, 174, 181; **1955**, 174; **1956-1957**, 176; **1958**, 177; **1959**, 205; **1960**, 190; **1961**, 184, 190, 205, 245; **1962**, 205; **1963**, 190, 196; **1964-1965**, 198; **1966**, 202-3, 222; **1967**, 203; **1970**, 221; **1971**, 222; **1972**, 227-28; **1973**, 228, 245; **1974**, 230; **1975**, 231; **1976**, 232; **1977**, 233; **1978**, 234; **1979**, 235; **1980**, 244; **1981**, 245; **1982**, 247; **1983**, 247, 248; **1984**, 250; **1985**, 260; **1986**, 262; **1987**, 264; **1988**, 265; **1989**, 267; **1990**, 271, 323; **1991**, 273; **1992**, 276; **1993**, 278; **1994**, 280, 334, 343; **1995**, 282, 344; **1996**, 284; **1997**, 292; **1998**, 294; **1999**, 297; **2000**, 300-301; **2001**, 303; **2002**, 305, 336; **2003**, 308; **2004**, 310-11, 332; **2005**, 313; **2006**, 316; **2007**, 332; **2008**, 334, 337; **2009**, 334, 337; **2011**, 401; **2012**, 402; **2013**, 405
U.S. Amateur Four-Ball Championship, 406
U.S.G.A. (U.S. Golf Association)
  on ball parameters, 36-37, 172
  and Curtis Cup, 419, 420
  founding of, 40-41
  Gulbis calendar banned by, 372
  and Jones's temper, 94
  letter to McDermott for "extreme discourtesy," 62-63
  loading the field for 1913 U.S. Open, 65
  and Macdonald, 44
  and Ouimet's sporting goods store, 80-81
  response to Shoal Creek discrimination, 271
  roping fairways, 174
  and W.W.I., 80-81
  See also Walker Cup
U.S.G.A. Championships, 284, 285, 297, 311
U.S.G.A. Senior Women's Amateur Championship, 125
U.S. Girls' Junior Championship: **1949**, 170; **1952**, 162; **1972**, 237; **1973**, 359; **1974**, 237; **1996**, 285; **1999**, 297; and Carner, 240; and Stacy, 250
U.S. Junior Championship: 1948, 169; 1991, 278, 343; 1992, 278; 1993, 278; and Woods, 284, 343
U.S. Mid-Amateur Championship, 245, 248, 294
U.S. Open: winners list, 422-26; **1895**, 44, 45; **1896**, 35; **1897**, 55; **1900**, 47, 55; **1901**, 55; **1903-1905**, 55; **1909**, 58, 61; **1910**, 61; **1911**, 61-62, 65; **1912**, 62, 65; **1913**, 60, 62-63, 64, 65-68, 72-73, 264, 307; **1914**, 69, 73-74, 75, 77-78; **1915**, 60, 78; **1916**, 78; **1919**, 73, 75; **1920**, 75, 82-83, 95; **1921**, 83, 95-96; **1922**, 83, 96; **1923**, 83, 97-99; **1924**, 99; **1925**, 69, 100; **1926**, 100; **1928-1929**, 101; **1930**, 106-7; **1931**, 127; **1932**, 84-86, 127; **1933**, 127; **1934**, 127-29; **1935**, 129; **1936**, 131; **1937**, 132, 140; **1938**, 132; **1939**, 135, 140, 151; **1940**, 86-87, 130, 140, 149; **1941**, 151; **1946**, 138, 144, 152; **1947**, 140-41, 153; **1948**, 144, 169; **1949**, 141, 170; **1950-1951**, 171; **1952**, 172; **1953**, 141, 146, 173; **1954**, 147, 174; **1955**, 147, 170, 174-75; **1956**, 147-48, 176; **1957**, 176; **1958**, 177; **1959**, 180, 189, 199-200; **1960**, 182, 190, 205; **1961**, 190, 195; **1962**, 184-85, 205-7; **1963**, 186, 195-96; **1964**, 197; **1965**, 192, 198; **1966**, 186-87, 196, 200, 202; **1967**, 203, 207-8, 211, 223-24, 242; **1968**, 219, 224; **1969**, 219; **1970**, 220, 244, 338; **1971**, 221-22, 224; **1972**, 208, 227, 245-46; **1973**, 228, 243; **1974**, 229-30,

270; **1975**, 230-31; **1976**, 231; **1977**, 232; **1978**, 233-34; **1979**, 235; **1980**, 211, 242-43; **1981**, 244, 314; **1982**, 212, 227, 245-46; **1983**, 244, 247-48; **1984**, 249, 271; **1985**, 259; **1986**, 261-62; **1987**, 263; **1988**, 264; **1989**, 266; **1990**, 261-62, 270-71; **1991**, 272; **1992**, 274-75; **1993**, 276-77; **1994**, 278, 318; **1995**, 280-81; **1996**, 283; **1997**, 290-91, 318; **1998**, 293, 402; **1999**, 295; **2000**, 298-99, 345; **2001**, 301-2; **2002**, 304, 313, 346; **2003**, 243, 307; **2004**, 309; **2005**, 312; **2006**, 314-15, 324-25, 347; **2007**, 325, 330, 335, 348; **2008**, 211, 333, 349, 350-51; **2009**, 335-36, 394; **2010**, 255, 326, 338, 401; **2011**, 389, 391, 400, 401; **2012**, 327, 389, 396, 402; **2013**, 327, 352, 404; **2014**, 406; **2015**, 389, 399, 407

U.S. Public Links, 311, 332
U.S. Senior Amateur, 198, 418
U.S. Senior Open: about, 187, 234; winners list, 447; **1980**, 187; **1981**, 187; **1983**, 201; **1990**, 271; **1991**, 213; **1993**, 213-14
See also Champions Tour
U.S. Senior Tour, 234
U.S. Women's Amateur: winners list, 444-45; **1895**, 44, 51, 52; **1896-1898**, 51; **1906-1907**, 419; **1911-1912**, 419; **1914-1915**, 54; **1916**, 54, 80; **1919-1920**, 80; **1922**, 54, 119; **1923-1927**, 119; **1928**, 120; **1929-1931**, 122; **1932**, 123; **1934**, 123; **1935**, 123-24, 158; **1937**, 158; **1938**, 124, 133, 158; **1939**, 167; **1940**, 150, 167, 168; **1941**, 151; **1946**, 152, 155-56; **1947**, 153, 164; **1948**, 151; **1962**, 195; **1968**, 219; **1969**, 220; **1971**, 51; **1975**, 360; **1977**, 360; **1980-1981**, 360; **1982**, 247, 360; **1992**, 362; **1996**, 285; **2003-2004**, 373; **2005**, 374; **2008**, 334; **2009**, 337; **2012**, 401
U.S. Women's Amateur Public Links Championship, 375, 380, 406
U.S. Women's Mid-Amateur, 278
U.S. Women's Open: winners list, 437-39; **1921**, 119; **1946**, 152, 158-59, 167; **1947**, 167; **1948**, 157; **1949**, 164; **1950**, 157, 171; **1951**, 166; **1953**, 166; **1954**, 157, 173; **1955**, 175; **1957**, 166; **1958**, 162; 1959, 162, 163; **1960**, 166, 166; **1961**, 162, 163; **1964**, 162; **1967**, 203, 220; **1971**, 240; **1976**, 240; **1980**, 359; **1981**, 240; **1984**, 250; **1986**, 240; **1987**, 361; **1989-1990**, 358; **1992**, 359; **1994**, 359; **1995**, 363; **1996**, 363, 371; **1997**, 238, 292-93; **1998**, 368, 380; **1999**, 360; **2000**, 367, 371; **2001**, 367, 374; **2002**, 361; **2004**, 373; **2005**, 374; **2006**, 365; **2007**, 365, 371, 376, 386; **2008**, 333, 405; **2009**, 387; **2010**, 373, 387; **2012**, 382; **2013**, 381, 404; 2014, 377, 386

V

Vanderbeck, Florence, 119
Vanderbilt, William K., 31
Van de Velde, Jean, 295-96

Van Wie, Virginia, 120, 122, 123
"Vardon Grip," 24-25
Vardon, Harry
  biographical information, 22, 23, *24*, 47
  British Open, 21, 248
  career summaries, 22
  gutta percha and Haskell balls, 36, 56
  influence on modern golf, 23-25
  tours of the United States, 46-47, 64-65
  U.S. Open, 60, 65-69, *66*, 95
Vardon Trophy
  Casper (5 times), 199
  McIlroy, 393, 399
  Palmer (4 times), 187
  Singh, 320
  Trevino (5 times), 226
  Watson (3 times), 233, 253, 255
  Woods (7 times), 346, 350
Vare, Glenna Collett, 54, 118-25, *121*
Vare Trophy
  about, 125, 168
  1953, Berg, 159
  1955, Berg, 159
  1956, Berg, 159
  1959, Rawls, 167
  1960-1964, Wright, 162, 198
  1965-1972, Whitworth, 239
  1986, Bradley, 240
  1990, Daniel, 271
  1995-1996, Sörenstam, 363
  1997, Webb, 366
  2000, Webb, 367
  2001-2002, Sörenstam, 364
  2003, Pak, 368
  2005, Sörenstam, 365
  2006, Ochoa, 370
  2014, Lewis, 386
  Carner (5 times), 240-41
Venturi, Ken, 169, 175, 180, 181, 182, 197-98
Verplank, Scott, 250, 261, 327
Victory Classic, 390
Vincenzo, Roberto De, 147
Vogues, Mitch, 273
Voigt, George, 104-5
Volvo Open Championship, 319
Von Elm, George, 99, 100, 127

W

Wachovia Championship, 348
Wachovia L.P.G.A. Classic, 370
Wadkins, Lanny
  The Masters, 272, 276
  P.G.A. Championship, 225, 233, 247, 250, 263, 278
  Ryder Cup, 274, 412
  U.S. Amateur, 221
  U.S. Open, 262
Walker Cup: about, 417; **1921**, 95; **1922**, 96; **1924**, 99; **1926**, 100; **1928**, 101; 1930, 103;

1936, 131; **1938**, 133; **1951**, 172; **1953**, 173; **1955**, 175; **1959**, 205; **1961**, 205; **1995**, 321, 343; **2011**, 401; Ouimet (11 times), 69
Walker, Cyril, 99
Wallace, James, 130
Wall, Art, 181, 189, 234
Wall, Art, Jr., 222, 224-25
Walmart NW Arkansas Championship, 386
Walzer, Winifred, 181
Wanamaker, Rodman, 74
Wanamaker Trophy, 74. *See also* P.G.A. Championship
Ward, E. Harvie, 174, 176, 248
Ward, Marvin, 149, 151
Watson, Bubba, 338, *378*, 395, 402, 406
Watson, Tom
 biographical information, 251
 British Open, 187, 210-11, 232-33, 243, 248, 249-50, 252, 253, 254, 255, 258, 265, 266, 279, 281, 336
 career summary, 233, 251-55, 254
 MasterCard Colonial, 255
 The Masters, 194, 232, 233, 235, 244, 247, 249, 252-53, 254, 272
 P.G.A. Championship, 234, 278
 Ryder Cup, 412-13
 U.S. Open, 212, *216*, 230-31, 232, 243, 245-46, 248, 251-53, 254, 255, 263, 277, 278-79
 Western Open, 252
Watt, G.O., 104
Watts, Bryan, 294
Weaver, Michael, 402
Webb, Karrie, 363, 364, 366-68, *367*, 370
WEC Cadillac Match Play Championship, 399
wedge development, 84
Wegman's Rochester L.P.G.A., 370
Weir, Mike, 196, 306-7
Weiskopf, Tom, 243
 British Open, 228
 The Masters, 193, 208, 209-10, 219, 229, 230
 as model for Singh, 319
 U.S. Open, 231, 242
Welch's Circle K Championship, 363
Wells Fargo Championship, 398, 399
Wendy's Three Tour Challenge, 214
Western Open: winners list, 443; **1913**, 62; **1916**, 75; **1921**, 75; **1926-1927**, 75; **1932**, 75; **1936-1938**, 132; **1940**, 149; **1963**, 185; **1975**, lightening hits players, 225; **1977**, 233; **1985**, 261; Hagen (five times), 75
Westland, Jack, 130
Westwood, Lee
 Abu Dhabi HSBC Golf Championship, 397
 British Open, 310, 328
 The Masters, 326, 338
 Race to Dubai, 394
 U.S. Open, 299, 326, 333
 WGC-Accenture Match Play Championship, 397

Wethered, Joyce, 54, 119, 120-22, *121*, 123
Wethered, Roger, 96, 105
WGC-Accenture Match Play Championship, 351, 390, 393-94, 397
WGC-Bridgestone Invitational, 321, 348, 352, 399
WGC-CA Championship, 326, 394
WGC-Cadillac Championship, 352, 389, 397
WGC-HSBC Championship, 396
Whitcomb, Reg, 310
White Sulphur Springs, West Virginia, 27
Whitworth, Kathy, 203, 238-39, 419
Wie, Michelle, *375*, 375-77, 380, 419
Wigham, H. J., 45
William IV, king of Scots, 14
Williams, Henry, Jr., 171
Williams, Steve, 350, 351
Wilson, Oliver, 394
Wilson Sporting Goods Company, 157, 158, 160
Wilson, Virginia, 119
Wittenberg, Casey, 308
Women's British Open: winners list, 442-43; **1995**, 366; **1997**, 366; **2001**, 368, 380; 2002, 367; **2003**, 364; **2006**, 371; **2007**, 370, 376; **2009**, 383; **2010**, 380; **2011**, 381; **2013**, 385, 386. *See also* du Maurier Classic
women's golf, 50-54
Women's Golf Association, 52
Women's Professional Golf Association (W.P.G.A.), 158, 160
Women's Public Links, 337
Women's Western Open: **1942**, 167; **1943**, 158; **1954**, 167; **1958**, 177; **1963**, 196; **1967**, 239; Berg (seven times), 159
Wongluekiet, Aree, 297
Wood, Craig, 86, 114, 127, 135, 150, 151
Woods, Tiger
 biographical information, *340*, 342-43, 352-54
 Abu Dhabi Golf Championship, 397
 Arnold Palmer International, 352, 403
 Arnold Palmer Invitational, 141-42, 349, 351, 352, 354-55
 AT&T National, 349, 355
 AT&T Pebble Beach National Pro-Am, 345, 351
 BMW Championship, 352
 Bridgestone Invitational, 349, 355
 British Open, 294, 299-300, 304, 307-8, 312-13, 315, 331, 345, 346-47, 348, 352, 405
 Byron Nelson Trophy, 350
 career Grand Slams, 198, 215, 300, 333, 345, 350-51
 career stats, 214, 310, 316, 333, 345, 347, 348-49, 349-50, 351, 352, 355, 399, 400, 403, 405, 406
 career summaries, 215, 284, 343-52, 354-55
 Championship, 299
 Chevron World Challenge, 349, 351, 354
 consecutive cuts made record, 350
 Deutsche Bank Championship, 325-26, 346

Emirates Australian Open, 351
endorsements, 344, 354
Farmers Insurance Open, 352, 355
FedEx Cup, 326, 332, 337, 350
golf course design career, 353
health challenges, 333, 350, 351, 352, 355
Honda Classic, 351
The Masters, 202, 242, 290, 301, 303–4, 306,
  311, 314, 326, 329, 332, 335, 338, 344, 345–46,
  347–48, 351, 352, 407
and McIlroy, 393
Memorial Tournament, 344, 349, 352, 355
N.C.A.A. Championship, 284, 344
P.G.A. Championship, 294, 296, 300, 305, 308,
  313, 315–16, 331–32, 337, 345, 346, 347, 349,
  352
Players Championship, 351, 352
Presidents Cup, 337, 354, 405–6, 416–17
Ryder Cup, 415
and Sörenstam, 364
Tiger Slam, 301, 345, 350
Tour Championship, 348, 350
U.S. Amateur, 280, 282, 284, 334
U.S. Junior Championship, 278
U.S. Open, 211, 295, 298–99, 304, 312, 330,
  333, 336, 345, 346, 348, 349, 350–51, 352, 396
WGC-Accenture Match Play Championship,
  351
WGC Bridgestone Invitational, 352
WGC-Cadillac Championship, 352
Woosnam, Ian, 272, 275, 302
Work, Bertram, 34, 35
World Amateur Team Championship, 205
World Championship, 173
"World Championship of Golf" (1922), 83
World Golf Hall of Fame
  about, 363
  Alcott, 359
  Ballesteros, 258
  Berg, 159
  Bradley, 240
  Carner, 241
  Casper, 201
  Daniel, 360
  Davies, 361
  Els, 318
  Evans, 79
  Faldo, 289
  Hagen, 76
  Hogan, 148
  Inkster, 361
  Jameson, 168

  Jones, 115
  King, 359
  Lopez, 238
  Mickelson, 328
  Nelson, 138
  Nicklaus, 209, 215
  Ochoa, 370–71
  Ouimet, 69
  Pak, 367, 368, 380
  Palmer, 188
  Player, 194
  Rawls, 167
  Sarazen, 87
  Sheehan, 359
  Singh, 320
  Snead, 142
  Sörenstam, 363
  Suggs, 165
  Travers, 60
  Travis, 58
  Trevino, 226
  Watson, 255
  Webb, 367
  Whitworth, 239
  Wright, 163
  -Zaharias, 157
World Match Play Championship, 194, 258, 318
World Series of Golf, 210, 243, 323
World War I, 80–81
World War II, 114, 136, 151, 158
Worsham, Bud, 181
Worsham, Lew, 141, 153, 173
Worsham, Lou, 153
Wragg, Mabel, 120
Wright, Mary Kathryn "Mickey," 162–63, *163*,
  177, 196, 198, 368
Wright, Mickey, 196
Wysong, Dudley, Jr., 202, 205

Y

Yang, Amy, 387
Yang, Y.E., 337, 349
Yates, Danny, 265
Yonkers, New York, 28–29, 30

Z

Zaharias, George, 155
Zaharias, Mildred Didrikson "Babe," 154–57, *156*,
  164, 168, 171, 173
Zerman, Manny, 271, 273, 323
Zoeller, Frank Urban "Fuzzy," 235, 249, 277, 279
Zurich Classic, 390